Fodor's

SAN
FRANCISCO

WELCOME TO SAN FRANCISCO

With its myriad hills and spectacular bay, San Francisco beguiles with natural beauty, vibrant neighborhoods, and contagious energy. From the hipster Mission District to the sassy Castro, from bustling Union Square to enduring Chinatown, this dynamic town thrives on variety. The city makes it wonderfully easy to tap into the good life, too: between San Francisco's hot arts scene, tempting boutiques, parks perfect for jogging or biking, and all those stellar locavore restaurants and cocktail bars, it's the ultimate destination for relaxed self-indulgence.

TOP REASONS TO GO

★ **Foodie heaven:** Top restaurants, hip ethnic favorites, farmers markets, food trucks.

★ **Distinctive neighborhoods:** Buzzing, walkable streets invite discovery.

★ **Golden Gate Bridge:** Electric orange and towering, this glorious span inspires awe.

★ **Waterfront activities:** Whether you hike, bike, or stroll it, the bay is magnetic.

★ **Accessible art:** From famous street murals to top-notch museums, art is everywhere.

Fodor's SAN FRANCISCO

Publisher: Amanda D'Acierno, *Senior Vice President*

Editorial: Arabella Bowen, *Editor in Chief*; Linda Cabasin, *Editorial Director*

Design: Tina Malaney, *Associate Art Director*; Chie Ushio, *Senior Designer*; Ann McBride, *Production Designer*

Photography: Jennifer Arnow, *Senior Photo Editor*; Jennifer Romains, *Photo Researcher*

Production: Linda Schmidt, *Managing Editor*; Evangelos Vasilakis, *Associate Managing Editor*; Angela L. McLean, *Senior Production Manager*

Maps: Rebecca Baer, *Senior Map Editor*; Mark Stroud (Moon Street Cartography), David Lindroth, *Cartographers*

Sales: Jacqueline Lebow, *Sales Director*

Marketing & Publicity: Heather Dalton, *Marketing Director*; Katherine Punia, *Publicity Director*

Business & Operations: Susan Livingston, *Vice President, Strategic Business Planning*; Sue Daulton, *Vice President, Operations*

Fodors.com: Megan Bell, *Executive Director, Revenue & Business Development*; Yasmin Marinaro, *Senior Director, Marketing & Partnerships*

Copyright © 2015 by Fodor's Travel, a division of Random House LLC

Writers: Michele Bigley, Christine Ciarmello, Denise M. Leto, Daniel Mangin, Fiona G. Parrott, Jerry James Stone

Lead Editor: Amanda Sadlowski

Editors: Stephen Brewer, Daniel Mangin

Production Editor: Elyse Rozelle

28th edition

ISBN 978–1–101–87840–8

ISSN 1525–1829

SPECIAL SALES

This book is available at special discounts for bulk purchases for sales promotions or premiums. For more information, e-mail specialmarkets@penguinrandomhouse.com

PRINTED IN THE UNITED STATES OF AMERICA

10 9 8 7 6 5 4 3 2 1

CONTENTS

CONTENTS

MAPS

ABOUT THIS GUIDE

Fodor's Recommendations

Everything in this guide is worth doing—we don't cover what isn't—but exceptional sights, hotels, and restaurants are recognized with additional accolades. **Fodor's** Choice ★ indicates our top recommendations; and **Best Bets** call attention to notable hotels and restaurants in various categories. Care to nominate a new place? Visit Fodors.com/contact-us.

Trip Costs

We list prices wherever possible to help you budget well. Hotel and restaurant price categories from **$** to **$$$$** are noted alongside each recommendation. For hotels, we include the lowest cost of a standard double room in high season. For restaurants, we cite the average price of a main course at dinner or, if dinner isn't served, at lunch. For attractions, we always list adult admission fees; discounts are usually available for children, students, and senior citizens.

Hotels

Our local writers vet every hotel to recommend the best overnights in each price category, from budget to expensive. Unless otherwise specified, you can expect private bath, phone, and TV in your room. For expanded hotel reviews, facilities, and deals visit Fodors.com.

Top Picks	Hotels &
★ **Fodor's** Choice	Restaurants
	🏨 Hotel
Listings	↧ Number of
✉ Address	rooms
✉ Branch address	❍ Meal plans
☎ Telephone	✕ Restaurant
🖷 Fax	⚲ Reservations
⊕ Website	👔 Dress code
✉ E-mail	▭ No credit cards
✉ Admission fee	$ Price
◷ Open/closed times	
	Other
Ⓜ Subway	⇨ See also
⊹ Directions or Map coordinates	☞ Take note
	🏌 Golf facilities

Restaurants

Unless we state otherwise, restaurants are open for lunch and dinner daily. We mention dress code only when there's a specific requirement and reservations only when they're essential or not accepted. To make restaurant reservations, visit Fodors.com.

Credit Cards

The hotels and restaurants in this guide typically accept credit cards. If not, we'll say so.

EUGENE FODOR

Hungarian-born Eugene Fodor (1905–91) began his travel career as an interpreter on a French cruise ship. The experience inspired him to write *On the Continent* (1936), the first guidebook to receive annual updates and discuss a country's way of life as well as its sights. Fodor later joined the U.S. Army and worked for the OSS in World War II. After the war, he kept up his intelligence work while expanding his guidebook series. During the Cold War, many guides were written by fellow agents who understood the value of insider information. Today's guides continue Fodor's legacy by providing travelers with timely coverage, insider tips, and cultural context.

EXPERIENCE
SAN FRANCISCO

SAN FRANCISCO TODAY

The quintessential boomtown, San Francisco has been alternately riding high and crashing since the gold rush. Those who lost out during the heady days of the dot-com bubble had barely finished dancing on the grave of the Internet economy when biotech rode into town, turning bust to boom. So which San Francisco will you find when you come to town? A reversal of fortune is always possible, but here's a snapshot of what the city's like—for now, anyway.

Revitalized Neighborhoods

Long the domain of drug addicts and homeless people smack-dab in the heart of downtown, **Mid-Market**—Market Street between 5th and 9th streets south to Mission Street—has resisted the best efforts of a string of San Francisco mayors to revitalize the area. But City Hall muscle is apparently no match for Twitter, the social media heavyweight lured here by the promise of a payroll tax break in 2013. A bevy of tech companies followed hot on its heels, and the retail and services that sprung up to serve their employees changed the vibe on the street, as did the long-awaited police substation that opened on embattled 6th Street the same year. After dark, hot new nightspots now draw a young crowd, real estate is suddenly on fire: the American Conservatory's new Strand Theater is set to open across from U.N. Plaza in 2015 while Hall, a pop-up indoor food market hopes to draw diners to one of the area's more stubborn blocks.

Elsewhere, city development skews southward, with long-sleepy quarters transforming into the latest hot neighborhoods. The renaissance of **Dogpatch**, the city's 19th-century industrial center at the bottom of Potrero Hill, is in high gear. Today artists and craftspeople reside in the lovely pre-1906 earthquake homes here, and a critical mass of restaurants, cafés, shops, and galleries are drawing folks from around town. In the coming years, watch for development of Pier 70, with a bay-front park bringing badly needed green space to this suddenly chic corner of the city.

Sports

When the 49ers abandoned Candlestick Park in 2014 for fancy new digs in Santa Clara, local fans were devastated. But a new professional sports franchise is coming to town: the NBA's **Golden State Warriors** are set to cross the bay from Oakland to San Francisco in 2018. Project boosters insist that the 12-acre complex, set to rise in Mission Bay down the waterfront from the Giants' AT&T Park, will catapult the long-neglected area into the league of destination neighborhoods, just like the baseball park did for South Beach. Most residents agree that the planned 5.5-acre bayfront park is a winner, but there's just one problem: popular opinion says the proposed arena itself looks like a giant toilet, and the bad jokes are flying. Here's hoping the design-review process flushes out the issue.

Google

Highly paid tech jobs are flooding the city and not everyone is thrilled about what that means for San Francisco: namely, stratospheric rents, gentrifying neighborhoods, and what many locals think of as an entitled vibe from the tech-elite. Growing frustration has found a target in the giant, unmarked, dark-windowed buses—all called Google buses, regardless of which tech companies' well-paid employees ride them—that shuttle riders

to jobs in Silicon Valley. Protests blocking the buses have become commonplace; they can occasionally be entertaining (one included a band of brightly clad acrobats), but others can unfortunately turn borderline violent. Activists are suing the city for allowing use of public bus lanes, saying the buses clog traffic for other commuters. In response to the criticism, Google donated $6.8 million to pay the bus fares of working-class youths, and are now picking up the tab for free Wi-Fi in public spaces.

Muni Development

Boondoggle alert: no one's enjoying the disruption caused by Muni's 1.7-mile **Central Subway extension,** designed to extend the T-Third line from SoMa under Union Square and into Chinatown. Aboveground hassles in North Beach are affecting the vacation vibe at the neighborhood's outdoor café tables. The controversial project is set to finish boring the tunnels by 2015, but with station construction ahead, don't expect to ride until 2019.

City Laws

Since 2013 all **parking meters** in the city must be fed on Sundays, and the hourly rate at 25% of meters now varies according to demand. In the Mission on Saturday, for example, you'll likely pay $6 per hour, while spots in less-busy areas may cost as little as $.25 per hour, which you can pay by credit card or by phone with a free app.

On the environmental front, San Francisco continues to value eco-friendly sustainability laws. Ever on the vanguard of the battle against climate change, in 2014 San Francisco banned the sale of single-use (21-ounce and under) water bottles on city property and at large nonsporting events as a step toward the city's plan to reach zero waste by 2020. Don't forget to pack your own reusable bottle, or pick up a SF one as a souvenir.

SAN FRANCISCO PLANNER

When to Go

You can visit San Francisco comfortably any time of year. Possibly the best time is September and October, when the city's summerlike weather brings outdoor concerts and festivals. The climate here always feels Mediterranean and moderate—with a foggy, sometimes chilly bite. The temperature rarely drops below 40°F, and anything warmer than 80°F is considered a heat wave. Be prepared for rain in winter, especially December and January. Winds off the ocean can add to the chill factor. That old joke about summer in San Francisco feeling like winter is true at heart, but once you move inland, it gets warmer. (And some locals swear that the thermostat has inched up in recent years.)

Weather

Thanks to its proximity to the Pacific Ocean, San Francisco has remarkably consistent weather throughout the year. The average high is 63°F and the average low is 51°F. Summer comes late in San Francisco, which sees its warmest days in September and October. On average, the city gets 20 inches of rainfall a year, most of it in the December-to-March period.

Getting Around

Walking: San Francisco rewards walking, and the areas that most visitors cover are easy (and safe) to reach on foot. However, many neighborhoods have steep—make that *steep*—hills. In some areas the sidewalk is carved into steps; a place that seems just a few blocks away might be a real hike, depending on the grade. When your calves ache, you're that much closer to being a local.

By Subway: BART is San Francisco's subway, limited to one straight line through the city. Within the city, it's a handy way to get to the Mission or perhaps Civic Center. BART is most useful for reaching the East Bay or SFO and Oakland's airport. There are no special visitor passes for BART; within town a ticket runs $1.85.

On Muni: Muni includes the city's extensive system of buses, electric streetcars, nostalgic F-line trolleys, and cable cars. The trolleys and cable cars are a pleasure for the ride alone, and they run in well-traveled areas like Market Street and, in the case of the cable cars, the hills from Union Square to Fisherman's Wharf. Basic fare for the bus, streetcars, and trolleys is $2.25; cable-car tickets cost $6 one-way. At $15, a one-day Muni Passport, which includes cable car rides, is a great deal.

By Car or Taxi: Considering its precipitous hills, one-way streets, and infuriating dearth of parking, San Francisco is not a good place to drive yourself. Taxis, however, can come in very handy. Call one or hail one on the street; they tend to cluster around downtown hotels. Ride companies like Lyft and Uber now do most of the taxi business in the city; hail one with their respective phone apps.

Festivals and Parades

San Francisco's major parades and festivals are notoriously creative, energetic, and often off-the-wall. Among the hundreds of events on the city's annual calendar, here are the ones that are especially characteristic and fun.

Chinese New Year, February. This celebration in North America's largest Chinatown lasts for almost three weeks. The grand finale is the spectacularly loud, crowded, and colorful Golden Dragon Parade, which rocks with firecrackers. If you don't want to stand on the sidewalk for hours in advance, buy bleacher seats. Contact the **Chinese Chamber of Commerce** (☎ 415/982–3071 ⊕ www. chineseparade.com) for more info.

St. Stupid's Day Parade, April. The First Church of the Last Laugh (⊕ www.saintstupid.com) holds this fantastically funny event on—when else?—April 1. Hundreds of people wander through the Financial District dressed in elaborate costumes (although there are fewer drag queens than on Halloween). Parade goers toss singular socks at the Stock Exchange, lob losing lottery tickets at the Federal Reserve, and sing their way down Columbus Avenue.

San Francisco International Film Festival, April and May. The country's longest-running film festival packs in audiences with premieres, international films, and rarities. Check the listings (☎ 415/561–5000 ⊕ festival.sffs.org) well in advance; screenings can sell out quickly.

Lesbian, Gay, Bisexual, and Transgender Pride Celebration, June. More than half a million people come to join the world's largest pride event, with a downtown parade roaring to a start by leather-clad Dykes on Bikes. If you're visiting around this time—usually the last weekend of June—book your hotel *far* ahead (☎ 415/864–0831 ⊕ www.sfpride.org).

San Francisco Open Studios, October. More than 700 artists open their studios to the public. It's a great window into the local fine-arts scene (☎ 415/861–9838 ⊕ www. artspan.org).

Dance-Along Nutcracker, December. This holiday tradition, part spoof and part warmhearted family event, was started by the San Francisco Lesbian/Gay Freedom Band (⊕ www. sflgfb.org). You can join the dancers onstage or simply toss snowflakes from the audience.

Helpful San Francisco Websites

Check out these online options—besides our own ⊕ www.fodors.com.

⊕ www.sanfrancisco.travel for the San Francisco visitor bureau.

⊕ www.sfgate.com from the major daily newspaper, especially ⊕ www.sfgate. com/sfguide (for city neighborhoods and events) and ⊕ www.sfgate.com/entertainment (for entertainment articles and listings).

⊕ www.sf.funcheap.com for a daily listing of free and inexpensive events in the city.

⊕ www.sfist.com for a daily feed of local news, gossip, and SF preoccupations.

⊕ www.sfstation.com for daily listings on all sorts of events, restaurants, clubs, and so on.

⊕ www.7x7.com for the skinny on shopping, eating, playing, and following art in the city.

⊕ www.thebolditalic.com for a photo-heavy, hip take on life in the city, from microhoods to microbrews.

⊕ www.burritojustice.com for opinionated takes on San Francisco burritos and some history thrown in for kicks.

⊕ www.sfgirlbybay.com, a design blog that spans the globe, but shows plenty of love to San Francisco attractions and shops.

WHAT'S WHERE

1 Union Square. Home to a tourism trifecta: hotels, public transportation, and shopping. There are more hotel beds here than in any other neighborhood in the city and several transit options converge, including the cable cars.

2 Chinatown. Live fish flopping around on ice; the scent of incense, cigarettes, and vanilla; bargains announced in myriad Chinese dialects . . . you'll feel like you should've brought your passport.

3 SoMa. Anchored by SFMOMA and Yerba Buena Gardens, SoMa is a once-industrial neighborhood that's in transition. Luxury condos and stylish restaurants abound and cool dance clubs draw the bridge-and-tunnel crowd, but some parts are still gritty.

4 Civic Center. Monumental city government buildings and performing arts venues dominate, but it's also a chronic homeless magnet. Locals love Hayes Valley, the chic little neighborhood west of City Hall.

5 Nob Hill. Topped by staid and elegant behemoths, hotels that ooze reserve and breeding, Nob Hill is old-money San Francisco.

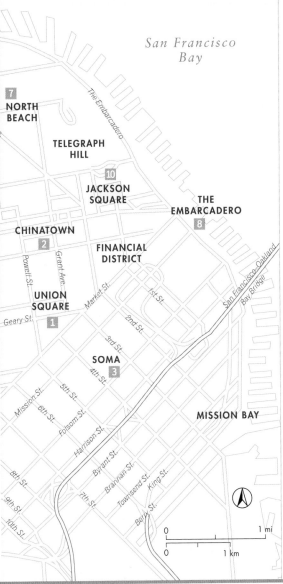

San Francisco Bay

7 NORTH BEACH

TELEGRAPH HILL

The Embarcadero

10 JACKSON SQUARE

THE EMBARCADERO

8

CHINATOWN

2

Powell St. *Grant Ave.*

FINANCIAL DISTRICT

UNION SQUARE

1

Geary St. *Market St.* *1st St.*

2nd St.

San Francisco–Oakland Bay Bridge

3rd St.

SOMA

3

4th St.

Mission St. *5th St.* *6th St.* *Folsom St.*

MISSION BAY

Harrison St.

8th St. *7th St.* *Bryant St.* *Brannan St.* *Townsend St.* *King St.* *Berry St.*

9th St.

10th St.

0   1 mi
0   1 km

6 Russian Hill. These steep streets hold a vibrant, classy neighborhood that's very au courant. Locals flock to Polk and Hyde streets, the hill's main commercial avenues, for excellent neighborhood eateries and fantastic window-shopping.

7 North Beach. The city's small Italian neighborhood makes even locals feel as if they're on holiday. In the morning, fresh focaccia beckons, and there are few better ways to laze away an afternoon than in one of North Beach's cafés.

8 Embarcadero. The city's northeastern waterfront is anchored at the foot of Market Street by the exquisite Ferry Building marketplace. The promenade that starts in back has great views of the bay and the Bay Bridge.

9 The Waterfront. Wandering the shops and attractions of Fisherman's Wharf, Pier 39, and Ghirardelli Square, the only locals you'll meet will be the ones with visitors in tow. Everything here is designed for tourists.

10 Jackson Square. For history buffs and antiques lovers, this upscale corner of the Financial District is a pleasant diversion.

WHAT'S WHERE

11 The Marina. With fine-wine shops, trendy boutiques, fashionable cafés and restaurants, and pricey waterfront homes, the Marina is San Francisco's yuppiest neighborhood. It's also home to the exquisite 1915 Palace of Fine Arts.

12 The Presidio. Locals come to the Presidio, the wooded shoreline park just west of the Marina, for a quick in-town getaway, the spirit lift only an amble on the sand in the shadow of the Golden Gate Bridge can provide.

13 Golden Gate Park. Covering more than 1,000 acres of greenery, with sports fields, windmills, museums, gardens, and a few bison thrown in for good measure, Golden Gate Park is San Francisco's backyard.

14 The Western Shoreline. A natural gem underappreciated by locals and visitors alike, the city's windswept Pacific shore stretches for miles.

15 The Haight. If you're looking for '60s souvenirs, you can find them here, along with some of the loveliest Victorians in town (and aggressive panhandling). Hip locals come for the great secondhand shops, cheap brunch, and low-key bars and cafés.

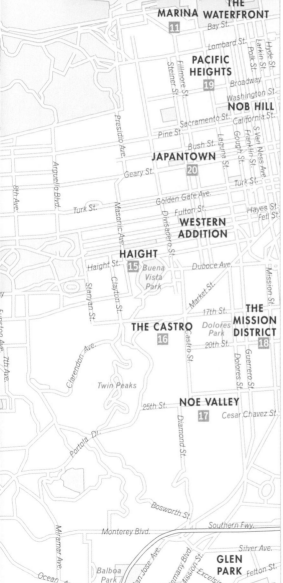

16 The Castro. Yes, it's proudly rainbow-flag-waving, in-your-face fab, but the Castro is a friendly neighborhood that welcomes visitors of all stripes. Shop the trendy boutiques, and catch a film at the truly noteworthy Castro Theatre.

17 Noe Valley. A cute, pricey neighborhood favored by young families. The main strip, 24th Street, is lined with coffee shops, eateries, and boutiques selling fancy bath products and trendy children's clothing.

18 The Mission District. When the sun sets, people descend on the Mission from all over the Bay Area for destination restaurants, excellent bargain-price ethnic eateries, and the hippest bar scene around.

19 Pacific Heights. This neighborhood has some of San Francisco's most opulent real estate—but in most cases you'll have to be content with an exterior view.

20 Japantown. A tight-knit Japanese-American population supports this area, of interest to outsiders mostly for the ethnic shopping and dining opportunities of the Japan Center and the small streets just north.

SAN FRANCISCO
TOP ATTRACTIONS

Golden Gate Bridge

(A) San Francisco's signature International Orange entryway is the city's majestic background, and about 10 million people a year head to the bridge for an up-close look. Walking the 1.7 miles to Marin County—inches from roaring traffic, steel shaking beneath your feet, and only a railing between you and the water 200 feet below—is much more than a superlative photo op (though it's that, too).

Alcatraz

(B) Considering how many movies have been set here, you might feel that you've already "been there, done that"—but you really shouldn't miss a trip to America's most infamous federal pen. Husky-throated onetime inmates and grizzled former guards bring the Rock to life on the wonderful audio tour; you'll hear yarns about desperate escape attempts and notorious crooks like Al Capone while you walk the cold cement cellblock.

But it's not all doom and gloom: you'll enjoy stunning views of the city skyline on the ferry ride to and from the island.

Golden Gate Park

(C) It may be world-famous, but first and foremost the park is the city's backyard. Come here any day of the week and you'll find a microcosm of San Francisco, from the Russian senior citizens feeding the pigeons at Stow Lake and the moms pushing strollers through the botanical gardens to school kids exploring the fabulous California Academy of Sciences and arts boosters checking out the latest at the de Young Museum. Be sure to visit the park's iconic treasures, including the serene Japanese Tea Garden and the beautiful Victorian Conservatory of Flowers. If you have the time to venture farther into this urban oasis, you'll discover less-accessible gems like the Beach Chalet and the wild western shores of Ocean Beach.

Cable Cars

(D) You've already seen them (on the big screen, in magazines, and, admit it, on the Rice-a-Roni box). And considering a ticket costs $6 a pop, do you really need to ride a cable car? Yes, you do, at least once during your visit. Flag down a Powell–Hyde car along Powell Street, grab the pole, and clatter and jiggle up mansion-topped Nob Hill. Crest the hill, and hold on for the hair-raising descent to Fisherman's Wharf, with sun glittering off the bay and Alcatraz bobbing in the distance. Don't deny it—this would be a deal at twice the price.

Ferry Building

(E) Foodies, rejoice! The historic Ferry Building is stuffed to the brim with all things tasty, including cafés, restaurants, a farmers' market, and merchants peddling everything from wine and olive oil to oysters and mushrooms. The building backs up to the bay, so the views are great—but they're even better from the decks of the departing ferries.

Wine Country

(F) You don't need to be a connoisseur to enjoy a trip to Napa or Sonoma . . . or both (hey, you're on vacation). But there's more to a Wine Country visit than vineyard tours and tastings: landmark restaurants, breathtaking scenery, fantastic artwork, hot-air-balloon rides, and secluded boutique hotels. And when you're ready for a break, a great glass of wine is never that far out of reach.

LOCAL FOR A DAY

Want to get a slice of local life by just hanging out and skipping the sightseeing? These experiences will let you pretend you're a San Franciscan, without a whopping rent check.

Shop the Ferry Plaza Farmers' Market
Roll out of bed and make your way to the Ferry Building—preferably on a Saturday—to join locals and celebrity chefs on a taste bud–driven raid. Out front, farmer-run stands showcase the Bay Area's finest organic, free-range, locavore goods. The indoor stalls will keep your mouth watering with artisanal cheeses, chocolates, and luscious pastries. Snag some takeaway food and perfectly ripe fruit for a picnic.

Stretch Your Legs in the Presidio
Spend a few hours wandering around this former military base at the foot of the Golden Gate Bridge. From gorgeous lookout points and the only campsite in the city to exhibition spaces and restaurants in restored military buildings, the Presidio has a sweeping natural beauty that brushes up against man-made diversions. Join people walking their dogs on the wooded hiking trails, or amble the paths along the sand of Crissy Field, then get in line for a cocoa at the Warming Hut.

Hang Out in Hayes Valley
Long beloved of artsy, cutting-edge locals, this quarter of cool cafés and high-design boutiques is finally on the radar of most San Franciscans. Browse your socks off, then grab a coffee from local cult microroasters Blue Bottle Coffee or a brew at the Biergarten and check out the latest temporary art installation in Patricia's Green, the petite community park.

Find a Quiet Beach
Leave the beach near Fisherman's Wharf far behind and seek out these two instead: Breezy Baker Beach, tucked against the cliffs just south of the Golden Gate Bridge, is known for its bridge and ocean views—and its nudists, those hardy souls. A bit farther south, nestled in ultrapricey Seacliff, is China Beach, a smaller, more secluded spot that's never crowded.

Linger over Breakfast
Notoriously food-centric San Franciscans are big on the most important meal of the day. The lines at popular breakfast places can be just as long as those at the hottest nightspots. Some favorites include:

Dottie's True Blue Café. The wait is worth it here for the blueberry cornmeal pancakes or smoked whiskey-fennel sausage, mushroom, and baby spinach scramble.

Kate's Kitchen. Heaping plates of Southern-inspired fare take the edge off a hairy-tongued Lower Haight morning after. Go for the cornmeal pancakes.

Mama's. The line forms early at this tried-and-true diner.

Sweet Maple. Famous for its Millionaire's Bacon (bacon with brown sugar, black pepper, and cayenne), this stylish diner also serves what many claim is the city's best French toast.

Nurse a Coffee
Spend a few hours in the right independent café or coffeehouse and you'll feel as if you're in a neighbor's living room. Come for a jolt of java, sometimes a reasonably priced meal, and usually Wi-Fi. Stay all afternoon—nobody minds—and you'll see the best reflection of a microcommunity.

SAN FRANCISCO WITH KIDS

On the Move

Adventure Cat Sailing. Them: playing on the trampoline at the bow of this 55-foot catamaran. You: enjoying a drink and the bay sunset on the stern deck.

Cable Cars. This one's a no-brainer. But don't miss the **Cable Car Terminus** at Powell and Market streets, where conductors push the iconic cars on giant turntables, and the **Cable Car Museum,** where you can see how cable cars work.

F-Line Trolleys. Thomas the Tank Engine fan in tow? Hop on one of the F-line's neat historic streetcars. ■TIP➔ Bonus: this line connects other kid-friendly sights, like Fisherman's Wharf, Pier 39, and the San Francisco Railway Museum.

Sneak in Some Culture

ODC/San Francisco. Best known for its holiday production of *The Velveteen Rabbit,* the dance troupe also holds other performances throughout the year.

San Francisco Mime Troupe. We know, it sounds lame. But these aren't your father's mimes, or mimes at all. In fact, they're a vocal political theater troupe that gives family-friendly outdoor performances.

Stern Grove Festival. Enjoying a delicious picnic in a eucalyptus grove and your kids might not even complain that they're listening to—gasp—classical music (or Latin jazz or opera).

The Great Outdoors

Aquatic Park Beach. Does your brood include a wannabe Michael Phelps? Then head to this popular beach, one of the few places around the city where it's safe to swim. ■TIP➔ Many other Bay Area beaches have powerful currents that make swimming dangerous.

Golden Gate Promenade. If your kids can handle a 3.3-mile walk, this one's a beauty—winding from Aquatic Park Beach, through the Presidio, to Fort Point Pier near the base of the Golden Gate Bridge.

Muir Woods. If these massive trees look tall to you, imagine seeing them from 2 or 4 feet lower.

Stow Lake. When feeding bread to the ducks gets old (like that's ever going to happen), you can rent a rowboat or pedal boat.

Just Plain Fun

AT&T Park. Emerald grass, a sun-kissed day, a hot dog in your hand . . . and suddenly, you're 10 again, too.

Dim Sum. A rolling buffet from which kids point and pick—likely an instant hit.

Fisherman's Wharf, Hyde Street Pier, Ghirardelli Square, and Pier 39. The phrase "tourist trap" may come to mind, but in this area you can get a shrimp cocktail, clamber around old ships, snack on chocolate, and laugh at the sea lions.

Musée Mécanique. How did people entertain themselves before Wii (or TV)? Come here to find out.

Rooftop @ Yerba Buena Gardens. Head here for ice-skating, bowling, a carousel, a playground, and the Children's Creativity Museum, a hands-on arts-and-technology center.

San Francisco Zoo. Between Grizzly Gulch, Lemur Forest, and Koala Crossing, you can make a day of it.

Learn a Thing or Two

California Academy of Sciences. Dinosaurs, penguins, free-flying rain-forest butterflies, giant snakes . . . what's not to like?

Exploratorium. A very hands-on science museum, including the full-immersion Tactile Dome.

TOP WALKING TOURS

All About Chinatown. A delightful "behind-the-scenes" look at the neighborhood, owner Linda Lee and her guides stop in Ross Alley and at a Buddhist temple. At herbal and food markets you'll learn the therapeutic benefits of fish stomachs and ponder uses for live partridges. ☎ 415/982–8839 ⊕ www.allaboutchinatown.com ✉ From $30.

Chinatown Alleyway Tours. To learn about the modern Chinatown community, join up with one of these young guides. Tour leaders, who all grew up here, discuss Chinatown's history and current social issues. ☎ 415/984–1478 ⊕ www.chinatownalleywaytours.org ✉ From $18.

Discover Walks. These free, hour-long tours of Chinatown, Fisherman's Wharf, and North Beach by enthusiastic young locals conveniently happen every day, so you can book one when it suits your schedule. The guides are paid in tips, so be sure to show them some love. Free tours run April through October; the rest of the year paid tours are available by reservation. ☎ 415/494–9255 ⊕ www.discoverwalks.com/san-francisco-walking-tours ✉ Free.

Don Herron's Dashiell Hammett Tour. Brush up on your noir slang and join trench-coated guide Herron for a walk by the mystery writer's haunts and the locations from some of Hammett's novels. At four hours for $20, it's one of the best deals going. See the website for tours or arrange one of your own. ⊕ www.donherron.com ✉ $20.

Foot! Comedy Walking Tours. You'll likely find yourself breathless with laughter, not just gasping after a steep hill. The tour leaders are all moonlighting pro comedians; they've got offerings like the Nob Hill tour "Hobnobbing With Gobs of Snobs."

☎ 415/793–5378 ⊕ www.foottours.com ✉ From $30.

Local Tastes of the City Tours. If you want to aggressively snack your way through a neighborhood as you walk it, consider hanging with cookbook author Tom Medin or one of his local guides. You'll learn why certain things just taste better in San Francisco—like coffee and anything baked with sourdough—and you'll get tips about how to find good food once you get back home. Along the way, you'll gorge yourself into oblivion: the North Beach tour, for instance, might include multiple stops for coffee and baked goods. ☎ 415/665–0480, 888/358–8687 ⊕ www.sffoodtour.com ✉ From $59.

Precita Eyes Mural Walks. For an insider's look at the Mission District's vibrant murals, this is the place to call. The nonprofit organization has nurtured this local art form from the get-go, and the folks here stay on top of the latest additions. ⇨ See the Mission District, Chapter 11, for more details. ☎ 415/285–2287 ⊕ www.precitaeyes.org ✉ From $15.

San Francisco City Guides. An outstanding free service supported by the San Francisco Public Library, these walking-tour themes range from individual neighborhoods to local history (the gold rush, the 1906 quake, ghost walks) to architecture. Each May and October additional walks are offered. Although the tours are free and the knowledgeable guides are volunteers, it's appropriate to make a $5 donation for these nonprofit programs. Tour schedules are available online, at library branches, and at the San Francisco Visitor Information Center at Powell and Market streets. ☎ 415/557–4266 ⊕ www.sfcityguides.org ✉ Free.

OFFBEAT SF

Looking for an unusual San Francisco experience that'll give you bragging rights? Try one of these quirky choices—even a local would be impressed.

16th Avenue Steps. Just standing at the base of this glorious mosaic of a stairway in the Inner Sunset is a treat: its underwater theme gives way to daytime dragonflies and butterflies, eventually transitioning to a starry, bat-studded night sky. Hike to the top, and you may have tiny Grand View Park all to yourself. The view (after a further climb) is, well, grand. (✉ *Moraga St., between 15th and 16th Aves.*)

ATA. Dedicated to getting anyone's art in front of an audience, Artists' Television Access has been showing films by local artists for more than 20 years. An open-minded crowd comes to ATA's tiny space, where $7 to $12 gets you a peek at what might be the next groundbreaker. ⊕ *www. atasite.org*

Audium. Billed as a "theater of sound-sculptured space," Audium is an experience like no other. Every Friday and Saturday a few dozen participants sit in concentric circles in a completely sound-proofed room in utter darkness, and music plays over the 169 speakers strategically placed, well, everywhere. ⊕ *www. audium.org*

Mt. Davidson. Ask San Franciscans what the highest point in town is and most will likely say Twin Peaks, but it's actually this "mountain," the next hill over. Visible from all over town but rarely visited, Mt. Davidson is topped with a eucalyptus-filled park. Finding the road up here is tricky (entrance at Dalewood and Myra ways), but once you get there you'll have amazing views—while all those tourists are still waiting for a parking space on Twin Peaks.

NightLife at the Cal Academy of Sciences. Supersize snakes, waddling penguins, and taxidermy are cool anytime, but throw in a cash bar and a DJ and this science club gets even cooler. Join the trendiest of geek crowds knocking back drinks and getting up close and personal with wild animals (with help from the academy's staffers) Thursdays from 6 pm to 10 pm; 21 and over. ⊕ *www.calacademy.org*

Nontraditional holiday celebrations. If you find yourself in town on a holiday, chances are the locals are commemorating it in an unorthodox way. Valentine's Day and you want to do something special with your honey? How about the mass pillow fight at Ferry Plaza? Easter Sunday after Mass? Check out BYOBW; at Bring Your Own Big Wheel—yes, those plastic ride-ons from grade-school days—often costumed grown-ups fly down the windy bit of Vermont Street with knees akimbo. Celebrations here are a bit of a non sequitur, but that's all part of the fun.

Red Hots Burlesque. Divey Mission hot spot El Rio is hopping most any night, but the saucy ladies of Red Hots Burlesque absolutely pack the house Friday evenings with their sexy, funny, body-positive show. You can even visit their School of Shimmy and take some new moves home with you.

Seward Street Slides. Wander a few blocks off the beaten path in the Castro to the unassuming Seward Minipark (Seward Street, off Douglass Street) and its unbelievably awesome, steep concrete slides. They may be intended for kids, but grownups are just as likely to hop on a cardboard box and take a ride.

A WATERFRONT WALK: THE FERRY BUILDING TO FISHERMAN'S WHARF

One of the great pleasures of San Francisco is a stroll along the bay, with its briny scent, the cry of the gulls, and boats bobbing on the waves. The flat, 2-mile walk along the Embarcadero from the Ferry Building offers a chance to take in some of the city's blockbuster sights along with spectacular bay vistas.

The Ferry Building: Foodie Mecca

Standing sentry at the foot of Market Street, the **Ferry Building** offers organic, seasonal delights from such local treasures as Cowgirl Creamery and Prather Ranch Meat Company. Take your picnic to a bench out back and take in the bay and the Bay Bridge.

Embarcadero: New Life for Old Piers

Heading north on the Embarcadero as the piers go up in number, watch for a mélange of historical info on black-and-white pillars, engraved in the sidewalk, and on plaques. These line **Pier 1**, where the giant paddle wheeler *San Francisco Belle* docks. **Pier 7** juts out far into the bay; an evening stroll here is lovely (if chilly) under the street lamps.

Just two blocks beyond at Pier 15 is the city's excellent hands-on science museum, the **Exploratorium.**

North Beach Detour: Levi's and Coit Tower

Near Pier 17, a left on Union and a right on Battery leads to **Levi Strauss headquarters,** where visitors can shop for jeans or peruse artifacts such as miners' jeans from the 1880s. Back across Battery, **Levi's Plaza** is one of the most manicured parks in town.

Consider heading west on Filbert or Greenwich and ascending one of the steep staircases clinging to **Telegraph Hill** for spectacular views and a peek into the lush stairway gardens along the way up to **Coit Tower.** Then return down the stairs to continue along the Embarcadero.

Embarcadero North End: Tourist San Francisco

Continuing north up the Embarcadero, **Alcatraz Landing** (Pier 33) is a good spot to pick up souvenirs even if you're not taking the highly recommended tour. **Pier 39** is just around the corner, with its cornucopia of souvenir vendors; thankfully, sea lion–watching is still free.

A few blocks farther north is **Fisherman's Wharf,** at Pier 45. Bypass the wax museum and make a beeline for the fabulous vintage arcade **Musée Mécanique** (at the foot of Taylor Street). For crab- and bunny-shape sourdough loaves, stop by Boudin Bakery, just down Taylor on Jefferson.

Last Stop: Historic Vessels at the Hyde Street Pier

Follow the towering masts to the foot of Hyde Street and the collection of exquisitely restored ships there. Afterward, head up Hyde to the **cable-car turnaround,** where you can grab an Irish coffee at the **Buena Vista.**

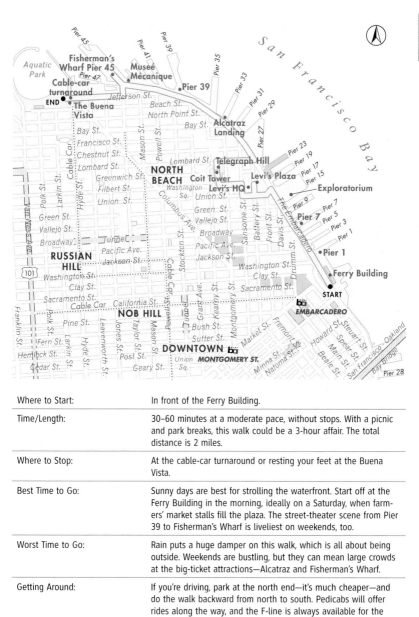

Where to Start:	In front of the Ferry Building.
Time/Length:	30–60 minutes at a moderate pace, without stops. With a picnic and park breaks, this walk could be a 3-hour affair. The total distance is 2 miles.
Where to Stop:	At the cable-car turnaround or resting your feet at the Buena Vista.
Best Time to Go:	Sunny days are best for strolling the waterfront. Start off at the Ferry Building in the morning, ideally on a Saturday, when farmers' market stalls fill the plaza. The street-theater scene from Pier 39 to Fisherman's Wharf is liveliest on weekends, too.
Worst Time to Go:	Rain puts a huge damper on this walk, which is all about being outside. Weekends are bustling, but they can mean large crowds at the big-ticket attractions—Alcatraz and Fisherman's Wharf.
Getting Around:	If you're driving, park at the north end—it's much cheaper—and do the walk backward from north to south. Pedicabs will offer rides along the way, and the F-line is always available for the weary.

GREAT ITINERARIES

SAN FRANCISCO IN 3 DAYS

Compared to other major cities, San Francisco is quite a small town, with just a handful of major sights and museums. Much of the city's charm is in its neighborhoods, so look beyond the big names and explore the stairways and alleyways that are the heart of the city.

Day 1: Union Square, Chinatown, and North Beach

Start your first day in **Union Square,** but don't be too early: the focus of this neighborhood is shopping, and most doors don't open until 10 am (11 am on Sundays). At the cable-car turnaround at Powell and Market streets, hop aboard either line and ride over Nob Hill and into **Chinatown.** Browse the produce stalls and markets, peruse herb shops, and explore alleyways. Have your camera ready as you pass from Chinatown into **North Beach,** the old Italian quarter: Broadway looking down Columbus and Grant is one of the most interesting cultural intersections of the city. Walk Columbus Avenue—stopping for espresso, of course—then head toward Coit Tower up Filbert Street, which becomes the Filbert Steps, one of the city's many stairways. Keep your eyes—and ears—open for **Telegraph Hill**'s famous wild parrots. Take in the views at the top and the tower's WPA-era murals of California's history, then head back into North Beach for dinner or cocktails.

Day 2: Ferry Building, Alcatraz, and Fisherman's Wharf

Get up early and head to the gourmet marketplace at the **Ferry Building;** Saturday morning's picture-perfect famers' market is the best time to visit. Gather provisions and head north along the Embarcadero to Pier 33, stopping to read the historical markers along the way. You should buy tickets to the next stop **Alcatraz,** in advance since tours frequently sell out; plan to spend a few hours exploring the former prison island. Afterward, head north to **Pier 39,** where you can browse through the overpriced stores if you're on a kitschy-souvenir hunt. Otherwise, follow the barking to the sea lions basking just north of the pier. At **Fisherman's Wharf,** return to early-20th-century San Francisco at the delightful **Musée Mécanique,** then grab an Irish coffee at the Buena Vista. As tempting as it might be to dine on the water, most restaurants here have less-than-spectacular food. A better and cheaper option is to pick up some to-go Dungeness crab from one of the outdoor vendors and eat as you stroll along the waterfront. Or hop on the Powell–Hyde or Powell–Mason cable-car line for better dining on Russian Hill or in North Beach, respectively.

Day 3: South of Market, Civic Center, Golden Gate Park, and Golden Gate Bridge

The San Francisco Museum of Modern Art (or SFMOMA, as it's known) is currently closed for construction, but there's still plenty of art in the **South of Market** neighborhood. Check out the striking **Contemporary Jewish Museum** or the **Museum of the African Diaspora,** and then consider a short stop at the **California Historical Society** or the **Cartoon Art Museum.** Take a break in expansive **Yerba Buena Gardens,** then hop a beautifully restored vintage F-Line streetcar down Market Street to **Civic Center** and the **Asian Art Museum.** Now head to the city's favorite green space: **Golden Gate Park.** Explore the park's eastern end, where you'll find the Conservatory of Flowers, the California Academy of

Sciences, the de Young Museum, and the San Francisco Botanical Garden. In the afternoon head north to the **Golden Gate Bridge** (wear layers—that wind can be brutal!) for a quick photo op. The adventurous may choose to bike or even walk across the bridge to Sausalito (a 5- to 6-mile trip), a Mediterranean jewel of a small town. Have drinks along the boardwalk then hop a ferry back to the city; be sure to check the schedule; the last ferry usually leaves before 7 pm.

SAN FRANCISCO IN 5 DAYS

Day 4: The Castro and the Mission

Ride the antique trolleys to the western end of the F-Line in the **Castro**. Stroll down Castro Street, under the giant rainbow flag and past the art-deco **Castro Theatre**, window-shopping and stopping at any café that might tempt you. You can north to the **Haight** and see its beautiful Victorians while treasure hunting in the many vintage shops. Otherwise, head east on 18th Street to the **Mission** and **Dolores Park,** one of the city's favorite hangouts, then visit Mission Dolores and wander rows of centuries-old gravestones in the tiny cemetery. Be sure to hit the "Valencia Corridor" (Valencia Street between 16th and 20th streets), dipping into independent bookstores, hipster cafés, and quirky shops. Don't miss the area's vibrant, often politically charged murals. Stay in the Mission for dinner and drinks; this is the city's best neighborhood for restaurants and watering holes.

Day 5: Other Neighborhoods

Not many visitors venture to these lesser-known spots, but you'll know the city better for having explored these hoods. In **Japantown,** visit the two-building Japan Center mall, with traditional Japanese restaurants, toy stores, and tea shops—the Kinokuniya Bookstore is a favorite. Contrast that with a visit to the J-Pop Center on Post Street, with funky shops that reflect modern Japanese pop culture. Head north on Fillmore and explore another world: swanky **Pacific Heights,** with its wine shops, high-end boutiques, and elegant home-decor stores. Cross Van Ness to Polk Street and see the transformation **Polk Gulch** is making, from gritty bars and donut shops to fancy lounges and unique stores. Continue north to **Russian Hill** and terraced Ina Coolbrith Park for broad vistas of the bay. Ascend the Vallejo Steps and you're within easy reach of the hill's best hidden lanes, including Macondray Lane. Continue north to zigzag down crooked Lombard Street. Finally, head back to Hyde Street for dinner at one of Russian Hill's trendy eateries.

If You Have More Time

With more than five days, you can begin to explore the Bay Area. Cross the bay to **Oakland;** take a quick swing through Jack London Square—new restaurants are giving it a lift—before heading into Chinatown and Old Oakland for shopping and dining. While waiting for Uptown's happening arts and nightlife scene, head into **Berkeley** and spend an afternoon scouting the university and touring the Gourmet Ghetto north of campus. Alternatively, you can head north from the city to majestic Muir Woods; if you've never seen the redwoods—the largest living things on earth—this is a must. Wine lovers will want to head to wine country: world-famous Napa Valley or lower-key Sonoma Valley both merit an overnight stay.

FREE AND ALMOST FREE

Despite—or perhaps because of—the astronomical cost of living here, San Francisco offers loads of free diversions. Here are our picks for the best free things to do in the city, in alphabetical order. Also check out ⊕ *sf.funcheap.com* for a calendar of random, offbeat, and often free one-offs.

Free Museums and Galleries

- Fort Point National Historic Site
- Octagon House
- San Francisco Cable Car Museum
- San Francisco Railway Museum
- Wells Fargo History Museum

Free Museum Times

The first week of every month brings a bonanza of free museum times.

- Asian Art Museum, first Sunday of every month
- Cartoon Art Museum, first Tuesday of every month is pay-what-you-wish
- Chinese Historical Society of America, first Thursday of every month
- Contemporary Jewish Museum, first Tuesday of every month
- de Young Museum, first Tuesday of every month
- Legion of Honor, first Tuesday of every month
- Yerba Buena Center for the Arts (galleries), first Tuesday of every month

Free Concerts

- The Golden Gate Park Band plays free public concerts on Sunday afternoon, April through October, on the Music Concourse in the namesake park.
- Stern Grove Festival concerts, held on Sunday afternoon from June through August, ranging from opera to jazz to pop music. The amphitheater is in a beautiful eucalyptus grove, so come early and picnic before the show.
- Yerba Buena Gardens Festival hosts many concerts and performances from May through October, including Latin jazz, global music, dance, and even puppet shows.

Free Tours

- The free San Francisco City Guides walking tours are easily one of the best deals going. Knowledgeable, enthusiastic guides lead walks that focus on a particular neighborhood, theme, or historical period, like Victorian architecture in Alamo Square or the bawdy days of the Barbary Coast.
- City Hall offers free tours of its grandiose HQ on weekdays.
- Discover Walks offers free daily tours of Chinatown, Fisherman's Wharf, and North Beach in summer.

More Great Experiences for $6 or Less

- See some baseball at AT&T Park, for free! Go to the stadium's Portwalk, beyond the outfield wall, and you'll have a standing-room view of the game through the open fence.
- Do your own walking tour of the Mission District's fantastic outdoor murals, then grab a bite at a taqueria or food truck.
- Choose a perfect treat at the Ferry Building's fabulous marketplace—maybe a scoop of Ciao Bella gelato or a croissant from Miette—and stroll the waterfront promenade.
- Hike up to the top of Telegraph Hill for sweeping city and bay views.

CABLE CARS

The moment it dawns on you that you severely underestimated the steepness of the San Francisco hills will likely be the same moment you look down and realize those tracks aren't just for show—or just for tourists.

Sure, locals rarely use the cable cars for commuting these days. (That's partially due to the $6 fare—hear that, Muni?) So you'll likely be packed in with plenty of fellow sightseers. You may even be approaching cable-car fatigue after seeing its image on so many souvenirs. But if you fear the magic is gone, simply climb on board, and those jaded thoughts will dissolve. Grab the pole and gawk at the view as the car clanks down an insanely steep grade toward the bay. Listen to the humming cable, the clang of the bell, and the occasional quip from the gripman. It's an experience you shouldn't pass up, whether on your first trip or your fiftieth.

HOW CABLE CARS WORK

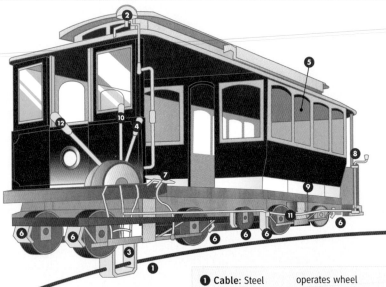

The mechanics are pretty simple: cable cars grab a moving subterranean cable with a "grip" to go. To stop, they release the grip and apply one or more types of brakes. Four cables, totaling 9 miles, power the city's three lines. If the gripman doesn't adjust the grip just right when going up a steep hill, the cable will start to slip and the car will have to back down the hill and try again. This is an extremely rare occurrence—imagine the ribbing the gripman gets back at the cable car barn!

Gripman: Stands in front and operates the grip, brakes, and bell. Favorite joke, especially at the peak of a steep hill: "This is my first day on the job folks…"

Conductor: Moves around the car, deals with tickets, alerts the grip about what's coming up, and operates the rear wheel brakes.

❶ Cable: Steel wrapped around flexible sisal core; 2 inches thick; runs at a constant 9½ mph.

❷ Bells: Used for crew communication; alerts other drivers and pedestrians.

❸ Grip: Vice-like lever extends through the center slot in the track to grab or release the cable.

❹ Grip Lever: Left-hand lever; operates grip.

❺ Car: Entire car weighs 8 tons.

❻ Wheel Brake: Steel brake pads on each wheel.

❼ Wheel Brake Lever: Foot pedal; operates wheel brakes.

❽ Rear Wheel Brake Lever: Applied for extra traction on hills.

❾ Track Brake: 2-foot-long sections of Monterey pine push down against the track to help stop the car.

❿ Track Brake Lever: Middle lever; operates track brakes.

⓫ Emergency Brake: 18-inch steel wedge, jams into street slot to bring car to an immediate stop.

⓬ Emergency Brake Lever: Right-hand lever, red; operates emergency brake.

ROUTES

Cars run at least every 15 minutes, from around 6 AM to about 1 AM.

Powell–Hyde line: Most scenic, with classic Bay views. Begins at Powell and Market streets, then crosses Nob Hill and Russian Hill before a white-knuckle descent down Hyde Street, ending near the Hyde Street Pier.

Powell–Mason line: Also begins at Powell and Market streets, but winds through North Beach to Bay and Taylor streets, a few blocks from Fisherman's Wharf.

California line: Runs from the foot of Market Street, at Drumm Street, up Nob Hill and back. Great views (and aromas and sounds) of Chinatown on the way up. Sit in back to catch glimpses of the Bay. ■TIP→ Take the California line if it's just the cable-car experience you're after—the lines are shorter, and the grips and conductors say it's friendlier and has a slower pace.

RULES OF THE RIDE

Tickets. There are ticket booths at all three turnarounds, or you can pay the conductor after you board (they can make change). Try not to grumble about the price—they're embarrassed enough as it is.

■TIP→ If you're planning to use public transit a few times, or if you'd like to ride back and forth on the cable car without worrying about the price, consider a one-day Muni passport. You can get passports online, at the Powell Street turnaround, the TIX booth on Union Square, or the Fisherman's Wharf cable-car ticket booth at Beach and Hyde streets.

All Aboard. You can board on either side of the cable car. It's legal to stand on the running boards and hang on to the pole, but keep your ears open for the gripman's warnings. ■TIP→ Grab a seat on the outside bench for the best views.

Most people wait (and wait) in line at one of the cable car turnarounds, but you can also hop on along the route. Board wherever you see a white sign showing a figure climbing aboard a brown cable car; wave to the approaching driver, and wait until the car stops.

Riding on the running boards can be part of the thrill.

CABLE CAR HISTORY

HALLIDIE FREES THE HORSES

In the 1850s and '60s, San Francisco's streetcars were drawn by horses. Legend has it that the horrible sight of a car dragging a team of horses downhill to their deaths roused Andrew Smith Hallidie to action. The English immigrant had invented the "Hallidie Ropeway," essentially a cable car for mined ore, and he was convinced that his invention could also move people. In 1873, Hallidie and his intrepid crew prepared to test the first cable car high on Russian Hill. The anxious engineer peered down into the foggy darkness, failed to see the bottom of the hill, and promptly turned the controls over to Hallidie. Needless to say, the thing worked . . . but rides were free for the first two days because people were afraid to get on.

SEE IT FOR YOURSELF

The **Cable Car Museum** is one of the city's best free offerings and an absolute must for kids. (You can even ride a cable car there, since all three lines stop between Russian Hill and Nob Hill.) The museum, which is inside the city's last cable-car barn, takes the top off the system to let you see how it all works.

Eternally humming and squealing, the massive powerhouse cable wheels steal the show. You can also climb aboard a vintage car and take the grip, let the kids ring a cable-car bell (briefly, please!), and check out vintage gear dating from 1873.

■ TIP→ The gift shop sells cable car paraphernalia, including an authentic gripman's bell for $600 (it'll sound like Powell Street in your house every day). For significantly less, you can pick up a key chain made from a piece of worn-out cable.

CHAMPION OF THE CABLE CAR BELL

Each September the city's best and brightest come together to crown a bell-ringing champion at Union Square. The crowd cheers gripmen and conductors as they stomp, shake, and riff with the rope. But it's not a popularity contest; the ringers are judged by former bell-ringing champions who take each ping and gong very seriously.

UNION SQUARE AND CHINATOWN

GETTING ORIENTED

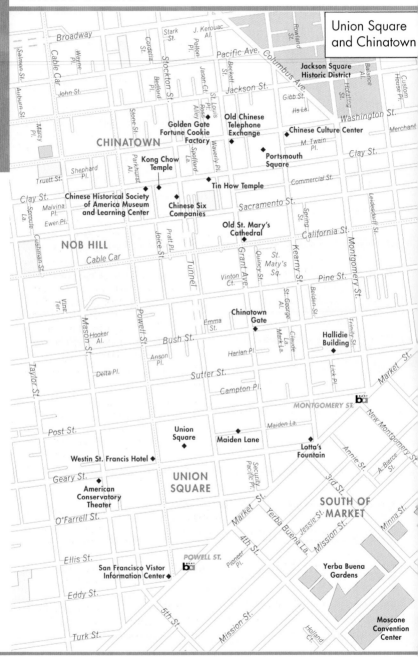

Union Square
and Chinatown

Broadway

Stark St.

J. Kerouac Al.

Pacific Ave.

Columbus Ave.

Jackson Square
Historic District

Jackson St.

Gibb St.

His La.

Washington St.

Old Chinese
Telephone
Exchange

Golden Gate
Fortune Cookie
Factory

Chinese Culture Center

Merchant

CHINATOWN

Kong Chow
Temple

Portsmouth
Square

Clay St.

Shephard Pl.

Truett St.

Chinese Historical Society
of America Museum
and Learning Center

Tin How Temple

Commercial St.

Clay St.

Chinese Six
Companies

Sacramento St.

Old St. Mary's
Cathedral

California St.

NOB HILL

Cable Car

St.
Mary's
Sq.

Pine St.

Chinatown
Gate

Hallidie
Building

Bush St.

Harlan Pl.

Sutter St.

Campton Pl.

MONTGOMERY ST.

Union
Square

Maiden La.

Maiden Lane

Lotta's
Fountain

Westin St. Francis Hotel ◆

Geary St.

UNION
SQUARE

American
Conservatory
Theater

SOUTH OF
MARKET

O'Farrell St.

Ellis St.

POWELL ST.

San Francisco Vistor
Information Center ◆

Yerba Buena
Gardens

Eddy St.

Turk St.

Mission St.

5th St.

Moscone
Convention
Center

TOP REASONS TO GO

Ross Alley, Chinatown: Breathe in the scented air as you watch the nimble hands at Golden Gate Fortune Cookie Factory, then kick back with a cocktail at Li Po around the corner, rumored to be haunted by the ghost of an opium junkie still looking to score.

Return to noir San Francisco: Have a late martini lunch under the gaze of the Maltese Falcon at John's Grill, then swing through the lobby of the Flood Building and nod to the other Maltese Falcon there.

Shop the square: Prime your credit cards and dive right in, from Bloomie's to the boutiques of Maiden Lane.

Tin How Temple: Climb the narrow stairway to this space with hundreds of red lanterns, then step onto the tiny balcony and take in the alley scene below.

Elevator at the St. Francis: Ride a glass elevator to the sky (or the 32nd floor) for a gorgeous view of the cityscape, especially in the evening when the lights come up.

QUICK BITES

Cako Bakery. Only the hardiest souls pass by Cako without succumbing to the siren call of the perfect cupcake. ⊠ 211 O'Farrell St., Union Sq. ☎ 415/404-7303 ⊕ www.cako.com.

Coffee Bar. Great coffee is hard to come by in Chinatown (and Union Square), so when you need some seriously good local roast, head to this tiny storefront in St. Mary's Square Garage. ⊠ 433 Kearny St., between Pine and California Sts., Chinatown ☎ 415/795-1214 ⊕ www.coffeebarsf.com.

Eastern Bakery. This packed space that claims to be Chinatown's oldest bakery has become a must-stop on the tourist trail. But Eastern isn't a tourist trap, because the goods back up the rep. The dirt-cheap steamed pork buns make a terrific lunch on the go. ⊠ 720 Grant Ave., Chinatown ☎ 415/433-7973.

GETTING THERE

In these two neighborhoods, cars equal hassle. Traffic is slow and parking is pricey. Save yourself the frustration and take advantage of the confluence of public transit at Powell and Market streets: buses, Muni light-rail vehicles and BART (Powell Street Station for both), cable cars, and F-line streetcars run here.

For the love of Buddha, don't drive in Chinatown! The steep, narrow, one-way streets are difficult to navigate by car. It's an easy walk from Union Square, and both Powell lines of the cable-car system pass through. You can also take the 30–Stockton bus; this route is a virtual "Chinatown Express," running from Fisherman's Wharf down Stockton Street through Chinatown to Union Square.

PLANNING YOUR TIME

Set aside at least an hour to scope out the stores and sights in and around Union Square— or most of the day if you're a shopper—but don't bother arriving before 10 am, when the first shops open. Sunday is a bit quieter.

Give yourself at least two hours to tour compact Chinatown. If possible, come on a weekday (it's less crowded) and before lunchtime (busiest with locals). You won't need more than 15 or 20 minutes at any of the sights themselves, but exploring the shops and alleys is, indeed, the whole point.

Sightseeing
★★★
Nightlife
★
Dining
★★★
Lodging
★★★★★
Shopping
★★★★★

The Union Square area bristles with big-city bravado, while just a stone's throw away is a place that feels like a city unto itself, Chinatown. The two areas share a strong commercial streak, although manifested very differently. In Union Square—a plaza but also the neighborhood around it—the crowds zigzag among international brands, trailing glossy shopping bags. A few blocks north, people dash between small neighborhood stores, their arms draped with plastic totes filled with groceries or souvenirs.

UNION SQUARE

Updated by
Denise M. Leto

The city's finest department stores put on their best faces in Union Square, along with such exclusive emporiums as Tiffany & Co. and Prada, and such big-name franchises as Nike, the Apple Store, H&M, Barney's, and UNIQLO. Visitors lay their heads at several dozen hotels within a three-block walk of the square, and the downtown theater district and many fine-arts galleries are nearby. Union Square is shopping-centric; nonshoppers will find fewer enticements here.

TOP ATTRACTIONS

Maiden Lane. Known as Morton Street in the raffish Barbary Coast era, this former red-light district reported at least one murder a week during the late 19th century. Things cooled down after the 1906 fire destroyed the brothels, and these days Maiden Lane is a chic, boutique-lined pedestrian mall (favored by brides to be) stretching two blocks, between Stockton and Kearny streets. Wrought-iron gates close the street to traffic most days between 11 and 5, when the lane becomes a patchwork of umbrella-shaded tables.

At **140 Maiden Lane** you can see the only Frank Lloyd Wright building in San Francisco. Walking through the brick archway and recessed entry feels a bit like entering a glowing cave. The interior's graceful, curving ramp and skylights are said to have been his model for the Guggenheim Museum in New York. Xanadu Gallery, which showcases expensive Baltic, Latin American, and African folk art, occupies the space and welcomes Frank Lloyd Wright fans. ⊠ *Between Stockton and Kearny Sts., Union Sq.*

Union Square. Ground zero for big-name shopping in the city and within walking distance of many hotels, Union Square is home base for many visitors. The Westin St. Francis Hotel and Macy's line two of the square's sides, and Saks, Neiman-Marcus, and Tiffany & Co. edge the other two. Four globular lamp sculptures by the artist R. M. Fischer preside over the landscaped, 2½-acre park, which has a café with outdoor seating, an open-air stage, and a visitor-information booth—along with a familiar kaleidoscope of characters: office workers sunning and brown-bagging, street musicians, shoppers taking a rest, kids chasing pigeons, and a fair number of homeless people. The constant clang of cable cars traveling up and down Powell Street helps maintain a festive mood.

The heart of San Francisco's downtown since 1850, the square takes its name from the violent pro-Union demonstrations staged here before the Civil War. At center stage, Robert Ingersoll Aitken's *Victory Monument* commemorates Commodore George Dewey's victory over the Spanish fleet at Manila in 1898. The 97-foot Corinthian column, topped by a bronze figure symbolizing naval conquest, was dedicated by Theodore Roosevelt in 1903 and withstood the 1906 earthquake. After the earthquake and fire of 1906, the square was dubbed "Little St. Francis" because of the temporary shelter erected for residents of the St. Francis Hotel. Actor John Barrymore (grandfather of actress Drew Barrymore and a notorious carouser) was among the guests pressed into volunteering to stack bricks in the square. His uncle, thespian John Drew, remarked, "It took an act of God to get John out of bed and the United States Army to get him to work."

The square sits atop a handy four-level garage, allegedly the world's first underground parking structure. Aboveground the convenient **TIX Bay Area** (☏ *415/433–7827* ⊕ *www.tixbayarea.com*) provides half-price, day-of-performance tickets to performing-arts events, as well as regular full-price box-office services. ■ **TIP→ Tired of shopping? Grab a coffee and pastry right in the square at Emporio Rulli, sit at a small outdoor table, and take in the action.** ⊠ *Bordered by Powell, Stockton, Post, and Geary Sts., Union Sq.*

CABLE CAR TERMINUS

Two of the three cable-car lines begin and end their runs at Powell and Market streets, a couple blocks south of Union Square. These two lines are the most scenic, and both pass near Fisherman's Wharf, so they're usually clogged with first-time sightseers. The wait to board a cable car at this intersection is longer than at any other stop in the system. If you'd rather avoid the mob, board the less-touristy California line at the bottom of Market Street, at Drumm Street. ⇨ *For more info on the cable cars, see the Experience San Francisco chapter.*

Union Square is the city's epicenter of high-end shopping.

WORTH NOTING

American Conservatory Theater. Celebrated local architects Bliss and Faville, also responsible for the nearby St. Francis Hotel, designed the neoclassical home of San Francisco's premier repertory theater company. The 1910 structure, which replaced one destroyed in the 1906 earthquake, sustained heavy damage in the 1989 quake but was beautifully restored. A.C.T. is renowned for productions by playwrights such as Tony Kushner (*Angels in America*) and Tom Stoppard (*The Invention of Love* premiered here), and cutting-edge works such as *The Black Rider* by Tom Waits, William S. Burroughs, and Robert Wilson. ⊠ *415 Geary St., box office at 405 Geary St., Union Sq.* ☎ 415/749–2228 ⊕ *www.act-sf.org.*

Hallidie Building. Named for cable-car inventor Andrew S. Hallidie, this 1918 structure is best viewed from across the street. Willis Polk's revolutionary glass-curtain wall—believed to be the world's first such facade—hangs a foot beyond the reinforced concrete of the frame. The reflecting glass, decorative exterior fire escapes that appear to be metal balconies, and Venetian Gothic cornice are notably lovely. ⊠ *130 Sutter St., between Kearny and Montgomery Sts., Union Sq.*

Lotta's Fountain. Saucy gold rush–era actress, singer, and dancer Lotta Crabtree so aroused the city's miners that they were known to shower her with gold nuggets and silver dollars after her performances. The peculiar, rather clunky fountain was her way of saying thanks to her fans. Given to the city in 1875, the fountain became a meeting place for survivors after the 1906 earthquake. Each April 18th, the anniversary of the quake, San Franciscans gather at this quirky monument. An image of redheaded Lotta herself, in a very pink, rather risqué dress, appears in one of the Anton Refregier murals in Rincon Center. ⊠ *Traffic triangle at intersection of 3rd, Market, Kearny, and Geary Sts., Union Sq.*

San Francisco Visitor Information Center. Head downstairs from the cable-car terminus to the visitor center, where multilingual staffers answer questions and provide maps and pamphlets. Muni Passports are sold here, and you can pick up discount coupons—the savings can be significant, especially for families. If you're planning to hit the big-ticket stops like the California Academy of Sciences and the Exploratorium and ride the cable cars, consider purchasing a CityPass (⊕ *www.citypass.com/san-francisco*) here. ■TIP➔ The CityPass ($86, $64 ages 5–11), good for nine days, including seven days of transit, will save you more than 40%. The pass is also available at the attractions it covers, though if you choose the pass that includes Alcatraz—an excellent deal—you'll have to buy it directly from Alcatraz Cruises. ⊠ *Hallidie Plaza, lower level, 900 Market St., at Market and Powell Sts., Union Sq.* ☎ *415/391–2000* ⊕ *www.sanfrancisco.travel* ☉ *Weekdays 9–5, Sat. 9–3; also May–Oct., Sun. 9–3.*

Westin St. Francis Hotel. Built in 1904 and barely established as the most sumptuous hotel in town before it was ravaged by fire following the 1906 earthquake, this grande-dame hotel designed by Walter Danforth Bliss and William Baker Faville reopened in 1907 with the addition of a luxurious Italian Renaissance–style residence designed to attract loyal clients from among the world's rich and powerful. The hotel's checkered past includes the ill-fated 1921 bash in the suite of the silent-film superstar Fatty Arbuckle, at which a woman became ill and later died. Arbuckle endured three sensational trials for rape and murder before being acquitted, by which time his career was kaput. In 1975 Sara Jane Moore, standing among a crowd outside the hotel, attempted to shoot then-president Gerald Ford. Of course, the grand lobby contains no plaques commemorating these events. Every November the hotel's pastry chef adds a new touch to his spectacular, rotating 12-foot-high gingerbread castle on display here; it's fun to compare it with the grand walk-through gingerbread house at the Fairmont. ■TIP➔ Some visitors make the St. Francis a stop whenever they're in town, soaking up the lobby ambience or enjoying a cocktail in Clock Bar or a meal at Michael Mina's Bourbon Steak. ⊠ *335 Powell St., at Geary St., Union Sq.* ☎ *415/397–7000* ⊕ *www.westinstfrancis.com.*

SAN FRANCISCO'S FANTASY FOUNTAIN

In front of the Grand Hyatt hotel at 345 Stockton St. gurgles an intricate bronze fountain depicting San Francisco. It's one of many local public works by Ruth Asawa, the city's "fountain lady." Look closely at this one and you can find an amorous couple behind one of the Victorian bay windows.

CHINATOWN

A few blocks uphill from Union Square is the abrupt beginning of dense and insular Chinatown— the oldest such community in the country. When the street signs have Chinese characters, produce stalls crowd pedestrians off the sidewalk, and folks scurry by with telltale pink plastic shopping bags, you'll know you've arrived. (The neighborhood huddles together in the 17 blocks and 41 alleys bordered roughly by Bush, Kearny, and Pow-

> **LOOK UP!**
>
> When wandering around China-town, don't forget to look up! Above the chintziest souvenir shop might loom an ornate balcony or a curly pagoda roof. The best examples are on the 900 block of Grant Avenue (at Washington Street) and at Waverly Place.

ell streets and Broadway.) Chinatown has been attracting the curious for more than 100 years, and no other neighborhood in the city absorbs as many tourists without seeming to forfeit its character. Join the flow and step into another world. Good-luck banners of crimson and gold hang beside dragon-entwined lampposts and pagoda roofs, while honking cars chime in with shoppers bargaining loudly in Cantonese or Mandarin.

TOP ATTRACTIONS

Chinatown Gate. This is the official entrance to Chinatown. Stone lions flank the base of the pagoda-topped gate; the lions, dragons, and fish up top symbolize wealth, prosperity, and other good things. The four Chinese characters immediately beneath the pagoda represent the philosophy of Sun Yat-sen (1866–1925), the leader who unified China in the early 20th century. Sun Yat-sen, who lived in exile in San Francisco for a few years, promoted the notion of friendship and peace among all nations based on equality, justice, and goodwill. The vertical characters under the left pagoda read "peace" and "trust," the ones under the right pagoda "respect" and "love." The whole shebang telegraphs the internationally understood message of "photo op." Immediately beyond the gate, dive into souvenir shopping on Grant Avenue, Chinatown's tourist strip. ⊠ *Grant Ave. at Bush St., Chinatown.*

Fodor'sChoice   **Tin How Temple.** Duck into the inconspicuous doorway, climb three flights
★   of stairs, and be assaulted by the aroma of incense in this tiny, altar-filled room. In 1852, Day Ju, one of the first three Chinese to arrive in San Francisco, dedicated this temple to the Queen of the Heavens and the Goddess of the Seven Seas, and the temple looks largely the same today as it did more than a century ago. In the entryway, elderly ladies can often be seen preparing "money" to be burned as offerings to various Buddhist gods or as funds for ancestors to use in the afterlife. Hundreds of red-and-gold lanterns cover the ceiling; the larger the lamp, the larger its donor's contribution to the temple. Gifts of oranges, dim sum, and money left by the faithful, who kneel mumbling prayers, rest on altars to different gods. Tin How presides over the middle back of the temple, flanked by one red and one green lesser god. Take a good look around, since taking photographs is not allowed. ⊠ *125 Waverly*

Locals snap up flowers from an outdoor vendor in Chinatown.

Pl., between Clay and Washington Sts., Chinatown 🖪 *Free, donations accepted* ⊘ *Daily 10–4.*

WORTH NOTING

Chinese Culture Center. Chiefly a place for the community to gather for calligraphy and Mandarin classes, the center operates a gallery with occasionally interesting temporary exhibits by Chinese and Chinese-American artists. Two different two-hour walking tours of Chinatown depart from the gallery on Wednesdays, Fridays, and Saturdays; call the center or visit its website for details. ⊠ *Hilton Hotel, 750 Kearny St., 3rd fl., Chinatown* 🕾 *415/986–1822* ⊕ *www.c-c-c.org* 🖪 *Center and gallery free ($5 suggested donation), tour $30* ⊘ *Tues.–Sat. 10–4.*

Chinese Historical Society of America Museum and Learning Center. The displays at this small, light-filled gallery document the Chinese-American experience—from 19th-century agriculture to 21st-century food and fashion trends—and include a thought-provoking collection of racist games and toys. The facility also has temporary exhibits of works by contemporary Chinese-American artists. ⊠ *965 Clay St., between Stockton and Powell Sts., Chinatown* 🕾 *415/391–1188* ⊕ *www.chsa. org* 🖪 *$5, free 1st Thurs. of month* ⊘ *Tues.–Fri. noon–5, Sat. 11–4.*

Chinese Six Companies. Once the White House of Chinatown, this striking building has balconies and lion-supported columns. Begun as an umbrella group for the many family and regional *tongs* (mutual-aid and fraternal organizations) that sprang up to help gold-rush immigrants, the Chinese Six Companies functioned as a government within Chinatown, settling disputes among members and fighting against anti-Chinese laws. The business leaders who ran the six companies (which

CLOSE UP

Chinatown Tongs

If you take it from Hollywood, Chinese *tongs* (secretive fraternal associations) rank right up there with the Italian Mafia and the Japanese yakuza. The general public perception is one of an honor-bound brotherhood with an impenetrable code of silence; fortunes amassed through prostitution and narcotics; and disputes settled in a hail of gunfire, preferably in a crowded restaurant. In fact, the tongs began as an innocent community service—but for roughly a century there's been more than a little truth to the sensational image.

When Chinese immigrants first arrived in San Francisco during the gold rush, they made a beeline for an appropriate tong. These benevolent organizations welcomed people from specific regions of China, or those with certain family names, and helped new arrivals get a foothold. For thousands of men otherwise alone in the city, these tongs were a vital social connection. It didn't take long, however, until offers of protection services ushered in a new criminal element, casting a sinister shadow over all the tongs, legitimate or not.

As gambling parlors, illegal lotteries, opium dens, and brothels took root, many tongs became the go-to sources for turf protection and retribution. Early on, the muscle behind the tongs

became known as "hatchet men" for their weapons of choice. (They believed guns made too much noise.)

"Tong wars" regularly broke out between competing groups, with especially blood-soaked periods in the 1920s and 1970s. Today the tongs are less influential than at the turn of the 20th century, but they remain a major part of Chinatown life, as they own large swaths of real estate and provide care for the elderly. The criminal side is alive and well, profiting from prostitution and drugs and doing a brisk business in pirated music and DVDs. Violence still erupts, too. In 2006 Allen Leung, a prominent community leader, was shot dead in his shop on Jackson Street. Among his activities, Leung was a very influential "dragon head" of the Hop Sing tong, a group involved in prostitution, the heroin trade, and other underground activities, and leader of the Chinese freemasons. Many suspect Raymond "Shrimp Boy" Chow, Leung's successor in the freemasons, committed the crime. Leung's murder sparked a racketeering and corruption investigation by the FBI that in 2014 took down longtime state senator Leland Yee. While Chow is under arrest (again) on money laundering charges, Leung's murder remains unsolved. And just as in the movies, no one's talking.

still exist) dominated the neighborhood's political and economic life for decades. The building is closed to the public. ⊠ *843 Stockton St., Chinatown.*

FAMILY   **Golden Gate Fortune Cookie Factory.** Follow your nose down Ross Alley to this tiny but fragrant cookie factory. Workers sit at circular motorized griddles and wait for dollops of batter to drop onto a tiny metal plate, which rotates into an oven. A few moments later out comes a cookie that's pliable and ready for folding. It's easy to peek in for a moment,

Continued on page 47

CHINATOWN

Chinatown's streets flood the senses. Incense and cigarette smoke mingle with the scents of briny fish and sweet vanilla. Rooflines flare outward, pagoda-style. Loud Cantonese bargaining and honking car horns rise above the sharp clack of mah-jongg tiles and the eternally humming cables beneath the street.

Most Chinatown visitors march down Grant Avenue, buy a few trinkets, and call it a day. Do yourself a favor and dig deeper. This is one of the largest Chinese communities outside Asia, and there is far more to it than buying a back-scratcher near Chinatown Gate. To get a real feel for the neighborhood, wander off the main drag. Step into a temple or an herb shop and wander down a flag-draped alley. And don't be shy: residents welcome guests warmly, though rarely in English.

Whatever you do, don't leave without eating something. Noodle houses, bakeries, tea houses, and dim sum shops seem to occupy every other storefront. There's a feast for your eyes as well: in the market windows on Stockton and Grant, you'll see hanging whole roast ducks, fish, and shellfish swimming in tanks, and strips of shiny, pink-glazed Chinese-style barbecued pork.

CHINATOWN'S HISTORY

Sam Brannan's 1848 cry of "Gold!" didn't take long to reach across the world to China. Struggling with famine, drought, and political upheaval at home, thousands of Chinese jumped at the chance to try their luck in California. Most came from the Pearl River Delta region, in the Guangdong province, and spoke Cantonese dialects. From the start, Chinese businesses circled around Portsmouth Square, which was conveniently central. Bachelor rooming houses sprang up, since the vast majority of new arrivals were men. By 1853, the area was called Chinatown.

The Street of Gamblers (Ross Alley), 1898 (top). The first Chinese telephone operator in Chinatown (bottom).

COLD WELCOME

The Chinese faced discrimination from the get-go. Harrassment became outright hostility as first the gold rush, then the work on the Transcontinental Railroad petered out. Special taxes were imposed to shoulder aside competing "coolie labor." Laws forbidding the Chinese from moving outside Chinatown kept the residents packed in like sardines, with nowhere to go but up and down—thus the many basement establishments in the neighborhood. State and federal laws passed in the 1870s deterred Chinese women from immigrating, deeming them prostitutes. In the late 1870s, looting and arson attacks on Chinatown businesses soared.

The coup de grace, though, was the Chinese Exclusion Act, passed by the U.S.

Chinatown's Grant Avenue.

Women and children flooded into the neighborhood after the Great Quake.

Congress in 1882, which slammed the doors to America for "Asiatics." This was the country's first significant restriction on immigration. The law also prevented the existing Chinese residents, including American-born children, from becoming naturalized citizens. With a society of mostly men (forbidden, of course, from marrying white women), San Francisco hoped that Chinatown would simply die out.

OUT OF THE ASHES

When the devastating 1906 earthquake and fire hit, city fathers thought they'd seize the opportunity to kick the Chinese out of Chinatown and get their hands on that desirable piece of downtown real estate. Then Chinatown businessman Look Tin Eli had a brainstorm of Disneyesque proportions.

He proposed that Chinatown be rebuilt, but in a tourist-friendly, stylized, "Oriental" way. Anglo-American architects would design new buildings with pagoda roofs and dragon-covered columns. Chinatown would attract more tourists—the curious had been visiting on the sly

for decades—and add more tax money to the city's coffers. Ka-ching: the sales pitch worked.

PAPER SONS

For the Chinese, the 1906 earthquake turned the virtual "no entry" sign into a flashing neon "welcome!" All the city's immigration records went up in smoke, and the Chinese quickly began to apply for passports as U.S. citizens, claiming their old ones were lost in the fire. Not only did thousands of Chinese become legal overnight, but so did their sons in China, or "sons," if they weren't really related. Whole families in Chinatown had passports in names that weren't their own; these "paper sons" were not only a windfall but also an uncomfortable neighborhood conspiracy. The city caught on eventually and set up an immigration center on Angel Island in 1910. Immigrants spent weeks or months being inspected and interrogated while their papers were checked. Roughly 250,000 people made it through. With this influx, including women and children, Chinatown finally became a more complete community.

A GREAT WALK THROUGH CHINATOWN

■ Start at the Chinatown Gate and walk ahead on Grant Avenue, entering the souvenir gauntlet. (You'll also pass Old St. Mary's Cathedral.)

■ Make a right on Clay Street and walk to Portsmouth Square. Sometimes it feels like the whole neighborhood's here, playing chess and exercising.

■ Head up Washington Street to the Old Chinese Telephone Exchange building, now the EastWest Bank. Across Grant, look left for Waverly Place. Here Free Republic of China (Taiwanese) flags flap over some of the neighborhood's most striking buildings, including Tin How Temple.

■ At the Sacramento Street end of Waverly Place stands the First Chinese Baptist Church of 1908. Just across the way, the Clarion Music Center is full of unusual instruments, as well as exquisite lion-dance sets.

■ Head back to Washington Street and check out the many herb shops.

■ Follow the scent of vanilla down Ross Alley (entrance across from Superior Trading Company) to the Golden Gate Fortune Cookie Factory. Then head across the alley to Sam Bo Trading Co., where religious

items are stacked in the narrow space. Tell the owners your troubles and they'll prepare a package of joss papers, joss sticks, and candles, and tell you how and when to offer them up.

■ Turn left on Jackson Street; ahead is the real Chinatown's main artery, Stockton Street, where most residents do their

grocery shopping. Vegetarians will want to avoid Luen Fat Market (No. 1135), with tanks of live frogs, turtles, and lobster as well as chickens and ducks. Look toward the back of stores for Buddhist altars with offerings of oranges and grapefruit. From here you can loop one block east back to Grant.

2

and hard to leave without a few free samples. A bagful of cookies—with mildly racy "adult" fortunes or more benign ones—costs under $5. You can also purchase the cookies "fortuneless" in their wafer-like unfolded state, which makes snacking that much more efficient. ■ TIP➔ Photographing the cookie makers at work will set you back 50¢. ⊠ *56 Ross Alley, off Washington or Jackson St. west of Grant Ave., Chinatown* ☎ *415/781–3956* ⊠ *Free* ⊙ *Daily 9–8.*

SPOT THE ALTARS

Walking down Chinatown's streets, peek into stores and try to spot the Buddhist altar. Often simple, these red, boxlike shrines include a statue of Buddha, candles or joss sticks, and offerings of fruit. Most common are oranges, which symbolize a prayer for good fortune and wealth—a shopkeeper's wish that transcends religion and culture.

Kong Chow Temple. This ornate temple sets a somber, spiritual tone right away with a sign warning visitors not to touch *anything*. The god to whom the members of this temple pray represents honesty and trust. Chinese stores and restaurants often display his image because he's thought to bring good luck in business. Chinese immigrants established the temple in 1851; its congregation moved to this building in 1977. Take the elevator up to the fourth floor, where incense fills the air. You can show respect by placing a dollar or two in the donation box and by leaving your camera in its case. Amid the statuary, flowers, and richly colored altars (red wards off evil spirits and signifies virility, green symbolizes longevity, and gold connotes majesty), a couple of plaques announce that "Mrs. Harry S. Truman came to this temple in June 1948 for a prediction on the outcome of the election . . . this fortune came true." ■ TIP➔ The temple's balcony has a good view of Chinatown. ⊠ *855 Stockton St., Chinatown* ⊠ *Free* ⊙ *Mon.–Sat. 9–4.*

Old Chinese Telephone Exchange. After the 1906 earthquake, many Chinatown buildings were rebuilt in Western style with pagoda roof and fancy balconies slapped on. This building—today East West Bank—is the exception, an example of top-to-bottom Chinese architecture. The intricate three-tier pagoda was built in 1909. To the Chinese, it's considered rude to refer to a person as a number, so the operators were required to memorize each subscriber's name. As the San Francisco Chamber of Commerce boasted in 1914: "These girls respond all day with hardly a mistake to calls that are given (in English or one of five Chinese dialects) by the name of the subscriber instead of by his number—a mental feat that would be practically impossible for most high-schooled American misses." ⊠ *East West Bank, 743 Washington St., Chinatown.*

Old St. Mary's Cathedral. Dedicated in 1854, this served as the city's Catholic cathedral until 1891. The verse below the massive clock face beseeched naughty Barbary Coast boys: "Son, observe the time and fly from evil." Across the street from the church in **St. Mary's Square,** a statue of Sun Yat-sen towers over the site of the Chinese leader's favorite reading spot during his years in San Francisco. ■ TIP➔ A surprisingly peaceful spot, St. Mary's Square also has a couple of small, well-kept playgrounds, perfect for a break from the hustle and bustle of Chinatown. ⊠ *660 California St., at Grant Ave., Chinatown* ⊕ *old-saintmarys.org.*

Portsmouth Square. Chinatown's living room buzzes with activity. The square, with its pagoda-shape structures, is a favorite spot for morning tai chi; by noon dozens of men huddle around Chinese chess tables, engaged in competition. Kids scamper about the square's two grungy playgrounds (warning: the bathrooms are sketchy). Back in the late 19th century this land was near the waterfront. The square is named for the USS *Portsmouth*, the ship helmed by Captain John Montgomery, who in 1846 raised the American flag here and claimed the then-Mexican land for the United States. A couple of years later, Sam Brannan kicked off the gold rush at the square when he waved his loot and proclaimed, "Gold from the American River!" Robert Louis Stevenson, the author of *Treasure Island,* often dropped by, chatting up the sailors who hung out here. Some of the information he gleaned about life at sea found its way into his fiction. A bronze galleon sculpture, a tribute to Stevenson, anchors the square's northwest corner. A plaque marks the site of California's first public school, built in 1847. ⊠ *Bordered by Walter Lum Pl. and Kearny, Washington, and Clay Sts., Chinatown.*

SOMA AND CIVIC CENTER

With the Tenderloin and Hayes Valley

GETTING ORIENTED

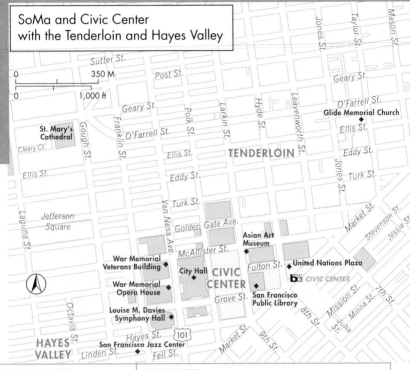

SoMa and Civic Center with the Tenderloin and Hayes Valley

GETTING THERE

QUICK BITES

For most SoMa visitors who stick close to the area around Yerba Buena Gardens and the Moscone Center, getting here is a matter of walking roughly 10 minutes from Union Square, less from Market Street transit.

It's best to reach the Civic Center by Muni light rail, bus, or F-line. Hoofing it from Union Square requires walking through the unsavory Tenderloin area, and from SoMa it's a long, ugly haul.

After dark, safety concerns dictate a cab for both of these neighborhoods.

Blue Bottle Coffee. If you're in Hayes Valley and see a clutch of people gathered around what looks like a garage, chances are you've stumbled upon the original kiosk of Blue Bottle Coffee, selling what many claim is the best organic coffee on the planet. ⊠ *315 Linden St., at Gough St., Hayes Valley* ☎ *415/252–7535* ⊕ *www.bluebottlecoffee.net.*

Morty's Delicatessen. Your search for an excellent Reuben ends here. The sandwiches and salads are piled high, the folks are friendly, and vegetarians have reasonable options at this super casual spot on the edge of the Tenderloin. ⊠ *280 Golden Gate Ave., at Hyde St., Civic Center* ☎ *415/567–3354* ⊕ *www.mortysdeli.com* ☼ *Closed weekends.*

Samovar Tea Lounge. Above the Martin Luther King Jr. memorial in the Yerba Buena Gardens, the lounge is a serene retreat with glass walls overlooking an infinity pool. Especially on a blustery day, the organic and fair-trade teas hit the spot. ⊠ *730 Howard St., at 4th St., SoMa* ☎ *415/227–9400* ⊕ *www.samovarlife.com.*

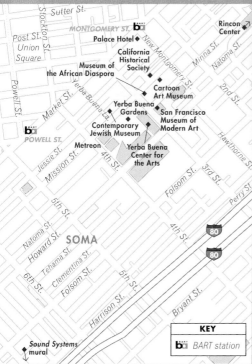

PLANNING YOUR TIME

You could spend all day museum-hopping in SoMa. An hour each should do it for the Museum of the African Diaspora, the Contemporary Jewish Museum, and the Center for the Arts, a little less than that for the smaller museums.

SoMa after dark is another adventure entirely. More interested in Merlot or megaclubs than Matisse? Start here around 8 pm for dinner, then move on to a bar or dance spot. ⇨ See Where to Eat and Nightlife for our top recommendations.

Plan on spending at least two hours at the Asian Art Museum and no more than a half hour at City Hall. Except for these two mainstays, you'll have little reason to visit the Civic Center area unless you have tickets to the opera, symphony, or other cultural event. Hayes Valley and its shops and boutiques merit a leisurely one-hour look-see.

KEY

bㅋ BART station

TOP REASONS TO GO

Asian Art Museum: Stand face-to-face with a massive gold Buddha in one of the world's largest collections of Asian art.

Club-hopping in SoMa: Shake it with the cool, friendly crowd that fills SoMa's dance clubs until the wee hours, and all weekend long at the EndUp.

Yerba Buena Gardens: Gather picnic provisions and choose a spot on the grass in downtown's oasis.

Hanging out at Patricia's Green: Grab a cup of coffee or an ice cream—Blue Bottle and Smitten Ice Cream are just around the corner—and head to the narrow swath of park that serves as hopping Hayes Valley's living room.

San Francisco Jazz Center: Experience the amazing acoustics at this intimate temple to jazz that opened in Hayes Valley in 2013.

Sightseeing
★★★
Nightlife
★★★★
Dining
★★★
Lodging
★★★★
Shopping
★

To a newcomer, SoMa (short for "south of Market") and the Civic Center may look like cheek-by-jowl neighbors—they're divided by Market Street. To locals, though, these areas are separate entities, especially since Market Street itself is considered such a strong demarcation line. Both neighborhoods have a core of cultural sights but more than their share of sketchy blocks. North of the Civic Center lies the western section of the frisky Tenderloin neighborhood, while to the east is hip Hayes Valley.

SOMA

Updated by
Denise M. Leto

SoMa is less a neighborhood than a sprawling area of wide, traffic-heavy boulevards lined with office skyscrapers and ultrachic condo high-rises. Aside from the fact that many of them work in the area, locals are drawn to the cultural offerings, smattering of destination restaurants, and concentration of dance clubs. In terms of sightseeing, SoMa holds a few points of interest—with SFMOMA closed until 2016, the specialty museums within a block or two of the Yerba Buena Gardens area top the list.

SoMa was once known as South of the Slot (read: the Wrong Side of the Tracks) in reference to the cable-car slot that ran up Market Street. Ever since gold-rush miners set up their tents here in 1848, SoMa has played a major role in housing immigrants to the city. The neighborhood's relatively reasonable prices through much of the 20th century made it a focal point of San Francisco's cultural life. In the 1960s, alternative artists and the gay leather crowd set up shop here; the legacy of that time is the still-raucous annual Folsom Street Fair.

The dot-com boom sent prices skyrocketing in the 1990s, when young prospectors flooded in to take their pick of well-paying jobs at high-tech startups. The most recent influx of techies (and their money) is changing

The glass-domed Garden Court contributes to the majestic feel of the Palace Hotel.

the neighborhood again: the skid row of Sixth Street, between Market and Mission streets, now coexists with trendy bars and cafés that cater to Twitter's workforce; once a scary alley in SoMa, the neighborhood is trying hard to rebrand itself as Mid-Market. The area may still have more than its share of seedy pockets, but even in earthquake town, the 20,000-square-foot penthouse atop the chic St. Regis sold for a record-breaking $28 million in 2011.

TOP ATTRACTIONS

Contemporary Jewish Museum. Daniel Liebeskind designed the postmodern CJM, whose impossible-to-ignore diagonal blue cube juts out of a painstakingly restored power substation. A physical manifestation of the Hebrew phrase *l'chaim* (to life), the cube may have obscure philosophical origins, but Liebeskind created a unique, light-filled space that merits a stroll through the lobby even if current exhibits don't entice you into the galleries. Be sure to check out the seam where old building meets new, and check the website for fun children's activities linked to exhibits. ■TIP→ San Francisco's best Jewish deli, Wise Sons, recently opened a counter in the museum, giving you a chance to sample the company's wildly popular smoked trout. ⊠ *736 Mission St., between 3rd and 4th Sts., SoMa* ☎ *415/655–7800* ⊕ *www.thecjm.org* ⊡ *$12; $5 Thurs. after 5 pm, free 1st Tues. of month* ☉ *Thurs. 1–8, Fri.–Tues. 11–5.*

San Francisco Museum of Modern Art. SFMOMA closed for a massive expansion project in 2013 and is scheduled to reopen in 2016. Until then, the museum will draw from its collection to create joint exhibitions with the Asian Art Museum, the Yerba Buena Center for the Arts,

Above the Yerba Buena Gardens, SFMOMA's striped "eye" can be spotted.

and other institutions. SFMOMA's store—known for its fun gadgets, artsy doodads, and superb art and kids' books—is relocating temporarily to 51 Yerba Buena Lane, off Mission and Market streets near 4th Street. ⊠ *151 3rd St., SoMa* ☏ *415/357–4000* ⊕ *www.sfmoma.org.*

FAMILY
Fodor's Choice
★

Yerba Buena Gardens. There's not much south of Market Street that encourages lingering outdoors—or indeed walking at all—with this notable exception. These two blocks encompass the Center for the Arts, the Metreon, Moscone Convention Center, and the convention center's rooftop Children's Creativity Museum, but the gardens themselves are the everyday draw. Office workers escape to the green swath of the East Garden, the focal point of which is the memorial to Martin Luther King Jr. Powerful streams of water surge over large, jagged stone columns, mirroring the enduring force of King's words that are carved on the stone walls and on glass blocks behind the waterfall. Moscone North is behind the memorial, and an overhead walkway leads to Moscone South and its rooftop attractions. ▮TIP➡ **The gardens are liveliest during the week and especially during the Yerba Buena Gardens Festival, from May through October (⊕ www.ybgf.org), with free performances of everything from Latin music to Balinese dance.**

Atop the Moscone Convention Center perch a few lures for kids. The historic Looff carousel (*$4 for two rides*) twirls daily 10–5. South of the carousel is the Children's Creativity Museum (☏ *415/820–3320* ⊕ *creativity.org*), a high-tech, interactive arts-and-technology center (*$12*) geared to children ages 3–12. Kids can make Claymation videos, work in a computer lab, check out new games and apps, and perform and record music videos. The museum is open year-round 10–4 from

Wednesday through Sunday, and on Tuesday during the summer. Just outside, kids adore the excellent slides, including a 25-foot tube slide, at the play circle. Also part of the rooftop complex are gardens, an ice-skating rink, and a bowling alley. ⊠ *Bordered by 3rd, 4th, Mission, and Folsom Sts., SoMa* ⊕ *www.yerbabuenagardens.com* ✉ *Free* ◷ *Daily sunrise–10 pm.*

WORTH NOTING

California Historical Society. If you're not a history buff, the CHS might seem like an obvious skip—who wants to look at fading old photographs and musty artifacts?—but these airy galleries are worth a stop. The shows here draw from the society's vast repository of Californiana—hundreds of thousands of photographs, publications, paintings, and gold-rush paraphernalia. Special exhibits have included *A Wild Flight of the Imagination: The Story of the Golden Gate Bridge* and *Hobos to Street People: Artists' Responses to Homelessness from the New Deal to the Present.* ■ TIP→ From out front, take a look across the street: this is the best view of the Museum of the African Diaspora's three-story photo mosaic. ⊠ *678 Mission St., SoMa* ☎ *415/357–1848* ⊕ *www.californiahistoricalsociety.org* ✉ *$5* ◷ *Tues.–Sun. noon–5; galleries close between exhibitions.*

Cartoon Art Museum. Krazy Kat, Zippy the Pinhead, Batman, and other colorful cartoon icons greet you at the Cartoon Art Museum, established with an endowment from cartoonist-icon Charles M. Schulz. The museum's strength is its changing exhibits, which explore such topics as America from the perspective of international political cartoons, and the output of women and African-American cartoonists. Serious fans of cartoons—especially those on the quirky underground side—will likely enjoy the exhibits; those with a casual interest may be bored. The store here carries cool titles to add to your collection. ⊠ *655 Mission St., SoMa* ☎ *415/227–8666* ⊕ *www.cartoonart.org* ✉ *$8, pay what you wish 1st Tues. of month* ◷ *Tues.–Sun. 11–5.*

Museum of the African Diaspora (MoAD). Dedicated to the influence that people of African descent have had all over the world, MoAD provokes discussion from the get-go with the question, "When did you discover you are African?" painted on the wall in the lobby. Recently renovated and reimagined for its 10th anniversary in 2015, MoAD is moving away from static historical displays toward temporary exhibits in its three new galleries over two upper floors. Its new status as a Smithsonian affiliate means access to resources, lecturers, and touring shows, and perhaps a higher profile for this institution, which has struggled to find its place. With floor-to-ceiling windows onto Mission Street, the museum fits perfectly into the cultural scene of Yerba Buena and is well worth a 30-minute foray. Happily, the museum retained its striking front-window exhibit: a three-story mosaic, made from thousands of photographs, that forms the image of a young girl's face. ■ TIP→ Walk up the stairs inside the museum to view the photographs up close—Malcolm X is there, Muhammad Ali, too, along with everyday folks—but the best view is from across the street. ⊠ *685 Mission St., SoMa* ☎ *415/358–7200* ⊕ *www.moadsf.org* ✉ *$10* ◷ *Wed.–Sat. 11–6, Sun. noon–5.*

Palace Hotel. The city's oldest hotel, a Sheraton property, has a storied past. It opened in 1875, but fire destroyed the original structure after the 1906 earthquake, despite the hotel's 28,000-gallon reservoir. The current building dates from 1909. President Warren Harding died here while still in office in 1923, and the body of King Kalakaua of Hawaii spent a night at the Palace after he died in San Francisco in 1891. The managers play up this ghoulish history with talk of a haunted guest room, but the opulent surroundings are this genteel hostelry's real draw. Glass cases off the main lobby contain memorabilia of the Palace's glory days; due to hotel renovation the memorabilia may relocate, so inquire on-site. ⊠ *2 New Montgomery St., SoMa* ☎ *415/512–1111* ⊕ *www. sfpalace.com.*

Rincon Center. The only reason to visit what is basically a modern office building is the striking Works Project Administration mural by Anton Refregier in the lobby of the streamlined Moderne–style former post office on the building's Mission Street side. The 27 panels depict California life from the days when Native Americans were the state's sole inhabitants through World War I. Completion of this significant work was interrupted by World War II (which explains the swastika in the final panel) and political infighting. The latter led to some alteration in Refregier's "radical" historical interpretations; they exuded too much populist sentiment for some of the politicians who opposed the artist. A permanent exhibit below the murals contains photographs and artifacts of life in the Rincon area in the 1800s. A sheer five-story column of water resembling a mini-rainstorm is the centerpiece of the indoor arcade around the corner from the mural. ⊠ *Bordered by Steuart, Spear, Mission, and Howard Sts., SoMa.*

Sound Systems mural. On a sound wall along the Caltrain tracks is Brian Barneclo's behemoth *Sound Systems* (2011), exploring everything from the nervous system to the ecosystem. At 24,000 square feet, the city's largest mural is also among its most high-profile artworks, visible from passenger trains and the freeway. ⊠ *7th and Townsend Sts., SoMa.*

Yerba Buena Center for the Arts. You never know what's going to be on display at this facility in Yerba Buena Gardens, but whether it's an exhibit of Mexican street art (graffiti to laypeople), innovative modern dance, or a baffling video installation, it's likely to be memorable. The productions here, which lean toward the cutting edge, tend to draw a young, energetic crowd. ■ TIP➔ Present any public library card to receive a $2 discount. ⊠ *701 Mission St., SoMa* ☎ *415/978–2787* ⊕ *www.ybca.org* 🎟 *Galleries $10, free 1st Tues. of month* ☉ *Wed. noon–6, Thurs.–Sat. noon–8, Sun. noon–6, 1st Tues. of month noon–8.*

CIVIC CENTER

The eye-catching, gold-domed City Hall presides over this patchy neighborhood bordered roughly by Franklin, McAllister, Hyde, and Grove streets. The optimistic "City Beautiful" movement of the early 20th century produced the Beaux Arts–style complex for which the area is named, including City Hall, the War Memorial Opera House, the Veterans Building, and the old public library, now the home of the Asian

Art Museum. The wonderful Main Library on Larkin Street between Fulton and Grove streets is a modern variation on the Civic Center's architectural theme.

The Civic Center area may have been set up on City Beautiful principles, but illusion soon gives way to reality. The buildings are grand, but there's a stark juxtaposition of the powerful and the powerless here. Many of the city's most destitute residents eke out an existence on the neighborhood's streets and plazas. Despite the evidence of social problems, there are areas of interest on either side of City Hall. East of City Hall are the Asian Art Museum, the Main Library, and United Nations Plaza, which twice weekly hosts a farmers' market that reflects the neighborhood's large Asian population. On the west side of City Hall are the War Memorial Opera House, Davies Symphony Hall, and other cultural institutions. A few upscale restaurants in the surrounding blocks cater to the opera and symphony crowd. Tickets to a show at one of the grand performance halls are the main reason many venture here, and major city events like the Pride parade and Giants' victory celebrations draw big crowds; the Asian Art Museum and City Hall are worthy sightseeing stops, too.

TOP ATTRACTIONS

Fodor's Choice
★
Asian Art Museum. You don't have to be a connoisseur of Asian art to appreciate a visit to this museum whose monumental exterior conceals a light, open, and welcoming space. The fraction of the Asian's collection on display (about 2,500 pieces out of 15,000-plus total) is laid out thematically and by region, making it easy to follow historical developments.

Begin on the third floor, where highlights of Buddhist art in Southeast Asia and early China include a large, jewel-encrusted, exquisitely painted 19th-century Burmese Buddha and clothed rod puppets from Java. On the second floor you can find later Chinese works, as well as pieces from Korea and Japan. The joy here is all in the details: on a whimsical Korean jar, look for a cobalt tiger jauntily smoking a pipe, or admire the delicacy of the Japanese tea implements. The ground floor is devoted to temporary exhibits, often traveling shows such as recent ones about Balinese art, and the transformation of yoga. ■ TIP➜ During spring and summer, visit the museum the first Thursday evening of the month for extended programs and sip drinks while a DJ spins tunes. ✉ *200 Larkin St., between McAllister and Fulton Sts., Civic Center* ☎ *415/581–3500* ⊕ *www.asianart.org* ⌦ *$15, free 1st Sun. of month; $10 Thurs. 5–9* ⊙ *Tues.–Sun. 10–5; Feb.–Oct., also Thurs. until 9.*

City Hall. This imposing 1915 structure with its massive gold-leaf dome— higher than the U.S. Capitol's—is about as close to a palace as you're going to get in San Francisco. (Alas, the metal detectors detract from the grandeur.) The classic granite-and-marble behemoth was modeled after St. Peter's Basilica in Rome. Architect Arthur Brown Jr., who also designed Coit Tower and the War Memorial Opera House, designed an interior with grand columns and a sweeping central staircase. San Franciscans were thrilled, and probably a bit surprised, when his firm built City Hall in just a few years. The 1899 structure it replaced had taken 27 years to erect, as corrupt builders and politicians lined their pockets with funds earmarked for it. That building collapsed in about 27 seconds during the 1906 earthquake, revealing trash and newspapers mixed into the construction materials.

City Hall was spruced up and seismically retrofitted in the late 1990s, but the sense of history remains palpable. Some noteworthy events that have taken place here include the marriage of Marilyn Monroe and Joe DiMaggio (1954); the hosing—down the central staircase—of civil-rights and freedom-of-speech protesters (1960); the murders of Mayor George Moscone and openly gay supervisor Harvey Milk (1978); the torching of the lobby by angry members of the gay community in response to the light sentence given to the former supervisor who killed both men (1979); and the registrations of scores of gay couples in celebration of the passage of San Francisco's Domestic Partners Act (1991). February 2004 has come to be known as the Winter of Love: thousands of gay and lesbian couples responded to Mayor Gavin Newsom's decision to issue marriage licenses to same-sex partners, turning City Hall into the site of raucous celebration and joyful nuptials for a month before the state Supreme Court ordered the practice stopped. That celebratory scene replayed during 2008, when scores of couples were wed between the court's June ruling that everyone enjoys the civil right to marry and the November passage of California's ballot proposition banning same-sex marriage. In 2013, the U.S. Supreme Court resolved the issue, ruling against the proposition.

On display in the South Light Court are artifacts from the collection of the **Museum of the City of San Francisco** (⊕ *www.sfmuseum.org*), including maps, documents, and photographs. That enormous, 700-pound iron head once crowned the *Goddess of Progress* statue, which topped the old City Hall building until it crumbled during the 1906 earthquake. City Hall's centennial in 2013 kicked off three years of exhibits—the same amount of time it took to raise the building.

Across Polk Street from City Hall is **Civic Center Plaza,** with lawns, walkways, seasonal flower beds, a playground, and an underground parking garage. This sprawling space is generally clean but somewhat grim. A large part of the city's homeless population hangs out here, so the plaza can feel dodgy. ⊠ *Bordered by Van Ness Ave. and Polk, Grove, and McAllister Sts., Civic Center* ☏ *415/554–6023 recorded tour info, 415/554–6139 tour reservations* ⊕ *sfgsa.org/index.aspx?page=1172* ☏ *Free* ⊗ *Weekdays 8–8 except holidays; free tours weekdays at 10, noon, and 2.*

WORTH NOTING

Louise M. Davies Symphony Hall. Fascinating and futuristic-looking, this 2,750-seat hall is the home of the San Francisco Symphony. The glass wraparound lobby and pop-out balcony high on the southeast corner are visible from outside, as is the Henry Moore bronze sculpture that sits on the sidewalk at Van Ness Avenue and Grove Street. The hall's 59 adjustable Plexiglas acoustical disks cascade from the ceiling like hanging windshields. Concerts range from typical symphonic fare to more unusual combinations, such as performers like Al Green and Arlo

Guthrie. Scheduled tours (about 75 minutes), which meet at the Grove Street entrance, take in Davies and the nearby War Memorial Opera House. ⊠ *201 Van Ness Ave., Civic Center* ☎ *415/552–8338* ⊕ *www. sfwmpac.org* ⊡ *Tours $7* ⊗ *Tours Mon. on the hr 10–2.*

War Memorial Opera House. During San Francisco's Barbary Coast days, operagoers smoked cigars, didn't check their revolvers, and expressed their appreciation with "shrill whistles and savage yells," as one observer put it. All the old opera houses were destroyed in the 1906 quake, but lusty support for opera continued. The San Francisco Opera didn't have a permanent home until the War Memorial Opera House was inaugurated in 1932 with a performance of *Tosca*. Modeled after its European counterparts, the building has a vaulted and coffered ceiling, marble foyer, two balconies, and a huge silver art-deco chandelier that resembles a sunburst. The San Francisco Opera performs here from September through December and in summer; the opera house hosts the San Francisco Ballet from February through May, with December *Nutcracker* performances. ⊠ *301 Van Ness Ave., Civic Center* ☎ *415/621–6600* ⊕ *www.sfwmpac.org.*

THE TENDERLOIN

Stretching west of Union Square and north of Civic Center, the Tenderloin could be the city's poster child for urban challenges: low-income families huddle in tiny apartments; single-room-occupancy hotels offer shelter a step up from living on the street; drug dealing and prostitution are rampant and visible; and very few green spaces break up the monotony of high-rises. So why in the world would anyone go out of the way to come here? Well, exceptional Vietnamese food, for one thing, but these days more than just the great *pho* is luring people to the Tenderloin. Trendy watering holes and coffee shops are springing up, with a handful of intrepid hipsters moving into the hood after them. The Tenderloin may be slowly on its way to becoming the next Mission, though for now it remains a gritty slice of San Francisco: come hungry and take a cab, especially at night.

■ TIP→ Some parts of the Tenderloin are more dangerous than others, and a single street can change from block to block. Little Saigon's Larkin Street corridor is relatively safe during the day, as are most streets north of Eddy (an area that realtors insist on calling the TenderNob for its proximity to Nob Hill). Absolutely avoid the last two blocks of Turk Street and Golden Gate Avenue before they meet Market Street.

EXPLORING

Glide Memorial Church. For a rockin' gospel concert and an inclusive, feel-good vibe, head to Glide, where Reverend Cecil Williams, a bear of a man and a local celeb do-gooder, leads a hand-clapping, shout-it-out, get-on-your-feet "celebration." The diverse crowd—gay and straight, all colors of the rainbow, religious and not—is large and enthusiastic. You might recognize the church from the Will Smith film *The Pursuit of Happyness.* ⊠ *330 Ellis St., at Taylor St., Tenderloin* ☎ *415/674–6000* ⊕ *www.glide.org* ⊗ *Gospel services Sun. morning at 9 and 11.*

HAYES VALLEY

An offbeat neighborhood due west of Civic Center, Hayes Valley has terrific eateries, cool watering holes, and great browsing in its funky clothing, home-decor, and design boutiques. Locals love this quarter, but without any big-name draws it remains off the radar for many visitors, though that may change with the opening of the SF Jazz Center on Franklin Street.

Bisected by the Central Freeway until the 1989 Loma Prieta earthquake, Hayes Valley was nondescript and not particularly safe, about as far from a destination neighborhood as you can get. Years of political and legal jockeying resulted in the demolition of the damaged freeway and the creation of Octavia Boulevard as a thoroughfare connecting the freeway with the city's main east–west arteries in Hayes Valley.

Freed of the shadow of the freeway, Hayes Valley has thrived. You feel it on a sunny day in Patricia's Green (Octavia Boulevard, between Hayes and Fell streets), with kids climbing the play dome, chic moms sipping Blue Bottle, and maybe a homeless guy taking a nap. You feel it in the *Great Adventure* mural over the community garden at Octavia and Page Street, and in the Biergarten (Octavia, near Fell Street) over a liter of German brew. This is a real neighborhood where real folks live and a favorite destination for locals. The hipsters have the Mission, the yuppies have the Marina, the edgy indie crowd has the Haight, and now the artsy-design people have modish Hayes Valley. Swing down main drag Hayes Street between Franklin and Laguna streets and you can hit this neighborhood's highlights, including the very popular restaurant, Suppenküche (⇨ *See Where to Eat*).

EXPLORING

SFJAZZ Center. Opened in 2013 to much fanfare, the center is devoted entirely to jazz. The debut week alone saw performances by McCoy Tyner, Joshua Redman, Regina Carter, Chick Corea, and Savion Glover, among others. Walk by and the street-level glass walls will make you feel as if you're inside; head indoors and the acoustics will knock your socks off. Celebrated artists Sandow Birk and Elyse Pignolet created the lobby murals. ■TIP→ Grab dinner at South, a rustic-Mexican restaurant developed by Charles Phan, the acclaimed chef of the Slanted Door; during showtime, you can listen to the musicians playing in the adjacent auditorium. ✉ *201 Franklin St., at Fell St., Hayes Valley* ☎ *866/920–5299* ⊕ *www.sfjazz.org.*

NOB HILL AND RUSSIAN HILL

With Polk Gulch

GETTING ORIENTED

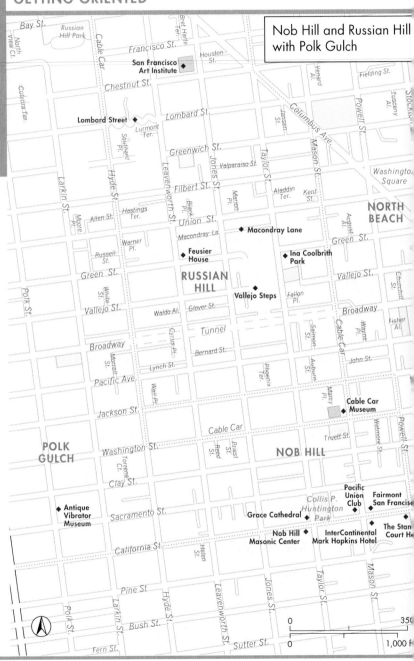

Nob Hill and Russian Hill
with Polk Gulch

Bay St.

Russian Hill Park

North View Ct.

Cable Car

Francisco St.

Bret Harte Ter.

Houston St.

San Francisco Art Institute ◆

Venard Al.

Fielding St.

Chestnut St.

Columbus Ave.

Powell St.

Tuscany Al.

Stockton

Lombard Street ◆

Lombard St.

Southard Pl.

Lurmont Ter.

Hyde St.

Jansen St.

Larkin St.

Cubrta Ter.

Greenwich St.

Valparaiso St.

Taylor St.

Mason St.

Washington Square

Leavenworth St.

Filbert St.

Jones St.

Aladdin Ter.

Kent St.

NORTH BEACH

Moore St.

Allen St.

Hastings Ter.

Black Pl.

Marion Pl.

Union St.

◆ Macondray Lane

August Al.

Green St.

Warner Pl.

Macondray La.

◆ Feusier House

◆ Ina Coolbrith Park

Russell St.

Green St.

White St.

RUSSIAN HILL

Vallejo St.

Church St.

Polk St.

Vallejo St.

Waldo Al.

Glover St.

Vallejo Steps ◆

Fallon Pl.

Broadway

Fisher Al.

Cyrus Pl.

Tunnel

Salmon St.

Wayne Pl.

Cable Car

Broadway

Bernard St.

John St.

Morrell St.

Lynch St.

Phoenix Ter.

Auburn St.

Pacific Ave.

Watt Pl.

Jackson St.

Marcy Pl.

Cable Car Museum ◆

Cable Car

Powell St.

Wetmore St.

POLK GULCH

Washington St.

Torrens Ct.

Reed St.

Priest St.

Truett St.

NOB HILL

Clay St.

Pacific Union Club

Fairmont San Francisc

◆ Antique Vibrator Museum

Sacramento St.

Collis P. Huntington Park

Grace Cathedral ◆

◆

The Stan Court He

California St.

Nob Hill Masonic Center ◆

InterContinental Mark Hopkins Hotel

Haven St.

Mason St.

Pine St.

Leavenworth St.

Jones St.

Taylor St.

Larkin St.

Hyde St.

Polk St.

Bush St.

Sutter St.

Fern St.

0   35(

0   1,000 f

TOP REASONS TO GO

Macondray Lane: Duck into this secret, lush garden lane and walk its narrow, uneven cobblestones.

Vallejo Steps area: Make the steep climb up to lovely Ina Coolbrith Park, then continue up along the glorious garden path of the Vallejo Steps to a spectacular view at the top.

San Francisco Art Institute: Contemplate a Diego Rivera mural and stop at the café for cheap organic coffee and a priceless view of the city and the bay. It may be the best—and cheapest—way to spend an hour in the neighborhood.

Cable Car Museum: Ride a cable car all the way back to the barn, hanging on tight as it clack-clack-clacks its way up Nob Hill, then go behind the scenes at the museum.

Play "Bullitt" on the steepest streets: For the ride of your life, take a drive up and down the city's steepest streets on Russian Hill. A trip over the precipice of Filbert or Jones will make you feel as if you're falling off the edge of the world.

QUICK BITES

Another Cafe. The name may not promise much, but this low-key, two-level café serves up yummy chicken-garlic and other panini, pours locally roasted Bicycle Coffee, and has awesome murals. ✉ *1191 Pine St., Nob Hill* ☎ *415/857–5770* ⊕ *www.anothercafesf.com.*

The Boy's Deli. Tucked in the back of a tiny produce market is a counter serving up some of the biggest, juiciest, best sandwiches in town—strictly to go—along with traditional sides. *2222 Polk St., Russian Hill* ☎ *415/776–3099* ⊕ *theboysdeli.com.*

Swensen's Ice Cream. The original Swensen's has been a neighborhood favorite since it opened in 1948. ✉ *1999 Hyde St., Russian Hill* ☎ *415/775–6818* ⊕ *www.swensensicecream.com.*

GETTING THERE

The thing about Russian Hill and Nob Hill is that they're both especially steep hills. If you're not up for the hike, a cable car is certainly the most exciting way to reach the top. Take the California line for Nob Hill and the Powell–Hyde line for Russian Hill. Buses serve the area as well, such as the 1–California bus for Nob Hill, but the routes only run east–west. Only the cable cars tackle the steeper north–south streets. Driving yourself is a hassle, since parking is a challenge on these crowded, precipitous streets.

PLANNING YOUR TIME

Since walking Nob Hill is (almost) all about gazing at exteriors, touring the neighborhood during daylight hours is a must. The sights here don't require a lot of visiting time—say a half hour each at the Cable Car Museum and Grace Cathedral—but allow time for the walk itself. An afternoon visit is ideal for Russian Hill, so you can browse the shops. You could cover both neighborhoods in three or four hours. If you time it just right, you can finish up with a sunset cocktail at a swanky hotel lounge or the retro-tiki Tonga Room.

4

In place of the quirky charm and cultural diversity that mark other San Francisco neighborhoods, Nob Hill exudes history and good breeding. Topped with some of the city's most elegant hotels, Gothic Grace Cathedral, and private blue-blood clubs, it's the pinnacle of privilege. One hill over, across Pacific Avenue, is another old-family bastion, Russian Hill. It may not be quite as wealthy as Nob Hill, but it's no slouch—and it's got jaw-dropping views.

NOB HILL

Updated by
Denise M. Leto

Nob Hill was officially dubbed during the 1870s when "the Big Four"—Charles Crocker, Leland Stanford, Mark Hopkins, and Collis P. Huntington, who were involved in the construction of the transcontinental railroad—built their hilltop estates. The lingo is thick from this era: those on the hilltop were referred to as "nabobs" (originally meaning a provincial governor from India) and "swells," and the hill itself was called Snob Hill, a term that survives to this day. By 1882 so many estates had sprung up on Nob Hill that Robert Louis Stevenson called it "the hill of palaces." But the 1906 earthquake and fire destroyed all the palatial mansions except for portions of the James Flood brownstone. History buffs may choose to linger here, but for most visitors, a casual glimpse from a cable car will be enough.

⇨ *For more details on the Cable Car Museum, see the Cable Cars feature in Experience San Francisco.*

TOP ATTRACTIONS

FAMILY **Cable Car Museum.** One of the city's best free offerings, this museum is an absolute must for kids. You can even ride a cable car here—all three lines stop between Russian Hill and Nob Hill. The facility, which is inside the city's last cable-car barn, takes the top off the system to let you see how it all works. Eternally humming and squealing, the massive powerhouse cable wheels steal the show. You can also climb aboard a vintage car and take the grip, let the kids ring a cable-car bell (briefly), and check out vintage gear dating from 1873.

The gift shop sells cable-car paraphernalia, including an authentic gripman's bell for $600—it'll sound like Powell Street in your house every day. For significantly less, you can pick up a key chain made from a piece of worn-out cable. ⊠ *1201 Mason St., at Washington St., Nob Hill* ☎ *415/474–1887* ⊕ *www.cablecarmuseum.org* ⊠ *Free* ⊙ *Oct.–Mar., daily 10–5; Apr.–Sept., daily 10–6.*

CLOSE UPS ON THE BROCKLEBANK

The grand Brocklebank Apartments, on the northeast corner of Sacramento and Mason streets across from the Fairmont hotel, might look eerily familiar. In 1958 the complex was showcasaed in Alfred Hitchcock's *Vertigo* (Jimmy Stewart starts trailing Kim Novak here) and in the 1990s it popped up in the miniseries *Tales of the City.*

Grace Cathedral. Not many churches can boast an altarpiece by Keith Haring and not one, but two labyrinths. The seat of the Episcopal Church in San Francisco, this soaring Gothic-style structure, erected on the site of the 19th-century railroad baron Charles Crocker's mansion, took 53 years to build, wrapping up in 1964. The gilded bronze doors at the east entrance were taken from casts of Lorenzo Ghiberti's incredible Gates of Paradise, which are on the Baptistery in Florence, Italy. A black-and-bronze stone sculpture of St. Francis by Beniamino Bufano greets you as you enter.

The 35-foot-wide limestone labyrinth is a replica of the 13th-century stone maze on the floor of Chartres Cathedral. All are encouraged to walk the ¼-mile-long labyrinth, a ritual based on the tradition of meditative walking. There's also a terrazzo outdoor labyrinth on the church's north side. The AIDS Interfaith Chapel, to the right as you enter Grace, contains a metal triptych by the late artist Keith Haring and panels from the AIDS Memorial Quilt. ■ TIP→ Especially dramatic times to view the cathedral are during Thursday-night evensong (5:15 pm) and during special holiday programs. ⊠ *1100 California St., at Taylor St., Nob Hill* ☎ *415/749–6300* ⊕ *www.gracecathedral.org* ⊠ *Free; tours $25* ⊙ *Weekdays 7–6, Sat. 8–6, Sun. 8–7; tour times vary.*

WORTH NOTING

Collis P. Huntington Park. The elegant park west of the Pacific Union Club and east of Grace Cathedral occupies the site of a mansion owned by the "Big Four" railroad baron Collis P. Huntington. He died in 1900, the mansion was destroyed in the 1906 fire, and in 1915 his widow—by then married to Huntington's nephew—donated the land to the city for use as a park. The Huntingtons' neighbors, the Crockers, once owned the *Fountain of the Tortoises,* based on the original in Rome's Piazza Mattei. ■ TIP→ The benches around the fountain offer a welcome break after climbing Nob Hill. ⊠ *Taylor and California Sts., Nob Hill.*

Fairmont San Francisco. The hotel's dazzling opening was delayed a year by the 1906 quake, but since then, the marble palace has hosted presidents, royalty, movie stars, and local nabobs. Things have changed

WALKING THE HILLS

Start a tour of Nob Hill and Russian Hill with a cable-car ride up to California and Powell Streets on Nob Hill (all lines go here). Walking two blocks east you can pass all the Big Four mansions-cum-hotels on the hill. Peek at the Keith Haring triptych in impressive Grace Cathedral; grab a Peet's coffee in the basement café if you need a lift. Next, head down to the Cable Car Museum to see the machinery in action. Then make your way to Russian Hill—a cable car is a fine way to reach the peak—to visit some of the city's loveliest hidden lanes and stairways. At Mason and Vallejo Streets, head up the Vallejo Steps, passing contemplative, terraced Ina Coolbrith Park and beautifully tended private gardens. Take in the sweeping city and bay view from the top of the hill, then head right on Jones Street and duck right under the trellis to wooded and shady Macondray Lane. From here it's a six-block hike to crooked Lombard Street. If you've still got some steam, be sure to go another block to see Diego Rivera's mural and the surprise panoramic view from the San Francisco Art Institute.

since its early days, however: on the eve of World War I, you could get a room for as low as $2.50 per night, meals included. Nowadays, prices go as high as $15,000, which buys a night in the eight-room, contemporary art–filled penthouse suite. Swing through the opulent lobby on your way to tea (served on weekends from 1:30 to 3) at the Laurel Court restaurant; peek through the foyer's floor-to-ceiling windows for a glimpse of the hotel's garden and beehives, where the honey served with tea is produced. Don't miss an evening cocktail (a mai tai is in order) in the kitschy Tonga Room, complete with tiki huts, a sporadic tropical rainstorm, and a floating bandstand. ⊠ *950 Mason St., Nob Hill* ☎ *415/772–5000* ⊕ *www.fairmont.com.*

InterContinental Mark Hopkins Hotel. Built on the ashes of railroad tycoon Mark Hopkins's grand estate (constructed at his wife's urging; Hopkins himself preferred to live frugally), this 19-story hotel went up in 1926. A combination of French château and Spanish Renaissance architecture, with noteworthy terra-cotta detailing, it has hosted statesmen, royalty, and Hollywood celebrities. The 11-room penthouse was turned into a glass-wall cocktail lounge in 1939: the Top of the Mark is remembered fondly by thousands of World War II veterans who jammed the lounge before leaving for overseas duty. Wives and sweethearts watching the ships depart gave the room's northwest nook its name—Weepers' Corner. ■TIP→ With its 360-degree views, the lounge is a wonderful spot for a nighttime drink. ⊠ *999 California St., at Mason St., Nob Hill* ☎ *415/392–3434* ⊕ *www.intercontinentalmarkhopkins.com.*

Nob Hill Masonic Center. Erected by Freemasons in 1957, the hall is familiar to locals mostly as a concert and lecture venue, where such notables as Van Morrison and Al Gore have appeared. An extensive 2014 renovation means more general-admission shows, like concerts by Chrissie Hynde and Cat Stevens. But you don't need a ticket to check out artist Emile Norman's impressive lobby mosaic. Mainly in rich greens and yellows, it depicts the Masons' role in California history. ⊠ *1111 California St., Nob Hill* ☎ *415/776–7457* ⊕ *sfmasonic.com* ☉ *Lobby weekdays 9–5.*

Pacific Union Club. The former home of silver baron James Flood cost a whopping $1.5 million in 1886, when even a stylish Victorian like the Haas-Lilienthal House cost less than $20,000. All that cash did buy some structural stability. The Flood residence (to be precise, its shell) was the only Nob Hill mansion to survive the 1906 earthquake and fire. The Pacific Union Club, a bastion of the wealthy and powerful, purchased the house in 1907 and commissioned Willis Polk to redesign it; the architect added the semicircular wings and third floor. (The ornate fence design dates from the mansion's construction.) It's hard to get the skinny on the club itself; its 700 or so members allegedly follow the directive "no women, no Democrats, no reporters." Needless to say, the club is closed to the public. ⊠ *1000 California St., Nob Hill.*

The Stanford Court Hotel. In 1876 trendsetter Leland Stanford, a California governor and founder of Stanford University, was the first to build an estate on Nob Hill. The only part that survived the earthquake was a basalt-and-granite wall that's been restored; check it out from the eastern side of the hotel. In 1912 an apartment house was built on the site of the former estate, and in 1972 the present-day hotel was constructed from the shell of that building. A stained-glass dome tops the carriage entrance. ⊠ *905 California St., Nob Hill* ☎ *415/989–3500* ⊕ *www.stanfordcourt.com.*

RUSSIAN HILL

Essentially a tony residential neighborhood of spiffy pieds-à-terre, Victorian flats, Edwardian cottages, and boxlike condos, Russian Hill has some of the city's loveliest stairway walks, hidden garden ways, and steepest streets—not to mention those bay views. Several stories explain the origin of Russian Hill's name. One legend has it that Russian farmers raised vegetables here for Farallon Islands seal hunters; another attributes the name to a Russian sailor of prodigious drinking habits who drowned when he fell into a well on the hill. A plaque at the top of the Vallejo Steps gives credence to the version that says sailors of the Russian-American company were buried here in the 1840s. Be sure to visit the sign for yourself—its location offers perhaps the finest vantage point on the hill.

TOP ATTRACTIONS

Fodor'sChoice
★

Ina Coolbrith Park. If you make it all the way up here, you may have the place all to yourself, or at least feel like you do. The park's terraces are carved from a hill so steep that it's difficult to see if anyone else is there or not. Locals love this park because it feels like a secret no one else knows about—one of the city's magic hidden gardens, with a meditative setting and spectacular views of the bay peeking out from among the trees. A poet, Oakland librarian, and niece of Mormon prophet Joseph Smith, Ina Coolbrith (1842–1928) introduced Jack London and Isadora Duncan to the world of books. For years she entertained literary greats in her Macondray Lane home near the park. In 1915 she was named poet laureate of California. ⊠ *Vallejo St. between Mason and Taylor Sts., Russian Hill.*

Lombard Street. The block-long "Crookedest Street in the World" makes eight switchbacks down the east face of Russian Hill between Hyde and Leavenworth streets. Residents bemoan the traffic jam outside their front doors, but the throngs continue. Join the line of cars waiting to drive down the steep hill, or avoid the whole mess and walk down the steps on either side of Lombard. You take in super views of North Beach and Coit Tower whether you walk or drive—though if you're the one behind the wheel, you'd better keep your eye on the road lest you become yet another of the many folks who ram the garden barriers. ■TIP→ **Can't stand the traffic? Thrill seekers of a different stripe may want to head two blocks south of Lombard to Filbert Street. At a gradient of 31.5%, the hair-raising descent between Hyde and Leavenworth streets is the city's steepest. Go slowly!** ⊠ *Lombard St. between Hyde and Leavenworth Sts., Russian Hill.*

Fodor's Choice
★

Macondray Lane. San Francisco has no shortage of impressive, grand homes, but it's the tiny fairy-tale lanes that make most want to move here, and Macondray Lane is the quintessential hidden garden. Enter under a lovely wooden trellis and proceed down a quiet, cobbled pedestrian lane lined with Edwardian cottages and flowering plants and trees. Watch your step—the cobblestones are quite uneven in spots. A flight of steep wooden stairs at the end of the lane leads to Taylor Street—on the way down you can't miss the bay views. If you've read any of Armistead Maupin's *Tales of the City* books, you may find the lane vaguely familiar. It's the thinly disguised setting for part of the series' action. ⊠ *Between Jones and Taylor Sts., and Union and Green Sts., Russian Hill.*

San Francisco Art Institute. A Moorish-tile fountain in a tree-shaded courtyard draws the eye as soon as you enter the institute. The number-one reason for a visit is Mexican master Diego Rivera's *The Making of a Fresco Showing the Building of a City* (1931), in the student gallery to your immediate left inside the entrance. Rivera himself is in the fresco—his broad behind is to the viewer—and he's surrounded by his assistants. They in turn are surrounded by a construction scene, laborers, and city notables such as sculptor Robert Stackpole and architect Timothy Pfleuger. *Making* is one of three San Francisco murals painted by Rivera. The number-two reason to come here is the café, or more precisely the eye-popping, panoramic view from the café, which serves surprisingly decent food for a song.

The older portions of the Art Institute, including the lovely Mission-style bell tower, were erected in 1926. To this day, otherwise pragmatic people claim that ghostly footsteps can be heard in the tower at night. Ansel Adams created the school's fine-arts photography department in 1946, and school directors established the country's first fine-arts film program. Notable faculty and alumni have included painter Richard Diebenkorn and photographers Dorothea Lange, Edward Weston, and Annie Leibovitz.

The **Walter & McBean Galleries** (☎ *415/749–4563 ⊙ Open Tues. 11–7, Wed.–Sat. 11–6*) exhibit the often provocative works of established artists. ⊠ *800 Chestnut St., North Beach* ☎ *415/771–7020* ⊕ *www.sfai.edu* ✉ *Galleries free ⊙ Hrs vary but building generally open Mon.–Sat. 9–7.*

WORTH NOTING

Feusier House. Octagonal houses were once thought to make the best use of space and enhance the physical and mental well-being of their occupants. A brief mid-19th-century craze inspired the construction of several in San Francisco. Only the Feusier House, built in 1857, and the Octagon House in Pacific Heights remain standing. A private residence, the Feusier House is easy to overlook unless you look closely—it's dwarfed by the large-scale apartments around it. Across from the Feusier House is the **1907 Firehouse** (⊠ *1088 Green St.*). Louise M. Davies, the local art patron for whom Symphony Hall is named, bought it from the city in 1957. The firehouse is closed to the public, but it's worth taking in the exterior. ⊠ *1067 Green St., Russian Hill.*

Fodor's Choice
★

Vallejo Steps area. Several Russian Hill buildings survived the 1906 earthquake and fire and remain standing. Patriotic firefighters saved what's become known as the **Flag House** (⊠ *1652–56 Taylor St.*) when they spotted the American flag on the property and doused the flames with seltzer water and wet sand. The owner, a flag collector, fearing the house would burn to the ground, wanted it to go down in style, with "all flags flying." The Flag House, at the southwest corner of Ina Coolbrith Park, is one of a number of California Shingle–style homes in this neighborhood, several of which the architect Willis Polk designed.

Polk drew up the plans for the nearby **Polk-Williams House** (⊠ *Taylor and Vallejo Sts.*) and lived in one of its finer sections, and he was responsible for **1034–1036 Vallejo,** across the street. He also laid out the Vallejo Steps themselves, which climb the steep ridge across Taylor Street from the Flag House. Though very steep, the walk up to Ina Coolbrith Park and beyond is possibly the most pleasurable thing to do while on Russian Hill, rewarding you as it does with glorious views. ▪ **TIP→ If the walk up the steps will be too taxing, park at the top of the steps by heading east on Vallejo from Jones and enjoy the scene from there.** ⊠ *Taylor and Vallejo Sts., steps lead up toward Jones St., Russian Hill.*

POLK GULCH

Polk Gulch, the microhood surrounding north–south Polk Street, hugs the western edges of Nob Hill and Russian Hill but is nothing like either. It's actually two microhoods: Upper Polk Gulch, fairly classy in its northern section, runs from about Union Street south to California Street; Lower Polk Gulch, the rougher southern part, continues south from California to Geary or so.

Polk Gulch was the Castro before the Castro. It was the city's gay neighborhood into the 1970s, hosting San Francisco's first pride parade in 1972 and several festive Halloween extravaganzas. The area became known for tranny bars and gay prostitution but has "straightened" out—lost its edge, some would say. Today the friendly saloon the Cinch, the last remnant of gay Polk, and stalwart holdovers from that earlier time—among them folksy Grubstake, where you can get a giant burger until 4 am nightly—share space with newer mid-range restaurants, a passel of bars and nightclubs, and some browsable, funky stores, not to mention two great doughnut shops and the Antique Vibrator Museum.

Downhill and down-market from its hilltop neighbors, Polk Gulch has been flirting with gentrification for almost a decade, but (female) prostitutes still walk the streets of the Lower Gulch, and the neighborhood feels closer in spirit to the Tenderloin, which it borders. Come to see a lively, scrappy, down-to-earth slice of the city that's forever in transition but rarely seems to change.

EXPLORING

Antique Vibrator Museum. In shapes ranging from rolling pins to eggbeaters and hair dryers, vibrators dating back to the 19th century are displayed in this fun and fascinating museum inside the sex-positive store Good Vibrations. Originally used by physicians to treat hysteria and later marketed as health and beauty aids, vibrators are sold in many mainstream outlets these days—but as "massage aids," not sex toys. Arranged chronologically from the 1880s (the electric vibrator was invented in 1869) to the 1970s, the examples here include the impressive, suitcase-size models of the 1930s, the Magic Fingers beds of the 1950s and '60s, and the more current Ecstasy 2000. ■TIP➜ **Visitors must be 18 or older to enter the store and museum.** ⊠ *1620 Polk St., at Sacramento St., Polk Gulch* ☎ *415/345–0400* ⊕ *antiquevibratormuseum.com* ☞ *Free* ⊙ *Daily 12:30–6:30, Thurs. until 8:30.*

NORTH BEACH

GETTING ORIENTED

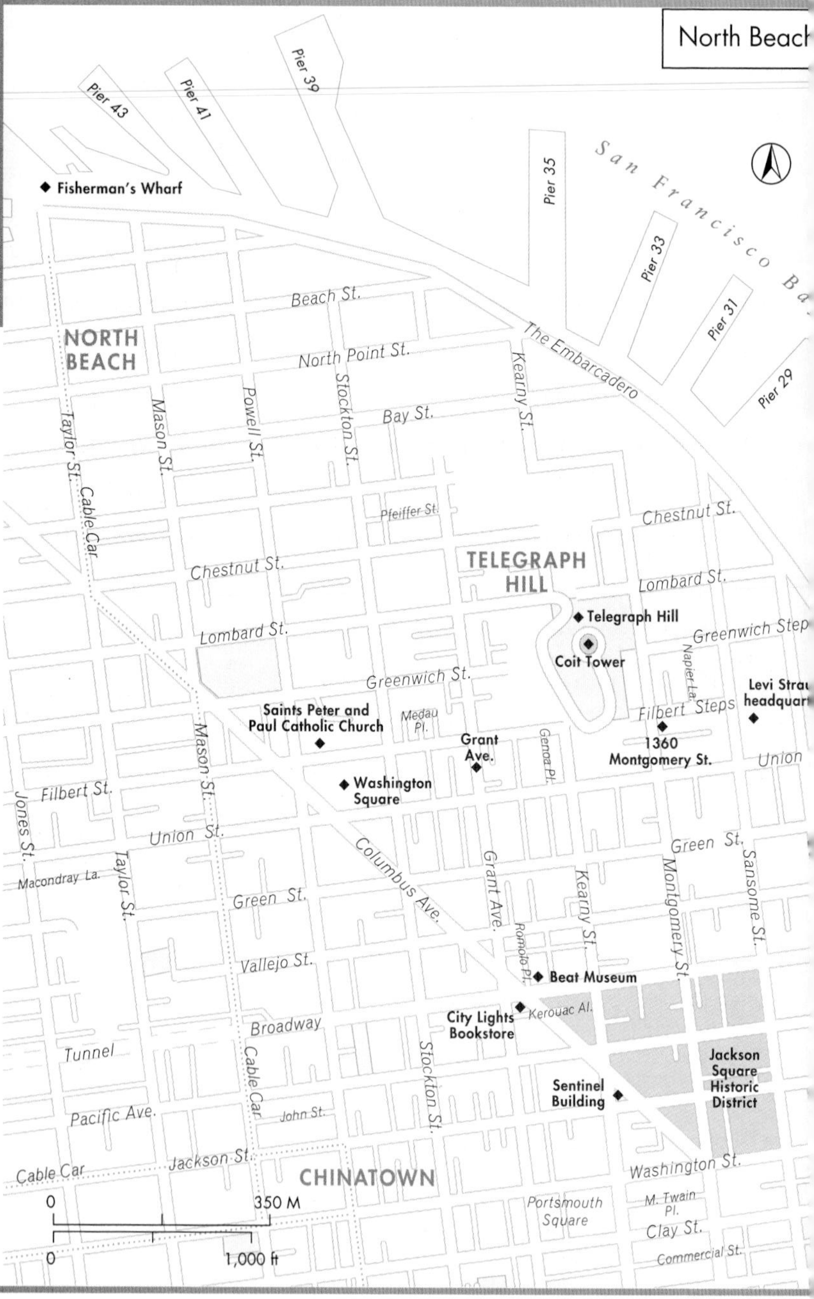

North Beach

Pier 43

Pier 41

Pier 39

Pier 35

San Francisco Bay

Pier 33

Pier 31

Pier 29

◆ Fisherman's Wharf

NORTH BEACH

Beach St.

North Point St.

The Embarcadero

Bay St.

Pfeiffer St.

Chestnut St.

TELEGRAPH HILL

Chestnut St.

Lombard St.

◆ Telegraph Hill

Greenwich Step

Lombard St.

Coit Tower

Greenwich St.

Greenwich St.

Filbert Steps

Levi Strau headquar

Saints Peter and Paul Catholic Church

Medau Pl.

Grant Ave.

1360 Montgomery St.

Union

◆ Washington Square

Filbert St.

Green St.

Union St.

Macondray La.

Green St.

Columbus Ave.

Grant Ave.

Kearny St.

Montgomery St.

Sansome St.

Vallejo St.

Rondo Pl.

◆ Beat Museum

Tunnel

Broadway

City Lights Bookstore

Kerouac Al.

Pacific Ave.

John St.

Stockton St.

Sentinel Building ◆

Jackson Square Historic District

Cable Car

Jackson St.

CHINATOWN

Washington St.

M. Twain Pl.

0 _____ 350 M

Portsmouth Square

Clay St.

0 _____ 1,000 ft

Commercial St.

Taylor St. Cable Car

Mason St.

Powell St.

Stockton St.

Kearny St.

Mason St.

Jones St.

Taylor St.

Cable Car

Napier La.

Genoa Pl.

TOP REASONS TO GO

Espresso, espresso, espresso: Or cappuccino, americano, mocha—however you take your caffeine, this is the neighborhood for it. Hanging out in a café constitutes sightseeing here, so find a chair and get to work.

Colorful watering holes: The high concentration of bars with character, like Tosca Café and Vesuvio, makes North Beach the perfect neighborhood for a pub crawl.

Filbert Steps: Walk down this dizzying stairway from Telegraph Hill's Coit Tower, past lush private gardens and jaw-dropping bay views—and listen for the hill's famous screeching parrots.

Grant Avenue: Check out vanguard boutiques, rambling antiques shops, and cavernous old-time bars, all chockablock on narrow Grant Avenue. The best stuff is crowded into the four blocks between Columbus Avenue and Filbert Street.

Browsing books at City Lights: Illuminate your mind at this Beat-era landmark. Its great book selection, author events, and keen staff make it just as cool as ever.

QUICK BITES

Liguria Bakery. The Soracco family has been baking focaccia in North Beach for more than a century, and many consider their fresh-from-the-oven bread the neighborhood's best. Arrive before noon: when the focaccia is gone, the bakery closes. ✉ *1700 Stockton St., at Filbert St., North Beach* ☏ *415/421–3786.*

Molinari Delicatessen. The friendly *paesans* behind the counter serve up the most delicious, and quite possibly the biggest, sandwiches in town. Take a number, grab your bread from the bin, and gaze upon the sandwich board. If you want to eat in, say a prayer to the patron saint of table nabbing— there are only a few tables, outside. Fortunately, Washington Square Park is close by. ✉ *373 Columbus Ave., at Vallejo St., North Beach* ☏ *415/421–2337.*

GETTING THERE

The Powell–Mason cable-car line can drop you within a block of Washington Square Park, in the heart of North Beach. The 30–Stockton and 15–3rd Street buses run to the neighborhood from Market Street. Once you're here, North Beach is a snap to explore on foot. Most of it is relatively flat—but climbing Telegraph Hill to reach Coit Tower is another story entirely.

PLANNING YOUR TIME

There's no bad time of day to visit this quarter. The cafés buzz from morning to night, the shops along main drags Columbus Avenue and Broadway tend to stay open until at least 6 or 7 pm, and late-night revelers don't start checking their watches until about 2 am. Sunday is quieter, since some shops close (though City Lights is open daily, until midnight).

Plan to spend a few hours here. It's all about lingering, and the only major "sightseeing" spot is Coit Tower. The walk up to the tower is strenuous but rewarding; if you can tough it, make time for it. If you're driving, keep in mind that parking is difficult, especially at night.

5

Sightseeing
★★
Nightlife
★★★★
Dining
★★★
Lodging
★
Shopping
★★★

San Francisco novelist Herbert Gold calls North Beach "the longest-running, most glorious, American bohemian operetta outside Greenwich Village." Indeed, to anyone who's spent some time in its eccentric old bars and cafés, North Beach evokes everything from the Barbary Coast days to the no-less-rowdy Beatnik era.

NORTH BEACH

Updated by
Denise M. Leto

Italian bakeries appear frozen in time, homages to Jack Kerouac and Allen Ginsberg pop up everywhere, and strip joints, the modern equivalent of the Barbary Coast's "houses of ill repute," do business on Broadway. With its outdoor café tables, throngs of tourists, and holiday vibe, this is probably the part of town Europeans are thinking of when they say San Francisco is the most European city in America.

The neighborhood truly was a beach at the time of the gold rush—the bay extended into the hollow between Telegraph and Russian hills. Among the first immigrants to Yerba Buena during the early 1840s were young men from the northern provinces of Italy. The Genoese started the fishing industry in the newly renamed boomtown of San Francisco, as well as a much-needed produce business. Later, Sicilians emerged as leaders of the fishing fleets and eventually as proprietors of the seafood restaurants lining Fisherman's Wharf. Meanwhile, their Genoese cousins established banking and manufacturing empires.

Once almost exclusively Italian American, today's North Beach has only a small percentage of Italians (many of them elderly), with growing Chinese and San Francisco yuppie populations. But walk down narrow Romolo Place (off Broadway east of Columbus) or Genoa Place (off Union west of Kearny) or Medau Place (off Filbert west of Grant) and you can feel the immigrant Italian roots of this neighborhood. Locals know that most of the city's finest Italian restaurants are elsewhere, but North Beach is the place that puts folks in mind of Italian food, and there are many decent options to choose from. Bakeries sell focaccia fresh from the oven; eaten warm or cold, it's the perfect portable food.

A NORTH BEACH WALK

To hit the highlights of the neighborhood, start off with a browse at Beat landmark **City Lights Bookstore.** For cool boutique shopping, head north up **Grant Avenue.** Otherwise, it's time to get down to the serious business of hanging out. Make a left onto **Columbus Avenue** when you leave the bookstore and walk the strip until you find a café table or pastry display that calls your name.

Fortified, continue down Columbus to **Washington Square,** where you can walk or take the 39 bus up **Telegraph Hill** to Coit Tower's views. Be sure to take in the gorgeous gardens along the **Filbert Steps** on the way down. Finally, reward yourself by returning to **Columbus Avenue** for a drink at one of the atmosphere-steeped watering holes like **Tosca** or **Specs.**

Many other aromas fill the air: coffee beans, deli meats and cheeses, Italian pastries, and—always—pungent garlic. ⇨ *For more on the North Beach food scene, see the Where to Eat chapter.*

TOP ATTRACTIONS

Fodor'sChoice
★
City Lights Bookstore. Take a look at the exterior of the store: the replica of a revolutionary mural destroyed in Chiapas, Mexico by military forces; the art banners hanging above the windows; and the sign that says "Turn your sell [sic] phone off. Be here now." This place isn't just doling out best sellers. Designated a city landmark, this hangout of Beat-era writers—Allen Ginsberg and store founder Lawrence Ferlinghetti among them—and independent publisher remains a vital part of San Francisco's literary scene. Browse the three levels of poetry, philosophy, politics, fiction, history, and local zines, to the tune of creaking wood floors. ■ TIP➜ **Be sure to check the calendar of literary events.**

Back in the day, the basement was a kind of literary living room, where writers like Ginsberg and Jack Kerouac would read and even receive mail. Ferlinghetti cemented City Lights' place in history by publishing Ginsberg's *Howl and Other Poems* in 1956. The small volume was ignored in the mainstream . . . until Ferlinghetti and the bookstore manager were arrested for obscenity and corruption of youth. In the landmark First Amendment trial that followed, the judge exonerated both men, declaring that a work that has "redeeming social significance" can't be obscene. *Howl* went on to become a classic.

Stroll Kerouac Alley, branching off Columbus Avenue next to City Lights, to read the quotes from Ferlinghetti, Maya Angelou, Confucius, John Steinbeck, and the street's namesake embedded in the pavement. ✉ *261 Columbus Ave., North Beach* ☎ *415/362–8193* ⊕ *www.citylights.com* ☾ *Daily 10 am–midnight.*

Coit Tower. Whether or not you agree that it resembles a fire-hose nozzle, this 210-foot tower is among San Francisco's most distinctive skyline sights. Although the monument wasn't intended as a tribute to firemen, it's often considered as such because of the donor's special attachment to the local fire company. As the story goes, a young gold rush–era girl, Lillie Hitchcock Coit (known as Miss Lil), was a fervent admirer of her

Lolling around Washington Square, postespresso, is a fine use of a sunny afternoon.

local fire company—so much so that she once deserted a wedding party and chased down the street after her favorite engine, Knickerbocker No. 5, while clad in her bridesmaid finery. She became the Knickerbocker Company's mascot and always signed her name "Lillie Coit 5." When Lillie died in 1929 she left the city $125,000 to "expend in an appropriate manner . . . to the beauty of San Francisco."

You can ride the elevator to the top of the tower—the only thing you have to pay for here—to enjoy the view of the Bay Bridge and the Golden Gate Bridge; due north is Alcatraz Island. Most visitors saunter right past the 19 fabulous Depression-era murals inside the tower that depict California's economic and political life, but take the time to appreciate the first New Deal art project supported by taxpayer money. The federal government commissioned the paintings from 25 local artists, and ended up funding a controversy. The radical Mexican painter Diego Rivera inspired the murals' socialist-realist style, with its biting cultural commentary, particularly about the exploitation of workers. At the time the murals were painted, clashes between management and labor along the waterfront and elsewhere in San Francisco were widespread. The elements, the thousands of visitors that pass by them every year, and the lack of climate control in the tower have taken their toll on the murals, but restoration work done on the tower in 2013 should help protect them. ■TIP→ The views from the tower's base are also expansive—and free. Parking at Coit Tower is limited; in fact, you may have to wait (and wait) for a space. Spare yourself the frustration and hike up, if you're in good shape, or take the 39 bus. ⊠ *Telegraph Hill Blvd. at Greenwich St. or Lombard St., North Beach* ☎ *415/362–0808*

CLOSE UP

Top 3 Espresso Spots in North Beach

Caffè Trieste. The Giotta family celebrates the art of a good espresso as well as a good tune at Caffè Trieste. Every Saturday from 2 pm to 4 pm, the family presents a weekly musical. Arrive early to secure seats. The program ranges from Italian pop and folk music to operas, and patrons are encouraged to participate. There's live music at other times during the week as well. If you're one of the few people in creation who hasn't begun a screenplay, here's some inspiration: legend has it that Francis Ford Coppola wrote *The Godfather* screenplay here. ⊠ *601 Vallejo St., at Grant Ave., North Beach* ☎ *415/392–6739* ⊕ *www.caffetrieste.com.*

Mario's Bohemian Cigar Store. Intimate, triangular Mario's Bohemian Cigar Store serves up great hot focaccia sandwiches and North Beach–worthy espresso at its few tables and beautiful antique oak bar under old-time posters. On sunny days,

take your order across the street to Washington Square for a classic San Francisco picnic. ⊠ *566 Columbus Ave., North Beach* ☎ *415/362–0536.*

Caffè Roma. A glance at the menu board—"Espresso: $1.80, Espresso with lemon: $20"—will clue you in that Caffè Roma takes its coffee a lot more seriously than it takes itself. And if you've got a problem with that, owner Tony Azzollini will convince you, from his refusal to make your coffee extra hot to his insistence that you drink your espresso the moment it's brewed. Airy and decidedly undistracting—black and white marble is the predominant theme—Roma is a no-nonsense coffee drinker's pit stop for a hot cup as well as coffee drinks, pastries, and wine. Spot the massive red roaster in the window and you'll know you're here. And if you insist on the lemon twist, you deserve to pay. ⊠ *526 Columbus Ave., North Beach* ☎ *415/296–7942.*

5

⌨ *Free; elevator to top $7* ☉ *Mar.–Sept., daily 10–5:30; Oct.–Feb., daily 9–4:30.*

Fodor's Choice ★ **Telegraph Hill.** Residents here have some of the city's best views, as well as the most difficult ascents to their aeries. The hill rises from the east end of Lombard Street to a height of 284 feet and is capped by Coit Tower. Imagine lugging your groceries up that! If you brave the slope, though, you can be rewarded with a "secret treasure" San Francisco moment. Filbert Street starts up the hill, then becomes the **Filbert Steps** when the going gets too steep. You can cut between the Filbert Steps and another flight, the **Greenwich Steps**, on up to the hilltop. As you climb, you can pass some of the city's oldest houses and be surrounded by beautiful, flowering private gardens. In some places the trees grow over the stairs so it feels like you're walking through a green tunnel; elsewhere, you'll have wide-open views of the bay. The cypress trees that grow on the hill are a favorite roost of local avian celebrities the wild parrots of Telegraph Hill; you'll hear the cries of the cherry-headed conures if they're nearby. And the telegraphic name? It comes from the hill's status as the first Morse code signal station back in 1853. ⊠ *Bordered by Lombard, Filbert, Kearny, and Sansome Sts., North Beach.*

CLOSE UP

The Birds

While on Telegraph Hill, you might be startled by a chorus of piercing squawks and a rushing sound of wings. No, you're not about to have a Hitchcock bird-attack moment. These small, vivid green parrots with cherry red heads number in the hundreds; they're descendants of former pets that escaped or were released by their owners. (The birds dislike cages, and they bite if bothered . . . must've been some disillusioned owners along the way.)

The parrots like to roost high in the aging cypress trees on the hill, chattering and fluttering, sometimes taking wing en masse. They're not popular with some residents, but they did find a champion in local bohemian Mark Bittner, a former street musician. Bittner began chronicling their habits, publishing a book and battling the homeowners who wanted to cut down the cypresses. A documentary, *The Wild Parrots of Telegraph Hill*, made the issue a cause célèbre. In 2007 City Hall, which recognizes a golden goose when it sees one, stepped in and brokered a solution to keep the celebrity birds in town. The city would cover the homeowners' insurance worries and plant new trees for the next generation of wild parrots.

WORTH NOTING

OFF THE BEATEN PATH

1360 Montgomery Street. In the 1947 film *Dark Passage* Humphrey Bogart plays an escaped prisoner from San Quentin convicted of killing his wife. His real-life wife, Lauren Bacall, befriends him and lets him hole up in her apartment, inside this fantastic art-deco building. From the street you can view the etched-glass gazelles and palms counterpointing a silvered fresco of a heroic bridge worker. ⊠ *Montgomery St. between Union and Filbert Sts., near top of Filbert Steps, North Beach.*

Beat Museum. "Museum" might be a stretch for this tiny storefront that's half bookstore, half memorabilia collection. You can see the 1949 Hudson from the movie version of *On the Road* and the shirt Neal Cassady wore while driving Ken Kesey's Merry Prankster bus, "Further." There are also manuscripts, letters, and early editions by Jack Kerouac, Allen Ginsberg, and Lawrence Ferlinghetti, but the true treasure here is the passionate and well-informed staff, which often includes the museum's founder, Jerry Cimino: your short visit may turn into an hours-long trip through the Beat era. ■ TIP→ The excellent two-hour walking tour goes beyond the museum to take in favorite Beat watering holes and hangouts in North Beach. ⊠ *540 Broadway, North Beach* ☎ *415/399–9626* ⊕ *www.thebeatmuseum.org* ☞ *$8; walking tours $30* ⊗ *Sun.–Thurs. 10–7, Fri. and Sat. 10–10.*

Grant Avenue. Originally called Calle de la Fundación, Grant Avenue is the oldest street in the city, but it's got plenty of young blood. Here dusty bars such as the Saloon and perennial favorites like the Savoy Tivoli mix with hotshot boutiques, odd curio shops like the antique jumble that is Aria, atmospheric cafés such as the boho haven Caffè Trieste, and authentic Italian delis. While the street runs from Union Square through Chinatown, North Beach, and beyond, the fun stuff in this neighborhood is crowded into the four blocks between Columbus Avenue and Filbert Street. ⊠ *North Beach*.

Levi Strauss headquarters. The carefully landscaped complex appears so collegiate that it's affectionately known as LSU—short for Levi Strauss University. Lawns complement the redbrick buildings, and gurgling fountains drown out the sounds of traffic, providing a perfect environment for brown-bag and picnic lunches. The Vault, the lobby exhibition space, has displays focusing on the history of the company, including jeans that saw the gold rush, videos about Levi's marketing and textile restoration, and temporary displays such as the jeans made for celebs like Lady Gaga and Elton John. ■TIP➔ You can purchase Levi's and Dockers straight from the source at the cozy lobby boutique. The wonderful Filbert Steps to Coit Tower are across the street. ⊠ *Levi's Plaza, 1155 Battery St., North Beach* ☎ *415/501–6000* ⊕ *www.levistrauss.com* ☒ *Free* ☉ *Weekdays 9–6, weekends noon–5.*

> **O PIONEERS!**
>
> The corner of Broadway and Columbus Avenue witnessed an unusual historic breakthrough. Here stood the Condor Club, where in 1964 Carol Doda became the country's first dancer to break the topless barrier. A bronze plaque honors the milestone (only in SF). And Doda, naturally, now owns a lingerie store in Cow Hollow.

Saints Peter and Paul Catholic Church. Camera-toting visitors focus their lenses on the Romanesque splendor of what's often called the Italian Cathedral. Completed in 1924, the church has Disneyesque stone-white towers that are local landmarks. Mass reflects the neighborhood; it's given in English, Italian, and Chinese. (This is one of the few churches in town where you can hear Mass in Italian.) Following their 1954 City Hall wedding, Marilyn Monroe and Joe DiMaggio had their wedding photos snapped here. ■TIP➔ On the first Sunday of October, a Mass followed by a parade to Fisherman's Wharf celebrates the Blessing of the (Fishing) Fleet. Also in October is the Italian Heritage Parade in North Beach. The country's oldest Italian celebration, it began in 1869. ⊠ *666 Filbert St., at Washington Sq., North Beach* ☎ *415/421–0809* ⊕ *www. sspeterpaulsf.org/church.*

Sentinel Building. A striking triangular shape and a gorgeous green patina make this 1907 flatiron building at the end of Columbus Avenue a visual knockout. In the 1970s local filmmaker Francis Ford Coppola bought the building to use for his production company. The ground floor houses Coppola's stylish wine bar, **Café Zoetrope.** Stop in for wines from the Coppola vineyards in Napa and Sonoma, simple Italian dishes, and foodie gifts. ⊠ *916 Kearny St., at Columbus Ave., North Beach.*

Washington Square. Once the daytime social heart of Little Italy, this grassy patch has changed character numerous times over the years. The Beats hung out here in the 1950s, hippies camped out in the 1960s and early '70s, and nowadays you're more likely to see kids of Southeast Asian descent tossing a Frisbee than Italian folks reminiscing about the old country. In the morning, elderly Asians perform the motions of tai chi. Then and later you might see homeless people hanging out on the benches, and by midday young locals sunbathing or running their dogs. Lillie Hitchcock Coit, in yet another show of affection for San Francisco's firefighters, donated the statue of two firemen with a child they rescued. ■ TIP➜ The North Beach Festival, the city's oldest street fair, celebrates the area's Italian culture here each June. ⊠ *Bordered by Columbus Ave. and Stockton, Filbert, and Union Sts., North Beach.*

ON THE
WATERFRONT

GETTING ORIENTED

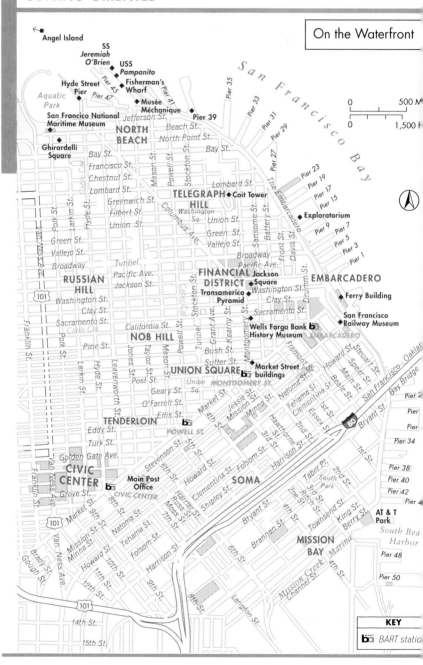

On the Waterfront

GETTING THERE

The Powell–Hyde and Powell–Mason cable-car lines both end near Fisherman's Wharf. The walk from downtown through North Beach to the northern waterfront is lovely, and if you stick to Columbus Avenue, the incline is relatively gentle. F-line trolleys run all the way down Market to the Embarcadero, then north to the wharf, but a packed trolley or two may pass by before one with room stops.

TOP REASONS TO GO

Ferry Building: Join locals eyeing luscious produce and foods prepared by some of the city's best chefs at San Francisco's premier farmers' market on Saturday morning.

Alcatraz: Go from a scenic bay tour to "the hole"—solitary confinement in absolute darkness—while inmates and guards tell you stories about what life was really like on the Rock.

F-line: Grab a polished wooden seat aboard one of the city's vintage streetcars and clatter down the tracks toward the Ferry Building's spire.

Exploratorium: Play with the ultimate marble run, touch your way through the pitch-black Tactile Dome, or explore yourself in the Science of Sharing at the city's beloved hands-on science museum, in its spectacular new bayside home.

QUICK BITES

The Ferry Building is a favorite spot for a bite on the Embarcadero.

Miette. If you need a sweet treat, head to pink Miette, where the cakes and pastries are absolute organic perfection. ☎ 415/837-0300 ⊕ www.miette.com.

Out the Door. Grab something to go from the beloved Vietnamese restaurant Slanted Door's takeout counter. ☎ 415/321-3740 ⊕ www.outthedoors.com.

PLANNING YOUR TIME

If you're planning to go to Alcatraz, be sure to buy your tickets in advance, as tours frequently sell out. Alcatraz ferries leave from Pier 33—so there isn't a single good reason to suffer Pier 39's tacky, overpriced attractions. If you're a sailor at heart, though, definitely spend an hour with the historic ships of the Hyde Street Pier.

FERRIES

The bay is a huge part of San Francisco's charm, and getting out on the water gives you an attractive and unique (though windy) perspective on the city. ■TIP➔ A ride on a commuter ferry is cheaper than a cruise, and just as lovely.

Blue & Gold Fleet. This ferry operator offers bay cruises and, in summer, high-speed Rocket-Boat rides, as well as commuter service to Oakland, Alameda, Tiburon, Sausalito, Vallejo, and Angel Island. ⊠ Pier 39, Fisherman's Wharf ☎ 415/705-5555 ⊕ www.blueandgoldfleet.com.

Red and White Fleet. Choose from among the widest range of tour options, including sunset cruises from April to October. ⊠ Pier 43½, Fisherman's Wharf ☎ 415/673-2900 ⊕ www.redandwhite.com.

6

San Francisco's waterfront neighborhoods have fabulous views and utterly different personalities. Kitschy, overpriced Fisherman's Wharf struggles to maintain the last shreds of its existence as a working wharf, while Pier 39 is a full-fledged consumer circus. The Ferry Building draws well-heeled locals with its culinary pleasures, firmly connecting the Embarcadero and downtown. Between the Ferry Building and Pier 39 a former maritime no-man's-land is filling in with the recently relocated Exploratorium, a new $90-million cruise-ship terminal, Alcatraz Landing, fashionable waterfront restaurants, and restored, pedestrian-friendly piers.

FISHERMAN'S WHARF

Updated by
Denise M. Leto

The crack of fresh Dungeness crab, the aroma of sourdough warm from the oven, the cry of the gulls—in some ways you can experience Fisherman's Wharf today as it has been for more than 100 years. Italians began fishing these waters in the 19th century as immigrants to booming Barbary Coast San Francisco. Family businesses established generations ago continue to this day—look for the Alioto-Lazio Fish Company, selling crab fresh off the boat here for more than 70 years, and Castagnola's restaurant, serving Italian food and seafood since 1916.

As the local fishing industry has contracted and environmental awareness has changed fishing regulations, Fisherman's Wharf has morphed. Fewer families make a living off the sea here, fewer fishing boats go out, and more of the wharf survives on tourist dollars. You'll see more schlock here than in any other neighborhood in town: overpriced food alongside discount electronics stores, bargain-luggage outlets, and cheap T-shirts and souvenirs.

It's enough to send locals running for the hills, but there are things here worth experiencing. Explore maritime history aboard the fabulous ships of the Hyde Street Pier, amuse yourself early-20th-century style with the mechanical diversions at Musée Mécanique, and grab a bowl of chowder or some Dungeness crab from one of the stands along Jefferson Street to get a taste of what made Fisherman's Wharf what it is in the first place. If you come early, you can avoid the crowds and get a sense of the Wharf's functional side: it's not entirely an amusement-park replica.

TOP ATTRACTIONS

FAMILY

Fodor's Choice

★

Hyde Street Pier. Cotton candy and souvenirs are all well and good, but if you want to get to the heart of the Wharf—boats—there's no better place to do it than at this pier, one of the Wharf area's best bargains. Depending on the time of day, you might see boatbuilders at work or children pretending to man an early-1900s ship.

Don't pass up the centerpiece collection of historic vessels, part of the **San Francisco Maritime National Historic Park,** almost all of which can be boarded. The *Balclutha,* an 1886 full-rigged three-masted sailing vessel that's more than 250 feet long, sailed around Cape Horn 17 times. Kids especially love the *Eureka,* a side-wheel passenger and car ferry, for her onboard collection of vintage cars. The *Hercules* is a steam-powered tugboat, and the *C.A. Thayer* is a beautifully restored three-masted schooner.

Across the street from the pier and a museum in itself is the maritime park's **Visitor Center** (✉ *499 Jefferson St.* ☎ *415/447–5000* ⊙ *Open June–Aug., daily 9:30–5:30; Sept.–May, daily 9:30–5*), whose fun, large-scale exhibits make it an engaging stop. See a huge First Order Fresnel lighthouse lens and a shipwrecked boat. Then stroll through time in the exhibit "The Waterfront," where you can touch the timber from a gold rush–era ship recovered from below the Financial District, peek into 19th-century storefronts, and see the sails of an Italian fishing vessel. ✉ *Hyde and Jefferson Sts., Fisherman's Wharf* ☎ *415/561–7100* ⊕ *www.nps.gov/safr* ✉ *Ships $5 (ticket good for 5 days)* ⊙ *June–Aug., daily 9:30–5:30; Sept.–May, daily 9:30–5.*

QUICK
BITES

Buena Vista Café. Locals love the cheery Buena Vista Café, which claims to be the first place in the United States to have served Irish coffee. The bartenders serve about 2,000 Irish coffees a day, so it's always crowded; try for a table overlooking Victorian Park and its cable-car turntable.

◼ TIP➔ The café dishes up great breakfasts, including crab omelets and crab Benedict. ✉ *2765 Hyde St., Fisherman's Wharf* ☎ *415/474–5044* ⊕ *thebuenavista.com* ⊙ *Weekdays 9 am–2 am, weekends 8 am–2 am.*

FAMILY

Fodor's Choice

★

Musée Mécanique. Once a staple at Playland-at-the-Beach, San Francisco's early 20th-century amusement park, the antique mechanical contrivances at this time-warped arcade—including peep shows and nickelodeons—make it one of the most worthwhile attractions at the Wharf. Some favorites are the giant and rather creepy "Laffing Sal," an arm-wrestling machine, the world's only steam-powered motorcycle,

6

and mechanical fortune-telling figures that speak from their curtained boxes. Note the depictions of race that betray the prejudices of the time: stoned Chinese figures in the "Opium-Den" and clown-faced African Americans eating watermelon in the "Mechanical Farm." ■TIP➔ Admission is free, but you'll need quarters to bring the machines to life. ✉ *Pier 45, Shed A, Fisherman's Wharf* ☎ *415/346–2000* ⊕ *www.museemechanique.org* 🎫 *Free* ⊙ *Weekdays 10–7, weekends 10–8.*

FAMILY   **Pier 39.** The city's most popular waterfront attraction draws millions of visitors each year who come to browse through its shops and concessions hawking every conceivable form of souvenir. The pier can be quite crowded, and the numerous street performers may leave you feeling more harassed than entertained. Arriving early in the morning ensures you a front-row view of the sea lions that bask here, but if you're here to shop—and make no mistake about it, Pier 39 wants your money—be aware that most stores don't open until 9:30 or 10 (later in winter).

Brilliant colors enliven the double-decker **San Francisco Carousel** (🎫 *$3 per ride*), decorated with images of such city landmarks as the Golden Gate Bridge and Lombard Street.

Follow the sound of barking to the northwest side of the pier to view the **sea lions** that flop about the floating docks. During the summer, orange-clad naturalists answer questions and offer fascinating facts about the playful pinnipeds—for example, that most of the animals here are males.

At the **Aquarium of the Bay** (☎ *415/623–5300 or 888/732–3483* ⊕ *www.aquariumofthebay.org* 🎫 *$19.95, hrs vary but at least 10–6 daily*) moving walkways transport you through a space surrounded on three sides by water filled with indigenous San Francisco Bay marine life, from fish and plankton to sharks. Many find the aquarium overpriced; if you can, take advantage of the family rate (🎫 *$64 for 2 adults and 2 kids under 12*).

Parking is across the street at the **Pier 39 Garage** (*with validation from a Pier 39 restaurant, 1 hr free before 6 pm, 2 hrs after 6 pm*), off Powell Street at the Embarcadero; look for the mural of the gray whales to spot it. ✉ *Beach St. at Embarcadero, Fisherman's Wharf* ⊕ *www.pier39.com.*

OFF THE
BEATEN
PATH
SS Jeremiah O'Brien. A participant in the D-Day landing in Normandy during World War II, this Liberty Ship freighter is one of two such vessels (out of more than 2,700 built) still in working order. Onboard you can peek at the crew's living quarters—bedding and personal items make it look as if they've just stepped away for a moment—and the officers' mess hall. The large display of the Normandy invasion, one of many exhibits onboard, was a gift from France, To keep the 1943 ship in sailing shape, the steam engine—which appears in the film *Titanic*—is operated dockside seven times a year on special "steaming weekends." Cruises take place several times a year between May and October, and the vessel is open to visitors daily. ✉ *Pier 45, Fisherman's Wharf* ☎ *415/544–0100* ⊕ *www.ssjeremiahobrien.org* 🎫 *$12 (family pass $25)* ⊙ *Daily 9–4.*

WORTH NOTING

Angel Island. For an outdoorsy adventure and some fascinating history, consider a day at this island northwest of Alcatraz. Discovered by Spaniards in 1775 and declared a U.S. military reserve 75 years later, the island was used as a screening ground for Asian, mostly Chinese, immigrants—who were often held for months, even years, before being granted entry—from 1910 until 1940. You can visit the restored Immigration Station, from the dock where detainees landed to the barracks where you can see the poems in Chinese script they etched onto the walls. In 1963 the government designated Angel Island a state park. Today people come for picnics, hikes along the scenic 5-mile path that winds around the island's perimeter, and tram tours that explain the park's history. Twenty-five bicycles are permitted on the ferry on a first-come, first-served basis, and you can rent mountain bikes for $10 an hour or $40 a day at the landing (daily April through October; call during other times). There are also a dozen primitive campsites. Blue & Gold Fleet is the only Angel Island ferry service with departures from San Francisco; boats leave from Pier 41. ⌧ *Pier 41, Fisherman's Wharf* ☎ *415/435–1915 park information and ferry schedules, 415/705–5555, 800/426–8687 tickets* ⊕ *www.parks.ca.gov, www.angelisland.com* ⌨ *$17 round-trip* ⊗ *Daily 8 am–sunset.*

Ghirardelli Square. Most of the redbrick buildings in this early-20th-century complex were once part of the Ghirardelli factory. Now tourists come here to pick up the famous chocolate, though you can purchase it all over town and save yourself a trip to what is essentially a mall. But this is the only place to watch the cool chocolate manufactory in action. Placards throughout the square describe the factory's history. ⌧ *900 North Point St., Fisherman's Wharf* ☎ *415/775–5500* ⊕ *www. ghirardellisq.com.*

FAMILY **San Francisco National Maritime Museum.** You'll feel as if you're out to sea when you step aboard, er, inside this sturdy, round, ship-shape structure dubbed the Bathhouse Building. The first floor of the recently renovated museum, part of the **San Francisco Maritime National Historical Park,** has stunningly restored undersea dreamscape murals and some of the museum's intricate ship models. Also on view is a piece of the *Niantic,* a whaling ship abandoned by its crew during the gold rush near the present-day site of the Transamerica Pyramid; an old-time diorama shows the *Niantic* serving as a hotel along the wharf where it docked. Upstairs and across the balcony, exhibit spaces feature rotating exhibitions on nautical topics. The first-floor balcony overlooks the beach and has lovely WPA-era tile designs. ■ TIP→ **If you've got young kids in tow, the museum makes a great quick, free stop. Then pick up ice cream at Ghirardelli Square across the street and enjoy it on the beach or next door in Victorian Park, where you can watch the cable cars turn around.** ⌧ *Aquatic Park, foot of Polk St., Fisherman's Wharf* ☎ *415/447–5000* ⊕ *www.nps.gov/safr* ⌨ *Donation suggested* ⊗ *Daily 10–4.*

USS *Pampanito.* Get an intriguing, if mildly claustrophobic, glimpse into life on a submarine during World War II on this small, 80-man sub, which sank six Japanese warships and damaged four others. ■ TIP→ **There's not much in the way of interpretive signs, so opt for**

6

DID YOU KNOW?

Cable cars have been running up and down the hills of San Francisco since 1873. For the first two days after they were introduced, rides were free because passengers were afraid to get on.

ESCAPE FROM ALCATRAZ

Federal-prison officials liked to claim that it was impossible to escape Alcatraz, and for the most part, that assertion was true. For seasoned swimmers, though, the trip has never posed a problem—in fact, it's been downright popular.

In the 1930s, in an attempt to dissuade the feds from convert-ing Alcatraz into a prison, a handful of schoolgirls made the swim to the city. At age 60, native son Jack LaLanne did it (for the second time) while shackled and towing a 1,000-pound rowboat. Every year a couple of thousand participants take the plunge during the annual Escape from Alcatraz Triathlon. Heck, a dog made the crossing in 2005 and finished well ahead of most of the (human) pack. And since 2006, seven-year-old Braxton Bilbrey remains the youngest "escapee" on record. Incidentally, those reports of shark-infested waters are true—but the sharks aren't a dangerous species.

the audio tour to learn about what you're seeing. ⊠ *Pier 45, Fisherman's Wharf* ☎ *415/775–1943* ⊕ *www.maritime.org/pamphome.htm* ⊡ *$12 (family pass $25)* ⊘ *Oct.–late May, Sun.–Thurs. 9–6, Fri. and Sat. 9–8; late May–Sept., daily 9–8.*

EMBARCADERO

Stretching from below the Bay Bridge to Fisherman's Wharf, San Fran-cisco's flat, accessible waterfront invites you to get close-up and personal with the bay, the picturesque and constant backdrop to this stunning city. For decades the Embarcadero was obscured by a terrible raised freeway and known best for the giant buildings on its piers that further cut off the city from the bay. With the freeway gone and a few piers restored for public access, the Embarcadero has been given a new lease on life. Millions of visitors may come through the northern waterfront every year, lured by Fisherman's Wharf and Pier 39, but locals tend to stop short of these, opting instead for the gastronomic pleasures of the Ferry Building. Between the two, though, you'll find tourists and San Franciscans alike soaking up the sun, walking out over the water on a long pier to see the sailboats, savoring the excellent restaurants and old-time watering holes, watching the street performers that crowd Justin Herman Plaza on a sunny day—these are the simple joys that make you happy you're in San Francisco, whether for a few days or a lifetime.

TOP ATTRACTIONS

Fodor'sChoice **Alcatraz.** ⊠ *Pier 33, Embarcadero* ☎ *415/981–7625* ⊕ *www.nps.gov/*
★ *alca* ⊡ *$30, including audio tour; $37 evening tour, including audio* ⊘ *Ferry departs every 30–45 mins Sept.–late May, daily 9:30–2:15, 4:20 for evening tour Thurs.–Mon. only; late May–Aug., daily 9:30–4:15 and 6:30 and 7:30 for evening tour*

⇨ *See the highlighted feature at the end of the chapter.*

FAMILY
Fodor'sChoice
★

Exploratorium. Walking into this fascinating "museum of science, art, and human perception" is like visiting a mad-scientist's laboratory. Most of the exhibits are supersize, and you can play with everything. After moving into larger digs on the Embarcadero in 2013, the Exploratorium has even more space for its signature experiential exhibits, including a brand-new Tinkering Studio and a glass Bay Observatory building, where the exhibits inside help visitors better understand what they see outside.

Quintessential exhibits remain: Get an *Alice in Wonderland* feeling in the distortion room, where you seem to shrink and grow as you walk across the slanted, checkered floor. In the shadow room, a powerful flash freezes an image of your shadow on the wall; jumping is a favorite pose. "Pushover" demonstrates cow-tipping, but for people: stand on one foot and try to keep your balance while a friend swings a striped panel in front of you (trust us, you're going to fall).

More than 650 other exhibits focus on sea and insect life, computers, electricity, patterns and light, language, the weather, and more. "Explainers"—usually high-school students on their days off—demonstrate cool scientific tools and procedures, like DNA sample-collection and cow-eye dissection. One surefire hit is the pitch-black, touchy-feely Tactile Dome ($15 extra; reservations required). In this geodesic dome strewn with textured objects, you crawl through a course of ladders, slides, and tunnels, relying solely on your sense of touch. Lovey-dovey couples sometimes linger in the "grope dome," but be forewarned: the staff will turn on the lights if necessary. ■ TIP➔ Patrons must be at least seven years old to enter the Tactile Dome, and the space is not for the claustrophobic. ⊠ *Piers 15–17, Embarcadero* ☎ *415/561–0360 general information, 415/561–0362 Tactile Dome reservations* ⊕ *www. exploratorium.edu* ⊠ *$29* ☉ *Tues.–Sun. 10–5, Thurs. 6 pm–10 pm ages 18 and over only.*

Fodor'sChoice
★

Ferry Building. The jewel of the Embarcadero, erected in 1896, is topped by a 230-foot clock tower modeled after the campanile of the cathedral in Seville, Spain. On the morning of April 18, 1906, the tower's four clock faces, powered by the swinging of a 14-foot pendulum, stopped at 5:17—the moment the great earthquake struck—and stayed still for 12 months.

Today San Franciscans flock to the street-level marketplace, stocking up on supplies from local favorites such as Acme Bread, Scharffen Berger Chocolate, Cowgirl Creamery, Blue Bottle Coffee, and Humphry Slocombe ice cream. Slanted Door, the city's beloved high-end Vietnamese restaurant, is here, along with highly regarded Bouli Bar. The seafood bar at Hog Island Oyster Company has fantastic bay view panoramas. On the plaza side, the outdoor tables at Gott's Roadside offer great people-watching with their famous burgers. On Saturday morning the plazas outside the building buzz with an upscale farmers' market where you can buy exotic sandwiches and other munchables. Extending south from the piers north of the building all the way to the Bay Bridge, the waterfront promenade out front is a favorite among joggers and picnickers, with a front-row view of sailboats plying the bay. True to its

6

name the Ferry Building still serves actual ferries: from its eastern flank they sail to Sausalito, Larkspur, Tiburon, and the East Bay. ⊠ *Embarcadero at foot of Market St., Embarcadero* ☎ *415/983–8030* ⊕ *www.ferrybuildingmarketplace.com.*

F-line. The city's system of vintage electric trolleys, the F-line, gives the cable cars a run for their money as a beloved mode of transportation. The beautifully restored streetcars—some dating from the 19th century—run from the Castro District down Market Street to the Embarcadero, then north to Fisherman's Wharf. Each car is unique, restored to the colors of its city of origin, from New Orleans and Philadelphia to Moscow and Milan. ■ TIP➔ Purchase tickets on board; exact change is required. ⊠ *San Francisco* ⊕ *www.streetcar.org* 🖮 *$2.25.*

WORTH NOTING

FAMILY **San Francisco Railway Museum.** A labor of love brought to you by the same vintage-transit enthusiasts responsible for the F-line's revival, this one-room museum and store celebrates the city's streetcars and cable cars with photographs, models, and artifacts. The permanent exhibit includes the replicated end of a streetcar with a working cab—complete with controls and a bell—for kids to explore; the cool, antique Wiley birdcage traffic signal; and models and display cases to view. Right on the F-line track, just across from the Ferry Building, this is a great quick stop. ⊠ *77 Steuart St., Embarcadero* ☎ *415/974–1948* ⊕ *www.streetcar.org* 🖮 *Free* ☉ *Daily 10–6; closed Mon. in winter.*

FINANCIAL DISTRICT

During the latter half of the 19th century, when San Francisco was a brawling, extravagant gold-rush town, today's Financial District was underwater. Yerba Buena Cove reached all the way up to Montgomery Street, and what's now Jackson Square was the heart of the Barbary Coast, bordering some of the roughest wharves in the world. These days, Jackson Square is a genteel and upscale neighborhood wedged between North Beach and the Financial District, but buried below Montgomery Street lies a remnant of these wild days: more than 100 ships abandoned by frantic crews and passengers caught up in gold fever lie under the foundations of buildings here.

The Financial District of the 21st century is a decidedly less exciting affair, and safer, too: no one's going to slip you a Mickey and ship you off to Shanghai. It's all office towers packed with mazes of cubicles now, and folks in suits and "office casual" fill the sidewalks at lunchtime. When the sun sets, this quarter empties out fast. The few sights here will appeal mainly to gold-rush history enthusiasts; others can safely steer clear.

EXPLORING

Jackson Square Historic District. This was the heart of the Barbary Coast of the Gay '90s—the 1890s, that is. Although most of the red-light district was destroyed in the fire that followed the 1906 earthquake, the remaining old redbrick buildings, many of them now occupied by advertising agencies, law offices, and antiques firms, retain hints of the romance and rowdiness of San Francisco's early days.

With its gentrified gold rush–era buildings, the 700 block of **Montgomery Street** just barely evokes the Barbary Coast days, but this was a colorful block in 19th century and on into the 20th. Writers Mark Twain and Bret Harte were among the contributors to the spunky *Golden Era* newspaper, which occupied No. 732 (now part of the building at No. 744). From 1959 to 1996 the late ambulance-chaser extraordinaire, lawyer Melvin Belli,

> ### WHISKEY RHYME
>
> The Italianate Hotaling building survived the disastrous 1906 quake and fire—a miracle considering the thousands of barrels of inflammable liquid inside. A plaque on the side of the structure repeats a famous query: "If, as they say, god spanked the town for being over frisky, why did he burn the churches down and save Hotaling's whiskey?"

had his headquarters at Nos. 722 and 728–730. There was never a dull moment in Belli's world; he represented clients from the actress Mae West to Gloria Sykes (who in 1964 claimed that a cable-car accident turned her into a nymphomaniac) to the disgraced televangelists Jim and Tammy Faye Bakker. Whenever he won a case, he fired a cannon and raised the Jolly Roger. Belli was also known for receiving a letter from the never-caught Zodiac killer.

Restored 19th-century brick buildings line Hotaling Place, which connects Washington and Jackson streets. The lane is named for the head of the **A.P. Hotaling Company whiskey distillery** (⊠ *451 Jackson St., at Hotaling Pl.*), the largest liquor repository on the West Coast in its day. (Anchor Distillery still makes an occasional Hotaling whiskey in the city, by the way; look for this single malt for a sip of truly local flavor.) ■TIP➔ The exceptional City Guides (☎415/557–4266 ⊕ www.sfcityguides.org) Gold Rush City walking tour covers this area and brings its history to life. ⊠ *Bordered by Columbus Ave., Broadway, and Washington and Sansome Sts., Jackson Square.*

Market Street buildings. The street, which bisects the city at an angle, has consistently challenged San Francisco's architects. One of the most intriguing responses to this challenge sits diagonally across Market Street from the Palace Hotel. The tower of the **Hobart Building** (No. 582) combines a flat facade and oval sides and is considered one of Willis Polk's best works in the city. East on Market Street is Charles Havens's triangular **Flatiron Building** (Nos. 540–548), another classic solution. At Bush Street, the **Donahue Monument** holds its own against the skyscrapers that tower over the intersection. This homage to waterfront mechanics, which survived the 1906 earthquake (a famous photograph shows Market Street in ruins around the sculpture), was designed by Douglas Tilden, a noted California sculptor. The plaque in the sidewalk next to the monument marks the spot as the location of the San Francisco Bay shoreline in 1848. Telltale nautical details such as anchors, ropes, and shells adorn the gracefully detailed **Matson Building** (No. 215), built in the 1920s for the shipping line Matson Navigation. ⊠ *Between New Montgomery and Beale Sts., Financial District.*

6

CLOSE UP

Alcatraz as Native Land

In the 1960s Native Americans attempted to reclaim Alcatraz, citing an 1868 treaty that granted Native Americans any surplus federal land. Their activism crested in 1969, when several dozen Native Americans began a 19-month occupation, supported by public opinion and friendly media.

The group offered to buy the island from the government for $24 worth of beads and other goods—exactly what Native Americans had been paid for Manhattan in 1626. In their Proclamation to the Great White Father and His People, the group laid out the 10 reasons why Alcatraz would make an ideal Indian reservation, among them: "There is no industry and so unemployment is very great," and "The soil is rocky and nonproductive, and the land does not support game." Federal agents removed the last holdouts in 1971, but each Thanksgiving Native Americans and others gather on the island to commemorate the takeover. In 2013 the park service restored the protesters' fading graffiti on the water tower, and today's visitors are still greeted with the huge message: "Indians Welcome. Indian Land."

Transamerica Pyramid. It's neither owned by Transamerica nor is it a pyramid, but this 853-foot-tall obelisk *is* the most photographed of the city's high-rises. Excoriated in the design stages as "the world's largest architectural folly," the icon was quickly hailed as a masterpiece when it opened in 1972. Today it's probably the city's most recognized structure after the Golden Gate Bridge. Visit the small, street-level visitor center to see the virtual view from the top, watch videos about the building's history, and perhaps pick up a T-shirt. ■ TIP➡ A fragrant redwood grove along the east side of the building, replete with benches and a cheerful fountain, is a placid patch in which to unwind. ⊠ *600 Montgomery St., Financial District* ⊕ *www.thepyramidcenter.com.*

Wells Fargo Bank History Museum. There were no formal banks in San Francisco during the early years of the gold rush, and miners often entrusted their gold dust to saloonkeepers. In 1852 Wells Fargo opened its first bank in the city on this spot, and the company soon established banking offices in mother-lode camps throughout California. At the fun and newly renovated two-story museum, you can pick up a free ticket and climb aboard a stagecoach—the projected driver will tell you about the ride and the scenery passing by on the wall—or take the reins and experience a trip out west. Have your picture taken in front of the gorgeous red Concord stagecoach (collect your souvenir photo at the desk), the likes of which carried passengers from St. Joseph, Missouri, to San Francisco in just three weeks during the 1850s. The museum also displays samples of nuggets and gold dust from mines, an old telegraph machine on which you can practice sending codes, and tools the '49ers used to coax the precious mineral from the ground. ⊠ *420 Montgomery St., Financial District* ☎ *415/396–2619* ⊕ *www.wellsfargohistory.com* ▭ *Free* ☉ *Weekdays 9–5.*

ALCATRAZ

"They made that place purely for punishment, where men would rot. It was designed to systematically destroy human beings . . . Cold, gray, and lonely, it had a weird way of haunting you—there were those dungeons that you heard about, but there was also the city . . . only a mile and a quarter away, so close you could almost touch it. Sometimes the wind would blow a certain way and you could smell the Italian cooking in North Beach and hear the laughter of people, of women and kids. That made it worse than hell."

—Jim Quillen, former Alcatraz inmate

Gripping the rail as the ferryboat pitches gently in the chilly breeze, you watch formidable Alcatraz rising ahead. Imagine making this trip shackled at the ankle and waist, the looming fortress on the craggy island ahead, waiting to swallow you whole. Thousands of visitors come every day to walk in the footsteps of Alcatraz's notorious criminals. The stories of life and death on "the Rock" may sometimes be exaggerated, but it's almost impossible to resist the chance to wander the cellblock that tamed the country's toughest gangsters and saw daring escape attempts of tremendous desperation.

LIFE ON THE ROCK

The federal penitentiary's first warden, James A. Johnston, was largely responsible for Alcatraz's (mostly false) hell-on-earth reputation. A tough but relatively humane disciplinarian, Johnston strictly limited the information flow to and from the prison when it opened in 1934. Prisoners' letters were censored, newspapers and radios were forbidden, and no visits were allowed during a convict's first three months in the slammer. Understandably, imaginations ran wild on the mainland.

A LIFE OF PRIVILEGE

Monotony was an understatement on Alcatraz; the same precise schedule was kept daily. The rulebook stated, "You are entitled to food, clothing, shelter, and medical attention. Anything else you get is a privilege." These privileges, from the right to work to the ability to receive mail, were earned by following the prison's rules. A relatively minor infraction meant losing privileges. A serious breach, like fighting, brought severe punishments like time in the Hole (a.k.a. the Strip Cell, since the prisoner had to strip) or the Oriental (an absolutely dark, silent cell with a hole in the ground for a toilet).

THE SPAGHETTI RIOT

Johnston knew that poor food was one of the major causes of prison riots, so he insisted that Alcatraz serve the best chow in the prison system. But the next warden at Alcatraz slacked off, and in 1950, one spaghetti meal too many sent the inmates over the edge. Guards deployed tear gas to subdue the rioters.

A PRISONER'S DAY

6:30 AM: Wake-up call. Prisoners get up, get dressed, and clean cells.

6:50 AM: Prisoners stand at cell doors to be counted.

7:00 AM: Prisoners march single-file to mess hall for breakfast.

7:20 AM: Prisoners head to work or industries detail; count.

9:30 AM: 8-minute break; count.

11:30 AM: Count; prisoners march to mess hall for lunch.

12:00 PM: Prisoners march to cells; count; break in cells.

12:20 PM: Prisoners leave cells, march single-file back to work; count.

2:30 PM: 8-minute break; count.

4:15 PM: Prisoners stop work, two counts.

4:25 PM: Prisoners march into mess hall and are counted; dinner.

4:45 PM: Prisoners return to cells and are locked in.

5:00 PM: Prisoners stand at their doors to be counted.

8:00 PM: Count.

9:30 PM: Count; lights out.

12:01 AM—5 AM: Three counts.

INFAMOUS INMATES

Fewer than 2,000 inmates ever did time on the Rock; though they weren't necessarily the worst criminals, they were definitely the worst prisoners. Most were escape artists, and others, like Al Capone, had corrupted the prison system from the inside with bribes.

Name Al "Scarface" Capone

On the Rock 1934–1939

In for Tax evasion

Claim to fame Notorious Chicago gangster and bootlegger who arranged the 1929 St. Valentine's Day Massacre.

Hard fact Capone was among the first transfers to the Rock and arrived smiling and joking. He soon realized the party was over. Capone endured a few stints in the Hole and Warden Johnston's early enforced-silence policy; he was also stabbed by a fellow inmate. The gangster eventually caved, saying "it looks like Alcatraz has got me licked," thus cementing the prison's reputation.

Name Robert "The Bird-man" Stroud

On the Rock 1942–1959

In for Murder, including the fatal stabbing of a prison guard

Claim to fame Subject of the acclaimed but largely fictitious 1962 film *Birdman of Alcatraz*.

Hard fact Stroud was actually known as the "Bird Doctor of Leavenworth." While incarcerated in Leavenworth prison through the 1920s and 30s, he became an expert on birds, tending an aviary and writing two books. The stench and mess in his cell discouraged the guards from searching it—and finding Stroud's homemade still. His years on the Rock were birdless.

Name George "Machine Gun" Kelly

On the Rock 1934–1951

In for Kidnapping

Claim to fame Became an expert with a machine gun at the urging of his wife, Kathryn. Kathryn also encouraged his string of bank robberies and the kidnapping for ransom of oilman Charles Urschel. While stashed in Leavenworth on a life sentence, Kelly boasted that he would escape and then free Kathryn. That got him a one-way ticket to Alcatraz.

Hard fact Was an altar boy on Alcatraz and was generally considered a model prisoner.

6

IN FOCUS ALCATRAZ

NO ESCAPE

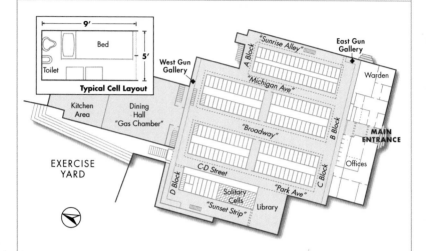

Alcatraz was a maximum-security federal penitentiary with one guard for every three prisoners. The biggest deterrent to escape, though, was the 1.4 miles of icy bay waters separating the Rock from the city. Only a few prisoners made it off the island, and only one is known to have survived. And that story about the shark-infested waters? There are sharks in the bay, but they're not the man-eating kind.

Bloodiest Attempt: In 1946, six prisoners hatched a plan to surprise a guard, seize weapons, and escape through the recreation yard. They succeeded up to a point, arming themselves and locking several guards into cells, but things got ugly when the group couldn't find the key that opened the door to the prison yard. Desperate, they opened fire on the trapped guards. Warden Johnston called in the Marines, who shelled the cell house for two days in the so-called Battle of Alcatraz. Three ringleaders were killed in the fighting; two were executed for murder; and one, who was just 19 years old, got 99 years slapped on to his sentence.

Craftiest Attempt: Over six months, three convicts stole bits and pieces from the kitchen and machine shop to make drills and digging pieces. They used these basic tools to widen a vent into the utility corridor. They also gathered bits of cardboard, toilet paper, and hair from the prison's barbershop to make crude models of their own heads. Then, like teenagers sneaking out, they put the decoy heads in their cots and walked away—up the pipes in the utility corridor to the roof, then down a drainpipe to the ground. They set sail in a raft made from prison raincoats, and are officially presumed dead.

Most Anticlimactic: In 1962, one prisoner spent an entire year loosening the bars in a window. Then he slipped through and managed to swim all the way to Fort Point, near the Golden Gate Bridge. He promptly fell asleep there and was found an hour later by some teenagers.

6 TIPS FOR ESCAPING TO ALCATRAZ

"Broadway," once the cell blocks' busiest corridor.

1. Buy your ticket in advance. Visit the website for Alcatraz Cruises (☎ 415/981–7625 ⊕ www.alcatrazcruises.com) to scout out available departure times for the ferry. Prepay by credit card—the ticket price covers the boat ride and the audio tour—and print your ticket at home. Bring it to Pier 33 up to an hour before sailing and experience just a touch of schadenfreude as you overhear attendants tell scores of too-late passengers that your tour is sold out.

2. Dress smart. Bring that pullover you packed to ward off the chill from the boat ride and Alcatraz Island. Also: sneakers. Some Alcatraz guides are fanatical about making excellent time.

3. Go for the evening tour. You'll get even more out of the experience if you do it at night. The evening tour has programs not offered during the day, the bridge-to-bridge view of the city twinkles at night, and your "prison experience" will be amplified as darkness mournfully falls while you shuffle around the cell block.

4. Unplug and go against the flow. If you miss a cue on the excellent audio tour and find yourself out of synch, don't sweat it—use it as an opportunity to switch off the tape and walk against the grain of the people following the tour. No one will stop you if you walk back through a cell block on your own, taking the time to listen to the haunting sound of your own footsteps on the concrete floor.

5. Be mindful of scheduled and limited-capacity talks. Some programs only happen once a day (the schedule is posted in the cell house). Certain talks have limited capacity seating, so keep an eye out for a cell house staffer handing out passes shortly before the start time.

6. Talk to the staff. One of the island's greatest resources is its staff, who practically bubble over with information. Pick their brains, and draw them out about what they know.

PRACTICALITIES

Visitors at the Alcatraz dock waiting to depart "Uncle Sam's Devil's Island."

GETTING THERE

All cruises are operated by Alcatraz Cruises, the park's authorized concessionaire.

TIMING

The boat ride to Alcatraz is only about 15 minutes long, but you should allow about three hours for your entire visit. The delightful F-line vintage streetcars are the most direct public transit to the dock; on weekdays the 10-Townsend bus will get you within a few blocks of Pier 33.

FOOD

The prisoners might have enjoyed good food on Alcatraz, but you won't—unless you pack a picnic. Food is not available on the island, so be sure to stock up before you board the boat. Sandwich fare is available at Alcatraz Landing, at Pier 33, and the Ferry Building's bounty is just a 20-minute walk from Pier 33. In a pinch, you can also pony up for the underwhelming snacks on the boat.

STORM TROOPER ALERT!

When he was filming *Star Wars*, George Lucas recorded the sound of Alcatraz's cell doors slamming shut and used the sound bite in the movie whenever Darth Vader's star cruiser closed its doors.

KIDS ON THE ROCK

Parents should be aware that the audio tour, while engaging and worthwhile, includes some startlingly realistic sound effects. (Some children might not get a kick out of the gunshots from the Battle of Alcatraz—or the guards' screams, for that matter.) If you stay just one minute ahead in the program, you can always fast forward through the violent moments on your little one's audio tour.

THE MARINA AND THE PRESIDIO

With Cow Hollow

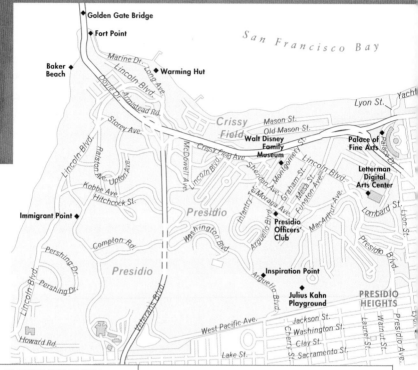

Golden Gate Bridge

Fort Point

San Francisco Bay

Baker Beach

Warming Hut

Marine Dr.

Long Ave.

Lincoln Blvd.

Doyle Dr.

Amistead Rd.

Lyon St.

Yacht

Storey Ave.

Crissy Field

Mason St.

Old Mason St.

Walt Disney Family Museum

Palace of Fine Arts

Lincoln Blvd.

Barton Ave.

Upton Ave.

Kobbe Ave.

Hitchcock St.

McDowell Ave.

Lincoln Blvd.

Crissy Field Ave.

Sheridan Ave.

Montgomery St.

Graham St.

Mesa St.

Funston Ave.

Lincoln Blvd.

Letterman Digital Arts Center

Lombard St.

Lyon St.

Immigrant Point

Presidio

Infantry

Te Moraga Ave.

Washington Blvd.

Arguello Blvd.

Presidio Officers' Club

MacArthur Ave.

Presidio Blvd.

Compton Rd.

Pershing Dr.

Pershing Dr.

Lincoln Blvd.

Presidio

Inspiration Point

Arguello Blvd.

Julius Kahn Playground

PRESIDIO HEIGHTS

Veterans Blvd.

Howard Rd.

West Pacific Ave.

Lake St.

Jackson St.

Washington St.

Clay St.

Sacramento St.

Laurel St.

Walnut St.

Presidio Ave.

Lyon

PLANNING YOUR TIME

Walking across the Golden Gate Bridge takes about 30 minutes, but leave some time to take in the view on the other side. If you aren't in a hurry, plan to spend at least two to three hours in the Presidio, and be sure to allow 15 minutes to stroll around the stunning Palace of Fine Arts. In a pinch, make a 30- to 45-minute swing-through for the views. Shoppers can burn up an entire day browsing the Marina's Chestnut Street and Cow Hollow's Union Street. Weekends are liveliest, while Mondays are quiet, since some shops close.

TOP REASONS TO GO

Golden Gate Bridge: Get a good look at the iconic span from the Presidio, then bundle up and walk over the water.

Shop Cow Hollow and the Marina: Browse hip boutiques and lavish antiques shops on Union Street, Cow Hollow's main drag. Then head north to Chestnut Street.

Palace of Fine Arts: Bring a picnic to this movingly beautiful faux-Greek remnant of the 1915 Panama-Pacific International Exposition and travel back in time to the city's post-earthquake-and-fire coming-out party.

Crissy Field: Join jogging, cycling, and kitesurfing locals along this beautifully restored strip of sand and marshland where the bay laps the shore, a stone's throw from the Golden Gate Bridge.

Presidio wanderings: Lace up your walking shoes and follow one of the wooded trails; the city will feel a hundred miles away.

The Marina, Cow Hollow, and The Presidio

Wave Organ ◆
Marina Small Craft Harbor
East Harbor
Aquatic Park
Marina Blvd.
Cervantes Blvd.
Ghirardelli Square
◆ Fort Mason Center
North Point St.
Beach St.
Bay St.
Francisco St.
MARINA
Bay St.
Francisco St.
Pierce St.
Scott St.
101
Filbert St.
Union St.
Green St.
Vallejo St.
Divisadero St.
Broderick St.
Vedanta Society Old Temple ◆
COW HOLLOW
Wedding Houses ◆
Octagon House
Chestnut St.
Lombard St.
Greenwich St.
Van Ness Ave.
Polk St.
Larkin St.
Octavia St.
Gough St.
Franklin St.
Broadway
Pacific Ave.
PACIFIC HEIGHTS
Jackson St.
Washington St.
Clay St.
Alta Plaza Park
Sacramento St.
California St.
Pine St.
FILLMORE
Steiner St.
Fillmore St.
Webster St.
Buchanan St.
Laguna St.
Lafayette Park
101

0   350 M
0   1,000 ft

QUICK BITES

Bereka Coffee. *Bereka* means blessing in Amharic and is fundamental to the Ethiopian coffee ceremony, which you'll appreciate after you taste the excellent, individualized pour-over served here—truly some of the best coffee in town. Add a couple of potato sambussas and you'll have the perfect snack. ⊠ *2320 Lombard St., Marina* ☎ *415/440–4438.*

Greens to Go. The take-out counter of the famous vegetarian restaurant carries mouthwatering premade salads, sandwiches, and soups. Eat at picnic tables outside or head up a steep flight of stairs to a grassy park with splendid Marina views. ⊠ *Fort Mason, Bldg. A, Marina* ☎ *415/771–6330* ⊕ *www.greensrestaurant.com.*

GETTING THERE

The Marina and the Presidio are great for biking and easily reached along the Embarcadero. The Presidio, vast and with plenty of parking, is one area where it pays to have a car. If you're driving to either the Marina or the Presidio, parking isn't too bad—the Palace of Fine Arts and Crissy Field both have lots. For those without wheels, the free year-round shuttle PresidiGo, which runs two routes through the Presidio every half hour, is a dream; ride both loops for a good one-hour overview. Pick up the shuttle at the transit center at Lincoln Boulevard and Graham Street. Weekdays from 9:30 to 4, a free shuttle runs from the Embarcadero BART/Muni station and the Transbay Temporary Terminal downtown to the Presidio (Muni Passport holders can ride this shuttle during commuter hours as well). For a map and schedule, check ⊕ *www.presidio.gov.* The only public transportation to this part of town is the bus; the 30–Stockton runs to Chestnut and Laguna in the Marina, two blocks south of Fort Mason.

Sightseeing
★★★★
Nightlife
★★
Dining
★★★
Lodging
★★★
Shopping
★★★★

Yachts bob at their moorings, satisfied-looking folks jog along the Marina Green, and multimillion-dollar homes overlook the bay in the picturesque, if somewhat sterile, Marina neighborhood. Does it all seem a bit too perfect? Well, it got this way after the hard knock of Loma Prieta—the current pretty face was put on after hundreds of homes collapsed in the 1989 earthquake. Just west of this waterfront area is a more natural beauty: the Presidio. Once a military base, this beautiful, sprawling park is mostly green space, with hills, woods, and the marshlands of Crissy Field.

THE MARINA

Updated by
Denise M. Leto

Well-funded postcollegiates and the nouveau riche flooded the Marina after the 1989 Loma Prieta earthquake had sent many residents running for more-solid ground, changing the tenor of this formerly low-key neighborhood. The number of yuppie coffee emporiums skyrocketed, a bank became a Williams-Sonoma store, and the local grocer gave way to a Pottery Barn. On weekends a young, fairly homogeneous, well-to-do crowd floods the cafés and bars. (Some things don't change—even before the quake, the Marina Safeway was a famed pickup place for straight singles, hence the nickname "Dateway.") South of Lombard Street is the Marina's affluent neighbor, Cow Hollow, whose main drag, Union Street, has some of the city's best boutique shopping and a good selection of restaurants and cafés. Joggers and kite-flyers head to the Marina Green, the strip of lawn between the yacht club and the mansions of Marina Boulevard.

TOP ATTRACTIONS

Fodor's Choice
★

Palace of Fine Arts. At first glance this stunning, rosy rococo palace seems to be from another world, and indeed, it's the sole survivor of the many tinted-plaster structures (a temporary classical city of sorts) built for the 1915 Panama-Pacific International Exposition, the world's fair that celebrated San Francisco's recovery from the 1906 earthquake and fire. The expo buildings originally extended about a mile along the shore. Bernard Maybeck designed this faux–Roman classic beauty, which was reconstructed in concrete and reopened in 1967. A victim of the elements, the Palace required a piece-by-piece renovation that was completed in 2008.

The pseudo-Latin language adorning the Palace's exterior urns continues to stump scholars. The massive columns (each topped with four "weeping maidens"), great rotunda, and swan-filled lagoon have been used in countless fashion layouts, films, and wedding photo shoots. After admiring the lagoon, look across the street to the house at 3460 Baker St. If the maidens out front look familiar, they should—they're original casts of the "garland ladies" you can see in the Palace's colonnade.

Inside the palace is a performance venue favored by local community groups and international musicians. ⊠ *3301 Lyon St., at Beach St., Marina* 🕾 *415/561–0364 Palace history tours* ⊕ *www.palaceoffinearts. org* 🗝 *Free* ⊙ *Daily 24 hrs.*

OFF THE BEATEN PATH

Wave Organ. Conceived by environmental artist Peter Richards and fashioned by master stonecutter George Gonzales, this unusual wave-activated acoustic sculpture gives off subtle harmonic sounds produced by seawater as it passes through 25 tubes. The sound is loudest at high tide. The granite and marble used for walkways, benches, and alcoves that are part of the piece were salvaged from a gold rush–era cemetery. ⊠ *North of Marina Green at end of jetty by Yacht Rd., park in lot north of Marina Blvd. at Lyon St., Marina.*

WORTH NOTING

Fort Mason Center. Originally a depot for the shipment of supplies to the Pacific during World War II, the fort was converted into a cultural center in 1977. Here you can find the vegetarian restaurant Greens and shops, galleries, and performance spaces, most of which are closed on Mondays. Below are three free arts venues of note.

The **Museo Italo-Americano** (⊠ *Bldg. C* 🕾 *415/673–2200* ⊕ *museoitaloamericano.org* ⊙ *Tues.–Sun. noon–4*) is a small gallery that hosts one exhibit at a time, worth a glance if you're already at Fort Mason.

The temporary exhibits downstairs at the **SFMOMA Artists Gallery** (⊠ *Bldg. A* 🕾 *415/441–4777* ⊕ *www.sfmoma.org/visit/artists_gallery* ⊙ *Tues.–Sat. 10:30–5*) can be great, but head upstairs and check out the paintings, sculptures, prints, and photographs for sale or rent. You won't find a Picasso or a Rembrandt, but where else can you get a $50,000 work of art to hang on your wall for $400 (a month)?

The **Mexican Museum** (⊠ *Bldg. D* 🕾 *415/202–9700* ⊕ *www.mexicanmuseum.org* ⊙ *Wed.–Sun. noon–4*) hosts temporary exhibits in its small space.

From May to October, Friday evenings at Fort Mason mean **Off the Grid** (⊕ *offthegridsf.com*); the city's food-truck gathering happens at locations around town, and this is one of the oldest and most popular.

7

Buchanan St. and Marina Blvd., Marina ☏415/345–7500 event information ⊕ www.fortmason.org.

COW HOLLOW

Between old-money Pacific Heights and the well-heeled, postcollegiate Marina lies comfortably upscale Cow Hollow. The neighborhood's name harks back to the 19th-century dairy farms whose owners eked out a living here despite the fact that there was more sand than grass. A patch of grass remains a scarce commodity in this mostly residential area, but Cow Hollow does have one heck of a commercial strip, centered around Union Street (⇨ *Chapter 18, Shopping*). To get a feel for this accessible bastion of affluence, stroll down Union.

> **DON'T LOOK DOWN!**
>
> Armed only with helmets, safety harnesses, and painting equipment, a full-time crew of 38 painters keeps the Golden Gate Bridge clad in International Orange. Contrary to a favorite bit of local lore, they don't actually sweep on an entire coat of paint from one end of the bridge to the other, but instead scrape, prime, and repaint small sections that have rusted from exposure to the elements.

Browse the cosmetics and jewelry stores, snazzy clothing boutiques, and shops selling home decor for every taste (if not budget), then rest your feet at one of the many good restaurants or sidewalk cafés.

EXPLORING

Octagon House. This eight-sided home sits across the street from its original site on Gough Street; it's one of two remaining octagonal houses in the city (the other is on Russian Hill), and the only one open to the public. White quoins accent each of the eight corners of the pretty blue-gray exterior, and a colonial-style garden completes the picture. The house is full of antique American furniture, decorative arts (paintings, silver, rugs), and documents from the 18th and 19th centuries, including the contents of a time capsule left by the original owners in 1861 that was discovered during a 1950s renovation. A deck of Revolutionary-era hand-painted playing cards takes an antimonarchist position: in place of kings, queens, and jacks, the American upstarts substituted American statesmen, Roman goddesses, and Indian chiefs. *2645 Gough St., near Union St., Cow Hollow ☏415/441–7512 ✉Free, donations encouraged ⊙ Feb.–Dec., 2nd Sun. and 2nd and 4th Thurs. of month noon–3; group tours weekdays by appointment.*

Vedanta Society Old Temple. A pastiche of colonial, Queen Anne, Moorish, and Hindu opulence, lavender with turrets battling red-top onion domes, and Victorian detailing everywhere, this 1905 structure was the first Hindu temple in the West. Vedanta, an underlying philosophy of Hinduism, maintains that all religions are paths to one goal. Although the Vedanta Society's main location is its New Temple at Vallejo and Fillmore streets, the Old Temple is the organization's heart. *2963 Webster St., Cow Hollow ☏415/922–2323 ⊕ www.sfvedanta.org.*

Wedding Houses. These identical white double-peak homes (joined in the middle) were erected in the late 1870s or early 1880s by dairy rancher

PARK IT HERE

Since 2009 San Francisco has been reclaiming parking spaces and turning them into parklets, tiny parks open to the public. These dot the city—more than three dozen and counting—from mobile, red-metal containers with built-in benches and plantings to Powell Street's eight-section high-design aluminum parklet. The Mission has the highest concentration, mostly along Valencia Street, but one of the most creative—an old Citroën van turned into seating and planters—is in front of the Rapha bike shop on Filbert near Fillmore in Cow Hollow. And even if everyone in that parklet in front of a café is clutching a to-go cup, remember these are public spaces; look for the "Public Parklet" sign and grab a seat. For a parklet map, visit ⊕ *pavementtoparks. sfplanning.org.*

James Cudworth as wedding gifts for his two daughters, down the street from his own house at 2040 Union Street. These days the buildings house a bar and a pizzeria. ⊠ *1980 Union St., Cow Hollow.*

PRESIDIO

At the foot of the Golden Gate Bridge, one of city residents' favorite in-town getaways is the 1,400-plus-acre Presidio, which combines accessible nature-in-the-raw with a window into the past. For more than 200 years and under the flags of three nations—Spain, Mexico, and the United States—the Presidio served as an army post, but in 1995 the U.S. Army officially handed over the keys to the National Park Service. The keys came without sufficient federal funding, though, and it seemed the Presidio would be sold piecemeal to developers.

An innovative plan combining public and private monies and overseen by the Presidio Trust, the federal agency created to run the park was hatched to help the Presidio become self-sufficient, which it did in 2013. The trust has found paying tenants such as George Lucas's Industrial Light and Magic, the Walt Disney Family Museum, and a few thousand lucky San Franciscans who live in restored army housing. Now this spectacular corner of the city—surrounded by sandy beaches and rocky shores, and with windswept hills of cypress dotted with historical buildings—is a thriving urban park. The Presidio has superb views and some of the best hiking and biking areas in San Francisco; even a drive through this lush area is a treat.

TOP ATTRACTIONS

FodorsChoice
★
Presidio. When San Franciscans want to spend a day in the woods, they come here. The Presidio has 1,400 acres of hills and majestic woods, two small beaches, and stunning views of the bay, the Golden Gate Bridge, and Marin County. Famed environmental artist Andy Goldsworthy's work greets visitors at the Arguello Gate entrance. The 100-plus-foot *Spire*, made of 37 cypress logs reclaimed from the Presidio, looks like a rough, natural version of a church spire. ■ TIP→ The Presidio's best lookout points lie along Washington Boulevard, which meanders through the park.

THE GOLDEN GATE BRIDGE

Two red towers reach into the sky, floating above the mist like ghost ships on foggy days. If there's one image that instantly conjures San Francisco, it's the majestic Golden Gate Bridge, one of the most recognizable sights in the world.

Spanning the Golden Gate—the mouth of the San Francisco Bay, after which the bridge was named—between San Francisco and pastoral Marin County, the bridge has won both popular and critical acclaim, including being named one of the seven wonders of the modern world. With its simple but powerful art-deco design, the 1.7-mile suspension span and its 750-foot towers were built to withstand winds of more than 100 mph. It's also not a bad place to be in an earthquake: designed to sway almost 28 feet, the Golden Gate Bridge (unlike the Bay Bridge) was undamaged by the 1989 Loma Prieta quake. If you're on the bridge when it's windy, stand still and you can feel it swaying a bit.

✉ *Lincoln Blvd. near Doyle Dr. and Fort Point, Presidio* ☎ *415/921–5858* ⊕ *www.goldengatebridge.org*

🕐 *Pedestrians: Mar.–Oct., daily 5 am–9 pm; Nov.–Feb., daily 5 am–6:30 pm; hrs change with daylight saving time. Bicyclists: daily 24 hrs.*

A DAY OVER THE BAY

Crossing the Golden Gate Bridge under your own power is a sensation that's hard to describe. Especially as you approach midspan, hovering more than 200 feet above the water makes you feel as though you're outside of time—exhilarating, a little scary, definitely chilly. From the bridge's eastern-side walkway, the only side pedestrians are allowed on, you can take in the San Francisco skyline and the bay islands; look west for the wild hills of the Marin Headlands, the curving coast south to Lands End, and the Pacific Ocean. On sunny days, sailboats dot the water, and brave windsurfers test the often-treacherous tides beneath the bridge. A vista point on the Marin County side provides a spectacular city panorama.

THE MAN WHO BUILT THE BRIDGE

In the early 1900s, San Francisco was behind the times. Sure, the city had the engineering marvel of the cable car and hundreds of streetcar lines, but as the largest U.S. city served mainly by ferries, this town needed a bridge. Enter Joseph Strauss, a structural engineer, dreamer, and poet who promised that not only could he build a bridge, but he could also do it on the cheap. At 5 feet 3 inches tall, Strauss was a force of nature. He worked tirelessly over the next 20-odd years, first as a bridge booster and then overseeing its design and construction. Though the final structure bore little resemblance to his original plan, Strauss guarded his legacy jealously, refusing to recognize the seminal contributions of engineer Charles A. Ellis. In 2007, the Golden Gate Bridge District finally recognized Ellis's role, though Strauss, who died less than a year after opening day in 1937, would

doubtless be pleased with the inscription on his statue, which stands sentry in the southern parking lot: "The Man Who Built the Bridge."

VISITING THE BRIDGE TODAY

The bridge has been standing for three-quarters of a century, but the visitor's experience got an upgrade to coincide with the 75th-anniversary celebration. You can grab a snack at the art deco–style Bridge Café. The recently erected Bridge Pavilion sells attractive, high-quality souvenirs and has a small display of historical artifacts: look for an original brush used to paint the bridge. At the outdoor exhibits, you can see the bridge rise before your eyes on hologram panels, learn about the features that make it art deco, and read about the personalities behind its design and construction. City Guides offers free walking tours of the bridge every Thursday and Sunday at 11 am.

Art in the Presidio

Fans of Andy Goldsworthy, the Scottish artist famed for his work with natural elements, will have a field day in the Presidio: the park contains four of his creations, all using materials reclaimed from the Presidio. *Spire*, created in 2008, is a 100-foot-high sculpture that reaches toward the sky in a grove near the Arguello Gate. Made of the trunks of 37 Monterey cypress trees cut down during reforestation work at the Presidio, it's currently surrounded by saplings that will one day be a forest. Near the intersection of Presidio Boulevard and West Pacific Avenue, Goldsworthy created *Wood Line* in 2011. Felled eucalyptus weave lines through a cypress grove in a work that the artist says "draws the place." In 2013 Goldsworthy moved inside for the installation *Tree Fall*, located in the Presidio's Powder Magazine.

Suspended above the historic structure's walls, he covered a tree trunk and dome above it with clay from the Presidio, which cracked into lovely patterns. The work is open for viewing on guided tours weekends 10–4. In 2014, Goldsworthy created *Earth Wall* in a wall around the patio at the Officers' Club. He collected curved eucalyptus branches from the site, affixed them in a sphere on the side of the concrete wall, then added a rammed-earth layer to the entire wall, burying the wood while thickening the wall. When it had dried, he used a chisel to reveal the ball, essentially excavating it in a nod to the layers of history at the Presidio: "Maybe this is where it all begins . . . with this really intense core. . . . That, to me, is what's happening: that contact, that earth, wood, growth . . . life. That's life."

Part of the **Golden Gate National Recreation Area,** the Presidio was a military post for more than 200 years. Don Juan Bautista de Anza and a band of Spanish settlers first claimed the area in 1776. It became a Mexican garrison in 1822, when Mexico gained its independence from Spain; U.S. troops forcibly occupied the Presidio in 1846. The U.S. Sixth Army was stationed here until 1994.

The Presidio is now a thriving community of residential and nonresidential tenants, who help to fund its operations by rehabilitating and leasing its more than 700 buildings. In 2005 Bay Area filmmaker George Lucas opened the **Letterman Digital Arts Center,** his 23-acre digital studio "campus," along the eastern edge of the land. Seventeen of those acres are exquisitely landscaped and open to the public. If you have kids in tow or are a *Star Wars* fan yourself, sidle over to the **Yoda Fountain** (Letterman Drive at Dewitt Road), between two of the arts-center buildings, then take your picture with the life-size Darth Vader statue in the lobby, open to the public on weekdays.

Especially popular is **Crissy Field,** a stretch of restored marshland along the sand of the bay. Kids on bikes, folks walking dogs, and joggers share the paved path along the shore, often winding up at the Warming Hut, a combination café and fun gift store at the end of the path, for a hot chocolate in the shadow of the Golden Gate Bridge. Midway along the Golden Gate Promenade that winds along the shore is the Gulf of the

Farallones National Marine Sanctuary Visitor Center, where kids can get a close-up view of small sea creatures and learn about the rich ecosystem offshore. Just across from the Palace of Fine Arts, Crissy Field Center offers great children's programs and has cool science displays. West of the Golden Gate Bridge is sandy **Baker Beach,** beloved for its spectacular views and laid-back vibe (read: you'll see naked people here). This is one of those places that inspires local pride. ⊠ *Between Marina and Lincoln Park, Presidio* ⊕ *www.presidio.gov.*

Presidio Officers' Club. An excellent place to begin a historical tour of the Presidio, the newly restored Officers' Club offers a walk through time from the Presidio's earliest days as the first non-native outpost in present-day San Francisco to more than a century as a U.S. army post. For a richer experience, visit the Presidio Heritage Gallery upstairs before exploring the building. Start with the excellent short film about life here from the time of the Ohlone to the present, then peruse the displays of artifacts including uniforms and weaponry. Head back downstairs to the Mesa Room, where you can literally see layers of history: part of the painstakingly preserved original adobe wall from the 1790s, the brick fireplace from the 1880s commander's office, and the mission revival fireplace from the 1930s billiard room. You can imagine the brass mingling under giant wrought-iron chandeliers in the Moraga Room. Excavation of the Presidio continues: outside, a canopy covers the Presidio Archaeology Field Station, where you can watch archaeologists at work from May to September. ■TIP→ Also at the club, the outdoor seating at Mexican-influenced Arguello, by local favorite chef Traci Des Jardins, is lovely on a sunny day. ⊠ *50 Moraga Ave., Presidio* ☎ *415/561–4400* ⊕ *www.presidioofficersclub.com* ⊠ *Free* ⊗ *Tues.–Sun. 10–6.*

WORTH NOTING

FAMILY **Fort Point.** Dwarfed today by the Golden Gate Bridge, this brick fortress constructed between 1853 and 1861 was designed to protect San Francisco from a Civil War sea attack that never materialized. It was also used as a coastal-defense fortification post during World War II, when soldiers stood watch here. This National Historic Site is now a sprawling museum of military memorabilia. The building, which surrounds a lonely, windswept courtyard, has a gloomy air and is suitably atmospheric. It's usually chilly, too, so bring a jacket. The top floor affords a unique angle on the bay. ■TIP→ Take care when walking along the front side of the building, as it's slippery, and the waves have a dizzying effect. On the days when Fort Point is staffed (on Friday and weekends), guided group tours and cannon drills take place. The popular, guided candlelight tours, available only in winter, book up in advance, so plan ahead. Living-history days take place throughout the year, when Union soldiers perform drills, a drum-and-fife band plays, and a Civil War–era doctor shows his instruments and describes his surgical technique (gulp). ⊠ *Marine Dr. off Lincoln Blvd., Presidio* ☎ *415/556–1693* ⊕ *www.nps.gov/fopo* ⊠ *Free* ⊗ *Fri.–Sun. 10–5.*

Walt Disney Family Museum. This beautifully refurbished brick barracks house is a tribute to the man behind Mickey Mouse, the Disney Studios, and Disneyland. The smartly organized displays include hundreds of family photos, and well-chosen videos play throughout. Disney's

CLOSE UP

The Presidio with Kids

If you're in town with children (and you have a car), the sprawling, bayside Presidio offers enough kid-friendly diversions for one very full day. Start off at **Julius Kahn Park,** on the Presidio's southern edge, which has a disproportionate number of structures that spin. Swing by George Lucas's **Letterman Digital Arts Center** to check out the Yoda fountain; then head to the **Immigrant Point Lookout** on Washington Boulevard, with views of the bay and the ocean. Children love the pet cemetery, with its sweet, leaning headstones; it's near the stables, where you might glimpse some of the park police's equestrian members. Older kids might enjoy a stop at the **Walt Disney**

Family Museum (✉ 104 Montgomery St. ☎ 415/345–6800) to see the model of Disneyland and a replica of the ambulance jeep Disney drove during World War I. The last stop is **Crissy Field,** where kids can ride bikes, skate, or run along the beach and clamber over the rocks; the view of the Golden Gate Bridge from below is captivating. Two nature centers here have fun, hands-on exhibits for kids. Finally, stop by the **Warming Hut,** at the western end of Crissy Field, for sandwiches and hot chocolate. You can also do a version of this day using the PresidiGo shuttle, but you'll need to adapt your route according to the shuttle stops.

legendary attention to detail becomes particularly evident in the cels and footage of *Fantasia, Sleeping Beauty,* and other animation classics. "The Toughest Period in My Whole Life" exhibit sheds light on lesser-known bits of history: the animators' strike at Disney Studios, the films Walt Disney made for the U.S. military during World War II, and his testimony before the House Un-American Activities Committee during its investigation of Communist influence in Hollywood. The glass-walled gallery showcasing Disney's wildlife films takes full advantage of the museum's location, with a lovely view of Presidio trees and the Golden Gate Bridge in the background. The liveliest exhibit and the largest gallery documents the creation of Disneyland with a fun, detailed model of what Disney imagined the park would be. Teacups spin, the Matterhorn looms, and that world-famous castle leads the way to Fantasyland. You won't be the first to leave humming "It's a Small World." In the final gallery, titled simply "December 16, 1966," a series of sweet cartoons chronicles the world's reaction to Disney's sudden death. The one-way flow of the galleries deposits you near the attractive gift shop, which carries cool Disney-related stuff, and a café serving sandwiches, salads, and drinks. The downstairs theater shows Disney films (free with admission, $7 without) most days. ✉ *Main Post, 104 Montgomery St., off Lincoln Blvd., Presidio* ☎ *415/345–6800* ⊕ *www.waltdisney.org* ⊠ *$20* ⊙ *Wed.–Mon. 10–6.*

THE WESTERN SHORELINE

GETTING ORIENTED

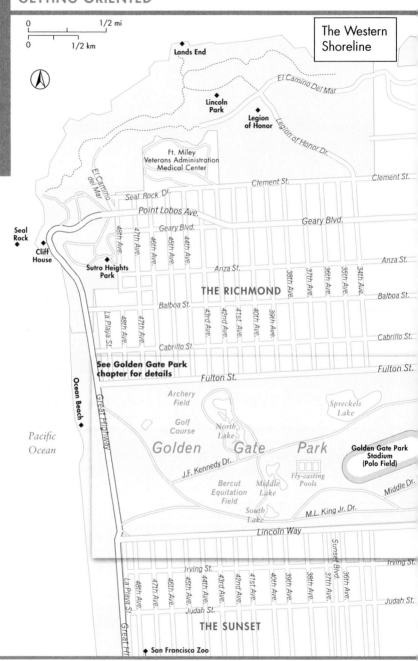

The Western
Shoreline

0   1/2 mi

0   1/2 km

Lands End

El Camino Del Mar

Lincoln
Park

Legion
of Honor

Legion of Honor Dr.

Ft. Miley
Veterans Administration
Medical Center

Clement St.

Clement St.

Seal Rock Dr.

Point Lobos Ave.

Geary Blvd.

Geary Blvd.

Seal
Rock

48th Ave.
47th Ave.
46th Ave.
45th Ave.
44th Ave.

Cliff
House

Sutro Heights
Park

Anza St.

Anza St.

38th Ave.
37th Ave.
36th Ave.
35th Ave.
34th Ave.

THE RICHMOND

Balboa St.

Balboa St.

La Playa St.
48th Ave.
47th Ave.

43rd Ave.
42nd Ave.
41st Ave.
40th Ave.
39th Ave.

Cabrillo St.

Cabrillo St.

**See Golden Gate Park
chapter for details**

Fulton St.

Fulton St.

Ocean Beach

Great Highway

Archery
Field

Spreckels
Lake

Golf
Course

North
Lake

*Pacific
Ocean*

Golden   *Gate*   *Park*

**Golden Gate Park
Stadium
(Polo Field)**

J.F. Kennedy Dr.

Bercut
Equitation
Field

Middle
Lake

Fly-casting
Pools

Middle Dr.

South
Lake

M.L. King Jr. Dr.

Lincoln Way

Sunset Blvd.

Irving St.

Irving St.

La Playa St.
48th Ave.
47th Ave.
46th Ave.
45th Ave.
44th Ave.
43rd Ave.
42nd Ave.
41st Ave.
40th Ave.
39th Ave.
38th Ave.
37th Ave.
36th Ave.

Judah St.

Great Hwy.

Judah St.

THE SUNSET

San Francisco Zoo

MAKING THE MOST OF YOUR TIME

Despite low-lying fog and often biting chill, the premier sights of the Western Shoreline are outdoors—gorgeous hiking trails and sandy stretches of coastline. Bundle up and start off on the Coastal Trail, which passes by the Legion of Honor. Continue west to catch the sunset from the Cliff House or the Beach Chalet. If you don't want to do the entire 3-mile hike, you can spend an hour touring the museum, catch the stunning views just below it, and head to the beach.

TOP REASONS TO GO

Lands End: Head down the freshly restored Coastal Trail near the Cliff House; you'll quickly find yourself in a forest with unparalleled views of the Golden Gate Bridge.

Toast the sunset at the Beach Chalet: Top off a day of exploring with a cocktail overlooking Ocean Beach.

Legion of Honor: Tear yourself away from the spectacular setting and eye-popping view and travel back to 18th-century Europe through the paintings, drawings, and porcelain collected here.

Ocean Beach: Wrap up warm and stroll along the strand on a brisk, cloudy day and you'll feel like a gritty local. Then thaw out over a bowl of steaming pho in the Richmond.

Old-time San Francisco: Wandering among the ruins of the Sutro Baths below the Cliff House, close your eyes and imagine vintage San Francisco: the monumental baths, popular amusement park Playland at the Beach, and that great, old, teetering, Victorian Cliff House of days gone by.

GETTING THERE

To reach the Western Shoreline from downtown by Muni light rail, take the N–Judah to Ocean Beach or the L–Taraval to the zoo. From downtown by bus, take the 38-Geary, which runs all the way to 48th and Point Lobos Avenues, just east of the Cliff House. Along the Western Shoreline, the 18–46th Avenue runs between the Legion of Honor and the zoo (and beyond).

QUICK BITES

Beach Chalet and Park Chalet. The gorgeous setting often overshadows the upscale comfort food at the upstairs Beach Chalet and its downstairs sister, Park Chalet, across from Ocean Beach, on the western edge of Golden Gate Park. ✉ *1000 Great Hwy., at JFK Dr., Golden Gate Park* ☎ *415/386–8439* ⊕ *www.beachchalet.com.*

Hunan Café 2. With its plain-wrap storefront, this mom-and-pop shop in the Outer Richmond may not look like much, but the friendly folks here serve delicious Chinese food; favorites include the ginger-and-onion chicken, Mongolian beef, and hot-and-sour soup. ✉ *4450 Cabrillo St., at 46th Ave., Richmond* ☎ *415/751–1283.*

8

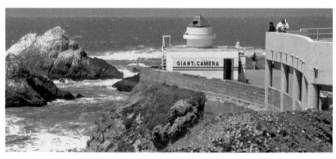

Sightseeing
★★★

Nightlife
—

Dining
★

Lodging
—

Shopping
—

Few American cities provide a more intimate and dramatic view of the power and fury of the surf attacking the shore than San Francisco does along its wild Western Shoreline. From Lincoln Park in the north, along Ocean Beach from the Richmond south to the Sunset, a different breed of San Franciscan chooses to live in this area: surfers who brave the heaviest fog to ride the waves; writers who seek solace and inspiration in this city outpost; and dog lovers committed to giving their pets a good workout each day.

THE RICHMOND

Updated by
Denise M. Leto

In the mid-19th century, the western section of town just north of Golden Gate Park was known as the Outer Lands, covered in sand dunes and seen fit for cemeteries and little else. Today it's the Richmond, comprised of two distinct neighborhoods: the Inner Richmond, from Arguello Boulevard to about 20th Avenue, and the Outer Richmond, from 20th to the ocean. Clement Street, packed with solid dining options, from French to Burmese, and with numerous Chinese groceries, is the Inner Richmond's favorite commercial strip. The street makes for great strolling and even better eating. The Outer Richmond has its share of restaurants—most along Geary Boulevard, some along Clement—including the city's highest concentration of Russian eateries and bakeries. But this mostly residential neighborhood is about the foggy hinterlands that stretch west to the coast: dramatic Lincoln Park with Golden Gate views, the Cliff House, and often-chilly, uncrowded Ocean Beach.

From Lands End in Lincoln Park you have some of the best views of the Golden Gate—the name was given to the opening of San Francisco Bay long before the bridge was built—and the Marin Headlands. From the historic Cliff House south to the sprawling San Francisco Zoo, the Great Highway and Ocean Beach run along the western edge of the city (south of Golden Gate Park, you're in the Sunset). If you're here in winter or spring, keep your eyes peeled for migrating gray whales. The wind is often strong along the shoreline, summer fog can blanket the ocean beaches, and the water is cold and usually too rough for swimming. Don't forget your jacket!

TOP ATTRACTIONS

Fodor'sChoice **Legion of Honor.** The old adage of real estate—location, location, loca-★ tion—is at full force here. You can't beat the site of this museum of European art atop cliffs overlooking the ocean, the Golden Gate Bridge, and the Marin Headlands. A pyramidal glass skylight in the entrance court illuminates the lower-level galleries, which exhibit prints and drawings, English and European porcelain, and ancient Assyrian, Greek, Roman, and Egyptian art. The 20-plus galleries on the upper level display the permanent collection of European art (paintings, sculpture, decorative arts, and tapestries) from the 14th century to the present day.

The noteworthy Auguste Rodin collection includes two galleries devoted to the master and a third with works by Rodin and other 19th-century sculptors. An original cast of Rodin's *The Thinker* welcomes you as you walk through the courtyard. As fine as the museum is, the setting and view outshine the collection and also make a trip here worthwhile.

The **Legion Café,** on the lower level, serves tasty light meals (soup, sandwiches, grilled chicken) inside and on a garden terrace. (Unfortunately, there's no view.) Just north of the museum's parking lot is George Segal's *The Holocaust,* a stark white installation that evokes life in concentration camps during World War II. It's haunting at night, when backlighted by lights in the Legion's parking lot. ■TIP➔ **Admission to the Legion is also good for same-day admission to the de Young Museum in Golden Gate Park.** ⊠ *34th Ave. at Clement St., Richmond* ☎ *415/750–3600* ⊕ *legionofhonor.famsf.org* ✉ *$10, $2 off with proof of Bay Area public transit, free 1st Tues. of month* ⊗ *Tues.–Sun. 9:30–5:15.*

Fodor'sChoice **Lincoln Park.** Although many of the city's green spaces are gentle and ★ welcoming, Lincoln Park is a wild, 275-acre park in the Outer Richmond with windswept cliffs and panoramic views. The newly renovated Coastal Trail, the park's most dramatic one, leads out to **Lands End;** pick it up west of the Legion of Honor (at the end of El Camino del Mar) or from the parking lot at Point Lobos and El Camino del Mar. Time your hike to hit Mile Rock at low tide, and you might catch a glimpse of two wrecked ships peeking up from their watery graves. ⚠ Be careful if you hike here; landslides are frequent, and people have fallen into the sea by standing too close to the edge of a crumbling bluff top.

On the tamer side, large Monterey cypresses line the fairways at Lincoln Park's 18-hole golf course, near the Legion of Honor. At one time this land was the Golden Gate Cemetery, where the dead were segregated by nationality; most were indigent and interred without ceremony in the potter's field. In 1900 the Board of Supervisors voted to ban burials within city limits, and all but two city cemeteries (at Mission Dolores and the Presidio) were moved to Colma, a small town just south of San

8

Visitors enjoy the rough beauty of the Pacific from the Cliff House.

Francisco. When digging has to be done in the park, bones occasionally surface again. ⊠ *Entrance at 34th Ave. at Clement St., Richmond.*

WORTH NOTING

Cliff House. A meal at the Cliff House isn't just about the food—the spectacular ocean view is what brings folks here—but the cuisine won't leave you wanting. The vistas, which include offshore Seal Rock (the barking marine mammals who reside there are actually sea lions), can be 30 miles or more on a clear day—or less than a mile on foggy days. ■TIP→ **Come for drinks just before sunset; then head back into town for dinner.**

Three buildings have occupied this site since 1863. The current building dates from 1909; a 2004 renovation has left a strikingly attractive restaurant and a squat concrete viewing platform out back. The complex, owned by the National Park Service, includes a gift shop.

Sitting on the observation deck is the **Giant Camera,** a camera obscura with its lens pointing skyward housed in a cute yellow-painted wooden shack. Built in the 1940s and threatened many times with demolition, it's now on the National Register of Historic Places. Step into the dark, tiny room inside (for a $3 fee); a fascinating 360-degree image of the surrounding area—which rotates as the "lens" on the roof rotates—is projected on a large, circular table. ■TIP→ **In winter and spring you may also glimpse migrating gray whales from the observation deck.**

To the north of the Cliff House lie the ruins of the once grand glass-roof **Sutro Baths,** which you can explore on your own (they look a bit like water-storage receptacles). Adolf Sutro, eccentric onetime San Francisco mayor and Cliff House owner, built the bath complex, including a train out to the site, in 1896, so that everyday folks could enjoy the benefits of swimming. Six enormous baths (some freshwater and some seawater), more than 500 dressing rooms, and several restaurants covered 3 acres north of the Cliff House and accommodated 25,000 bathers. Likened to Roman baths in a European glass palace, the baths were for decades the favorite destination of San Franciscans in search of entertainment. The complex fell into disuse after World War II, was closed in 1952, and burned down (under questionable circumstances) during demolition in 1966. ⊠ *1090 Point Lobos Ave., Richmond* ☎ *415/386–3330* ⊕ *www.cliffhouse.com* 🍴 *Free* ☉ *Weekdays 9 am–9:30 pm, weekends 9 am–10 pm.*

Ocean Beach. Stretching 3 miles along the western side of the city from the Richmond to the Sunset, this sandy swath of the Pacific coast is good for jogging or walking the dog—but not for swimming. The water is so cold that surfers wear wet suits year-round, and riptides are strong, so only brave the waves if you are a strong swimmer or surfer—drownings are not infrequent. As for sunbathing, it's rarely warm enough here; think meditative walking instead of sun worshipping.

Paths on both sides of the Great Highway lead from Lincoln Way to Sloat Boulevard (near the zoo); the beachside path winds through landscaped sand dunes, and the paved path across the highway is good for biking and in-line skating (though you have to rent bikes elsewhere). The **Beach Chalet** restaurant and brewpub is across the Great Highway from Ocean Beach, about five blocks south of the Cliff House. ⊠ *Along Great Hwy. from Cliff House to Sloat Blvd. and beyond.*

Sutro Heights Park. Crows and other large birds battle the heady breezes at this cliff-top park on what were once the grounds of the home of Adolph Sutro, an eccentric mining engineer and former San Francisco mayor. An extremely wealthy man, Sutro may have owned about 10% of San Francisco at one point, but he couldn't buy good taste: a few remnants of his gaudy, faux-classical statue collection still stand (including the lions at what was the main gate). Monterey cypresses and Canary Island palms dot the park, and photos on placards depict what things looked like before the house burned down in 1896, from the greenhouse to the ornate carpet-bed designs.

All that remains of the main house is its foundation. Climb up for a sweeping view of the Pacific Ocean and the Cliff House below (which Sutro owned), and try to imagine what the perspective might have been like from one of the upper floors. San Francisco City Guides (☎ *415/557–4266*, ⊕ *www.sfcityguides.org*) runs a free Saturday tour of the park that starts at 2 (meet at the lion statue at 48th and Point Lobos avenues). ⊠ *Point Lobos and 48th Aves., Richmond.*

THE SUNSET

Hugging the southern edge of Golden Gate Park and built atop the sand dunes that covered much of western San Francisco into the 19th century, the Sunset is made up of two distinct neighborhoods—the popular Inner Sunset, from Stanyan Street to 19th Avenue, and the foggy Outer Sunset, from 19th to the beach. The Inner Sunset is perhaps the

8

perfect San Francisco "suburb": not too far from the center of things, reachable by public transit, and home to main streets—Irving Street and 9th Avenue just off Golden Gate Park—packed with excellent dining options, with Asian food particularly well represented. Along the domain of surfers and others who love the laid-back beach vibe and the fog, the slow-paced Outer Sunset finds itself newly on the radar of locals, with high-quality cafés and restaurants and quirky shops springing up along Judah Street between 42nd and 46th avenues. The zoo is the district's main tourist attraction.

EXPLORING

FAMILY **San Francisco Zoo.** Occupying prime oceanfront property, the zoo is touting its metamorphosis into the "New Zoo," a wildlife-focused recreation center that inspires visitors to become conservationists. Integrated exhibits group different species of animals from the same geographic areas together in enclosures that don't look like cages. More than 250 species reside here, including endangered species such as the snow leopard, Sumatran tiger, grizzly bear, and a Siberian tiger.

The zoo's superstar exhibit is **Grizzly Gulch,** where orphaned grizzly bear sisters Kachina and Kiona enchant visitors with their frolicking and swimming. When the bears are in the water, the only thing between you and them is (thankfully thick) glass. Grizzly feedings are at 11:30 am daily.

The **Lemur Forest** has four varieties of the bug-eyed, long-tailed primates from Madagascar. You can help hoist food into the lemurs' feeding towers and watch the fuzzy creatures climb up to chow down. African Kikuyu grass carpets the circular outer area of **Gorilla Preserve,** one of the largest and most natural gorilla habitats of any zoo in the world. Trees and shrubs create communal play areas.

Ten species of rare primates—including black howler monkeys, emperor tamarins, and lion-tailed macaques—live and play at the two-tier **Primate Discovery Center,** which contains 23 interactive learning exhibits on the ground level.

Magellanic penguins waddle about the rather sad concrete **Penguin Island,** splashing and frolicking in its 200-foot pool. Feeding times are 10:30 and 3:30. Koalas peer out from among the trees in **Koala Crossing,** and kangaroos and wallabies headline the **Australian Walkabout** exhibit. The 7-acre **Puente al Sur** (Bridge to the South) re-creates habitats in South America, replete with giant anteaters and capybaras.

An **African Savanna** exhibit mixes giraffes, zebras, kudus, ostriches, and many other species, all living together in a 3-acre section with a central viewing spot accessed by a covered passageway.

The 6-acre **Children's Zoo** has about 300 mammals, birds, and reptiles, plus an insect zoo, a meerkat and prairie-dog exhibit, a nature trail, a nature theater, a huge playground, a restored 1921 Dentzel carousel, and a mini–steam train. A ride on the train costs $5, and you can hop astride one of the carousel's 52 hand-carved menagerie animals for $3. ⊠ *Sloat Blvd. and 47th Ave., Sunset* ☎ *415/753–7080* ⊕ *www.sfzoo.org* 🎫 *$17, $1 off with Muni transfer (take Muni L–Taraval streetcar from downtown)* ☉ *Mid-Mar.–Oct., daily 10–5; Nov.–mid-Mar., daily 10–4.*

GOLDEN GATE PARK

Visit Fodors.com for advice, updates, and bookings

A GREEN RETREAT

Stretching more than 1,000 acres from the ocean to the Haight, Golden Gate Park is a place to slow down and smell the eucalyptus. Stockbrokers and gadget-laden parents stroll the Music Concourse, while speedy tattooed cyclists and wobbly, training-wheeled kids cruise along shaded paths. Stooped seniors warm the garden benches, hikers search for waterfalls, and picnickers lounge in the Rhododendron Dell. San Franciscans love their city streets, but the park is where they come to breathe.

PLANNING A PARK VISIT

ORIENTATION

The park breaks down naturally into three chunks. The eastern end attracts the biggest crowds with its cluster of blockbuster sights. It's also the easiest place to dip into the park for a quick trip. Water hobbyists come to the middle section's lake-speckled open space. Sporty types head west to the coastal end for its soccer fields, golf course, and archery range. This windswept western end is the park's least visited and most naturally landscaped part. ☉ Daily 6 am–10 pm ⊕ www.sfrecpark.org.

WALKING TOURS

San Francisco Botanical Garden (☎ 415/661–1316) has free botanical tours every day (admission not included). Tours start near the main gate daily at 1:30 pm. Additional tours meet at the Friend Gate (at the northern entrance) Apr.–Sept., Fri.–Sun. at 2 pm.
San Francisco City Guides (☎ 415/557–4266) offers free year-round tours of the eastern end and the western end of the park and two different

tours of the Japanese Tea Garden.

BEST TIMES TO VISIT

Time of day: It's best to arrive early at the Conservatory of Flowers, the de Young Museum, and the Japanese Tea Garden to avoid crowds. At sunset, the only place to be is the park's western end, watching the sun dip into the Pacific.

Time of year: Visit during the week if you can. The long, Indian summer days of September and October are the warmest times to visit, and many special weekend events are held then.

Blooms: The rhododendrons bloom between February and May. The Queen Wilhelmina Tulip Garden blossoms in February and March. Cherry trees in the Japanese Tea Garden bloom in April, and the Rose Garden is at its best from mid-May to mid-June, in the beginning of July, and during September

(opposite) Conservatory of Flowers. (top left) The San Francisco Botanical Garden in bloom.

TIPS

■ Carry a map—the park's sightlines usually prevent you from using city landmarks as reference points. Posted maps are few and far between, and they're often out of date. Paths aren't always clear, so stick to well-marked trails.

■ In Golden Gate Park, free public restrooms are fairly common and mostly clean, especially around the eastern end's attractions. Facilities are available behind the Conservatory of Flowers or in the de Young Museum at the sculpture garden and café patio. Farther west, behind Stow Lake's boathouse and near the Koret Children's Quarter are facilities.

■ Check out www. goldengate-park.com for a calendar of park events. This unofficial site also has maps and parking info.

BEST WAYS TO SPEND YOUR TIME

The park stretches 3 miles east to west and is a half-mile wide, so it's possible to cover the whole thing in a day—by car, public transportation, bike, or even on foot. But to do so might feel more like a forced march than a pleasure jaunt. Weigh your time and your interests, choose your top picks, then leave at least an extra hour to just enjoy being outdoors.

Two hours: Swing by the exquisite Conservatory of Flowers for a 20-minute peek, then head to the de Young Museum. Spend a few minutes assessing its controversial exterior and perhaps glide through some of the galleries before heading to the observation tower for a panoramic view of the city. Cross the music concourse to the spectacular Academy of Sciences.

Half day: Spend a little extra time at the sights described above, then head to the nearby Japanese Tea Garden to enjoy its perfectionist landscape. Next, cross the street to the San Francisco Botanical Garden at Strybing Arboretum and check out the intriguing Primitive Garden. If you brought supplies, this is a great place for a picnic; you can also grab lunch at the de Young Café.

Full day: After the half-day tour (above) continue on to the children's playground if you have kids in tow. Once your little ones see the playground's tree house–like play structures and climbing opportunities, you may be here for the rest of the day. Alternatively, make your way to the serene National AIDS Memorial Grove. Then head west, stopping at Stow Lake to climb Strawberry Hill. Wind up at the Beach Chalet for a sunset drink.

(top) Amateur musicians entertain passersby. (middle) Sundays are ideal biking days. (bottom) The meandering paths are perfect for strolling.

GETTING AROUND THE PARK

WALKING

The most convenient entry point is on the eastern edge at Stanyan Street, continuing into the park on JFK Drive, which points you directly toward the Conservatory of Flowers. It's a 10-minute walk there; allow another 10–15 minutes to reach the California Academy of Sciences, de Young Museum, Japanese Tea Garden, and San Francisco Botanical Garden. Stow Lake is another 10 minutes west from these four sights.

BY BIKE

The park is fantastic for cycling, especially on Sunday when cars are barred from John F. Kennedy Drive. Biking the park round trip is about a 7-miles trip, which usually takes 1–2 hours. The route down John F. Kennedy Drive takes you past the prettiest, well-maintained sections of the park on a mostly flat circuit. The most popular route continues all the way to the beach. Keep in mind that the ride is downhill toward the ocean, uphill heading east.

BY CAR

If you have a car, you'll have no trouble hopping from sight to sight. (But remember, the main road, John F. Kennedy Drive, is closed to cars on Sunday.) Parking within the park is often free and is usually easy to find especially beyond the eastern end. On Sundays or anytime the eastern end is crowded, head for the residential streets north of the park or the underground parking lot; enter on 10th and Fulton (northern edge of the park) or MLK and Concourse (in the park).

BY SHUTTLE

The free Golden Gate Park shuttle runs 9-6 weekends and holidays. It loops through the park every 15-20 minutes, stopping at 14 sights from McLaren Lodge to the Dutch Windmill. If you're driving, leave your car in the free spaces along Ocean Beach (Great Hwy. between Lincoln and Fulton) and wait at the green shuttle stop sign.

(top) Water lilies adorn the Japanese Tea Garden.

WHERE TO RENT

Parkwide Bike Rentals & Tours (☎ 415/671–8989). The only rental shop in the park is behind the band-shell on the music concourse. For an extra $10 you can return your bike to the Embarcadero/ Ferry Building, the Marina, or Union Square. **Golden Gate Park Bike & Skate** (✉ 3038 Fulton St. ☎ 415/668–1117). On the northern edge of the park; good deals on rentals. **San Francisco Bicycle Rentals** (✉ 425 Jefferson St. ☎ 415/922–4537). Customers rave about excellent service and good deals at this Fisherman's Wharf outfit. **Bike and Roll** (✉ 2800 Leavenworth St. ☎ 415/229–2000). This business operates out of Fisherman's Wharf, North Beach, and the Embarcadero, but you can take their bikes to the park, too.

BEST PLACES TO PICNIC ON WEEKENDS

■ Lawn in front of the Conservatory of Flowers.

■ By the pond in the San Francisco Botanical Garden.

■ The benches overlooking the Rustic Bridge at Stow Lake.

■ Rhododendron Dell.

DON'T-MISS SIGHTS

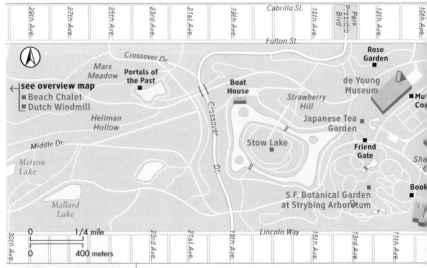

Conservatory of Flowers

✉ John F. Kennedy Dr. at Conservatory Dr.

☎ 415/666-7001

💲 $8, free 1st Tues. of month

🕐 Tues.–Sun. 9–5; 10–4:30 in winter

🌐 www.conservatoryofflowers.org

CONSERVATORY OF FLOWERS

Whatever you do, be sure to at least drive by the Conservatory of Flowers—it's just too darn pretty to miss. The gorgeous, white-framed, 1878 glass structure is topped with a 14-ton glass dome. Stepping inside the giant greenhouse is like taking a quick trip to the rainforest; it's humid, warm, and smells earthy. The undeniable highlight is the Aquatic Plants section, where lily pads float and carnivorous plants dine on bugs to the sounds of rushing water. On the east side of the conservatory (to the right as you face the building), cypress, pine, and redwood trees surround the **Dahlia Garden,** which blooms in summer and fall. To the west is the **Rhododendron Dell,** which contains 850 varieties, more than any other garden in the country. It's a favorite local Mother's Day picnic spot.

STOW LAKE

Russian seniors feed the pigeons, kids watch turtles sunning themselves, and joggers circle this placid body of water, Golden Gate Park's largest lake. Early park superintendent John McLaren may have snarked that manmade Stow Lake was "a shoestring around a watermelon," but for more than a century visitors have come to walk its paths and bridges, paddle boats, and climb Strawberry Hill (the "watermelon"). Cross one of the bridges—the 19th-century stone bridge on the southwest side is lovely—and ascend the hill; keep your eyes open for the waterfall and an elaborate Chinese Pavilion.

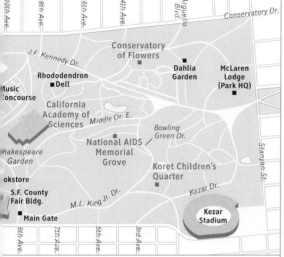

Stow Lake

✉ Off John F. Kennedy Dr.

☎ Boat rental 415/752–0347

🕐 Boat rentals daily 10–4.

San Francisco Japanese Tea Garden

✉ Hagiwara Tea Garden Dr.

☎ 415/752–4227

🎟 $8, free Mon., Wed., and Fri. with entry by 10 am

🕐 Mar.–Oct., daily 9–6; Nov.–Feb., daily 9–4:45.

🌐 www.japaneseteagardensf.com

Koret Children's Quarter

✉ Bowling Green Dr., off Martin Luther King Jr. Dr

☎ 415/831–2700

🎟 Playground free, carousel $2, kids 6–12 $1

🕐 Playground daily dawn–dusk; carousel Memorial Day–Labor Day, daily 10–4:30, Labor Day–Memorial Day, Fri.–Sun. 10–4:30.

SAN FRANCISCO JAPANESE TEA GARDEN

As you amble through the manicured landscape, past Japanese sculptures and perfect miniature pagodas, over ponds of huge, ancient carp, you may be transported to a more peaceful plane. Or maybe the shrieks of kids clambering over the almost vertical "humpback" bridges will keep you firmly in the here and now. Either way, this garden is one of those tourist spots that's truly worth a stop (a half-hour will do). And at 5 acres, it's large enough that you'll always be able to find a bit of serenity, even when the tour buses drop by. ◼ TIP➜ The garden is especially lovely in April, when the cherry blossoms are in bloom.

KORET CHILDREN'S QUARTER

The country's first public children's playground reopened in 2007 after a spectacular renovation, with wave-shaped climbing walls, old-fashioned cement slides, and a 20-plus-foot rope climbing structure that kids love and parents fear. Thankfully, one holdover is the beautiful, handcrafted 1912 Herschell-Spillman Carousel. The lovely stone Sharon Building, next to the playground, offers kids' art classes. Bring a picnic or pick up grub nearby on 9th Avenue and you could spend the entire day here. Be aware that the playground, which has separate areas for toddlers and bigger kids, is unenclosed and sightlines can be obstructed.

DE YOUNG MUSEUM

✉ 50 Hagiwara Tea Garden Dr.

☎ 415/750–3600

🌐 deyoung.famsf.org

💲 $10; free 1st Tues. of month

🕐 Tues.–Sun. 9:30–5:15

TIPS

■ Admission at the de Young is good for same-day admission to the Legion of Honor and vice-versa.

■ The de Young is famous these days first and foremost for its striking and controversial building and tree-topping tower. These are accessible to the public for free, so if it's not the art you're interested in seeing, save the cost of admission and head up the elevator to 360-degree views from the glass-walled observation floor.

■ When it's time for a nosh, head to the de Young Café and dine in the lovely outdoor sculpture garden on tableware fit for MOMA.

Everyone in town has a strong opinion about the de Young. Some adore the striking copper façade, while others grimace and hope that the green patina of age will mellow the effect. The building almost overshadows the museum's respected collection of American, African, and Oceanic art.

HIGHLIGHTS

Head through the sprawling concourse level and begin your visit on the upper level, where you'll find textiles; art from Africa, Oceana, and New Guinea; and highlights of the 20th-century American painting collection (such as Wayne Thiebaud, John Singer Sargent, Winslow Homer, and Richard Diebenkorn). These are the don't-miss items, so take your time. Then head back downstairs to see art from the Americas and contemporary work.

The de Young has had some major international coups, scoring exhibits such as *Tutankhamun and the Golden Age of the Pharoahs*; *Van Gogh, Gaugin, Cezanne, and Beyond: Post-Impressionist Masterpieces from the Musée d'Orsay*; and *Picasso: Masterpieces from the Musée National Picasso, Paris*. Be sure to check for traveling exhibits while you're visiting. Recent shows have included the stunning Jean Paul Gaultier exhibition (extra fees apply).

CALIFORNIA ACADEMY OF SCIENCES

With its native plant–covered living roof, retractable ceiling, three-story rainforest, gigantic planetarium, living coral reef, and frolicking penguins, the Cal Academy is one of the city's most spectacular treasures. Dramatically designed by Renzo Piano, it's an eco-friendly, energy-efficient adventure in biodiversity and green architecture. The roof's large mounds and hills mirror the local topography, and Piano's audacious design completes the dramatic transformation of the park's Music Concourse. Moving away from a restrictive role as a backward-looking museum that catalogued natural history, the new academy is all about sustainability and the future, but you'll still find those beloved dioramas in African Hall.

HIGHLIGHTS

By the time you arrive, hopefully you've decided which shows and programs to attend, looked at the academy's floorplan, and designed a plan to cover it all in the time you have. And if not, here's the quick version: Head left from the entrance to the wooden walkway over otherworldly rays in the Philippine Coral Reef, then continue to the Swamp to see Claude, the famous albino alligator. Swing through African Hall and gander at the penguins, take the elevator up to the living roof, then return to the main floor and get in line to explore the Rainforests of the World, ducking free-flying butterflies and watching for other live surprises. You'll end up below ground in the Amazonian Flooded Rainforest, where you can explore the academy's other aquarium exhibits. Phew.

✉ 55 Music Concourse Dr.

☎ 415/379–8000

🌐 www.calacademy.org

💳 $34, free one Sun. per quarter, $3 off for visitors who walk, bike, or take public transit.

🕐 Mon.–Sat. 9:30–5, Sun. 11–5

TIPS

■ The academy often hosts gaggles of schoolchildren. Arrive early and allow plenty of time to wait in line.

■ Plan ahead: check Planetarium show times, animal feeding times, etc, before you arrive.

■ Visitors complain about the high cost of food here; consider bringing a picnic.

■ Free days are tempting, but the tradeoff includes extremely long lines and the possibility that you won't get in.

■ With antsy kids, visit Early Explorers Cove and use the academy's in-and-out privileges to run around outside.

■ Take time to examine the structure itself, from denim insulation to weather sensors.

ALSO WORTH SEEING

San Francisco Botanical Garden at Strybing Arboretum

SAN FRANCISCO BOTANICAL GARDEN AT STRYBING ARBORETUM

One of the best picnic spots in a very picnic-friendly park, the 55-acre arboretum specializes in plants from areas with climates similar to that of the Bay Area. Walk the Eastern Australian garden to see tough, pokey shrubs and plants with cartoon-like names, such as the hilly-pilly tree. Kids gravitate toward the large shallow fountain and the pond with ducks, turtles, and egrets. Free tours meet at the main gate daily at 1:30. ⊠ *Enter the park at 9th Ave. at Lincoln Way* ☎ *415/661-1316* ⊕ *www.sfbotanicalgarden.org* 🎫 *$7* ⊙ *Mar.–Sept., daily 9–7; Oct.–early Nov. and Feb.–Mar., daily 9–5. Nov.–Jan., daily 9–4.*

NATIONAL AIDS MEMORIAL GROVE

This lush, serene 7-acre grove was conceived as a living memorial to the disease's victims. Coast live oaks, Monterey pines, coast redwoods, and other trees flank the grove. There are also two stone circles, one recording the names of the dead and their loved ones, the other engraved with a poem. Free 20-minute tours are available some Saturdays. ⊠ *Middle Dr. E, west of tennis courts* ☎ *415/765-0497* ⊕ *www.aidsmemorial.org.*

Beach Chalet

BEACH CHALET

Hugging the park's western border, this 1925 Willis Polk–designed structure houses gorgeous depression-era murals of familiar San Francisco scenes, while verses by local poets adorn niches here and there. Stop by the ground-floor visitors center on your way to indulge in a microbrew upstairs, ideally at sunset. ⊠ *1000 Great Hwy.* ☎ *restaurant 415/386-8439* ⊕ *www.beachchalet.com* ⊙ *Restaurant Mon.–Thurs. 9 am–10 pm, Fri. 9 am–11 pm, Sat. 8 am–11 pm, Sun. 8 am–10 pm.*

Dutch Windmill

DUTCH WINDMILL

It may not pump water anymore, but this carefully restored windmill, built in 1903 to irrigate the park, continues to enchant visitors. The Queen Wilhelmina Tulip Garden here is a welcoming respite, particularly lovely during its February and March bloom. The Murphy Windmill is just south of the Dutch Windmill and has a refurbished copper dome; swing by for an interesting comparison. ⊠ *Northwest corner of the park* ☎ *No phone* ⊙ *Dawn–dusk.*

THE HAIGHT, THE CASTRO, AND NOE VALLEY

GETTING ORIENTED

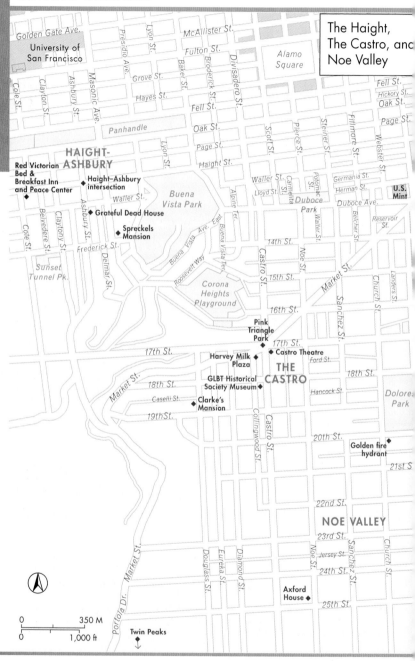

The Haight,
The Castro, and
Noe Valley

PLANNING YOUR TIME

The Upper Haight is only a few blocks long, and although there are plenty of shops and amusements, an hour or so should be enough unless you're into vintage shopping. Many restaurants here cater to the morning-after crowd, so this is a great place for brunch. With the prevalence of panhandling in this area, you may be most comfortable here during the day.

The Castro, with its fun, sometimes adult-theme storefronts, invites unhurried exploration; allot at least 60 to 90 minutes. Visit in the evening to check out the lively nightlife, or in the late morning—especially on weekends—when the street scene is hopping.

A loop through Noe Valley takes about an hour. With its popular breakfast spots and cafés, this neighborhood is a good place for a morning stroll. After you've filled up, browse the shops along 24th and Church streets.

TOP REASONS TO GO

Castro Theatre: Take in a film at this gorgeous throwback and join the audience shouting out lines, commentary, and songs. Come early and let the Wurlitzer set the mood.

Sunday brunch in the Castro: Recover from Saturday night (with the entire community) at one of the area's favorite brunch spots.

Vintage shopping in the Haight: Find the perfect chiffon dress at La Rosa, a pristine faux-leopard coat at Held Over, or the motorcycle jacket of your dreams at Buffalo Exchange.

24th Street stroll: Take a leisurely ramble down lovable Noe Valley's main drag, lined with unpretentious cafés, comfy eateries, and cute one-of-a-kind shops.

Cliff's Variety: Stroll the aisles of the Castro's "hardware" store (⊠ 479 Castro St.) for light bulbs, hammers, and pipes (as well as false eyelashes, tiaras, and feather boas) to get a feel for this neighborhood's full-tilt flair.

QUICK BITES

Flywheel Coffee Roasters. Family-owned, this light-filled cafe with a view of Golden Gate Park roasts its beans in-house for a great cuppa. ⊠ 672 Stanyan St., Haight ☎ 415/682–4023 ⊕ www.flywheelcoffee.com.

Lovejoy's Tea Room. The tearoom is a homey jumble, with its lace-covered tables, couches, and mismatched chairs set among the antiques for sale. High tea and cream tea are served, along with traditional English-tearoom "fayre." ⊠ 1351 Church St., at Clipper St., Noe Valley ☎ 415/648–5895 ⊕ www.lovejoystearoom.com.

Philz Coffee. The aroma alone might lure you into Philz, just off Castro Street. Its cramped space gives off a casual vibe, but don't be fooled: it serves up the strongest handcrafted cup of joe in town. ⊠ 4023 18th St., Castro ☎ 415/875–9656 ⊕ www.philzcoffee.com.

GETTING THERE

F-line trolleys serve the Castro; Muni light rail K-Ingleside, L-Taraval, M-Ocean View, and T-Third cars stop at Castro station; and the J–Church Metro serves the Castro and Noe Valley. The 71–Haight/Noriega bus from Union Square and the 6–Parnassus from Market and Van Ness serve the Haight. If on foot, know that the hill between the Castro and Noe Valley is steep.

10

Sightseeing
★

Nightlife
★★★

Dining
★★★

Lodging
★

Shopping
★★★

These distinct neighborhoods wear their personalities large and proud, and all are perfect for just strolling around. Like a slide show of San Franciscan history, you can move from the Haight's residue of 1960s counterculture to the Castro's connection to 1970s and '80s gay life to 1990s gentrification in Noe Valley. Although historic events thrust the Haight and the Castro onto the international stage, both are anything but stagnant—they're still dynamic areas well worth exploring.

THE HAIGHT

Updated by
Denise M. Leto

During the 1960s the siren song of free love, peace, and mind-altering substances lured thousands of young people to the Haight, a neighborhood just east of Golden Gate Park. By 1966 the area had become a hot spot for rock artists, including the Grateful Dead, Jefferson Airplane, and Janis Joplin. Some of the most infamous flower children, including Charles Manson and People's Temple founder Jim Jones, also called the Haight home.

Today the '60s message of peace, civil rights, and higher consciousness has been distilled into a successful blend of commercialism and progressive causes: the Haight Ashbury Free Clinic, founded in 1967, survives at the corner of Haight and Clayton, while throwbacks like Bound Together Books (the anarchist book collective), the head shop Pipe Dreams, and a bevy of tie-dye shops all keep the Summer of Love alive in their own way. The Haight's famous political spirit—it was the first neighborhood in the nation to lead a freeway revolt, and it continues to host regular boycotts against chain stores—survives alongside some of the finest Victorian-lined streets in the city. And the kids continue to come: this is where young people who end up on San Francisco's streets most often gather. Visitors tend to find the Haight either edgy

Hippie History

The eternal lure for twentysome-things, cheap rent, first helped spawn an indelible part of SF's history and public image. In the early 1960s young people started streaming into the sprawling, inexpensive Victorians in the area around the University of San Francisco, earnestly seeking a new era of communal living, individual empowerment, and expanded consciousness.

Golden Gate Park's Panhandle, a green strip on the Haight's northern edge, was their gathering spot—the site of protests, concerts, food giveaways, and general hanging out. In 1967 George Harrison strolled up the park's Hippie Hill, borrowed a guitar, and played for a while before being recognized. He led the crowd, Pied Piper–style, into the Haight.

A HIPPIE STATE OF MIND

At first the counterculture was all about sharing and taking care of one another—a good thing, consider-ing most hippies were either broke or had renounced money. The daily free "feeds" in the Panhandle were a staple for many. The Diggers, an anarchist street-theater group, were known for handing out bread shaped like the big coffee cans they baked it in. (The Diggers also gave us immortal phrases such as "Do your own thing.")

At the time, the U.S. government, Harvard professor Timothy Leary, a Stanford student named Ken Kesey, and the kids in the Haight were all experimenting with LSD. Acid was legal, widely available, and usually given away for free. At Kesey's all-night parties, called "acid tests," a buck got you a cup of "electric" Kool-Aid, a preview of psychedelic art, and an earful of the house band, the

Grateful Dead. When LSD was made illegal in 1966, the kids responded by staging a Love Pageant Rally, where they dropped acid tabs en masse and rocked out to Janis Joplin and the Dead.

THE PEAK OF THE PARTY

Things crested early in 1967, when between 10,000 and 50,000 people ("depending on whether you were a policeman or a hippie," according to one hippie) gathered at the Polo Field in Golden Gate Park for the Human Be-In of the Gathering of the Tribes. Allen Ginsberg and Timothy Leary spoke, the Dead and Jefferson Airplane played, and people costumed with beads and feathers waved flags, clanged cymbals, and beat drums. A parachutist dropped onto the field, tossing fistfuls of acid tabs to the crowd. America watched via satellite, gape-mouthed—it was every conser-vative parent's nightmare.

BURN OUT

Later that year, thousands heeded Scott McKenzie's song "San Francisco," which promised "For those who come to San Francisco, Summertime will be a love-in there." The Summer of Love swelled the Haight's population from 7,000 to 75,000; people came both to join in and to ogle. But degenerates soon joined the gentle people, heroin replaced LSD, crime became rampant, and the Haight began a fast slide.

Hippies will tell you the Human Be-In was the pinnacle of their scene, while the Summer of Love came from outside—a media creation that turned their movement into a monster. Still, the idea of that fictional summer still lingers, and to this day pilgrims from all over the world come to the Haight to search for a past that never was.

10

TWO HAIGHTS

The Haight is actually composed of two distinct neighborhoods: the Lower Haight runs from Divisadero to Webster; the Upper Haight, immediately east of Golden Gate Park, is the part people tend to call Haight-Ashbury (and the part that's covered here). San Franciscans come to the Upper Haight for the myriad vintage clothing stores concentrated in its few blocks, bars with character, restaurants where huge break-fast portions take the edge off a hangover, and Amoeba, the best place in town for new and used CDs and vinyl. The Lower Haight is a lively, grittier stretch with several well-loved pubs and a smattering of niche music shops.

and exhilarating or scummy and intimidating (the panhandling here can be aggressive).

TOP ATTRACTIONS

Haight-Ashbury Intersection. On October 6, 1967, hippies took over the intersection of Haight and Ashbury streets to proclaim the "Death of Hip." If they thought hip was dead then, they'd find absolute confirmation of it today, what with the only tie-dye in sight on the famed corner being Ben & Jerry's storefront.

Everyone knows the Summer of Love had something to do with free love and LSD, but the drugs and other excesses of that period have tended to obscure the residents' serious attempts to create an America that was more spiritually oriented, more environmentally aware, and less caught up in commercialism. The Diggers, a radical group of actors and populist agitators, for example, operated a free shop a few blocks off Haight Street. Everything really was free at the free shop; people brought in things they didn't need and took things they did.

Among the folks who hung out in or near the Haight during the late 1960s were writers Richard Brautigan, Allen Ginsberg, Ken Kesey, and Gary Snyder; anarchist Abbie Hoffman; rock performers Marty Balin, Jerry Garcia, Janis Joplin, and Grace Slick; LSD champion Timothy Leary; and filmmaker Kenneth Anger. If you're keen to feel something resembling the hippie spirit these days, there's always Hippie Hill, just inside the Haight Street entrance of Golden Gate Park. Think drum circles, guitar players, and whiffs of pot smoke. ⊠ *Haight.*

WORTH NOTING

Buena Vista Park. If you can manage the steep climb, this eucalyptus-filled park has great city views. Dog walkers and homeless folks make good use of the park, the only green area in the Haight. Be sure to scan the stone rain gutters lining many of the park's walkways for inscribed names and dates; these are the remains of gravestones left unclaimed when the city closed the Laurel Hill cemetery around 1940. You might also come across used needles and condoms; definitely avoid the park after dark, when these items are left behind. ⊠ *Haight St. between Lyon St. and Buena Vista Ave. W, Haight.*

A colorful mosaic mural in the Castro

Cha Cha Cha. Boisterous Cha Cha Cha serves island cuisine, a mix of Cajun, Southwestern, and Caribbean influences. The decor is Technicolor tropical plastic, and the food is hot and spicy. Try the fried calamari or chili-spiked shrimp, and wash everything down with a pitcher of Cha Cha Cha's signature sangria. Reservations are not accepted, so expect a wait for dinner. ✉ *1801 Haight St., at Shrader St., Haight* ☎ 415/386–7670 ⊕ *www.cha3. com.*

Grateful Dead House. On the outside, this is just one more well-kept Victorian on a street that's full of them, but true fans of the Dead may find some inspiration at this legendary structure. The three-story house (closed to the public) is tastefully painted in sedate mauves, tans, and teals—no bright tie-dye colors here. ✉ *710 Ashbury St., just past Waller St., Haight.*

Red Victorian Bed & Breakfast Inn and Peace Center. By even the most generous accounts, the Summer of Love quickly crashed and burned, and the Haight veered sharply away from the higher goals that inspired that fabled summer. In 1977 Sami Sunchild acquired the Red Vic, built as a hotel in 1904, with the aim of preserving the best of 1960s ideals. She decorated her rooms with 1960s themes—one chamber is called the Flower Child Room—and opened the Peace Arts Gallery on the ground floor. Here you can buy her paintings, T-shirts, and "meditative art," along with books about the Haight and prayer flags. Simple, cheap vegan and vegetarian fare is available in the Peace Café, and there's also a meditation room. The whole space is shiny after a recent,

10

The Evolution of Gay San Francisco

San Francisco's gay community has been a part of the city since its earliest days. As a port city and a major hub during the 19th-century gold rush, San Francisco became known for its sexual openness along with all of its other liberalities. But a major catalyst for the rise of a gay community was World War II.

STATIONED IN SAN FRANCISCO

During the war, hundreds of thousands of servicemen cycled through "Sodom by the Sea," and for most, San Francisco's permissive atmosphere was an eye-opening experience. The army's "off-limits" lists of forbidden establishments unintentionally (but effectively) pointed the way to the city's gay bars. When soldiers were dishonorably discharged for homosexual activity, many stayed on.

MAKING THE CITY HOME

Scores of these newcomers found homes in what was then called Eureka Valley. When the war ended, the predominantly Irish-Catholic families in that neighborhood began to move out, heading for the 'burbs. The new arrivals snapped up the Victorians on the main drag, Castro Street.

OPENING THE CLOSET A CRACK

The establishment pushed back. In the 1950s San Francisco's police chief vowed to crack down on "perverts," and the city's gay, lesbian, bisexual, and transgender residents lived in fear of getting caught in police raids. (Arrest meant being outed in the morning paper.) But harassment helped galvanize the community. The Daughters of Bilitis lesbian organization was founded in the city in 1955; the gay male Mattachine Society,

started in Los Angeles in 1950, followed suit with a San Francisco branch.

THE TIDE BEGINS TO TURN

By the mid-1960s these clashing interests gave the growing gay population a national profile. The police upped their policy of harassment but overplayed their hand. In 1965 they dramatically raided a New Year's benefit event, and the tide of public opinion began to turn. The police were forced to appoint the first-ever liaison to the gay community. Local gay organizations began to lobby openly. As one gay participant noted, "We didn't go back into the woodwork."

THE 1970S AND HARVEY MILK

The 1970s—thumping disco, raucous street parties, and gay bashing—were a tumultuous time for the gay community. Thousands from across the country flocked to San Francisco's gay scene. Eureka Valley had more than 60 gay bars, the bathhouse scene in SoMa (where the leather crowd held court) was thriving, and graffiti around town read "Save San Francisco—Kill a Fag." When the Eureka Valley Merchants Association refused to admit gay-owned businesses in 1974, camera shop owner Harvey Milk founded the Castro Valley Association, and the neighborhood's new moniker was born. Milk was elected to the city's Board of Supervisors in 1977, its first openly gay official (and the inspirational figure for the Oscar-winning film *Milk*).

San Francisco's gay community was getting serious about politics, civil rights, and self-preservation, but it still loved a party: 350,000 people attended the 1978 Gay Freedom Day Parade, where the rainbow flag debuted. But on November 27, 1978, Milk and Mayor George Moscone were gunned down in City Hall by enraged former city council member Dan White. Thousands marched in silent tribute out of the Castro down to City Hall.

When the killer got a relatively light conviction of manslaughter, the next march was not silent. Another crowd of thousands converged on City Hall, this time smashing windows, burning 12 police cars, and fighting with police in what became known as the White Night Riot. The police retaliated by storming the Castro.

THE ADVENT OF AIDS

The gay community recovered, even thrived—especially economically—but in 1981 the first medical and journalistic reports of a dangerous new disease surfaced. A notice appeared in a Castro pharmacy's window warning people about "the gay cancer," later named AIDS. By 1983 the populations most vulnerable to the burgeoning epidemic were publicly identified as gay men in San Francisco and New York City.

San Francisco gay activists were quick to mobilize, starting foundations as early as 1982 to care for the sick, along with public memorials to raise awareness nationwide. By 1990 the disease had killed 10,000 San Franciscans. Local organizations lobbied hard to speed up drug development and FDA approvals. Since then, the city's network of volunteer organizations and public outreach has been recognized as one of the best global models for combating the disease.

TODAY'S CASTRO

Today the Castro is still the heart of San Francisco's gay life—though many young hetero families have also moved in. As the gay mecca becomes diluted, debate about the neighborhood's character and future continues. But the legacy remains, evident in the giant rainbow flag above Castro and Market streets and the Harvey Milk bust unveiled in City Hall on May 22, 2008, Milk's birthday.

10

much needed restoration. ⊠ *1665 Haight St., Haight* ☎ *415/864–1978* ⊕ *www.redvic.com.*

Spreckels Mansion. Not to be confused with the Spreckels Mansion of Pacific Heights, this house was built for sugar baron Richard Spreckels in 1887. Jack London and Ambrose Bierce both lived and wrote here, while more recent residents included musician Graham Nash and actor Danny Glover. The boxy, putty-color Victorian—today a private home—is in mint condition. ⊠ *737 Buena Vista Ave. W, Haight.*

THE CASTRO

The brash and sassy Castro district—the social, political, and cultural center of San Francisco's thriving gay (and, to a much lesser extent, lesbian) community—stands at the western end of Market Street. This neighborhood is one of the city's liveliest and most welcoming, especially on weekends. Streets teem with folks out shopping, pushing political causes, heading to art films, and lingering in bars and cafés. Hard-bodied men in painted-on T-shirts cruise the cutting-edge clothing and novelty stores, and pairs of all genders and sexual persuasions hold hands. Brightly painted, intricately restored Victorians line the streets here, making the Castro a good place to view striking examples of the architecture San Francisco is famous for.

TOP ATTRACTIONS

Fodor'sChoice **Castro Theatre.** Here's a classic way to join in the Castro community: ★ grab some popcorn and catch a flick at this 1,500-seat art-deco theater; opened in 1922, it's the grandest of San Francisco's few remaining movie palaces. The neon marquee, which stands at the top of the Castro strip, is the neighborhood's great landmark. The Castro was the fitting host of 2008's red-carpet preview of Gus Van Sant's film *Milk*, starring Sean Penn as openly gay San Francisco supervisor Harvey Milk. The theater's elaborate Spanish baroque interior is fairly well preserved. Before many shows the theater's pipe organ rises from the orchestra pit and an organist plays pop and movie tunes, usually ending with the Jeanette McDonald standard "San Francisco" (go ahead, sing along). The crowd can be enthusiastic and vocal, talking back to the screen as loudly as it talks to them. Classics such as *Who's Afraid of Virginia Woolf?* take on a whole new life, with the assembled beating the actors to the punch and fashioning even snappier comebacks for Elizabeth Taylor. Head here to catch sing-along classics like *Mary Poppins*, a Fellini film retrospective, or the latest take on same-sex love. ⊠ *429 Castro St., Castro* ☎ *415/621–6120* ⊕ *www.castrotheatre.com.*

10

WORTH NOTING

Clarke's Mansion. Built for attorney Alfred "Nobby" Clarke, this 1892 off-white baroque Queen Anne home was dubbed Clarke's Folly. (His wife refused to inhabit it because it was in an unfashionable part of town—at the time, anyone who was anyone lived on Nob Hill.) The greenery-shrouded house (now apartments) is a beauty, with dormers, cupolas, rounded bay windows, and huge turrets topped by gold-leaf spheres. ⊠ *250 Douglass St., between 18th and 19th Sts., Castro.*

QUICK BITES

Dinosaurs. Most folks think of the Tenderloin or the Richmond for Vietnamese sandwiches, but this small Castro storefront serves up exceptionally fresh bánh mì and rockin' spring rolls. Service is quick, and a couple of outdoor tables take in the scene on Market Street. ⊠ *2275 Market St., near 16th St., Castro* ☎ *415/503–1421* ⊕ *eatdinosaurs.com.*

SISTER ACT!

If you're lucky enough to happen upon a cluster of cheeky cross-dressing nuns while in the Castro, meet the legendary Sisters of Perpetual Indulgence. They're decked out in white face-paint, glitter, and fabulous jewels. Renowned for their wit and charity fund-raising bashes, the Sisters—Sister Mary MaeHimm, Sister Bea Attitude, Sister Farrah Moans, and the gang—are the pinnacle of Castro color.

GLBT Historical Society Museum. The two-gallery Gay, Lesbian, Bisexual, and Transgender (GLBT) Historical Society Museum, the first of its kind, presents multimedia exhibits from its vast holdings covering San Francisco's queer history. In the remodeled main gallery, you might hear the audiotape Harvey Milk made for the community in the event of his assassination; explore artifacts from "Gayborhoods," lost landmarks of the city's gay past; or flip through a memory book with pictures and thoughts on some of the more than 20,000 San Franciscans lost to AIDS. Though certainly not for the faint of heart (those offended by sex toys and photos of lustily frolicking naked people may, well, be offended), the museum offers an inside look at these communities so integral to the fabric of San Francisco life. ⊠ *4127 18th St., near Castro St., Castro* ☎ *415/621–1107* ⊕ *www.glbthistory.org* ⊠ *$5, free 1st Wed. of month* ☉ *Mon. and Wed.–Sat. 11–7, Sun. noon–5.*

Harvey Milk Plaza. An 18-foot-long rainbow flag, the symbol of gay pride, flies above this plaza named for the man who electrified the city in 1977 by being elected to its Board of Supervisors as an openly gay candidate. In the early 1970s Milk had opened a camera store on the block of Castro Street between 18th and 19th streets. The store became the center for his campaign to open San Francisco's social and political life to gays and lesbians.

The liberal Milk hadn't served a full year of his term before he and Mayor George Moscone, also a liberal, were shot in November 1978 at City Hall. The murderer was a conservative ex-supervisor named Dan White, who had recently resigned his post and then became enraged when Moscone wouldn't reinstate him. Milk and White had often been at odds on the board, and White thought Milk had been part of a cabal to keep him from returning to his post. Milk's assassination shocked the gay community, which became infuriated when the infamous "Twinkie defense"—that junk food had led to diminished mental capacity—resulted in a manslaughter verdict for White. During the so-called White Night Riot of May 21, 1979, gays and their allies stormed City Hall, torching its lobby and several police cars.

CASTRO AND NOE WALK

The Castro and Noe Valley are both neighborhoods that beg to be walked—or ambled through, really, without time pressure or an absolute destination. Hit the Castro first, beginning at **Harvey Milk Plaza** under the gigantic rainbow flag. If you're going on to Noe Valley, first head east down **Market Street** for the cafés, bistros, and shops, then go back to **Castro Street** and head south, past the glorious art-deco **Castro Theatre**, checking out boutiques and cafés along the way (Cliff's Variety, at 479 Castro Street, is a must). To tour Noe Valley, go east down **18th Street** to Church (at Dolores Park), and then either strap on your hiking boots and head south over the hill or hop the J–Church to **24th Street**, the center of this rambling neighborhood.

Milk, who had feared assassination, left behind a tape recording in which he urged the community to continue the work he had begun. His legacy is the high visibility of gay people throughout city government; a bust of him was unveiled at City Hall on his birthday in 2008, and the 2008 film *Milk* gives insight into his life. A plaque at the base of the flagpole lists the names of past and present openly gay and lesbian state and local officials. ⊠ *Southwest corner of Castro and Market Sts., Castro.*

Pink Triangle Park. On a median near the Castro's huge rainbow flag stands this memorial to the gays, lesbians, bisexual and transgender people whom the Nazis forced to wear pink triangles. Fifteen triangular granite columns, one for every 1,000 gays, lesbians, bisexual, and transgender people estimated to have been killed during and after the Holocaust, stand at the tip of a pink-rock-filled triangle—a reminder of the gay community's past and ongoing struggle for civil rights. ⊠ *Corner of Market, Castro, and 17th Sts., Castro.*

NOE VALLEY

10

This upscale but relaxed enclave just south of the Castro (also known as Stroller Valley for its relatively high concentration of little ones) is among the city's most desirable places to live, with laid-back cafés, kid-friendly restaurants, and comfortable, old-time shops along Church Street and 24th Street, its main thoroughfares. You can also see remnants of Noe Valley's agricultural beginnings: Billy Goat Hill (at Castro and 30th streets), a wild-grass hill often draped in fog and topped by one of the city's best rope-swinging trees, is named for the goats that grazed here right into the 20th century.

EXPLORING

Axford House. This mauve house was built in 1877 by William Axford, a Scottish immigrant and metalsmith whose Mission Iron Works made cannonballs for the Union Army during the Civil War. The house, perched several feet above the sidewalk, was built when Noe Valley was still a rural area, as evidenced by the hayloft in the gable of the adjacent carriage house. The original iron fence, made in Axford's foundry, remains. ⊠ *1190 Noe St., at 25th St., Noe Valley.*

Golden fire hydrant. When all the other fire hydrants went dry during the fire that followed the 1906 earthquake, this one kept pumping. Noe Valley and the Mission District were thus spared the devastation wrought elsewhere in the city, which explains the large number of pre-quake homes here. Every year on April 18th (the anniversary of the quake) folks gather here to share stories about the earthquake, and the famous hydrant gets a fresh coat of gold paint. ⊠ *Church and 20th Sts., southeastern corner, across from Dolores Park, Noe Valley.*

OFF THE
BEATEN
PATH

Twin Peaks. Windswept and desolate Twin Peaks yields sweeping vistas of San Francisco and the neighboring East and North Bay counties. You can get a real feel for the city's layout here, but you'll share it with busloads of other admirers; in summer, arrive before the late-afternoon fog turns the view into pea soup. To drive here, head west from Castro Street up Market Street, which eventually becomes Portola Drive. Turn right (north) on Twin Peaks Boulevard and follow the signs to the top. Muni Bus 37–Corbett heads west to Twin Peaks from Market Street. Catch this bus above the Castro Street Muni light-rail station on the island west of Castro at Market Street. ⊠ *Twin Peaks.*

MISSION
DISTRICT

GETTING ORIENTED

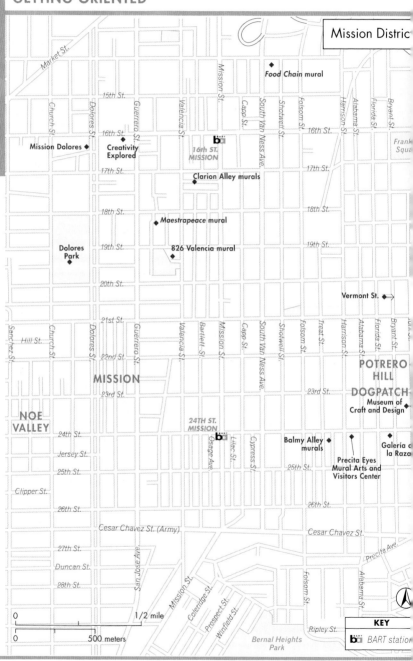

Mission Distric

Market St.

15th St.

Food Chain mural

Church St.

Dolores St.

Guerrero St.

Valencia St.

Mission St.

Capp St.

South Van Ness Ave.

Shotwell St.

Folsom St.

Harrison St.

Alabama St.

Florida St.

Bryant St.

16th St.

Frank Squa

16th St.

Mission Dolores ◆

Creativity Explored

16th ST. MISSION

17th St.

17th St.

Clarion Alley murals

18th St.

18th St.

Maestrapeace mural

Dolores Park

19th St.

826 Valencia mural

19th St.

20th St.

Vermont St. ◆

21st St.

Sanchez St.

Hill St.

Church St.

Dolores St.

Guerrero St.

Valencia St.

Bartlett St.

Mission St.

Capp St.

South Van Ness Ave.

Shotwell St.

Folsom St.

Treat St.

Harrison St.

Alabama St.

Florida St.

Bryant St.

22nd St.

MISSION

POTRERO HILL

23rd St.

23rd St.

DOGPATCH

Museum of Craft and Design ◆

NOE VALLEY

24th St.

24TH ST. MISSION

Balmy Alley murals ◆

Galeria a la Raza

Jersey St.

Osage Ave.

Lilac St.

Cypress St.

Precita Eyes Mural Arts and Visitors Center

25th St.

25th St.

Clipper St.

26th St.

26th St.

Cesar Chavez St. (Army)

Cesar Chavez St.

27th St.

Duncan St.

San Jose Ave.

Precita Ave.

28th St.

Mission St.

Coleridge St.

Prospect St.

Winfield St.

Folsom St.

Alabama St.

0   1/2 mile

0   500 meters

Ripley St.

Bernal Heights Park

KEY

b̄ BART station

TOP REASONS TO GOV

Bar-hop: Embrace your inner (or not-so-inner) hipster. Grab a cocktail at Trick Dog, whose mixologists mix up some of the Mission's finest drinks, then head over to the stylish Nihon Whisky Lounge or stop by the Chapel, where live music often accompanies the cocktails.

Chow down on phenomenal, cheap ethnic food: Keen appetites and thin wallets will meet their match here. Just try to decide between deliciously fresh burritos, garlicky falafel, thin-crust pizza, savory samosas, and more.

One-of-a-kind shopping: Barter for buried treasure at 826 Valencia and its Pirate Supply Store, then hop next door and say hello to the giraffe's head at the mad taxidermy–cum–garden store hodgepodge that is Paxton Gate.

Vivid murals: Check out dozens of energetic, colorful public artworks in alleyways and on building exteriors.

Hang out in Dolores Park: Join Mission locals and their dogs on this hilly expanse of green that has a glorious view of downtown and, if you're lucky, the Bay Bridge. On sunny days the whole neighborhood comes out to play.

QUICK BITES

Four Barrel Coffee. The pastries may be fresh and the space may be light and inviting, but come to Four Barrel for the coffee: house-roasted beans make for one of the best cups of coffee in town, and you'll be in and out while others are still in line at Tartine. ⊠ *375 Valencia St., Mission* ☏ *415/252–0800* ⊕ *fourbarrelcoffee.com.*

Tartine Bakery and Cafe. It may not be quick—the line often snakes out the door—but if you're hankering for the perfect croque monsieur or frangapine, Tartine is certainly worth the wait. Skip the line and head to the register in the back right corner if you're just ordering drinks. ⊠ *600 Guerrero St., at 18th St., Mission* ☏ *415/487–2600* ⊕ *www. tartinebakery.com.*

GETTING THERE

After climbing the hills downtown, you'll find the Mission to be welcomingly flat. BART's two Mission District stations drop you right in the heart of the action. Get off at 16th Street for Mission Dolores, shopping, nightlife, and restaurants, or 24th Street to see the neighborhood murals and a street that's turning into the next Valencia Corridor. The busy 14–Mission bus runs all the way from downtown into the neighborhood, but BART is a much faster and more direct route. Parking can be a drag, especially on weekend evenings. If you're heading out in the evening, your safest bet would be taking a cab, since some blocks are sketchy.

PLANNING YOUR TIME

A walk that includes Mission Dolores and the neighborhood's murals takes about two hours. If you plan to go on a mural walk with the Precita Eyes organization, or if you're a window-shopper, add at least another hour. The Mission is a neighborhood that sleeps in. In the afternoon and evening, the main drags—Mission, Valencia, and 24th streets—really come to life.

From Sunday through Tuesday it's relatively quiet here, especially in the evening—a great time to get a café table with no wait.

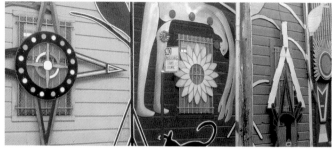

Sightseeing
★★

Nightlife
★★★★★

Dining
★★★★★

Lodging
–

Shopping
★★★

The Mission has a number of distinct personalities: it's the Latino neighborhood, where working-class folks raise their families and where gangs occasionally clash; it's the hipster hood, where tattooed and pierced twenty- and thirty-somethings hold court in the coolest cafés and bars in town; it's a culinary epicenter, with the strongest concentration of destination restaurants and affordable ethnic cuisine; it's the face of gentrification, where high-tech money prices out longtime commercial and residential renters; and it's the artists' quarter, where murals adorn literally blocks of walls long after the artists have moved to cheaper digs. It's also the city's equivalent of the Sunshine State—this neighborhood's always the last to succumb to fog.

MISSION DISTRICT

Updated by
Denise M Leto

Packed with destination restaurants, hole-in-the-wall ethnic eateries, and hip watering holes—plus taquerias, pupuserias, and produce markets—the city's hottest hood strikes an increasingly precarious balance between cutting-edge hot spot and working-class enclave. With long-time businesses being forced out by astronomical rents and even the merchants' association begging the city to stem the tide of restaurants into the neighborhood, the Mission is in flux once again, a familiar state for almost 100 years.

The eight blocks of Valencia Street between 16th and 24th streets—what's become known as the Valencia Corridor—typify the Mission District's diversity. Businesses on the block between 16th and 17th streets, for instance, include an upscale Peruvian restaurant, a tattoo parlor, a Belgian eatery beloved for its fries, the yuppie-chic bar

Blondie's, a handful of funky home-decor stores, a pizzeria, a Vietnamese kitchen, a trendy Italian place, a sushi bar, bargain and pricey thrift shops, and the Puerto Alegre restaurant, a near dive with pack-a-punch margaritas locals revere. As prices rise, this strip is losing some of its edge as even international publications proclaim its hipness. At the same time, nearby Mission Street is morphing from a down-at-the-heels row of check-cashing parlors, dollar stores, and residential hotels into overflow for the Valencia Corridor's restaurant explosion.

Italian and Irish in the early 20th century, the Mission became heavily Latino in the late 1960s, when immigrants from Mexico and Central America began arriving. Since the 1970s, groups of muralists have transformed walls and storefronts into canvases, creating art accessible to everyone. Following the example set by the Mexican liberal artist and muralist Diego Rivera, many of the Latino artists address political and social justice issues in their murals. More recently, artists of varied backgrounds, some of whom simply like to paint on a large scale, have expanded the conversation.

The actual conversations you'll hear on the street these days might unfold in Chinese, Vietnamese, Arabic, and other tongues of the non-Latino immigrants who began settling in the Mission in the 1980s and 1990s along with a young bohemian crowd enticed by cheap rents and the burgeoning arts-and-nightlife scene. These newer arrivals made a diverse and lively neighborhood even more so, setting the stage for the Mission's current hipster cachet. With the neighborhood flourishing, rents have gone through the roof, but the Mission remains scruffy in patches, so as you plan your explorations, take into account your comfort zone.

■TIP➜ Be prepared for homelessness and drug use around the BART stations, prostitution along Mission Street, and raucous bar-hoppers along the Valencia Corridor. The farther east you go, the sketchier the neighborhood gets.

TOP ATTRACTIONS

Balmy Alley murals. Mission District artists have transformed the walls of their neighborhood with paintings, and Balmy Alley is one of the best-executed examples. Many murals adorn the one-block alley, with newer ones continually filling in the blank spaces. In 1971, artists began teaming with local children to create a space to promote peace in Central America, community spirit, and (later) AIDS awareness; since then dozens of artists have added their vibrant works. ■TIP➜ Be alert here: the 25th Street end of the alley adjoins a somewhat dangerous area. ✉ 24th St. between and parallel to Harrison and Treat Sts., alley runs south to 25th St., Mission.

Clarion Alley murals. Inspired by the work in Balmy Alley, a new generation of muralists began creating a fresh alley-cum-gallery here in 1992. The works by the loosely connected artists of the Clarion Alley Mural Project (CAMP) represent a broad range of styles and imagery, an exuberant, flowery exhortation to Tax the Rich; a lesbian celebration including donkey heads, skirts, and rainbows; and some of the first black-and-white murals in the city. The alley's murals offer a quick

DID YOU KNOW?

San Francisco is chockablock with murals—around 2,000—and the Mission District is the epicenter of all the artistic fervor.

but dense glimpse at the Mission's contemporary art scene. ⊠ *Between Valencia and Mission Sts. and 17th and 18th Sts., Mission.*

Fodor's Choice **Dolores Park.** A two-square-block microcosm of life in the Mission,
★ Dolores Park is one of San Francisco's liveliest green spaces: dog lovers and their pampered pups congregate, kids play at the extravagant, recently reconstructed playground, and hipsters hold court, drinking beer on sunny days. During the summer, the park hosts movie nights; performances by Shakespeare in the Park, the San Francisco Mime Troupe, and the San Francisco Symphony; and any number of pop-up events and impromptu parties. Spend a warm day here—maybe sitting at the top of the park with a view of the city and the Bay Bridge—surrounded by locals and that laid-back San Francisco energy, and you may well find yourself plotting your move to the city. The park continues to be well visited during a major renovation expected to continue through 2015. ⊠ *Between 18th and 20th Sts. and Dolores and Church Sts., Mission.*

Maestrapeace mural. The towering mural that seems to enclose the Women's Building celebrates women around the world who work for peace. Created by seven main artists and numerous helpers, this is one of the city's don't-miss murals. Head inside to pick up a key to the mural's figures and symbols or to purchase T-shirts, postcards, and other mural-related items. ⊠ *Women's Bldg., 3543 18th St., between Valencia and Guerrero Sts., Mission* ☎ *415/431–1180* ⊕ *www.womensbuilding.org* ⊙ *Bldg. Mon.–Thurs. 9–5, Fri. 10–6.*

Mission Dolores. Two churches stand side by side here, including the small adobe **Mission San Francisco de Asís,** which, along with the Presidio's Officers' Club is the oldest standing structure in San Francisco. Completed in 1791, it's the sixth of the 21 California missions founded by Franciscan friars in the 18th and early 19th centuries. Its ceiling depicts original Ohlone Indian basket designs, executed in vegetable dyes. The tiny chapel includes frescoes and a hand-painted wooden altar.

There's a hidden treasure here, too. In 2004 an archaeologist and an artist crawling along the ceiling's rafters opened a trapdoor behind the altar and rediscovered the mission's original mural, painted with natural dyes by Native Americans in 1791. The centuries have taken their toll, so the team photographed the 20-by-22-foot mural and began digitally restoring the photographic version. Among the images is a dagger-pierced Sacred Heart of Jesus.

The small museum here covers the mission's founding and history, and the pretty little cemetery—which appears in Alfred Hitchcock's film *Vertigo*—contains the graves of mid-19th-century European immigrants. (The remains of an estimated 5,000 Native Americans lie in unmarked graves.) Services are held in both the old mission and next door in the handsome multidome basilica. ⊠ *Dolores and 16th Sts., Mission* ☎ *415/621–8203* ⊕ *www.missiondolores.org* ✉ *$5, audio tour $7* ⊙ *Nov.–Apr., daily 9–4; May–Oct., daily 9–4:30.*

Vivid public art provides a backdrop for the Mission District.

WORTH NOTING

826 Valencia mural. Fans of graphic novelist Chris Ware will want to take a good look at the facade of 826 Valencia, the nonprofit organization established by writer Dave Eggers and educator Nínive Calegari to help students in elementary, middle, and high school develop their writing skills. Ware designed the intricate mural for the group's storefront as a meditation on the evolution of human communication. ⊠ *826 Valencia St., between 19th and 20th Sts., Mission* ⊕ *826valencia.org.*

Creativity Explored. Joyous, if chaotic, creativity pervades the workshops of this art-education center and gallery for developmentally disabled adults. Several dozen adults work at the center each day—guided by a staff of working artists—painting, working in the darkroom, producing videos, and crafting prints, textiles, and ceramics. On weekdays you can drop by and see the artists at work. The art produced here is striking, and some of it is for sale; this is a great place to find a unique San Francisco masterpiece to take home. ⊠ *3245 16th St., Mission* ☎ *415/863–2108* ⊕ *www.creativityexplored.org* ⌫ *Free* ⊙ *Mon.–Wed. and Fri. 10–3, Thurs. 10–7, weekends noon–5.*

***Food Chain* mural.** Brian Barneclo's gigantic *Food Chain* is a retro, 1950s-style celebration of the city's many neighborhoods—and the food chain—complete with an ant birthday party and worms finishing off a human skull. But in a cute way. Barneclo fans can see more of his work at Rye bar and the restaurants Nopa and farmerbrown (as well as the Facebook headquarters in Menlo Park). ⊠ *Foods Co, 1800 Folsom St., Shotwell St. side of store between 14th and 15th Sts., Mission.*

CLOSE UP

San Francisco on Film

11

With its spectacular cityscape, atmospheric fog, and a camera-ready iconic bridge, it's little wonder that San Francisco has been the setting for hundreds of films. While you're running around town, you might have the occasional sense of déjà vu, sparked by a scene from a Hitchcock or Clint Eastwood thriller. *Here are a few of the city's favorite cinematic sites:*

■ *Zodiac*, a 2007 drama about a legendary Bay Area serial killer, filmed scenes at the real-life locations where victims were gunned down. It also re-created the *San Francisco Chronicle* offices, but down south in L.A.

■ City Hall shows up in the Clint Eastwood cop thrillers *Dirty Harry* and *Magnum Force*, and is set aflame in the James Bond flick *A View to a Kill*. Its interior became a nightclub for Robin Williams' *Bicentennial Man* and a courthouse in *Tucker: The Man and His Dream*.

■ Streets in Russian Hill, Potrero Hill, and North Beach were used for the supreme car-chase sequence in *Bullitt*. The namesake detective, played by Steve McQueen, lived in Nob Hill at 1153–57 Taylor Street. And the "King of Cool" did much of his own stunt driving, thank you very much.

■ Brocklebank Apartments, at Mason and Sacramento streets in Nob Hill, appears in several films, most notably as the posh residence of Kim Novak in Alfred Hitchcock's *Vertigo*. Other key *Vertigo* locations include the cemetery of Mission Dolores and the waterfront at Fort Point.

■ The great Bogie-and-Bacall noir film *Dark Passage* revolves around the art-deco apartment building at 1360 Montgomery Street and the nearby Filbert Steps.

■ Dashiell Hammett's *Thin Man* characters, Nick and Nora Charles, do much of their sleuthing in the city, especially in films like *After the Thin Man*, in which the base of Coit Tower stands in as the entrance to the Charles' home.

■ North Beach's Tosca Café, at 242 Columbus Avenue, is the bar where Michael Douglas unwinds in *Basic Instinct.*

■ The Hilton Hotel at 333 O'Farrell Street became the "Hotel Bristol," the scene of much of the mayhem caused by Barbra Streisand in *What's Up, Doc?*

■ At 2640 Steiner Street in Pacific Heights is the elegant home that Robin Williams infiltrates while disguised as a nanny in *Mrs. Doubtfire.*

■ The Castro of the 1970s comes alive in *Milk*, Gus Van Sant's film starring Sean Penn as slain San Francisco supervisor Harvey Milk.

■ And, of course, there are plenty of movies about the notorious federal prison on Alcatraz Island, including Burt Lancaster's redemption drama *Birdman of Alcatraz*, Clint Eastwood's suspenseful *Escape from Alcatraz*, the goofy *So I Married an Axe Murderer*, and the Sean Connery and Nicolas Cage action flick, *The Rock.*

Galería de la Raza. San Francisco's premier showcase for contemporary Latino art, the gallery exhibits the works of mostly local artists. Events include readings and spoken word by local poets and writers, screenings of Latin American and Spanish films, and theater works by local minority theater troupes. The gallery may close between exhibits, so call ahead. Just across the street, murals and mosaics festoon the 24th Street/York Street Minipark, a tiny urban playground. A mosaic-covered Quetzalcoatl serpent plunges into the ground and rises, creating hills for little ones to clamber over, and mural-covered walls surround the space. ⊠ *2857 24th St., at Bryant St., Mission* 🕾 *415/826–8009* ⊕ *www.galeriadelaraza.org* 🕙 *Gallery Wed.–Sat. noon–6, Sun. noon–5.*

Precita Eyes Mural Arts and Visitors Center. The muralists of this nonprofit arts organization design and create murals and lead guided walks of area murals. The Classic Mission Mural Walk ($20) starts with a 45-minute slide presentation before participants head outside to view murals on Balmy Alley and 24th Street. The Mission Trail Mural Walk ($15) includes some of the same murals and impressive ones at Cesar Chavez Elementary School. You can pick up a map of 24th Street's murals at the center and buy art supplies, T-shirts, postcards, and other mural-related items. ⊠ *2981 24th St., Mission* 🕾 *415/285–2287* ⊕ *www.precitaeyes.org* 🔳 *Center free, tours $15–$20* 🕙 *Center weekdays 10–5, Sat. 10–4, Sun. noon–4; walks: weekends at 1:30 (Classic), Sat. at 11 (Mission Trail).*

DOGPATCH

East of the Mission District and Potrero Hill and a short T-Third Muni light-rail ride from SoMa, the Dogpatch neighborhood has been on the rise for the last decade. Artisans, designers, and craftspeople eager to protect the area's historical industrial legacy have all moved here in recent years, providing a solid customer base for shops, galleries, and boutique restaurants and artisanal food producers. At or near the intersection of 3rd and 22nd streets, you'll find neighborhood breakfast favorite Just for You Café, locally sourced Italian food at sunny yellow Piccino, small-batch organic ice cream at Mr. and Mrs. Miscellaneous, and artisanal chocolates at Michael Recchiuti's Chocolate Lab, which has a small café, too. The Museum of Craft and Design moved to Dogpatch in 2013 and instantly became the neighborhood's cultural anchor.

EXPLORING

Museum of Craft and Design. Right at home in this once-industrial neighborhood now bursting with creative energy, this small, four-room space—definitely a quick view—mounts temporary art and design exhibitions. The focus might be sculpture, metalwork, furniture, or jewelry—or industrial design, architecture, or other topics. The MakeArt Lab gives kids the opportunity to create their own exhibit-inspired work, and the beautifully curated shop sells tempting textiles, housewares, jewelry, and other well-crafted items. ⊠ *2569 3rd St., near 22nd St., Dogpatch* 🕾 *415/773–0303* ⊕ *sfmcd.org* 🔳 *$8, free 1st Tues. of month* 🕙 *Tues.–Sat. 11–6 (Thurs. until 7), Sun. noon–5.*

PACIFIC HEIGHTS
AND JAPANTOWN

GETTING ORIENTED

Pacific Heights
and Japantown

TOP REASONS TO GO

Chic shopping on Fillmore Street: Browse the superfine shops along Pacific Heights' main drag.

Picnic with a view at Lafayette Park: Gather supplies along Fillmore Street and climb to the top of this park. It's surrounded by grand homes and has a sweeping view of the city.

Asian shops galore in the Japan Center: Graze your way through the mall—grab a quick bean-paste snack at May's Coffee Shop, decked out like an open-air Japanese restaurant—then browse the wonderful Kinokuniya Bookstore and the tea implements at Asakichi.

Spa serenity at Kabuki Springs: Enter the peaceful lobby and prepare to be transported at the Japanese-style communal baths.

See how the other half lives: Check out the grand, historic homes along the tree-lined streets of Pacific Heights.

QUICK BITES

Jane on Fillmore. Stop in this bright, two-story spot for a loaded panino, mile-high quiche, and a cup of Stumptown coffee. You're still likely to surrender to the homemade baked goods, created with locally sourced ingredients. ⊠ *2123 Fillmore St., Pacific Heights* ☎ *415/931–5263* ⊕ *janeonfillmore.com.*

Yasukochi's Sweet Stop. A Japantown anchor, this counter tucked inside the Super Mira market has been baking up mouthwatering cakes for 40 years. Generations of locals swear by the coffee crunch cake—layers of cake and light, airy frosting, all covered in crispy, coffee-flavored candy—but even if you don't arrive early enough to get a piece, you'll still have plenty of options. ⊠ *1790 Sutter St., Japantown* ☎ *415/931–8165.*

GETTING THERE

12

Steep streets in Pacific Heights make for impressive views and rough walking; unless you're in decent shape, consider taking a car or taxi to this neighborhood.

The only public transit that runs through the area is the bus. For Pacific Heights proper, take the 12–Folsom to its terminus at Van Ness and Pacific avenues and walk west. For shopping on Union Street in Cow Hollow (lower Pacific Heights), catch the 41–Union or the 45–Union bus.

Buses that run to Japantown from downtown include the 2–Clement, 3–Jackson, and the very busy 38–Geary.

PLANNING YOUR TIME

Give yourself an hour to wander Fillmore Street, more if you're planning to have a meal here or picnic in Lafayette or Alta Plaza parks. Checking out the stunning homes in Pacific Heights is best done by car, unless you have serious stamina; a half hour should be enough.

Shops and restaurants are the highlights of Japantown, so plan a daytime visit for a meal and some window-shopping; lunchtime is ideal.

Sightseeing
★★
Nightlife
★★
Dining
★★★
Lodging
★
Shopping
★★★

Pacific Heights and Japantown are something of an odd couple: privileged, old-school San Francisco and the workaday commercial center of Japanese American life in the city, stacked virtually on top of each other. The sprawling, extravagant mansions of Pacific Heights gradually give way to the more modest Victorians and unassuming housing tracts of Japantown. The most interesting spots in Japantown huddle in the Japan Center, the neighborhood's two-block centerpiece, and along Post Street. You can find plenty of authentic Japanese treats in the shops and restaurants.

PACIFIC HEIGHTS

Updated by
Denise M. Leto

Pacific Heights defines San Francisco's most expensive and dramatic real estate. Grand Victorians line the streets, mansions and town houses are priced in the millions, and there are magnificent views from almost any point in the neighborhood. Old money and new, personalities in the limelight and those who prefer absolute media anonymity live here, and few outsiders see anything other than the pleasing facades of Queen Anne charmers, English Tudor imports, and baroque bastions. Nancy Pelosi and Dianne Feinstein, Larry Ellison, and Gordon Getty all own impressive homes here, but not even pockets as deep as those can buy a large garden—space in the city is simply at too much of a premium. The boutiques and restaurants along Fillmore Street, which range from glam to funky, have become a draw for the whole city.

TOP ATTRACTIONS

Haas-Lilienthal House. A small display of photographs on the bottom floor of this elaborate, gray 1886 Queen Anne house makes clear that despite its lofty stature and striking, round third-story tower, the house was modest compared with some of the giants that fell victim to the 1906 earthquake and fire. The Foundation for San Francisco's Architectural

A PACIFIC HEIGHTS WALK

Start at **Broadway and Webster Street**, where four notable estates stand within a block of one another. Two are on the north side of Broadway west of the intersection, one is on the same side to the east, and the last is half a block south on Webster. Head south down Webster and hang a right onto Clay to **Alta Plaza Park**, or skip the park and turn left on Jackson to the **Whittier Mansion**, at Jackson and Laguna streets. Head south down Laguna and cross Washington Street to **Lafayette Park**. Walk on Washington along the edge of the park, past the formal French **Spreckels Mansion** at the corner of Octavia Street, and continue east two more blocks to Franklin Street. Turn left (north); halfway down the block stands the handsome **Haas-Lilienthal House.** Head back south on Franklin Street, stopping to view several **Franklin Street buildings.** At California Street, turn right (west) to see two **Italianate Victorians** and the **Atherton House.** Continue west to Laguna Street and turn left (south); past Pine Street sits a sedate block of **Laguna Street Victorians.**

Heritage operates the home, whose carefully kept rooms provide a glimpse into late-19th-century life through period furniture, authentic details (antique dishes in the kitchen built-in), and photos of the family that occupied the house until 1972. ■TIP→ You can admire hundreds of gorgeous San Francisco Victorians from the outside, but this is the only one that's open to the public, and it's worth a visit. Volunteers conduct one-hour house tours three days a week, and informative two-hour walking tours of Pacific Heights on Sunday afternoon (call or check website for schedule). ⊠ *2007 Franklin St., between Washington and Jackson Sts., Pacific Heights* 🕾 *415/441–3004* ⊕ *www.sfheritage.org* 🎫 *Tours $8* ⊘ *1-hr tour Wed. and Sat. noon–3, Sun. 11–4; 2-hr tour Sun. at 12:30.*

WORTH NOTING

FAMILY **Alta Plaza Park.** Golden Gate Park's longtime superintendent, John McLaren, designed Alta Plaza in 1910, modeling its terracing on that of the Grand Casino in Monte Carlo, Monaco. From the top you can see Marin to the north, downtown to the east, Twin Peaks to the south, and Golden Gate Park to the west. ■TIP→ Kids love the many play structures at the large, enclosed playground at the top; everywhere else is dog territory. ⊠ *Bordered by Clay, Steiner, Jackson, and Scott Sts., Pacific Heights.*

Atherton House. The mildly daffy design of this Victorian-era house incorporates Queen Anne, Stick-Eastlake, and other architectural elements. Many claim the house—now apartments—is haunted by the ghosts of its 19th-century residents, who regularly whisper, glow, and generally cause a mild fuss. ⊠ *1990 California St., Pacific Heights.*

SAN FRANCISCO'S ARCHITECTURE

San Francisco's architecture scene underwent a dramatic growth spurt in the first decade of the new millennium. Boldface international architects spearheaded major projects like the de Young Museum, the California Academy of Sciences, and the Contemporary Jewish Museum. And with those additions came heated local debates.

The development flurry is thrown into sharp relief by the previous decades spent carefully preserving the city's historic buildings. Genteel Victorian homes are a city signature, and this residential legacy is fiercely protected.

Residents aren't shy about voicing opinions on the "starchitect" plans, either. As high-profile designs unfold and new condo neighborhoods break ground, criticism will surely escalate. One thing that gratifies everyone: the impressive advances made in eco-friendly building practices. As *Chronicle* columnist John King put it, San Francisco has gotten "a crash course in contemporary architecture. One that is long, long overdue."

SAN FRANCISCO MUSEUM OF MODERN ART (SFMOMA)

Renowned Swiss architect Mario Botta's first shot at designing a museum resulted in the distinctive, sturdy geometrical forms that reflected his signature style. Here a black-and-white cylindrical tower anchors the brick structure. Botta called the huge, slanted skylight the "city's eye, like the Cyclops." A new wing, designed by Snøhetta, a Norwegian architecture firm noted for its cultural projects, is slated to open in 2016. The expansion, which adds more than

12

100,000 square feet of gallery and public space, will accommodate the recently acquired modern art collection of late Gap founder, Don Fisher, a must for modern art lovers.

DE YOUNG MUSEUM OF FINE ART

Love it or hate it, the structure is a must-see destination in Golden Gate Park. After the original Egyptian-revival edifice was deemed seismically unsafe following the Lowa Prieta quake in 1989, the Pritzker-winning Swiss team Herzog & de Meuron won the commission to rebuild. Their design's copper facade and, in particular, the 144-foot observation tower—a twisted parallelogram grazing the treetops—drew fire from critics, who compared the design to a "rusty aircraft carrier." But the copper hue is mellowing with age, and the panoramic view from the ninth-floor observation deck is a hit—shifting any controversy to the museum's internal politics.

CALIFORNIA ACADEMY OF SCIENCES

An eco-friendly, energy-efficient adventure in biodiversity, Renzo Piano's audacious design for this natural history museum comes equipped with a rain forest, a planetarium, skylights, and a retractable ceiling over the central courtyard. But it's the "living roof," covered in native plants, that's generating the most comment.

MISSION BAY, RINCON HILL, AND THE TRANSBAY DISTRICT

San Francisco's cityscape is undergoing tremendous change, especially moving south from Market Street along the waterfront. Don't expect old-school gingerbread here. Instead, glass-sheathed, condo-crammed high-rises are taking over what was a working-class area of warehouses and lofts, studded by the AT&T Ballpark. An ultramodern Transbay Terminal is slated for 2017. A new University of California, San Francisco (UCSF) campus is springing up in Mission Bay, with a blocky Campus Community Center by Mexican architect Ricardo Legorreta now open for business.

PRESIDIO

The development of this parkland continues at a relatively slow pace. Its historic military-base buildings are being put to new uses—everything from a printing press to a spa. Additions include a digital arts center by George Lucas; a Walt Disney Museum; and the hip Inn at the Presidio boutique hotel.

Top left: California Academy of Sciences; top right: Painted Ladies; bottom right: de Young Museum of Fine Arts

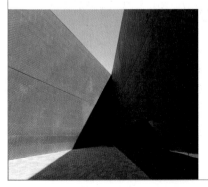

Broadway and Webster Street estates. Broadway uptown, unlike its garish North Beach stretch, has plenty of prestigious addresses. The three-story palace at 2222 Broadway, which has an intricately filigreed doorway, was built by Comstock silver-mine heir James Flood and later donated to a religious order. The Convent of the Sacred Heart purchased the **Grant House** at 2220 Broadway. These two buildings, along with a Flood property at 2120 Broadway, are used as school quarters. A gold-mine heir, William Bourn II, commissioned Willis Polk to build the nearby brick mansion at 2550 Webster Street. ⊠ *Pacific Heights.*

Franklin Street buildings. The three blocks south of the Haas-Lilienthal House contain a few curiosities of interest to architecture buffs. What at first looks like a stone facade on the **Golden Gate Church** (⊠ *1901 Franklin St.*) is actually redwood painted white. A handsome Georgian-style residence built in the early 1900s for a coffee merchant sits at 1735 Franklin. On the northeast corner of Franklin and California streets is a **Christian Science church**; built in the Tuscan revival style, it's noteworthy for its terra-cotta detailing. The **Coleman House** (⊠ *1701 Franklin St.*) is an impressive twin-turret Queen Anne mansion that was built for a gold-rush mining and lumber baron. Don't miss the large, brilliant-purple stained-glass window on the house's north side. ⊠ *Franklin St. between Washington and California Sts., Pacific Heights.*

Italianate Victorians. Two Italianate Victorians stand out on the 1800 block of California. The beauty at 1834, the Wormser-Coleman house, was built in the 1870s. Coleman bought the lot next door, giving this property an unusually spacious yard for the city, even in this luxurious neighborhood. ⊠ *1818 and 1834 California St., Pacific Heights.*

Lafayette Park. Clusters of trees dot this four-block-square oasis for sunbathers and dog-and-Frisbee teams. On the south side of the park, squat but elegant **2151 Sacramento,** a private condominium, is the site of a home occupied by Sir Arthur Conan Doyle in the late 19th century. Coats of arms blaze in the front stained-glass windows. The park itself is a lovely neighborhood space, where Pacific Heights residents laze in the sun or exercise their pedigreed canines while gazing at downtown's skyline in the distance. ⊠ *Bordered by Laguna, Gough, Sacramento, and Washington Sts., Pacific Heights.*

Laguna Street Victorians. On the west side of the 1800 block of Laguna Street, these oft-photographed houses cost between $2,000 and $2,600 when they were built in the 1870s. No bright colors here, though—most of the paint jobs are in soft beiges or pastels. ⊠ *Between Bush and Pine Sts., Pacific Heights.*

Spreckels Mansion. Shrouded behind tall juniper hedges at the corner of winding, redbrick Octavia Street, overlooking Lafayette Park, the estate was built for sugar heir Adolph Spreckels and his wife Alma. Mrs. Spreckels was so pleased with her house that she commissioned George Applegarth to design another building in a similar vein: the Legion of Honor. One of the city's great iconoclasts, Alma Spreckels was the model for the bronze figure atop the Victory Monument in Union Square. These days an iconoclast of another sort owns the mansion: romance novelist Danielle Steel, whose dust-up with local columnists

over the size of those hedges entertained aficionados of local gossip in 2014. ⊠ *2080 Washington St., at Octavia St., Pacific Heights.*

Whittier Mansion. With a Spanish-tile roof and scrolled bay windows on all four sides, this is one of the most elegant 19th-century houses in the state. Unlike other grand mansions lost in the 1906 quake, the Whittier Mansion was built so solidly that only a chimney toppled over during the disaster. Built by William Franklin Whittier, the founder of (what became) PG&E, the house served as the German consulate during the Nazi period. Legend has it that the house is haunted. ⊠ *2090 Jackson St., Pacific Heights.*

JAPANTOWN

Though still the spiritual center of San Francisco's Japanese American community, Japantown feels somewhat adrift. The Japan Center mall, for instance, comes across as rather sterile, and whereas Chinatown is densely populated and still largely Chinese, Japantown struggles to retain its unique character.

Also called Nihonmachi, Japantown is centered on the southern slope of Pacific Heights, north of Geary Boulevard between Fillmore and Laguna streets. The Japanese community in San Francisco started around 1860; after the 1906 earthquake and fire many of these newcomers settled in the Western Addition. By the 1930s they had opened shops, markets, meeting halls, and restaurants and established Shinto and Buddhist temples. But during World War II the area was virtually gutted when many of its residents, including second- and third-generation Americans, were forced into so-called relocation camps. During the 1960s and 1970s redevelopment further eroded the neighborhood, and most Japanese Americans now live elsewhere in the city.

Still, when several key properties in the neighborhood were sold in 2007, a group rallied to "save Japantown," and some new blood finally infused the area with energy: Robert Redford's Sundance corporation revived the Kabuki Theatre; the local, hip hotel group Joie de Vivre took over the Hotel Kabuki; and the J-Pop Center, New People, has brought Japanese pop culture and a long-missing youthful vibe. ■ TIP➔ **Japantown is a relatively safe area, but the Western Addition, south of Geary Boulevard, can be dangerous even during the daytime. Also avoid going too far west of Fillmore Street on either side of Geary.**

TOP ATTRACTIONS

Japan Center. Cool and curious trinkets, noodle houses and sushi joints, a destination bookstore, and a peek at Japanese culture high and low await at this 5-acre complex designed in 1968 by noted American architect Minoru Yamasaki. The Japan Center includes the shop- and restaurant-filled Kintetsu and Kinokuniya buildings; the excellent Kabuki Springs & Spa; the Hotel Kabuki; and the Sundance Kabuki, Robert Redford's fancy, reserved-seating cinema/restaurant complex.

The Kinokuniya Bookstore, in the Kinokuniya Building, has an extensive selection of Japanese-language books, *manga* (graphic novels), books on design, and English-language translations and books on

Japanese topics. Just outside, follow the Japanese teenagers to Pika Pika, where you and your friends can step into a photo booth and then use special effects and stickers to decorate your creation. On the bridge connecting the center's two buildings, check out Shige Antiques for *yukata* (lightweight cotton kimonos) for kids and lovely silk kimonos, and Asakichi and its tiny incense shop for tinkling wind chimes and display-worthy teakettles. Continue into the Kintetsu Building for a selection of Japanese restaurants.

Between the Miyako Mall and Kintetsu Building are the five-tier, 100-foot-tall **Peace Pagoda** and the Peace Plaza, where seasonal festivals are held. The pagoda, which draws on the 1,200-year-old tradition of miniature round pagodas dedicated to eternal peace, was designed in the late 1960s by Yoshiro Taniguchi to convey the "friendship and goodwill" of the Japanese people to the people of the United States. The plaza itself is a shadeless, unwelcoming space with little seating. Continue into the Miyako Mall to Ichiban Kan, a Japanese dollar store where you can pick up fun Japanese kitchenware, tote bags decorated with hedgehogs, and erasers shaped like food. ☒ *Bordered by Geary Blvd. and Fillmore, Post, and Laguna Sts., Japantown.*

Fodor's Choice   **Kabuki Springs & Spa.** This serene spa is one Japantown destination that
★   draws locals from all over town, from hipster to grandma, Japanese-American or not. Balinese urns decorate the communal bath area of this house of tranquility.

The massage menu has also expanded well beyond traditional shiatsu technique. The experience is no less relaxing, however, and the treatment regimen includes facials, salt scrubs, and mud and seaweed wraps. You can take your massage in a private room with a bath or in a curtained-off area.

The communal baths ($25) contain hot and cold tubs, a large Japanese-style bath, a sauna, a steam room, and showers. Bang the gong for quiet if your fellow bathers are speaking too loudly. The clothing-optional baths are open for men only on Monday, Thursday, and Saturday; women bathe on Wednesday, Friday, and Sunday. Bathing suits are required on Tuesday, when the baths are coed.

Men and women can reserve private rooms daily. An 80-minute massage-and-private-bath package costs $125 weekdays, $140 weekends; a package that includes a 50-minute massage and the use of the communal baths costs $105 weekdays, $114 weekends. ☒ *1750 Geary Blvd., Japantown* ☎ *415/922–6000* ⊕ *www.kabukisprings.com* ☉ *Daily 10–10.*

WORTH NOTING

Buchanan Mall. The shops lining this open-air mall are geared more toward locals—travel agencies, electronics shops—but there are some fun Japanese-goods stores here, too. Arrive early in the day and you may score some fabulous *mochi* (a soft, sweet Japanese rice treat) at **Benkyodo Company** (☒ *1747 Buchanan St.* ☎ *415/922–1244* ⊕ *www.benkyodocompany.com*). It's easy to spend hours among the fabulous origami and craft papers at **Paper Tree** (☒ *1743 Buchanan St.* ☎ *415/921–7100* ⊕ *paper-tree.com*). Have a seat on local artist Ruth

Asawa's twin origami-style fountains, which sit in the middle of the mall. ⊠ *Buchanan St. between Post and Sutter Sts., Japantown.*

New People. The kids' counterpart to the Japan Center, this fresh shopping center combines a cinema, a tea parlor, and shops with a successful synergy. The downstairs cinema shows classic and cutting-edge Asian (largely Japanese) films and is home to the San Francisco Film Society. Upstairs you can peruse Japanese pop-culture items and anime-inspired fashion, like handmade, split-toe shoes at Sou Sou and Lolita fashion at Baby, the Stars Shine Bright. ⊠ *1746 Post St., Japantown* ⊕ *www. newpeopleworld.com* ⊘ *Mon.–Sat. noon–7, Sun. noon–6.*

WHERE TO EAT

HOW TO EAT LIKE A LOCAL

San Francisco may well be the most piping-red-hot dining scene in the nation now. After all, with a booming tech industry, there are mouths to feed. Freedom to do what you want. Innovation. Eccentricity. These words define the culture, the food, and the cuisine of the city by the bay. Get in on what locals know by enjoying their favorite foods.

FOOD TRUCKS

This is where experimentation begins, where the overhead is low, and risk-taking is fun. From these mobile kitchens careers are launched. A food meet-up called "Off the Grid" happens in season at Fort Mason where you can do a progressive dinner among the 25 or so trucks. Year round the convoy roams to different locations, selling things like Korean poutine, Indian burritos, and Vietnamese burgers. Each dish seems to reflect a refusal to follow the norm.

DIM SUM

The tradition of dim sum took hold in San Francisco when Chinese immigrants from Guangdong Province arrived with Cantonese cuisine. These earlier settlers eventually established teahouses and bakeries that sold dim sum, like the steamed dumplings stuffed with shrimp (*har gow*) or pork (*shao mai*). Now carts roll from table to table in Chinatown restaurants—and other parts of the city. Try the grilled and fried bite-size savories but also the sweets like *dan tat*, an egg custard tart.

BARBEQUE

Whaaa? San Francisco barbecue? And what would that be? You can bet it's meat from top purveyors nearby. The city is surrounded by grazing lands,

13

where the animals and their minders, the ranchers, are king. Until now, meats came simply plated. Now it's messy, with smokiness, charred crusts, and gorgeous marbling. But you may never hear of a San-Fran-style barbecue, because, in the words of one chef, we're "nondenominational." You'll see it all: Memphis, Texas, Carolina, and Kansas City.

ICE CREAM

How ice cream became so popular in a place that probably spends many of its 365 days below the 75 degree mark is a mystery. But the lines attest to the popularity of the frozen dessert that gets its own San Francisco twist. This is the vanilla-bean vanilla and Tcho chocolate crowd. Bourbon and cornflakes? Reposado tequila? Cheers to that. Diversity and local produce is blended into flavors like ube (purple yam), yuzu, and Thai latte. Vegans, we got you covered, too.

BURRITOS

This stuffed tortilla got its Bay Area start in the 1960s in the Mission District. Because the size and fillings distinguish it from other styles, it became known as the Mission burrito. Look for rice (Southern Californians are cringing), beans, salsa, and enough meat in the burrito for two meals. The aluminum foil keeps the interior neat, in theory. Popular choices are *carne asada* (beef) and *carnitas* (pork). But then

there's *lengua* (beef tongue) and *birria* (goat). This is a hands-on meal. No utensils, please.

COFFEE

Coffee roasters here are like sports teams in other cities. You pick one of the big five or six to be loyal to, and defend it tirelessly. San Francisco favorites source impeccably and blend different beans as if they were winemaking. In addition, a few of the big names—Four Barrel, Sightglass, Ritual, Blue Bottle—roast their own to control what they grind and pour at their outlets across the city—and now nationally and internationally.

FARMERS' MARKETS

These are our new grocery stores. They're the places to discover the latest in fruits, vegetables, and dried beans—much of it grown within a 60-mile radius. Cheeses, cured salami, breads, and nuts are sampled. Then there are the local ready-to-eat snacks, like pizza and *huevos rancheros*. The most popular market is the one on Saturday at the Ferry Plaza.

Top left: Several farmers' markets occupy the Ferry Building; top right: Dim sum being served at a local restaurant; bottom right: Farmer's Market on Pier 39

Updated
by Christine
Ciarmello

Make no mistake, San Francisco is one of America's top food cities. Some of the biggest landmarks are restaurants; and for some visitors, chefs like Daniel Patterson are just as big a draw as Alcatraz. In fact, on a Saturday, the Ferry Building—a temple to local eating—may attract more visitors than the Golden Gate Bridge: cheeses, breads, "salty pig parts," homemade delicacies, and sensory-perfect vegetables and fruits attract rabidly dedicated aficionados. You see, San Franciscans are a little loco about their edibles. If you ask them what their favorite season is, don't be surprised if they respond, "tomato season."

Chefs are drawn to the superb ingredients plucked from the soils. Chances are that the Meyer lemons, fava beans, or strawberries on your plate that are preserved, pureed, or pickled were harvested this morning or within the last 48 hours. The briny abalone, crab, oysters, squid, and tuna that are poached, seared, smoked, or carpaccio'ed are caught just off shore. You will also get to taste unusual varieties, like lollipop kale, agretti greens, and Yuzu citrus. (The biggest downside is that some San Francisco menus come across as precious not delicious, a name-dump of ingredients.) But this is definitely post-carrot-and-peas paradise, unless, of course, you're talking heirloom carrot sorbet.

Today the most interesting kitchens are using these ingredients in regional cuisines, like Korean, Japanese, Italian, or South American. So get ready to dig into kung pao pastrami, porcini doughnuts with raclette béchamel, and yucca gnocchi. That fig-on-a-plate reputation? That's so last decade—as is foie gras, the sale of which is incredibly controversial throughout the state.

But the playground isn't just in haute cuisine kitchens. Culinary hot spots are just as likely to be a burger, pizza, or barbecue joint—with a few classically trained chefs dedicating their lives to making a better

Margherita. And you can just as easily find superb *bahn mi,* ramen noodles, and juicy *al pastor* tacos in the kitchens of Little Saigon, Japantown, or the Mission District, with allegiances running strong. A *carnitas* burrito can cause serious family feuds (especially, say, if your husband likes El Farolito and you're more a La Taqueria diehard).

And for the record, we do like our wine. Sure, Napa Cab is sold here, but these days wine lists are filling with French organic wines and making room for craft beers, ciders, and sakes, with a strong cocktail movement using herbs and regionally distilled spirits. Whatever you pair with your brisket, let's drink to San Francisco's best food decade yet.

13

SAN FRANCISCO DINING PLANNER

RESERVATIONS

Snagging reservations at restaurants with a lot of buzz has gotten notoriously difficult, with 5:30 and 9:30 often the pick. These choices aren't terrible if you plan on it. For a reservation at peak eating hours, though, our best advice is to call as far in advance as possible—try dining there earlier in the week if the Friday and Saturday tables are all full. You can also try calling a restaurant in the early afternoon the day of, because that's when they're making their reservation confirmation calls. If you're calling a few days ahead of time, ask if you can be put on a waiting list. Also, ask whether there's a bar or counter you can dine at—these are usually offered first-come, first-served. It's worth noting that several places set aside many tables for walk-in business (and not for advance reservations), in which case you can just show up and make the most of the waits. Often, the host will take your cell number and call you when the table is ready. Meanwhile, you can enjoy a predinner walk or a drink at a nearby bar. Occasionally, an eatery may ask you to call the day before your scheduled meal to reconfirm: don't forget, or you could lose out. As a last resort, don't forget many popular San Francisco restaurants are also open for lunch.

HOURS

Unless otherwise noted, the restaurants listed in this guide are open daily for lunch and dinner. Prime time for dinner is around 7:30 or 8 pm, and although there are places for night owls to fuel up, most restaurants stop serving around 10 pm. Restaurants, along with bars and clubs, may serve alcohol between the hours of 6 am and 2 am. The legal age to buy alcoholic beverages in California is 21.

WHAT TO WEAR

In general, San Franciscans are neat but casual dressers; only at the top-notch dining rooms do you see a more formal style. But the way you look can influence how you're treated—and where you're seated. Generally speaking, jeans will suffice at most table-service restaurants in the $ to $$$ range. A few pricier restaurants require jackets, and some insist on ties. In reviews, we mention dress only when men are required to wear a jacket or a jacket and tie. Note that shorts, sweatpants, and sports jerseys are rarely appropriate. When in doubt, call the restaurant and ask.

13

PRICES

If you're watching your budget, be sure to ask the price of daily specials. The charge for these dishes can sometimes be out of line with the menu. If you eat early or late, you may be able to take advantage of a prix-fixe deal not offered at peak hours. Many upscale restaurants offer lunch deals with special menus at bargain prices. Credit cards are widely accepted, but some restaurants (particularly smaller ones) accept only cash. Also, keep in mind that a restaurant listed as $$$ may actually have a good deal or two, such as an early prix-fixe dinner or a great bar scene and good, reasonably priced bar food to go with it.

WHAT IT COSTS				
	$	$$	$$$	$$$$
Restaurants	under $15	$15–$22	$23–$30	over $30

Restaurant prices are the average cost of a main course at dinner, or if dinner is not served, at lunch.

TIPPING AND TAXES

In most restaurants, tip the waiter 18%–20%. (To figure out a 20% tip quickly, just move the decimal spot one place to the left and double that.) Bills for parties of six or more sometimes include the tip. A few restaurants in the Bay Area are experimenting with a gratuity-included policy for all parties. There are only about six such places, and the movement is led by some of the best chefs.

Tip at least $1 per drink at the bar; $2 if it's a labor-intensive cocktail. Also be aware that some restaurants, now required to fund the city's new universal health-care ordinance, are passing these costs along to their customers instead of raising prices—usually in the form of a 3%–4% surcharge or a $1–$3.50-per-head charge. (San Francisco sales tax is currently at 8.5%.)

CHILDREN

Dining with youngsters in the city does not have to mean culinary exile. *Many of the restaurants reviewed in this chapter are excellent choices for families and are marked in the margins as such.*

SMOKING

Smoking is banned in all city restaurants and bars, and is now banned in all restaurant outdoor areas, from sidewalk seating to patios.

PARKING

Most high-end restaurants offer valet parking—worth considering in crowded neighborhoods such as North Beach, Russian Hill, Union Square, and the Mission. There's often a nominal charge and a time restriction on validated parking.

USING THE MAPS

Throughout the chapter, you'll see mapping symbols and coordinates (✛ 3:F2) after property names or reviews. To locate the property on a map, turn to the San Francisco Dining and Lodging Atlas at the end of the chapter. The first number after the ✛ symbol indicates the map number. Following that is the property's coordinate on the map grid.

RESTAURANT REVIEWS

Listed alphabetically within neighborhood.

UNION SQUARE

Tourists are attracted to this neighborhood for its many hotels and theater houses but primarily for its first-rate shopping. What is harder to find here is authentic San Francisco eating (locals dislike battling the crowds). But if you know where to look, you can find good places tucked away into narrow side alleys or in the lobbies of hotels.

$$$$
SEAFOOD
✕**Farallon.** Even though San Francisco is right on the Bay, it can be surprisingly hard to find great menus that focus on fish. But this white-linen restaurant delivers. Platters of *fruits de mer* are shucked right at the raw bar, scallop carpaccio is tender, and pan-roasted fish sustainably caught. The main dining room is in a 1920s original with Spanish Gothic influences and a domed hand-painted ceiling. While the bar is more modern, with jelly-fish chandeliers and kelp-covered columns, it is a busy happy hour spot. Regional oysters and truffled fries are the happy-hour bargain (from 3 until 6 pm), even on Saturdays. $ *Average main: $32* ✉ *450 Post St., Union Sq.* ☎ *415/956–6969* ⊕ *www. farallonrestaurant.com* ✛ *4:E3.*

$
JAPANESE
✕**Katana-Ya.** From the moment it opens, there's a line in front of this hole-in-the-wall ramen house across from the American Conservatory Theater. Hand-drawn pictures of specials punctuate a colorful interior with too-close tables and a couple of stools around the bar. There's nothing fancy, but the ramen is among the most authentic in town, and the place stays open late (till 2 am). Add a couple sushi rolls and gyozas to your order and be on your way. $ *Average main: $8* ✉ *430 Geary St., Union Sq.* ☎ *415/771–1280* ✍ *Reservations not accepted* ✛ *4:E4.*

$$
THAI
Fodor'sChoice
★
✕**Kin Khao.** Casual eaters of Thai food probably won't see much they recognize in these modern environs with homespun touches. However, Bangkok travelers—the chef is a native—might see a few familiars on the short, focused menu. The yum kai dao, a spicy fried egg salad, runs with yolk and is spiked with cilantro. Dry-fried kua kling ribs burst with curry and chili flavors. Ingredients are sourced—more accurately, tracked down with dedication—from regional purveyors. Cocktails are just as alluring, especially Hua Hin Beach—rum, coconut cream, and Kaffir lime over crushed ice. $ *Average main: $18* ✉ *55 Cyril Magnin, corner of Mason and Ellis Sts., Union Sq.* ☎ *415/362–7456* ⊕ *kinkhao. com* ☉ *Closed lunch weekends* ✛ *4:E5.*

$$$
VEGETARIAN
✕**Millennium.** Vegetarians and vegans who tire of being an afterthought (here's the sides menu!) will find a welcoming spot here. Not only is the menu meatless, but the dining room, inside the Hotel California, is a stately wood-paneled affair. Organic and seasonal ingredients include wordly-influenced dishes such as rice flour and coriander seed–crusted oyster mushrooms; pumpkin tamales; and, a gnocchi dish with an Alfredo-esque eggplant cashew cream sauce. ■TIP➔ The "Frugal Foodie" three-course menu is available Sunday through Wednesday (raw also available with advance notice). $ *Average main: $24*

⊠ *Hotel California, 580 Geary St., Union Sq.* ☏*415/345–3900* ⊕ *www. millenniumrestaurant.com* ◎ *No lunch* ✛ *4:D4.*

$$$ ✕ **M.Y. China.** At the show palace of star chef Martin Yan, noodles are

CHINESE stretched for yards—and eventually dropped into a beef short-rib soup flavored with star anise. Whether or not M.Y.'s there, you're sure to see the feat. Scissors and knives are also wielded for about nine noodle bowls nightly. The swank restaurant on the fourth floor of Market Street's Westfield Mall has a megaton bronze bell from China as the bar centerpiece, and opium bottles from China on display in glass cases. The tea selection is nice, with an oolong fermented with milk. ■**TIP➔ A special Dungeness crab menu highlights six styles of Chinese cooking.** Ⓢ *Average main: $25* ⊠ *Westfield Mall, 845 Market St., Union Sq.* ☏ *415/580–3001* ⊕ *tastemychina.com* ✛ *4:F5.*

CHINATOWN

Once you step beneath the gateway on Grant Street and meander the alleyways, into the restaurants and bakeries along Jackson, Clay, and Washington streets, you might be surprised at what you'll find. A food market, along Stockton, is a riot of exotic fruits, vegetables, and other delicacies. Restaurants feature the cuisine of (mostly) China's Guangdong Province, or Cantonese style. A lot of the Chinese, though, have moved out and into the Richmond and Sunset neighborhoods. This is a trek from downtown, set against the breakers and not the bay, but if you want the real deal, venture there. Not far from Chinatown is also Little Saigon, in the Tenderloin—many restaurants are run by ethnic Chinese who emigrated from Vietnam.

$$ ✕ **Great Eastern.** The fresh, simply prepared seafood, quickly cooked

CHINESE vegetables and meats, with no fiery chilies, is signature Cantonese-

FAMILY style cuisine, and the reason to dine here (as notables such as President Obama have done). Tanks filled with freshwater- and saltwater creatures occupy a corner of the street-level main dining room. Kids will find their Chinese-restaurant favorites here: stir-fried noodles, cashew chicken, fried rice. The dim sum starts at 10 am, but there aren't any carts, however—you order off a paper sheet, and the dumplings come out of the kitchen piping hot. Avoid the basement dining room if possible, which is brightly lit but claustrophobic. Ⓢ *Average main: $19* ⊠ *649 Jackson St., Chinatown* ☏ *415/986–2500* ⊕ *www.greateasternsf. com* ✛ *1:D4.*

$$ ✕ **R&G Lounge.** Cravings for salt-and-pepper Dungeness crab are deli-

CHINESE ciously sated at this bright, three-level Cantonese eatery that excels in

FAMILY the crustacean. A menu with photographs will help you sort through other HK specialties, including Peking duck and shrimp-stuffed tofu. Much of the seafood is fresh from the tank. Expect a packed dining room during peak hours. Dim sum is also served. ■**TIP➔ Crab portions are easily splittable by three, especially when accompanied by appetizers and another dish.** Ⓢ *Average main: $16* ⊠ *631 Kearny St., Chinatown* ☏ *415/982–7877* ⊕ *www.rnglounge.com* ✛ *1:E4.*

BEST BETS FOR SAN FRANCISCO DINING

Fodor's writers and editors have selected their favorite restaurants by price, cuisine, and experience in the Best Bets lists below. In the first column, Fodor's Choice designations represent the "best of the best" in every price category. You can also search by neighborhood for excellent eats—just peruse the following pages.

13

CHINESE

Chino, $$, p. 202
Mission Chinese Food, $, p. 204
R&G Lounge, $$, p. 175
San Tung, $$, p. 197
Ton Kiang, $$, p. 197
Yank Sing, $$, p. 193

ITALIAN

A16, $$$, p. 195
Acquerello, $$$$, p. 185
Cotogna, $$$, p. 191
Delfina, $$$, p. 202
La Ciccia, $$$, p. 201
Locanda, $$$, p. 204
SPQR, $$$, p. 208
Trou Normand, $$$, p. 181
Zero Zero, $$, p. 181

JAPANESE

Nojo, $$, p. 183
Orenchi Beyond, $, p. 205
Pink Zebra, $$, p. 205

LATIN AMERICAN

La Mar Cebicheria Peruana, $$$, p. 190
La Santaneca de la Mission, $, p. 203
Limón Rotisserie, $$, p. 204
Lolinda, $$, p. 204
Mijita Cocina Mexicana, $, p. 190

MEXICAN

Mijita Cocina Mexicana, $, p. 190

Nopalito, $$, p. 199
SanJalisco, $, p. 206
Tacolicious, $$, p. 195

THAI

Kin Khao, $$, p. 174
Lers Ros, $, p. 182

VEGETARIAN

Greens, $$, p. 195
Millennium, $$$, p. 174

VIETNAMESE

Bodega Bistro, $$, p. 182
Out the Door, $$$, p. 207
Slanted Door, $$$, p. 190

By Experience

BRUNCH

Bar Jules, $$$, p. 183
Bar Tartine, $$$, p. 202
Foreign Cinema, $$$, p. 203
Plow, $, p. 207
Rose's Café, $$$, p. 196

CHILD-FRIENDLY

Chino, $$, p. 202
Gott's Roadside, $, p. 189
Magnolia Brewing Co.'s Smokestack, $$, p. 207
Mijita Cocina Mexicana, $, p. 190
Nopalito, $$, p. 199
Park Chow, $, p. 197

Plow, $, p. 207
San Tung, $$, p. 197
Roam Artisan Burgers, $, p. 208
Tommaso's, $$, p. 188
Yank Sing, $$, p. 193

HISTORIC INTEREST

Boulevard, $$$$, p. 189
Swan Oyster Depot, $$, p. 185
Tadich Grill, $$$, p. 193
Tommaso's, $$, p. 188
Tosca Cafe, $$$, p. 188
Trou Normand, $$$, p. 181
Wayfare Tavern, $$$, p. 193

HOT SPOTS

Beretta, $$, p. 202
Central Kitchen, $$$, p. 202
Cotogna, $$$, p. 191
Delfina, $$$, p. 202
Dosa on Fillmore, $$, p. 208
Flour + Water, $$$, p. 203
Frances, $$$, p. 200
Locanda, $$$, p. 204
Nopa, $$$, p. 199
Nopalito, $$, p. 199
Park Tavern, $$$, p. 187
Plow, $, p. 207
The Progress, $$$$, p. 199
Rich Table, $$$, p. 184
SPQR, $$$, p. 208

State Bird Provisions, $$$, p. 200
Zero Zero, $$, p. 181

LATE-NIGHT BITES

Chow, $, p. 200
Locanda, $$$, p. 204
Nopa, $$$, p. 199
Zuni Café, $$$, p. 184

OCEAN VIEWS

Greens, $$, p. 195
Mijita Cocina Mexicana, $, p. 190
Slanted Door, $$$, p. 190

PRETHEATER MEAL

Alta CA, $$$, p. 182
Farallon, $$$$, p. 174
Nojo, $$, p. 183
Rich Table, $$$, p. 184

QUIET MEAL

Acquerello, $$$$, p. 185
Coi, $$$$, p. 186
Quince, $$$$, p. 192

SPECIAL OCCASION

Acquerello, $$$$, p. 185
Benu, $$$$, p. 179
Boulevard, $$$$, p. 189
Central Kitchen, $$$, p. 202
Gary Danko, $$$$, p. 188
Jardinière, $$$, p. 183
Quince, $$$$, p. 192
Saison, $$$$, p. 180

Around Union Square, hotels pull in diners for pricey lunches and even pricier dinners, sometimes with people-watching included.

SOMA

Hip SoMa covers a large area that swings from chic residential lofts and 19th-century warehouses turned trendy eatery to slightly dingy sidewalk scenes, particularly near the police station and in the higher numbers (7th through 10th nearer to Market). It has the rowdy ballpark and the genteel South Park within its fold. And restaurants near here fuel the mostly young and single local crowd who work in tech (Pinterest, Yelp, Twitter, and Adobe are nearby and so is the train to Silicon Valley). Also, interesting chef-owned restaurants are finding their footing here, like AQ, Una Pizza Napoletana, Benu, Saison, and Citizen's Band.

$$$$ ECLECTIC 🍴 **Ame.** Japanese specialties are the stars at this sleek, modern (though somewhat stuffy) dining room in the St. Regis. While the menu offers French and American dishes, skip to the well-loved *chawan mushi* (egg custard) with sea urchin, mushrooms, and lobster, and the sake-marinated black cod with shrimp dumplings. The sashimi bar is a particular delight, so be sure to sample. Co-owner and pastry chef Lissa Doumani handles the sweet portions, like molten chocolate bread pudding with caramel popcorn ice cream. [$] *Average main: $39* ✉ *St. Regis Hotel, 689 Mission St., SoMa* ☎ *415/284–4040* 🌐 *www.amerestaurant.com* ⏲ *No lunch* ⊕ *1:E6.*

$$$ MODERN AMERICAN 🍴 **AQ.** This chic spot on a sketchy stretch of Mission attracts those drawn to ingredients impeccably sourced, from the bitters in the handcrafted cocktails to the squab, swordfish, and vegetables on the plate. The food is California progressive, which translates to ingredients often unheard of and many tastes and textures served in a smallish portion

four-course tasting menu each night. Dishes may include buttery carrots with salmon roe or beef tenderloin. The decor, too, is seasonal, changing looks every quarter. ■TIP➡ The menu offers a four-course prix fixe or seven-to-nine-course tasting. However, you may also order à la carte. $ *Average main: $25* ✉ *1085 Mission St., SoMa* ☎ *415/341–9000* ⊕ *www.aq-sf.com* ⊗ *Closed Sun. and Mon. No lunch* ✦ *3:H1.*

$$$ ✕**Bar Agricole.** This modern spot, set back from the street in a LEED-
MODERN certified warehouse, first attracted cocktail hounds because of well-
AMERICAN known bartender/owner Thad Vogler. Definitely partake in creative rum libations. Then get comfy at a table, set with recycled denim napkins, either on the planty-perfect patio or in the real looker of a dining room that uses reclaimed whisky barrels as wall slats. The Italian-inspired cuisine with farmers ingredients excels at breadline items, like flatbread and farinata (a chicpea cake). Plates are meant for sharing, except for the pumpkin whoopie pie. Hands off. The bar gets boisterous at night, but the sophistication of the space entices everyone all age groups, including Sunday brunch. ■TIP➡ A downstairs room can seat larger groups. $ *Average main: $27* ✉ *355 11th St., SoMa* ☎ *415/355–9400* ⊕ *www.baragricole.com* ⊗ *Closed Mon. No lunch Tues.–Fri.* ✦ *3:G3.*

$$$$ ✕**Benu.** Chef Corey Lee's modern Californian Mecca is a must-stop for
MODERN those who hop from city to city, collecting memorable meals. Each dish
AMERICAN in the 15- to 19-course tasting menu is a marvel of textures and flavors,
Fodor's Choice presented meticulously enough to make this one of only two restau-
★ rants in the city to earn three Michelin stars (the other is Saison). Lee, formerly of French Laundry, handles Asian ingredients—a thousand-year-old quail egg, *xiao long bao* dumplings, and sea cucumber—with a Western touch. You may find dishes like Hokkaido sea cucumber stuffed with lobster, pork belly, eggplant, fermented pepper or eel. An extremely professional staff is behind the quick pacing and on-point wine pairings. Bare-wood tables and a minimalistic interior guarantees concentration on the plate. The tasting menu is mandatory. $ *Average main: $195* ✉ *22 Hawthorne St., SoMa* ☎ *415/685–4860* ⊕ *www.benusf.com* ⌂ *Reservations essential* ⊗ *Closed Sun. and Mon. No lunch* ✦ *1:F6.*

$$$ ✕**The Cavalier.** This Anna Weinberg–Jennifer Puccio production is no
MODERN different than the two others (Marlowe and Park Tavern): insanely
AMERICAN popular and loud, yet deliciously comforting. Chef Puccio gives British Pub grub a Nor Cal makeover (fresh ingredients rightly cooked). The darkly painted space, with high ceilings and large arched windows, is decorated with stuffed animal heads, horses, and clusters of paintings imparting a decidedly British temperament that attracts the clubby tech crowd. The gin-based cocktails pair well with starters such as deviled quail eggs, Brussels sprouts chips, and hearty mains like the Sunday chicken—bathed in a bacon-mustard *jus.* $ *Average main: $23* ✉ *Hotel Zetta, 360 Jessie St., SoMa* ☎ *415/321–6000* ⊕ *thecavaliersf. com* ✦ *4:F6.*

$$ ✕**Citizen's Band.** This fresh take on the classic American diner always
DINER seems to pack its coveted 40 seats. The draw: one of the city's tastiest versions of mac and cheese (topped with onion rings), and fried chicken with red-eye gravy. Other "fine diner" dishes—among them seasonal salads and pan-roasted rock cod—further reveal chef-owner Chris Beerman's

13

experience in upscale restaurants. The vibe is very SoMa, with an edgy and eclectic crowd that can match the rock-and-roll playing (sometimes loudly) on the stereo or at the club next door, but the well-chosen wine list keeps things elevated. The restaurant shares restrooms with the rock club next door. [$] *Average main: $22* ✉ *1198 Folsom St., at 8th St., SoMa* ☎ *415/556–4901* 🌐 *www.citizensbandsf.com* ✥ *3:H2.*

$$$ MEDITERRANEAN 🍴 **The Fly Trap.** The pistachio meatballs put this place on the San Francisco culinary map. It continues to attract SOMA crowds with Persian influenced dishes, like eggplant dip *kashkeh bademjan,* and calamari stuffed with Persian-spiced pork. Both the bar and communal table fill up with an after-work crowd getting cocktails and digging into flavorful Mediterranean bites. A sit-down dinner here is ideal for dates, a meal with friends or the parents, or a casual business meeting—the non-tablecloth environment keeps things comfortable. The frozen *faloodeh* dessert is like a citrusy shave ice with noodles. [$] *Average main: $27* ✉ *606 Folsom St., SoMa* ☎ *415/243–0580* 🌐 *flytrapsf.com* ⏲ *Closed Sun. No lunch* ✥ *1:F6.*

$$$ MEDITERRANEAN 🍴 **LuLu.** A former magnet for dot-commers is now a go-to option for business diners and conventioneers from nearby Moscone Center. It is convenient for lunch and turns out succulent rotisserie chicken from the kitchen centerpiece: a giant oak-fired wood oven. A few pastas and pizzas round out the menu. Friday brings spit-roasted suckling pig. Wine drinkers will appreciate the long list of choices by the glass. Note: when LuLu is packed, service can suffer. [$] *Average main: $27* ✉ *816 Folsom St., SoMa* ☎ *415/495–5775* 🌐 *www.restaurantlulu.com* ✥ *1:F6.*

$$$ AMERICAN Fodor's Choice ★ 🍴 **Marlowe.** A new location doubles the number of diners who can get a piece of chef Jennifer Puccio's hearty American bistro fare, like roasted chicken, steak tartare, and one of the city's best burgers. In hip SoMa, near the main Caltrain station, this spot has a lighter, airy touch with white penny tile floors, marble countertops, and butcher paper emblazoned with the day's specials—including cocktails like the tequila-based la cuchilla. An outdoor patio is jam-packed in good weather. Chief pastry chef Emily Luchetti takes care of the kitchen's sweet side, and makes us wonder why no one has thought of a farmers' market sundae till now. **TIP→ Avoid the crowds and order a burger off the bar menu.** [$] *Average main: $24* ✉ *500 Brannan St., SoMa* ☎ *415/777–1413* 🌐 *www.marlowesf.com* ⏲ *No lunch weekends* ✥ *1:E6.*

$$$$ MODERN AMERICAN 🍴 **Saison.** This award-winning, starred restaurant in a 19th-century, brick-and-timber building always begs the question, what exactly do you get for $248 per person? The answer is a culinary adventure of 18 to 20 courses impeccably prepared by chef Joshua Skenes, who teases from premium ingredients their deepest flavors, mostly using fire, embers, and ash. You might taste Monterey abalone roasted over embers, or fresh fish seared on a log. An extra $248 includes wine pairings by wine director Mark Bright; cocktails are a new addition, served in glass hand-blown in Japan. This is definitely a unique, splurgy dining experience. [$] *Average main: $248* ✉ *178 Townsend St., SoMa* ☎ *415/828–7990* 🌐 *www.saisonsf.com* ✍ *Reservations essential* ⏲ *Closed Sun. and Mon.* ✥ *1:G6.*

$$$ MODERN AMERICAN 🍴 **Town Hall.** Well-known chefs Mitchell and Steven Rosenthal are the culinary brains behind this power broker's pit stop. The fare is American with Southern flair—cornmeal-fried oysters with an Herbsaint spinach puree, juicy fried chicken, butterscotch-and-chocolate *pot de crème*—with plenty of variety to satisfy nearly everyone, and the portions ensure no one leaves hungry. The converted-warehouse space, with dark-wood floors, exposed brick walls, white wainscoting, and contemporary art comfortably blends old with new. You can curl up with a cocktail on the heated patio (like a perfect Sazerac) while you wait for your table. The decibel level here can wear down your vocal chords, so ask for a quieter spot. [$] *Average main: $26* ✉ *342 Howard St., SoMa* ☎ *415/908–3900* 🌐 *www.townhallsf.com* 🕓 *No lunch weekends* ✥ *1:F5.*

13

$$$ ITALIAN Fodor's Choice ★ 🍴 **Trou Normand.** Walk through the door of the 1925 Timothy Pflueger-designed building and it's like entering the art deco period, greeted as you are with soaring ceilings, marble, and an enormous painted illustration of a nude. Welcome to the Roaring 2010s. Thad Vogler's latest endeavor (Bar Agricole was the first) delivers on a fun boozy evening, introducing the French tradition known as *trou normand*—drinking a brandy between courses to settle your stomach. There are also about 40 house-cured salumi and charcuterie. Arancini, seasonal salads and pickles, and mains of pasta and roasted black cod round out offerings. An enclosed patio reads like a Parisian garden conservatory. Unfortunately, noise is a real issue out there, because it's an after-work escape. **■ TIP→ A small café within the restaurant serves up espresso and breakfast sandwiches in the mornings.** [$] *Average main: $25* ✉ *140 New Montgomery St., SoMa* ☎ *415/975–0876* 🌐 *www.trounormandsf.com* ✍ *Reservations essential* 🕓 *Closed Sun.* ✥ *1:E6.*

$$$$ MODERN AMERICAN 🍴 **Twenty Five Lusk.** With blinis made in a skillet from St. Petersburg, Russia, yellowtail from Kona, and Kobe beef from Washington, this bastion of contemporary American cuisine geeks out on well-sourced ingredients and implements. For mains, the perfectly cooked Louisiana prawns on spicy grits is a perennial favorite. The wines are very well chosen, and the lime posset for dessert is a can't-miss. Tucked off an alley, the soaring space seems more New York than San Francisco, with a rockin' downstairs lounge, gleaming surfaces, and raw-wood beams. **■ TIP→ For a quiet dinner, try to get a booth on the top level near the kitchen.** [$] *Average main: $32* ✉ *25 Lusk St., SoMa* ☎ *415/495–5875* 🌐 *www.twentyfivelusk.com* ✥ *1:G6.*

$$ PIZZA 🍴 **Una Pizza Napoletana.** Inside this bare-bones location in SoMa you'll find one of the best Neapolitan-style pizzas outside of Italy. Chef-owner and Manhattan transplant Anthony Mangieri is an obsessive artisan, carefully making each and every pizza by hand. The menu lists five kinds of pies (all versions of mozzarella and tomato). The crust exhibits a particular kind of perfection (the imported wood-fired oven is a beauty). There isn't much else on the menu (just some beverages and wines), so it really is all about the pizza. Don't come in a large group (couples get seated more quickly). [$] *Average main: $20* ✉ *210 11th St., SoMa* ☎ *415/861–3444* 🌐 *www.unapizza.com/sf* 🕓 *Closed Sun.–Tues.* ✥ *3:G3.*

$$ ITALIAN 🍴 **Zero Zero.** This popular and comfortable California-Italian place is where you can go almost any time of day, whether you're craving a

thin-crust "Cali-politan" pizza for lunch with a cocktail, an order of Taleggio-stuffed arancini after work, or house-made pasta for dinner. Ingredients are fresh and seasonal, and portions are affordable and easy to share. A few wines are available, as are Negronis. The mistake diners make is not saving room for dessert, a choose-your-own-toppings soft serve. There's a lengthy downstairs bar and lounge, with another second smaller bar upstairs; both are packed in the evenings. $ *Average main: $17* ✉ *826 Folsom St., SoMa* ☎ *415/348–8800* ⊕ *www. zerozerosf.com* ✛ *1:F6.*

TENDERLOIN

A land of dive bars, package-liquor stores, panhandlers, and . . . some of the best pho and bahn mi in the city, this seedy district of low rents encompasses Little Saigon. Locals know to come here for great cheap eats, including not just Vietnamese but naans and masalas. This is San Francisco's rougher neighborhood—one of the last holdouts.

$$
VIETNAMESE

✕ **Bodega Bistro.** Located on the sketchy edge of the Tenderloin, this casual Vietnamese bistro brims at lunchtime with savvy eaters from Civic Center offices who come in for steaming bowls of pho (the beef versions are particularly good). For dinner, groups of diners overload round tables with green papaya salad, roast squab, *bun cha Hanoi* (broiled pork, herbs, rice vermicelli, and lettuce wrapped in rice paper), and salt-and-pepper Dungeness crab with garlic noodles, the latter priced for a special occasion. You'll see many French touches on the extensive menu. $ *Average main: $18* ✉ *607 Larkin St., Tenderloin* ☎ *415/921–1218* ⊕ *www.bodegabistrosf.net* ✛ *4:A6.*

$
THAI

✕ **Lers Ros.** Diners who navigate the sketchy neighborhood are richly rewarded with authentic Thai. Skip the "same old" pad thai and try something new—Thai herb sausage and papaya salad with salted egg are good appetizers to share. The pork belly with crispy rind and basil leaves and *duck larb* (meat salad) come packed with flavor—speaking of which, be sure to specify how hot you can really handle it. The room is a bit nondescript, but clean, and the food has been such a hit that the restaurant has expanded to spots in the Mission and Hayes Valley. ■ TIP➔ There are nightly late hours and free delivery. $ *Average main: $14* ✉ *730 Larkin St., Tenderloin* ☎ *415/931–6917* ⊕ *www. lersros.com* ✛ *4:A5.*

HAYES VALLEY

Hayes Valley is sprouting several hip and haute dining destinations around its main stem, Hayes Street, upping choices for pretheater dining. The low-key vibe in the wine bars and cafés makes it easy to feel like a local.

$$$
AMERICAN
Fodor'sChoice
★

✕ **Alta CA.** With a location across the street from the HQs of Twitter and Uber, this pretty restaurant *could* phone it in. Alta is the creation of Daniel Patterson, whose talents have been well documented at the Michelin-starred Coi. Creativity is on par, but the vibe is *waaay* less formal. At its nucleus is the 25-seat large circular bar. Small plates dominate the menu, and the beef tendon puffs are pure chicharrónes-like bliss, while the delicate homemade pierogi is a mainstay but with seasonal accents, like pumpkin. As expected the hoodies descend, but so, too, do the pretheater crowd. ■TIP➜ **This is one of the city's few great food experiences after midnight on weekends.** $ *Average main: $30* ✉ *1420 Market St., Van Ness/Civic Center* ☎ *415/590–2585* ⊕ *altaca. co* ⊗ *Closed for lunch on weekends* ✛ *3:F2.*

$$$ ✕ **Bar Jules.** This sunny storefront oozes with Parisian charm, with
FRENCH an open kitchen, wicker bistro chairs, and a changing menu du jour scribbled on a blackboard. You may find dishes like Dungeness crab salad with chives, avocado, and chervil; or cauliflower and sunchoke gratin with Gruyère and thyme. The Meyer lemon panna cotta is a delicate finish. On the downside: service can be slow, and the sea of hard surfaces make it a loud dining experience. $ *Average main: $28* ✉ *609 Hayes St., Hayes Valley* ☎ *415/621–5482* ⊕ *www.barjules.com* ⊗ *Closed Mon. No dinner Sun.* ✛ *3:E2.*

$$$ ✕ **Hayes Street Grill.** Arrive here just as music lovers are folding their
SEAFOOD napkins and heading off for an 8 pm show at the nearby Opera House or SF JAZZ Center, and you'll snag a table and some fresh, sustainable, often local seafood. Much of the fish—sea bass, steelhead, swordfish—is grilled and served with a choice of sauces from beurre blanc to lemon-and-caper butter. Brass coat hooks, white tablecloths, a long bar, and a mix of banquettes and tables define the traditional San Francisco look of this four-decades-old seafood stronghold. $ *Average main: $26* ✉ *320 Hayes St., Hayes Valley* ☎ *415/863–5545* ⊕ *www.hayesstreetgrill.com* ⊗ *No lunch weekends* ✛ *3:F2.*

$$$ ✕ **Jardinière.** Famed chef Traci Des Jardins' restaurant is so sophisti-
MODERN cated you may as well be eating at the nearby Opera House. An eye-
AMERICAN catching curving staircase leads to an oval atrium, where locals and out-of-towners alike indulge in French-Californian dishes, such as bacon-wrapped rabbit or trout amandine. It's also a draw for pasta lovers—a nice selection (agnolotti, tajarin, garganelli) are available as an appetizer or main. Downstairs is the lounge menu, with smaller plates and smaller price points. $ *Average main: $27* ✉ *300 Grove St., Hayes Valley* ☎ *415/861–5555* ⊕ *www.jardiniere.com* ⌂ *Reservations essential* ⊗ *No lunch* ✛ *3:F2.*

$$ ✕ **Nojo.** For a little bonhomie before the symphony, this buzzy yaki-
JAPANESE tori and izakaya spot serves stellar Japanese pub food, made from Bay Area ingredients. The menu is divided into items "on a stick" and "not on a stick." Much of the "stick" is *yakitori* (grilled chicken), like chicken skin with matcha sea salt and *tsukune* (a chicken meatball) with egg yolk sauce. Not on a stick is the savory, rich custard, *chawan mushi,* with Dungeness crabmeat and shiitake mushrooms. Seating is at bamboo tables in a mod-Japanese-slash-San Franciscan setting with windows overlooking Hayes Valley's main thoroughfare of Franklin. There are 20 sakes by the glass. ■TIP➜ **Nojo requires a credit card number to hold a reservation.** $ *Average main: $20* ✉ *231 Franklin St., Hayes Valley* ☎ *415/896–4587* ⊕ *www.nojosf.com* ⊗ *Closed Tues. No lunch.* ✛ *3:F2.*

$$$ ✕ **Pläj.** The only Swedish restaurant in San Francisco is tucked behind
SWEDISH the lobby of the Inn at the Opera and serves refreshing cuisine—fishes

pickled, smoked, and cured in-house. A dill puree with lemon crème fraîche and a homemade spicy mustard complement the delicate salmon gravlax. Chef Roberth Sundell is from Stockholm, and the Swedish meatballs with lingonberry gravy is a treasured family recipe. The money spot is the table in front of the fireplace. FYI, Pläj is pronounced "play" and has no Swedish translation. It's just pläjing with you. **TIP→ There's a gluten-free menu.** [$] *Average main: $30* ✉ *333 Fulton St., Hayes Valley* ☎ *415/294–8925* 🌐 *www.plajrestaurant.com* 🕓 *No lunch* ⊕ *3:E2.*

$$$ MODERN AMERICAN Fodor's Choice ★

🍴 **Rich Table.** To leave co-chefs Evan and Sarah Rich's popular place without ordering the porcini doughnuts, served with a raclette béchamel sauce, is a dining sin. That and the sardines in chip format are the two most popular bites, and you should wander to the mains half of the menu for one of the half-dozen pastas or proteins, like a seared black cod with crunchy skin. The room's weathered-wood wallboards repurposed from a Northern California sawmill give it a homey vibe. There's a nice selection of wines by the glass and artisanal cocktails. All seats are by reservation only and are not an easy acquisition. **TIP→ Ten bar seats are available for walk-ins.** [$] *Average main: $30* ✉ *199 Gough St., at Oak St., Hayes Valley* ☎ *415/355–9085* 🌐 *www.richtablesf.com* ✍ *Reservations essential* 🕓 *No lunch* ⊕ *3:E3.*

$$ GERMAN

🍴 **Suppenküche.** Nobody goes hungry—and no beer drinker goes thirsty—at this lively, hip outpost of simple German cooking in Hayes Valley. When the room gets crowded, which it regularly does, strangers sit together at unfinished pine tables. Servers are quick and efficient, and keep the pace moving along. The hearty food—bratwurst and red cabbage, potato pancakes with house-made applesauce, meat loaf, braised beef, pork loin, schnitzel, strudel—is tasty and kind to your pocketbook, and the imported brews are first-rate. **TIP→ The same management runs Biergarten (424 Octavia Street), a charming outdoor spot just a block away that serves bratwurst, pretzels, and German beers.** [$] *Average main: $18* ✉ *525 Laguna St., Hayes Valley* ☎ *415/252–9289* 🌐 *www.suppenkuche.com* 🕓 *No brunch Mon.–Sat.* ⊕ *3:E2.*

$$$ MEDITERRANEAN Fodor's Choice ★

🍴 **Zuni Café.** After one bite of Zuni's succulent brick-oven-roasted whole chicken with Tuscan bread salad, you'll understand why the two-floor café is a perennial star. At the long copper bar a disparate mix of patrons communes over oysters on the half shell and cocktails and wine. Nearly as famous as the chicken are the Caesar salad with house-cured anchovies and the chocolatey flourless *gâteau Victoire*. The most cheerful spot to sit is at the tip of the "pyramid window" near the bar, easier to score if you plan a late lunch. Zuni's world-famous chef-owner, Judy Rodgers, passed away in 2013, but thanks to her strong guidance, the food remains outstanding. [$] *Average main: $28* ✉ *1658 Market St., Hayes Valley* ☎ *415/552–2522* 🌐 *www.zunicafe.com* 🕓 *Closed Mon.* ⊕ *3:F3.*

NOB HILL AND RUSSIAN HILL

NOB HILL

Nob Hill, the most famous hill in a city of hills, is known for its iconic hotels—the Fairmont, the Mark, the Ritz-Carlton, the Huntington—and for its views. Unfortunately, the food isn't as unparalleled as the scenic outlooks. Real estate is expensive so it's not the place for chefs to roll the dice on a new venture. But what you will find are hotel dining rooms and established institutions.

$$$$ ✕**Acquerello.** Devotees of chef-owner Suzette Gresham-Tognetti's high-
ITALIAN end but soulful Italian cooking have swooned for years over her Parme-
Fodor's Choice san *budino* (pudding). Classics pepper the menu but there are also some
★ cutting-edge touches, techniques, and flavors. Dinners are prix-fixe, with three, four, or five courses and at least four choices within each course. Co-owner Giancarlo Paterlini oversees the service and his son Gianpaolo presides over the roughly 1,900-bottle list of Italian wines. The room, in a former chapel, with vaulted ceiling and terra-cotta and pale-ocher palette, is refined but never stuffy. This true San Francisco dining gem is worth every penny. Ⓢ *Average main: $87* ⊠ *1722 Sacramento St., Van Ness/Polk* ☏ *415/567–5432* ⊕ *www.acquerello.com* ⌔ *Reservations essential* ⊙ *Closed Sun. and Mon. No lunch* ✛ *2:H5.*

$$ ✕**Swan Oyster Depot.** Half fish market and half diner, this small, slim,
SEAFOOD family-run seafood operation, open since 1912, has no tables, just a nar-
Fodor's Choice row marble counter with about a dozen-and-a-half stools. Most people
★ come in to buy perfectly fresh salmon, halibut, crabs, and other seafood to take home. Everyone else hops onto one of the rickety stools to enjoy a dozen oysters, other shellfish, or a bowl of clam chowder—the only hot food served. It's all served up with a side of big personality from the jovial folks behind the counter who make you feel like a regular. ■TIP➜ **Come before 11 am or after 2 pm to avoid a long wait, and bring a full wallet: old-school Swan only takes cash.** Ⓢ *Average main: $18* ⊠ *1517 Polk St., Nob Hill* ☏ *415/673–1101* ⌔ *Reservations not accepted* ▭ *No credit cards* ⊙ *Closed Sun. No dinner* ✛ *2:H5.*

RUSSIAN HILL
Despite its name, don't expect Russian food here. Instead, this area bordering Nob Hill caters to the postcollege crowds, who want to live near the buzzy Polk and Larkin streets. They mix in with the upper-crust San Franciscans who live in the art-deco high-rises with views. Many romantic bistros are tucked away on tree-lined Hyde Street.

$$ ✕**Helmand Palace.** This handsomely outfitted spot will introduce you to
AFGHAN the aromas and tastes of Afghan cooking. While the sauces and spices are reminiscent of India's cuisine, the lamb focus is very Turkish and Greek. Highlights of the reasonably priced menu include *aushak* (leek-filled ravioli served with yogurt and ground beef), and *kaddo* (a sweet savory dish of sugared pumpkin in a beef tomato sauce). Basmati rice pudding, perfumed with cardamom and pistachio, is an exotic finish. The subdued restaurant, with white tableclothes and real Afghan rugs, does a quick-paced delivery service. Ⓢ *Average main: $16* ⊠ *2424 Van Ness Ave., Russian Hill* ☏ *415/345–0072* ⊕ *www.helmandpalacesf.com* ⊙ *No lunch* ✛ *2:H3.*

$$$$ ✕**La Folie.** The small, *très* Parisian establishment is smartly designed
FRENCH in warm woods and copper tones to let chef-owner Roland Passot's whimsical cuisine take center stage. Passot is often seen greeting return customers. Choose from prix-fixe menus of three, four, or five courses that may include butter-poached lobster with truffle beurre fondue and

parsnip ravioli, or rôti of squab and quail wrapped in crisp and thin potato. Vegetarians will be happy to discover a menu of their own. **TIP→ La Folie Lounge next door has cocktails and small plates on the menu—you can also order à la carte off La Folie's menu.** [$] *Average main: $50* ✉ *2316 Polk St., Russian Hill* ☎ *415/776–5577* 🌐 *www.lafolie.com* 🕑 *Closed Sun. No lunch* ✥ *2:H3.*

$$ MODERN AMERICAN 🍴 **Verbena.** This sister of the highly praised Gather restaurant in Berkeley manages to do the impossible: woo carnivores, pescaterians, and vegetarians with equal success. To the meat-eater, for example, spreadable salami is a dream come true. Flavorful sauces, like spiced moles, nutty pesto, and lemongrass-spiked broths bring out the best of the main ingredient, whether it's a pork rib, duck wing, or sunchoke. Farm-fresh produce are placed on a pedestal, with dramatic presentation—as well as a backlit wall of vegetables pickling and fermenting that is altar-like. Large hanging panels in the buzzy dining room may look painted, but they are the pigment of soil. This is a valuable addition to Russian Hill, bereft of good dining options. [$] *Average main: $22* ✉ *2323 Polk St., Russian Hill* ☎ *415/441–2323* 🌐 *www.verbenarestaurant.com* ✍ *Reservations essential* 🕑 *No lunch weekdays* ✥ *1:A3.*

$$ TAPAS 🍴 **Zarzuela.** Full-blooded Spaniards swear by the paella at this tiny Old World–style bistro, complete with matador art on the wall, not far from the crookedest street in the world (Lombard). Also not to be missed is the homemade sangria—or the goat cheese baked in tomato sauce or poached octopus, all prepared by chef Lucas Gasco, who grew up in Madrid. Arched windows overlook Hyde Street and the cable cars rolling by. Riding the Powell–Hyde line to and from dinner adds to the romance of the evening and saves you the nightmare of parking in this neighborhood. [$] *Average main: $21* ✉ *2000 Hyde St., Russian Hill* ☎ *415/346–0800* ✍ *Reservations not accepted* 🕑 *Closed Sun. and Mon. No lunch* ✥ *1:B3.*

NORTH BEACH

One of the city's oldest neighborhoods, North Beach continues to speak Italian, albeit in fewer households than it did when Joe DiMaggio was hitting home runs at the local playground.

Columbus Avenue, North Beach's primary commercial artery, and nearby side streets boast dozens of moderately priced Italian restaurants and coffee bars that San Franciscans flock to for a dose of strong community feeling. But beware, there are a few tourist traps that are after the college crowd who flock here for cheap drinks then want to fill up on cheap food.

$$$$ MODERN AMERICAN Fodor's Choice ★ 🍴 **Coi.** Chef Daniel Patterson is one of the biggest names in the food circuit, and his destination restaurant shows you, via an eight-course tasting, just how he's gotten a golden reputation. Highly seasonal ingredients are obsessively sourced—some of it foraged. One example, the Dungeness crab raviolo with sheep sorrel and butter crab broth. A more casual front dining room is followed by a formal space, with natural linens, soft lighting, and hand-crafted pottery. Patterson is always brining, curing, and innovating, including Coi's pay-in-advance, nonrefundable

ticketing system for reservations. ■TIP➔ A vegetarian tasting menu is available with advance notice. Couldn't get a reservation? Call. Tables do open up. $ *Average main: $195* ✉ *373 Broadway, North Beach* ☎ *415/393–9000* ⊕ *www.coirestaurant.com* ♨ *Reservations essential* ⊙ *Closed Mon. No lunch* ✛ *1:E3.*

$$ ✕**L'Osteria del Forno.** Pass through the door of this modest storefront
ITALIAN and you'll feel as if you've stumbled into a trattoria in Italy, with the staff chattering in Italian and seductive aromas drifting from the kitchen through the sunny yellow dining room. Each day the kitchen produces small plates including a few baked pastas, a roast of the day, and thin-crust pizzas—including a memorable "white" pie topped with porcini mushrooms and mozzarella. (All the hot dishes come out of an oven—no stove here.) Wine drinkers will find an all-Italian list, which showcases gems from limited-production vineyards. ■TIP➔ The space is not suitable for large groups. $ *Average main: $15* ✉ *519 Columbus Ave., North Beach* ☎ *415/982–1124* ⊕ *www.losteriadelforno.com* ♨ *Reservations not accepted* ═ *No credit cards* ⊙ *Closed Tues.* ✛ *1:D3.*

$$ ✕**Maykadeh.** The authentic Persian cooking has a large and faithful
MIDDLE EASTERN following of homesick Iranian émigrés—and locals in-the-know. Lamb dishes with rice are the specialties, served in a warm and attractive dining room. Appetizers include the traditional eggplant with mint sauce, pickled vegetables, and saffron-and-lime-spiced lamb tongue. Kebabs, like the chicken joojeh, and other marinated meats are great for sharing. To satisfy heartier appetites is the *ghorme sabzee*, lamb shank braised with a bouquet of Middle Eastern spices. The room is full of families and friends dining together. Give yourself plenty of time here, as service occasionally slows to a crawl. ■TIP➔ The affordable valet parking is a bonus. $ *Average main: $22* ✉ *470 Green St., North Beach* ☎ *415/362–8286* ⊕ *www.maykadehrestaurant.com* ✛ *1:D3.*

$$ ✕**Original Joe's.** You'll fall for the charm of this *retro* North Beach
AMERICAN institution, where the nostalgia isn't just in the decor but on the menu. Forget everything you know about health post-1955, because, really, how often can you order a hamburger steak seasoned to perfection? Pot roast and five different veal dishes add to the mid-century meat-heavy menu. The butterscotch pudding, an all-cream confection, is topped with whipped mascarpone and sea salt. Black Formica tabletops, checkerboard floors, and red leather booths provide the backdrop at this 1937 institution (only in this location since 2012.) $ *Average main: $21* ✉ *601 Union St., North Beach* ☎ *415/775–4877* ⊕ *www.originaljoessf.com* ✛ *1:D3.*

$$$ ✕**Park Tavern.** This upscale American tavern on pretty Washington
AMERICAN Square has been a hit from the day it opened. It appeals to those who want to sit at the dark-wood bar and nibble on delicious little things like the deviled eggs (with bacon and jalapeños) or who are looking for a proper sit-down complete with a twice-baked potato and grass-fed rib eye (although the roasted chicken is not to be missed). The dining room is classic bistro with an urban touch. $ *Average main: $28* ✉ *1652 Stockton St., North Beach* ☎ *415/989–7300* ⊕ *www.parktavernsf.com* ♨ *Reservations essential* ⊙ *No lunch Mon.–Thurs.* ✛ *1:D3.*

$$ ✕ **Tommaso's.** San Francisco's first wood-fired pizza oven was installed here
PIZZA   in 1935. The oven is still here, and the pizzas' delightfully chewy crusts,
FAMILY   creamy mozzarella, and full-bodied house-made sauce have kept legions
returning for decades. Pair one of the hearty pies with broccoli dressed
in lemon juice and olive oil and a bottle of the house wine. There are
also a variety of old-school pasta dishes (think: ravioli, spaghetti, mani-
cotti), and old-school favorite dessert, tiramisu. $ *Average main: $21*
⊠ *1042 Kearny St., North Beach* ☎ *415/398–9696* ⊕ *www.tommasos.*
com ⟲ *Reservations not accepted* ⊘ *Closed Mon. No lunch* ✛ *1:D3.*

$$ ✕ **Tony's Pizza Napoletana.** Locals hotly debate who makes the city's
PIZZA   best pizza, and for many Tony Gemignani takes the prize. His reputa-
FAMILY   tion extends well beyond the city: at the World Pizza Cup in Naples he
eclipsed the Italians for the title of World Champion Pizza Maker. The
dough at his restaurant is flavorful and fired just right, with multiple
wood-burning ovens in his casual, modern pizzeria turning out many
different pies—the famed Neapolitan-style Margherita, but also Sicil-
ian, Romana, and Detroit styles. Salads, antipasti, homemade pastas,
and calzone, round out the menu. You can grab a slice next door.
■ TIP➜ If you're dining with kids, ask for some pizza dough to keep
them entertained. $ *Average main: $20* ⊠ *1570 Stockton St., North*
Beach ☎ *415/835–9888* ⊕ *www.tonyspizzanapoletana.com* ⟲ *Reserva-*
tions not accepted ⊘ *Closed Tues.* ✛ *1:D3.*

$$$ ✕ **Tosca Cafe.** A revamped 1919 boho classic attracts edgy celebs (the
MODERN ITALIAN   Sean Penns and Lena Dunhams of the world) and they eat quite well
on Italian wedding soup with meatballs, crispy pork-fat fries, and pas-
tas. A rainbow trout, one of the three mains, is flavored with anchovy,
garlic, and peppers. An espresso machine dispenses a cappuccino with
local Dandelion chocolate, and a shot of bourbon. A jukebox belts
out tunes. You can eat at the bar, which is first come, first served. The
leather booths and chairs are in higher demand. $ *Average main: $28*
⊠ *242 Columbus Ave., North Beach* ☎ *415/986–9651* ⊕ *toscacafesf.*
com/food ⊘ *No lunch* ✛ *1:D3.*

THE WATERFRONT

FISHERMAN'S WHARF

To the north of the Ferry Building lies Fisherman's Wharf, a jumbled
mix of seafood dining rooms, sidewalk vendors, and trinket shops that
visitors religiously trudge through and San Franciscans invariably dis-
miss as a tourist trap. But even locals may come for a cracked crab.

$$$$ ✕ **Gary Danko.** In high season plan on reserving two months ahead at
MODERN   Chef Danko's namesake restaurant—his legion of fans typically keep
AMERICAN   the reservation book full. The cost of a meal is pegged to the number of
courses, from three to five, and the menu spans a classic yet Californian
style that changes seasonally. Dishes might include risotto with lobster
and rock shrimp, or herb-crusted lamb loin. A diet-destroying chocolate
soufflé with two sauces is usually among the desserts. The wine list is
the size of a small-town phone book, and the banquette-lined rooms,
with beautiful wood floors and stunning (but restrained) floral arrange-
ments, are as memorable as the food and impeccable service. $ *Average*

main: $76 ✉ 800 N. Point St., Fisherman's Wharf ☎ 415/749–2060 🌐 www.garydanko.com ✍ Reservations essential 👔 Jacket required ⏲ No lunch ✣ 1:A1.

EMBARCADERO

Locals and visitors alike flock here for gorgeous bay views, a world-class waterfront esplanade, and a Ferry Building that's much better known for its food than its boat rides. Some of the best bakers and cooks in the city have their satellites here, or this is where they start up.

13

$$$$ AMERICAN 🍴 **Boulevard.** Two local restaurant celebrities—chef Nancy Oakes and designer Pat Kuleto—are behind this high-profile, high-priced eatery in the 1889 Audiffred Building, a Parisian look-alike that survived the 1906 quake. The Belle-Époque interior and sophisticated American food with a French accent attract well-dressed locals and flush out-of-towners. Count on generous portions of mains such as grilled king salmon, Maine lobster ravioli, and a wood-grilled pork prime rib chop. Save room for one of the dynamite desserts, among them the dark-chocolate brioche custard. There's counter seating for folks too hungry to wait for a table, and an American Wagyu beef burger with Cowgirl Creamery cheese at lunchtime. [$] *Average main: $36 ✉ 1 Mission St., Embarcadero ☎ 415/543–6084 🌐 www.boulevardrestaurant.com ✍ Reservations essential ⏲ No lunch weekends ✣ 1:G4.*

$$$ SPANISH 🍴 **Coqueta.** With its Embarcadero perch, Bay Bridge views, and stellar Spanish tapas, celebrity chef Michael Chiarello's San Francisco debut has been an instant hit. Equal parts rustic and chic, his dining room's bold decor—stained wooden beams, cowhide rugs, marble bar—sends out the visual message that Chiarello is on top of his game, and it's fun to see him mingling with diners as they enjoy toothpicked *pintxos* (small snacks) such as quail egg with Serrano ham. The real draws, though, are the inventive cocktails, luscious paella, and dazzling variation on the cut of pork *secreto Ibérico* (Iberian secret). The desserts are also small bites, so you'll likely have room to end your experience on a sweet note. ■ **TIP→ Book well in advance for dinner.** [$] *Average main: $30 ✉ Pier 5, on the Embarcadero, near Broadway, Embarcadero ☎ 415/704–8866 🌐 coquetasf.com ✍ Reservations essential ⏲ No lunch Mon. ✣ 1:F3.*

$$$ AMERICAN FAMILY 🍴 **Fog City.** Just about anything from the wood-fired oven and grill at this 21st-century diner is worth ordering: crispy-skinned chicken in a skillet, Wagyu flank-steak frites, or oak-grilled pork chops. A classic, deviled eggs, is spun Californian with crunchy bits of quinoa. For those who favor the meal's end, a custard machine churns out the frozen treat with Cali toppings like the frothy egg-yolk caramel. A stellar bourbon milk punch is but one of too many to choose from. An inviting U-shape bar and tables-with-a-view attract a mix of FiDi locals and tourists who've wandered right into a gold mine. [$] *Average main: $25 ✉ 1300 Battery St., Embarcadero ☎ 415/982–2000 🌐 www.fogcitysf.com ✣ 1:E2.*

$ BURGER 🍴 **Gott's Roadside.** How many burger chains can claim a view of Coit Tower? That's not even the biggest selling point—it's the house-made dressings tossed into the salads, the Mary's chicken buttermilk-dipped for tenders, and Niman Ranch beef ground daily for burgers, washed down with a Napa Cab. Gott's has made the concept of fast food pleasurable (though, technically, this isn't that fast; it takes about 10 to 15 minutes). Gleaming metal countertops and hand-lettered boards recall the prime burger era. $ *Average main: $12* ✉ *1 Ferry Bldg., Suite 6, Embarcadero* ☎ *415/318–3423* ⊕ *www.gotts.com* ✛ *1:G4.*

$$ ✕ **Hog Island Oyster Company.** A thriving oyster farm north of San Fran-
SEAFOOD cisco in Tomales Bay serves up its harvest at this newly expanded raw bar and restaurant in the Ferry Building. Devotees come here for impeccably fresh oysters and clams on the half shell. Other mollusk-centered options include a first-rate oyster stew, baked oysters, clam chowder, and "steamer" dishes atop of a bed of local greens. The bar also turns out one of the city's best grilled-cheese sandwiches, made with three artisanal cheeses on artisanal bread. $ *Average main: $20* ✉ *Ferry Bldg., Embarcadero at Market St., Embarcadero* ☎ *415/391–7117* ⊕ *www.hogislandoysters.com* ⚭ *Reservations not accepted* ✛ *1:G4.*

$$$ ✕ **La Mar Cebicheria Peruana.** Right on the water's edge, this casually chic
PERUVIAN outpost, the chain's first outside Peru, imports real Peruvian flavors to San Francisco. Your waiter will start you out with a pile of potato and plantain chips with three dipping sauces, but after that you're on your own, choosing from a long list of ceviches, can't-miss *causas* (whipped potatoes topped with a choice of fish, shellfish, or vegetable salads), and everything from crisp, lightly deep-fried fish and shellfish to soups and stews. The view of the water is especially enjoyable during lunch or a warm evening. $ *Average main: $25* ✉ *Pier 1½, between Washington and Jackson Sts., Embarcadero* ☎ *415/397–8880* ⊕ *lamarsf.com* ✛ *1:F3.*

$ ✕ **Mijita Cocina Mexicana.** Famed local chef Traci Des Jardins honors her
MEXICAN Latin roots at this casual taqueria. The tacos here feature handmade
FAMILY corn tortillas and fillings like *carnitas* (slow-cooked pork), mahimahi, and *carne asada* (grilled strips of marinated meat). The weekend brings breakfast favorites like *chilaquiles* and *huevos rancheros.* Kid-size burritos (beans and cheese) and quesadillas will keep your niños happy. Seating is simple—wooden tables and benches—but some outside tables offer a perfect perch for bay views. Plan to eat dinner early (Mijita closes at 7 on weekdays, 8 on weekends) and avoid the madness of peak weekday lunch hours. $ *Average main: $9* ✉ *Ferry Bldg., Embarcadero at Market St., Embarcadero* ☎ *415/399–0814* ⊕ *www.mijitasf.com* ☾ *No dinner Sun.* ✛ *1:G4*

$$$ ✕ **Slanted Door.** If you're looking for homey Vietnamese food served in
VIETNAMESE a down-to-earth dining room at a decent price, *don't* stop here. Celebrated chef-owner Charles Phan has mastered the upmarket, Western-accented Vietnamese menu. To showcase his cuisine, he built a big space with sleek wooden tables and chairs, a cocktail lounge, a bar, and an enviable bay view. His popular dishes include green-papaya salad, daikon rice cakes, cellophane crab noodles, chicken clay pot, and shaking beef (tender beef cubes with garlic and onion). They don't come cheap, but they're made with quality ingredients. ■TIP➜ **To avoid the midday and evening crowds, dine at the bar, drop by for afternoon tea (2:30–4:30), or visit Out the Door, Phan's take-out counter around the corner, which is less expensive.** $ *Average main: $29* ✉ *Ferry Bldg., Embarcadero at Market St., Embarcadero* ☎ *415/861–8032* ⊕ *www. slanteddoor.com* ⚭ *Reservations essential* ✛ *1:G4.*

FINANCIAL DISTRICT

The center of commerce, with some very good restaurants (housed in old Barbary Coast buildings), FiDi caters to the business elite with prices to match. But there are some new faces in San Francisco's economy: engineers and software developers looking for a fast lunch head to modest Indian and Chinese places as well as superb sandwich shops.

13

$$ ITALIAN 🍴 **Barbacco.** The busy sister restaurant to neighboring Perbacco offers affordable small plates to let you try a little of this and a little of that: it's like grazing through the different regions of Italy. Start with the *ascolane* (stuffed olives; in this instance with short rib filling) and move on to chicken "under a brick" or a pasta. There are plenty of Italian wines to explore by the glass and a well-informed staff to explain them. Financial District workers crowd in for lunch or happy hour at the communal tables and long counter. The room has a chic Milanese look to it, but the food is soulful and rustic. [$] *Average main: $18* ✉ *220 California St., Financial District* ☎ *415/955–1919* 🌐 *www.barbaccosf.com* ⏲ *No lunch weekends. Closed Sun.* ✢ *1:E4.*

$$ SPANISH 🍴 **Bocadillos.** The name means "sandwiches," but that's only half the story here. You'll find a baker's dozen bocadillos at lunchtime: plump rolls (pick two for $12) filled with everything from Serrano ham to Catalan sausage with arugula. At night are two dozen choices of tapas, including roasted Monterey Bay squid, bavette empanadas, and corn fritters with housemade chorizo. There are ample wines by the glass but also a few sherries. A youngish crowd typically piles into the red-brick dining space, whose aesthetic includes wire chairs and small, square light fixtures. ■ **TIP→ Breakfast is served here, too.** [$] *Average main: $18* ✉ *710 Montgomery St., Financial District* ☎ *415/982–2622* 🌐 *www.bocasf.com* ✍ *Reservations not accepted* ⏲ *Closed Sun. No lunch Sat.* ✢ *1:E4.*

$$$ FRENCH 🍴 **Café Claude.** Francophiles congregate here for that *je ne sais quoi,* right down to the delicious croque monsieur, escargots, steak tartare, and coquilles Saint-Jacques. If you think this place looks straight out of Paris, it mostly is. The banquettes, the zinc bar, the light fixtures, and cinema posters were shipped from a defunct café in the City of Light to this atmospheric downtown alley. Stop by Thursday, Friday, and Saturday nights starting at 7:30 pm to enjoy live jazz with your meal. A second Café Claude has brought Paris to the Marina neighborhood. [$] *Average main: $30* ✉ *7 Claude La., Financial District* ☎ *415/392–3505* 🌐 *www.cafeclaude.com* ⏲ *No lunch Sun.* ✢ *4:H2.*

$$$ ITALIAN 🍴 **Cotogna.** This urban trattoria is just as in demand as its fancier big sister, Quince, next door. Chef Michael Tusk's flavorful, rustic Italian dishes are driven by the seasons, with such irresistible dishes as *raviolo di ricotta,* warm housemade ricotta with wild mushrooms, and juicy spit-roasted pork. The look is comfortably chic, with wood tables, quality stemware, and fantastic Italian wines by the bottle and glass to match. [$] *Average main: $24* ✉ *490 Pacific Ave., Financial District* ☎ *415/775–8508* 🌐 *www.cotognasf.com* ✍ *Reservations essential* ✢ *1:E3.*

$$$ MEDITERRANEAN 🍴 **Gitane.** The name comes from a gypsy, and the boho-ness shines through in the one-of-a-kind decor—lush red lamps, tuffeted curved

seats, and vibrant, oversized art. More importantly, this is a great place for a romantic dinner with conversation, sangrias, and Basque-inspired cooking. Tops are the bacon bonbons (prunes stuffed with goat cheese and wrapped in smoked bacon) and slow-cooked short ribs. The downstairs bar makes inventive and flavorful cocktails (many of them are sherry-based), with seats in demand. While there is outdoor seating, the interior is a seductive part of the experience here. $ *Average main: $30* ⊠ *6 Claude La., Financial District* ☎ *415/788–6686* ⊕ *www.gitanerestaurant.com* ⊗ *Closed Sun. No lunch* ✛ *4:H2.*

$$$$　✕ **Kokkari.** Satisfy your craving for outstanding Greek taverna food—
GREEK　albeit at steak-house prices. Most savvy diners start off with a trio of dips—eggplant, yogurt, and cucumber—and *taramosalata,* fish roe pureed with olive oil and bread crumbs. Main courses showcase Athenian standards as *moussaka,* lemon-oregano chicken, and notable grilled lamb chops. Desserts like semolina custard wrapped in phyllo (it has a dedicated following) make for a light, sweet finish. There's a lively after-work scene in this chic farmhouse setting with wood beamed ceilings, a roaring wood oven, and candlelight. ■ TIP➔ **If the incredible goat stew with orzo is available, get it.** $ *Average main: $35* ⊠ *200 Jackson St., Financial District* ☎ *415/981–0983* ⊕ *www.kokkari.com* ⊰ *Reservations essential* ⊗ *No lunch weekends* ✛ *1:F3.*

$$$$　✕ **Michael Mina.** The refined flagship outpost for this acclaimed chef
ECLECTIC　remains a treat, with luxurious renditions of shabu-shabu (boiled beef) and lobster potpie with Meyer lemons and smoked potatoes. There's a prix fixe–only menu for dinner, while lunch is the time to sample the mastery of Mina at half the price. $ *Average main: $38* ⊠ *252 California St., Financial District* ☎ *415/397–9222* ⊕ *www.michaelmina.net* ⊗ *No lunch Sat. and Sun.* ✛ *1:E4.*

$$$　✕ **Perbacco.** The arrival of skinny, brittle breadsticks is the first sign that
ITALIAN　the kitchen understands the cuisine of northern Italy, specifically Piedmont. And if the breadbasket doesn't convince you, try the antipasto of house-made cured meats (chef Staffan Terje is known for making some of the city's finest *salumi*) or *burrata* with seasonal vegetables, the delicate *agnolotti dal plin* (veal-stuffed pasta with a cabbage-laced meat sauce), or *pappardelle* with short rib *ragù.* With a long marble bar and open kitchen, this brick-lined two-story space oozes big-city charm, attracting business types and Italian food aficionados. $ *Average main: $25* ⊠ *230 California St., Financial District* ☎ *415/955–0663* ⊕ *www.perbaccosf.com* ⊗ *Closed Sun. No lunch Sat.* ✛ *1:E4.*

$$$$　✕ **Quince.** Beloved chef-owner Michael Tusk turns out Italian-inspired
ITALIAN　cuisine with the finest local ingredients. But to enjoy it, you'll have to splurge on a nine-course chef's tasting menu. You'll definitely get to taste a delicious selection of pastas then seasonal items such as suckling pig and sweetbreads, and Bosc pear with Medjool date genoise. The 800-bottle-strong wine list is top-notch, but can get pricey (a steep corkage fee means you won't save much by bringing your own bottle), and the seamless service is both refined and welcoming. ■ TIP➔ **Just get a taste with the à la carte menu in the lounge.** $ *Average main: $95* ⊠ *470 Pacific Ave., Financial District* ☎ *415/775–8500* ⊕ *www.quincerestaurant.com* ⊰ *Reservations essential* ⊗ *No lunch. Closed Sun.* ✛ *1:E3.*

$ ✕ **The Ramen Bar.** Ramen has taken hold of the city, and acclaimed chef
RAMEN Michael Mina is in on the action, his conduit being Tokyo-native and chef Ken Tominaga. The two have collaborated on this FiDi spot. A popular choice is the seafood, which bobs with shrimp and crab dumplings in an aromatic ginger clam broth. Although ramen is in the name, the menu also veers into salad territory, with such ingredients as slow-cooked salmon. Lunch is a rockin' scene, with the FiDi set queuing up to order at the counter. The light, casual setting has sit-down service only at dinner. Prices tend to add up; this is not your strip-mall bowl of ramen joint. ■TIP→ Gluten-free noodles are available. $ *Average main: $14* ✉ *101 California St., Financial District* ☎ *415/684–1570* ⊙ *Closed weekends* ✛ *1:F4.*

$$$ ✕ **Tadich Grill.** Locations and owners have changed more than once since
SEAFOOD this old-timer started as a coffee stand on the waterfront in 1849, but the crowds keep coming. Try the Dungeness crab cocktail, crab Louie, and cioppino during crab season (usually November to May), the Pacific halibut between January and May, and iconic San Francisco sand dabs year-round. In any season, finish the meal with the Tadich rice custard pudding, topped with cream. The private booths (complete with a bell to summon the crusty, white-coated waiters) are a coveted spot. A long line of business types at noon is inevitable. $ *Average main: $27* ✉ *240 California St., Financial District* ☎ *415/391–1849* ⊕ *www.tadichgrill. com* ⚱ *Reservations not accepted* ⊙ *Closed Sun.* ✛ *1:E4.*

$$$ ✕ **Wayfare Tavern.** This energetic and upscale American tavern owned
AMERICAN by TV chef and personality Tyler Florence has a good-looking style that's rich with turn-of-the-century Americana, including brick walls, comfortable booths, wood tables, multiple levels, and even a billiards room. The approachable menu has deviled eggs, fresh seafood, excellent salads (the Green Goddess dressing is particularly good), and the decadent burger and fried chicken are both favorites. The volume can be loud, so this won't be a good fit if you're wanting to hear your dinner companion, but the upstairs is slightly quieter. Reservations are highly recommended. $ *Average main: $27* ✉ *558 Sacramento St., Financial District* ☎ *415/722–9060* ⊕ *www.wayfaretavern.com* ✛ *1:E4.*

$$ ✕ **Wexler's.** Four words: bourbon banana cream pie. Of course, there's
BARBECUE a slew of tempting barbecue items that threaten whether you'll have room at the end of the meal. The interior is chic minimalist, with a couple of red chandeliers to liven up the place. Barbecue traditionalists should come with an open mind. The crispy Scotch eggs, fork-tender short ribs, and smoked wings (with Point Reyes blue cheese dressing) wander into more creative territory—chef Charlie Kleinman earns accolades. $ *Average main: $22* ✉ *568 Sacramento St., Financial District* ☎ *415/983–0102* ⊕ *www.wexlerssf.com* ⊙ *Closed Sun. No dinner Mon. No lunch weekends* ✛ *1:E4.*

$$ ✕ **Yank Sing.** This granddaddy of teahouses in a quiet location on Ste-
CHINESE venson Street—there's also a big, brassy branch in the Rincon Cen-
FAMILY ter—serves some of San Francisco's best dim sum to office workers on weekdays and boisterous families on weekends. The several dozen varieties prepared daily include both the classic (steamed pork buns, shrimp dumplings, egg custard tartlets) and the creative (scallion-skewered

CLOSE UP

Eating with Kids

Kids can be fussy eaters, and parents can be, too. Fortunately, there are plenty of excellent options in the city that will satisfy both.

Barney's Gourmet Burgers. With locations all over the Bay Area, including this one not far from Fort Mason, this chain caters to older kids and their parents with mile-high burgers and giant salads. But Barney's doesn't forget "kids under 8," who have their own menu featuring a burger, an all-beef frank, and chicken strips. And they don't forget parents, offering a nice selection of wines by the glass and beer on tap. ✉ *3344 Steiner St., near Union St.* ☎ *415/563–0307* ⊕ *www.barneyshamburgers.com.* *(✛ 3:C6)*

City View Restaurant. Nearby in Chinatown, City View Restaurant serves a varied selection of dim sum, with tasty pork buns for kids and more-exotic fare for adults. ✉ *662 Commercial St., near Kearny St.* ☎ *415/398–2838. (✛ 1:E4)*

The Ferry Building *(✛ 1:G4)* on the Embarcadero has plenty of kid-friendly options, from **Mijita Cocina Mexicana,** which has its own kids' menu, to **Gott's Roadside,** for burgers, shakes, and more. (And the outdoor access can help keep the little ones entertained.)

La Corneta. The Mission has dozens of no-frills taco-and-burrito parlors; especially worthy is bustling La Corneta, which has a baby burrito and well-made quesadillas. ✉ *2731 Mission St., between 23rd and 24th Sts.* ☎ *415/643–7001. (✛ 3:F6)*

Park Chalet. Finally, both kids and adults love to be by the ocean, and the Park Chalet, hidden behind the two-story Beach Chalet, offers pizza, mac and cheese, sticky ribs, and a big banana split. ✉ *1000 Great Hwy., at Fulton St.* ☎ *415/386–8439. (✛ 3:A3)*

Rosamunde Sausage Grill. In Lower Haight, the small Rosamunde Sausage Grill serves just that—a slew of different sausages, from Polish to duck to *Weisswurst* (Bavarian veal). You get your choice of two toppings, like grilled onions, sauerkraut, and chili, and since there are only six stools, plan on take-out. ■TIP➜ **Head to nearby Duboce Park, with its cute playground.** ✉ *545 Haight St., between Steiner and Fillmore Sts.* ☎ *415/437–6851. (✛ 3:D3)*

Sears Fine Food. If you're downtown for breakfast, stop at the touristy but venerable Sears Fine Food, home of "the world-famous Swedish pancakes." Eighteen of the silver-dollar-size beauties cost less than a movie ticket. ✉ *439 Powell St., near Post St.* ☎ *415/986–0700. (✛ 4:F3)*

St. Francis Fountain. Banana splits and hot-fudge sundaes are what St. Francis Fountain is known for, along with its vintage decor (and popularity with hipsters for weekend brunch). Opened in 1918, it recalls the early 1950s, and the menu, with its burgers, BLTs, grilled-cheese sandwiches, and chili with corn bread, is timeless. ✉ *2801 24th St., at York St.* ☎ *415/836–4210. (✛ 3:H6)*

prawns tied with bacon, lobster and *tobiko* roe dumplings, basil seafood dumplings). The tab can rise quickly, so pace yourself. The take-out counter makes a meal on the run a satisfying compromise when office duties—or touring—won't wait. ■ TIP→ **The Shanghai soup dumplings are perfection.** Ⓢ *Average main: $16* ⊠ *49 Stevenson St., Financial District* ☎ *415/541–4949* ⊕ *www.yanksing.com* ⊙ *No dinner* ✛ *1:E5.*

THE MARINA

On a sunny day, the Marina is perhaps one of the most cheerful places in the city, with sweeping views of Marin and the Golden Gate Bridge and plenty of joggers and bicyclists. Residents tend to be a mix of the just-graduated who are still very much into the nightclub scene. Mixed in are the affluent of the spectacular waterfront properties who hit Chestnut Street after dark for good food.

$$$ ✕ **A16.** Marina residents—and, judging from the crowds, everybody
ITALIAN   else—gravitate to this trattoria named for a highway that runs past Naples into surrounding Campania and specializing in the food from that region, done very, very well. Rustic pasta favorites such as *maccaronara* with *ragu napoletana* and house-made salted ricotta might show up on the menu, and for an entrée perhaps petrale sole with crispy black trumpet mushrooms. The pizzas are also a highlight. The selection of primarily southern Italian wines, augmented by some California vintages, supports the food perfectly, and there's a substantial beer list. ■ TIP→ **The animated bar scene near the door sets the tone; for a quieter time request a table in the alcove or try for the patio.** Ⓢ *Average main: $27* ⊠ *2355 Chestnut St., Marina* ☎ *415/771–2216* ⊕ *www.a16sf.com* ⌔ *Reservations essential* ⊙ *No lunch Mon. and Tues.* ✛ *2:D2.*

$$ ✕ **Greens.** Owned and operated by the San Francisco Zen Center, this
VEGETARIAN   nonprofit vegetarian restaurant gets some of its fresh produce from the center's organic Green Gulch Farm. Despite the lack of meat, hearty dishes from chef Annie Somerville—shepherd's pie with wild mushrooms, for example, or the vegetable brochette plate—really satisfy. An à la carte menu is offered on Sunday and weeknights, but on Saturday a four-course prix-fixe dinner is served. Floor-to-ceiling windows give diners a sweeping view of the Marina and the Golden Gate Bridge. ■ TIP→ **A small counter by the front door stocks sandwiches, soups, and sweets for easy takeout, open in the morning.** Ⓢ *Average main: $19* ⊠ *Bldg. A, Fort Mason, off Marina Blvd., Marina* ☎ *415/771–6222* ⊕ *www.greensrestaurant.com* ⌔ *Reservations essential* ⊙ *No lunch Mon.* ✛ *2:G1.*

$$ ✕ **Tacolicious.** This Marina hot spot draws a young and energetic crowd
MEXICAN   that fuels up on equal parts tacos and tequila, or on chilaquiles and Bloody Marias during weekend brunch. Tables are usually laden with made-to-order guacamole and platters of well-stuffed tacos (the carnitas and short-rib versions are especially full of flavor). You'll also see groups ordering rounds of "chupitos," easy-to-drink shots of tequila mixed with juices, from prickly pear to passion fruit. If you don't want to speak in a raised voice, this is not the restaurant for you, unless you land one of the few outside tables. Their equally bustling Mission

13

District outpost has a tequila bar, Mosto. $ *Average main: $15* ✉ *2031 Chestnut St., Marina* ☎ *415/346–1966* ⊕ *www.tacolicious.com* ✛ *2:E2.*

COW HOLLOW

Just up the hill from the Marina—and slightly quieter with more young families—is Cow Hollow. Union Street is the main strip, dense with restaurants, cafés, and boutiques that mostly cater to the trendy A-list crowd. Wander even farther up the hills and you'll be in the thick of the manses of Pacific Heights.

$$$ ✕ **Rose's Café.** Sleepy-headed locals turn up for the breakfast pizza of
ITALIAN   smoked ham, eggs, and fontina; poached eggs with Yukon Gold potato
FAMILY   and mushroom hash; and soft polenta with mascarpone and jam. Midday is time for pizza with wild nettles, or linguine with clams. Evening hours find customers eating their way through more pizza and pasta, or skirt steak and a glorious roasted chicken. The ingredients are top-notch, the service is friendly, and the seating is in comfortable booths and at tables and a counter. Heaters above the outdoor tables keep things toasty when the temperature dips. ■ TIP➜ Expect long lines for Sunday brunch. $ *Average main: $27* ✉ *2298 Union St., Cow Hollow* ☎ *415/775–2200* ⊕ *www.rosescafesf.com* ✛ *2:E3.*

THE RICHMOND AND SUNSET DISTRICT

THE RICHMOND

The Richmond encompasses the land on the north side of Golden Gate Park, running to the ocean's edge. As for architecture eye-candy, there isn't much, but this is the land of authentic Asian food, particularly in Inner Richmond, known as the new Chinatown, covering Clement Street from about 2nd to 13th avenues. On the main thoroughfares of Clement, Balboa, and Geary streets, you'll find bargain dim sum, Burmese, Korean barbecue, and noodle soups of all persuasions.

$ ✕ **Burma Superstar.** Locals make the trek to the "Avenues" for the
ASIAN   extraordinary tea-leaf salad, a combo of spicy, salty, crunchy, and sour that is mixed table-side, with fermented tea leaves from Burma, fried garlic, and peanuts. Another hit is the hearty vegetarian *samusa* soup. The modestly decorated, no-reservations restaurant is small, so lines can be long during peak times. Leave your number and wait for the call. ■ TIP➜ Walk a couple blocks east to B-Star, owned by the same people but lesser known and often less crowded. $ *Average main: $14* ✉ *309 Clement St., The Richmond* ☎ *415/387–2147* ⊕ *www.burmasuperstar. com* ⬧ *Reservations not accepted* ✛ *2:A6.*

$ ✕ **Good Noodle.** The menu at this no-frills Formica-and-linoleum spot is
VIETNAMESE   big and remarkably cheap. You can order everything from Vietnamese
FAMILY   salads to rice dishes and noodle plates. But the soups are what take up the most space on the menu, from the two dozen varieties of *pho*, rice noodles in beef broth, to a dozen types of *hu tieu*, seafood and pork noodle soups. Regulars, many of whom hail from Southeast Asia, favor the shrimp, fish ball, and pork slices soup with clear noodles and the special combo pho with rare steak, well-done brisket, tendon, and tripe.

$ *Average main: $8* ⊠ *239 Clement St., The Richmond* ☎ *415/379–9008* ⊹ *2:A6.*

$ ✕ **Pizzetta 211.** This shoebox-size spot puts together thin-crust pies

PIZZA topped with the kinds of ingredients that are worth the (almost) constant wait. The selection changes daily: the tomato-basil-and-mozzarella pizza and the Sardinian-cheese-pine nut-and-rosemary pie are a couple of the only constants on the menu (the white anchovies that top the pizzas here are also stellar). Pizzetta doesn't take reservations, so go early to avoid a long wait. $ *Average main: $13* ⊠ *211 23rd Ave., The Richmond* ☎ *415/379–9880* ⊕ *www.pizzetta211.com* ⊹ *3:A1.*

13

$ ✕ **Tenglong.** Two former restaurant owners from Hong Kong opened this

CHINESE tidy space with pale-yellow walls only to give everyone in the neighborhood an addiction to their dry chicken wings, fried in garlic and roasted red peppers. The place specializes in mostly Southern-style Chinese like Cantonese and has a few Sichuan specialties, too. Other good choices are the honey-walnut prawns, thinly sliced Mongolian beef, spicy seafood noodles, and *dan dan* noodles. The service is remarkably friendly and welcoming, though English is spotty. $ *Average main: $12* ⊠ *208 Clement St., The Richmond* ☎ *415/666–3515* ⊕ *www.tenglongsf.com* ☽ *Closed Tues.* ⊹ *2:A6*

$$ ✕ **Ton Kiang.** This local favorite introduces the lightly seasoned Hakka

CHINESE cuisine of southern China, rarely found in this country and even obscure

FAMILY to many Chinese. Salt-baked chicken, stuffed bean curd, steamed fresh

Fodor's Choice bacon with dried mustard greens, chicken in wine sauce, and clay pots

★ of meats and seafood are among the hallmarks. Ton Kiang opens in the morning for dim sum, serving delicate dumplings of pea shoots and shrimp, scallops and shrimp, and pork and greens; a small selection of dim sum is available at night, too. Expect a noontime rush. $ *Average main: $18* ⊠ *5821 Geary Blvd., The Richmond* ☎ *415/387–8273* ⊕ *www.tonkiang.net* ⊹ *2:A6.*

SUNSET DISTRICT

The Sunset neighborhood encompasses the land south of Golden Gate Park, running all the way to the ocean's edge, and has a surf-town or small-town vibe. It's known for its fog, yes, but also bargain eats (UCSF is here) that range from pizzas and salads to Eritrean *injera* (flatbread) and Chinese dumplings, concentrated along Irving Street.

$ ✕ **Park Chow.** What do spaghetti and meatballs, Thai noodles with chicken

AMERICAN and shrimp, salads in three sizes, and big burgers have in common?

FAMILY They're all on the eclectic comfort-food menu here, and all are made with sustainable ingredients yet offered at unbeatable prices. This neighborhood standby is also known for its desserts: the fresh-baked pies and ginger cake with pumpkin ice cream are among the standouts. Kids get their own menu. In cool weather fires roar in the dining-room fireplaces; in warm weather, the outdoor tables are the place to be. There's another Chow in the Castro neighborhood. ■ **TIP➜ You can call ahead to put your name on the waiting list.** $ *Average main: $13* ⊠ *1240 9th Ave., Inner Sunset* ☎ *415/665–9912* ⊕ *www.chowfoodbar.com* ⊹ *3:A5.*

$$ ✕ **San Tung.** Many of the best chefs in Beijing's imperial kitchens hailed

CHINESE from China's northeastern province of Shandong, and San Franciscans

FAMILY regularly enjoy dishes of the same province at this bare-bones storefront restaurant. Specialties include steamed dumplings—shrimp and leek dumplings are the most popular—and hand-pulled noodles, in soup or stir-fried. Parents and kids regularly fight over platters of dry-fried chicken wings, a cult dish in the city. To get a table without a wait, come before or after the noon or dinner rush. [$] *Average main: $16* ✉ *1031 Irving St., Inner Sunset* ☎ *415/242–0828* ⏲ *Closed Wed.* ✥ *3:A5.*

THE HAIGHT, THE WESTERN ADDITION, THE CASTRO, AND NOE VALLEY

THE HAIGHT

The Haight-Ashbury was home base for the country's famed 1960s counterculture, and its café scene still reflects that colorful past. For ethnic flavors, go to the neighborhoods on either side of Golden Gate Park.

Over time, the Haight has become two distinct neighborhoods. The Upper Haight is an energetic commercial stretch from Masonic Avenue to Stanyan Street, where head shops and tofu-burger joints still thrive.

Meanwhile, the modestly gritty Lower Haight has emerged as a lively bohemian quarter of sorts, with mostly ethnic eateries lining the blocks between Webster and Pierce streets.

$$ THAI

🍴 **Thep Phanom.** Long ago, local food critics and restaurant-goers began singing the praises of Thep Phanom and the tune hasn't stopped. Duck is deliciously prepared deep-fried with a plum sauce. Seafood is another specialty, along with warm eggplant salad, fried tofu with peanut sauce, spicy beef salad, fried quail, and rich Thai curries. The lengthy regular menu is supplemented by a list of daily specials, which only makes it harder to make a decision. You'll be pondering your choices in comfortable surroundings: the cozy dining room is lined with Thai art and artifacts that owner Pathama Parikanont has collected over the years. [$] *Average main: $15* ✉ *400 Waller St., Lower Haight* ☎ *415/431–2526* 🌐 *www.thepphanom.com* ⏲ *No lunch* ✥ *3:D3.*

$$ ITALIAN

🍴 **Uva Enoteca.** This casual Italian wine bar hits all the right notes: It's convivial, food is solidly good, and there's plenty of wine—more than 15 by the glass (available in 2- or 8-ounce pours) and a long list of bottles. The menu is straightforward: assortments of Italian cured meats and cheeses, about 10 salads and vegetable dishes, and four to five pastas or pizzas. Even the gelato is special, made by a local artisan. A young, savvy staff right fits into the upbeat surroundings, with a marble counter, a handful of banquettes, and tables for two and four. There's a weekend brunch. [$] *Average main: $16* ✉ *568 Haight St., Lower Haight* ☎ *415/829–2024* 🌐 *www.uvaenoteca.com* ⏲ *No lunch weekdays. Closed Sun. dinner.* ✥ *3:D3.*

THE WESTERN ADDITION

This is a patchwork of culturally and economically diverse neighborhoods bordering the Lower Haight, the Fillmore District, and Japantown, where you can find Italian, Japanese, and Indian restaurants housed in 1950s and Victorian buildings in the span of a couple city blocks. Tucked between some cheap-knockoff stores and national chains are a couple of dining heavies (and one of the most well-known city parks, Alamo Square).

$$ ✕ **4505 Burgers & BBQ.** Those who have ever wondered how a butcher
BARBECUE would prepare meat will find the answer in the tender brisket here. The crust is deliciously charred, and the meat flavorful, spending 18 to 24 hours in a smoker as part of a process perfected by the butcher/owners. Every plate comes with two sides, and you should choose frankaroni as one of them. Possibly the work of the devil, this is macaroni-and-cheese with pieces of hot dog . . . deep fried. You order at the counter in this chic-hipster shack on a rapidly evolving stretch of Divis that attracts long lines, though they move quickly. Seating is mostly outside at communal picnic tables. The restaurant's sign, "Pig N or Pig Out" truly means it. They do takeout and delivery (via Try Caviar). Ⓢ *Average main: $15* ✉ *705 Divisadero, at Grove St., Western Addition* ☎ *415/231–6993* ✛ *3:B2.*

$$$ ✕ **Nopa.** This is the good-food granddaddy of the hot corridor of the
AMERICAN same name (NoPa equals North of the Panhandle). The Cali-rustic fare includes an always winning flatbread topped with fennel sausage and caramelized onions; smoky, crisp-skin rotisserie chicken; and a juicy hamburger with thick-cut fries. This place is so lively—and high ceilings and concrete floors contribute to the noise factor—that raised voices are sometimes the only way to communicate. The weekend brunch is among the city's best. ■ TIP➔ **Late-night cravings can be satisfied until 1 am.** Ⓢ *Average main: $24* ✉ *560 Divisadero St., Western Addition* ☎ *415/864–8643* ⊕ *www.nopasf.com* ☾ *No lunch weekdays* ✛ *3:B3.*

$$ ✕ **Nopalito.** Those in the mood for Mexican will get some of the most
MEXICAN authentic flavors here—and at the same time, be surprised by the cre-
FAMILY ativity and fresh ingredients on the plate. All the tortillas are made from
Fodor's Choice organic house-ground *masa* (dough), and Mexico's peppers find their
★ way into many of the offerings. The spicy beef empanada and succulent pork carnitas are skillfully prepared—not a goopy mess. The casual atmosphere is popular with families yet pleasing to adults lured by the well-selected tequilas. Expect a substantial wait in the evening, though you can call ahead to be put on the list. If you're feeling truly impatient, order from the take-out window; or the second location in Inner Sunset may be less crowded. Ⓢ *Average main: $15* ✉ *306 Broderick St., Western Addition* ☎ *415/437–0303* ⊕ *www.nopalitosf.com* ✛ *3:B3.*

$$$$ ✕ **The Progress.** Tables are coveted at this restaurant by the chef-owners
MODERN of the Michelin-starred State Bird Provisions, and for good reason: the
AMERICAN inventive dishes, marrying Californian and Japanese cuisine, are a culi-
nary adventure served family-style. Dumplings are filled with Mt. Tam cheese and porcini, and Cali beef comes with a mustard miso-oyster sauce, all served on eye-popping ceramics. For $65 per person, tables collectively decide on six items to get off the 18-item menu (which includes three desserts). Next door to the revered State Bird Provisions and equally signless, the space is airy with soaring ceilings, a mezzanine, and exposed beams and concrete. Foodies of all ages come out in droves. ■ TIP➔ **Nab one of the 12 bar stools, and you can forego the $65 prix-fixe menu, and order à la carte.** Ⓢ *Average main: $65* ✉ *1525*

13

Fillmore St., Western Addition ☎ *415/673–1294* 🌐 *www.theprogress-sf.com/* ⏲ *No lunch* ✣ *3:C2.*

$$$ MODERN AMERICAN Fodor's Choice ★

🍴 **State Bird Provisions.** A reservation here is practically impossible to get, but if you do walk in and commit to a 90-plus minute wait you'll eventually be treated to a festive parade of bites that roll around on carts dim-sum style. Choices include half dollar–size thick savory pancakes stuffed with sauerkraut; giant nori chips topped with Hamachi, radishes, and avocados; and about 15 or so other nightly creations, often with a Japanese slant. The colorful dining room with pegboard walls has a high school art-room vibe. The staff remains super friendly, even though they turn away dozens. **TIP→ Get here an hour before opening and wait in line, or come at 5:30, leave your number, and the host will page you when the table is ready.** [$] *Average main: $30* ✉ *1529 Fillmore St., Western Addition* ☎ *415/795–1272* 🌐 *www.statebirdsf.com* ⏲ *No lunch* ✣ *3:C1.*

THE CASTRO

The Castro neighborhood, the epicenter of the city's gay community, is chockablock with restaurants and bars. Market Street between Church and Castro streets is a great stretch for people-watching and café- or bistro-hopping.

$ AMERICAN FAMILY Fodor's Choice ★

🍴 **Chow.** This consistently popular and consciously unpretentious, funky-yet-savvy diner serves soporific standards like hamburgers, pizzas, and spaghetti with meatballs, all treated with culinary respect. A magnet for penny-pinchers, the restaurant has built its reputation on honest and approachable fare made with local ingredients. Diners will discover Asian dishes mixed in with the primarily American/Italian menu (the silky wontons are popular) and a nice list of salads. Don't even think about leaving without trying the ginger cake with caramel sauce. The wine list has some well-chosen picks. [$] *Average main: $13* ✉ *215 Church St., Castro* ☎ *415/552–2469* 🌐 *www.chowfoodbar.com* ✣ *3:D4.*

$$$ FRENCH

🍴 **Frances.** Still one of the hottest tickets in town, this small space belts out a delicious bacon beignet. You come to see what chef/owner Melissa Perello will execute. Standouts on the California-French menu are the savory bavette steak, duck confit, and baked clams with bacon cream. The apple galette for dessert hits all the right notes. The space is simply designed with a limited number of tables, so it can be extraordinarily difficult to get a reservation, except at 10 pm. Service is professional and warm. [$] *Average main: $27* ✉ *3870 17th St., Castro* ☎ *415/621–3870* 🌐 *www.frances-sf.com* ✍ *Reservations essential* ⏲ *Closed Mon. No lunch* ✣ *3:C5.*

$$ SEAFOOD

🍴 **Woodhouse Fish Co.** New Englanders hungry for a lobster roll fix need look no further than this super-friendly spot, where the rolls are utterly authentic and accompanied with slaw and fries. But then this is California. So go for the Dungeness crab roll. The V-shape storefront, which stands on a busy Market Street corner, is all worn wood and paint and comfortably funky. It seems like everyone in the neighborhood turns out for one-dollar West Coast oysters on Tuesday afternoons, all day. A second branch is in Lower Pacific Heights. [$] *Average main: $18* ✉ *2073 Market St., Castro* ☎ *415/437–2722* 🌐 *www.woodhousefish.com* ✍ *Reservations not accepted* ✣ *3:D4.*

NOE VALLEY

Also called Stroller Valley for its high quota of young families, Noe has seen a change in demographic lately, with many newly minted Facebook millionaires moving into this area and neighboring Mission Dolores (heard of Mark Zuckerberg?). Despite hungry, wealthy residents, Noe has been mysteriously slow to welcome good restaurants. A few stand-outs are along the main strip of 24th Street from Church to Castro streets, and on Church Street from 24th to 30th streets.

$$$ ✕ **La Ciccia.** This charming neighborhood trattoria is the only restaurant
ITALIAN in the city exclusively serving Sardinian food. The island's classics are all represented—octopus stew in a spicy tomato sauce; spaghetti with spicy oil and *bottarga* (salted mullet roe); and *fregola* (pebble-shape pasta) with sea urchin, tomato, and cured tuna heart. One-fourth of the choices on the extensive wine list are Sardinian. The staff is both friendly and efficient. This is not only a local's favorite, but a restaurant industry favorite as well, so tables in this unassuming spot, with homespun decor, are usually booked well in advance. $ *Average main: $25* ⊠ *291 30th St., Noe Valley* ☎ *415/550–8114* ⊕ *www.laciccia.com* ⊙ *Closed Sun. and Mon. No lunch* ✛ *3:D6.*

$$$ ✕ **La Nebbia.** Because sister restaurant, the cultish La Ciccia, is nearly
ITALIAN always booked, the convivial owners opened La Nebbia (which means fog) a block away. Here, you can sit back and linger over plates of pro-sciutto and other antipasti, like the gorgeously done combo of Spanish anchovies dusted with cocoa, the saltiness balancing the bitter sweet. Or how about a salumi flight? Pizzas, hearty meatballs, lasagna, and lamb skewers have all been added recently to make this a full-on trattoria. However, the enoteca roots show on the Italian wine list of about 70 bottles. Neighbors gather in this simple setting that was once a furniture showroom and is now big on bonhomie and great food. $ *Average main: $25* ⊠ *1781 Church St., Noe Valley* ☎ *415/874–9924* ⊕ *www.lanebbia.com* ⊙ *Closed Mon. No lunch* ✛ *3:D6.*

MISSION DISTRICT AND POTRERO HILL

MISSION DISTRICT

You'll never go hungry here, in San Francisco's most jam-packed restaurant neighborhood. From dirt-cheap taquerias to hip tapas joints, city dwellers know this sector as the go-to area for a great meal. The Valencia Street corridor has been particularly hot, opening new restaurants at a milestone pace, with many declaring this to be the best food neighborhood in the city.

$ ✕ **Angkor Borei.** Aromatic Thai basil, lemongrass, and softly sizzling
CAMBODIAN chilies perfume this modest neighborhood favorite, opened by Cambodian refugees in the late 1980s. The menu includes an array of curries; salads of squid or cold noodles with ground fish; and lightly curried fish mousse cooked in a banana leaf basket. Chicken grilled on skewers and served with mild pickled vegetables is a house specialty. Vegetarians will be happy to discover two full pages of selections. Service is friendly though sometimes languid, so don't stop here when you're in a hurry. $ *Average main: $11* ⊠ *3471 Mission St., Bernal Heights*

☎ *415/550–8417* ⊕ *www.cambodiankitchen.com* ⊗ *No lunch Sun.* ✛ *3:F6.*

$$$ ✕ **Bar Tartine.** An offshoot of the cultlike Tartine Bakery, this artsy space
MODERN provides a way to taste the bakery's famed (and nearly always sold-
AMERICAN out) country loaf. Flavor-packed cuisine is eclectic, influenced by East-
ern Europe, Scandinavia, and Japan with California sensibility. The
menu includes many house-pickled items, tempting *langos* (fried potato
bread), and seasonal salads such as smoked potatoes with black garlic.
Chicken *paprikas* and fisherman's stew are among the homey dishes.
Weekend brunch is one of the city's more distinct offerings in that
category, with buckwheat blintzes, and a beef-brisket hash with celery
root, parsnip, Yukon Gold potatoes, and fried eggs. Ⓢ *Average main:*
$25 ⊠ *561 Valencia St., Mission* ☎ *415/487–1600* ⊕ *www.bartartine.*
com ⊗ *Closed for lunch weekdays* ✛ *3:F5.*

$$ ✕ **Beretta.** The formula here basically works: excellent cocktails, an array
ITALIAN of affordable antipasti, solid pizzas, *piatti del giorno* (daily mains), and
late dining until 1 am. The bartenders are both serious and friendly.
The pizzas respect their Italian heritage (thin crusts, traditional and
contemporary toppings) and the antipasti are an appealing mix of vegetables (cauliflower with capers), fish (a light fritto misto), and artisanal
salumi. The long room with tin ceiling and bare-wood tables is casual
and smart, and typically filled with a young crowd. What doesn't work
here? Conversation. ■**TIP→ Come on the weekends for a late lunch**
or brunch, and you'll probably cruise right in. Ⓢ *Average main: $18*
⊠ *1199 Valencia St., Mission* ☎ *415/695–1199* ⊕ *www.berettasf.com*
⊗ *No lunch weekdays* ✛ *3:E6.*

$$$ ✕ **Central Kitchen.** Californian cuisine in all of its freshness is on display in
MODERN this offshoot of Flour + Water. You might taste raw Hamachi topped with
AMERICAN fennel, or one of chef Thomas McNaughton's famous pastas. A planked-
Fodor'sChoice and-concrete tea-light strung courtyard, with a retractable awning, shares
★ space with Salumeria (a deli and larder) and Trick Dog (an energetic
cocktail bar). Ⓢ *Average main: $30* ⊠ *3000 20th St., Mission* ☎ *415/826–*
7004 ⊕ *www.centralkitchensf.com* ⊗ *No lunch weekdays* ✛ *3:H6.*

$$ ✕ **Chino.** If you think Chinese food needs to loosen up, here's your
CHINESE FUSION dream destination. Chino has all the playfulness of its sister restaurant
FAMILY Tacolicious, only it's wandered into dumpling territory. There are about
a half dozen of those choices, like shanghai soup dumplings, and the
nicely spiced steamed shrimp wontons. The yuba noodle salad bursts
with cilantro and sesame oil. The decor is whimsical, with balloon-
sized paper lanterns and sneakers hanging from light fixtures. This
is all paired with boba drinks gone boozy. The place is very loud and
popular with the Mission District bar-crawling crowd, but takeout is
offered; and there's even a dumpling-centric menu for kids. Ⓢ *Average*
main: $20 ⊠ *3198 16th St., Mission* ☎ *415/552–5771* ⊕ *chinosf.com*
⊗ *No lunch Mon.–Thurs.* ✛ *3:E5.*

$$$ ✕ **Delfina.** "Irresistible." That's how countless die-hard fans describe
ITALIAN Craig and Anne Stoll's Northern Italian spot. Don't even think about an
Fodor'sChoice eye roll should we recommend you order the spaghetti with plum toma-
★ toes. It's been dialed to perfection. If Piemontese fresh white truffles
have made their way to San Francisco, you are likely to find hand-cut

tagliarini dressed with butter, cream, and the pricey aromatic fungus on the menu. The panna cotta is the best in its class. Tables are squeezed into an urban interior, with hardwood floors, aluminum-top tables, and a tile bar, that seems to radiate with happiness. $ *Average main: $25* ✉ *3621 18th St., Mission* ☎ *415/552–4055* ⊕ *www.delfinasf.com* ⚑ *Reservations essential* ⊗ *No lunch* ✛ *3:E6.*

$$ ✕ **Dosa on Valencia.** If you like Indian food but crave more than chicken
INDIAN   tikka masala and naan, this cheerful temple of South Indian cuisine
Fodor'sChoice is for you. Aside from the large, thin savory namesake pancake, the
★   kitchen also perpare curries, *uttapam* (open-face pancakes), and various starters, breads, rice dishes, and chutneys. Dosa fillings range from traditional potatoes, onions, and cashews to spinach and fennel stems. Tamil lamb curry with fennel and tomatoes and poppy seed prawns are popular, as are the Indian street-food additions, among them *vada pav* (a vegetarian slider). A second, splashier branch is in Japantown. $ *Average main: $18* ✉ *995 Valencia St., at 21st St., Mission* ☎ *415/642–3672* ⊕ *www.dosasf.com* ⊗ *No lunch weekdays* ✛ *3:F6.*

$$$ ✕ **Flour + Water.** Diners used to flood into this hot spot for the blistery
ITALIAN   thin-crust Neapolitan pizza, but these days it's the pasta that holds attention. The grand experience here is the seven-course pasta-tasting menu (extra for wine pairings). The homemade mustard tagliatelle with smoked lamb's tongue is surprisingly zippy, with lemon zest lifting and extracting flavors. A whimsical interior includes tabletop beakers as candleholders, a moth-wing wall mural, and a cabinet of taxidermy in the bathroom. Expect a noisy, boisterous scene. Trying to get a reservation at Flour + Water is one of the longest-running jokes in town. Your best bet is to come when the doors open. $ *Average main: $26* ✉ *2401 Harrison St., Mission* ☎ *415/826–7000* ⊕ *www.flourandwater. com* ⊗ *No lunch* ✛ *3:G6.*

$$$ ✕ **Foreign Cinema.** Forget popcorn. In this hip, loftlike space "dinner
MODERN   and a movie" become one joyous event. Classic films are projected on
AMERICAN   a wall in a large inner courtyard while you're served perfectly shucked
FAMILY   oysters on the half shell, warm brandade, house-cured sardines, bavette steak, or seafood stew. Avid filmgoers should keep in mind that it's really more about dining than movie watching here. Kids aren't forgotten, with a special meal of celery and carrot sticks, pasta with butter and cheese, and two scoops of ice cream. The weekend brunch brings throngs of people fighting for a spot on the patio for some of the city's best egg dishes and Bloody Marys. $ *Average main: $25* ✉ *2534 Mission St., Mission* ☎ *415/648–7600* ⊕ *www.foreigncinema.com* ⊗ *No lunch weekdays* ✛ *3:F6.*

$ ✕ **La Santaneca de la Mission.** El Salvadorans who live in the Mission
LATIN AMERICAN head here for *pupusas*, stuffed cornmeal rounds that are more or less
FAMILY   the hamburger of their homeland, usually filled with beans, cheese, or meat—sometimes in combination—and eaten with seasoned shredded cabbage (and is less than $2 apiece). The kitchen at this friendly, family-run place also makes the more unusual rice-flour pupusa, as well as other dishes popular in Central America, including seafood soup, tamales, *chicharrones* (fried pork skins), and yucca. Pupusas are made to order, so don't come here when you're in a rush. $ *Average*

main: $7 ☒ *2815 Mission St., Mission* ☏ *415/285–2131* ⊟ *No credit cards* ⊕ *3:F6.*

$$$$ ✕ **Lazy Bear.** There's no end to the buzz of chef David Barzelay's pop-
MODERN up turned permanent, or the quest for a ticket to one of his modern
AMERICAN American dinners. A reservation for the 12- to 18-course prix-fixe menu
that changes monthly is required. You might see Delta crawfish, hen
jus, or duck with cracklins. An ode to the Western lodge, the two-level
dining room includes a modern fireplace, charred wood walls, wooden
rafters and tables made of American elm. You're basically going to
a dinner party for 40, with cocktails and bites enjoyed upstairs and
dinner downstairs at two communal tables. Everyone is thoughtfully
given a passbook for writing their notes. Ⓢ *Average main: $120* ☒ *3416
19th St., Mission* ☏ *415/874–9921* ⊕ *Closed Tues. and Wed. No lunch*
⌲ *Reservations essential* ☉ *www.lazybearsf.com* ⊕ *3:F6.*

$$ ✕ **Limón Rotisserie.** Cooks in Peru and Ecuador have long argued over
PERUVIAN which country invented ceviche. Most diners at Limón would probably
line up with the Peruvians after eating the myriad, delicious versions
here, like the red snapper, calamari, octopus, and shrimp, accompanied
by yucca and corn. This restaurant with three locations also gets a big
nod for the marinated roasted chicken (a whole chicken is a popular
to-go item); although flavorful on its own, explore dipping pieces into
the aji sauces. Everything is served family-style. Choose from a list of
pisco-based sour cocktails for sipping. The crowd and atmosphere are
a bit all over the map, depending on the location. There are two in the
Mission and one near the ballpark. Ⓢ *Average main: $22* ☒ *524 Valen-
cia St., Mission* ☏ *415/252–0918* ⊕ *www.limonsf.com* ⊕ *3:E5, 3:F6.*

$$$ ✕ **Locanda.** The owners of lauded Delfina have bestowed another culi-
ITALIAN nary gift on the city. Only this time the muse for the menu is Rome. An
addictive starter is *pizza bianca*: chewy, hot bread that holds mini pud-
dles of olive oil and is sprinkled with sea salt. The peppery and creamy
pasta, *tonnarelli cacio e pepe*, is a signature. A good strategy here is to
double down on pastas and antipasti, then share a main. Finely made
cocktails arrive at dark-wood tables on a candlelit tray, and white Heath
wall tiles lend a Mission vibe. This is a busy place with the bar stools
constantly occupied. Ⓢ *Average main: $26* ☒ *557 Valencia St., Mission*
☏ *415/863–6800* ⊕ *www.locandasf.com* ☉ *No lunch* ⊕ *3:F5.*

$$ ✕ **Lolinda.** For a convivial atmosphere, with some of the better bartend-
ARGENTINE ers in the city working the room, Lolinda fits the bill for those who
want to share Argentine fare, including the country's famed grilled
meats. This former sprawling-nightclub space has been transformed
into a welcoming two-level, 220-seat dining room, with two bars and
a scene-y-with-a-capital-S rooftop deck (El Techo), particularly capti-
vating for views galore and weekend brunch. Don't miss the chicken
empanadas with flakey pastry and a slight sweetness. The crowd swings
young and noisy. Ⓢ *Average main: $22* ☒ *2518 Mission St., Mission*
☏ *415/550–6970* ⊕ *www.lolindasf.com* ☉ *No lunch weekdays* ⊕ *3:F6*

$ ✕ **Mission Chinese Food.** While the setting is somewhat one-star, the food
CHINESE draws throngs for its wildly different and bold take on Chinese. MCF
has become so popular that it now has a satellite in New York. The
kitchen pumps out some fine and superfiery kung pao pastrami as well

as other Chinese dishes made with quality meats and ingredients, like salt cod fried rice with mackerel confit, and braised lamb cheek with shanghai noodles. Some of the dishes spike hot (ma po tofu) while milder dishes (Westlake rice porridge) are homey and satisfying. Because of long waits, we recommend lunchtime. Many locals rely on delivery for their fix. $ *Average main: $14* ✉ *2234 Mission St., Mission* ☎ *415/863–2800* ⊕ *www.missionchinesefood.com* ♨ *Reservations not accepted* ☺ *Closed Wed.* ✛ *3:F6*

$$
KOREAN FUSION
FAMILY

✕ **Namu Gaji.** At this primo location across from Dolores Park, Korean-American food emerges from the kitchen in surprising ways—sometimes sprinkled with Japanese elements, often with a bit of kitsch, and always using fresh ingredients from their farm. Indonesian-style *mie ayam* handmade noodles are in an aromatic chicken broth with fried garlic. The *gamja* fries reinvent poutine, with kimchi relish, chili paste, Japanese mayo, teriyaki sauce, and short ribs. Delicate items are plentiful, too, like shiitake dumplings. The shave ice with coconut milk and crumbled Oreos is a refreshing closer. Most seats are bar-style, lined up in neat rows facing 18th Street. Waits can be long, but the host will text you when a table is ready. Also, during happy hour, a kids' menu is available. $ *Average main: $16* ✉ *499 Dolores St., Mission* ☎ *415/431–6268* ⊕ *www.namusf.com* ☺ *Closed Mon. No lunch Tues.* ✛ *3:E6*

13

$
RAMEN

✕ **Orenchi Beyond.** For years, San Franciscans headed an hour south down the peninsula to satisfy their cravings for authentic ramen at the nondescript Orenchi. Those days are over, because the restaurant has now opened here with a decidedly more hipster look to match the Valencia Street location. The namesake ramen bowl still has the tonkotsu broth base that cooks for 18 hours, and chewy noodles that attract the harshest of critics. The wait of about 90 minutes is remedied (slightly) by the small front bar that sells sakes and beers. The space is airy and geometric, and service is quick and friendly. $ *Average main: $12* ✉ *174 Valencia St., at Duboce, Mission* ⊕ *www.orenchi-beyond. com* ♨ *Reservations not accepted* ☺ *Closed Mon. No lunch* ✛ *3:E4.*

$$
JAPANESE
FUSION

✕ **Pink Zebra.** A former chef of MCF masterminds California ingredients into *izakaya*-like dishes, reinventing with a bold, zany San Francisco outlook. You might see Japanese pickles, hurricane popcorn with nori and crispy pigs ears, and *oshizushi* (sushi made into rectangles by pressing it with a mold). *Omakase* (chef's choice) is a memorable experience here, eaten at the five seats at the sushi counter. The decor is cheery, with Japanese artwork. ■**TIP➔ You can reserve for omakase only.** $ *Average main: $18* ✉ *3515 20th St., Mission* ⊕ *www.pinkzebrasf.com* ☺ *Closed Tues. and Wed. No lunch* ✛ *3:F6.*

$$
PIZZA

✕ **Pizzeria Delfina.** As one of the contenders for making the best pizzas in this city, this offshoot of Delfina has its defenders (several of whom wear logo'd T-shirts). The European-style pizzeria, sandwiched between Tartine Bakery and Delfina, has a few sidewalk tables that can be sublime on a nice day (if you can score one). Besides six regular pizzas and two seasonal ones, the menu also offers superfresh salads and antipasti. You can also order takeout and carry the pizza to Dolores Park. A second, equally busy, location is in Pacific Heights. $ *Average main: $16*

✉ *3611 18th St., Mission* ☎ *415/437–6800* 🌐 *www.pizzeriadelfina.com* ✍ *Reservations not accepted* ⏲ *No lunch Mon.* ✥ *3:E6.*

$$$ AMERICAN 🍴 **Range.** This small Valencia Street restaurant is a nice mix of high-end and homey, with chicken liver mousse or egg pasta with smoked trumpet mushrooms sharing space with California rainbow trout with German butterball potatoes and sautéed puntarelle. Adventurous cocktail drinkers will want to take advantage of the skilled bar. On the sweeter side, you'll find some excellent seasonal desserts, plus a bittersweet chocolate soufflé with prune-walnut ice cream. The name may sound strictly down-home, but this place looks and feels big-city. [$] *Average main: $25* ✉ *842 Valencia St., Mission* ☎ *415/282–8283* 🌐 *www.rangesf.com* ⏲ *No lunch* ✥ *3:F6.*

$ DELI 🍴 **Salumeria.** When chef Thomas McNaughton isn't hosting dinner guests at Central Kitchen, that restaurant's courtyard turns into a casual hangout for lunch-goers who order from this larder and deli. Should they ever take the pretzel roll sandwich off the menu (with roast beef), there may truly be a revolt. A half-dozen sandwiches as well as salads are on the menu, with daily specials. The pasta salad is made with famed Flour + Water pasta (another McNaughton enterprise). You can also provision up at the larder and deli, which serves as a specialty grocer. A new location a few blocks away (1550 Bryant Street) stays just as crowded. [$] *Average main: $12* ✉ *3000 20th St., Mission* ☎ *415/471–2998* 🌐 *salumeriasf.com* ✍ *Reservations not accepted* ⏲ *No dinner* ✥ *3:E6.*

$ MEXICAN FAMILY 🍴 **SanJalisco.** This old-time, sun-filled, colorful, family-run restaurant is a neighborhood gem, and not only because it serves breakfast all day—though the hearty *chilaquiles* hit the spot. On weekends, adventurous eaters may opt for *birria,* a spicy goat stew, or *menudo,* a tongue-searing soup made from tripe, calf's foot, and hominy. The latter is a time-honored hangover cure—but don't come expecting margaritas (though you will find beer and sangria). Bring plenty of change for the jukebox loaded with Latin hits. [$] *Average main: $11* ✉ *901 S. Van Ness Ave., Mission* ☎ *415/648–8383* 🌐 *www.sanjalisco.com* ✥ *3:F6.*

$ BAKERY Fodor's Choice ★ 🍴 **Tartine Bakery & Café.** Chad Robertson is America's first modern cult baker, and this tiny Mission District outpost—neighboring Pizzeria Delfina—is where to experience the loaves of tangy country bread that sell out insanely quickly, and/or a morning bun dusted with brown sugar, cinnamon, and orange zest. Lines are long in the morning when locals need a pastry-punch to start the day, and at 4:30 pm when the 250 famed loaves emerge. The small bakery has a coffee counter, but seating can be difficult to find. [$] *Average main: $10* ✉ *600 Guerrero St., at 18th St., Mission* ☎ *415/487–2600* 🌐 *www.tartinebakery.com* ✍ *Reservations not accepted* ✥ *3:E6.*

$ DELI Fodor's Choice ★ 🍴 **Wise Sons Jewish Delicatessen.** At this tiny deli counter with some simple tables, walls are hung with old family portraits, and corned beef hash and bialy egg sandwiches are standard fare on the breakfast menu. For other meals, no one can stop gushing about the pastrami delicately smoked and heaped between two slabs of house-baked rye. Satellite locations are in the Ferry Building and in the Contemporary Jewish Museum (museum admission is not required). **TIP→ Vegetarians need** not skip the Reuben: in one version, a smoked trumpet-mushroom takes the place of pastrami (well, sort of). $ *Average main: $12* ⊠ *3150 24th St., at Shotwell, Mission* ☎ *415/787–3354* ⊕ *wisesonsdeli.com* ⚱ *Reservations not accepted* ◷ *Closed Mon.* ✛ *3:F6.*

POTRERO HILL AND DOGPATCH

East of the Mission, Potrero Hill is home to a cluster of casual, often reasonably priced, dining rooms in the blocks around Connecticut and 18th streets and is one of the more elevated places in the city (like Nob Hill) so be prepared to work your calves. Hot now is historic Dogpatch—a neighborhood of dilapidated warehouses and the Hell's Angels headquarters. Because the 22nd Street Caltrain Station is here, the terminus for trains that go south to Silicon Valley, the neighborhood is filling up with transplanted techies, along with restaurants and bars to feed and water them.

$$ ✕ **The Magnolia Brewing Co.'s Smokestack.** One of the city's best Wagyu
BARBECUE beef briskets is served in an unassuming (from the exterior) former fac-
FAMILY tory in trendy Dogpatch. Several American styles—Kansas City, Texas, and the Carolinas—are showcased on an extra-large chalkboard that lists daily specials, priced by the pound. The 10,000-square-foot warehouse has been strikingly redone by New York design firm Nothing: Something, who have thoughtfully elevated the old in a steampunk-ish vibe. The lion's share of footage is for Magnolia Brewery, with tanks in the back room. When the tech set descends, the volume cranks, which can be a plus for families—frankly, a tantrum would probably go unnoticed. $ *Average main: $15* ⊠ *2505 3rd St., Dogpatch* ☎ *415/864–7468* ⊕ *www.magnoliasmokestack.com* ⚱ *Reservations not accepted* ✛ *3:H6.*

$ ✕ **Plow.** In a former architect's studio, one of the hottest tickets for
MODERN breakfast creates lines that are as constant as the excellent fluffy lemon-
AMERICAN ricotta pancakes, chia puddings, and scrambles with Dungeness crab.
FAMILY But also the atmosphere is winning—bright and pastoral, with rustic, diagonally laid wood floors and windows framing trees. A Little Plowers menu dishes out smaller-portioned pancakes, French toast, and grilled cheese. $ *Average main: $14* ⊠ *1299 18th St., Potrero Hill* ☎ *415/821–7569* ⊕ *www.eatatplow.com* ⚱ *Reservations not accepted* ◷ *Closed Mon. No dinner* ✛ *3:H6.*

PACIFIC HEIGHTS AND JAPANTOWN

PACIFIC HEIGHTS

Pacific Heights may well be one of the city's better-known neighborhoods, thanks to Hollywood movies and jaw-dropping mansions. More down-to-earth, and down the hill, is Lower Pac Heights, which attracts professionals and postgrads who flock to Fillmore Street's many casual eateries.

$$$ ✕ **Out the Door.** A casual offshoot of Charles Phan's Slanted Door, this
VIETNAMESE spot is actually where locals prefer to go for his version of Vietnam-
FAMILY ese. The look is chic and simple, with an open kitchen, a communal table, counter seating, and an eclectic crowd. You can find all the Phan classics (daikon rice cake, crab and cellophane noodles, shaking beef),

but there are plenty of other standout dishes on the menu, like fried chicken. And the weekend brunch is truly delicious (hello, beignets). There's excellent Vietnamese coffee made with Blue Bottle's brew, and plenty of quality wines and beers on tap to choose from. $ *Average main: $24* ✉ *2232 Bush St., Lower Pacific Heights* ☎ *415/923–9575* ⊕ *www.outthedoors.com* ✚ *2:F6.*

$ | ✕ **Roam Artisan Burgers.** For those who think turkey burgers are dry
BURGER | and ho-hum, meet the Tejano turkey burger—a juicy rendition topped
FAMILY | with pepper jack, avocado, and white corn chips. All burgers at this laidback, woodcraft-looking spot, are well sourced, and the beef is 100% grass-fed. Choose a patty (beef, bison, vegetarian, and turkey are standard), then apply preset toppings, such as the aforementioned Tejano, or invent your own. Often specialty patties (elk) appear on the menu, too. A markets salad rotates weekly, and sodas are made with all-natural fruits like Meyer lemon and prickly pear. Kombucha, beers, and wines are also available, as is a kids' menu. $ *Average main: $10* ✉ *1923 Fillmore St., Lower Pacific Heights* ☎ *415/800–7801* ⊕ *roamburgers.com* ✚ *2:F5.*

$$$ | ✕ **SPQR.** Brought to you by the same team that operates the Marina's
ITALIAN | wildly popular A16, SPQR is a modern Italian friendly spot known for the antipasti and *piccolo* plates (the chicken liver is a favorite), eight superlative pastas (many of them are stuffed), and savory mains, like suckling pork. The casualness, with travel posters on the wall, attracts a dedicated neighborhood following of all ages, which means a wait. Singles and walk-in couples can opt for a seat at the two counters (one looks into the galley kitchen). The Italian wine list is also full of gems. This is a comfortable brunch destination on the weekends, when it's tough to snag one of the few outdoor tables. $ *Average main: $26* ✉ *1911 Fillmore St., Lower Pacific Heights* ☎ *415/771–7779* ⊕ *www. spqrsf.com* ⊗ *No lunch weekdays* ✚ *2:F6.*

JAPANTOWN

The epicenter of Japantown, which covers about six city blocks, may well be the Kintetsu Mall, with kitschy Japanese gift shops (a Hello Kitty shop and a bookstore) and restaurants dishing out ramen, donburi, and mochi. There's also a glut of restaurants, sushi shops, and izakayas along Buchanan Street's pedestrian way, between Post and Sutter.

$$ | ✕ **Dosa on Fillmore.** As soon as the large door swings open to this hap-
INDIAN | pening two-level space, diners are greeted with a sexy atmosphere with
Fodor's Choice | bright colors, a lively bar, and the smell of spices in the air. This is the
★ | second location of the popular Dosa on Valencia, but it's definitely the glamorous younger sister, with an expanded menu and much more room. The menu entices with savory fish dishes, fall-off-the-bone pepper chicken, and papery dosas. The restaurant handles group dining often. At lunch, indulge in the Indian street-food selections, and the famed *pani puri* (little crisp puffs you fill with mint and tamarind water and pop all at once into your mouth). $ *Average main: $17* ✉ *1700 Fillmore St., Japantown* ☎ *415/441–3672* ⊕ *www.dosasf.com* ⊗ *No lunch Mon. and Tues.* ✚ *2:F6.*

DINING AND
LODGING ATLAS

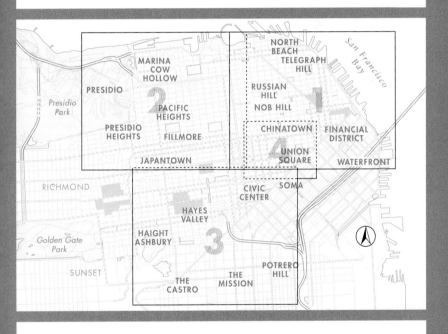

San Francisco Bay

NORTH
BEACH
TELEGRAPH
HILL

MARINA
COW
HOLLOW

PRESIDIO

RUSSIAN
HILL

NOB HILL

2

PACIFIC
HEIGHTS

CHINATOWN

FINANCIAL
DISTRICT

PRESIDIO
HEIGHTS

FILLMORE

4

UNION
SQUARE

Presidio
Park

Presidio

JAPANTOWN

WATERFRONT

RICHMOND

CIVIC
CENTER

SOMA

1

HAYES
VALLEY

HAIGHT
ASHBURY

3

Golden Gate
Park

SUNSET

POTRERO
HILL

THE
CASTRO

THE
MISSION

KEY

☐   *Hotels*
■   *Restaurants*
■   *Restaurant in Hotel*

b▮ *Embarcadero*
BART Station
Bay Area Rapid Transit

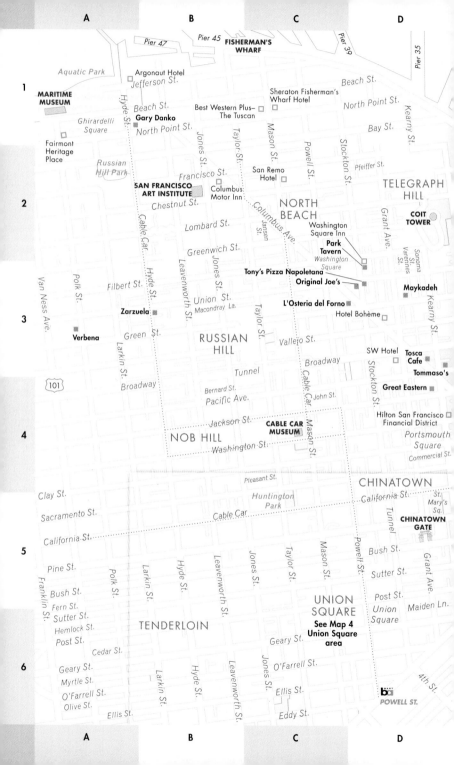

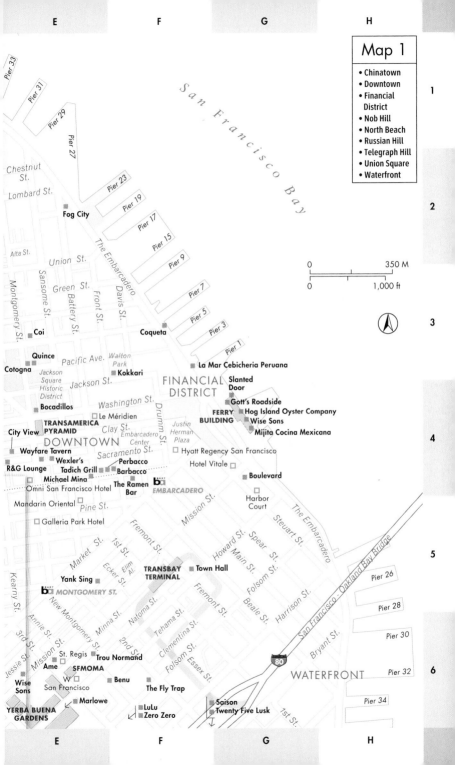

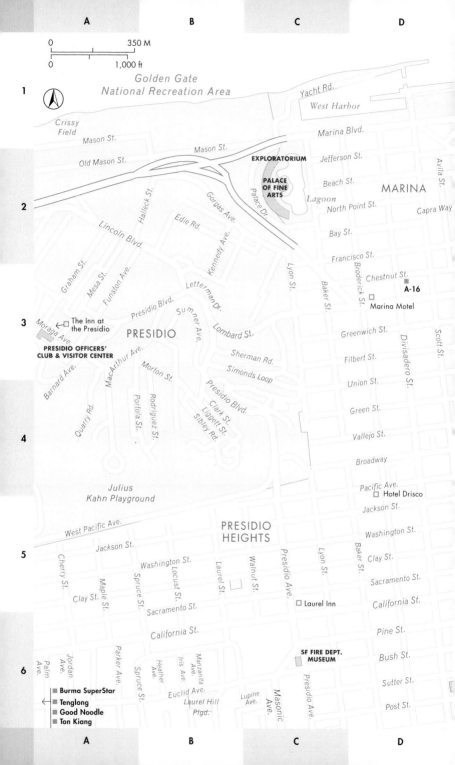

A   **B**   **C**   **D**

0   350 M

0   1,000 ft

1

Golden Gate
National Recreation Area

Yacht Rd.

West Harbor

Crissy
Field

Mason St.

Mason St.

Old Mason St.

Marina Blvd.

Jefferson St.

EXPLORATORIUM

Beach St.

**PALACE
OF FINE
ARTS**

Lagoon

North Point St.

MARINA

Avila St.

2

Halleck St.

Gorgas Ave.

Edie Rd.

Kennedy Ave.

Palace Dr.

Bay St.

Capra Way

Lincoln Blvd.

Francisco St.

Broderick St.

Chestnut St.

A-16

Graham St.

Mesa St.

Funston Ave.

Letterman Dr.

Lyon St.

Baker St.

Marina Motel

3

The Inn at
the Presidio

Presidio Blvd.

Sumner Ave.

Lombard St.

Greenwich St.

Divisadero St.

Scott St.

Moraga Ave.

**PRESIDIO OFFICERS'
CLUB & VISITOR CENTER**

PRESIDIO

MacArthur Ave.

Sherman Rd.

Filbert St.

Barnard Ave.

Morton St.

Simonds Loop

Union St.

Portola St.

Rodriguez St.

Presidio Blvd.

Green St.

Quarry Rd.

Clark St.

Liggett St.

Sibley Rd.

Vallejo St.

4

Broadway

Julius
Kahn Playground

Pacific Ave.

Hotel Drisco

Jackson St.

West Pacific Ave.

**PRESIDIO
HEIGHTS**

Washington St.

5

Jackson St.

Washington St.

Walnut St.

Presidio Ave.

Lyon St.

Baker St.

Clay St.

Cherry St.

Maple St.

Spruce St.

Locust St.

Laurel St.

Sacramento St.

Clay St.

Sacramento St.

Laurel Inn

California St.

California St.

Pine St.

6

Palm Ave.

Jordan Ave.

Parker Ave.

Spruce St.

Heather Ave.

Iris Ave.

Manzanita Ave.

Masonic Ave.

Presidio Ave.

**SF FIRE DEPT.
MUSEUM**

Bush St.

Sutter St.

Euclid Ave.

Lupine Ave.

Post St.

Laurel Hill
Ptgd.

■ Burma SuperStar
■ Tenglong
■ Good Noodle
■ Ton Kiang

A   **B**   **C**   **D**

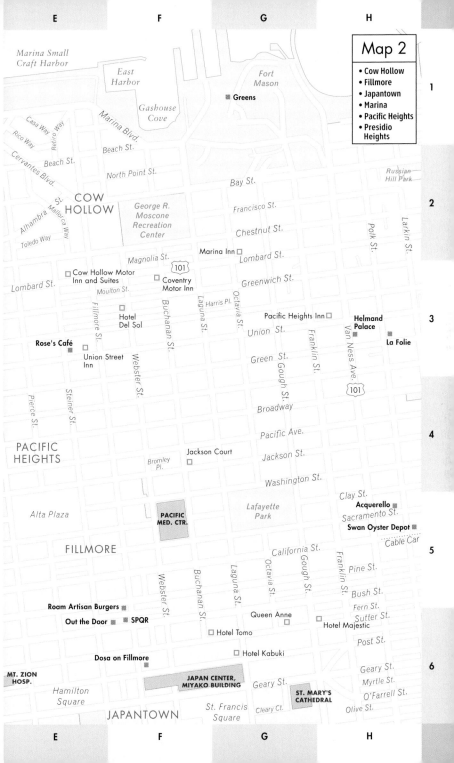

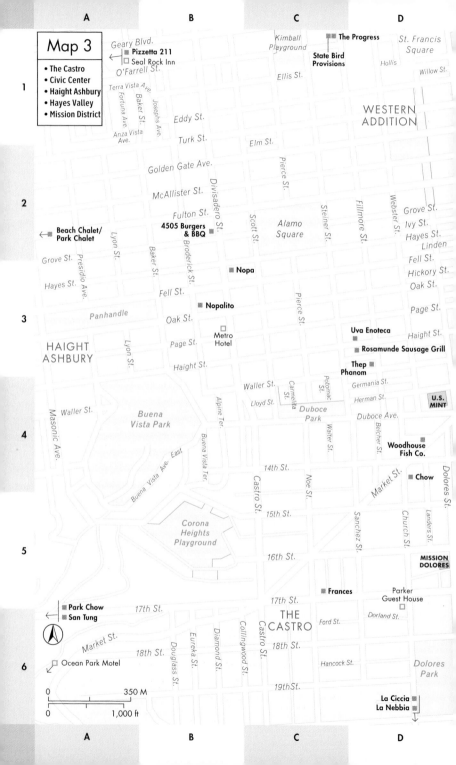

Map 3

- The Castro
- Civic Center
- Haight Ashbury
- Hayes Valley
- Mission District

Geary Blvd. ←
■ Pizzetta 211
□ Seal Rock Inn
O'Farrell St.

Kimball Playground

■■ The Progress

St. Francis Square

State Bird Provisions

Hollis

Willow St.

Ellis St.

WESTERN ADDITION

Terra Vista Ave.

Fortuna Ave.

Baker St.

Josephs Ave.

Eddy St.

Anza Vista Ave.

Turk St.

Elm St.

Golden Gate Ave.

McAllister St.

Pierce St.

Fulton St.

Divisadero St.

■ 4505 Burgers & BBQ

Scott St.

Alamo Square

Steiner St.

Fillmore St.

Webster St.

Grove St.

Ivy St.

Hayes St.

Linden

Beach Chalet/ Park Chalet ←

Lyon St.

Grove St.

Presidio Ave.

Baker St.

Broderick St.

■ Nopa

Fell St.

Hickory St.

Oak St.

Hayes St.

Fell St.

■ Nopalito

Page St.

Pierce St.

HAIGHT ASHBURY

Panhandle

Oak St.

Lyon St.

Page St.

□ Metro Hotel

Uva Enoteca ■

Haight St.

Haight St.

■ Rosamunde Sausage Grill

Thep Phanom ■

Germania St.

Waller St.

Carmelita St.

Potomac St.

U.S. MINT

Masonic Ave.

Waller St.

Buena Vista Park

Alpine Ter.

Lloyd St.

Duboce Park

Herman St.

Duboce Ave.

Belcher St.

Walter St.

Woodhouse Fish Co. ■

Buena Vista Ave. East

Buena Vista Ter.

14th St.

Castro St.

Noe St.

Market St.

■ Chow

Dolores St.

Corona Heights Playground

15th St.

Sanchez St.

Church St.

Landers St.

16th St.

MISSION DOLORES

■ Park Chow
■ San Tung

17th St.

■ Frances

Parker Guest House

□

17th St.

THE CASTRO

Ford St.

Dorland St.

Market St.

Eureka St.

Diamond St.

Collingwood St.

Castro St.

18th St.

□ Ocean Park Motel

Douglass St.

18th St.

Hancock St.

Dolores Park

0   350 M

19th St.

La Ciccia ■
La Nebbia ■

0   1,000 ft

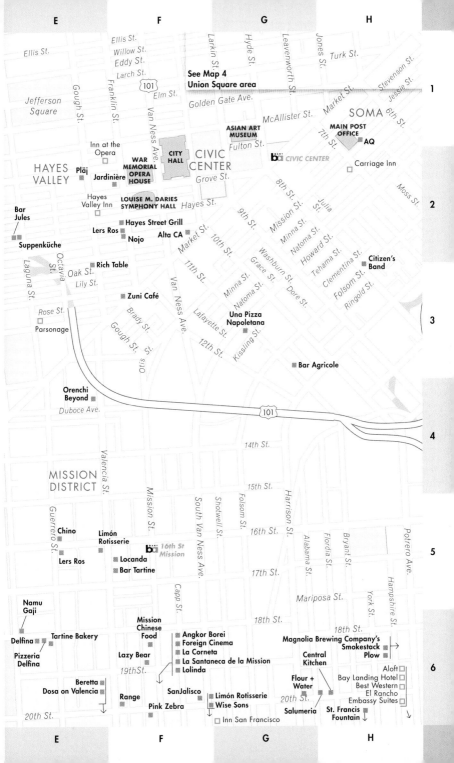

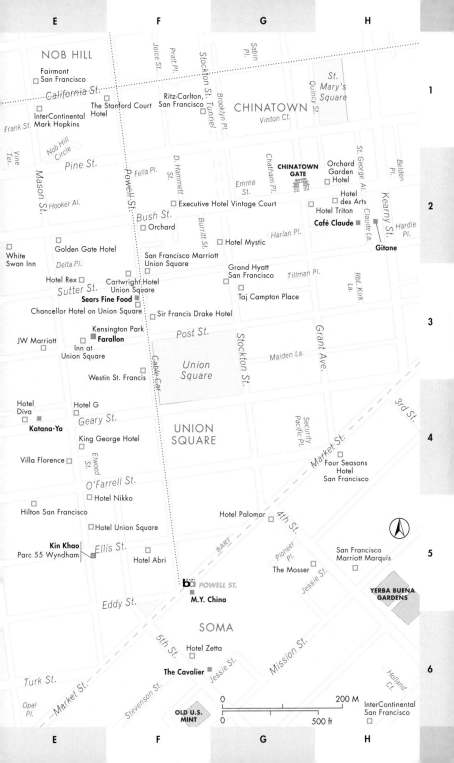

Dining

4505 Burgers & BBQ, 3:B2
A16, 2:D2
AQ, 3:H1
Acquerello, 2:H5
Alta CA, 3:F2
Ame, 1:E6
Angkor Borei, 3:F6
Bar Agricole, 3:G3
Bar Jules, 3:E2
Bar Tartine, 3:F5
Barbacco, 1:E4
Beach Chalet, 3:A2
Benu, 1:F6
Beretta, 3:E6
Bocadillos, 1:E4
Bodega Bistro, 4:A6
Boulevard, 1:G4
Burma Superstar, 2:A6
Café Claude, 4:H2
The Cavalier, 4:F6
Central Kitchen, 3:H6
Chino, 3:E5
Chow, 3:D4
Citizen's Band, 3:H2
City View, 1:E4
Coi, 1:E3
Coqueta, 1:F3
Cotogna, 1:E3
Delfina, 3:E6
Dosa on Fillmore, 2:F6
Dosa on Valencia, 3:F6
Farallon, 4:E3
Flour + Water, 3:G6
The Fly Trap, 1:F6
Fog City, 1:E2
Foreign Cinema, 3:F6
Frances, 3:C5
Gary Danko, 1:A1
Gitane, 4:H2
Good Noodle, 2:A6
Gott's Roadside, 1:G4
Great Eastern, 1:D4
Greens, 2:G1
Hayes Street Grill, 3:F2
Helmand Palace, 2:H3
Hog Island Oyster Company, 1:G4
Jardinière, 3:F2
Katana-Ya, 4:E4
Kin Khao, 4:E5
Kokkari, 1:F3
L'Osteria del Forno, 1:D3
La Ciccia, 3:D6
La Corneta, 2:F6
La Folie, 2:H3
La Mar Cebicheria Peruana, 1:F3
La Nebbia, 3:D6
La Santaneca de la Mission, 3:F6
Lazy Bear, 3:F6
Lers Ros, 3:F2, 4:A5
Limón Rotisserie, 3:E5, 3:F6
Locanda, 3:F5
Lolinda, 3:F6
LuLu, 1:F6
The Magnolia Brewing Company's Smokestack, 3:H6
Marlowe, 1:E6
Maykadeh, 1:D3
Michael Mina, 1:E4
Mijita Cocina Mexicana, 1:G4
Millennium, 4:D4
Mission Chinese Food, 3:F6
M.Y. China, 4:F5
Namu Gaji, 3:E6
Nojo, 3:F2
Nopa, 3:B3
Nopalito, 3:B3
Orenchi Beyond, 3:E4
Original Joe's, 1:D3
Out the Door, 2:F6
Park Chalet, 3:A2
Park Chow, 3:A5
Park Tavern, 1:D3
Perbacco, 1:E4
Pink Zebra, 3:F6
Pizzeria Delfina, 3:E6
Pizzetta 211, 3:A1
Pläj, 3:E2
Plow, 3:H6
The Progress, 3:C1
Quince, 1:E3
R&G Lounge, 1:E4
The Ramen Bar, 1:F4
Range, 3:F6
Rich Table, 3:E3
Roam Artisan Burgers, 2:F5
Rosamunde Sausage Grill, 3:D3
Rose's Café, 2:E3
Saison, 1:G6
Salumeria, 3:H6
San Tung, 3:A5
SanJalisco, 3:F6
Sears Fine Food, 4:F3
Slanted Door, 1:G4
SPQR, 2:F6
St. Francis Fountain, 3:H6
State Bird Provisions, 3:C1
Suppenküche, 3:E2
Swan Oyster Depot, 2:H5
Tacolicious, 2:E2
Tadich Grill, 1:E4
Tartine Bakery, 3:E6
Tenglong, 2:A6
Thep Phanom, 3:D3
Tommaso's, 1:D3
Ton Kiang, 2:A6
Tony's Pizza Napoletana, 1:D3
Tosca Café, 1:D3
Town Hall, 1:F5
Trou Normand, 1:E6
Twenty Five Lusk, 1:G6
Una Pizza Napoletana, 3:G3
Uva Enoteca, 3:D3
Verbena, 1:A3
Wayfare Tavern, 1:E4
Wexler's, 1:E4
Wise Sons, 1:G4, 1:E6, 3:F6
Woodhouse Fish Co, 3:D4
Yank Sing, 1:E5
Zarzuela, 1:B3
Zero Zero, 1:F6
Zuni Café, 3:F3

Lodging

Aloft San Francisco Airport, 3:H6
The Andrews Hotel, 4:D3
Argonaut Hotel, 1:A1
Bay Landing Hotel, 3:H6
Beresford Arms, 4:C3
Best Western El Rancho Inn and Suites, 3:H6
Best Western Plus–The Tuscan, 1:C1
Carriage Inn, 3:H2
The Cartwright Hotel, 4:F3
Chancellor Hotel on Union Square, 4:F3
Clift San Francisco, 4:D4
Columbus Motor Inn, 1:B2
Coventry Motor Inn, 2:F3
Cow Hollow Motor Inn and Suites, 2:E3
Embassy Suites San Francisco Airport–Waterfront, 3:H6
Executive Hotel Vintage Court, 4:F2
Fairmont Heritage Place, Ghirardelli Square, 1:A1
Fairmont San Francisco, 4:E1
Four Seasons Hotel, 4:H4
Galleria Park Hotel, 1:E5
Golden Gate Hotel, 4:E2
Grand Hyatt, 4:G3
Harbor Court Hotel, 1:G5
Hayes Valley Inn, 3:E2
Hilton San Francisco, 4:E5
Hilton San Francisco Financial District, 1:D4
Hotel Adagio, 4:D4
Hotel Beresford, 4:D3
Hotel Bohème, 1:D3
Hotel Carlton, 4:A3
Hotel Del Sol, 2:F3
Hotel des Arts, 4:H2
Hotel Diva, 4:E4
Hotel Drisco, 2:D4
Hotel G, 4:E4
Hotel Kabuki, 2:G6
Hotel Majestic, 2:G6
Hotel Monaco, 4:D4
Hotel Mystic, 4:G2
Hotel Nikko, 4:E5
Hotel Palomar, 4:G5
Hotel Rex, 4:F3
Hotel Tomo, 2:G6
Hotel Triton, 4:H2
Hotel Union Square, 4:E5
Hotel Vertigo, 4:B3
Hotel Vitale, 1:G4
Hotel Zetta, 4:F6
Hyatt Regency, 1:G4
Inn at the Opera, 3:E2
Inn at the Presidio, 2:A3
The Inn San Francisco, 3:G6
Inn at Union Square, 4:E3
InterContinental Mark Hopkins, 4:E1
InterContinental San Francisco, 4:H6
JW Marriott, 4:E3
Jackson Court, 2:F4
Kensington Park, 4:E3
King George Hotel, 4:E4
Laurel Inn, 2:C5
Le Méridien, 1:E4
Mandarin Oriental, 1:E4
Marina Inn, 2:G2
Marina Motel, 2:D3
Metro Hotel, 3:B3
The Mosser Hotel, 4:G5
Ocean Park Motel, 3:A6
Omni San Francisco Hotel, 1:E4
Orchard Garden Hotel, 4:H2
Orchard Hotel, 4:F2
Pacific Heights Inn, 2:H3
Parc 55 Wyndham, 4:F5
The Parker Guest House, 3:D5
The Parsonage, 3:E3
Petite Auberge, 4:D2
Phoenix Hotel, 4:A6
Queen Anne Hotel, 2:G6
Renaissance San Francisco Stanford Court, 4:F1
Ritz-Carlton, 4:F1
San Francisco Marriott Marquis, 4:H5
San Francisco Marriott Union Square, 4:F3
San Remo Hotel, 1:C2
The Scarlet Huntington Hotel, 4:D1
Seal Rock Inn, 3:A1
Sheraton Fisherman's Wharf Hotel, 1:C1
Sir Francis Drake Hotel, 4:F3
The St. Regis San Francisco, 1:E6
Stanford Court Hotel, 4:F1
SW Hotel, 1:D3
Taj Campton Place San Francisco, 4:G3
Union Street Inn, 2:E3
Villa Florence, 4:E4
W San Francisco, 1:E6
Warwick San Francisco, 4:D4
Washington Square Inn, 1:D2
Westin St. Francis, 4:F3
White Swan Inn, 4:E2

WHERE TO STAY

Updated by
Michele Bigley

San Francisco accommodations are diverse, ranging from cozy inns and kitschy motels, to chic little inns and true grande dames, housed in century-old structures and sleek high-rises. While the tech boom has skyrocketed the prices of even some of the most dependable low-cost options, luckily, some Fodor's faves still offer fine accommodations without the jaw-dropping prices to match those steep hills. In fact, the number of reasonably priced accommodations is impressive.

Not only have many city stalwarts been spruced up recently (including the Ritz Carlton, Hotel Monaco, Mandarin Oriental, Scarlet Huntington, Argonaut, and the Palace), but also this edition includes many exciting new properties: Hotel G, The Parker Guest House, and The Parsonage among them.

Also exciting is that new and established properties are trending toward the eco-friendly—San Francisco hotels are "going green" in a big way. The Orchard Garden boasts San Francisco's first all-new green construction, and many other properties are installing ecological upgrades. Also worth noting: almost all of the city's hotels are nonsmoking.

When contemplating a hotel stay in San Francisco, consider timing: if you're flexible on dates, ask the reservationist if there's a cheaper time to stay in your preferred travel window—for many hotels, weekends can offer better deals. Be sure to ask what's included in your room rate—one big unexpected extra might be parking fees, which are off the charts in San Francisco. Once you settle into your perfect room, remember this advice: when in doubt, ask the concierge. This holds true for almost any request, whether you have special needs or burning desires (if anyone can get you tickets to a sold-out show at the ACT or a table at the hard-to-come-by State Bird Provisions, it's the concierge). You'll likely be impressed by the lengths hoteliers are willing to go to please their guests.

WHERE SHOULD I STAY?

	Neighborhood Vibe	Pros	Cons
Union Square/ Downtown	Union Square is a hub for visitors; you'll find a wide range of choices—and prices—for lodging.	Excellent shopping. Home to the theater district, great transit access to other neighborhoods.	Often crowded and noisy. Many panhandlers. Close to Tenderloin, a still-seedy part of town. Take cabs at night.
SoMa	Square one for the business set. Offers luxury high-rises, old classics, and a few bargains.	Near the museums and Yerba Buena Gardens. Steps from the convention center. Many fine eateries.	Construction in the area may mean traffic snarls. As with many changing neighborhoods, street life takes many forms. Be cautious walking around at night.
Financial District	A mini Midtown Manhattan where properties cater to business travelers.	Excellent city and bay views, which are spectacular by night. Easy access to restaurants and nightclubs.	Some streets are iffy at night. Hotels are on the pricey side. Many businesses close at night and on weekends.
Nob Hill	Synonymous with San Francisco's high society, this area contains some of the city's best-known luxury hotels.	Many hotels boast gorgeous views and notable restaurants. Easy access to Union Square and Chinatown.	Hotels here will test your wallet, while the area's steep hills may try your endurance.
Civic Center/ Van Ness	A wide mix of lodgings scattered throughout this area.	Many cultural offerings and government offices surround this central hub. Not too far from Union Square.	Away from touristy areas. A large homeless population lives in the area.
Fisherman's Wharf/North Beach	Mostly chain hotels by the wharf; lodgings get funkier and smaller in North Beach.	Near attractions like Ghirardelli Square and Pier 39. Cable-car lines and bay-cruise piers are nearby.	City ordinances limit wharf hotels to four stories, so good views are out. Very touristy.
Pacific Heights/Cow Hollow/The Marina	A few tony accommodations in quietly residential Pacific Heights. Mostly motels along Lombard Street, a busy traffic corridor.	Away from the more tourist-oriented areas; visitors have a chance to explore where locals eat and shop. Lots of free parking.	Getting downtown can be challenging via public transportation. Some complain of the fraternity-like bar scene.

14

SAN FRANCISCO LODGING PLANNER

RESERVATIONS

Reservations are always advised, especially during the peak seasons—August through November, during the Oracle Convention week in fall, weekends in December, and celebrations like gay pride, Mother's Day, Bay to Breakers, and Chinese New Year. The San Francisco Convention and Visitors Bureau publishes a free lodging guide with a map and listings of San Francisco and Bay Area hotels. You can reserve a room, by phone or via the Internet, at more than 60 Bureau-recommended hotels. San Francisco Reservations can arrange reservations at more than 200 Bay Area hotels, often at discounted rates.

Booking Bed & Breakfast San Francisco ☎ *415/899–0060* ⊕ *www.bbsf.com.* **San Francisco Convention and Visitors Bureau** ☎ *415/391–2000 general information,* 888/782–9673 *lodging service* ⊕ *www.onlyinsanfrancisco.com.* **San Francisco Reservations** ☎ *800/677–1500* ⊕ *www.hotelres.com.*

FACILITIES

When pricing accommodations, always ask what facilities are included and what entails an additional charge (parking is often extra, and expensive). All the hotels listed have private baths, central heating, and private phones unless otherwise noted. (On that note, many lower-cost options have shared baths.) Many places don't have air-conditioning, but you probably won't need it. Even in September and October, when the city sees its warmest days, the temperature rarely climbs above 70°F.

Many hotels now have wireless Internet (Wi-Fi) available, although many are trending to offer free Wi-Fi, they sometimes do charge for quicker connections for multiple devices. Larger hotels often have video or high-speed checkout capability. Pools are a rarity, but most large properties have gyms or health clubs, and sometimes full-scale spas; hotels without facilities usually have arrangements for guests at nearby gyms, sometimes for a fee. At the end of each review, we state whether any meals (and in San Francisco, this means breakfast) are included in the room rate.

PARKING

Several properties on Lombard Street and in the Civic Center area have free parking (but not always in a covered garage). Hotels in the Union Square and Nob Hill areas almost invariably charge $25 to $50-plus per day for a spot in their garages; many hotels charge extra fees for SUVs. Occasionally hotel package deals include parking. Some B&Bs have limited free parking available, but many don't, and require you to park on the street. Depending on the neighborhood and the time, this can be easy or quite difficult (and require a pass), so ask for realistic parking information when you call. Some hotels with paid parking offer a choice of valet parking with unlimited in-out privileges or self-parking (where the fee is less expensive and there's no tipping). Given the cost of parking, and the ease of getting around San Francisco on public transportation, you may well want to leave the car at home or wait to rent one until you're ready to leave town.

FAMILY TRAVEL

San Francisco has gone to great lengths to attract family vacationers, and hotels have followed the family-friendly trend. Some properties provide diversions like in-room video games, suites with kitchenettes, and foldout sofa beds; some, like Hotel Diva, have even decked out special kids' suites with toys, games, and karaoke machines. Many full-service San Francisco hotels provide roll-away beds, babysitting recommendations, and stroller rentals, but be sure to make arrangements when booking the room, not when you arrive.

PRICES

San Francisco hotel prices, among the highest in the United States, may come as an unpleasant surprise. Weekend rates for double rooms in high season average about $250 a night citywide. On the other hand, lower-cost accommodations are relatively plentiful, especially in comparison to New York, Washington, and some other big cities. Rates may vary widely according to room availability; always inquire about special rates and packages when making reservations. Call the property directly, but also check its website (often the source for the lowest rates) and try Internet booking agencies. The lodgings we list are the cream of the crop in each price category.

14

WHAT IT COSTS				
	$	$$	$$$	$$$$
Hotels	under $150	$150–$249	$250–$350	over $350

Prices are the lowest cost of a standard double room in high season.

USING THE MAPS

Throughout, you'll see mapping symbols and coordinates (✥ 3:F2) after property names or reviews. To locate the property on a map, turn to the San Francisco Dining and Lodging Atlas at the end of Where to Eat. The first number after the ✥ symbol indicates the map number. Following that is the property's coordinate on the map grid.

LODGING REVIEWS

Listed alphabetically within neighborhoods. Hotel reviews have been shortened. For full information, visit Fodors.com.

UNION SQUARE AND CHINATOWN

UNION SQUARE

$$ HOTEL 🏨 **The Andrews Hotel.** Two blocks west of Union Square, this Queen Anne–style abode began its life in 1904 as the Sultan Turkish Baths; today rooms are tight but well decorated with Victorian reproductions, ceiling fans, old-fashioned floral curtains with lace sheers, and iron bedsteads draped with soft bedding. **Pros:** intimate; decor has character; moderately priced; free Wi-Fi. **Cons:** small rooms. [$] *Rooms from: $189* ✉ *624 Post St., Union Sq.* ☎ *415/563–6877, 800/926–3739* 🌐 *www.andrewshotel.com* 🛏 *48 rooms, 5 suites* 🍴 *Breakfast* ✥ *4:D3.*

$$ HOTEL FAMILY 🏨 **Beresford Arms.** Fancy molding and 10-foot-tall windows grace the red-carpeted lobby of this brick Victorian listed on the National Register of Historic Places, while rooms have dark-wood antique-reproduction furniture and vary in size and setup. **Pros:** moderately priced; suites with kitchenettes and Murphy beds are a plus for families with kids; excellent service. **Cons:** no air-conditioning; cramped, out-of-date standard rooms; can be noisy at night. [$] *Rooms from: $179* ✉ *701 Post St., Union Sq.* ☎ *415/673–2600, 800/533–6533* 🌐 *www.beresford.com* 🛏 *83 rooms, 12 suites* 🍴 *Breakfast* ✥ *4:C3.*

BEST BETS FOR SAN FRANCISCO LODGING

Fodor's offers a selective listing of quality lodging experiences at every price range, from the city's best budget motel to its most sophisticated luxury hotel. *Here we've compiled our top recommendations by price and experience. The very best properties—in other words, those that provide a particularly remarkable experience in their price range—are designated in the listings with the Fodor's Choice logo.*

Fodor's Choice ★

Argonaut Hotel, $$$, p. 237

Cow Hollow Motor Inn and Suites, $, p. 241

Four Seasons Hotel San Francisco, $$$$, p. 232

Golden Gate Hotel, $, p. 225

Hotel Diva, $$, p. 227

Hotel Drisco, $$$$, p. 242

Hotel Nikko, San Francisco, $$$$, p. 227

Hotel Palomar, San Francisco, $$$, p. 232

Hotel Triton, $$, p. 228

Hotel Vitale, $$$$, p. 238

Hotel Zetta, $$$, p. 232

Inn at the Presidio, $$, p. 240

Metro Hotel $, p. 234

The Parker Guest House, $$, p. 242

The Parsonage, $$, p. 234

Ritz-Carlton, San Francisco $$$$, p. 236

San Remo Hotel, $, p. 237

The St. Regis San Francisco, $$$$, p. 233

Union Street Inn, $$, p. 241

Westin St. Francis, $$$, p. 230

By Price

$

Columbus Motor Inn, p. 237

Cow Hollow Motor Inn and Suites, p. 241

Golden Gate Hotel, p. 225

Metro Hotel, p. 234

San Remo Hotel, p. 237

$$

Hotel Diva, p. 227

Hotel Triton, p. 228

Inn at the Presidio, p. 240

The Parker Guest House, p. 242

The Parsonage, p. 234

Union Street Inn, p. 241

$$$

Argonaut Hotel, p. 237

Hotel Palomar, San Francisco, p. 232

Hotel Zetta, p. 232

Westin St. Francis, p. 230

$$$$

Four Seasons Hotel San Francisco, p. 232

Hotel Drisco, p. 242

Hotel Nikko, San Francisco, p. 227

Hotel Vitale, p. 238

Ritz-Carlton, San Francisco, p. 236

The St. Regis San Francisco, p. 233

By Experience

BUSINESS TRAVELERS

Hotel Nikko San Francisco, $$$$, p. 227

Hotel Vitale, $$$$, p. 238

Le Méridien San Francisco, $$$, p. 239

Westin St. Francis, $$$, p. 230

HISTORIC INTEREST

Fairmont San Francisco, $$$$, p. 234

Inn at the Presidio, $$, p. 240

The Parsonage, $$, p. 234

Westin St. Francis, $$$, p. 230

MOST KID-FRIENDLY

Argonaut Hotel, $$$, p. 237

Four Seasons Hotel San Francisco, $$$$, p. 232

Hotel Del Sol, $$, p. 241

Hotel Diva, $$, p. 227

MOST ROMANTIC

Fairmont San Francisco, $$$$, p. 234

Hotel Drisco, $$$$, p. 242

Inn at the Presidio, $$, p. 240

Union Street Inn, $$, p. 241

W San Francisco, $$$$, p. 233

$$ HOTEL **The Cartwright Hotel Union Square.** A coup for historians, this 1913 Edwardian hotel near Union Square retains the original period feel throughout the lobby, its lively Bar 1915, and rooms that come with FeatherBorne beds and flat-screen TVs. **Pros:** great location; spacious closets; clean; homey lobby. **Cons:** airless, cramped rooms and hallways; small baths. [$] *Rooms from: $219* ✉ *524 Sutter St., Union Sq.* ☎ *415/421–2865, 866/823–4669* 🌐 *www.cartwrightunionsquare.com* *109 rooms, 5 suites* 🍴 *No meals* ✥ *4:F3.*

$$$ HOTEL **Chancellor Hotel on Union Square.** Built to accommodate visitors to the 1915 Panama-Pacific International Exposition, these moderate-sized Edwardian-style rooms, some with huge walk-in closets, have high ceilings and are considered by many to be among of the best bets on Union Square for comfort without extravagance. **Pros:** huge walk-in closets; free Wi-Fi; great value for Union Square; clean rooms. **Cons:** older building with dark hallways and rooms; small bathrooms; noise from cable cars. [$] *Rooms from: $279* ✉ *433 Powell St., Union Sq.* ☎ *415/362–2004, 800/428–4748* 🌐 *www.chancellorhotel.com* *135 rooms, 2 suites* 🍴 *No meals* ✥ *4:F3.*

$$$ HOTEL **Clift San Francisco.** The entrance here is so nondescript, you could walk right past without a hint of what's inside—a seriously sexy hotel, the brainchild of entrepreneur Ian Schrager and artist-designer Philippe Starck, where spacious rooms sport translucent orange Plexiglas tables, high ceilings, and two huge "infinity" wall mirrors. **Pros:** good rates compared to similar top-tier hotels in San Francisco; surreal, moody interior design; ideal location for shopping and theaters; close to public transportation; discreet and helpful staff. **Cons:** some guests note thin walls; street noise (book on upper floors to avoid). [$] *Rooms from: $348* ✉ *495 Geary St., Union Sq.* ☎ *415/775–4700, 800/606–6090* 🌐 *www.clifthotel.com* *337 rooms, 26 suites* 🍴 *No meals* ✥ *4:D4.*

$$ HOTEL **Executive Hotel Vintage Court.** These Napa Valley–inspired rooms, just two blocks from Union Square, are named after California wineries and feature large writing desks and dark-wood venetian blinds; some have sunny window seats. **Pros:** complimentary local wines; corner rooms offer plenty of light. **Cons:** small (but newly refreshed) bathrooms, some with stall showers only; a bit of an uphill walk from downtown and many tourist spots. [$] *Rooms from: $229* ✉ *650 Bush St., Union Sq.* ☎ *415/392–4666, 800/654–1100* 🌐 *www.executivehotels.net/vintagecourt* *106 rooms, 1 suite* 🍴 *Breakfast* ✥ *4:F2.*

$ B&B/INN FAMILY Fodor's Choice ★ **Golden Gate Hotel.** Budget seekers looking for accommodations around Union Square will enjoy this four-story Edwardian with bay windows, an original birdcage elevator, hallways lined with historical photographs, and rooms decorated with antiques, wicker pieces, and Laura Ashley bedding and curtains. **Pros:** friendly staff; free Wi-Fi; spotless rooms; comfortable bedding; good location if you're a walker. **Cons:** some rooms without private bath. [$] *Rooms from: $135* ✉ *775 Bush St., Union Sq.* ☎ *415/392–3702, 800/835–1118* 🌐 *www.goldengatehotel.com* *25 rooms, 14 with bath* 🍴 *Breakfast* ✥ *4:E2.*

$$ HOTEL FAMILY **Grand Hyatt San Francisco.** Rooms done in warm autumnal tones, with textured custom furniture, original artwork, and teak beds, are all high-tech: windows can be blacked out from your bed, while a "jack

pack" projects your laptop on a swiveling flat-screen. **Pros:** deals on weekends; stellar views from upper floors. **Cons:** small bathrooms; some guests complain about the Internet fee, which you must pay per device. [$] *Rooms from: $209* ✉ *345 Stockton St., Union Sq.* ☎ *415/398–1234* 🌐 *grandsanfrancisco.hyatt.com* 🛏 *659 rooms* 🍴 *No meals* ✥ *4:G3.*

$$ HOTEL 🏨 **Hilton San Francisco.** With 1,908 rooms and suites, this is the largest hotel in California—and sometimes the lobby feels like downtown at rush hour, but there is a positive side to all that size: many handsome rooms in the silvery tower that rises 46 floors to a penthouse event space enjoy awe-inspiring 360-degree panoramic views that rank among the finest in San Francisco. **Pros:** super views; excellent service; full-service spa. **Cons:** area is dodgy after dark; there can be a wait at check-in. [$] *Rooms from: $249* ✉ *333 O'Farrell St., Union Sq.* ☎ *415/771–1400* 🌐 *www.hiltonsanfranciscohotel.com* 🛏 *1,824 rooms, 84 suites* 🍴 *No meals* ✥ *4:E5.*

$$$ HOTEL 🏨 **Hotel Abri.** Near Union Square shops, theaters, and restaurants, this stylish hotel (formerly the Monticello Inn) offers small but well appointed rooms, with flat-screen TVs, iPod docking stations, comfy bedding, and L'Occitane bath products. **Pros:** tasteful rooms; free Wi-Fi; shouting distance from the cable-car turnaround, shops, and eateries. **Cons:** most rooms have showers only; on-street parking nearly impossible. [$] *Rooms from: $275* ✉ *127 Ellis St., Union Sq.* ☎ *866/823–4669, 415/392–8800* 🌐 *www.hotel-abri.com* 🛏 *63 rooms, 28 suites* 🍴 *No meals* ✥ *4:F5.*

$$$ HOTEL 🏨 **Hotel Adagio.** The Spanish-colonial facade of this 16-story, theater-row hotel complements its chic interior, where decent-size rooms play on hues of fog, spring grasses, and Merlot grapes, with a dose of modern chrome and glass; half have city views, and two penthouse suites boast terraces overlooking the neighborhood. **Pros:** backing of trusted Marriott brand paired with boutique-hotel charm; close to theater district; on a bus route; many deals online. **Cons:** street noise; area can be dodgy at night; expensive parking; adjacent to a popular outdoor bar. [$] *Rooms from: $289* ✉ *550 Geary St., Union Sq.* ☎ *415/775–5000, 800/228–8830* 🌐 *www.hoteladagiosf.com* 🛏 *169 rooms, 2 suites* 🍴 *No meals* ✥ *4:D4.*

$$ HOTEL 🏨 **Hotel Beresford.** Less than two blocks from Union Square, these relatively inexpensive but well-maintained rooms feature traditional furniture, floral wallpaper, earth-toned linens, flat-screen TVs, and dark-wood beds. **Pros:** reasonably priced; close to Union Square; friendly staff; free Wi-Fi. **Cons:** no air-conditioning; small rooms; traditional decor can be stuffy. [$] *Rooms from: $159* ✉ *635 Sutter St., Union Sq.* ☎ *415/673–9900, 800/533–6533* 🌐 *www.beresford.com* 🛏 *114 rooms* 🍴 *Breakfast* ✥ *4:D3.*

$ HOTEL 🏨 **Hotel des Arts.** You'll need to climb a narrow, nondescript staircase to discover this small, funky hotel that doubles as an art gallery: the hallways and rooms have been transformed by international artists who painted splashy murals and installed site-specific small sculptures. **Pros:** art-gallery atmosphere; good location. **Cons:** only about half the rooms have private baths; small rooms. [$] *Rooms from: $149* ✉ *447 Bush St.,*

Union Sq. ☎ *415/956–3232, 800/956–4322* 🌐 *www.sfhoteldesarts.com* 🛏 *43 rooms* 🍴 *Breakfast* ✥ *4:H2.*

$$ HOTEL FAMILY Fodor's Choice ★ **Hotel Diva.** Entering this magnet for hip urbanites craving modern decor requires stepping over footprints, handprints, and autographs embedded in the sidewalk by visiting stars; in the rooms, designer carpets complement Harry Bertoia chairs and brushed-steel headboards whose shape mimics that of ocean waves. **Pros:** punchy design; in the heart of the theater district; accommodating service. **Cons:** few frills; tiny bathrooms (but equipped with eco-friendly bath products). [$] *Rooms from: $199* ✉ *440 Geary St., Union Sq.* ☎ *415/885–0200, 800/553–1900* 🌐 *www.hoteldiva.com* 🛏 *115 rooms, 3 suites* 🍴 *No meals* ✥ *4:E4.*

$$ HOTEL **Hotel G.** Union Square's newest hotel manages to be both homey and innovative, with an ensemble of woven Indian rugs, denim headboards, black-and-white wallpapered closets, floating light fixtures, and throw pillows shaped like the Golden State. **Pros:** fun design; on-site restaurants and bars; great central location. **Cons:** new hotel is still working out some kinks; wooden or concrete flooring can be loud. [$] *Rooms from: $229* ✉ *386 Geary St., Union Sq.* ☎ *877/828–4478* 🌐 *www.hotelgsanfrancisco.com* 🛏 *121 rooms, 30 suites* 🍴 *No meals* ✥ *4:E4.*

$$ HOTEL **Hotel Monaco, San Francisco.** Behind a cheery 1910 Beaux-Arts facade and snappily dressed doormen, a major renovation has raised the Monaco's notable style a notch, and individually cut, multicolor, striped wallpaper on bedroom walls accent bold pillows and furnishings straight out of a globetrekker's collection. **Pros:** amazing service; stylish; full of character; near theater district. **Cons:** close to the Tenderloin; some discount-rate rooms are small. [$] *Rooms from: $209* ✉ *501 Geary St., Union Sq.* ☎ *415/292–0100, 866/622–5284* 🌐 *www.monaco-sf.com* 🛏 *181 rooms, 20 suites* 🍴 *No meals* ✥ *4:D4.*

$$ HOTEL **Hotel Mystic.** This historic property that survived the 1906 earthquake serves up a healthy dose of art, cuisine, and style—the latter even in compact guest rooms enlivened with brick walls. **Pros:** decent price; fun restaurant and bar on-site; artsy decor. **Cons:** smallish rooms (but large suites with soaking tubs); city noise. [$] *Rooms from: $249* ✉ *417 Stockton St., Union Sq.* ☎ *415/400–0500* 🌐 *www.mystichotel.com* 🛏 *57 rooms, 25 suites* 🍴 *Breakfast* ✥ *4:G2.*

$$$$ HOTEL FAMILY Fodor's Choice ★ **Hotel Nikko, San Francisco.** The vast surfaces of gray-flecked white marble that dominate the Nikko's neoclassical lobby have the starkness of an airport, but the crisply designed rooms please the business-traveler clientele with soothing muted tones, Bluetooth-enabled headboards, and modern bathrooms with sinks atop granite bases. **Pros:** friendly multilingual staff; tastefully designed rooms; large indoor pool; very clean. **Cons:** lobby lacks color; atmosphere feels cold to some patrons; expensive parking. [$] *Rooms from: $399* ✉ *222 Mason St., Union Sq.* ☎ *415/394–1111, 800/248–3308* 🌐 *www.hotelnikkosf.com* 🛏 *510 rooms, 22 suites* 🍴 *No meals* ✥ *4:E5.*

$$ HOTEL **Hotel Rex.** At this stylish, literary-themed hotel—named after San Francisco Renaissance poet, translator, and essayist Kenneth Rexroth and frequented by artists and writers—paintings and shelves of antiquarian books line the a homey lobby lounge and small, somewhat dark

rooms with restored period furnishings and striped carpeting evoke the spirit of salon society. **Pros:** convenient location; literary pedigree. **Cons:** cramped, airless rooms; tiny baths and closets; musty hallways. [$] *Rooms from: $239* ✉ *562 Sutter St., Union Sq.* ☎ *415/433–4434, 800/433–4434* 🌐 *www.thehotelrex.com* 🛏 *92 rooms, 2 suites* 🍴 *No meals* ✥ *4:E3.*

$$ HOTEL Fodor's Choice ★ 🏨 **Hotel Triton.** A spirit of fun has taken up full-time residence in this Kimpton property with a youngish, super-friendly staff and smallish but colorful rooms that boast Chinese dragons stenciled over excerpts of Beat literature, striking yellow headboards, vintage chairs, and chalkboard doors donned with quotes from famed writers. **Pros:** attentive service; refreshingly funky atmosphere; hip arty environs; good location. **Cons:** rooms and baths are on the small side (with sinks positioned outside the bathrooms). [$] *Rooms from: $189* ✉ *342 Grant Ave., Union Sq.* ☎ *415/394–0500, 800/800–1299* 🌐 *www.hoteltriton.com* 🛏 *133 rooms, 7 suites* 🍴 *No meals* ✥ *4:H2.*

$$ HOTEL 🏨 **Hotel Union Square.** Tucked beside a money-exchange business along bustling Powell Street, this century-old hotel was erected for the 1915 Pan Pacific Exposition; behind the nondescript facade, design-centric interiors provide a dash of art deco–by-way-of-Egypt. **Pros:** stylish rooms; central location; free Wi-Fi; creative suites. **Cons:** rooms on the small side; street noise can be loud in the evenings. [$] *Rooms from: $239* ✉ *114 Powell St., Union Sq.* ☎ *415/397–3000* 🌐 *www.hotelunionsquare.com* 🛏 *124 rooms, 7 suites* 🍴 *No meals* ✥ *4:E5.*

$$$ B&B/INN 🏨 **Inn at Union Square.** A friendly staff, along with reasonably sized rooms decked out in maroon and gold, poster beds, oversized pillows, and tubs, provide a retreat from the hustle of Union Square while being located in the heart of it all. **Pros:** helpful staff; comfortable rooms; lounges with complimentary snacks; in the center of Union Square. **Cons:** some rooms can be noisy; interiors feel stuffy; cramped hallways. [$] *Rooms from: $299* ✉ *440 Post St., Union Sq.* ☎ *800/288–4346* 🌐 *www.unionsquare.com* 🛏 *30 rooms* 🍴 *Breakfast* ✥ *4:E3.*

$$$ HOTEL 🏨 **JW Marriott San Francisco.** Bullet elevators whisk guests skyward from the marble foyer of this John Portman–designed hotel, formerly the Pan Pacific, to guest rooms outfitted with gold, olive, and rosy bedding, large flat-screen TVs, and versatile desks for dining or working. **Pros:** convenient location; large rooms; luxurious bathrooms with deep soaking tubs. **Cons:** comfortable but lacking character; some readers complain that the showers are too small. [$] *Rooms from: $289* ✉ *500 Post St., Union Sq.* ☎ *415/771–8600* 🌐 *www.jwmarriottunionsquare.com* 🛏 *329 rooms, 8 suites* 🍴 *No meals* ✥ *4:E3.*

$$ HOTEL 🏨 **Kensington Park Hotel.** Built in the 1920s in a Moorish and Gothic style, this former Elks Club retains its distinctive period feel and features, with rich marble and dark-wood accents, crystal chandeliers, vaulted ceilings, and antique furnishings in the lobby and art-deco touches in the comfortable guest rooms. **Pros:** friendly personal service; guests rave about great location. **Cons:** some rooms have street noise; standard rooms are on the smallish side; bathrooms are small but sparkling. [$] *Rooms from: $199* ✉ *450 Post St., Union Sq.* ☎ *415/788–6400,*

800/553–1900 🌐 *www.kensingtonparkhotel.com* 🛏 *92 rooms, 1 suite* 🍴 *No meals* ✥ *4:E3.*

$$ HOTEL 🏨 **King George Hotel.** Compact rooms, though attractively furnished in classic English style, can feel a bit stuffy, dark, and cramped, and baths and closets are minuscule, but service and hospitality have been points of pride at this hotel since its 1914 opening. **Pros:** friendly service; quiet, convenient location; most rooms were refreshed in 2015. **Cons:** no tubs; low ceilings in hallways; small closets; on the edge of the Tenderloin. [$] *Rooms from: $249* ✉ *334 Mason St., Union Sq.* ☎ *415/781–5050, 800/288–6005* 🌐 *www.kinggeorge.com* 🛏 *153 rooms* 🍴 *No meals* ✥ *4:E4.*

$$$ HOTEL 🏨 **Orchard Garden Hotel.** Feel virtuous and eco-friendly while enjoying a junior terrace room with private outdoor space and views of downtown at the first San Francisco hotel built to environmentally stringent LEED specifications. **Pros:** clean rooms; great location close to the Financial District and Chinatown. **Cons:** a bit on the pricy side. [$] *Rooms from: $275* ✉ *46 Bush St., Union Sq.* ☎ *415/399–9807, 888/717–2881* 🌐 *www.theorchardgardenhotel.com* 🛏 *86 rooms* 🍴 *Breakfast* ✥ *4:H2.*

$$$ HOTEL 🏨 **Orchard Hotel.** Rooms done in a soft palette of relaxing colors are a refuge from Union Square and nicely mix cutting-edge Silicon Valley chic with classic European touches. **Pros:** cutting-edge technology; sizable rooms; green pedigree. **Cons:** can be pricey. [$] *Rooms from: $250* ✉ *665 Bush St., Union Sq.* ☎ *415/362–8878, 888/717–2881* 🌐 *www.theorchardhotel.com* 🛏 *104 rooms, 9 suites* 🍴 *No meals* ✥ *4:F2.*

$$$ HOTEL 🏨 **Parc 55 Wyndham San Francisco-Union Square.** The fourth-largest hotel in town bustles with activity, but its size is by no means overwhelming. **Pros:** close to public transportation, shops, and restaurants; comfortable rooms, some with nice views. **Cons:** the immediate area can be seedy at night; panhandlers abound; street parking is a challenge. [$] *Rooms from: $299* ✉ *55 Cyril Magnin St., near 5th and Market Sts., Union Sq.* ☎ *800/595–0507, 415/392–8000* 🌐 *www.parc55hotel.com* 🛏 *1,024 rooms* 🍴 *No meals* ✥ *4:F5.*

$$ B&B/INN 🏨 **Petite Auberge.** Provincial room decor—the small rooms have bright flowered wallpaper, an old-fashioned writing desk, and a much-needed armoire (there's little or no closet space)—recalls an intimate French country inn and pleases Francophiles looking for a retreat from hectic downtown. **Pros:** European charm; breakfast buffet. **Cons:** virtually no closet space. [$] *Rooms from: $229* ✉ *863 Bush St., Union Sq.* ☎ *415/928–6000, 800/365–3004* 🌐 *www.jdvhotels.com* 🛏 *25 rooms, 1 suite* 🍴 *Breakfast* ✥ *4:D2.*

$$$ HOTEL 🏨 **San Francisco Marriott Union Square.** Business travelers appreciate the Marriott's attention to their needs (as in easily accessible plugs, movable desks, ergonomic chairs, and laptop connectors to flat-screen TVs) and its prime location near shopping, restaurants, nightspots, and public transportation. **Pros:** convenient location; a slew of in-room amenities for business travelers. **Cons:** noisy street; feels corporate. [$] *Rooms from: $334* ✉ *480 Sutter St., Union Sq.* ☎ *415/398–8900* 🌐 *www.marriott.com* 🛏 *447 rooms, 53 suites* 🍴 *No meals* ✥ *4:F3.*

$$$$ HOTEL 🏨 **Sir Francis Drake Hotel.** Beefeater-costumed doormen welcome you into the regal lobby of this 1928 landmark property, fresh off a $30-million

face-lift, while guest quarters are fitted with typical technological amenities yet evoke the era with regal headboards atop beds draped in blue, white, red, and gray. **Pros:** can't beat the location; free in-room Wi-Fi; renovation added needed zip to a formerly faded queen. **Cons:** small baths; some complaints about unresponsive service and questionable cleanliness. $ *Rooms from: $409* ✉ *450 Powell St., Union Sq.* ☎ *415/392–7755, 800/795–7129* ⊕ *www.sirfrancisdrake.com* ⤳ *412 rooms, 4 suites* ⭕ *No meals* ✛ *4:F3.*

$$$$
HOTEL

ⓣ **Taj Campton Place San Francisco.** Beauty and highly attentive service remain the hallmarks of this exquisite jewel-like, top-tier hotel where small but updated rooms are elegantly decorated in a contemporary Italian style, with sandy earth tones and handsome pearwood paneling and cabinetry. **Pros:** attentive service; first-class restaurant; abundant natural light; the most lavish robes in town. **Cons:** pricey (but worth it). $ *Rooms from: $425* ✉ *340 Stockton St., Union Sq.* ☎ *415/781–5555, 866/332–1670* ⊕ *www.tajhotels.com* ⤳ *101 rooms, 9 suites* ⭕ *No meals* ✛ *4:G3.*

$$$
HOTEL

ⓣ **Villa Florence.** This little bit of Italy on Powell Street houses guests in traditional rooms that, though not large, feel comfortable, upbeat, and expansive. **Pros:** great location for those who want to be in the center of things; easy access to shopping, theater, and public transport; town cars drive guests around the city throughout the day. **Cons:** excess fees; noise from cable cars; crowded street. $ *Rooms from: $256* ✉ *225 Powell St., Union Sq.* ☎ *415/397–7700* ⊕ *www.villaflorence.com* ⤳ *154 rooms, 28 suites* ⭕ *No meals* ✛ *4:E4.*

$$$
HOTEL

ⓣ **The Warwick San Francisco.** A century-old classic is one of San Francisco's newest *it* hotels, where handsome, though small rooms evoke an aristocratic feel with geometric wallpaper, black-and-white framed historic photos curated by the San Francisco Public Library, and hearty wooden furnishings. **Pros:** artsy rooms; great location in the heart of Union Square; on-site restaurant and bar. **Cons:** elderly hotel with thin walls; small rooms. $ *Rooms from: $269* ✉ *490 Geary St., Union Sq.* ☎ *415/928–7900* ⊕ *www.warwickhotels.com* ⤳ *54 rooms, 20 suites* ⭕ *No meals* ✛ *4:D4.*

$$$
HOTEL
Fodor's Choice
★

ⓣ **Westin St. Francis.** The survivor of two major earthquakes, some headline-grabbing scandals, and even an attempted presidential assassination, this grande dame that dates to 1904 remains ever above the fray—richly appointed, serenely elegant, and superbly located. **Pros:** fantastic beds; prime Union Square location; spacious rooms, some with great views. **Cons:** some guests comment on the long wait at check-in; rooms in original building can be small. $ *Rooms from: $325* ✉ *335 Powell St., Union Sq.* ☎ *415/397–7000, 800/917–7458* ⊕ *www. westinstfrancis.com* ⤳ *1,157 rooms, 38 suites* ⭕ *No meals* ✛ *4:F3.*

$$
B&B/INN

ⓣ **White Swan Inn.** A cozy library with a crackling fireplace and comfortable chairs and sofas is the heart of this inviting English-style B&B, while the sizable rooms have floral carpeting and wallpaper, reproduction Edwardian furniture, and gas fireplaces topped by book-lined mantels. **Pros:** cozy B&B antidote to sterile chain hotels; nice lounge and patio area. **Cons:** thin walls can make for noisy rooms; nearby streets can be rough at night. $ *Rooms from: $249* ✉ *845 Bush St., Union Sq.*

Room for the Kids

With some luck and a little planning, the family trip to San Francisco will be something you and your kids will always remember, in a good way. Finding the right lodgings can go a long way toward making your vacation a success.

Start with the practical stuff. You'll want to find something with enough room, so look for places with full suites or junior suites so the kids can play on their own without getting underfoot. Cow Hollow Motor Inn and Suites has apartment-size quarters, and the Fairmont Heritage Place's spacious apartments can fit a large family. Hotel Diva tapped into the hip kiddo market by crafting luxe quarters for the playground set; imagine a bunk bed draped with colorful bedding, stuffed animals, toys, a Wii, and a karaoke machine. If you can't afford a suite, places with big closets can help with the clutter of toys, strollers, and the like.

Motels with parking right outside your door (like those on Lombard Street) can help you clear clutter, too, as well as reduce the schlep factor coming and going. Many hotels contract with babysitting services, and some have child-friendly furnishings in certain rooms. Places with kitchens or kitchenettes (such as the Beresford Arms and the Laurel Inn) will make meals and snacks easier, and if you can afford it, room service is a great mess-free way to feed the group— just shove the dirty dishes into the hallway and call down to have them removed. Some expensive hotels, such as the Ritz-Carlton, have Club Levels with continuous food service all day. This option costs extra but can actually save you money on meals and snacks.

Now for the fun! Any place with a pool will probably be a hit if your kids can swim. Video games can also while away the hours if absolutely necessary. Ask if your hotel has special welcome amenities for kids, such as the toys and games offered by the Hilton, Four Seasons, Argonaut, and Omni; complimentary kids' snacks (such as cookies and milk at the Omni and the Hotel Del Sol); or a library of games, movies, and snacks for kiddos at the Fairmont Heritage Place.

The Fairmont has a wonderful "Doorman for a Day" program that lets kids don an official pint-size doorman's cap to greet guests and blow a whistle to hail a taxi while mom and dad capture the moment with a camera supplied free by the hotel (kids get to keep the whistle). Kids staying at the Golden Gate Hotel like to ride up and down on the antique "birdcage" elevator and play with Pip the cat or Humphrey the friendly golden retriever.

14

☎ *415/775–1755, 800/999–9570* ⊕ *www.jdvhotels.com* ⤵ *25 rooms, 1 suite* ❋ *Breakfast* ✛ *4:E2.*

CHINATOWN

$$
HOTEL
☐ **SW Hotel.** Opened in 1913 as the Columbo Hotel, this lodging on the bustling border between Chinatown and North Beach has rooms and suites decorated in a blend of Italian and Chinese styles, with Florentine wall coverings and Ming-style furniture. **Pros:** top-floor views of Coit Tower; multilingual staff; self-serve parking under building.

Cons: cramped closets and bathrooms; some guests complain breakfast is disappointing. [$] *Rooms from: $169* ✉ *615 Broadway, Chinatown* ☎ *415/362–2999, 888/595–9188* 🌐 *www.swhotel.com* 🛏 *81 rooms, 2 suites* 🍴 *Breakfast* ✥ *1:D3.*

SOMA

$$ HOTEL

🏨 **Carriage Inn.** This welcoming inn reminisces about San Francisco's literary, subversive, and comedic history by paying homage to city legends: in each spacious room, decked out in a funky mix of antique furnishings, Asian-themed throw pillows, and contemporary touches, the bio of a local celebrity is typed out on an antique typewriter. **Pros:** plenty of character; spacious rooms; hot tub; free Wi-Fi and continental breakfast. **Cons:** not the safest neighborhood; thin walls. [$] *Rooms from: $169* ✉ *140 7th St., SoMa* ☎ *415/552–8600, 866/539–0036* 🌐 *www.carriageinnsf.com* 🛏 *48 rooms* 🍴 *Breakfast* ✥ *3:H2.*

$$$$ HOTEL Fodor's Choice ★

🏨 **Four Seasons Hotel San Francisco.** Occupying floors 5 through 17 of a skyscraper, these elegant rooms with contemporary artwork and fine linens have floor-to-ceiling windows overlooking either Yerba Buena Gardens or downtown; all have deep soaking tubs and glass-enclosed showers. **Pros:** near museums, galleries, restaurants, shopping, and clubs; terrific fitness facilities; luxurious rooms and amenities; MKT restaurant is worth the splurge. **Cons:** pricey; rooms can feel sterile. [$] *Rooms from: $595* ✉ *757 Market St., SoMa* ☎ *415/633–3000, 800/332–3442, 800/819–5053* 🌐 *www.fourseasons.com/sanfrancisco* 🛏 *231 rooms, 46 suites* 🍴 *No meals* ✥ *4:H4.*

$$$ HOTEL Fodor's Choice ★

🏨 **Hotel Palomar San Francisco.** Favored by celebrities, this lair on the top five floors of the green-tile 1908 Pacific Place Building offers a luxurious oasis above the busiest part of town, where spacious rooms offer muted alligator-pattern carpeting, drapes with bold taupe-and-cream stripes, and sleek furniture echoing a 1930s sensibility. **Pros:** in-room spa service available; much hyped restaurant and bar; good location; refuge from downtown. **Cons:** pricey. [$] *Rooms from: $270* ✉ *12 4th St., SoMa* ☎ *415/348–1111, 866/373–4941* 🌐 *www.hotelpalomar-sf.com* 🛏 *184 rooms, 11 suites* 🍴 *No meals* ✥ *4:G5.*

$$$ HOTEL Fodor's Choice ★

🏨 **Hotel Zetta.** With a playful lobby lounge, the lively Cavalier restaurant, and slick-yet-homey tech-friendly rooms, this trendy redo behind a stately 1913 neoclassical facade is a leader in the SoMa hotel scene. **Pros:** hip, arty design; eco-friendly; great location close to shopping and museums; fine restaurant and lounges; free basic Wi-Fi; state-of-the-art tech amenities. **Cons:** lots of hubbub and traffic; no bathtubs. [$] *Rooms from: $289* ✉ *55 5th St., SoMa* ☎ *415/543–8555* 🌐 *www.viceroyhotelgroup.com/zetta* 🛏 *116 rooms, 1 suite* 🍴 *No meals* ✥ *4:F6.*

$$$$ HOTEL

🏨 **InterContinental San Francisco.** The arctic-blue glass exterior and subdued, Zen-like lobby may be as bland as an airport concourse, but they're merely a prelude to the spectacularly light, expansive, thoughtfully laid-out guest rooms, which have all the ultramodern conveniences. **Pros:** a stone's throw from Moscone Center; well-equipped gym; near hip clubs and restaurants. **Cons:** decor is short on character; borders a rough neighborhood; a few blocks off the major tourist path. [$] *Rooms from: $387* ✉ *888 Howard St., SoMa* ☎ *415/616–6500,*

866/781–2364 ⊕ *www.intercontinentalsanfrancisco.com* ⤴ *536 rooms, 14 suites* |○| *No meals* ✚ *4:H6.*

$ ⊞ **The Mosser Hotel.** A compatible pairing of contemporary decor and
HOTEL original 1913 architectural elements caters to a hip clientele, with double-pane windows in the guest rooms, plush bedding and sofas, and spruced-up color schemes. **Pros:** convenient location; reasonably priced; music-themed rooms; lively SoMa location. **Cons:** a third of the rooms are without private baths; can be loud. **$** *Rooms from: $134* ⊠ *54 4th St., SoMa* ☎ *415/986–4400, 800/227–3804* ⊕ *www.themosser.com* ⤴ *166 rooms, 112 with bath* |○| *Breakfast* ✚ *4:G5.*

$$$ ⊞ **San Francisco Marriott Marquis.** The distinctive design of this 40-story
HOTEL hotel has been compared to a parking meter and a jukebox, though guest rooms are all about practical comfort—decorated in tasteful neutrals consistent with the Marriott brand, they cater to the business set with a host of technological amenities, ergonomic chairs, city views, and wide desks. **Pros:** stunning views from some rooms; in the cultural district; centered on business travelers. **Cons:** pricey parking; noisy lobby; rooms fill quickly during conferences. **$** *Rooms from: $344* ⊠ *780 Mission St., SoMa* ☎ *415/896–1600* ⊕ *www.marriott.com/sfodt* ⤴ *1,498 rooms, 134 suites* |○| *No meals* ✚ *4:H5.*

$$$$ ⊞ **The St. Regis San Francisco.** Across from Yerba Buena and the MOMA,
HOTEL the city's most luxurious property, favored by celebrities such as Lady
Fodor's Choice Gaga and Al Gore, is at once luxurious and modern, pampering guests
★ in rooms and suites with subdued cream colors, leather-textured walls, and window seats offering city views. **Pros:** tasteful, yet current; lap pool; good location; luxe spa; views; two on-site restaurants. **Cons:** very expensive; hallway noise; long waits for room service and valet parking. **$** *Rooms from: $895* ⊠ *125 3rd St., SoMa* ☎ *415/284–4000* ⊕ *www.stregis.com/sanfrancisco* ⤴ *214 rooms, 46 suites* |○| *No meals* ✚ *1:E6.*

$$$$ ⊞ **W San Francisco.** At this epitome of cool urban chic, compact and
HOTEL colorful guest rooms come with such homey comforts as upholstered
FAMILY window seats, comfy pillow-top mattresses, and goose-down comforters and pillows; sleek baths sport green-glass countertops and shiny steel sinks. **Pros:** hip energy; sophisticated digs; in the heart of the cultural district. **Cons:** hotel's signature scents could pose a problem for sensitive noses. **$** *Rooms from: $429* ⊠ *181 3rd St., SoMa* ☎ *415/777–5300* ⊕ *www.wsanfrancisco.com* ⤴ *404 rooms, 9 suites* |○| *No meals* ✚ *1:E6.*

THE TENDERLOIN

$ ⊞ **Phoenix Hotel.** A magnet for the hip at heart and ultracool is a bit
HOTEL retro and low-key, with bamboo furniture, fresh white bedspreads, and original pieces by local artists, as well as modern amenities like iPad/iPod docking stations. **Pros:** boho atmosphere; cheeky design; popular with musicians; hip restaurant/bar; free parking. **Cons:** somewhat seedy location; no elevators; can be loud in the evenings. **$** *Rooms from: $149* ⊠ *601 Eddy St., Tenderloin* ☎ *415/776–1380, 800/248–9466* ⊕ *www.thephoenixhotel.com* ⤴ *41 rooms, 3 suites* |○| *Breakfast* ✚ *4:A6.*

14

HAYES VALLEY

$
B&B/INN
Hayes Valley Inn. Offering "European charm in the heart of Hayes Valley," the modest, clean rooms of this hotel come with sinks and vanities; a couple of spotless shared bathrooms are down the hall. **Pros:** inexpensive; free local calls and Wi-Fi; close to shopping, restaurants, and theater. **Cons:** no in-room bathrooms; no elevator; some street noise. $ *Rooms from: $129* ✉ *417 Gough St., Hayes Valley* ☎ *415/431–9131, 800/930–7999* ⊕ *www.hayesvalleyinn.com* ➦ *28 rooms with shared baths* ⫚ *Breakfast* ✛ *3:E2.*

$$
B&B/INN
Inn at the Opera. Within walking distance of Davies Symphony Hall and the War Memorial Opera House, these small, homey rooms with dark wood furnishings cater to season-ticket holders for the opera, ballet, and symphony; they've also been the choice for stars of the music, dance, and opera worlds, from Luciano Pavarotti to Mikhail Baryshnikov. **Pros:** staff goes the extra mile; intimate restaurant. **Cons:** smallish rooms and bath; sold out far in advance during opera season. $ *Rooms from: $169* ✉ *333 Fulton St., Hayes Valley* ☎ *415/863–8400, 800/325–2708* ⊕ *www.shellhospitality.com* ➦ *30 rooms, 18 suites* ⫚ *Breakfast* ✛ *3:E2.*

$
HOTEL
Fodor's Choice
★
Metro Hotel. These tiny rooms, with simple yet modern decor and equipped with private (though small) bathrooms, are within walking distance to the lively Haight, Hayes Valley, Panhandle, NoPa, and Castro districts. **Pros:** can't beat the price; great location for those wanting to be out of downtown; friendly staff. **Cons:** small rooms and bathrooms; street noise. $ *Rooms from: $88* ✉ *319 Divisadero St., Hayes Valley* ☎ *415/861–5364* ⊕ *www.metrohotelsf.com* ➦ *24 rooms* ⫚ *No meals* ✛ *3:B3.*

$$
B&B/INN
Fodor's Choice
★
The Parsonage. Stay in a National Historic Landmark Victorian, constructed in 1883, with many of the original mantelpieces, fireplaces, mirrors, and ornate molding gracing the 14-foot ceilings above 17th century beds and other antique treasures. **Pros:** step back in time and sleep on antique beds; outstanding breakfast; kind and intuitive hosts; walking distance to many attractions and restaurants. **Cons:** street parking only. $ *Rooms from: $240* ✉ *198 Haight St., Hayes Valley* ☎ *415/863–3699* ⊕ *www.theparsonage.com* ➦ *5 rooms* ⫚ *Breakfast* ✛ *3:E3.*

NOB HILL

$$$$
HOTEL
Fairmont San Francisco. Dominating the top of Nob Hill like a European palace, the Fairmont is steeped in a rich history and pampers guests in luxury—rooms in the main building are done in conservative color schemes and have high ceilings, colorful Chinese porcelain lamps, decadent beds, and marble bathrooms; rooms in the newer Tower are generally larger and have better views. **Pros:** huge bathrooms; stunning lobby; great location. **Cons:** some guests have complained about spotty service; older rooms can be quite small; hills can be challenging for those on foot. $ *Rooms from: $429* ✉ *950 Mason St., Nob Hill* ☎ *415/772–5000, 800/257–7544* ⊕ *www.fairmont.com/sanfrancisco* ➦ *591 rooms, 65 suites* ⫚ *No meals* ✛ *4:E1.*

LODGING ALTERNATIVES

VACATION RENTALS

If you want an alternative to a hotel—one that gives a more authentically San Francisco experience (or at least a slightly more spacious one)—vacation rentals are the way to go. Many families and long-term visitors have found great apartments for reasonable rates by searching online in specific neighborhoods using websites like 🌐 *www.airbnb.com* and 🌐 *www.vrbo.com*. There are few reputable local vacation rental companies, but you can't go wrong by visiting the San Francisco Convention and Visitors Bureau (🌐 *www.onlyinsanfrancisco.com*), where some property owners list their rentals.

CAMPING

While most travelers don't equate camping with an urban experience, those nutty San Franciscans have toppled that belief. **The Presidio of San Francisco** has recently renovated its **Rob Hill Campground** (☎ *415/561–5444* 🌐 *www.presidio.gov/explore/pages/rob-hill-campground.aspx*), the only place to pitch a tent in the city. Perched atop the highest hill in San Francisco's largest green space, beneath a canopy of eucalyptus trees, and with views of Baker Beach, this site may be small (there are two sites that house 30 people each) and expensive ($125 a night with a maximum of two nights), but you can imagine the bragging rights earned for a night spent outdoors in the fog. Book well in advance: as you might expect, sites fill fast. The season closes on November 30.

HOSTELS

No matter your age (or style of luggage), staying at a hostel saves cash. San Francisco's three hostels are members of **Hostelling International** (the massive umbrella organization of thousands of properties all over the world). While members receive priority reservations (and discounts), you don't have to pay to join in order to stay the night. The San Francisco City Center and San Francisco Downtown hostels offer reasonable rates in the heart of the action. But the real steal is the San Francisco Fisherman's Wharf Hostel, as some rooms offer bay views. 🌐 *www.norcalhostels.org.*

14

$$ HOTEL 🏨 **Hotel Vertigo.** Scenes in Alfred Hitchcock's classic thriller *Vertigo* were shot in this ornate hotel (it was a speakeasy during Prohibition), and designer Thomas Schoos has infused the guest rooms with a reckless, whimsical tribute—consider the tangerine highlights and the horse-head lamps, not to mention the classic *Vertigo* swirl logo along the walls. **Pros:** tons of personality; artsy decor. **Cons:** borderline neighborhood; no air-conditioning. [$] *Rooms from: $209* ✉ *940 Sutter St., between Leavenworth and Hyde Sts., Nob Hill* ☎ *415/885–6800, 800/553–1900* 🌐 *www.hotelvertigosf.com* 🛏 *102 rooms, 8 suites* 🍴 *No meals* ✥ *4:B3.*

$$$ HOTEL 🏨 **InterContinental Mark Hopkins.** The circular redbrick drive of this towering Nob Hill architectural landmark leads to an opulent, mirrored, marble-floor lobby that is the gateway to luxurious rooms, with Frette linens and goose-down duvets, glowing with gold, cream, and yellow tones. **Pros:** spectacular views; steeped in history; you can often find last-minute deals online. **Cons:** some guests have complained about stuffy, indifferent service and noisy rooms—especially for the price. $ *Rooms from: $314* ✉ *1 Nob Hill, Nob Hill* ☎ *415/392–3434, 800/662–4455* ⊕ *www.intercontinentalmarkhopkins.com* ⤳ *340 rooms, 40 suites* ⅼ⊙ⅼ *No meals* ✛ *4:E1.*

$$$$
HOTEL
Fodor's Choice
★

☷ **Ritz-Carlton, San Francisco.** This stunning tribute to beauty and attentive, professional service offers a modern twist on that classic Ritz style with luxurious, fog-hued guest rooms that are geared to solid comforts, such as featherbeds outfitted with 300-thread-count, Egyptian-cotton Frette sheets, and down comforters. **Pros:** terrific service; all-day food available on Club Level; beautiful surroundings; fantastic new restaurant and Lobby Lounge; renovated fitness center. **Cons:** expensive; hilly location; no pool. $ *Rooms from: $599* ✉ *600 Stockton St., at California St., Nob Hill* ☎ *415/296–7465* ⊕ *www.ritzcarlton.com* ⤳ *276 rooms, 60 suites* ⅼ⊙ⅼ *No meals* ✛ *4:F1.*

$$$$
HOTEL

☷ **The Scarlet Huntington Hotel.** Stars from Bogart and Bacall to Picasso and Pavarotti have stayed in this venerable hotel, famed for its spacious rooms and suites, most of which have great views of Grace Cathedral, the bay, or the fog rolling across the city skyline. **Pros:** city icon; spacious rooms; the aura of old San Francisco; first-rate spa with city views; cable cars pass by right out front. **Cons:** up a steep hill from downtown. $ *Rooms from: $459* ✉ *1075 California St., Nob Hill* ☎ *415/474–5400, 800/227–4683* ⊕ *www.huntingtonhotel.com* ⤳ *96 rooms, 40 suites* ⅼ⊙ⅼ *No meals* ✛ *4:D1.*

$$$
HOTEL

☷ **Stanford Court Hotel.** A stained-glass dome dominates the lobby of this stately but comfortable hotel, where the mansion of railroad baron Leland Stanford once stood, and rooms are decorated in warm tones and furnished with handsome leather chairs and tasteful modern accessories. **Pros:** focus on comfort; classic elegance; great location on historic Nob Hill. **Cons:** up a steep hill from most popular tourist sights; some guests complain that rooms are small. $ *Rooms from: $300* ✉ *905 California St., Nob Hill* ☎ *415/989–3500* ⊕ *www.stanfordcourt.com* ⤳ *389 rooms, 4 suites* ⅼ⊙ⅼ *No meals* ✛ *4:F1.*

VAN NESS/POLK

$$
HOTEL

☷ **Hotel Carlton.** "International vintage" aptly describes the eclectic collection of textiles, masks, globes, games, maps, postcards, and other ephemera from around the world that decorates this 1927 hotel, in which the simply furnished guest quarters—with ceiling fans and views from upper floors—are reminiscent of an apartment that would belong to a globe-trotting bohemian aunt. **Pros:** decent prices; decor with character; helpful staff; pet beds upon request. **Cons:** on the edge of a seedy area; several blocks from Union Square and restaurants; can be cold in winter (ask for a space heater). $ *Rooms from: $179* ✉ *1075 Sutter St., Van Ness/Polk* ☎ *415/673–0242, 800/922–7586* ⊕ *www.hotelcarltonsf.com* ⤳ *161 rooms, 1 suite* ⅼ⊙ⅼ *No meals* ✛ *4:A3.*

NORTH BEACH

$ **Columbus Motor Inn.** Fodorites sing the praises of this affordable
HOTEL   motor inn, calling it "a good family hotel if you have a car to park"
FAMILY   and basic rooms decked out with oversize pillows, earth-toned bedding, and large flat-screen TVs. **Pros:** free parking; affordable rooms; lively location; rooms are deep-cleaned every three months. **Cons:** lacks amenities; decor is not stylish; street-facing accommodations can be noisy. $ *Rooms from: $125* ⊠ *1075 Columbus Ave., North Beach* ☎ *415/885–1492* ⊕ *www.columbusmotorinn.com* ⇴ *45 rooms* ⦿ *No meals* ✚ *1:B2.*

$$ **Hotel Bohème.** This small hotel in historic North Beach takes you
HOTEL   back in time with cast-iron beds, large mirrored armoires, and memorabilia recalling the Beat generation—whose leading light, Allen Ginsberg, often stayed here (legend has it that in his later years he could be seen sitting in a window, typing away on his typewriter). **Pros:** North Beach location with literary pedigree; stylish rooms; helpful staff. **Cons:** street parking is scarce; lots of traffic congestion; no air-conditioning; small rooms. $ *Rooms from: $194* ⊠ *444 Columbus Ave., North Beach* ☎ *415/433–9111* ⊕ *www.hotelboheme.com* ⇴ *15 rooms* ⦿ *No meals* ✚ *1:D3.*

$ **San Remo Hotel.** A few blocks from Fisherman's Wharf, this three-
HOTEL   story 1906 Italianate Victorian—once home to longshoremen and Beat
Fodor's Choice   poets—has a narrow stairway from the street leading to the front desk
★   and labyrinthine hallways; rooms are small but charming, with lace curtains, forest-green-painted wood floors, and brass beds and other antique furnishings. **Pros:** inexpensive; historic; cozy. **Cons:** some rooms are dark; only the penthouse suite has a private bath; spartan amenities. $ *Rooms from: $104* ⊠ *2237 Mason St., North Beach* ☎ *415/776–8688, 800/352–7366* ⊕ *www.sanremohotel.com* ⇴ *64 rooms with shared baths, 1 suite* ⦿ *No meals* ✚ *1:C2.*

$$ **Washington Square Inn.** Overlooking the namesake tree-lined park,
B&B/INN   these gracious rooms are individually decorated with Venetian and French accents and many have gas fireplaces. **Pros:** lovely rooms; fun location; reasonably priced parking fees for San Francisco. **Cons:** no air-conditioning; street parking is difficult to come by. $ *Rooms from: $199* ⊠ *1660 Stockton St., at Filbert St., North Beach* ☎ *415/981–4220, 800/388–0220* ⊕ *www.wsisf.com* ⇴ *15 rooms* ⦿ *Breakfast* ✚ *1:D2.*

THE WATERFRONT

FISHERMAN'S WHARF

$$$ **Argonaut Hotel.** These spacious guest rooms, many with a sofa bed in
HOTEL   the sitting areas, have exposed-brick walls, wood-beam ceilings, and
FAMILY   best of all, windows that open to the sea air and the sounds of the water-
Fodor's Choice   front; many rooms enjoy views of Alcatraz and the Golden Gate Bridge.
★   **Pros:** bay views; near Hyde Street cable car; sofa beds; toys for the kids. **Cons:** nautical theme isn't for everyone; cramped public areas; service can be hit or miss; location requires a bit of a trek to many attractions. $ *Rooms from: $309* ⊠ *495 Jefferson St., at Hyde St., Fisherman's*

14

Wharf ☎ *415/563–0800, 866/415–0704* 🌐 *www.argonauthotel.com* 🛏 *239 rooms, 13 suites* 🍴 *No meals* ✣ *1:A1.*

$$$ HOTEL 🏨 **Best Western Plus–The Tuscan.** The redbrick facade of this hotel some Fodors.com users describe as a "hidden treasure" barely hints at the Tuscan country villa style that lies within—Italianate rooms feature delightful bedding, kingly studded headboards, and wine-colored textiles. **Pros:** wine and beer hour; cozy feeling; great location near Fisherman's Wharf. **Cons:** congested touristy area; small rooms. [$] *Rooms from: $265* ✉ *425 North Point St., at Mason St., Fisherman's Wharf* ☎ *415/561–1100, 800/648–4626* 🌐 *www.tuscaninn.com* 🛏 *212 rooms, 12 suites* 🍴 *No meals* ✣ *1:C1.*

$$$$ RENTAL FAMILY 🏨 **Fairmont Heritage Place, Ghirardelli Square.** Housed in the former Ghirardelli chocolate factory, these one- to-three-bedroom serviced apartments supply comfort and style without being stuffy—fully equipped gourmet kitchens, brick walls, marble soaking tubs, plush bedding, in-room iPads, laundry facilities, modern furniture in chocolate and lavender hues, and views of Alcatraz (in the bay-view residences) are standard. **Pros:** luxury at its finest; gigantic apartments; many amenities; bay views from most accommodations; free car service within a 2-mile radius. **Cons:** a bit of a trek from downtown; expensive. [$] *Rooms from: $899* ✉ *950 North Point St., Fisherman's Wharf* ☎ *415/268–9900* 🌐 *www.fairmont.com/ghirardelli* 🛏 *53 rooms* 🍴 *Breakfast* ✣ *1:A1.*

$$ HOTEL FAMILY 🏨 **Sheraton Fisherman's Wharf Hotel.** It might not look like much from outside, but this is one festive gal—from the fire pits lining the parking area to the contemporary teal mood lighting in the lobby, and the fun extends to the guest quarters: sloped walls let in plenty of sunshine through large windows, highlighting candy-colored throw pillows atop Signature beds, plush leather chair, and geometric lamps. **Pros:** in the heart of Fisherman's Wharf; newly renovated with fun colors; outdoor pool. **Cons:** touristy area; feels corporate. [$] *Rooms from: $239* ✉ *2500 Mason St., Fisherman's Wharf* ☎ *415/362–5500, 888/627–7024* 🌐 *www.sheratonatthewharf.com* 🛏 *524 rooms, 7 suites* 🍴 *No meals* ✣ *1:C1.*

EMBARCADERO

$$$ HOTEL 🏨 **Harbor Court Hotel.** A friendly staff earn high marks for this cozy hotel, which overlooks the Embarcadero, and all sorts of nice touches enliven the tight guest quarters, from double sets of soundproof windows to brightly colored throw pillows adorning beds with 320-thread-count sheets. **Pros:** convenient location; quiet; some rooms have views of the Bay Bridge and the Ferry Building. **Cons:** small rooms. [$] *Rooms from: $275* ✉ *165 Steuart St., Embarcadero* ☎ *415/882–1300, 866/792–6283* 🌐 *www.harborcourthotel.com* 🛏 *130 rooms, 1 suite* 🍴 *No meals* ✣ *1:G5.*

$$$$ HOTEL FAMILY Fodor's Choice ★ 🏨 **Hotel Vitale.** "Luxury, naturally," the theme of this eight-story, terraced bay-front hotel, is apparent in every thoughtful detail: little vases of lavender mounted outside each handsome room; limestone-lined baths; the penthouse-level day spa with soaking tubs set in a rooftop bamboo forest. **Pros:** family-friendly studios; great views of the Bay Bridge, Embarcadero, Treasure Island, or the skyline; twice-daily maid service. **Cons:** some rooms can feel cramped or be noisy; "urban

retreat fee" adds another charge to an already pricy property; some guests report inconsistent service. $ *Rooms from: $350* ⊠ *8 Mission St., Embarcadero* ☎ *415/278–3700, 888/890–8688* ⊕ *www.hotelvitale. com* ⤳ *190 rooms, 9 suites* ⊺⊙⊺ *No meals* ✛ *1:G4.*

$$$$ ⍟ **Hyatt Regency San Francisco.** The spectacular 17-story atrium lobby,
HOTEL reportedly the largest hotel lobby in North America, is a marvel, with sprawling trees, a shimmering stream, a huge fountain, and the sleek Eclipse restaurant and bar, while all the businesslike rooms have city or bay views; 134 come with bay-view balconies. **Pros:** convenient location; elegant modernist design; great views. **Cons:** some may find it cool rather than cozy; wait for check-in can be long; geared toward business travelers; soaring room rates for high season. $ *Rooms from: $699* ⊠ *5 Embarcadero Center, Embarcadero* ☎ *415/788–1234, 800/233–1234* ⊕ *sanfranciscoregency.hyatt.com* ⤳ *802 rooms, 51 suites* ⊺⊙⊺ *No meals* ✛ *1:G4.*

14

FINANCIAL DISTRICT

$$$ ⍟ **Galleria Park Hotel.** While rooms are small, they offer all the typical
HOTEL technological amenities, and this green-certified hotel manages to be both hip and welcoming, inviting guests to lounge in the lobby on soft couches, enjoy the garden and jogging track, and even to bring Fido. **Pros:** a can't-beat location one block from BART; friendly management. **Cons:** small rooms and bathrooms (but nice tiled showers); plenty of city noise. $ *Rooms from: $319* ⊠ *191 Sutter St., Financial District* ☎ *415/781–3060, 800/792–9639* ⊕ *www.galleriapark.com* ⤳ *177 rooms, 8 suites* ⊺⊙⊺ *No meals* ✛ *1:E5.*

$$ ⍟ **Hilton San Francisco Financial District.** A bridge over Kearny Street con-
HOTEL nects this giant hotel with Chinatown's Portsmouth Square, while the airy guest rooms are furnished with blond-wood Signature Serenity beds and large work desks with ergonomic chairs; spring for a balcony facing the bay for million-dollar views. **Pros:** abundant parking; bay and city views; playground across the street. **Cons:** congested downtown area. $ *Rooms from: $209* ⊠ *750 Kearny St., Financial District* ☎ *415/433–6600* ⊕ *www.sanfranciscohiltonhotel.com* ⤳ *537 rooms, 7 suites* ⊺⊙⊺ *Breakfast* ✛ *1:D4.*

$$$ ⍟ **Le Méridien San Francisco.** Lacewood paneling, polished granite sinks,
HOTEL contemporary furniture, handy in-room safes with outlets for recharging laptops and cell phones, and wall-size maps of San Francisco outfit the guest rooms, while the early-20th-century lobby is a showplace for rotating art installations. **Pros:** excellent service; ultraconvenient for the Embarcadero Center complex; spacious rooms; great views; top-notch concierge; interesting artwork throughout. **Cons:** after dark this Financial District neighborhood grows sleepy. $ *Rooms from: $319* ⊠ *333 Battery St., Financial District* ☎ *415/296–2900* ⊕ *www.lemeridien.com/ sanfrancisco* ⤳ *281 rooms, 79 suites* ⊺⊙⊺ *No meals* ✛ *1:E4.*

$$$$ ⍟ **Mandarin Oriental, San Francisco.** Two towers connected by glass-
HOTEL enclosed sky bridges compose the top 11 floors of one of San Francisco's tallest buildings, offering spectacular panoramas from every room; the windows open so you can hear that trademark San Francisco sound: the "ding ding" of the cable cars some 40 floors below (and rooms

include binoculars). **Pros:** spectacular "bridge-to-bridge" views; attentive service; in the running for the most comfy beds in the city. **Cons:** in a business area that's quiet on weekends; extremely pricey. [$] *Rooms from: $595* ✉ *222 Sansome St., Financial District* ☎ *415/276–9600, 800/622–0404* 🌐 *www.mandarinoriental.com/sanfrancisco* 🛏 *151 rooms, 7 suites* 🍴 *No meals* ✥ *1:E4.*

$$$$ HOTEL 🏨 **Omni San Francisco Hotel.** This 1926 redbrick-and-stone building, a former bank, is now home to a luxury hotel with lots of historical flavor in guest rooms graced with 9-foot-high ceilings and crown moldings, San Francisco-themed photographs, and carved-mahogany furniture. **Pros:** outstanding personalized service; cookies and milk for the kids; immaculately clean; historical flavor. **Cons:** so-so air-conditioning; rooftop views are less than inspiring. [$] *Rooms from: $355* ✉ *500 California St., Financial District* ☎ *415/677–9494* 🌐 *www.omnisanfrancisco.com* 🛏 *347 rooms, 15 suites* 🍴 *No meals* ✥ *1:E4.*

THE MARINA AND THE PRESIDIO

THE MARINA

$ B&B/INN 🏨 **Marina Inn.** In this four-story 1924 building five blocks from the Marina, spacious rooms are snazzy, with Urban Outfitters–inspired bedding, fresh wallpaper and carpets, and TVs with DVD players and CD players. **Pros:** affordable; daybed option for kids; great location near Marina and Fisherman's Wharf. **Cons:** street-side rooms can be noisy. [$] *Rooms from: $149* ✉ *3110 Octavia St., at Lombard St., Marina* ☎ *415/928–1000, 800/274–1420* 🌐 *www.marinainn.com* 🛏 *40 rooms* 🍴 *Breakfast* ✥ *2:G2.*

$$ HOTEL 🏨 **Marina Motel.** Reminiscent of the motor courts of yesteryear, this family-owned motel is an inexpensive option within walking distance of restaurants, bars, and shops in the Marina District, and units have fresh French country–style furnishings and thick windows; some have kitchenettes with eating areas, and all have spotless baths and small shower stalls. **Pros:** staff accommodates guests with pets and kids; more character than the chain motels on the same strip. **Cons:** located on a busy street; rooms can be noisy and stuffy; staff can be gruff. [$] *Rooms from: $199* ✉ *2576 Lombard St., Marina* ☎ *415/921–9406, 800/346–6118* 🌐 *www.marinamotel.com* 🛏 *39 rooms* 🍴 *No meals* ✥ *2:D3.*

THE PRESIDIO

$$ B&B/INN Fodor's Choice ★ 🏨 **The Inn at the Presidio.** Built in 1903 and opened as a hotel in 2012, this two-story, Georgian Revival–style building served as officers' quarters in military days past and now has 26 guest rooms—17 of them suites—complete with gas fireplaces and modern-meets-salvage-store finds, such as wrought-iron beds, industrial-inspired task lamps, historic black-and-white photos, and Pendleton blankets. **Pros:** playful design; only hotel in the Presidio; spacious rooms; views of Golden Gate Bridge. **Cons:** no on-site restaurant; no elevator; challenging to get a taxi; very far from downtown attractions. [$] *Rooms from: $220* ✉ *42 Moraga Ave., Presidio* ☎ *415/800–7356* 🌐 *www.innatthepresidio.com* 🛏 *8 rooms, 18 suites* 🍴 *Breakfast* ✥ *2:A3.*

COW HOLLOW

$$ HOTEL **Coventry Motor Inn.** Among the many motels on busy Lombard Street, this is one of the cleanest and quietest, and the unusually spacious rooms have Posturepedic beds and well-lit dining and work areas, which makes this a favorite with visitors hunting for comfort without a hefty price tag. **Pros:** clean; friendly; good value; lots of eateries nearby; free parking in building. **Cons:** busy street; few amenities. [$] *Rooms from: $160* ✉ *1901 Lombard St., Cow Hollow* ☎ *415/567–1200* 🌐 *www.coventrymotorinn.com* 🛏 *69 rooms* 🍴 *No meals* ✥ *2:F3.*

$ HOTEL Fodor's Choice ★ **Cow Hollow Motor Inn and Suites.** The suites at this large, family-owned, modern motel resemble typical San Francisco apartments and are more spacious than average, featuring big living rooms, one or two bedrooms, hardwood floors, sitting and dining areas, marble wood-burning fireplaces, and fully equipped kitchens. **Pros:** good for families; free covered parking in building for one vehicle. **Cons:** congested neighborhood has a college-rush-week feel; standard rooms are on a loud street. [$] *Rooms from: $120* ✉ *2190 Lombard St., Cow Hollow* ☎ *415/921–5800* 🌐 *www.cowhollowmotorinn.com* 🛏 *117 rooms, 12 suites* 🍴 *No meals* ✥ *2:E3.*

$$ HOTEL FAMILY **Hotel Del Sol.** The proximity of this beach-themed, three-story 1950s motor lodge to Fort Mason, the Walt Disney Family Museum, the Presidio, Crissy Field, and Chestnut Street's munchkin-favored shops already qualify it as kid-friendly, but the toys, games, DVDs, outdoor saltwater heated pool with plenty of inflatable playthings, snow cones on summer weekends, and afternoon cookies and milk make it a real haven for little ones. **Pros:** kid-friendly; plenty of nearby places to eat and shop; recently renovated; relatively inexpensive parking. **Cons:** far from downtown and the landmark attractions around Fisherman's Wharf; faces a busy thoroughfare. [$] *Rooms from: $189* ✉ *3100 Webster St., Cow Hollow* ☎ *415/921–5520, 877/433–5765* 🌐 *www.thehoteldelsol.com* 🛏 *47 rooms, 10 suites* 🍴 *Breakfast* ✥ *2:F3.*

$ HOTEL **Pacific Heights Inn.** Rooms are unassuming and simple at this two-story motor court near the busy intersection of Union and Van Ness, but this must be one of the most genteel-looking motels in town, dressed up with wrought-iron railings and benches, hanging plants, and pebbled exterior walkways facing the parking lot. **Pros:** some kitchenettes; free parking; reasonable rates; close walk to the Marina shopping and dining areas. **Cons:** can be noisy; crowded parking area. [$] *Rooms from: $109* ✉ *1555 Union St., Cow Hollow* ☎ *415/776–3310, 800/523–1801* 🌐 *www.pacificheightsinn.com* 🛏 *28 rooms, 12 suites* 🍴 *Breakfast* ✥ *2:H3.*

$$ B&B/INN Fodor's Choice ★ **Union Street Inn.** Precious family antiques, unique artwork, and such touches as candles, fresh flowers, wineglasses, and fine linens make rooms in this green-and-cream 1902 Edwardian popular with honeymooners and those looking for a romantic getaway with an English countryside ambience. **Pros:** personal service; Jane's excellent full breakfast; romantic setting. **Cons:** parking is difficult; no air-conditioning; no elevator. [$] *Rooms from: $249* ✉ *2229 Union St., Cow Hollow* ☎ *415/346–0424* 🌐 *www.unionstreetinn.com* 🛏 *6 rooms* 🍴 *Breakfast* ✥ *2:E3.*

14

MISSION AND CASTRO DISTRICTS

$ B&B/INN

🏨 **The Inn San Francisco.** No other San Francisco bed-and-breakfast is as steeped in local lore as this Italianate Victorian mansion decked out in ornate poster beds, opulent Oriental rugs, and precious Victorian artifacts. **Pros:** charming antiques; helpful staff; location on city's sunny side; extensive library of books about Northern California history; free street parking; pets welcome. **Cons:** neighborhood can be sketchy at night; some rooms are a tight squeeze; a couple rooms lack a private bathroom. [$] *Rooms from: $145* ✉ *943 S. Van Ness Ave., Mission* ☎ *415/641–0188, 800/359–0913* 🌐 *www.innsf.com* 🛏 *21 rooms* 🍴 *Breakfast* ✥ *3:G6.*

$$ B&B/INN Fodor's Choice ★

🏨 **The Parker Guest House.** Two yellow 1909 Edwardian houses enchant travelers wanting an authentic San Francisco experience; dark hallways and steep staircases lead to bright earth-toned rooms with private tiled baths (most with tubs), comfortable sitting areas and cozy linens. **Pros:** handsome affordable rooms; just steps from Dolores Park and the vibrant Castro District on a Muni line; free Wi-Fi; elaborate gardens. **Cons:** stairs can be challenging for those with limited mobility. [$] *Rooms from: $169* ✉ *520 Church St., Mission* ☎ *415/621–4139* 🌐 *parkerguesthouse.com* 🛏 *21 rooms* 🍴 *Breakfast* ✥ *3:D5.*

PACIFIC HEIGHTS AND JAPANTOWN

PACIFIC HEIGHTS

$$$$ HOTEL Fodor's Choice ★

🏨 **Hotel Drisco.** Pretend you're a resident of one of the wealthiest residential neighborhoods in San Francisco at this understated, elegant 1903 Edwardian hotel, where the pale yellow-and-white rooms are genteelly furnished and some have sweeping city views. **Pros:** great service and many amenities; comfortable rooms; quiet residential retreat; 24-hour room service. **Cons:** far from downtown (but free car service). [$] *Rooms from: $425* ✉ *2901 Pacific Ave., Pacific Heights* ☎ *415/346–2880, 800/634–7277* 🌐 *www.hoteldrisco.com* 🛏 *29 rooms, 19 suites* 🍴 *Breakfast* ✥ *2:D4.*

$$ HOTEL

🏨 **Hotel Majestic.** Built in 1902 as a private residence, this five-story white Edwardian is the city's oldest continually operating hotel—movie-star sisters Joan Fontaine and Olivia de Havilland once lived in these spacious rooms with poster beds and claw-foot tubs. **Pros:** quintessential San Francisco hotel; destination café; Victorian flavor; quiet neighborhood; spacious rooms; perfect for a romantic getaway; better rates for extended stays. **Cons:** to get downtown, take the bus or walk 15 minutes. [$] *Rooms from: $162* ✉ *1500 Sutter St., Pacific Heights* ☎ *415/441–1100, 800/869–8966* 🌐 *www.thehotelmajestic.com* 🛏 *47 rooms, 9 suites* 🍴 *No meals* ✥ *2:G6.*

$$ B&B/INN

🏨 **Jackson Court.** At this B&B and time share in a converted 1900 brownstone mansion on a tony residential block, light, spacious rooms, some with fireplaces and window seats, blend antiques with contemporary furnishings and fresh flowers. **Pros:** pleasant residential area; games for rainy days; rooms are constantly refreshed. **Cons:** no air-conditioning; small and dated bathrooms; no tubs. [$] *Rooms from: $229* ✉ *2198*

Jackson St., Pacific Heights ☎ *415/929–7670* 🌐 *www.jacksoncourt.com* 🛏 *10 rooms* 🍴 *Breakfast* ✥ *2:F4.*

$$ HOTEL FAMILY **Laurel Inn.** The blue-and-tan facade of this stylish inn suggests its 1963 urban-motel origins, yet the spacious rooms themselves are quite modern, decorated in simple earth tones; some have fold-out sofas, and 18 offer kitchenettes. **Pros:** spacious; family- and pet-friendly rooms; fun design; close to Sacramento Street shopping and dining. **Cons:** no air-conditioning; quite a distance from downtown. [$] *Rooms from: $209* ✉ *444 Presidio Ave., Pacific Heights* ☎ *415/567–8467, 800/552–8735* 🌐 *www.jdvhotels.com/hotels/california/san-francisco-hotels/laurel-inn* 🛏 *49 rooms* 🍴 *Breakfast* ✥ *2:C5.*

$$ B&B/INN **Queen Anne Hotel.** Built in the 1890s as a girls' finishing school, this Victorian mansion has a large comfortable parlor and guest rooms with such touches as painted cherub murals and, in some, wood-burning fireplaces. **Pros:** lots of character; free weekday car service. **Cons:** 15-minute walk to downtown; slightly dated; some guests complain of stuffy, airless rooms. [$] *Rooms from: $249* ✉ *1590 Sutter St., Pacific Heights* ☎ *415/441–2828, 800/227–3970* 🌐 *www.queenanne.com* 🛏 *41 rooms, 7 suites* 🍴 *Breakfast* ✥ *2:G6.*

14

JAPANTOWN

$$ HOTEL **Hotel Kabuki.** Rooms at this pagoda-style Japantown retreat rely on Asian furnishings, and they wow guests with silk-lined kimono robes, Asian kettles, rice-paper shoji screens, ornamental alcoves, and in most, soaking rooms that come with Japanese-style tubs (one foot deeper than Western tubs); 14 boast redwood saunas. **Pros:** serene environment; locally favored restaurant; great neighborhood. **Cons:** a bit of a schlep from downtown. [$] *Rooms from: $249* ✉ *1625 Post St., at Laguna St., Japantown* ☎ *415/922–3200, 800/533–4567* 🌐 *www.jdvhotels.com* 🛏 *204 rooms, 14 suites* 🍴 *No meals* ✥ *2:G6.*

$$$ HOTEL FAMILY **Hotel Tomo.** Inspired by the comic phenomena manga and anime, the Tomo draws hipsters and Japanophiles eager to immerse themselves in Japanese pop culture (or J-Pop as it is known across the pond) in cozy quarters with Scandinavian wood furnishings and low Japanese-style beds. **Pros:** cool J-Pop style; anime playing on the lobby TV; manga in your room; great price in a fun neighborhood. **Cons:** tight quarters; away from downtown; staff can be icy at times. [$] *Rooms from: $299* ✉ *1800 Sutter St., Japantown* ☎ *415/921–4000* 🌐 *www.hoteltomo.com* 🛏 *125 rooms, 1 suite* 🍴 *No meals* ✥ *2:G6.*

THE RICHMOND AND SUNSET

$$ HOTEL FAMILY **Ocean Park Motel.** This 1930s art-deco motel lures families, dog lovers, surfers, and locals wanting to escape the hustle of the city and retreat to these quiet, spacious, wood-paneled rooms in the Outer Sunset—one of San Francisco's most promising new neighborhoods. **Pros:** free parking; kitchens in many rooms; reasonable rates; quiet neighborhood. **Cons:** far from tourist sites and downtown; in the foggy part of town. [$] *Rooms from: $155* ✉ *2690 46th Ave., The Richmond* ☎ *415/566–7020* 🌐 *www.oceanparkmotel.com* 🛏 *14 rooms; 11 suites* 🍴 *No meals* ✥ *3:A6.*

$$ HOTEL FAMILY **Seal Rock Inn.** About as far west as you can go in San Francisco without falling into the Pacific, these large rooms with accordion-style dividers separating a queen bed from two twins are a good choice for families with kids. **Pros:** close to the beach; lots of activities for kids. **Cons:** aging rooms; far from the action of the city; in the foggy part of town. [$] *Rooms from: $185* ✉ *545 Point Lobos Ave., The Richmond* ☎ *415/752–8000, 888/732–5762* 🌐 *www.sealrockinn.com* 🛏 *27 rooms* 🍴 *No meals* ✣ *3:A1.*

BY THE AIRPORT

Reasonably priced—and occasionally posh—digs can make this area a fine choice for budget seekers or travelers who disdain the urban bustle.

$ HOTEL **Aloft San Francisco Airport.** On the southern edge of SFO's runway, these compact rooms are comfy enough (and have triple-paned windows with blackout curtains to help dim the noise) but the place to be is the glass-front lobby, taking advantage free Wi-Fi, live music, artful cocktails, and a pool table and house games. **Pros:** hip affordable hotel; indoor heated pool; jogging trail; airport shuttle. **Cons:** can be noisy; a bit pricy for smallish rooms outside of the city. [$] *Rooms from: $149* ✉ *401 E. Millbrae Ave., Millbrae* ☎ *650/443–5500* 🌐 *www.starwoodhotels.com/alofthotels* 🛏 *255 rooms* 🍴 *No meals* ✣ *3:H6.*

$$ HOTEL **Bay Landing Hotel.** The European country style, complete with poster beds and heavy wooden furnishings, is pleasing, but the selling point is the bay-front address, promising unsurpassed views out of the double-paned windows. **Pros:** spectacular bay-front views; friendly staff; breakfast included in rate. **Cons:** a trek from the city; decor feels a bit stuffy. [$] *Rooms from: $249* ✉ *1550 Bayshore Hwy., Burlingame* ☎ *650/259–9000* 🌐 *www.baylandinghotel.com* 🛏 *130 rooms, 3 suites* 🍴 *Breakfast* ✣ *3:H6.*

$$ HOTEL FAMILY **Best Western El Rancho Inn and Suites.** The finest of California landscaping, with redwoods, bougainvilleas and palms, decorates the public spaces, while retro paintings of California postcards enliven otherwise smallish quarters, each with a work desk, wingback chairs, and tiled baths with showers. **Pros:** friendly staff; affordable rooms; outdoor pool; airport shuttle; great Sleep & Fly package for guests to park at the hotel for up to 14 days while traveling. **Cons:** Caltrain noise; about 20 minutes from San Francisco. [$] *Rooms from: $155* ✉ *1100 El Camino Real, Millbrae* ☎ *800/780–7234* 🌐 *www.elranchoinn.com* 🛏 *219 rooms* 🍴 *Breakfast* ✣ *3:H6.*

$$ HOTEL **Embassy Suites San Francisco Airport–Waterfront.** Set on the bay, with clear vistas of airplanes flying above San Francisco in the distance, each refurbished suite has a living room with work area, microwave, sleeper sofa, and bedroom; kitchenettes are conveniently located between the suite's two rooms. **Pros:** low rates; pleasant accommodations. **Cons:** no standard rooms; no concierge. [$] *Rooms from: $249* ✉ *150 Anza Blvd., Burlingame* ☎ *650/342–4600, 800/362–2779* 🌐 *www.sfoburlingame.embassysuites.com* 🛏 *340 suites* 🍴 *Breakfast* ✣ *3:H6.*

PERFORMING
ARTS

Updated by
Jerry James
Stone

Sophisticated, offbeat, and often ahead of the curve, San Francisco's performing arts scene supports world-class opera, ballet, and theater productions, along with alternative-dance events, avant-garde plays, groundbreaking documentaries, and a slew of spoken-word and other literary happenings.

The heart of the mainstream theater district lies on or near Geary Street, mostly west of Union Square, though touring Broadway shows land a little farther afield at big houses like the Orpheum and Golden Gate. But theater can be found all over town. For a bit of culture shock, slip out to eclectic districts like the Mission or Haight, where smaller theater companies reside and short-run and one-night-only performances happen on a regular basis.

The city's opera house and symphony hall present the musical classics, and venues like the Fillmore and the Warfield host major rock and jazz talents, but the city's extensive festival circuit broadens the possibilities considerably. Stern Grove is the nation's oldest summer music festival that remains free still to this day; Noise Pop is the premier alt-rock showcase putting such acts like Modest Mouse on the map; and Hardly Strictly Bluegrass is a beloved celebration of bluegrass, country, and roots music, attracting hundreds of thousands of attendees from all over the nation every year.

The range of offerings is just as eclectic on the film front. San Francisco moviegoers love blockbuster hits like everyone else, but they also champion little-known indie and art-house flicks and flock to the interactive sing-along musicals presented at Castro Theatre. Nearly every month an important film festival takes place. During warmer months, many of the city's parks host free movie nights outdoors showcasing film classics or pop-culture favorites.

San Francisco also has a rich dance scene, from classical dancers to jugglers. And it doesn't take stadium seating to make a performance space. Cafés, clubs, and bookstores often host poetry readings or author lectures.

PERFORMING ARTS PLANNER

TICKETS 101

The opera, symphony, the San Francisco Ballet's *The Nutcracker,* and touring hit musicals are often sold out in advance. Tickets are usually available for other shows within a day of the performance.

City Box Office. This charge-by-phone service sells tickets for many performances and lectures. You can also buy tickets online, or in person on weekdays from 9:30 to 5:30. ✉ *180 Redwood St., Suite 100, off Van Ness Ave., between Golden Gate Ave. and McAllister St., Civic Center* ☎ *415/392–4400 ⊕ www.cityboxoffice.com.*

San Francisco Performances. SFP brings an eclectic array of top-flight global music and dance talents to various venues—mostly the Yerba Buena Center for the Arts, Davies Symphony Hall, and Herbst Theatre. Artists have included Yo-Yo Ma, Edgar Meyer, the Paul Taylor Dance Company, and Midori. Tickets can be purchased in person through City Box Office, online, or by phone. ✉ *500 Sutter St., Suite 710, Financial District* ☎ *415/392–2545 ⊕ www.performances.org.*

Tickets.com. You can charge tickets for everything from jazz concerts to Giants games by phone or online. ☎ *800/955–5566 ⊕ www.tickets. com.*

TIX Bay Area. Half-price, same-day tickets for many local and touring shows go on sale (cash only) at the TIX booth in Union Square, which is open daily from 10 to 6. Discount purchases can also be made online. ✉ *Powell St. between Geary and Post Sts., Union Sq.* ☎ *415/433–7827 ⊕ www.tixbayarea.com.*

LISTING INFORMATION

The best guide to the arts is printed in the "Datebook" section and the "96 Hours" section of the *San Francisco Chronicle* (⊕ *www.sfgate. com*). Also check out the city's free alternative weeklies, including *SF Weekly* (⊕ *www.sfweekly.com*) and the *San Francisco Bay Guardian* (⊕ *www.sfbg.com*).

Online, SF Station (⊕ *www.sfstation.com*) has a frequently updated arts and nightlife calendar. *San Francisco Arts Monthly* (⊕ *www.sfarts. org*), which is published at the end of the month, has arts features and events listings, plus a helpful "Visiting San Francisco?" section. For offbeat, emerging-artist performances, consult CounterPULSE (⊕ *www. counterpulse.org*).

DANCE

San Francisco has always been a hotbed of dance. Local groups such as Alonzo King's LINES Ballet tour extensively and are well regarded by national dance critics. Robert Moses' Kin Dance Company uses everything from ballet to hip-hop as a means for social commentary. But classical-ballet lovers won't be left out; the highly regarded San Francisco Ballet excels at both traditional and contemporary repertoires. **Dancers' Group** (⊕ *www.dancersgroup.org*) is a website with events and resource listings for dancers and dance aficionados. The

15

Web-only **DanceView Times** (⊕ *www.danceviewtimes.com*) reviews productions and events.

Alonzo King LINES Ballet. Since 1982 this company has been staging the fluid and gorgeous ballets of choreographer and founder Alonzo King, sometimes in collaboration with top-notch world musicians such as Zakir Hussain and Hamza El Din. Ballets incorporate both classical and modern techniques, with experimental set design, costumes, and music. The San Francisco season is in spring. ⊠ *26 7th St., SoMa* ☎ *415/863–3040* ⊕ *www.linesballet.org.*

FAMILY **ODC/San Francisco.** Highly popular with kids, this 10-person dance troupe holds an annual Yuletide version of *The Velveteen Rabbit* (mid-November to mid-December), at the Yerba Buena Center for the Arts, that ranks among the city's best holiday-season performances. The group's main repertory season generally runs intermittently between January and June. ⊠ *351 Shotwell St., Mission* ☎ *415/863–6606* ⊕ *www.odcdance.org.*

RAWdance Concept Series. A modern-day salon is made for both dance aficionados and those just ballet-curious. The semiregular series takes places in a small and awkward space, but it's perfect for making new friends. The choreography is colorful and "outside the lines" of your usual dance troupe. In true bohemian spirit, admission is pay-what-you-can, and sometimes food is served as well. ⊠ *105 Sanchez St., Lower Haight* ☎ *415/686–0728* ⊕ *www.rawdance.org.*

Robert Moses' Kin Dance Company. Founded in 1995 by choreographer Robert Moses and known for its provocative themes, the Kin makes a study of race, class, culture, and gender with the use of eclectic movements, such as jazz, hip-hop, and ballet. ⊠ *870 Market St., SoMa* ☎ *415/252–8384* ⊕ *www.robertmoseskin.org.*

Fodor'sChoice **San Francisco Ballet.** For ballet lovers the nation's oldest professional
★ company is reason alone to visit the Bay Area. SFB's performances, for the past three decades under direction of Helgi Tomasson, have won critical raves. The primary season runs from February through May. The repertoire includes full-length ballets such as *Don Quixote* and *Sleeping Beauty*; the December presentation of *The Nutcracker* is truly spectacular. The company also performs bold new dances from star choreographers such as William Forsythe and Mark Morris, alongside modern classics by George Balanchine and Jerome Robbins. Tickets are available at the **War Memorial Opera House.** ⊠ *War Memorial Opera House, 301 Van Ness Ave., at Grove St., Civic Center* ☎ *415/865–2000* ⊕ *www.sfballet.org.*

Smuin Ballet/SF. Former San Francisco Ballet director Michael Smuin founded this company, whose works are renowned for their gorgeous fluidity. The company regularly integrates popular music—everything from Gershwin to the Beatles and Elton John—into performances, most of which take place at the Yerba Buena Center for the Arts. ⊠ *44 Gough St., Lower Haight* ☎ *415/556–5000* ⊕ *www.smuinballet.org.*

FILM

Films of every stripe—3-D blockbusters, art-house indies, classic revivals—find an audience in the Bay Area. The region is also a filmmaking center, where documentaries and experimental works are produced on modest budgets, feature films and television programs are shot on location, and pioneering animation companies like Pixar Animation Studios are just across the bay.

MOVIE THEATERS

Balboa Theatre. This historic theater, which just celebrated its 88th birthday, features a combination of classic movies, second-run hits, local documentaries, and art-house favorites. ✉ *3630 Balboa St., at 37th St., The Richmond* ☎ *415/221–8184* ⊕ *www.balboamovies.com.*

Fodor's Choice **Castro Theatre.** A large neon sign marks the exterior of this 1,400-plus
★ seat art-deco movie palace whose exotic interior transports you back to 1922, when the theater first opened. High-profile festivals present films here, and classic revivals and foreign flicks also unfold. ■ TIP→ **Lines for the Castro's popular sing-along movie musicals often trail down the block.** ✉ *429 Castro St., near Market St., Castro* ☎ *415/621–6350* ⊕ *www.castrotheatre.com.*

Embarcadero Center Cinemas. Shows often sell out at this extremely popular five-screen theater, which screens the best in first-run independent, art house, and foreign films. ✉ *1 Embarcadero Center, promenade level, Embarcadero* ☎ *415/352–0835.*

Opera Plaza Cinemas. The four theaters and their screens are small, but this is often the last place you can see an independent or foreign film before it ends its run in the city. It's great for indie-film-loving procrastinators, but if you arrive late for the show, you may have to sit in the front row of the tiny screening room. ✉ *601 Van Ness Ave., between Turk St. and Golden Gate Ave., Civic Center* ☎ *415/771–0183.*

Roxie Theater. This is San Francisco's oldest continually operating theater, which turned 100 back in 2009. Film noir and indie features and documentaries, as well as first-run movies and classic foreign cinema, are the specialties. ■ TIP→ **Monday nights are discounted.** ✉ *3117 16th St., between Valencia and Guerrero Sts., Mission* ☎ *415/863–1087* ⊕ *www. roxie.com.*

San Francisco Cinematheque. In the spotlight are experimental film and digital media, with many screenings at the Yerba Buena Center for the Arts. ✉ *Yerba Buena Center for the Arts, 701 Mission St., SoMa* ☎ *415/552–1990* ⊕ *www.sfcinematheque.org.*

Sundance Kabuki Cinema. Moviegoing here is a first-class experience. The seating is comfy and spaced out, and you can reserve your seat in advance online, so you don't need to arrive an hour early to snag one. The standard concession items are available, along with food options that are borderline gourmet. Beer and wine—which you can take into the theater!—are also served. Film screenings run the gamut from mainstream blockbusters to offbeat indies. ✉ *1881 Post St., at Fillmore St., Japantown* ☎ *415/346–3243* ⊕ *www.sundancecinemas.com.*

15

FILM FESTIVALS

Area film festivals, especially the popular San Francisco International Film Festival, often attract sell-out crowds; many screenings feature Q&A sessions with directors and actors from around the world. Smaller niche events duplicate the format on a more intimate scale. During the summer months, you can even catch festival screenings outdoors in the city's many parks.

American Indian Film Festival. Presented by the American Indian Film Institute, this event has been based in San Francisco since 1977. Each November the festival takes over various venues, including the Palace of Fine Arts Theatre. ☎ *415/554–0525* ⊕ *www.aifisf.com.*

Film Night in the Park. One of the best times you can have watching a movie in San Francisco—and it's free—the Film Night in the Park is wildly popular. Put on by the San Francisco Neighborhood Theater Foundation, the event shows free films throughout the city from mid- to late summer. Films like *The Graduate, JAWS 3 in 3D, Sixteen Candles,* and *Citizen Cane* are screened in outdoor spaces such as Union Square or Dolores Park. All shows begin at dusk. ■ **TIP**→ **Bring a picnic, but chairs are not welcome.** ☎ *415/465–3456* ⊕ *www.sfntf.org.*

San Francisco Independent Film Festival (Indiefest and Docfest). This popular event presents a slate of movies that are defiantly out of the mainstream. Indiefest caters to a younger demographic and specializes in oddball fare rarely programmed at other festivals; Docfest performs the same service for documentaries that you won't find at the local multiplex. ☎ *415/820–3907* ⊕ *www.sfindie.com.*

San Francisco International Asian American Film Festival. Asian and Asian-American cinema is the focus of this March festival, presented by the Center for Asian American Media. The lineup includes feature and short films and videos—everything from animation to documentaries. ☎ *415/863–0814* ⊕ *www.caamedia.org.*

San Francisco International Film Festival. For two weeks at the end of spring, the San Francisco Film Society—which also sponsors year-round screenings and film series—takes over several theaters, including the Castro Theatre, the Sundance Kabuki Cinemas, and Pacific Film Archive to launch this festival. The event schedules about 300 films, documentaries, and videos from 50 countries; many are U.S. premieres. ⊕ *www.sffs.org.*

San Francisco International Lesbian & Gay Film Festival. The world's oldest and largest festival honoring gay and lesbian films takes place at various venues for two weeks in late June. ☎ *415/703–8655* ⊕ *www.frameline.org/festival.*

San Francisco International South Asian Film Festival. Documentaries, feature films, and Bollywood movies are shown at this weeklong festival in November. ⊕ *www.thirdi.org/festival.*

San Francisco Jewish Film Festival. In late July and early August, the Castro Theatre and other Bay Area venues screen films as part of this event. Parties on the opening and closing nights of the festival celebrate the films and filmmakers. ☎ *415/621–0556* ⊕ *www.sfjff.org.*

MUSIC

San Francisco's symphony and opera perform in the Civic Center area, but musical ensembles can be found all over the Bay Area in smaller spaces, churches, museums, restaurants, and parks.

CONCERTS

42nd Street Moon. This group produces delightful "semistaged" concert performances of rare chestnuts from Broadway's golden age of musical theater, such as *L'il Abner* and *The Boys From Syracuse*. ⊠ *Eureka Theatre, 215 Jackson St., Financial District* ☎ *415/255–8207* ⊕ *www.42ndstmoon.org.*

Eureka Theatre. The Eureka Theatre hosts most 42nd Street Moon shows. ⊠ *215 Jackson St., between Front and Battery Sts., Financial District.*

Chanticleer. A Bay Area treasure, this all-male a-cappella ensemble stages lively and technically flawless performances that show off a repertoire ranging from sacred medieval music to show tunes to contemporary avant-garde works. ☎ *415/252–8589* ⊕ *www.chanticleer.org.*

Kronos Quartet. Twentieth-century works and a number of premieres make up the programs for this always entertaining, Grammy Award–winning string ensemble, which spends much of the year traveling throughout the United States and abroad. ⊕ *www.kronosquartet.org.*

Noontime Concerts at Old St. Mary's Cathedral. This Gothic Revival church, completed in 1872 and rebuilt after the 1906 earthquake, hosts a notable chamber-music series on Tuesday at 12:30. ⊠ *660 California St., Financial District* ☎ *415/777–3211* ⊕ *www.noontimeconcerts.org.*

Old First Concerts. The well-respected Friday-evening and Sunday-afternoon series includes chamber music, choral works, vocal soloists, new music, and jazz. ⊠ *Old First Presbyterian Church, 1751 Sacramento St., at Van Ness Ave., Van Ness/Polk* ☎ *415/474–1608* ⊕ *www.oldfirstconcerts.org.*

Fodor's Choice
★ **San Francisco Symphony.** One of America's top orchestras performs from September through May, with additional summer performances of light classical music and show tunes. The orchestra and its charismatic music director, Michael Tilson Thomas, known for his daring programming of 20th-century American works, often perform with soloists of the caliber of Andre Watts, Gil Shaham, and Renée Fleming. The symphony's adventurous projects include its collaboration with the heavy metal band Metallica. ■TIP→ **Deep discounts on tickets are often available through Travelzoo, Groupon, and other vendors.** ⊠ *Davies Symphony Hall, 201 Van Ness Ave., at Grove St., Civic Center* ☎ *415/864–6000* ⊕ *www.sfsymphony.org.*

SFJAZZ Center. Jazz legends Branford Marsalis and Herbie Hancock have performed at the snazzy center, as have Rosanne Cash and world-music favorite Esperanza Spaulding. The sightlines and acoustics here impress. Shows often sell out quickly. ⊠ *201 Franklin St., Hayes Valley* ☎ *866/920–5299* ⊕ *www.sfjazz.org.*

15

MUSIC FESTIVALS

Hardly Strictly Bluegrass Festival. The city's top free music event, as well as one of the greatest gatherings for bluegrass, country, and roots music in the country, takes place in late September or early October. Roughly 50,000 fans turn out to see the likes of Willie Nelson, Emmylou Harris, Jimmie Dale Gilmore, and Del McCoury at Hellman Hollow (formerly Speedway Meadows) in Golden Gate Park. ⊠ *Hellman Hollow, 50 Overlook Dr., San Francisco* ⊕ *www.strictlybluegrass.com.*

How Weird Street Faire. Home to 10-plus music stages, ranging from drum and bass to techno-pop, this music festival for up-and-coming DJs is part Mardis Gras, part Burning Man, and *all* San Francisco. ⊠ *Howard St., near 2nd St., SoMa* ⊕ *www.howweird.org.*

Noise Pop Festival. This weeklong festival in February or March is widely considered to be one of the country's top showcases for what's new in indie-pop and alt-rock and is held at Slim's, the Great American Music Hall, The Independent, and other cool clubs. Founded in 1993, the low-key festival has helped local fans discover such talented acts as Modest Mouse, Kristin Hersh, and Bettie Serveert. (Phone info about the event is best obtained by calling the individual venues.) ☎ *415/375–3370* ⊕ *www.noisepop.com.*

San Francisco Jazz Festival. Every year starting in October, concert halls, clubs, and churches throughout the city host this acclaimed two-week festival. The popular event, which got its start in 1983, has featured such big-name acts as Ornette Coleman, Sonny Rollins, and McCoy Tyner, as well as newer jazz stars like Brad Mehldau and Chris Botti. ☎ *415/398–5655* ⊕ *www.sfjazz.org.*

Fodor'sChoice
★
Stern Grove Festival. The nation's oldest continual free summer music festival hosts Sunday-afternoon performances of symphony, opera, jazz, pop music, and dance. The amphitheater is in a beautiful eucalyptus grove, perfect for picnicking before the show. World-music favorites such as Ojos de Brujas, Seu Jorge, and Shuggie Otis get the massive crowds dancing. ■ TIP➔ Shows generally start at 2 pm, but arrive hours earlier if you want to see the performances up close—and dress for cool weather, as the fog often rolls in. ⊠ *Sloat Blvd. at 19th Ave., Sunset* ☎ *415/252–6252* ⊕ *www.sterngrove.org.*

OPERA

Pocket Opera. A lively, modestly priced alternative to grand opera, this company's concert performances of popular and seldom-heard works are mostly in English. Offenbach's operettas are frequently on the bill during the season, which runs from February through July. Concerts are held at various locations, including the Legion of Honor. ☎ *415/972–8934* ⊕ *www.pocketopera.org.*

Fodor'sChoice
★
San Francisco Opera. Founded in 1923, this internationally recognized organization has occupied the War Memorial Opera House since the building's completion in 1932. From September through January and June through July, the company presents a dozen or so operas. SF opera frequently collaborates with European companies and presents

unconventional, sometimes edgy projects designed to attract younger audiences. Translations are projected above the stage during most non-English productions. ⊠ *War Memorial Opera House, 301 Van Ness Ave., at Grove St., Civic Center* ☎ *415/864–3330 tickets* ⊕ *www.sfopera.com* ☞ *Box office: 199 Grove St., at Van Ness Ave.; open Mon. 10–5, Tues.–Fri. 10–6.*

PERFORMING ARTS CENTERS

Fodor's Choice ★ **War Memorial Opera House.** With its soaring vaulted ceilings and marble foyer, this elegant 3,146-seat venue, built in 1932, rivals the Old World theaters of Europe. Part of the San Francisco War Memorial and Performing Arts Center, which also includes Davies Symphony Hall and Herbst Theatre, this is the home of the San Francisco Opera and the San Francisco Ballet. ⊠ *301 Van Ness Ave., at Grove St., Civic Center* ☎ *415/621–6600* ⊕ *www.sfwmpac.org.*

Fodor's Choice ★ **Yerba Buena Center for the Arts.** Across the street from the San Francisco Museum of Modern Art and abutting a lovely urban garden, this performing arts complex schedules interdisciplinary art exhibitions, touring and local dance troupes, music, film programs, and contemporary theater events. You can depend on the quality of the productions at Yerba Buena. Film buffs often come here to check out the San Francisco Cinematheque (⊕ *www.sfcinematheque.org*), which showcases experimental film and digital media. And dance enthusiasts can attend concerts by a roster of city companies that perform here, including Smuin Ballet/SF (⊕ *www.smuinballet.org*), ODC/San Francisco (⊕ *www.odc-dance.org*), the Margaret Jenkins Dance Company (⊕ *www.mjdc.org*), and Alonzo King's Lines Ballet (⊕ *www.linesballet.org*). The Lamplighters (⊕ *www.lamplighters.org*), an alternative opera that specializes in Gilbert and Sullivan, also performs here. ⊠ *3rd and Howard Sts., SoMa* ☎ *415/978–2787* ⊕ *www.ybca.org.*

SPOKEN WORD AND READINGS

Aspiring and established writers, poets, and performers step up to the mike all over town and put their words and egos on the line. Check listings in the alternative weeklies or the *San Francisco Sunday Chronicle* (⊕ *www.sfgate.com*).

Cafe International. An open-mike session follows one or more featured readers here every Friday night at 8. Spoken-word performances are interspersed with acoustic musical acts. ⊠ *508 Haight St., at Fillmore St., Lower Haight* ☎ *415/552–7390.*

Fodor's Choice ★ **City Arts & Lectures.** Each year this program includes more than 20 fascinating conversations with writers, composers, actors, politicians, scientists, and others. The Nourse Theater, in the Performing Arts Center, is usually the venue. Past speakers have included Salman Rushdie, Ken Burns, and Linda Ronstadt. ⊠ *Nourse Theater, 275 Hayes St., Lower Haight* ☎ *415/392–4400* ⊕ *www.cityarts.net.*

Commonwealth Club of California. The nation's oldest public-affairs forum hosts speakers as diverse as Erin Brockovich and Bill Gates;

15

every president since Teddy Roosevelt has addressed the club. Topics range from culture and politics to economics and foreign policy. Events are open to nonmembers; contact the club for the current schedule of events. Venues vary by speaker. Lectures are broadcast on NPR. ⊠ *595 Market St., at 2nd St., Financial District* ☎ *415/597–6700* ⊕ *www. commonwealthclub.org.*

West Coast Live. Billed as "San Francisco's Live Radio Show to the World," the program invites an audience to its weekly broadcasts, many from the San Francisco Ferry Building or the Freight & Salvage Coffeehouse in Berkeley. The eclectic guest list includes personalities such as Craig Newmark, Rita Moreno, Jamaica Kincaid, and Adam Savage and Jamie Hyneman (the *Mythbusters* guys). ☎ *415/664–9500* ⊕ *www.wcl.org.*

Writers with Drinks. This quirky, oft-madcap, and hilariously funny spoken-word event is part reading, part circus variety show. Writers range from unknowns to rising stars and the occasional well-known author. Writers with Drinks usually takes place at the Make-Out Room, at 3225 22nd Street in the Mission. ⊠ *Usually takes place at Make-Out Room, 3225 22nd St., Mission* ⊕ *www.writerswithdrinks.com.*

THEATER

The three major commercial theaters—the Curran, Golden Gate, and Orpheum—are operated by the Shorenstein-Nederlander organization, which books touring plays and musicals, some before they open on Broadway. Theatre Bay Area (⊕ *www.theatrebayarea.org*) lists most Bay Area performances online.

American Conservatory Theater. One of the nation's leading regional theater companies presents about eight plays a year, from classics to contemporary works, often in repertory. The season runs from early fall to late spring. In December ACT stages a beloved version of Charles Dickens's *A Christmas Carol.* ⊠ *415 Geary St., Union Sq.* ☎ *415/749–2228* ⊕ *www.act-sf.org.*

Curran Theater. Some of the biggest touring shows come to this theater, which has hosted classical music, dance, and stage performances since its 1925 opening. Shows are of the long-running Broadway musical variety, such as *Stomp* and *Jersey Boys,* and the seasonal *A Christmas Carol.* ⊠ *445 Geary St., at Mason St., Union Sq.* ☎ *415/551–2000* ⊕ *www.shnsf.com.*

Exit Theatre. *The* place for absurdist and experimental theater, this three-stage venue also presents the annual **Fringe Festival** in September. ⊠ *156 Eddy St., between Mason and Taylor Sts., Union Sq.* ☎ *415/931–1094* ⊕ *www.theexit.org.*

Golden Gate Theater. This stylishly refurbished movie theater is now primarily a musical house. Touring productions of popular Broadway shows and revivals are its mainstays. ⊠ *Golden Gate Ave. at Taylor St., Tenderloin* ☎ *415/551–2000* ⊕ *www.shnsf.com.*

Lorraine Hansberry Theatre. The performance of plays by black writers such as August Wilson and Langston Hughes is the raison d'être of this

Arts and Culture Beyond the City

Although most folks from outlying areas drive *into* San Francisco to enjoy the performing arts, there are plenty of reasons to head *out* of the city.

FILM

Pacific Film Archive. Affiliated with the University of California, this theater screens a comprehensive mix of classics, American, and foreign films. ⊠ *2575 Bancroft Way, near Bowditch St., Berkeley* ☎ *510/642-0808* ⊕ *www.bampfa.berkeley.edu.*

Paramount Theatre. The spectacular art-deco Paramount screens a few vintage flicks (*The Sting, Casablanca*) every month and presents live events. ⊠ *2025 Broadway, near 19th St. BART station, Oakland* ☎ *510/465-6400* ⊕ *www.paramounttheatre.com.*

MUSIC

Berkeley Symphony Orchestra. The Berkeley Symphony Orchestra rose to prominence under Kent Nagano's baton and continues to prosper with Joana Carneiro at the helm. The emphasis is on 20th-century composers. The orchestra plays a few concerts each year, in the University of California–Berkeley's Zellerbach Hall and elsewhere in Berkeley. ■ TIP→ The acoustics in Zellerbach Hall are poor; sit in the front or middle orchestra for the best sound. ☎ *510/841-2800* ⊕ *www.berkeleysymphony.org.*

Freight & Salvage Coffeehouse. Some of the most talented practitioners of folk, blues, Cajun, and bluegrass perform at the alcohol-free venue. ⊠ *2020 Addison St., Berkeley* ☎ *510/644-2020* ⊕ *www.thefreight.org.*

Yoshi's. This popular Oakland club is one of the nation's best jazz venues. ⊠ *510 Embarcadero St., between Washington and Clay Sts., Oakland* ☎ *510/238-9200* ⊕ *www.yoshis.com.*

THEATER

Berkeley Repertory Theatre. This Tony Award–winning group is the American Conservatory Theater's major rival for leadership among the region's resident professional companies. It performs an adventurous mix of classics and new plays from fall to spring in its theater complex, near BART's Downtown Berkeley Station. Parking is difficult, so arrive early if you're coming by car. ⊠ *2025 Addison St., Berkeley* ☎ *510/647-2949* ⊕ *www.berkeleyrep.org.*

Cal Performances. Held at various venues on the University of California–Berkeley campus from September through May, this popular series offers the Bay Area's most varied bill of internationally acclaimed artists in all disciplines. ☎ *510/642-9988* ⊕ *www.calperformances.org.*

company, which performs at various venues throughout the city. ⊠ *777 Jones St, at Sutter St., San Francisco* ☎ *415/474-8800* ⊕ *www.lhtsf.org.*

Magic Theatre. Once Sam Shepard's favorite showcase, the pint-size Magic presents works by rising American playwrights such as Matthew Wells, Karen Hartman, and Claire Chafee. ⊠ *Fort Mason, Bldg. D, Laguna St. at Marina Blvd., Marina* ☎ *415/441–8822* ⊕ *www.magictheatre.org.*

The Marsh. Experimental works, including one-man and one-woman shows, works in progress, and new-vaudeville shows can be seen here. ✉ *1062 Valencia St., at 22nd St., Mission* ☎ *415/282–3055* ⊕ *www. themarsh.org.*

New Conservatory Theatre Center. This three-stage complex hosts the annual **Pride Season,** focusing on contemporary gay- and lesbian-themed works, as well as other events, including educational plays for young people. ✉ *25 Van Ness Ave., between Fell and Oak Sts., Civic Center* ☎ *415/861–8972* ⊕ *www.nctcsf.org.*

FAMILY **New Pickle Circus.** The acrobatically inclined group generally performs at the Circus Center around Christmastime, with fire-breathing jugglers and high-flying trapeze artists. There are a few smaller productions in San Francisco and the Bay Area throughout the year. ✉ *755 Frederick St., San Francisco* ☎ *415/759–8123* ⊕ *www.circuscenter.org.*

Orpheum Theater. The biggest touring shows, such as *Hairspray* and *The Lion King,* are performed at this gorgeously restored 2,500-seat venue. The theater, opened in 1926 as a vaudeville stage, is as much an attraction as the shows. It was modeled after the Spanish baroque palaces and is considered one of the most beautiful theaters in the world; the interior walls have ornate cathedral-like stonework, and the gilded plaster ceiling is perforated with tiny lights. ✉ *1192 Market St., at Hyde St., Tenderloin, San Francisco* ☎ *415/551–2000* ⊕ *www.shnsf.com.*

FAMILY **San Francisco Mime Troupe.** The politically leftist, barbed satires of this Tony Award–winning troupe are hardly mime in the Marcel Marceau sense. The group performs afternoon musicals at area parks from the July 4 weekend through September, and taking one in is a perfect way to spend a sunny summer day. ☎ *415/285–1717* ⊕ *www.sfmt.org.*

Fodor's Choice **Teatro ZinZanni.** In a fabulous antique Belgian dance-hall tent, contor-★ tionists, chanteuses, jugglers, illusionists, and circus performers entertain audiences who dine on a surprisingly good five-course dinner. The show, which ran for 11 years on a waterfront pier, is scheduled to debut in its new permanent home in 2015. During summer and on most weekends, reservations are essential. ✉ *Broadway and the Embarcadero, Northern Waterfront* ☎ *415/438–2668* ⊕ *www.zinzanni.org.*

Theatre Rhinoceros. Gay and lesbian performers and playwrights are showcased at various venues. ✉ *1 Sansome St., Suite 3500, Financial District* ☎ *800/838–3006 tickets, 415/552–4100 offices* ⊕ *www. therhino.org.*

NIGHTLIFE

Updated by
Jerry James
Stone

After hours, the city's business folk and workers give way to costume-clad partygoers, hippies and hipsters, downtown divas, frat boys, and those who prefer something a little more clothing-optional. Downtown and the Financial District remain pretty serious even after dark, and Nob Hill is staid, though you can't beat views from penthouse lounges, the most famous being the Top of the Mark (Hopkins). Nearby North Beach is an even better starting point for an evening out.

Always lively, North Beach's options include family-friendly dining spots, historic bars from the city's bohemian past (among them Jack Kerouac's old haunts), and even comedy clubs where stars such as Robin Williams and Jay Leno cut their teeth. In SoMa there are plenty of places to catch a drink before a Giants game and brewpubs to celebrate in afterward. SoMa also hosts some of the hottest dance clubs, along with some saucy gay bars. While Union Square can be a bit trendy, even the swanky establishments have loosened things up in recent years.

Heading west to Hayes Valley, a more sophisticated crowd dabbles in the burgeoning "culinary cocktail movement." Up-and-coming singles gravitate north of here to Cow Hollow and the Marina. Polk Street was the gay mecca before the Castro and still hosts some wild bars, but things get downright outlandish in the Castro district. Indie hipsters of all persuasions populate the Mission and Haight districts by night. Keep in mind, though, that some of the best times San Francisco has to offer can be found off the beaten path. And a good party can still be found in even the sleepiest of neighborhoods, such as Bernal Heights and Dogpatch.

NIGHTLIFE PLANNER

HOURS

Sports bars and hotel bars tend to be open on Sundays, but others may be closed. A few establishments—especially wine bars and restaurant bars—also close on Monday. Last call is typically at 1:30 am; Financial District bars catering to the after-work crowd, however, may stop serving as early as 9 or 10 pm, and generally close by midnight at the latest. Bands and performers usually take the stage between 8 and 11 pm. A few after-hours clubs are open until 4 am or all night.

MONEY

While larger establishments will take everything from Visa to Apple Pay, payment options can vary by neighborhood. It's easy to get by on plastic in Union Square or the Marina, but the Castro and Mission are hard cash only.

LATE-NIGHT TRANSPORTATION

You're better off taking public transportation or taxis on weekend nights, unless you're heading downtown (Financial District or Union Square) and are willing to park in a lot. There's only street parking in North Beach, the Mission, Castro, and the Haight, and finding a spot can be practically impossible. Muni stops running between 1 am and 5 am but has its limited Owl Service on a few lines—including the K, N, L, 90, 91, 14, 24, 38, and 22—every 30 minutes. Service cuts have put a dent in frequency; check ⊕ *www.sfmuni.com* for current details. You can sometimes hail a taxi on the street in well-trodden nightlife locations like North Beach or the Mission, but you can also call for one (☎ *415/626–2345 Yellow Cab, 415/648–3181 Arrow*). The best option by far is booking a taxi with a smartphone-based app (⊕ *www.uber. com, www.lyft.com*). ■ TIP→ Cabs in San Francisco are more expensive than in other areas of the United States; expect to pay at least $15 to get anywhere within the city. Keep in mind that BART service across the bay stops shortly after midnight.

LOCAL LISTINGS

Entertainment information is printed in the "Datebook" section and the more calendar-based "96 Hours" section of the *San Francisco Chronicle* (⊕ *www.sfgate.com*). Also consult any of the free alternative weeklies, notably the *SF Weekly* (⊕ *www.sfweekly.com*), which blurbs nightclubs and music, and the *San Francisco Bay Guardian* (⊕ *www.sfbg.com*), which lists neighborhood, avant-garde, and budget events. SF Station (⊕ *www.sfstation.com*; online only) has an up-to-date calendar of entertainment goings-on.

SMOKING

By law, bars and clubs are smoke-free, except for the very few that are staffed entirely by the owners.

TICKETS AND COVERS

The cover charge at smaller, less popular clubs ranges from $5 to $10, and credit cards are rarely accepted for this. Covers at larger venues may spike to $30, and tickets usually can be purchased through ⊕ *www.*

16

TOP 5 BARS

■ **Cliff House:** Granted, it's pricey and the interior is ho-hum, but huge picture windows with views of the rolling Pacific remind you why you came here in the first place.

■ **El Rio:** The perfect dive, with inexpensive drink specials, a stellar patio, and an ever-changing calendar of events (free oysters on Friday, salsa Sunday).

■ **Smuggler's Cove:** Despite the gaudy (and distracting) pirate theme, this joint serves superb cocktails.

Rum is king, with more than 200 different styles available.

■ **Vesuvio Café:** This is one of those rare bars with a fleet of regulars but is also a place that everyone knows about. It's in one of the most touristy parts of town, but still manages to be cool.

■ **Yield:** Planet-friendly wines and reclaimed decor, plus small plates using locally sourced ingredients are just a few reasons to visit this off-the-beaten-path wine bar.

tickets.com or ⊕ *www.ticketweb.com*. Bars often have covers for live music—usually $5 to $15.

WHAT TO WEAR

Except for a few skyline lounges, you're not expected to dress up. Still, San Franciscans are a stylish bunch. For women, dressed-up jeans with heels and cute tops are one popular uniform; for guys it's button-up shirts or designer tees and well-tailored jeans. Of course, stylish means a black designer outfit at one place and funky thrift-store togs at another, so you have to use your judgment.

UNION SQUARE AND CHINATOWN

UNION SQUARE

Known mostly for high-end shopping and the surrounding theater district, the square has its own share of nightlife. You'll find places pouring interesting cocktails, a good mix of locals and tourists, and nods to nightspots and eras past. Cantina is the perfect stop for cocktails crafted from locally grown ingredients.

BARS

Cantina. Let the skull and crossbones over the entryway of this intimate Latin hangout provide fair warning, because the magic the bartenders perform here is pure voodoo. The drinks are handcrafted with fresh ingredients, homemade bitters, and even homegrown citrus fruits. Because of this the service can be slow during busy times; fortunately, many cocktails are served in pitchers. ■ TIP→ **The most popular cocktail is the vibrant laughing buddha—vodka, lime, ginger, and Serrano chilies.** ⊠ *580 Sutter St., at Mason St., Union Sq.* ☎ *415/398–0195* ⊕ *www.cantinasf.com* ☾ *Closed Sun.*

Harry Denton's Starlight Room. Forget low-key drinks—the only way to experience Harry Denton's is to go for a show. Cough up the cover charge and enjoy the opulent, over-the-top decor and entertainment (some of the best cover bands in the business, usually playing Top

40 hits from the '60s, '70s, and '80s). Velvet booths and romantic lighting help re-create the 1950s high life on the 21st floor of the Sir Francis Drake Hotel, and the small dance floor is packed on Friday and Saturday nights. Jackets are preferred for men. Call ahead—the room is sometimes closed for private events on weekdays. ⊠ *Sir Francis Drake Hotel, 450 Powell St., between Post and Sutter Sts., Union Sq.* ☏ *415/395–8595* ⊕ *www.starlightroomsf.com.*

Le Colonial. Down an easy-to-miss alley off Taylor Street is what appears to be a two-story plantation house in the center of the city. Without being kitschy, the top-floor bar successfully evokes French-colonial Vietnam, thanks to creaky wooden floors, Victorian sofas, a patio with potted palms, and tasty French-Vietnamese food and tropical cocktails. You'll find local jazz bands playing early in the week, but come the weekend this is a full-on DJ-driven dance party. When you arrive, sweep past the café tables and the hostess and head up the stairs to your left. ⊠ *20 Cosmo Pl., off Taylor St., between Post and Sutter Sts., Union Sq.* ☏ *415/931–3600* ⊕ *www.lecolonialsf.com.*

Redwood Room. Opened in 1933 and updated by designer Philippe Starck in 2001, this lounge at the Clift Hotel is a San Francisco icon. The entire room, floor to ceiling, is paneled with the wood from a single redwood tree, giving the place a rich, monochromatic look. The gorgeous original art-deco sconces and chandeliers still hang, but bizarre video installations on plasma screens also adorn the walls. It's packed on weekend evenings after 10, when young scenesters swarm in; for maximum glamour, visit on a weeknight. ⊠ *Clift Hotel, 495 Geary St., at Taylor St., Union Sq.* ☏ *415/929–2372 for table reservations, 415/775–4700 for hotel* ⊕ *www.clifthotel.com.*

Romper Room. If you weren't of legal drinking age during the '80s, now's your chance to experience the era's ambience. The Romper Room, bubbling over with neon pink and leopard print, is a funky little bar and quasi-dance club located in the city's somewhat cookie-cutter and label-driven Union Square district. The cocktail menu is small and simple, but they guarantee you won't have to wait longer than 90 seconds to get one. ⊠ *25 Maiden La., at Kearny St., Union Sq.* ☏ *415/275–3418* ⊕ *www.romperroom.com.*

Slide. During Prohibition, one of the city's more notorious speakeasies was accessible only via a secret-wall passage and a 15-foot slide that whisked patrons into the basement "restaurant" known as Coffee Dan's (it wasn't really a restaurant). That space has been reclaimed, restored, and aptly renamed Slide. A swanky, modern version of its former self, the place still has a slide, though stairs are also available. On the weekends, DJs spin a mix of hip-hop, downtempo, and Rat Pack–era hits from a 1920s baby grand piano that has been converted to a DJ booth. Like similar-themed bars within the city (⇨ *See Bourbon & Branch*), the facility is completely unmarked. ⊠ *430 Mason St., at Geary St., Union Sq.* ☏ *415/421–1916* ⊕ *www.slidesf.com.*

CHINATOWN

Chinatown's streets are fast-paced and teeming with people, which makes the district's famous alleyways so charming and welcoming. Away from the bustle (and the hustle), you'll find sake bars and beer pubs filled with locals and tourists.

GAY NIGHTLIFE

Bow Bow Cocktail Lounge. At this quirky, inclusive, divey karaoke bar, you can get your kicks performing in front of a sometimes rowdy but nearly always supportive audience of hip young things and Asian business-men. ⊠ *1155 Grant Ave., near Broadway, Chinatown* ☎ *415/421–6730.*

SOMA AND CIVIC CENTER

SOMA

In modern, industrial SoMa you'll find everyone from loyal Giants fans celebrating with locally made brews at 21st Amendment to the gay biker crowd that explodes onto the patio of the Lone Star Saloon, with everyone else apt to wind up at one of The Stud's diverse dance parties. The headliners head to Slim's or the DNA Lounge.

BARS

21st Amendment Brewery. This popular brewery is known for its range of beer types, with multiple taps going at all times. In the spring, the Hell or High Watermelon—a wheat beer—gets rave reviews. ■TIP➔ Serious beer drinkers should try the Back in Black, a black IPA-style beer this brewpub helped pioneer. The space has an upmarket warehouse feel, though exposed wooden ceiling beams, framed photos, whitewashed brick walls, and hardwood floors make it feel cozy. It's a good spot to warm up before a Giants game and an even better place to party after they win. ⊠ *563 2nd St., between Federal and Brannan Sts., SoMa* ☎ *415/369–0900* ⊕ *www.21st-amendment.com.*

City Beer Store. Called CBS by locals, this friendly tasting room cum liquor mart has a wine-bar's sensibility. Perfect for connoisseurs and the merely beer curious, CBS stocks more than 300 different bottled beers, and more than a dozen are on tap. The indecisive can mix and match six-packs to go. ■TIP➔ Come early: The small space fills up quickly on event nights. ⊠ *1168 Folsom St., at 8th St., SoMa* ☎ *415/503–1033* ⊕ *www.citybeerstore.com.*

The Hotel Utah Saloon. This funky hipster spot presents a mix of local bands and young national touring acts performing rock, indie pop, alt-country, and everything in between. The low-ceiling performance space is small, with a few tables grouped around the stage. Be sure to grab a Cuban sandwich from the bar before the show. The bar area takes up about half of this joint and is just as popular as the music. Monday is open-mike night. ⊠ *500 4th St., at Bryant St., SoMa* ☎ *415/546–6300* ⊕ *www.thehotelutah.com.*

MoMo's. This stylish American restaurant and trendy bar has an outdoor patio perfect for sunny days; it's the most popular pre- and postgame bar. The individual pizzas are tasty—and big enough to share. ⊠ *760 2nd St., at King St., SoMa* ☎ *415/227–8660* ⊕ *www.sfmomos.com.*

Nova Bar and Restaurant. Fans thirsty for chic cocktails and hungering for hearty servings of mac-and-cheese pack this bar before and after Giants games. Year-round the Sunday brunch (many eggs Benedict options) is a good bet. ⊠ *555 2nd St., near Bryant St., SoMa* ☎ *415/543–2282* ⊕ *www.novabar.com.*

Pied Piper Bar. The Palace Hotel's clubby, wood-paneled watering hole takes its name from the Maxfield Parrish mural *The Pied Piper of Hamelin,* which covered most of the wall behind the bar for a century. Until 2013, that is, when the hotel management put it up for auction (tsk, tsk) before backing down after locals on up to the mayor howled in protest. The painting then went to a restorer with promises that it would return to the hotel, if not the bar, which draws and upscale clientele for two-olive martinis, Manhattans, and other trad libations. ⊠ *Palace Hotel, 2 New Montgomery St., at Market St., SoMa* ☎ *415/512–1111* ⊕ *www.sfpalace.com/pied-piper.*

Terroir. The focus at this quaint wine bar is on natural (and mostly Old World) vintages, though it's not impossible to find local offerings, too. And while the space may be small, the selection is not: more than 700 different wines, stacked literally to the ceiling, compete for your attention. Don't let the owners' French accents intimidate you: the staff here is helpful. Terroir serves a small selection of artisanal cheeses and charcuterie to pair with the wines. ■TIP➔ Go on a weekday and head to the candlelit loft above the bar. It's the best seat in the house. ⊠ *1116 Folsom St., at 7th St., SoMa* ☎ *415/558–9946* ⊕ *www.terroirsf.com.*

Thirsty Bear. This eco-friendly brewpub is the perfect pit stop for those on a budget who don't want to compromise. Thirsty Bear is the only certified organic brewery within the city limits, and the beers here are handcrafted variations on traditional styles. ■TIP➔ If you can't decide which beer to start with, sample all on tap. The bar's tapas menu features seasonal meats and produce (mostly local) and sustainably harvested seafood. The upstairs pool hall is ideal for large groups. ⊠ *661 Howard St., at Hawthorne St., SoMa* ☎ *415/974–0905* ⊕ *www.thirstybear.com.*

View Lounge. Art-deco-influenced floor-to-ceiling windows frame superb views on the 39th floor of the San Francisco Marriott. You won't feel out of place here just getting a drink or two rather than dinner. It can get crowded here on weekends. ⊠ *San Francisco Marriott, 55 4th St., between Mission and Market Sts., SoMa* ☎ *415/896–1600.*

CABARET

AsiaSF. Saucy, sexy, and fun, this is one of the hottest places in town for a drag-show virgin. The entertainment, as well as gracious food service, is provided by some of the city's most gorgeous "gender illusionists," who strut in impossibly high heels on top of the catwalk bar, vamping to tunes like "Cabaret" and "Big Spender." The creative Asian-influenced cuisine is surprisingly good. ■TIP➔ Go on a weekday to avoid the bachelorette parties. Make reservations, or risk being turned away. Oh, and bring a camera. ⊠ *201 9th St., at Howard St., SoMa* ☎ *415/255–2742* ⊕ *www.asiasf.com.*

16

DANCE CLUBS

111 Minna Gallery. Gallery by day, bar–dance club by night, this warehouse space on a small side street just south of Mission Street is usually full of hipsters and artsy youngsters. Dance events typically take place on Fridays and Saturdays from 9 pm until 2 am, though the bar opens around 5. ⊠ *111 Minna St., between 2nd and New Montgomery Sts., SoMa* ☎ *415/974–1719* ⊕ *www.111minnagallery.com* ⊗ *Gallery closed weekends.*

DNA Lounge. The music changes nightly at the venerable DNA Lounge, and one of the highlights is **Bootie.** Every Saturday night, this popular mash-up unites hard-core and indie rockers, hip-hop devotees, and emo fans. Three bars and dance floors on two levels mean that DNA is rarely uncomfortably crowded. ■TIP➜ **The action spills into the pizza joint next door, so you don't have to stop dancing if you suddenly get hungry.** ⊠ *375 11th St., between Harrison and Folsom Sts., SoMa* ☎ *415/626–1409* ⊕ *www.dnalounge.com.*

The EndUp. Sometimes 2 am is way too early. And with a 30-hour dance party starting at 10 pm on Saturday, the EndUp is by far SF's most popular after-hours place, with possibly the best sound system in the city. ■TIP➜ **Said system is cranked. Even the cool kids wear earplugs.** It's open nonstop from 10 pm Saturday until 4 am Monday, and generally 10 pm–4 am weekdays. It can be a bit of a meat market, but this San Francisco institution doesn't adhere to any particular scene. ⊠ *401 6th St., at Harrison St., SoMa* ☎ *415/646–0999* ⊕ *www.theendup.com.*

GAY NIGHTLIFE

Lone Star Saloon. This watering hole is popular with bikers, bears, and the men who love them. The inside bar has an old-style-tavern feel, with barrels (not bowls) of peanuts, a pool table, a tiny dance floor, and a long wooden bar you half expect the bartender to sling a beer down. Weekend "Beer Busts" unfold on the great outdoor patio bar. Expect a big crowd on a sunny day. The scene here isn't particularly female-friendly, and the action can get steamy during events like gay-pride day or the Folsom Street Fair. ⊠ *1354 Harrison St., at 9th St., SoMa* ☎ *415/863–9999* ⊕ *www.lonestarsf.com.*

SF Eagle. This spacious indoor-outdoor leather bar is a holdover from the days before AIDS and SoMa's gentrification. The Sunday-afternoon "Beer Busts" (3 pm–6 pm) remain a high point of the leather set's week, and Thursday nights are given over to live music. This remains a welcoming place for people from all walks of life. ⊠ *398 12th St., at Harrison St., SoMa* ⊕ *www.sf-eagle.com.*

The Stud. Glam trannies, gay bears, tight-teed pretty boys, ladies and their ladies, and a handful of straight onlookers congregate here to dance to live DJ sounds and watch world-class drag performers on the small stage. The entertainment is often campy, pee-your-pants funny, and downright fantastic. Each night's music is different—from funk, soul, and hip-hop to '80s tunes and disco favorites. ■TIP➜ **At Frolic, the Stud's most outrageous party (second Saturday of the month), club goers dance the night away dressed as bunnies, kittens, and even**

stranger creatures. ⊠ *1284 Harrison St., at 9th St., SoMa* ☎ *415/863–6623* ⊕ *www.studsf.com* ☽ *Closed Mon.*

MUSIC CLUBS

Slim's. National touring acts—mostly along the pop-punk and hard- and alt-rock lines but including metal and bluegrass—are the main draws at this venue, one of SoMa's most popular nightclubs. Co-owner Boz Scaggs helps bring in the crowds and famous headliners like Dressy Bessy and Dead Meadow. ⊠ *333 11th St., between Harrison and Folsom Sts., SoMa* ☎ *415/255–0333* ⊕ *www.slimspresents.com.*

CIVIC CENTER

Lawyers, politicians, and others in the government biz populate this neighborhood by day, and at night the scene tends to remain buttoned-up.

MUSIC CLUBS

Warfield. This former movie palace—a "palace" in every sense of the word—is now one of the city's largest rock-and-roll venues, with tables and chairs downstairs and theater seating upstairs. The historic venue has booked everyone from Prince and the Grateful Dead to the Pretenders and the Killers. ⊠ *982 Market St., at Taylor St., Civic Center* ☎ *415/345–0900* ⊕ *thewarfieldtheatre.com.*

16

THE TENDERLOIN

This neighborhood is best known for its grit and realism, but despite this The Loin is centrally located and, depending on your reservation time at Bourbon & Branch, the perfect place to start (or end) your night on the town.

BARS

Fodor's Choice ★ **Bourbon & Branch.** The address and phone are unlisted, the black outer door unmarked, and when you make your reservation (required), you get a password for entry. In short, Bourbon & Branch reeks of Prohibition-era speakeasy cool. It's not exclusive, though: everyone is granted a password. The place has sex appeal, with tin ceilings, bordello-red silk wallpaper, intimate booths, and low lighting; loud conversations and cell phones are not allowed. The menu of expertly mixed cocktails and quality bourbon and whiskey is substantial, though the servers aren't always authorities. ∎TIP➔ **Your reservation dictates your exit time, which is strictly enforced.** There's also a speakeasy within the speakeasy called Wilson & Wilson, which is more exclusive, but just as funky. ⊠ *501 Jones St., at O'Farrell St., Tenderloin* ⊕ *www.bourbonandbranch.com.*

Edinburgh Castle. Work off your fish-and-chips and Scottish brew with a turn at the dartboard or pool table at this cavernous pub. It's popular with locals and Brits who congregate at the long bar or in the scattered seating areas, downing single-malt Scotch or pints of Fuller's. The pub holds weekly trivia nights (the toughest in town) and occasional Scottish cultural events (January's Robert Burns celebration is a favorite). Be aware that the surrounding neighborhood is gritty. ⊠ *950 Geary St., between Larkin and Polk Sts., Tenderloin* ☎ *415/885–4074.*

Built as a bordello in 1907, the Great American Music Hall now pulls in top-tier performers.

MUSIC CLUBS

Fodor's Choice ★ **Great American Music Hall.** You can find top-drawer entertainment at this eclectic nightclub. Acts range from the best in blues, folk, and jazz to up-and-coming college-radio and American-roots artists to indie rockers such as OK Go, Mates of State, and the Cowboy Junkies. The colorful marble-pillared emporium (built in 1907 as a bordello) also accommodates dancing at some shows. Pub grub is available on most nights. ✉ *859 O'Farrell St., between Polk and Larkin Sts., Tenderloin* ☎ *415/885–0750* ⊕ *www.slimspresents.com.*

HAYES VALLEY

Chic Hayes Valley takes nighttime seriously but not at the expense of having a good time. Look for fine wines at Hôtel Biron, learn a thing or three about rum at Smuggler's Cove, and compete at karaoke at The Mint.

BARS

Absinthe. The popular restaurant's 30-plus specialty cocktails—or even just a plain old Manhattan—make a trip just to the bar worthwhile. ✉ *398 Hayes St., at Gough St., Hayes Valley* ☎ *415/551–1590.*

Hôtel Biron Wine Bar and Art Gallery. Sharing an alleylike block with the backs of Market Street restaurants, this tiny, cavelike (in a good way) spot displays artworks of the Mission School aesthetic on its brick walls. The well-behaved twenty- to thirtysomething clientele enjoys the off-the-beaten-path quarters, the wines from around the world, the soft lighting, and the hip music. ✉ *45 Rose St., off Market St. near Gough St., Hayes Valley* ☎ *415/703–0403* ⊕ *www.hotelbiron.com.*

Fodor's Choice
★

Smuggler's Cove. With the decor of a pirate ship and a slew of rum-based cocktails, you half expect Captain Jack Sparrow to sidle up next to you at this offbeat, Disney-esque hangout. But don't let the kitschy ambience fool you. The folks at Smuggler's Cove take rum so seriously they even make their own, which you can sample along with more than 200 other offerings, some of them vintage and very hard to find. A punch card is provided so you can try all 70 cocktails and remember where you left off without getting shipwrecked. The small space fills up quickly, so arrive early. ⊠ *650 Gough St., at McAllister St., Hayes Valley* ☎ *415/869–1900* ⊕ *www.smugglerscovesf.com.*

GAY NIGHTLIFE

The Mint Karaoke Lounge. A mixed gay-straight crowd that's drop-dead serious about its karaoke—to the point where you'd think an *American Idol* casting agent was in attendance—comes here seven nights a week. Regulars sing everything from Simon and Garfunkel songs to disco classics in front of an attentive audience. Do *not* walk onstage unprepared! Check out the songbook online to perfect your debut before you attempt to take the mike. ⊠ *1942 Market St., between Duboce Ave. and Laguna St., Hayes Valley* ☎ *415/626–4726* ⊕ *www.themint.net.*

San Francisco Lesbian, Gay, Bisexual, and Transgender Community Center. Night and day, the center hosts many social activities, from mixers and youth dances to holiday parties and yoga classes. ⊠ *1800 Market St., at Octavia St., Hayes Valley* ☎ *415/865–5555* ⊕ *www.sfcenter.org.*

16

NOB HILL

Whether you're out on the streets or inside a bar, Nob Hill serves up fantastic city views, the very best of which can be experienced from the Top of the Mark.

BARS

Big 4 Bar. Dark-wood paneling and green leather banquettes lend a masculine feel to the bar at the recently remodeled Scarlet Huntington Hotel, where the over-30 crowd orders Scotch and Irish coffee. To accompany your whiskey, try the potpies or Irish stew. This place is a San Francisco history lesson. To get more out of the experience, read up on the Big Four railroad barons—Stanford, Hopkins, Crocker, and the hotel's namesake—before you go. ⊠ *The Huntington Hotel, 1075 California St., at Mason St., Nob Hill* ☎ *415/771–1140* ⊕ *www. big4restaurant.com.*

Tonga Room and Hurricane Bar. Since the 1940s the Tonga Room has supplied its city with high Polynesian kitsch. Fake palm trees, grass huts, a lagoon (three-piece combos play pop standards on a floating barge), and faux monsoons—courtesy of sprinkler-system rain and simulated thunder and lightning—grow more surreal as you quaff the bar's signature mai tais and other too-too fruity cocktails. ■ TIP➔ **Looking for an evening chock-full of bad decision making? Order the Scorpion Bowl and let the drunk dialing begin!** ⊠ *Fairmont San Francisco, 950 Mason St., at California St., Nob Hill* ☎ *415/772–5278* ⊕ *www.tongaroom.com.*

Top of the Mark. A famous magazine photograph immortalized the bar atop the Mark Hopkins as a hot spot for World War II servicemen on leave or about to ship out. The view remains sensational. Entertainment ranges from solo jazz piano to six-piece jazz ensembles. Cover charges vary, and shows begin at 7 pm weekdays and 9 pm weekends. ⊠ *Mark Hopkins InterContinental, 999 California St., at Mason St., Nob Hill* 🕿 *415/616–6916* ⊕ *www.topofthemark.com.*

The Wreck Room. Shuffleboard, arcade basketball, a jukebox, and plenty of flat-screen TVs make this spacious yet divey place feel like a time machine back to your college days. On weekends the crowd is a sea of popped collars, baseball caps, and chest bumps, so get there early if you yearn for a turn at one of the games. ⊠ *1390 California St., at Hyde St., Nob Hill* 🕿 *415/932–6715* ⊕ *www.thewreckroomsf.com.*

POLK GULCH

Sassy, vibrant, and even a little crass, Lower Gulch, the southern half of this neighborhood—Polk Street from Geary Street to a little beyond California Street—was the heart of San Francisco's pre-Castro gay mecca. Things mostly settle down north of California in the Upper Gulch section, though even straight bars like Kozy Kar live up to this hood's feisty reputation.

BARS

Amélie. A slice of modern French life, this cozy and romantic wine bar is an ideal spot for European oenophiles. Vintage-theater seating is available up front—perfect for mingling with strangers. The prices are reasonable, the pours handsome. ■**TIP**➜ Sit at the red-lacquer bar to learn about wine and pick up a French phrase or two. ⊠ *1754 Polk St., at Washington St., Polk Gulch* 🕿 *415/292–6916* ⊕ *www.ameliesf.com.*

Kozy Kar. Outrageous and full of sexual energy, this tiny space with an even tinier dance floor may be the heterosexual equivalent of San Francisco's gay bar scene. The drinks are stiff, but if they overwhelm you—or you just want to have fun—there's a waterbed for you to lounge on. Cartoons and '80s movies play on various televisions. Pay attention and you'll catch frames of porn mixed in for good measure, but if you miss them, don't worry: the bar and the floors are lined with vintage centerfolds. It may all be on the racy side, but it's never creepy or uncomfortable. ⊠ *1548 Polk St., at Sacramento St., Van Ness/Polk* 🕿 *415/346–5699* ⊕ *www.kozykar.com.*

GAY NIGHTLIFE

The Cinch. This Wild West–themed neighborhood bar has pinball machines, pool tables, and a smoking patio. It's not the least bit trendy, which is part of the charm for regulars. ⊠ *1723 Polk St., between Washington and Clay Sts., Polk Gulch* 🕿 *415/776–4162.*

NORTH BEACH

The heterosexual counterpart to the gay Castro, North Beach contains a suave mixture of watering holes, espresso cafés, late-night gelato ops, and strip clubs. Vesuvio Cafe is a must-visit for literary fans.

BARS

15 Romolo. Easy to miss and overshadowed by the neighboring girlie shows, this watering hole serves up "artisinal" drinks—including riffs off your own suggestions—and intriguing fare like hot dogs stuffed with cheddar and wrapped in tortillas. With a non-Internet jukebox and a photo booth, we're talking strictly old school. ⊠ *15 Romolo Pl., between Broadway St. and Fresno St., North Beach* ☎ *415/398–1359* ⊕ *www.15romolo.com.*

Bubble Lounge. Champagne is the specialty at this dark, upscale spot; the selection of bubbly is excellent, with more than 300 types to choose from. Upstairs, young executives nestle into wing chairs and overstuffed couches, and downstairs there's a re-created Champagne cellar. A full bar is available, as are sushi, caviar, desserts, and other delicate nibbles. You won't feel out of place in a suit or slinky dress and heels here. Make table reservations on weekends, or you'll be relegated to the tiny bar area. ⊠ *714 Montgomery St., at Washington St., North Beach* ☎ *415/434–4204* ⊕ *www.bubblelounge.com* ☉ *Closed Sun.–Tues.*

Specs Twelve Adler Museum Cafe. If you're bohemian at heart, you can groove on this hidden hangout for artists, poets, and heavy-drinking lefties. It's one of the few remaining old-fashioned watering holes in North Beach that still smack of the Beat years and the 1960s. Though it's just off a busy street, Specs is strangely immune to the hustle and bustle outside. ⊠ *12 William Saroyan Pl., off Columbus Ave., between Pacific Ave. and Broadway St., North Beach* ☎ *415/421–4112.*

Tosca Café. Like Specs and Vesuvio nearby, this historic charmer holds a special place in San Francisco lore. It has an Italian flavor, with opera, big-band, and Italian standards on the jukebox, an antique espresso machine that's nothing less than a work of art, and lived-in red leather booths. With Francis Ford Coppola's Zoetrope just across the street, celebrities and hip film-industry types often stop by when they're in town; locals, like Sean Penn, have been known to shoot pool in the back room. ⊠ *242 Columbus Ave., near Broadway, North Beach* ☎ *415/986–9651* ⊕ *toscacafesf.com.*

Fodor's Choice ★ **Vesuvio Cafe.** If you're only hitting one bar in North Beach, it should be this one. The low-ceiling second floor of this raucous boho hangout, little altered since its 1960s heyday (when Jack Kerouac frequented the place), is a fine vantage point for watching the colorful Broadway Street and Columbus Avenue intersection. Another part of Vesuvio's appeal is its diverse clientele, from older neighborhood regulars and young couples to Bacchanalian posses. ⊠ *255 Columbus Ave., at Broadway St., North Beach* ☎ *415/362–3370* ⊕ *www.vesuvio.com.*

CABARET

Fodor's Choice ★ **Club Fugazi.** The claim to fame here is *Beach Blanket Babylon,* a wacky musical send-up of San Francisco moods and mores that has been going strong since 1974, making it the longest-running musical revue anywhere. Although the choreography is colorful, the singers brassy, and the satirical songs witty, the real stars are the comically exotic costumes and famous ceiling-high "hats"—which are worth the price of admission alone. The revue sells out as early as a month in advance, so order tickets as far ahead as possible. Those under 21 are admitted only to the Sunday matinee. ■ TIP➜ If you don't shell out the extra money for reserved seating, you won't have an assigned seat—so get your cannoli to go and arrive at least 30 minutes prior to showtime to get in line. ✉ *678 Green St., at Powell St., North Beach* ☎ *415/421–4222* ⊕ *www. beachblanketbabylon.com.*

COMEDY

Cobb's Comedy Club. Stand-up comics such as Bill Maher, Paula Poundstone, and Sarah Silverman have appeared at this club. You can also see sketch comedy and comic singer-songwriters here. No one under 18 is admitted. ✉ *915 Columbus Ave., at Lombard St., North Beach* ☎ *415/928–4320* ⊕ *www.cobbscomedyclub.com.*

Purple Onion. This funny house ranks right up there with Bimbo's and the Fillmore on the list of San Francisco's most famous clubs, and people seem to love it or hate it. Regardless, the Onion is a historic, quintessential San Francisco institution that provided an early platform for both folk-music troubadours such as the Kingston Trio and comedic acts like Robin Williams. In addition to stand-up, you can catch sketch comedy, open mike, and improv shows. ✉ *530 Jackson St., between Kearny St. and Columbus Ave., North Beach* ☎ *415/730–2359* ⊕ *purpleonionatkells.com.*

MUSIC CLUBS

Bimbo's 365 Club. The plush main room and adjacent lounge of this club, here since 1951, retain a retro vibe perfect for the "Cocktail Nation" programming that keeps the crowds entertained. For a taste of the old-school San Francisco nightclub scene, you can't beat it. Indie low-fi and pop bands such as Stephen Malkmus and the Jicks and Camera Obscura play here. ✉ *1025 Columbus Ave., at Chestnut St., North Beach* ☎ *415/474–0365* ⊕ *www.bimbos365club.com.*

The Saloon. Hard-drinkin' in-the-know locals favor this raucous spot, known for great blues. Built in the 1860s, the onetime bordello is purported to be the oldest bar in the city. This is not the place to order a mixed drink. You've been warned. ✉ *1232 Grant Ave., near Columbus Ave., North Beach* ☎ *415/989–7666* ⊕ *www.sfblues.net/Saloon.html.*

THE WATERFRONT

FISHERMAN'S WHARF

Come nightfall, the crowds that throng the northern waterfront during the day tend to thin out, and the nightlife scene here is almost quaint.

BARS

Buena Vista Café. At the end of the Hyde Street cable-car line, the Buena Vista packs 'em in for its famous Irish coffee—which, according to owners, was the first served stateside (in 1952). The place oozes nostalgia, drawing devoted locals as well as out-of-towners relaxing after a day of sightseeing. It's narrow and can get crowded, but this spot provides a fine alternative to the overpriced tourist joints nearby. ✉ *2765 Hyde St., at Beach St., Fisherman's Wharf* ☎ *415/474–5044* ⊕ *www. thebuenavista.com.*

Knuckles at the Wharf. This bar toned down its sports motif in an effort to attract more female patrons, but it's still in its historic location, the early-20th-century Joseph Musto Marble Works building. The original exposed beams and brick remain part of the decor. Because it's in Fisherman's Wharf, this lively spot draws a healthy stream of tourists who can view the venue's 28 TVs, including a jumbo screen. ⊠ *555 North Point St., at Taylor St., Fisherman's Wharf* ☎ *415/486–4346.*

EMBARCADERO

The waterfront's eastern section stays busy at night, not a surprise given its expansive bay views and proximity to Union Square, Chinatown, the Financial District, and SoMa.

BARS

Hard Water. This waterfront restaurant and bar with stunning bay views pays homage to America's most iconic spirit—bourbon—with a wall of whiskeys and a lineup of specialty cocktails. The menu, crafted by Charles Phan of Slanted Door fame, includes spicy pork-belly cracklings, cornbread-crusted alligator, and other fun snacks. ⊠ *Pier 3, Suite 3–102, at Embarcadero, Embarcadero* ☎ *415/392–3021* ⊕ *www.hardwaterbar.com.*

16

Hog Island Oyster Bar. On a sunny day, is there anything better than sipping wine and eating oysters? Only if it's here, on a waterside patio, with the looming Bay Bridge and the Oakland and Berkeley hills as a backdrop. The oysters are from Marin County, and many of the wines are from Sonoma and Napa. ⊠ *Ferry Bldg., 1 Embarcadero Plaza, Embarcadero* ☎ *415/391–7117* ⊕ *www.hogislandoysters.com.*

Pier 23 Cafe. Beer arrives at your table in buckets at this waterfront bar, which has ample seating at plastic tables on a wooden deck. Although you'd expect to sit elbow-to-elbow with fishermen, you're more likely to share the space with twenty- and thirtysomethings drawn by the beer and food specials. ⊠ *Pier 23, The Embarcadero, Embarcadero* ☎ *415/362–5125* ⊕ *www.pier23cafe.com.*

FINANCIAL DISTRICT

Not surprisingly, the nightlife scene here revolves around suits recovering from extended workdays or still trying to seal the deal. Wiggle in among the shop talkers and enjoy a stiff martini.

BARS

Harrington's Bar and Grill. The epicenter for downtown festivities on St. Patrick's Day, this family-owned Irish saloon (closed Sunday) is an attitude-free place for the well-tailored-suit set to have an after-work drink the rest of the year. The restaurant serves American fare, with the occasional Irish special, and has a good selection of imported beers. Another local favorite, the Royal Exchange, is next door and eerily similar. ⊠ *245 Front St., near Sacramento St., Financial District* ☎ *415/392–7595* ⊕ *www.harringtonsbarandgrill.com.*

The Hidden Vine. True to its name, this cozy wine bar is in a little alley (just north of Market Street) and the location is part of the appeal, but the wines and amuse-bouches make it truly worthwhile. A jumble of velvet chairs and love seats fills the space, and the owner, who serves most nights, acts as your sommelier. The space also features its very own boccie court. ⊠ *408 Merchant St., at Battery St., Financial District* ☎ *415/674–3567* ⊕ *www.thehiddenvine.com.*

COMEDY

Punchline. A launch pad for the likes of Jay Leno and Whoopi Goldberg, this place books some of the nation's top talents. Headliners have included Dave Chappelle, Margaret Cho, and Jay Mohr. No one under 18 is admitted. ⊠ *444 Battery St., between Clay and Washington Sts., Financial District* ☎ *415/397–7573* ⊕ *www.punchlinecomedyclub.com.*

THE MARINA

The young up-and-comers of the Marina district check each other out over high-end cocktails at a few semifancy, see-and-be-seen establishments.

BARS

Circa. This classy lounge with shimmering chandeliers is dimly lighted, but fellow patrons will still notice the logo on your purse, so dress appropriately here (and elsewhere in the Marina). At the central, square bar, attractive yuppies sip cosmos and nibble pan-seared scallops, while skilled DJs spin down-tempo electronica. This place takes tongue-in-cheek chic seriously, down to the lobster-and-truffle mac-and-cheese. As expected, there's a strong list of specialty cocktails. ⊠ *2001 Chestnut St., at Fillmore St., Marina* ☎ *415/351–0175* ⊕ *www.circasf.com.*

MatrixFillmore. Don a pair of Diesel jeans and a Michael Kors sweater and sip cosmos or cabernet with the Marina's bon vivants. This is the premier spot in the "Triangle" (short for Bermuda Triangle, named for all of the singles who disappear in the bars clustered at Greenwich and Fillmore streets). Although there's a small dance floor where some folks bump and grind to high-energy DJ-spun dance tracks, the majority of the clientele usually vies for the plush seats near the central open fireplace, flirts at the bar, or huddles for romantic tête-à-têtes in the back. The singles scene can be overwhelming on weekends. ⊠ *3138 Fillmore St., between Greenwich and Filbert Sts., Marina* ☎ *415/563–4180* ⊕ *www.matrixfillmore.com.*

Nectar. This small, classy, storefront lounge has reasonable tasting flights (around $20) and decent food that looks more impressive than it tastes. No complaints about the wine choices, though, which are consistently excellent. Warm lighting accents modern furnishings, including a signature beehive-shape wine display. On weekends the decibel level rises considerably and space is at a premium. ⊠ *3330 Steiner St., between Chestnut and Lombard Sts., Marina* ☎ *415/345–1377* ⊕ *www. nectarwinelounge.com.*

COW HOLLOW

In between the Marina and Pacific Heights, this small yet affluent neighborhood has a similar scene to the bordering Marina district but without the hefty price tags.

BARS

Balboa Cafe. Here you'll spy young (thirtysomething) and upwardly mobile former frat boys and sorority girls munching on tasty burgers—considered by some to be the best in town—while trying to add a few new names to their Blackberrys. ✉ *3199 Fillmore St., at Greenwich St., Cow Hollow* ☎ *415/921–3944* ⊕ *www.balboacafe.com.*

Bus Stop. Popular with frat boys and stockbrokers alike, this Marina/Cow Hollow favorite has 18 screens and two pool tables. If you want to meet the local diehards, this is the place. It's also one of the few spots in this neighborhood where you'll feel comfortable dressed down. Order food from neighboring restaurants; the bar provides menus. ✉ *1901 Union St., at Laguna St., Cow Hollow* ☎ *415/567–6905.*

Perry's. One of San Francisco's oldest singles bars still packs 'em in. You can dine on great hamburgers (and a stellar Reuben) as well as more-substantial fare while gabbing about the game with the well-scrubbed, khaki-clad, baseball-cap-wearing crowd. ✉ *1944 Union St., at Laguna St., Cow Hollow* ☎ *415/922–9022* ⊕ *www.perryssf.com.*

THE WESTERN SHORELINE

16

THE RICHMOND

The nightlife in this practical, comfy neighborhood centers more on reasonably priced restaurants—including Clement Street's good Chinese, Thai, Burmese, and Vietnamese ones—than on bars and nightclubs. What bar scene there is, you'll find low-key and welcoming. Fierce waves and mesmerizing sunsets are just a few of the reasons to make your way to the district's western reaches.

BARS

Fodor'sChoice ★ **Cliff House.** Classier than the nearby Beach Chalet, with a more impressive view of Ocean Beach, this is our pick if you must choose just one oceanfront restaurant/bar. Sure, it's the site of many high-school prom dates, and you could argue that the food and drinks are overpriced, and some say the sleek facade seems more suitable for a mausoleum—but the views are terrific. The best window seats are reserved for diners, but there's a small upstairs lounge where you can watch gulls sail high above the vast blue Pacific. ■TIP➜ Come before sunset. ✉ *1090 Point Lobos, at Great Hwy., Lincoln Park* ☎ *415/386–3330* ⊕ *www.cliffhouse.com.*

MUSIC CLUBS

The Plough and Stars. This decidedly unglamorous pub, where crusty old-timers swap stories over pints of Guinness, is the city's best bet for traditional Irish music. Bay Area musicians (and, once in a while, big-name bands) perform every night except Monday. Talented locals gather to play on Tuesday and Sunday *seisiúns,* informal "sessions" where musicians sit around a table and drink and eat while chiming in; anyone skilled at Irish traditional music can join in. ✉ *116 Clement St., at 2nd Ave., The Richmond* ☎ *415/751–1122* ⊕ *www.theploughandstars.com.*

GOLDEN GATE PARK

Often shrouded by the city's famous fog and always scented by crisp eucalyptus, Golden Gate Park provides a suitably mellow nightlife experience.

BARS

Beach Chalet. This restaurant-microbrewery, on the second floor of a historic building filled with 1930s Works Project Administration murals, has a stunning view of the Pacific Ocean, so you may want to time your visit to coincide with the sunset. ■TIP→ Arrive at least 30 minutes before sunset to beat the dinner crowd. If you come right at dinnertime or even at lunchtime on weekends, diners with reservations will be given first dibs on the window seats (and on tables in general). The bar is toward the back, with a so-so view of the action. The American bistro food—which, for appetizers, includes ahi tuna tartare and fried calamari—is decent, the house brews are rich and flavorful, and there's a good selection of California wines by the glass. The seasonal Oktoberfest brew is a highlight of the beer menu. The cheaper Park Chalet on the ground floor has park, rather than ocean, views. ⊠ *1000 Great Hwy., near John F. Kennedy Dr., Golden Gate Park* 🕾 *415/386–8439* ⊕ *www.beachchalet.com.*

Park Chalet. You'll feel like you're in a cabin in the woods as you relax in an Adirondack chair under a heat lamp, enclosed by the greenery of Golden Gate Park. In addition to serving pub food such as burgers, salads, steaks, and fish-and-chips, the brewery churns out its own beer. The Park Chalet shares a building with the Beach Chalet—but it isn't waterside, so you won't freeze if it's overcast. ⊠ *1000 Great Hwy., near John F. Kennedy Dr., Golden Gate Park* 🕾 *415/386–8439* ⊕ *www.parkchalet.com.*

THE HAIGHT AND THE CASTRO

THE HAIGHT

The hippie joints that made the Haight famous may be long gone, but this neighborhood retains a countercultural vibe. Beer connoisseurs should head directly to the Toronado.

BARS

The Alembic. This dark-wood and low-lit space has a certain swagger that is at once charming and classy. It serves full meals but is also a good choice for cocktails and small plates—the jerk-spiced duck hearts, pork-belly sliders, and pickled quail eggs are all winners. ■TIP→ Carnivores: check out the bone-marrow plate. ⊠ *1725 Haight St., at Cole St., Haight* 🕾 *415/666–0822* ⊕ *www.alembicbar.com.*

Noc Noc. A cross between a Tim Burton film and an Oingo Boingo album, this funky cavelike bar has been making every day Halloween since 1986. Noc Noc's bartenders serve up about 20 or so beers on tap, sake (even unfiltered), and unique twists on traditional drinks, like the P&P, a blend of hefeweizen and pear cider. The house DJ plays acid jazz, industrial, and ambient tunes. When the nearby Toronado gets too busy, head over here. ✉ *557 Haight St., at Steiner St., Lower Haight* ☏ *415/861–5811* ⊕ *nocnocs.com.*

Fodor's Choice **Toronado.** You come to what may be the city's most popular dive bar
★ for one thing and one thing only: the reasonably priced beers, about
four dozen of them on tap. The menu, which hangs from the ceiling,
will put a kink in your neck as you try to decide. The bar opens in the
late morning and has a good-size crowd by early afternoon, so show up
early to sit at one of the highly coveted tables. ■**TIP➜ Don't worry about
eating beforehand. It's okay to bring in outside food.** ✉ *547 Haight St.,
at Fillmore St., Lower Haight* ☏ *415/863–2276* ⊕ *www.toronado.com.*

THE CASTRO

The gay district is as outrageous as one might expect, if not more so.
Leather daddies, costumed club kids, and those who defy recently
passed "no nudity" laws are among the characters you'll stumble across
day or night. The party never seems to stop at popular Badlands.

BARS

Blackbird. This neighborhood hangout tries too hard to be hip and cool,
but it's a lot of fun. The crowd is less casual than others in the Castro,
though no one will judge you for wearing Chuck Taylors. Blackbird
serves up a good selection of craft beers, along with seasonal cocktails.
The chipotle Bloody Mary is a must-try. ✉ *2124 Market St., at Church
St., Castro* ☏ *415/503–0630* ⊕ *www.blackbirdbar.com.*

Lucky 13. Greasers, hipsters, Betty Page wannabes, anyone looking for
a good beer in the Castro, and assorted other patrons make Lucky 13
a fun place indeed. The drink prices are reasonable, the beer selection
is huge, and there's high-end root beer on tap for the designated driver
with a discriminating palate. The best seats are upstairs overlooking
the crowd. ✉ *2140 Market St, at Church St., Castro* ☏ *415/487–1313.*

GAY NIGHTLIFE

Badlands. Shirts off! If a sweaty muscle sandwich sounds like your idea
of a good time, head to Badlands, where serious party boys come to
grind to throbbing music on a packed dance floor. The lines can be
ridiculous on weekends; those in the know go on Wednesday or Thursday. Tight-teed patrons range from twenties to forties. ✉ *4121 18th
St., between Castro and Collingwood Sts., Castro* ☏ *415/626–9320*
⊕ *www.sfbadlands.com.*

The Café. Always comfortable and often packed with a mixed gay, lesbian, and straight crowd, this is a place where you can dance to house
or disco music, shoot pool, or meet guys in their twenties at the bar. The
outdoor deck—a rarity—makes it a favorite destination for smokers.
There's a small weekend cover; expect a line to get in. ✉ *2369 Market
St., at 17th St., Castro* ☏ *415/834–5840* ⊕ *www.cafesf.com.*

THE MISSION

Once a vibrant mix of Latino street culture and twentysomething dot-
com action, the Mission is defined these days by its hipster crowd. This
neighborhood rarely sleeps.

16

Gay and Lesbian Nightlife

In the days before the gay liberation movement, bars were more than mere watering holes—they also served as community centers where members of a mostly underground minority could network and socialize. In the 1960s the bars became hotbeds of political activity; by the 1970s other social opportunities had become available to gay men and lesbians, and the bars' importance as centers of activity decreased.

Old-timers may wax nostalgic about the vibrancy of pre-AIDS, 1970s bar life, but you can still have plenty of fun. The one difference is the one-night-a-week operation of some of the best clubs, which may cater to a different (sometimes straight) clientele on other nights. This type of club tends to come and go, so it's best

to pick up one of the two main gay papers to check the latest happenings.

Bay Area Reporter. The weekly *Bay Area Reporter* covers gay and lesbian events in its entertainment pages and calendar and has a nightlife website (⊕ www.bartabsf.com).

San Francisco Bay Times. The biweekly *Bay Times* (⊕ www.sfbaytimes.com) runs features and extensive calendar listings of lesbian and gay events.

For a place known as a gay mecca, San Francisco has always suffered from a surprising drought of lesbian bars. The Lexington Club, in the nightlife-filled Mission District, is the best-known bar. The Café is probably the most lesbian-friendly Castro bar, though you'll find queer gals (and many more queer guys) at the Mint and The Stud, too.

BARS

Elixir. The cocktails are well crafted and affordable at the city's second-oldest saloon location—various watering holes have operated on this site since 1858. ■TIP→ Sunday's do-it-yourself Bloody Mary bar is a local favorite. ✉ 3200 16th St., at Guerrero St., Mission ☎ 415/552–1633 ⊕ www.elixirsf.com.

Fodor's Choice   **El Rio.** A dive bar in the best sense has a calendar chock-full of events,
★   from free bands and films to Salsa Sunday (seasonal), all of which keep Mission kids coming back. Bands play several nights a week, and there are plenty of other events. No matter what day you attend, expect to find a diverse gay-straight crowd. When the weather's warm, the large patio out back is especially popular and the midday dance parties are *the* place to be. ✉ 3158 Mission St., between César Chavez and Valencia Sts., Mission ☎ 415/282–3325 ⊕ www.elriosf.com.

Elbo Room. This popular two-story space has a little something for everyone. The main bar downstairs is quaint and swanky with tables, booths, and classic arcade games. Hit the upstairs to see up-and-coming artists before they hit the bigtime. The music includes Afro-Cuban, indie rock, jazz, and more. ✉ 647 Valencia St., between 17th St. and 18th St., Mission ☎ 415/552–7788 ⊕ www.elbo.com.

Laszlo. Attached to the Foreign Cinema restaurant, Laszlo is a cavernous, classy space with an open, bi-level design; movies are projected onto the walls. Dim lighting, candles, and an upscale selection of cocktails and single-malts make it suitable for romance, but the loud music and cacophonic levels of conversation keep it lively. DJs spin most nights after 9. ⊠ *2526 Mission St., between 21st and 22nd Sts., Mission* ☎ *415/401–0810* ⊕ *www.laszlobar.com.*

Nihon. Whiskey lovers *need* to check this place out, if only to drool over the 150 or so bottles behind the bar. Nihon attracts a superswank, youngish crowd for decent (if pricey) Japanese tapas; the whiskeys pair with sushi surprisingly well. The dramatic lighting, close quarters, and blood-red tuffets make the bar more suitable for romance than business. ⊠ *1779 Folsom St., near 14th St., Mission* ☎ *415/552–4400* ⊕ *dajanigroup.net/establishments/nihon-whisky-lounge.*

Rite Spot Cafe. A Mission tradition for more than 50 years, this classy and casual charmer is like a cabaret club in an aging mobster's garage. Quirky lounge singers and other musicians entertain most nights. A small menu of affordable sandwiches and Italian food beats your average bar fare. Rite Spot is in a mostly residential and somewhat desolate part of the Mission, so you may feel like you're entering a no-man's-land. ⊠ *2099 Folsom St., at 17th St., Mission* ☎ *415/552–6066* ⊕ *www.ritespotcafe.net.*

Urban Putt. While the city's only miniature golf course is kid-friendly during the day, this 14-hole indoor course really lights up at night. The bar features cocktails inspired by Bay Area attractions, as does the fairway. So you'll be putting through the Transamerica Pyramid and those famous Painted Ladies. And Urban Put is complete with theme park cuisine, such as corn dogs and organic soft-serve ice cream. Those seeking more substantial eats should head upstairs to the restaurant. ⊠ *1096 S. Van Ness Ave., at 22nd St., Mission* ☎ *415/341–1080* ⊕ *www.urbanputt.com.*

Zeitgeist. It's a bit divey, a bit rock and roll, but a good place to relax with a cold one or an ever-popular (and ever-strong) Bloody Mary in the large beer "garden" (there's not much greenery) on a sunny day. Grill food is available, and if you're lucky one of the city's most famous food-cart operators, the Tamale Lady, will drop by. If you own a trucker hat, a pair of Vans, and a Pabst Blue Ribbon T-shirt, you'll fit right in. ⊠ *199 Valencia St., at Duboce Ave., Mission* ☎ *415/255–7505* ⊕ *www.zeitgeistsf.com.*

DANCE CLUBS

Make-Out Room. Are you ready to dance? At this tiny Latin club the beats are always fresh, if not downright nasty—this place is called the Make-Out Room for a reason. With the small bar and just a few cushiony booths, don't expect to sit for long. Most nights are free, but expect a small cover charge on weekends when bands like Thee Swank Bastards or Grave Bros Deluxe play. ⊠ *3225 22nd St., at Mission St., Mission* ☎ *415/647–2888* ⊕ *www.makeoutroom.com.*

GAY NIGHTLIFE

Martuni's. A mixed crowd enjoys cocktails in the semi-refined environment of this bar where the Castro, the Mission, and Hayes Valley intersect; variations on the martini are a specialty. In the intimate back room

16

a pianist plays nightly, and patrons take turns boisterously singing show tunes. Martuni's often gets busy after symphony and opera performances—Davies Hall and the Opera House are both within walking distance. ■TIP→ The Godiva Chocolate Martini is a crowd favorite. ✉ 4 *Valencia St., at Market St., Mission* ☎ *415/241–0205.*

JAZZ CLUBS

Savanna Jazz. Deep in the Outer Mission, this is one of SF's best jazz joints, an unexpected find in a hood filled with hipster bars. Loungey booths and low lighting set the mood for consistently good old-school Latin and Brazilian jazz acts. ✉ *2937 Mission St., between 25th and 26th Sts., Mission* ☎ *415/285–3369* ⊕ *www.savannajazz.com.*

DOGPATCH

The historic Dogpatch neighborhood was once mostly residential, but some of the city's best off-the-beaten-path joints can be found here. Yield Wine Bar is one of several shining stars at or near 3rd and 22nd streets. If dinner is on the agenda, consider Serpentine. Directly across 3rd from Yield, it serves up amazing food and even better cocktails.

BARS

Magnolia Pub & Brewery. Outfitted in industrial-chic, this brewhouse has a little something for everyone, except maybe hungry vegetarians. Its huge on-site brewing system can produce up to 30 barrels of beer and is equally matched by Magnolia's unique cocktail menu, featuring off-the-wall ingredients like beef bouillon. The love affair with meat doesn't stop there, as they even craft their own sausages. ✉ *2505 3rd St., between 22nd and 23rd Sts., Dogpatch* ☎ *415/864–7468* ⊕ *www. magnoliapub.com.*

Fodor's Choice ★ **Yield.** A stone's throw from the bay, the city's greenest wine bar serves up sustainable, organic, and biodynamic wines from around the world. Small plates are also available, usually vegetarian, and change weekly, as does the wine menu. The commitment to a healthier planet isn't only reflected in the food and drink, but also the decor, a mixture of reused wine bottles and wood reclaimed from nearby piers. ■TIP→ Public transportation shuts down early at night, so expect to need a taxi back and to wait about 30 minutes for it to arrive. ✉ *2490 3rd St., at 22nd St., Dogpatch* ☎ *415/401–8984* ⊕ *www.yieldsf.com.*

POTRERO HILL

One of the city's less walkable neighborhoods and far from the center of the nightlife scene sometimes feels downright sleepy. But a strip of 18th Street near Connecticut Street has good food and cocktails, and the Bottom of the Hill music club has a loyal clientele.

DANCE CLUBS

Bottom of the Hill. This is a great live-music dive—in the best sense of the word—and truly the epicenter for Bay Area indie rock. The club has hosted some great acts over the years, including the Strokes and the Throwing Muses. Rap and hip-hop acts occasionally make it to

SAFETY AFTER DARK

San Franciscans sometimes seem to get a perverse thrill out of the grittiness of their city. Some of the best nightlife options are in sketchy locations; in the areas we've listed below you're better off cabbing it. Bartenders can call you a ride when you're ready to leave.

■ **The Tenderloin:** Many locals walk to Tenderloin bars, but take a cab if addicts and lowlifes loitering in front of hourly rate hotels give you the jitters. The edges east of Jones Street and north of Sutter Street aren't too bad.

■ **SoMa:** More than five blocks or so south of Market Street is an industrial no-man's-land, though this area becomes more developed and inhabited by flashy residential skyscrapers with each passing year.

■ **Civic Center:** Don't stray north, east, or south of the performing arts venues. The one safe corridor is west to Gough Street, which will bring you into Hayes Valley. Avoid Market Street between 6th and 10th streets.

■ **Western Addition:** If coming to this neighborhood's music clubs, take a cab or opt for valet parking if it's available.

■ **The Outer Mission (south of 24th Street):** On Mission Street, don't stray below 24th. If you're feeling nervous between 16th and 24th streets, walk a block west to Valencia Street.

It's safe to walk around the Financial District, Union Square, Haight Street and Cole Valley, Nob Hill, the Mission (above 24th Street), and SoMa north of Howard.

the stage. ⊠ *1233 17th St., at Texas St., Potrero Hill* ☎ *415/621–4455* ⊕ *www.bottomofthehill.com.*

PACIFIC HEIGHTS

One of the city's most exclusive enclaves has city and bay views, though most of these are from posh residences. The nightlife here is generally tasteful and discreet.

GAY NIGHTLIFE

Lion Pub. With big comfy chairs, cascades of potted plants, and a small fireplace, this bar is so welcoming that—even though it's one of the oldest gay bars in the city—it tends to draw every sort of San Franciscan, young and old, gay and straight. Specialty drinks made with fresh-squeezed fruit juices attract cocktail connoisseurs. ⊠ *2062 Divisadero St., at Sacramento St., Pacific Heights* ☎ *415/567–6565.*

WESTERN ADDITION

The Western Addition was among San Francisco's earliest multicultural neighborhoods, and it remains ethnically and economically diverse, if also pretty rough in many spots. The jazz, rock, and blues clubs here book high-profile performers.

BARS

Tsunami Sushi Panhandle. This place next to a jointly owned sake shop has a small but very good sushi menu, as well as a list of more than 100 sakes. The staffers know their stuff—including how to make killer sake-tinis. ⊠ *1306 Fulton St., at Divisadero St., Western Addition* ☎ *415/567–7664* ⊕ *dajanigroup.net.*

MUSIC CLUBS

BooM BooM RooM. John Lee Hooker's old haunt has been an old-school blues haven for years, attracting top-notch acts from all around the country. Luck out with legendary masters like James "Super Chikan" Johnson, or discover new blues and funk artists. ⊠ *1601 Fillmore St., at Geary Blvd., Western Addition* ☎ *415/673–8000* ⊕ *www. boomboomblues.com.*

The Fillmore. This is *the* club that all the big names, from Coldplay to Clapton, want to play. San Francisco's most famous rock-music hall presents national and local acts: rock, reggae, grunge, jazz, folk, acid house, and more. Go upstairs to view the amazing collection of rock posters lining the walls. At the end of each show, free apples are set near the door, and staffers hand out collectible posters. ■ TIP➔ **Avoid steep service charges by purchasing tickets at the club's box office on Sunday from 10 to 4.** ⊠ *1805 Geary Blvd., at Fillmore St., Western Addition* ☎ *415/346–6000* ⊕ *www.thefillmore.com.*

The Independent. Originally called the Box for its giant cube-shape interior, this off-the-beaten-path music venue showcases rock, heavy metal, folk, soul, reggae, hip-hop, and even comedy acts. There's a big dance floor. Recent shows have included the Limousines, Mos Def, Ted Nugent, Dave Chappelle, Foster the People, and Cyndi Lauper. ⊠ *628 Divisadero St., at Hayes St., Western Addition* ☎ *415/771–1421* ⊕ *www.theindependentsf.com.*

BERNAL HEIGHTS

Atop a steep hill, Bernal Heights is a section of town many San Franciscans have yet to visit. Its few bars have a cozy, neighborhood feel.

GAY NIGHTLIFE

Wild Side West. A friendly pool game is always going on at this mellow, slightly out-of-the-way hangout, where all are welcome. Outside is a large deck and one of San Francisco's best bar gardens, where acoustic-guitar sing-alongs are not uncommon. Rumor has it that Janis Joplin was a regular here. Ask the bartender for the scoop. ⊠ *424 Cortland Ave., at Wool St., Bernal Heights* ☎ *415/647–3099.*

SPORTS AND
THE OUTDOORS

Updated by
Fiona G.
Parrott

San Francisco's surroundings—the bay, ocean, mountains, and forests—make getting outdoors away from the city a no-brainer. Muir Woods, Point Reyes, and Stinson Beach in Marin County offer dozens of opportunities for exploring the natural beauty of the Bay Area. But the peninsular city—with its many green spaces, steep inclines, and breathtaking views—has plenty to offer itself.

Bikers and hikers traverse the majestic Golden Gate Bridge, bound for the Marin Headlands or the winding trails of the Presidio. Runners, strollers, in-line skaters, and cyclists head for Golden Gate Park's wooded paths, and water lovers satisfy their addictions by kayaking, sailing, or kite-surfing in the bay and along the rugged Pacific coast.

Prefer to watch from the sidelines? The Giants (baseball) and the 49ers (football) are San Francisco's professional sports teams; the A's (baseball) and the Golden State Warriors (basketball) play in Oakland. But the city has plenty of other periodic sporting events to watch, including that roving costume party, the Bay to Breakers race in May. For events listings and local perspectives on Bay Area sports, pick up a copy of the *San Francisco Chronicle* (⊕ *www.sfgate.com*) or the *Examiner* (⊕ *www. examiner.com*), both of which list schedules and scores.

BASEBALL

FAMILY   **San Francisco Giants.** Three World Series titles (2010, 2012, and 2014)
Fodor'sChoice   and the classic design of AT&T Park lead to sellouts for nearly every
★   home game the National League team plays. ⊠ *AT&T Park, 24 Willie Mays Plaza, between 2nd and 3rd Sts., SoMa* ☏ *415/972–2000, 800/734–4268* ⊕ *sanfrancisco.giants.mlb.com.*

GETTING TICKETS
The park is small and there are 30,000 season-ticket holders (for 43,000 seats), so Giants tickets for popular games routinely sell out the day they go on sale. If tickets aren't available at Tickets.com, try

the team-approved reseller StubHub! (⊕ *www.stubhub.com*) or even try showing up on game day—there are usually plenty of scalpers, some selling at reasonable prices.

Giants Dugout. The Giants sell tickets at the ballpark and numerous Dugout locations, among them 4 Embarcadero Center and 337 Geary Street in Union Square. A surcharge is added at locations other than the ballpark. ✉ *AT&T Park, 24 Willie Mays Plaza, at 3rd St., SoMa* ☎ *415/947–3419, 800/734–4268* ⊕ *sanfrancisco.giants.mlb.com/sf/ ballpark/dugout_stores.jsp.*

Tickets.com. This service sells game tickets online and charges a per-ticket service charge. ☎ *877/473–4849* ⊕ *www.tickets.com.*

BEACHES

Taking in a beachside sunset is the perfect way to end a busy day—assuming the fog hasn't blown in for the afternoon. Always bring a sweater because even the sunniest of days can turn cold and foggy without warning. Icy temperatures and treacherous currents make most waters too dangerous for swimming without a wet suit, but with a Frisbee, picnic fixings, and some good walking shoes, you can have a fantastic day at the beach.

FAMILY **Aquatic Park Beach.** This urban beach surrounded by Fort Mason, Ghirardelli Square, and Fisherman's Wharf is a ¼-mile-long strip of sand. The gentle waters near shore are shallow, safe for kids to swim or wade, and fairly clean. Locals—including the seemingly ubiquitous older-man-in-Speedo—come out for quick dips in the frigid water. Members of the **Dolphin Club** come every morning for a swim, and a large and raucous crowd braves the cold on New Year's Day. **Amenities:** restrooms; showers; restaurants. **Best for:** walking; sunsets; swimming. ✉ *San Francisco Maritime National Historic Park, 499 Jefferson St., at Hyde St., Northern Waterfront* ⊕ *www.nps.gov/safr.*

Baker Beach. With its gorgeous views of the Golden Gate Bridge and the Marin Headlands, Baker Beach is a local favorite and an established nudist spot. (Never seen nude Frisbee? This is the place.) The pounding surf and strong currents make swimming a dangerous prospect, but the mile-long shoreline is ideal for fishing, building sand castles, or watching sea lions at play. On warm days the entire beach is packed with bodies—including those nudists, who hang out at the north end. Picnic tables, grills, restrooms, and drinking water are available. Rangers give tours of the 95,000-pound cannon at Battery Chamberlin, overlooking the beach, on the first weekend of every month. **Amenities:** parking (no fee); toilets. **Best for:** nudists; sunsets; jogging. ✉ *Gibson Rd. off Bowley St., southwest corner of Presidio.*

FAMILY **China Beach.** One of the city's safest swimming beaches was named for the impoverished Chinese fishermen who once camped here. (Some maps label it James D. Phelan Beach.) This 600-foot strip of sand, south of the Presidio and Baker Beach, has gentle waters as well as changing rooms, restrooms, showers, grills, drinking water, and picnic tables. Despite its humble beginnings, China Beach today is bordered

17

CLOSE UP

AT&T Park: Where Giants Tread

The size of AT&T Park hits you immediately—the field, McCovey Cove, and the Lefty O'Doul drawbridge all look like miniature models. At only 13 acres, the San Francisco Giants' ballpark is one of the country's smallest. After Boston's Fenway, AT&T Park has the shortest distance to the wall; from home plate it's just 309 feet to the right field. But there's something endearing about its petite stature—not to mention its location, with yacht masts poking up over the outfield and the blue bay sparkling beyond.

From 1960 to 2000 the Giants played at Candlestick Park, which is in one of the coldest, windiest parts of the city. (Giants' pitcher Stu Miller was famously "blown off the mound" here during the 1961 All-Star Game.)

In 2000 the Giants played their first game at AT&T Park (then called Pacific Bell Park and later SBC Park—in fact, some locals jokingly call it the Phone Company Park). All told, $357 million was spent on the privately funded facility, and it shows in the retro redbrick exterior, the quaint clock tower, handsome bronze statues and murals, above-average food, and tiny details like baseball-style lettering on no-smoking signs. There isn't a bad seat in the house, and the park has an unusual level of intimacy and access. Concourses circle the field on two levels—on the field level you can stand inches from players as they exit the locker rooms. On the street level non-ticket-holders can get up close, too, outside a gate behind the visiting team's dugout. The giant Coke bottle and mitt you see beyond the outfield are part of the Coca-Cola Fan Lot playground. Diehards may miss the grittiness of Candlestick, but it's hard not to love this park. It still feels new but has an old-time aura and it's already a San Francisco institution. Park tours are led daily at 10:30 and 12:30 and cost $22.

THE FAMOUS "SPLASH HIT"
Locals show up in motorboats and inflatable rafts, with fishing nets ready to scoop up home-run balls that clear the right field wall and land in McCovey Cove. Hitting one into the water isn't easy: the ball has to clear a 26-foot wall, the elevated walkway, and the promenade outside. Barry Bonds had the first splash hit on May 1, 2000.

GETTING THERE
Parking is pricey ($30 and up), and 5,000 spaces for 43,000 seats doesn't add up. Take public transportation. Muni line N (to CalTrain/Mission Bay) stops right in front of the park, and Muni bus lines 10, 15, 30, 42, 45, and 47 stop a block away. Or you can arrive in style—take the ferry from Jack London Square in Oakland (⊕ www.eastbayferry.com).

by the multimillion-dollar homes of the Seacliff neighborhood. The hike down to the beach is steep. **Amenities:** showers; toilets; parking (no fee). **Best for:** grilling; picnics; tide pools. ⊠ *Sea Cliff Ave. and El Camino del Mar, Presidio.*

FAMILY
Fodor's Choice
★

Ocean Beach. The city's largest beach stretches for more than 3 miles along the Great Highway south of the Cliff House, making it ideal for long walks and runs. This isn't the cleanest shore, but it's an easy-to-reach place to chill; spot sea lions sunning themselves atop Seal Rock at the north end of the beach; or watch daredevil surfers riding the rolling waves. Because of extremely dangerous currents, swimming isn't recommended. After sunset, bonfires form a string of lights along the beach in summer. (Fires are prohibited north of Fulton Street or south of Lincoln Way, the northern and southern edges of Golden Gate Park.) Restrooms are at the north end. **Amenities:** parking (no fee); lifeguards; toilets. **Best for:** bonfires; kite flying; long walks. ⊠ *Great Hwy. between Point Lobos Ave. and Sloat Blvd.*

BICYCLING

San Francisco is known for its treacherously steep hills, so it may be surprising to see so many cyclists. This is actually a great city for biking—there are ample bike lanes, it's not hard to find level ground with great scenery (especially along the water), and if you're willing to tackle a challenging uphill climb, you're often rewarded with a fabulous view—and a quick trip back down.

BikeMapper. The regional **511 SF Bay** transit website has an online app that allows you to plot your ride on a map and choose either the shortest or the flattest bike-friendly route. ☎ *511* ⊕ *bicycling.511.org/maps.*

San Francisco Bicycle Coalition. The San Francisco Bicycle Coalition has extensive information about the policies and politics of riding and lists local events for cyclists on its website. You can download (but not print) a PDF version of the *San Francisco Bike Map and Walking Guide.* ⊠ *833 Market St., 10th fl.* ☎ *415/431–2453* ⊕ *www.sfbike.org.*

WHERE TO RENT

Angel Island. A former military garrison and a beautiful wildlife preserve has some steep roads and great views of the city and the bay. Bicycles must stay on roadways; there are no single-track trails on the island. The café is open weekends only mid-November through February, so if you visit weekdays you'll need to bring your own grub. From April through October you can rent mountain bikes on the island for $12.50 an hour or $40 a day. Segway tours are also available for $68 per person. ⊠ *Tiburon* ☎ *415/435–5390* ⊕ *www.angelisland.org.*

Bay City Bike. With three Fisherman's Wharf locations, Bay City Bike isn't hard to find. The shop has an impressive fleet of bikes—many sizes and types—and friendly staff to help you map your biking adventure. ⊠ *2661 Taylor St., at Beach St., Fisherman's Wharf* ☎ *415/346–2453* ⊕ *baycitybike.com.*

Bike and Roll. You can rent bikes at this national outfit's locations $32 per day to $58; discounted weekly rates are available, and complimentary maps are provided. ⊠ *899 Columbus Ave., at Lombard St., North Beach* ☎ *415/229–2000* ⊕ *www.bikethegoldengate.com.*

Bike Hut. Known for its mom-and-pop–style service, the Hut is a small rental, repair, and used-bike shop. Rentals begin at $6 an hour. ⊠ *Pier 40, SoMa* ☎ *415/543–4335* ⊕ *www.thebikehut.org* ⊙ *Closed Mon. and Tues.*

17

Blazing Saddles. This outfitter with branches all around San Francisco rents bikes for $8 to $9 an hour ($32 to $60 a day), depending on the type of bike, and shares tips on sights to see along the paths. ⊠ *2715 Hyde St., at Beach St., Fisherman's Wharf* ☎ *415/202–8888* ⊕ *www.blazingsaddles.com.*

WHERE TO BIKE

THE EMBARCADERO

A completely flat, sea-level route, the Embarcadero hugs the eastern and northern bay and gives a clear view of open waters, the Bay Bridge, and sleek high-rises. The

> **NO UPHILL BATTLE**
>
> Don't want to get stuck slogging up 30-degree inclines? Then pick up a copy of the foldout *San Francisco Bike Map and Walking Guide* ($4), which indicates street grades by color and delineates bike routes that avoid major hills and heavy traffic. You can pick up a copy in bicycle shops, some bookstores, or at the San Francisco Bicycle Coalition's website (⊕ *www.sfbike.org*).

route from Pier 40 to Aquatic Park takes about 30 minutes to ride, and there are designated bike lanes the entire way. As you ride west, you'll pass the Bay Bridge, the Ferry Building, Coit Tower (look inland near Pier 19), and historic ships at the Hyde Street Pier. At Aquatic Park there's a nice view of Golden Gate Bridge. If you're not tired yet, continue along the Marina and through the Presidio's Crissy Field. You may want to time your ride so you end up at the Ferry Building, where you can refuel with a sandwich, a gelato, or—why not?—fresh oysters.
■ TIP➜ Keep your eyes open along this route—cars move quickly here, and streetcars and tourist traffic can cause congestion. Near Fisherman's Wharf you can bike on the promenade, but take it slow and watch out for pedestrians.

GOLDEN GATE PARK

FAMILY A beautiful maze of roads and hidden bike paths crisscrosses San Francisco's most famous park, winding past rose gardens, lakes, waterfalls, museums, horse stables, bison, and, at the park's western edge, spectacular views of the Pacific Ocean. John F. Kennedy Drive is closed to motor vehicles on Sunday (and sometimes Saturday), when it's crowded with people-powered wheels. ■ TIP➜ Get a map of the park before you go—it's huge.

As Fell Street intersects Stanyan Street at the park's eastern entrance, veer right to begin a 30- to 45-minute, 3-mile ride down John F. Kennedy Drive to the Great Highway, where land meets ocean. Take a break and watch the waves roll in at Ocean Beach, or cross the street for a drink or a bite to eat at the casual, tree-shrouded Park Chalet (behind the Beach Chalet). Extend your ride a few more miles by turning left, riding a few blocks, and connecting with a raised bike path that runs parallel to the Pacific, winds through fields of emerald-green ice plant, and, after 2 miles, leads to Sloat Boulevard and the San Francisco Zoo.

THE MARINA GREEN AND GOLDEN GATE BRIDGE

FAMILY The Marina Green, a vast lawn at the edge of the northern bay front, stretches along Marina Boulevard, adjacent to Fort Mason. It's the starting point of a well-used, paved bike path that runs through the

Presidio along Crissy Field's waterfront wetlands, then heads for the Golden Gate Bridge and beyond. To do this ride, first take the path from Aquatic Park through Fort Mason to the Marina Green. Continue into the Presidio, and you'll eventually reach the base of the bridge, a 60-minute ride round-trip. To view the bridge from underneath, stay at water level and ride to Fort Point (where Kim Novak leaped into the drink in the film *Vertigo*).

If you want to cross the bridge, take Lincoln Boulevard to reach the road-level viewing area and continue across the bridge (signs indicate which side you must use). Once you're across, turn right on the first road leading northeast, Alexander Avenue. After a 10-minute all-downhill ride, you'll arrive on Bridgeway in downtown Sausalito, where you can rest at a café. After a little shopping, board the Blue & Gold Fleet's ferry (the ferry terminal is at the end of Bridgeway) with your bike for the half-hour ride back to Fisherman's Wharf. ■TIP➔ If it's overcast, foggy, or windy, don't bother doing the Golden Gate Bridge bike ride—the wind can feel downright dangerous on the bridge, and the trip is only awe-inspiring when you can take in the view.

BOATING AND SAILING

San Francisco Bay has year-round sailing, but tricky currents and strong winds make the bay hazardous for inexperienced navigators. However, on group sails you can enjoy the bay while leaving the navigating to experienced sailors.

17

FAMILY **Adventure Cat Sailing Charters.** Near Fisherman's Wharf, from spring through fall, Adventure Cat takes passengers aboard a 55-foot-long catamaran. The kids can play on the trampoline-like net between the two hulls while you sip drinks on the wind-protected sundeck. A 90-minute bay cruise costs $40; sunset sails with drinks and hors d'oeuvres are $50. ⊠ *Pier 39, Dock J, Fisherman's Wharf* ☎ 800/498–4228, 415/777–1630 ⊕ *www.adventurecat.com.*

Rendezvous Charters. This operator offers individually ticketed trips on large sailing yachts, including sunset sails ($35) and Sunday brunch cruises on a schooner ($50). Ticketed trips tend to close from mid-October through March (although they continue to do private chartered sails throughout the year), so call in advance to confirm availability. ⊠ *Pier 40, South Beach Harbor, Embarcadero* ☎ 415/543–7333 ⊕ *www.rendezvouscharters.com.*

SF Bay Adventures. Nautical tours, such as full-moon sails, are the specialty here, along with Friday night sails and sunset cruises. This outfit is based in Sausalito, but some boats depart from San Francisco. ⊠ *85 Liberty Ship Way, at Marinship Way, Sausalito* ☎ 415/331–0444 ⊕ *www.sfbayadventures.com.*

FAMILY **Stow Lake.** If you prefer calm freshwater, you can rent rowboats and pedal boats at Stow Lake in Golden Gate Park. Remember to bring bread for the ducks. ■TIP➔ The lake is open daily from 10 to 4 for boating, weather permitting. ⊠ *50 Stow Lake Dr., off John F. Kennedy Dr., Golden Gate Park* ☎ 415/386–2531 ⊕ *www.stowlakeboathouse.com.*

FOOTBALL

San Francisco 49ers. The city's NFL team recently debuted its new Levi's Stadium. The state-of-the-art facility, 44 miles south of San Francisco, has more than 13,000 square feet of HD video boards. The 49ers may have left town, but the team hasn't forgotten SF cuisine: restaurateur and season-ticket holder Michael Mina opened Tailgate, based on his Bourbon and Steak restaurants, within the stadium's towering walls. Home games usually sell out far in advance. **Ticketmaster** (⊕ *www. ticketmaster.com*) and **StubHub!** (⊕ *www.stubhub.com*) are sources for single-game tickets. ⊠ *Levi's Stadium, 4949 Marie P. DeBartolo Way, from San Francisco, take U.S. 101 south to Lawrence Expressway and follow signs, Santa Clara* ☏ *800/745–3000 Ticketmaster, 866/788–2482 StubHub!, 415/464–9377 Santa Clara stadium* ⊕ *www.49ers.com.*

HIKING

Hiking options in and around San Francisco include everything from the easygoing Golden Gate Promenade along the city's waterfront to the more rigorous sections the Bay Area Ridge Trail. And there are plenty of great hikes to be had in the Presidio.

Bay Area Ridge Trail. Hills and mountains—including Mt. Tamalpais in Marin County and Mt. Diablo in the East Bay, which has the second-longest sight lines anywhere in the world after Mt. Kilimanjaro—form a ring around the Bay Area. The newest completed stretch of Ridge Trail connects the Pacific Overlook and the Golden Gate Overlook in the Presidio area of San Francisco, offering up the most spectacular views. The Bay Area Ridge Trail is an ongoing project to connect all of the region's ridgelines. The trail is currently more than 340 miles long, but when finished it will extend more than 550 miles, stretching from San Jose to Napa and encompassing all nine Bay Area counties. One of the trail's most impressive ridgelines can be found on Mt. Tamalpais, in Marin County (⇨ *see Mt. Tamalpais State Park, in Chapter 19*). ⊕ *ridgetrail.org.*

FAMILY **Golden Gate National Recreation Area (GGNRA).** This huge, protected area encompasses the San Francisco coastline, the Marin Headlands, and Point Reyes National Seashore. It's veined with hiking trails, and many guided walks take place. You can find current schedules at visitor centers in the Presidio and Marin Headlands; they're also online at ⊕ *www.nps.gov/goga/parknews.* For descriptions of locations within the recreation area—along with rich color photographs, hiking information, and maps—pick up a copy of *Guide to the Parks*, available in local bookstores or online from the **Golden Gate National Parks Conservancy** (⊕ *www.parksconservancy.org*). ⊠ *Bldg. 201, Fort Mason* ☏ *415/561–4700* ⊕ *www.nps.gov/goga.*

FAMILY
Fodor's Choice
★
Golden Gate Promenade. This great walk passes through Crissy Field, taking in marshlands, kite-flyers, beachfront, and windsurfers, with the Golden Gate Bridge as a backdrop. The 3.3-mile walk is flat and easy—it should take about two hours round-trip. If you begin at Aquatic Park, you'll end up practically underneath the bridge at Fort Point Pier.

■TIP→ **If you're driving, park at Fort Point and do the walk from west to east.** It can get blustery, even when it's sunny, so be sure to layer.

FAMILY **Presidio.** Hiking and biking trails wind through nearly 1,500 acres of woods and hills in the Presidio, past old redbrick military buildings and jaw-dropping scenic overlooks with bay and ocean views. Rangers and docents lead guided hikes and nature walks throughout the year. For a current schedule, pick up a copy of the quarterly *Park News* at the Presidio Visitor Center, in the park's Main Post area, or go online. The promenade at Crissy Field leads north past views of Golden Gate Bridge. If it's open, fortify yourself with coffee or snacks at the **Warming Hut** (⊠ *983 Marine Dr., off Long Ave.*) before following the paved road that continues on to the Civil War–era Fort Point, which sits under the bridge. ⊠ *Presidio Visitors Center, 105 Montgomery St. at Lincoln Blvd.* ☎ *415/561–4323* ⊕ *www.nps.gov/prsf.*

KAYAKING

Surrounded by water on three sides, San Francisco has plenty of opportunities for kayaking enthusiasts of all skill levels.

City Kayak. City Kayak operates bay tours along the waterfront and beneath the Bay Bridge starting from $50; the company also runs full-moon night paddles and trips to Alcatraz. Rentals are $40 per hour for a single, and $70 for a double. Half-day trips depart daily. No prior experience is necessary, but you must watch an instructional video. ⊠ *Pier 40* ⊕ *citykayak.com.*

Sea Trek Kayaking and SUP Center. This company offers trips around Angel Island and the Golden Gate Bridge, moonlight paddles, and many trips in Marin County. Three-hour trips cost from $65 to $75, full-day trips from $85 to $130. Most excursions leave from Sausalito (⇨ *see Chapter 19*), but Angel Island tours leave from the island. ⊠ *Bay Model, Sausalito* ☎ *415/332–8494* ⊕ *www.seatrek.com.*

RUNNING

San Francisco is spectacular for running. There are more than 7 miles of paved trails in and around **Golden Gate Park**; circling **Stow Lake** and then crossing the bridge and running up the path to the top of Strawberry Hill is a total of 2½ miles. An enormously popular route is the 2-mile raised bike path that runs from Lincoln Way along the ocean, at the southern border of Golden Gate Park, to Sloat Boulevard, which is the northern border of the San Francisco Zoo. (Stick to the park's interior when it's windy, as ocean gusts can kick up sand.) From Sloat Boulevard you can pick up the **Lake Merced** bike path, which loops around the lake and the golf course, to extend your run another 5 miles.

The paved path along the **Marina** provides a 1½-mile (round-trip) run along a flat, well-paved surface and has glorious bay views. Start where Laguna Street crosses Marina Boulevard, then run west along the Marina Green toward the Golden Gate Yacht Club, which is close to the docks at the northern end of Marina Boulevard. On weekends

17

beware: you'll have to wind through the crowds—but those views are worth it. You can extend your Marina run by jogging the paths through the restored wetlands of Crissy Field, just past the yacht harbor, then up the hill to the Golden Gate Bridge.

The *San Francisco Bike Map and Walking Guide (⇨ see Bicycling)*, which indicates hill grades on city streets by color, is a great resource. Online, check the **San Francisco Road Runners Club** site (⊕ *www.sfrrc. org*) for some recommended routes and links to several local running clubs.

EVENTS

Fodor's Choice ★ **Bay to Breakers.** First run in 1912, the 12K Bay to Breakers race, held on the third Sunday in May, is one of the world's oldest footraces—but in true San Francisco fashion there's nothing typical about it. About a third of the 50,000 to 100,000 runners are serious athletes; the rest are "fun runners" who wear famously wacky costumes—or attempt to wear no costumes at all. The race makes its way from the Embarcadero at the bay to the Pacific Ocean, passing through Golden Gate Park. ☎ *415/231–3130* ⊕ *www.baytobreakers.com.*

San Francisco Marathon. The marathon, usually held on a Sunday in late July, starts and finishes at the Embarcadero. Up to 7,000 runners pass through downtown, the Marina, the Presidio, and Golden Gate Park and cross the Golden Gate Bridge, tackling some of the city's milder hills along the way. ☎ *888/958–6668* ⊕ *www.thesfmarathon.com.*

WHALE-WATCHING

Between January and April, hundreds of gray whales migrate along the coast; the rest of the year humpback and blue whales feed offshore at the Farallon Islands. The best place to watch them from shore is Point Reyes, in Marin County (⇨ *see Chapter 19*).

For a better view, head out on a whale-watching trip. Seas around San Francisco can be rough, so pack motion-sickness tablets. You should also dress warmly, wear sunscreen, and pack rain gear and sunglasses; binoculars come in handy, too. Tour companies don't provide meals or snacks, so bring your own lunch and water. Make reservations at least a week ahead.

California Whale Adventures. California Whale Adventures has year-round whale-watching trips ($100), weekends only. In October you can take a great-white-shark tour, and seabird tours run July through October; these tours range between $90 and $150 per person, and are operated on weekends only. All trips leave from Fisherman's Wharf. ☎ *650/579–7777* ⊕ *www.californiawhaleadventures.com.*

SHOPPING AND SPAS

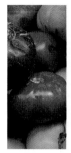

Updated by
Fiona G.
Parrott

With its grand department stores and funky secondhand boutiques, San Francisco summons a full range of shopping experiences. From the anarchist bookstore to the mouthwatering specialty-food purveyors at the gleaming Ferry Building, the local shopping opportunities reflect the city's various personalities. Visitors with limited time often focus their energies on the high-density Union Square area, where several major department stores tower over big-name boutiques. But if you're keen to find unique local shops, consider moving beyond the square's radius.

Each neighborhood has its own distinctive finds, whether it's 1960s housewares, cheeky stationery, or vintage Levi's. If shopping in San Francisco has a downside, it's that real bargains can be few and far between. Sure, neighborhoods such as the Lower Haight and the Mission have thrift shops and other inexpensive stores, but you won't find many discount outlets in the city, where rents are sky-high and space is at a premium.

Seasonal sales, usually in late January and late July or August, are good opportunities for finding deep discounts on clothing. The *San Francisco Chronicle* and *San Francisco Examiner* advertise sales. For smaller shops, check the free *SF Weekly*, which can be found on street corners every Wednesday. Sample sales are usually held by individual manufacturers, so check your favorite company's website before visiting.

SHOPPING

UNION SQUARE AND CHINATOWN

UNION SQUARE

Serious shoppers head straight to Union Square, San Francisco's main shopping area and the site of most of its department stores, including Macy's, Neiman Marcus, Barneys, and Saks Fifth Avenue. Nearby are such platinum-card international boutiques as Yves Saint Laurent, Cartier, Emporio Armani, Gucci, Hermès, and Louis Vuitton.

The **Westfield San Francisco Shopping Centre,** anchored by Bloomingdale's and Nordstrom, is notable for its gorgeous atriums and its top-notch dining options.

■TIP→ Most retailers in the square don't open until 10 am or later, so there isn't much advantage to getting an early start unless you're grabbing breakfast nearby. If you're on the prowl for art, be aware that many galleries are closed on Sundays and Mondays.

ART GALLERIES

The Bond Latin Gallery. The charming owners of this Latin American art gallery will alone make you want to return. Cozy yet light, some of the vibrant works on show come from such artists as Diego Rivera, Laura Hernandez, and Francisco Toledo. ⊠ *251 Post St., Suite 610, Union Sq.* ☎ *415/362–1480* ⊕ *www.bondlatin.com* ◷ *Closed Sun.*

Fodor's Choice
★

Fraenkel Gallery. This renowned gallery represents museum-caliber photographers or their estates, including Nicholas Nixon, Nan Goldin, Richard Misrach, and Garry Winogrand. Recent shows have included work by Robert Adams, Idris Khan, and Hiroshi Sugimoto. Most shows feature one or two artists, but the annual "Several Exceptionally Good Recently Acquired Pictures" showcases the range of works the gallery exhibits. ⊠ *49 Geary St., 4th fl., between Kearny St. and Grant Ave., Union Sq.* ☎ *415/981–2661* ⊕ *fraenkelgallery.com* ◷ *Closed Sun. and Mon.*

Hackett-Mill Gallery. This gallery prides itself on its friendly staffers who will educate you about the art or leave you alone, whichever you prefer. Some of the artists here include Conrad Marca-Relli, Esteban Vincente, Kenzo Okada, and Robert De Niro Sr. The specialties here are American modern, postwar abstract expressionist, and Bay Area figurative art. ⊠ *201 Post St., Suite 1000, at Grant Ave., Union Sq.* ☎ *415/362–3377* ⊕ *www.hackettmill.com* ◷ *Closed Sat.–Mon.*

Hang Art. A spirit of fun imbues this inviting space that showcases emerging artists. Prices range from a few hundred dollars to several thousand, making it an ideal place for novice collectors to get their feet wet. ⊠ *567 Sutter St., 2nd fl., near Mason St., Union Sq.* ☎ *415/434–4264* ⊕ *www.hangart.com.*

Hespe Gallery. Priced between $3,000 and $50,000, the paintings and sculptures here by midcareer artists, many of them Californians, are primarily representational. Owner Charles Hespe is an instantly likable art enthusiast who delights buyers and browsers. ⊠ *251 Post St., Suite*

18

210, between Stockton St. and Grant Ave., Union Sq. ☎415/776–5918 ⊕ www.hespe.com ⊗ Closed Sun. and Mon.

John Berggruen Gallery. Twentieth-century American and European paintings are displayed throughout three airy floors. Some recent exhibitions have included the works of Robert Kelly and Isca Greenfield-Sanders. Look for thematic shows here too; past exhibits have had titles such as Summer Highlights and Four Decades. ✉ 228 Grant Ave., at Post St., Union Sq. ☎415/781–4629 ⊕ www.berggruen.com ⊗ Closed Sun.

Meyerovich Gallery. Sculpture and works on paper by masters such as Pablo Picasso, Robert Motherwell, David Sultan, and Helen Frankenthaler are the attraction. Guy Dill's whimsical contemporary sculptures draw the eye from across the room. ✉251 Post St., Suite 400, 4th fl., between Stockton St. and Grant Ave., Union Sq. ☎415/421–7171 ⊕ www.meyerovich.com ⊗ Closed Sun.

Modernism. Multimodal exhibits are on a seven-week rotation and span an impressive arc of multimedia, photography, performance, painting, and sculpture. Featured artists have included Le Corbusier and Erwin Blumenfeld. ✉ Monadnock Bldg., 685 Market St., Suite 290, Union Sq. ☎415/541–0461 ⊕ www.modernisminc.com.

Robert Tat Gallery. Old meets new in Robert Tat's meticulously selected photography collection. Early 20th-century modernist works hang adjacent to contemporary pieces. A visit takes you back in time and around the world as well. ✉49 Geary St., Suite 410, Union Sq. ☎415/781–1122 ⊕ www.roberttat.com ⊗ Closed Sun. and Mon.; Tues. by appointment only.

Serge Sorokko Gallery. This big, bright open space is a welcoming retreat from the racing pulse of Geary Street. The friendly, knowledgeable staff will answer your questions as you stroll past walls and podiums decorated by the works of some very famous contemporary artists, including the paintings of Hunt Slonem and porcelain flowers of Vladimir Kanevsky. It's the perfect place to get lost, and to spend a few thousand to tens of thousands of dollars, if you're so inclined. ✉55 Geary St., between Kearny St. and Grant Ave., Union Sq. ☎415/421–7770 ⊕ www.sorokko.com.

BEAUTY

The Art of Shaving. Looking for a silver-tip badger brush? A polished-teak shaving-soap bowl? Or even sandalwood-infused pre-shave oil? You can pick up all of these items here, while the master barbers in the back provide anything from a moustache trim to the 45-minute "Royal Shave" (including hot towel and after-shave mask). ✉287 Geary St., at Powell St., Union Sq. ☎415/677–0871 ⊕ www.theartofshaving.com.

Fresh. The cosmetics line's only Northern California store occupies a quaint historic structure built just after the 1906 earthquake. Indulge in oval milk soaps from France, sugar-lemon lotion, and pomegranate conditioner. Fresh is most popular for its body-care sets, the Umbrian Clay being one of them. During the holiday season, the Seaberry Restorative Body Cream can be hard to come. ✉301 Sutter St., at Grant Ave., Union Sq. ☎415/248–0210 ⊕ www.fresh.com.

Lush. Towers of bulk soap, which can be cut to order, and mountains of baseball-size fizzing "bath bombs" are some of the first items you'll see in this tightly packed and extremely fragrant little boutique, which resembles a cheese shop more than a Sephora. Some potions are so fresh (and perishable) that they're stored in a refrigerator and come with an expiration date. ⊠ *240 Powell St., between O'Farrell and Geary Sts., Union Sq.* ☎ *415/693–9633* ⊕ *www.lushusa.com.*

CLOTHING: MEN AND WOMEN

Anne Fontaine. Brazilian-born designer Anne Fontaine's meticulously detailed button-up white shirts put a feminine touch on the menswear staple, with flounces at the neckline, impossibly tiny pleats, or ruching at the waist. The spare little store also stocks pants, skirts, and jackets to complement her famous tops. ⊠ *118 Grant Ave., at Maiden La., Union Sq.* ☎ *415/677–0911* ⊕ *www.annefontaine.com.*

The Archive. The closest thing to Savile Row in San Francisco, this small, cutting-edge, men-only boutique has everything from handmade suits to large handmade silver belt buckles from top-shelf Japanese and Italian designers. ⊠ *317 Sutter St., near Grant Ave., Union Sq.* ☎ *415/391– 5550* ⊕ *archivesf.com* ☾ *Closed Sun.*

Cable Car Clothiers/Robert Kirk Ltd. This classic British menswear store, open since 1939, is so fully stocked that a whole room is dedicated to hats, pants are cataloged like papers in file cabinets, and entire displays showcase badger-bristle shaving brushes. ■ TIP→ **The cable-car logo gear, from silk ties to pewter banks, makes for dashing souvenirs.** ⊠ *110 Sutter St., Suite 108, Union Sq.* ☎ *415/397–4740* ⊕ *www. cablecarclothiers.com* ☾ *Closed Sun.*

Gucci. The gold-label designer exudes luxe elegance in a palatial temple of black lacquer, bronze, and marble. Fine jewelry, handbags, and luggage dominate the first floor, and shoes rule the second. If you make it to the third floor without maxing out your credit card, you'll be rewarded with a flute of champagne for trying on an evening gown or dinner coat. ⊠ *200 Stockton St., Union Sq.* ☎ *415/392–2808* ⊕ *www.gucci.com.*

Levi's. A massive flagship for 501s, this is quite possibly the biggest place to buy your favorite pair of five-pocket jeans. Every style, size, color, and cut of the original denim brand is here. You can even get a custom fitting if you book ahead of time. ⊠ *815 Market St., at 4th St., Union Sq.* ☎ *415/501–0100* ⊕ *us.levi.com.*

Marc Jacobs. Fashion's wunderkind peddles his buckled leather bags, bright patent-leather shoes, and shrunken cashmere sweaters at his designer outpost—minus the expected pretense. The less expensive Marc by Marc Jacobs line, at 2142 Fillmore Street in Pacific Heights, includes plastic knickknacks, key chains, and buttons that make for quirky souvenirs. ⊠ *125 Maiden La., at Grant Ave., Union Sq.* ☎ *415/362–6500* ⊕ *www.marcjacobs.com.*

Fodor'sChoice **Margaret O'Leary.** If you can only buy one piece of clothing in San Francisco, make it a hand-loomed, cashmere sweater by this Irish-born local ★ legend. The perfect antidote to the city's wind and fog, the sweaters are so beloved by San Franciscans that some of them never wear anything else. Pick up an airplane wrap for your trip home, or a media cozy

18

to keep your iPod toasty. Another store is in Pacific Heights, at 2400 Fillmore Street. ⊠ *1 Claude La., at Sutter St., just west of Kearny St., Union Sq.* ☎ *415/391–1010* ⊕ *www.margaretoleary.com.*

Metier. For boutique shopping that's anything but hit or miss, browse through this unusual selection of jewelry by artists like Arielle de Pinto, Philip Crangi, and Gillian Conroy. The one-of-a-kind rings, charms, and pendants have won this boutique an obsessively loyal following. ⊠ *546 Laguna St., between Linden St. and Hayes St., Union Sq.* ☎ *415/590–2998* ⊕ *www.metiersf.com.*

Scotch & Soda. With clean tailored lines and deep solid colors, there is something elegant yet cutting-edge for every age here. Based on Amsterdam couture, and carrying European labels, this hive of a shop is cool but friendly; it also has an old but new feel to it. The Bodycon Peplum dress is a classic, as is the men's stretch wool blazer. This is a good place to visit if you're looking for a new pair of denims, or a cool shirt for a night out. ⊠ *59 Grant Ave., between Geary and O'Farrell Sts., Union Sq.* ☎ *415/644–8334* ⊕ *www.scotch-soda.com.*

Tory Burch. The East Coast socialite–turned–designer has brightened staid Maiden Lane with her outpost for Bergdorf Blondes, inspired by designs from the '60s and '70s. The carpet is a rich avocado, walls are magenta among other colors, and velvet curtains frame floor-to-ceiling mirrors in other candy colors. In addition to her ubiquitous ballet flats, Burch's signature tunics, silk blouses, and suits are on offer. ⊠ *50 Maiden La., between Kearny St. and Grant Ave., Union Sq.* ☎ *415/398–1525* ⊕ *www.toryburch.com.*

DEPARTMENT STORES

Barneys New York. Fashion is taken seriously here (a pair of distressed shoes that look like they've been mowed down on the highway can cost you over a grand), but it's always offered with a wink and a smile. Witty touches abound, from the infamous store windows to the design details throughout. As you enter Barneys' six-story corner locale, a flight of stairs extends to the mezzanine, with its salon displaying thousands of shoes. Below street level, cosmetics and fragrances reign. ⊠ *77 O'Farrell St., at Stockton St., Union Sq.* ☎ *415/268–3500* ⊕ *www.barneys.com.*

Bloomingdale's. The black-and-white checkerboard theme, the abundance of glass, and the sheer size might remind you of Vegas. This department store emphasizes American labels like Diane von Furstenberg and Jack Spade. The well-planned layout defines individual departments without losing the grand and open feel. ⊠ *845 Market St., between 4th and 5th Sts., Union Sq.* ☎ *415/856–5300* ⊕ *www.bloomingdales.com.*

Fodor's Choice
★

Gump's. It's a San Francisco institution, dating to the 19th century, and it's a strikingly luxurious one. The airy store exudes a museumlike vibe, with its large decorative vases, sumptuous housewares, and Tahitian-pearl display. It's a great place to pick up gifts, such as the Golden Gate Bridge note cards or silver-plated butter spreaders in a signature Gump's box. ⊠ *135 Post St., near Kearny St., Union Sq.* ☎ *415/982–1616* ⊕ *www.gumps.com.*

Macy's. The city's biggest department store has become so vast by absorbing spaces abdicated by competitors that it stocks just about everything you could want—if you have the patience to find it. The main location, with entrances on Geary, Stockton, and O'Farrell streets, houses the women's, children's, furniture, and housewares departments. With its emphasis on American designers like DKNY and Marc Jacobs, the department for young women stands out. Menswear occupies its own building across Stockton Street. ■ TIP → The Union Square views from the Cheesecake Factory's eighth-floor balcony are breathtaking. ✉ *170 O'Farrell St., at Stockton St., Union Sq.* ☎ *415/397–3333* ⊕ *www.macys.com.*

Neiman Marcus. The surroundings, which include a Philip Johnson–designed checkerboard facade, a gilded atrium, and a stained-glass skylight, are as ritzy as the goods showcased within. The mix includes designer men's and women's clothing and accessories as well as posh household wares. ■ TIP → Although the prices may raise an eyebrow or two, the Last Call sales—in January and July—draw big crowds. After hitting the vast handbag salon, those who lunch daintily can order consommé and bread laden with strawberry butter in the Rotunda Restaurant. ✉ *150 Stockton St., at Geary St., Union Sq.* ☎ *415/362–3900* ⊕ *www.neimanmarcus.com.*

Nordstrom. Somehow Nordstrom manages to be all things to all people, and this location, with spiral escalators circling a four-story atrium, is no exception. Whether you're an elegant lady of a certain age shopping for a new mink coat or a teen on the hunt for a Roxy hoodie, the salespeople are known for being happy to help. Nordstrom carries the best selections in town of designers such as Tory Burch, but its own brands have loyal followings, too. ■ TIP → The café upstairs is a superb choice for a shopping break. ✉ *Westfield Shopping Centre, 865 Market St., at 5th St., Union Sq.* ☎ *415/243–8500* ⊕ *shop.nordstrom.com.*

Saks Fifth Avenue. The West Coast branch of the New York legend claims a prime chunk of Union Square territory and it's chockablock with women swinging the latest "it" handbag. Where the store really outshines the competition, though, is at the incredibly well-stocked Men's Store down the street at 220 Post. The staff's service is so impeccable that even casual guys enjoy dressing up. ✉ *384 Post St., at Powell St., Union Sq.* ☎ *415/986–4300* ⊕ *www.saksfifthavenue.com.*

ELECTRONICS

Apple Store San Francisco. A shiny, stainless-steel box is the setting for Apple's flagship San Francisco store, a high-tech temple to Macs and the people who use them. Play around with iPhones, laptops, and hundreds of geeky accessories, then watch a theater presentation or attend an educational workshop. ✉ *1 Stockton St., at Market St., Union Sq.* ☎ *415/392–0202* ⊕ *www.apple.com.*

FOOD AND DRINK

William Glen. The more than 400 whiskies arranged along the back wall—mostly single-malt Scotches—are organized by their region of origin, so you can easily distinguish those made in Islay from those from Speyside or Lowland. The charming Scottish proprietor can tell

18

you about his favorites, help you with the selection of tartan scarves or cashmere sweaters, or even equip you with a kilt. ⊠ *360 Sutter St., between Grant Ave. and Stockton St., Union Sq.* ☎ *415/989–5458* ⊕ *www.wmglen.com.*

FURNITURE, HOUSEWARES, AND GIFTS

Fodor'sChoice **Diptyque.** The original Diptyque boutique in Paris has attracted a long
★ line of celebrities. You can find the full array of scented candles and fragrances in this chic shop that would be at home on the boulevard St-Germain. Trademark black-and-white labels adorn the popular L'eau toilet water, scented with geranium and sandalwood. Candles come in traditional and esoteric scents, including lavender, basil, leather, and fig tree. Also available are Mariage Frères teas. ⊠ *171 Maiden La., near Stockton St., Union Sq.* ☎ *415/402–0600* ⊕ *www.diptyqueparis.com.*

Samuel Scheuer. Designers and other fans make their way here for luxurious bed and bath items and linens. The pretty tablecloths, runners, and napkins, fragrant candles, and luxurious bath accessories are popular gifts. ⊠ *340 Sutter St., between Grant Ave. and Stockton St., Union Sq.* ☎ *415/392–2813* ⊕ *www.scheuerlinens.com.*

Williams-Sonoma. Behind striped awnings and a historic facade lies the massive mother ship of the Sonoma-founded kitchen-store empire. La Cornue custom stoves beckon you inward, and two grand staircases draw you upward to the world of dinnerware, linens, and chefs' tools. Antique tart tins, eggbeaters, and pastry cutters from the personal collection of founder Chuck Williams line the walls. ⊠ *340 Post St., between Powell and Stockton Sts., Union Sq.* ☎ *415/362–9450* ⊕ *www. williams-sonoma.com.*

HANDBAGS, LUGGAGE, AND LEATHER GOODS

Ghurka Trading and Design. The rich aroma of leather wraps around you as you walk through the doors; vintage chestnut leather duffel bags, olive twill briefcases, and leather poker sets wait patiently for you to take them home. Prices range from a few hundred to a few thousand dollars, but the quality here is worthy of such a price tag. ⊠ *245 Post St., between Stockton and Grant Sts., Union Sq.* ☎ *415/986–2250* ⊕ *www.ghurka.com.*

Goyard. After more than a century of selling trunks, handbags, and pet leashes to Parisians, Goyard opened its second store here to offer San Franciscans a discreet alternative to Louis Vuitton. Rather than splash its name everywhere, the store signals luxury with a signature chevron pattern. Even if you walk away empty-handed, you'll be reminded of what travel used to mean. ⊠ *345 Powell St., between Post and Geary Sts., Union Sq.* ☎ *415/398–1110* ⊕ *www.goyard.com.*

HANDICRAFTS AND FOLK ART

Britex Fabrics. Walls of Italian wool in deep rich colors, yards of Faille striped silk, and neat stacks of fresh cotton prints await your creative touch. A San Francisco institution, the multifloor Britex also sells a wide array of buttons, thread, and trim. If sewing is your thing, this will be a visit to paradise. ⊠ *146 Geary St., between Grant Ave. and Stockton St., Union Sq.* ☎ *415/392–2910* ⊕ *www.britexfabrics.com.*

Fodor's Choice **Xanadu Gallery San Francisco.** The spectacular international art and antiq-
★ uities displayed here include Latin American folk art and masks, sculp-
tures, woven baskets, tapestries, and textiles from Africa, Oceania, and
Indonesia. Museum-quality pieces such as a gilt bronze figure of a lama
(Tibetan Buddhist holy man) can go for nearly $100,000, but beautiful
books on subjects such as Tibetan art make more-affordable souvenirs.
■ TIP→ The shop is worth a visit to see its Frank Lloyd Wright-designed
space, whose spiral ramp recalls New York City's Guggenheim Museum.
⊠ *140 Maiden La., between Grant Ave. and Stockton St., Union Sq.*
☎ *415/392–9999* ⊕ *www.xanadugallery.us* ☉ *Closed Sun. and Mon.*

JEWELRY AND COLLECTIBLES

Lang Antiques and Estate Jewelry. Dozens of diamond bracelets in the
window attract shoppers to one of the city's best vintage jewelry shops,
where rings, brooches, and other glittering items represent various eras
and styles, from Victorian and Edwardian to art nouveau and Arts and
Crafts. The shop has been selling fine jewelry, including engagement
rings and a few vintage watches, since 1969. ⊠ *323 Sutter St., at Grant
Ave., Union Sq.* ☎ *415/982–2213* ⊕ *www.langantiques.com.*

Shreve & Co. Along with gems in dazzling settings, San Francisco's oldest
retail store—it's been at this location since 1852—carries watches by
Jaeger-LeCoultre and others. On weekends well-heeled couples scope
out hefty diamond engagement rings. ⊠ *200 Post St., at Grant Ave.,
Union Sq.* ☎ *415/421–2600* ⊕ *www.shreve.com.*

Tiffany & Co. This gray marble beauty towers over Union Square with
almost as much leverage as its signature blue box. The company that all
but invented the modern engagement ring makes more than just brides
swoon with Elsa Peretti's sinuous silver and architect Frank Gehry's collection using materials like Pernambuco wood and black gold. ⊠ *350
Post St., between Powell and Stockton Sts., Union Sq.* ☎ *415/781–7000*
⊕ *www.tiffany.com.*

18

SHOES

Camper. The Spanish brand's whimsical footwear is wildly popular with
young adults. Unexpected embroidered patterns (leaves, butterflies)
adorn many of the pairs, sometimes beginning on one shoe and continuing on the other. Other styles are reminiscent of bowling and boxing
shoes. ⊠ *39 Grant Ave., between O'Farrell and Geary Sts., Union Sq.*
☎ *415/296–1005* ⊕ *www.camper.com.*

SPORTING GOODS

Niketown. More glitzy multimedia extravaganza than true sporting-
goods store, this emporium is nevertheless the best place in town to
find anything and everything with the famous swoosh. ⊠ *278 Post St.,
at Stockton St., Union Sq.* ☎ *415/392–6453* ⊕ *store.nike.com.*

The North Face. The Bay Area–based national retailer is famous for its
tents, sleeping bags, backpacks, and outdoor apparel, including rugged
Gore-Tex jackets and pants. ⊠ *180 Post St., at Grant Ave., Union Sq.*
☎ *415/433–3223* ⊕ *www.thenorthface.com.*

CHINATOWN

The intersection of Grant Avenue and Bush Street marks the gateway to Chinatown. The area's 24 blocks of shops, restaurants, and markets are a nonstop tide of activity. Dominating the exotic cityscape are the sights and smells of food: crates of bok choy, tanks of live crabs, cages of live partridges, and hanging whole chickens. Racks of Chinese silks, colorful pottery, baskets, and carved figurines are displayed chockablock on the sidewalks, alongside fragrant herb shops where your bill might be tallied on an abacus. And if you need to knock off souvenir shopping for the kids and coworkers in your life, the dense and multiple selections of toys, T-shirts, mugs, magnets, decorative boxes, and countless other trinkets make it a quick, easy, and inexpensive proposition.

FOOD AND DRINK

Golden Gate Fortune Cookies. Nestled in a narrow alleyway, this tiny destination is impossible to find unless you have directions. This is the place to watch fortune cookies being made; an intricate process involves flattening, folding, and pressing patches of dough. You can purchase big bags of cookies in various flavors, shapes, and sizes to take home. ⊠ *56 Ross Alley, Chinatown* ☎ *415/781–3956.*

Great China Herb Co. Since 1922, this aromatic shop has been treating the city with its wide selection of ginseng, tea, and other herbs. You might even hear the click of an abacus as a purchase is tallied up. A Chinese doctor (who speaks English) is always on hand to recommend the perfect remedy. ⊠ *857 Washington St., between Grant Ave. and Stockton St., Chinatown* ☎ *415/982–2195.*

Fodor'sChoice ★ **Vital Tea Leaf.** Tea enthusiasts will feel at peace in this bright, spacious, hardwood-floor haven for sipping. You'll find more than 400 different varieties of tea here, and the staff is extremely knowledgeable on the health benefits of each and every one. ⊠ *1044 Grant Ave., between Jackson St. and Pacific Ave., Chinatown* ☎ *415/981–2388* ⊕ *www. vitaltealeaf.net.*

FURNITURE, HOUSEWARES, AND GIFTS

The Wok Shop. The store carries woks, of course, but also anything else you could need for Chinese cooking—bamboo steamers, ginger graters, wicked-looking cleavers—plus accessories for Japanese cooking, including sushi paraphernalia and tempura racks. ⊠ *718 Grant Ave., at Sacramento St., Chinatown* ☎ *415/989–3797* ⊕ *www.wokshop.com.*

TOYS AND GADGETS

Chinatown Kite Shop. The kites sold here range from basic diamond shapes to box- and animal-shape configurations. ■ TIP➔ Colorful dragon kites make great souvenirs. ⊠ *717 Grant Ave., near Sacramento St., Chinatown* ☎ *415/989–5182* ⊕ *www.chinatownkite.com.*

SOMA AND CIVIC CENTER

SOMA

ANTIQUES

Antonio's Antiques. This SoMa maze of museum-quality English and French antiques and objets d'art might include an 18th-century French harp or delicate tortoise-shell miniatures. The shop's inventory leans toward items from the 17th and 18th centuries. ⊠ *701 Bryant St., at 5th St., SoMa* ☎ *415/781–1737.*

Grand Central Station Antiques. This large, three-story space stocks mostly 19th- and early-20th-century European and American storage pieces—armoires, highboys, buffets, and the occasional barrister bookcase—with an emphasis on the small and practical. Service is affable. ⊠ *353 9th St., between Ringold and Sheridan Sts., SoMa* ☎ *415/252–8155* ⊕ *www.gcsantiques.com.*

ART GALLERIES

Arthaus. This one-story gallery south of Market provides an intimate space for both local and New York artists to display their contemporary work. Gallery owners Annette Schutz and James Bacchi are very approachable and include a diverse range of mediums as well as rotating shows beneath their roof. ⊠ *411 Brannan St., between 3rd and 4th Sts., SoMa* ☎ *415/977–0223* ⊕ *www.arthaus-sf.com* ☾ *Closed Sun. and Mon.*

Crown Point Press. What started as a print workshop in 1962 now includes studios as well as a large, airy gallery where etchings, intaglio prints, engravings, and aquatints by local and internationally renowned artists are displayed. ⊠ *20 Hawthorne St., between 2nd and 3rd Sts., SoMa* ☎ *415/974–6273* ⊕ *www.crownpoint.com* ☾ *Closed weekends.*

San Francisco Camerawork. This nonprofit organization mounts thematic exhibits and has a well-stocked bookstore and a reference library. The lecture program includes noted photographers and critics. ⊠ *1011 Market St., 2nd fl., at 6th St., SoMa* ☎ *415/487–1011* ⊕ *www.sfcamerawork.org* ☾ *Closed Sun. and Mon.*

Varnish Fine Art. Jen Rogers and Kerri Stephens' gallery specializes in thought-provoking works such as those by San Francisco based artist Brian Goggin, known for his public art piece Defenestration. Ransom & Mitchell, two other noteworthy locals the gallery represents, blend photography and set design together to create a truly surreal visual experience. This gallery is open by appointment only, Tuesday through Saturday from 11 am to 6 pm. ⊠ *16 Jessie St., Suite C120, near 1st St., SoMa* ☎ *415/433–4400* ⊕ *www.varnishfineart.com* ☾ *Closed Sun. and Mon.*

BOOKS

Alexander Book Co. The three floors here are stocked with literature, poetry, and children's books, with a focus on hard-to-find works by men and women of color. ⊠ *50 2nd St., between Jessie and Stevenson Sts., SoMa* ☎ *415/495–2992* ⊕ *www.alexanderbook.com.*

Fodor's Choice ★ **Chronicle Books.** This local beacon of publishing produces inventively designed fiction, cookbooks, art books, and other titles, as well as

18

diaries, planners, and address books—all of which you can purchase at three airy and attractive spaces. The other stores are at 680 2nd Street, near AT&T Park, and 1846 Union Street, in Cow Hollow. ⊠ *Metreon Westfield Shopping Center, 165 4th St., near Howard St., SoMa* ☎ *415/369–6271* ⊕ *www.chroniclebooks.com.*

CLOTHING: OUTLET AND DISCOUNT

Jeremy's. A discount store for people who usually wouldn't be caught dead discount shopping, this store offers steep markdowns (generally 20% to 50%, with occasional clearance items going priced even lower) on top-notch men's and women's apparel by designers such as Prada and Jil Sander. The space is tidily organized, so you won't need to rack-rake. ⊠ *2 South Park St., at 2nd St., SoMa* ☎ *415/882–4929* ⊕ *www. jeremys.com.*

Nordstrom Rack. Items from the Nordstrom department store are discounted between 30% and 75% here. The goods include fragrances, bath and body products, and a few housewares, as well as a good selection of men's and women's clothing and accessories displayed on well-organized racks. Call for the dates of new-arrival events, when savvy shoppers arrive promptly at opening time for the best selection. ⊠ *555 9th St., at Brannan St., SoMa* ☎ *415/934–1211* ⊕ *shop.nordstrom.com.*

FOOD AND DRINK

Blue Bottle Coffee. The revered microroaster's practitioners brew their sacred beans in a $20,000 siphon bar from Japan with halogen-lighted glass globes that resemble a science experiment. A stop here makes for a perfect reprieve from shopping. ⊠ *66 Mint Plaza, off Mission St., SoMa* ☎ *415/495–3394* ⊕ *www.bluebottlecoffee.com.*

Bluxome Street Winery. Wine shops exist all over the city, but this is the only winery within city limits. Grapes are brought in from Russian River Valley, and all production takes place on-site, reviving an industry that was once thriving a hundred years ago in SoMa before Napa and Sonoma took it over. Come to the tasting room to sample light summery Rosés, rich Pinot Noirs, or refreshing Sauvignon Blancs. On the last Saturday of each month, the space becomes a farmers' market with local vendors selling honey and eggs alongside the wine. ⊠ *53 Bluxome St., SoMa* ☎ *415/543–5353* ⊕ *www.bluxomewinery.com* ☉ *Closed Mon.*

City Beer. More than 450 beers (many refrigerated) are for sale here, and with six on tap that you can imbibe while you shop. You'll get 10% off when you mix and match your six-pack with everything from Allagash Curieux, a dark beer aged in Jim Beam barrels, to Dogfish Head, a light pilsner with pear juice. ⊠ *1168 Folsom St., Suite 101, near 8th St., SoMa* ☎ *415/503–1033* ⊕ *www.citybeerstore.com.*

K&L Wine Merchants. More than any other wine store, this one has an ardent cult following around town. The friendly staffers promise not to sell what they don't taste themselves, and weekly events—on Thursday from 5 pm to 6:30 pm and Saturday from noon to 3 pm—open the tastings to customers. The best-seller list for varietals and regions for both the under- and over-$30 categories appeals to the wine lover in everyone. ⊠ *638 4th St., between Brannan and Townsend Sts., SoMa* ☎ *415/896–1734* ⊕ *www.klwines.com.*

Wine Club. The large selection and great prices make up for this wine shop's bare-bones ambience. At the self-serve wine bar you can taste wines for a modest fee, a great boon if you want to try before you buy. Caviar and wine paraphernalia, including Riedel wineglasses, books, openers, and decanters, are also sold here. ⊠ *953 Harrison St., between 5th and 6th Sts., SoMa* ☏ *415/512–9086* ⊕ *www.thewineclub.com.*

FURNITURE, HOUSEWARES, AND GIFTS

Mscape. The shop sells sleek furniture and accessories, such as low-slung couches with nary a curve in sight, and a variety of platform beds. Many items can be custom ordered. ⊠ *521 6th St., between Bryant and Brannan Sts., SoMa* ☏ *415/543–1771* ⊕ *mscapesf.com.*

HANDBAGS, LUGGAGE, AND LEATHER GOODS

Kate Spade. Punchy colors, retro shapes, and a cheeky sense of humor have made Kate Spade purses wildly popular among ladies of all ages. Case in point: the Over the Moon Rocket clutch is actually shaped as a rocket and contains 14-karat gold plated hardware. The shop also stocks shoes, cosmetics cases, datebooks, and note cards. ⊠ *865 Market St., SoMa* ☏ *415/222–9638* ⊕ *www.katespade.com.*

JEWELRY AND COLLECTIBLES

San Francisco Museum of Modern Art Museum Store. The shop is known for its exclusive line of watches and jewelry, as well as artists' monographs and artful housewares. Posters, calendars, children's art sets and books, and art books for adults round out the merchandise. ⊠ *Temporary location (until 2016) during SFMOMA's renovations, 51 Yerba Buena La., between Mission and Howard Sts., SoMa* ☏ *415/357–4035* ⊕ *museumstore.sfmoma.org.*

18

SPORTING GOODS

REI. In addition to carrying a vast selection of clothing and outdoor gear of the Seattle-based co-op, the store rents camping equipment and repairs snowboards and bikes. ⊠ *840 Brannan St., between 7th and 8th Sts., SoMa* ☏ *415/934–1938* ⊕ *www.rei.com.*

CIVIC CENTER

FARMERS' MARKETS

Heart of the City Farmers' Market. Three times a week vendors sell heaps of cheap produce, along with baked goods, potted herbs, and the occasional live chicken. ⊠ *United Nations Plaza, between 7th and 8th Sts., Civic Center* ☏ *415/558–9455* ⊕ *heartofthecity-farmersmar. squarespace.com* ♡ *Wed. 7–5:30, Fri. 7–2:30, Sun. 7–5.*

FURNITURE, HOUSEWARES, AND GIFTS

Sur la Table. Everything the home chef could need is here, along with round aspic cutters, larding needles, and other things many cooks never knew existed. The store hosts cooking classes and jaw-dropping demonstrations. ⊠ *San Francisco Centre, 845 Market St., at 5th St., Civic Center* ☏ *415/814–4691* ⊕ *www.surlatable.com.*

THE TENDERLOIN

ART GALLERIES

John Pence Gallery. The 8,000-square-foot facility, San Francisco's largest gallery, exhibits drawings, paintings, and sculpture. Many of the works are by important contemporary academic realists. ⊠ *750 Post St., between Leavenworth and Jones Sts., Tenderloin* ☎ *415/441–1138* ⊕ *www.johnpence.com* ⊘ *Closed Sun.*

Silverman Gallery. Fashion, music, performance, paintings, and photography collide here—literally. Every four to six weeks a new exhibit enters the space pushing the boundaries of content, concept, and form. The gallery also hosts talks with local and international artists. ⊠ *488 Ellis St., between Jones and Leavenworth Sts., Tenderloin* ☎ *415/255–9508* ⊕ *jessicasilvermangallery.com* ⊘ *Closed Sun. and Mon.*

HAYES VALLEY

ANTIQUES

Another Time. Specializing in beautifully restored furniture from the 1930s through the 1960s, this store sells Heywood Wakefield tambour buffets, art-deco bars, and French art-deco desks. Jewelry, glassware, and lamps are on display, too. ⊠ *1710 Market St., at Gough St., Hayes Valley* ☎ *415/553–8900* ⊕ *www.anothertimesf.com* ⊘ *Closed Mon. and Tues.*

BEAUTY

Nancy Boy. This sparse white-on-white locally owned store sells indulgent skin- and hair-care products for men, as well as a small selection of aromatherapy items, such as soy travel candles scented with essential oils. ⊠ *347 Hayes St., between Franklin and Gough Sts., Hayes Valley* ☎ *415/552–3636* ⊕ *www.nancyboy.com.*

BOOKS

The Green Arcade. For environmental, political, sustainable, and über-green books, look no further. With deep roots in the community, energetic artwork, and an atmosphere that encourages reading, this is a good place to hide away; the comfy chairs and warm vibe make it hard to leave. ⊠ *1680 Market St., at Gough St., Hayes Valley* ☎ *415/431–6800* ⊕ *www.thegreenarcade.com.*

CLOTHING: MEN AND WOMEN

Acrimony. A handblown-glass chandelier winks at you through the store's front window, while DJs do their thing in the back. Sandwiched in between are styles like Cameo miniskirts or Shona Joy's hip-hugging skinny pants. There's something special for men, too: double-layered muscle tees and Gitman Bros. blue oxfords and vintage chambray shirts. Think progressive and of-the-moment. ⊠ *333 Hayes St., between Franklin and Gough Sts., Hayes Valley* ☎ *415/861–1025* ⊕ *www.shopacrimony.com.*

Azalea Boutique. With a dose of global flair, this boutique blends art, fun, and fashion. The deep-red walls provide a flattering backdrop both for patrons and the extensive denim collection (more than 100 different styles). Designers from Ariana Bohling to Freda Salvador and

Pamela Love offer a true alternative from the ubiquitous department-store brands. At the nail bar here, you can indulge in natural services that include formaldehyde-free polish and organic cuticle creams. ✉ *411 Hayes St., at Gough St., Hayes Valley* ☎ *415/861–9888* ⊕ *www.azaleasf.com.*

Dish. Many of the women's clothes displayed within this spare space are romantic, minus the frills. Look for the chic dresses of local designer Kathryn McCarron, as well as clothing and accessories by more widely known brands like Etten Eller and Zoe Chicco. ✉ *541 Hayes St., between Laguna and Octavia Sts., Hayes Valley* ☎ *415/252–5997* ⊕ *www.dishboutique.com.*

Ver Unica. Though you can find a few items from the psychedelic '60s, beautifully preserved fashions from the '40s and '50s are the best reason for visiting. You can even track down purses and hard-to-find vintage shoes to go with that fur-trimmed jacket. ✉ *437B Hayes St., between Gough and Octavia Sts., Hayes Valley* ☎ *415/431–0688.*

Welcome Stranger. Azalea's stylish sister store for men carries designer brands like Ontour, Filson, and Eastland Shoes. The styles range from rugged outdoors to urban chic, but somehow it all works—locals can't get enough of them. ✉ *460 Gough St., between Hayes and Grove Sts., Hayes Valley* ☎ *415/864–2079* ⊕ *www.welcomestranger.com.*

FOOD AND DRINK

Arlequin Wine Merchant. If you like the wine list at Absinthe Brasserie, you can walk next door and pick up a few bottles from its highly regarded sister establishment. This small, unintimidating shop carries hard-to-find wines from small producers. Why wait to taste? Crack open a bottle on the patio out back. ✉ *384 Hayes St., at Gough St., Hayes Valley* ☎ *415/863–1104* ⊕ *www.arlequinwinemerchant.com.*

Miette Confiserie. There is truly nothing sweeter than a cellophane bag tied with blue-and-white twine and filled with malt balls or chocolate sardines from this European-style apothecary. Grab a gingerbread cupcake or a tantalizing macaroon or some shortbread. The pastel-color cake stands make even window-shopping a treat. ✉ *449 Octavia Blvd., between Hayes and Fell Sts., Hayes Valley* ☎ *415/626–6221* ⊕ *www.miette.com.*

True Sake. Though it would be reasonable to expect a Japanese aesthetic at the first store in the United States dedicated entirely to sake, you might instead hear dance music thumping quietly in the background while you browse. Each of the many sakes is displayed with a label describing the drink's qualities and food-pairing suggestions. ✉ *560 Hayes St., between Laguna and Octavia Sts., Hayes Valley* ☎ *415/355–9555* ⊕ *www.truesake.com.*

FURNITURE, HOUSEWARES, AND GIFTS

Flight 001. Ultra-stylish travel accessories—retro-looking flight bags, supersoft leather passport wallets, and tiny Swiss travel alarm clocks—line the shelves of this brightly lighted shop, which vaguely resembles an airplane interior. High-tech travel gear and a small collection of guidebooks speed you on your way. ✉ *525 Hayes St., between Laguna and Octavia Sts., Hayes Valley* ☎ *415/487–1001* ⊕ *www.flight001.com.*

18

Zonal. You'll find refurbished authentic American sofas and recycled and reclaimed cabinets here. The antique pieces date from the 1800s up to 1945. Works by local artists are also on display. ⊠ *568 Hayes St., at Laguna St., Hayes Valley* ☎ *415/255–9307* ⊕ *www.zonalhome.com.*

HANDICRAFTS AND FOLK ART

F. Dorian. In addition to cards, jewelry, and other crafts from Central and South America, Africa, Asia, and the Middle East—a carved wooden candleholder from the Ivory Coast is one example—this store carries brightly colored glass and ceramic works by local artisans and whimsical mobiles. ⊠ *370 Hayes St., between Franklin and Gough Sts., Hayes Valley* ☎ *415/861–3191.*

Polanco. Devoted to showcasing the arts of Mexico, this gallery sells everything from antiques and traditional folk crafts to fine contemporary paintings. Brightly painted animal figures and a virtual village of Day of the Dead figures share space with religious statues and modern linocuts and paintings. ⊠ *393 Hayes St., between Franklin and Gough Sts., Hayes Valley* ☎ *415/252–5753* ⊕ *www.polancogallery.com.*

SHOES

Gimme Shoes. From the chunky to the sleek, the shoes carried here—including those by Chie Mihara, Dries Van Noten, Loeffler Randall, and Sydney Brown —are top-notch. And if $600 seems steep for a pair of black books, perhaps you haven't seen the perfect pair by Fiorentini + Baker. ⊠ *416 Hayes St., at Gough St., Hayes Valley* ☎ *415/864–0691* ⊕ *www.gimmeshoes.com.*

Paolo Shoes. Looking for gorgeous handcrafted Italian leather shoes? (Who isn't?) This is *the* place in San Francisco to find them. From knee-high boots to contoured heel pumps, Paolo Iantorno's designs will make your heart miss a beat. The prices might as well; they hover around the $300 mark, but all shoes are made in quantities of 25 pieces or fewer. ⊠ *524 Hayes St., between Octavia and Laguna Sts., Hayes Valley* ☎ *415/552–4580* ⊕ *paoloshoes.com.*

NOB HILL AND POLK GULCH

CLOTHING: OUTLET AND DISCOUNT

Christine Foley. Discounts of up to 50% apply to the hand-loomed cotton sweaters with fanciful, intricate designs. There's also a large selection of colorful sweaters for children. Pillows, stuffed animals, and assorted knickknacks are also on offer in this small showroom. ⊠ *Fairmont Hotel, 950 Mason St., at California St., Nob Hill* ☎ *415/399–9938* ⊕ *www.christinefoley.com.*

CLOTHING: WOMEN'S

Cris. This upscale designer consignment shop (the locals' best kept secret) is full of nearly new items for a lot less than new prices. Chloe and Chanel are a couple of the many designers to grace the racks. Not only is this shop brimming with one-of-a-kind tops, dresses, and coats, but it smells like a spring garden. And to top it all off, they include a fresh flower with every purchase. ⊠ *2056 Polk St., at Broadway St., Polk Gulch* ☎ *415/474–1191* ⊕ *www.crisconsignment.com.*

JEWELRY AND COLLECTIBLES

Velvet da Vinci. Each contemporary piece of jewelry here is one-of-a-kind or limited edition. The beautiful, unusual items might be sculpted out of resin, hammered from copper, or woven with silver wires. ✉ *2015 Polk St., between Broadway St. and Pacific Ave., Polk Gulch* ☎ *415/441-0109* 🌐 *www.velvetdavinci.com.*

NORTH BEACH

ANTIQUES

Aria Antiques. Get a gift for your favorite globe-trotter at this oasis for the unordinary. You'll find maps, boxes, vases, and vintage furniture, as well as European artifacts. ✉ *1522 Grant Ave., between Union and Filbert Sts., North Beach* ☎ *415/433-0219* 🌐 *Closed Sun.*

Schein & Schein. This tiny spot sells antique maps and engraved prints, many with a local focus, from inexpensive prints to genuine collectors' pieces. Whether you're looking for a chart of the world from the 13th century or a map of the Barbary Coast, this shop just might have it. The helpful owners will enthrall you with their historical anecdotes and vast knowledge. ✉ *1435 Grant Ave., between Green and Union Sts., North Beach* ☎ *415/399-8882* 🌐 *www.scheinandschein.com* ⏲ *Closed Sun.; open by appointment only Mon. and June–Aug.*

BOOKS

Fodor's Choice ★ **City Lights Bookstore.** The city's most famous bookstore is where the Beat movement of the 1950s was born. Neal Cassady and Jack Kerouac hung out in the basement, and now regulars and tourists while hours away in this well-worn space. The upstairs room holds impressive poetry and Beat literature collections. Poet Lawrence Ferlinghetti, the owner, remains involved in the workings of this three-story shop. City Lights Publishers, which issued the poet Allen Ginsberg's *Howl* in 1956, publishes a dozen new titles each year. ✉ *261 Columbus Ave., at Broadway St., North Beach* ☎ *415/362-8193* 🌐 *www.citylights.com.*

18

CLOTHING: MEN AND WOMEN

AB fits. The friendly staff can help guys and gals sort through the jeans selection, one of the hippest in the city (check out the Dope & Drakker organic denim). Salespeople pride themselves on being able to match the pants to the person. ✉ *1519 Grant Ave., between Filbert and Union Sts., North Beach* ☎ *415/982-5726* 🌐 *abfits.com* ⏲ *Closed Mon.*

FOOD AND DRINK

Graffeo Coffee Roasting Company. Forget those fancy flavored coffees if you're ordering from this emporium, open since 1935 and one of the best-loved coffee stores in a city devoted to its java. The shop sells dark roast, light roast, and dark roast–decaf beans only. ✉ *735 Columbus Ave., at Filbert St., North Beach* ☎ *415/986-2420* 🌐 *www.graffeo.com.*

Fodor's Choice ★ **Molinari Delicatessen.** This store has been making its own salami, sausages, and cold cuts since 1896. Other homemade specialties include meat and cheese ravioli, tomato sauces, and fresh pastas. **■ TIP→ Do like the locals: grab a made-to-order sandwich for lunch and eat it at one of the sidewalk tables or over at Washington Square Park.** ✉ *373 Columbus Ave., at Vallejo St., North Beach* ☎ *415/421-2337.*

Victoria Pastry Co. In business since the early 1900s and a throwback to the North Beach of old, this bakery has display cases full of Italian pastries, cookies, and St. Honoré cakes. ⊠ *700 Filbert St., between Columbus Ave. and Powell St., North Beach* ☏ *415/781–2015.*

Fodor's Choice **XOX Truffles.** The decadent confection comes in 27 bite-size flavors here,
★ from the traditional (cocoa-powder-coated Amaretto) to the unusual (flavored with rum-coconut liqueur and coated with coconut flakes or enrobing a bit of caramel). There's something yummy for everyone, even vegans (soy truffles). ⊠ *754 Columbus Ave., between Greenwich and Filbert Sts., North Beach* ☏ *415/421–4814* ⊕ *www.xoxtruffles.com.*

FURNITURE, HOUSEWARES, AND GIFTS

Biordi Art Imports. Hand-painted Italian pottery, mainly imported from Tuscany and Umbria, has been shipped worldwide by this family-run business since 1946. Dishware sets can be ordered in any combination. ⊠ *412 Columbus Ave., at Vallejo St., North Beach* ☏ *415/392–8096* ⊕ *www.biordi.com* ⊙ *Closed Sun.*

MUSIC: MEMORABILIA

San Francisco Rock Posters and Collectibles. The huge selection of rock-and-roll memorabilia, including posters, handbills, and original art, takes you back to the 1960s. Also available are posters from more recent shows—many at the legendary Fillmore Auditorium—featuring such musicians as George Clinton and the late Johnny Cash. ⊠ *1851 Powell St., between Filbert and Greenwich Sts., North Beach* ☏ *415/956–6749* ⊕ *rockposters.com.*

PAPER AND STATIONERY

Lola of North Beach. A section of this intimate North Beach store is devoted to the various stages of a relationship: friendship, I like you, I love you, I miss you, I'm sorry, and I'm here for you. The shop also carries an impressive collection of baby clothes, including some adorable tees. ⊠ *1415 Grant Ave., at Green St., North Beach* ☏ *415/781–1817* ⊕ *lolaofnorthbeach.com.*

THE WATERFRONT

FISHERMAN'S WHARF

CLOTHING: MEN AND WOMEN

Helpers' Bazaar. Arguably the city's best-dressed philanthropist, Joy Bianchi, along with other volunteers, runs this store to benefit the mentally disabled. A red Bill Blass cocktail dress, a Chanel suit, or a Schiaparelli hat are among the vintage masterpieces you might expect to find here—to see the good stuff, all you have to do is ask nicely. Don't miss a look at Bianchi's "mouse couture," a clever fund-raiser display in which designers like Armani and Carolina Herrera dress up 4-inch stuffed mice. ⊠ *Ghirardelli Sq., 900 North Point St., Fisherman's Wharf* ☏ *415/441–0779.*

SPORTING GOODS

Patagonia. Technical wear for serious outdoors enthusiasts is the specialty. Along with sportswear and casual clothing, the store carries active wear for backpacking, fly-fishing, kayaking, and other activities.

✉ *770 North Point St., at Hyde St., Fisherman's Wharf* ☎ *415/771–2050* ⊕ *www.patagonia.com.*

EMBARCADERO

Four sprawling buildings of shops, restaurants, offices, and a popular independent movie theater—plus the Hyatt Regency hotel—make up the Embarcadero Center, downtown at the end of Market Street. Most of the stores are branches of upscale national chains, such as Ann Taylor and Banana Republic. Also in this area is the Ferry Building, with its food and other vendors.

BOOKS

Book Passage. Windows at this modest-size bookstore frame close-up views of the docks and San Francisco Bay. Commuters snap up magazines by the front door as they rush off to their ferries, while shoppers leisurely thumb through the thorough selection of cooking and travel titles. Author events take place several times a month. ✉ *Ferry Building Marketplace, 1 Ferry Bldg. #42, at foot of Market St., Embarcadero* ☎ *415/835–1020* ⊕ *www.bookpassage.com.*

FARMERS' MARKETS

Fodor's Choice ★ **Ferry Plaza Farmers' Market.** The partylike Saturday edition of the city's most upscale and expensive farmers' market places baked goods, gourmet cheeses, smoked fish, and fancy pots of jam alongside organic basil, specialty mushrooms, heirloom tomatoes, handcrafted jams, and juicy-ripe locally grown fruit. On Saturday about 100 vendors pack along three sides of the building, and sandwiches and other prepared foods are for sale in addition to fruit, vegetable, and other samples free for the nibbling. Smaller markets take place on Tuesday and Thursday. (The Thursday one doesn't operate from about late December through March.) ✉ *Ferry Plaza, at Market St., Embarcadero* ☎ *415/291–3276* ⊕ *www.ferrybuildingmarketplace.com* ⊗ *Tues. and Thurs. 10–2, Sat. 8–2.*

FOOD AND DRINK

Fodor's Choice ★ **Cowgirl Creamery Artisan Cheese.** Fantastic organic-milk cheeses—such as the mellow, triple-cream Mt. Tam and *bocconcini* (small balls of fresh mozzarella)—are produced at a creamery an hour's drive north of the city. These and other carefully chosen artisanal cheeses and dairy products, including a luscious, freshly made crème fraîche, round out the selection at the in-town store. ✉ *Ferry Building Marketplace, 1 Ferry Bldg. #17, at foot of Market St., Embarcadero* ☎ *415/362–9354* ⊕ *www.cowgirlcreamery.com.*

McEvoy Ranch. This is the only retail outpost of this Sonoma County ranch, a producer of outstanding organic, extra-virgin olive oil. ■TIP➔ **If you stop by in fall or winter, don't miss the Olio Nuovo, the days-old green oil produced during the harvest.** ✉ *Ferry Building Marketplace, 1 Ferry Bldg. #16, at foot of Market St., Embarcadero* ☎ *415/291–7224* ⊕ *www.mcevoyranch.com.*

Recchiuti Confections. Michael and Jacky Recchiuti began making otherworldly chocolates in 1997, using traditional European techniques. Now considered among the best confectioners in the world, they stock their store here (there's also a smaller one in the Dogpatch neighborhood) with their full chocolate line, including several unique items inspired by the surrounding gourmet markets. ⊠ *Ferry Building Marketplace, 1 Ferry Bldg., Suite 30, Embarcadero at foot of Market St., Embarcadero* ☎ *415/834–9494* ⊕ *www.recchiuti.com.*

FURNITURE, HOUSEWARES, AND GIFTS

The Gardener. Artful, functional home and garden accessories are the lure here, from woven baskets and teak salad bowls to beautifully illustrated books. Although there's only a small selection of actual gardening items, such as seeds, bulbs, and tools, there are plenty of bath and body items with which to pamper yourself after a day in the yard. ⊠ *Ferry Building Marketplace, 1 Ferry Bldg., Suite 26, at foot of Market St., Embarcadero* ☎ *415/981–8181* ⊕ *www.thegardener.com.*

SPORTING GOODS

FAMILY **Exploratorium.** The educational gadgets and gizmos sold here are so much fun that your kids—whether they're in grade school or junior high—might not realize they're learning while they're playing with them. Space- and dinosaur-related games are popular, as are science videos and CD-ROMs. ⊠ *Piers 15/17, at Embarcadero at Green St., Embarcadero* ☎ *415/528–4390* ⊕ *www.exploratorium.edu.*

FINANCIAL DISTRICT

ANTIQUES

Kathleen Taylor The Lotus Collection. The handmade pillows, tapestries depicting iconic events in Europe, and Japanese brocades make this one of the finest collections of decorative antique textiles in the States. It's also a secret source for the city's interior designers outfitting Pacific Heights mansions. ⊠ *445 Jackson St., between Montgomery and Sansome Sts., Financial District* ☎ *415/398–8115* ⊕ *www.ktaylor-lotus. com* ⊙ *Closed Sun.; Sat. by appointment only.*

BOOKS

William Stout Architectural Books. Architect William Stout began selling books out of his apartment 25 years ago. Today the store is a source for Bay Area professionals looking for serious-minded tomes on architecture and design. Head down into the crumbling whitewashed basement for beautifully illustrated coffee-table books. Stout is the sole distributor of the popular IDEO method cards, which offer and inspire design solutions. ⊠ *804 Montgomery St., between Gold and Jackson Sts., Financial District* ☎ *415/391–6757* ⊕ *www.stoutbooks.com* ⊙ *Closed Sun.*

THE MARINA

The Marina is an outstanding shopping nexus, with stylish boutiques and mainstream and specialty housewares stores. On sunny weekends on the main commercial drag, Chestnut Street, the point seems to be as much about seeing and being seen as shopping—at least among the neighborhood's grown-up sorority sisters and frat boys.

CLOTHING: MEN AND WOMEN

dress. This quaint boutique offers up fashions by dozens of brands, among them Kathy Kamei and Ulla Johnson. The clothes have been thoughtfully selected with entire wardrobes in mind. Items don't crowd the racks, and the service is friendly without being overwhelming. ■TIP➜ You can sometimes find good bargains here. ✉ *2271 Chestnut St., between Scott and Avila Sts., Marina* ☎ *415/440–3737* ⊕ *www.shopdressonline.com.*

CLOTHING: OUTLET AND DISCOUNT

My Roommate's Closet. Fed by more than 25 boutiques in San Francisco, New York, and Los Angeles, the Closet carries clothing and accessories by designers like BB Dakota, Current Elliot, and Alexander McQueen, all at least 50% off the retail price. ✉ *3044 Fillmore St., at Union St., Marina* ☎ *415/447–7703* ⊕ *myroommatescloset.com.*

COW HOLLOW

CLOTHING

Blues Jean Bar. At this Western-theme shop with more than a dozen different brands of jeans on tap, simply tell the "bartender" the size and style you seek, and you'll be loaded with trendy pairs you can try on in a "Him," "Her," or "Them" dressing room. ✉ *1827 Union St., between Laguna and Octavia Sts., Cow Hollow* ☎ *415/346–4280* ⊕ *thebluesjeanbar.com.*

Fodor's Choice ★ **Marmalade.** Filled with bright dresses and patterned tops, this Cow Hollow beacon of style has a real Californian feel. Designers both local and from Southern California are represented, and the owner and her staff are happy to help you match things, including earrings and sweaters and jeans and simple T-shirts. ✉ *1843 Union St., between Octavia and Laguna Sts., Cow Hollow* ☎ *415/400–4027* ⊕ *marmaladesf.com.*

18

FOOD AND DRINK

PlumpJack Wines. A small selection of imported wines complements the well-priced, well-stocked collection of hard-to-find California wines here. Gift baskets—such as the Italian market basket, containing wine, Italian foods, and a cookbook—are popular hostess gifts. Noe Valley has a sister store. ✉ *3201 Fillmore St., at Greenwich St., Cow Hollow* ☎ *415/346–9870* ⊕ *www.plumpjackwines.com.*

FURNITURE, HOUSEWARES, AND GIFTS

Fatto a Mano. Owned by a husband and wife team who met and lived in Italy, this corner store is filled with Italian antiques and old and new works by Italian artisans. You'll find hand-painted Tuscan ceramics, olive-wood knife sets, rustic Tuscan pine benches, and even Consigli cutlery. ✉ *1800 Union St., at Octavia St., Cow Hollow* ☎ *415/525–4348* ⊕ *www.fattoamanosf.com.*

Itoya Topdrawer. The Japanese company's first U.S. store sells everything from patterned *furoshiki* (a Japanese wrapping cloth) to bright, and very realistic, cupcake-shaped erasers. There's an extensive selection of colorful stationery, leather-bound journals, daisy-printed masking tape, and cards, many of which are made by local artists. ✉ *1840 Union*

St., between Octavia and Laguna Sts., Cow Hollow ☎ *415/771–1108* ⊕ *itoyatopdrawer.tumblr.com.*

JEWELRY AND COLLECTIBLES

Dianne's Old and New Estates. Fine watches and platinum wedding and engagement rings are the specialties of this store that also sells antique and estate jewelry, crystal, objets d'art, and silver items. ✉ *2181A Union St., at Fillmore St., Cow Hollow* ☎ *415/346–7525* ⊕ *www.shopdej. com.*

Union Street Goldsmith. This local favorite prides itself on its selection of rare gemstones, such as golden sapphires and violet tanzanite. Custom work is a specialty: the no-pressure design consultants are happy to discuss how to make the jewelry of your dreams a reality. ✉ *1909 Union St., at Laguna St., Cow Hollow* ☎ *415/776–8048* ⊕ *www. unionstreetgoldsmith.com.*

PET FASHIONS

Moulin Pooch. Button-down sweaters, lace-trimmed dresses, sunhats, sequined leashes—who knew dogs could dress this well? This shop also sells gourmet canine cookies, some with liver-flavored icing. The staffers will help you find just the right outfit for your pooch and can direct you to the full-service grooming facility in back. ✉ *1750 Union St., between Gough and Octavia Sts., Cow Hollow* ☎ *415/440–7007.*

SPORTING GOODS

Lululemon Athletica. This yoga-inspired company makes all kinds of athletic gear out of Luon fabric—it's nonchafing, moisture-wicking, pre-shrunk, and best of all it can be washed in warm water. The pants have a rep as the best thing in town for a yogi's derriere. ✉ *1981 Union St., between Laguna and Buchanan Sts., Cow Hollow* ☎ *415/776–5858* ⊕ *www.lululemon.com.*

TOYS AND GADGETS

ATYS. Gadgets with a sleek modern design are imported from Scandinavia, Italy, Germany, and Japan. Among the eye-catching items are fancy German watches that tell time in words and Japanese knives that could pass for sculptures. ✉ *2149B Union St., between Fillmore and Webster Sts., Cow Hollow* ☎ *415/441–9220* ⊕ *www.atysdesign.com.*

THE RICHMOND

BOOKS

Fodor's Choice ★ **Green Apple Books.** This local favorite with a huge used-book department also carries new books in every field. It's known for its history room and rare-books collection. Two doors down, at 520 Clement Street, is a fiction annex that also sells CDs, DVDs, comic books, and graphic novels. ✉ *506 Clement St., at 6th Ave., The Richmond* ☎ *415/387–2272* ⊕ *www.greenapplebooks.com.*

SUNSET DISTRICT

FOOD AND DRINK

San Francisco Wine Trading Company. Owner and noted wine expert Gary Marcaletti stocks hard-to-find wines and hosts Saturday-afternoon tastings that usually start at 2 pm. ✉ *250 Taraval St., at Funston Ave., Sunset* ☎ *415/731–6222* ⊕ *www.sfwtc.com.*

FURNITURE, HOUSEWARES, AND GIFTS

General Store. New and vintage goods sit stylishly side by side in this fun, well-lit, Outer Sunset space that sells books, lotions, hats, cups, dog leashes, and other items, most of them designed by local artists. Don't miss the greenhouse in back. ✉ *4035 Judah St., between 45th and 46th Aves., Sunset* ☎ *415/682–0600* ⊕ *shop-generalstore.com.*

Urban Bazaar. This warm and friendly shop specializes in fair-trade goods, local jewelry, and even has a small nursery full of adorable little plants in hand-painted pots. You'll find bars of Golden Gate soap here, and cards made out of newspaper headlines. ✉ *1371 9th Ave., near Judah St., Sunset* ☎ *415/664–4422* ⊕ *urbanbazaarsf.com.*

Wishbone. If you're into the quirky and whimsical—bacon-flavored lip gloss, daisy pushpins, wacky snow globes, and cutesy toys and games— you'll enjoy browsing through Wishbone, which also has an extensive selection of unusual cards. ✉ *601 Irving St., at 7th Ave., Sunset* ☎ *415/242–5540* ⊕ *wishbonesf.com.*

THE HAIGHT, THE CASTRO, AND NOE VALLEY

THE HAIGHT

It's a sign of the times (and has been for a while) that a Gap store sits at the corner of Haight and Ashbury streets, the geographic center of the Flower Power movement. Don't be discouraged: it's still possible to find high-quality vintage clothing, funky shoes, folk art from around the world, and used records and CDs in this always-busy neighborhood.

BOOKS

Booksmith. This fine bookshop sells current releases, children's titles, and offbeat periodicals. Authors passing through town often make a stop at this neighborhood institution. ✉ *1644 Haight St., between Cole and Clayton Sts., Haight* ☎ *415/863–8688* ⊕ *www.booksmith.com.*

Bound Together Anarchist Book Collective. This old-school collective, around since 1976, stocks books on anarchist theory and practice, as well as titles about gender issues, radicalism, and various left-leaning topics. A portion of the revenue supports anarchist projects and the Prisoners' Literature Project. ✉ *1369 Haight St., between Masonic and Central Aves., Haight* ☎ *415/431–8355* ⊕ *boundtogetherbooks.wordpress.com.*

CLOTHING: MEN AND WOMEN

Buffalo Exchange. Men and women can find fashionable, high-quality, used clothing at this national chain. Among the items: Levi's, leather jackets, sunglasses, and vintage lunch boxes. Some new clothes are available, too. ✉ *1555 Haight St., between Clayton and Ashbury Sts., Haight* ☎ *415/431–7733* ⊕ *www.buffaloexchange.com.*

Colorful Haight Street offers secondhand clothing shops, music stores, and funky accessories.

Held Over. The extensive collection of clothing from the 1920s through 1980s is organized by decade, saving those looking for flapper dresses from having to wade through lime-green polyester sundresses of the '70s. Shoes, hats, handbags, and jewelry complete the different looks. ✉ *1543 Haight St., between Ashbury and Clayton Sts., Haight* ☎ *415/864–0818.*

MUSIC

Fodor's Choice
★

Amoeba Music. With more than 2.5 million new and used CDs, DVDs, and records at bargain prices, this warehouselike offshoot of the Berkeley original carries titles you can't find on Amazon. No niche is ignored—from electronica and hip-hop to jazz and classical—and the stock changes daily. ■ **TIP→ Weekly in-store performances attract large crowds.** ✉ *1855 Haight St., between Stanyan and Shrader Sts., Haight* ☎ *415/831–1200* ⊕ *www.amoeba.com.*

Recycled Records. A Haight Street landmark, this store buys, sells, and trades used records, including hard-to-find imports and sides by obscure alternative bands. The CD collection is large, but the vinyl is the real draw. ✉ *1377 Haight St., between Masonic and Central Aves., Haight* ☎ *415/626–4075* ⊕ *www.recycled-records.com.*

SHOES

Fodor's Choice
★

John Fluevog. The trendy but sturdily made footwear for men and women are among the best in the city. Club girls go gaga over the Double Dutch boots, handing over a pretty penny. They have another small store near Union Square, at 253 Grant Avenue. ✉ *1697 Haight St., at Cole St., Haight* ☎ *415/436–9784* ⊕ *www.fluevog.com.*

THE CASTRO
CLOTHING: MEN
Rolo. Selling hard-to-find men's denim, sportswear, shoes, and accessories with a distinct European influence, this store includes clothes designed by Fred Perry, James Tudor, and Tre Noir. There's another location in SoMa at 1301 Howard Street. ⊠ *2351 Market St., at Castro St., Castro* ☎ *415/578–7139* ⊕ *www.rolo.com.*

JEWELRY AND COLLECTIBLES
Brand X Antiques. The vintage jewelry, mostly from the early part of the 20th century, includes a wide selection of estate pieces and objets d'art. With rings that range in price from $5 to $30,000, there's something for everyone. ⊠ *570 Castro St., between 18th and 19th Sts., Castro* ☎ *415/626–8908* ⊙ *Closed Sun.*

MUSIC
Streetlight Records. Thousands of used CDs, with an emphasis on rock, jazz, soul, and R&B, are bought and sold here. But there's plenty of vinyl for purists. ⊠ *2350 Market St., at Castro St., Castro* ☎ *888/396–2350* ⊕ *streetlightrecords.com* ⊙ *Closed Mon.*

NOE VALLEY
BOOKS
Omnivore Books on Food. Love to eat? Love to read? Then this place is paradise. The shelves are bursting with books on growing and cooking food. The store stocks cookbooks on such diverse subjects as Colonial Jamaican and Victorian England cuisine or 1940s Creole cooking. And if you're after a signed first edition by Julia Child or James Beard, you'll find that, too. ⊠ *3885A Cesar Chavez St., at Church St., Noe Valley* ☎ *415/282–4712* ⊕ *www.omnivorebooks.com.*

CHILDREN'S CLOTHING
Small Frys. The colorful cottons carried here are mainly for infants, with some articles for older children. Brands include OshKosh and many Californian and French labels. A few shelves of organic and eco-friendly toys as well as whimsical finger puppets round out the selection. ⊠ *4066 24th St., between Castro and Noe Sts., Noe Valley* ☎ *415/648–3954* ⊕ *www.smallfrys.com.*

CLOTHING: WOMEN'S
Ambiance. A well-loved destination for fashion-conscious locals, this is a fun place to find 1920s-inspired dresses, velvet scarves, and dangling silver jewelry. The store has some jaw-dropping sales. There are additional locations on 9th Avenue, Union, Haight, and Irving streets. ⊠ *3979 24th St., between Sanchez and Noe Sts., Noe Valley* ☎ *415/647–7144* ⊕ *www.ambiancesf.com.*

Two Birds. A fresh place to find a lacy top or the soft pair of jeans, Two Birds stocks Erin Kleinberg, Tracy Reese, and Frame Denim. Staying in touch with their city roots, owners Susanna Taylor and Audrey Yang carry sleek jewelry, handbags, and dresses by local designers, too. ⊠ *1309 Castro St., between Jersey and 24th Sts., Noe Valley* ☎ *415/285–1840* ⊕ *www.2birds1store.com.*

18

FURNITURE, HOUSEWARES, AND GIFTS

Common Scents. A cozy destination for all things bath-related, this place stocks sweet-smelling soaps, lotions, candles, and bath salts. The aromas wash over you like a spring garden; scents of lavender, rose, honeysuckle, and jasmine will follow you all the way home. ⊠ *3920a 24th St., near Sanchez St., Noe Valley* ☎ *415/826–1019.*

Wink. Cards, toasters, aprons, books, candles, and even superhero Pez candy line the shelves. You'll also find fridge magnets, wisdom-spouting bags, and bakery-shape pencil erasers. And if you've misplaced your stainless-steel water bottle, the shop stocks a rainbow of colors. ⊠ *4107 24th St., at Castro St., Noe Valley* ☎ *415/401–8881* ⊕ *www.winksf.com.*

HANDICRAFTS AND FOLK ART

Xela Imports. Africa, Southeast Asia, and Central America are the sources for the handicrafts sold at Xela (pronounced *shay*-la). They include jewelry, religious masks, fertility statuary, and decorative wall hangings. ⊠ *3925 24th St., between Sanchez and Noe Sts., Noe Valley* ☎ *415/695–1323* ⊕ *xelaimports.com.*

TOYS AND GADGETS

Ark Toys, Books & Crafts. The emphasis here is on high-quality toys with an educational bent or that encourage imaginative play with dress-up costumes, message-in-a-bottle kits, and the like. Many of the toys are manufactured in Europe. ⊠ *3845 24th St., between Church and Sanchez Sts., Noe Valley* ☎ *415/821–1257* ⊕ *www.thearktoys.com.*

MISSION DISTRICT

The aesthetic of the hipsters and artist types who reside in the Mission contribute to the individuality of shopping here. These night owls keep the city's best thrift stores, vintage-furniture shops, alternative bookstores, and increasingly, small clothing boutiques afloat. As the Mission gentrifies though, bargain hunters find themselves trekking farther afield in search of truly local flavor.

ANTIQUES AND COLLECTIBLES

The Touch. If you've been searching hard for a 1920s double shelf or a Danish teak table, this could be the place you find it. Owner David Chen is always scouring the city for new relics, and his collection of midcentury American furniture is particular noteworthy. You'll also find retro lamps, solid-iron wine holders, and even classic electric typewriters. ⊠ *2221 Mission St., between 19th and 18th Sts., Mission* ☎ *415/550–2640.*

Viracocha. This eclectic but well-conceived community-operated space is part art gallery, part furniture store, part antiques showroom, and even part music store. The ceilings are high and the floor paved in sea-washed wood. There's an organ in back, near an old record player with LPs, and across the room sits a baby grand piano. Elsewhere are a red bathtub layered with faux-fur blankets, jewelry that's sold out of a 1920s suitcase, and a bulging old wedding-registry book from Louisiana. A fat, black cat greets everyone who walks through the door. Everything is for sale except the cat. ⊠ *998 Valencia St., at 21st*

St., Mission ☏ *415/374–7048* ⊕ *www.viracochasf.com* ⊘ *Closed Mon. and Tues.*

ART GALLERIES

Morgan Oakes Tribal. Sun-drenched Morgan Oakes specializes in tribal art, including masks, sculptures, and jewelry imported from Africa, Indonesia, Asia, and the Americas. New work is constantly arriving, so you never know what you'll find from one day, or week, to the next. ✉ *3328 22nd St., near Valencia St., Mission* ☏ *415/317–1777* ⊕ *www. morganoakestribal.com* ⊘ *Closed Mon. and Tues.*

Southern Exposure. An artist-run, nonprofit gallery, this is an established venue for cutting-edge art. In addition to exhibitions, lectures, performances, and film, video screenings take place. ✉ *3030 20th St., at Alabama St., Mission* ☏ *415/863–2141* ⊕ *soex.org* ⊘ *Closed Sun. and Mon.*

BOOKS

Dog Eared Books. An eclectic group of shoppers—gay and straight, fashionable and practical—wanders the aisles of this pleasantly ramshackle bookstore. The diverse stock, about 85% of it used, includes quirky selections like vintage children's books, remaindered art books, and local 'zines. A bin of free books just outside the front door is fun to browse. ✉ *900 Valencia St., at 20th St., Mission* ☏ *415/282–1901* ⊕ *www.dogearedbooks.com.*

Modern Times Bookstore. Named after Charlie Chaplin's politically subversive film, the left-leaning store stocks high-quality literary fiction and nonfiction, much of it with a political bent. There are also sections for children's books, Spanish-language titles, and magazines and local subversive 'zines. Author readings and public forums are held regularly. ■ TIP➜ If you're looking to kill a little time in the Mission before hooking up with dinner companions, this is a low-key and inviting place to hide out in the stacks. ✉ *2919 24th St., between Alabama and Florida Sts., Mission* ☏ *415/282–9246* ⊕ *moderntimesbookstore.com.*

CLOTHING: MEN AND WOMEN

Bell Jar. This diverse shop's tag line is "Gorgeous Little Things," and the items for sale—flowing dresses, dangling turquoise earrings, cat prints, pineapple vases, and more—live up to the billing. The owner is former art director Sasha Wingate, and she's made the atmosphere romantic, bright, and whimsically beautiful. ✉ *3187 16th St., at Guerrero St., Mission* ☏ *415/626–1749* ⊕ *belljarsf.com.*

Dema. Dema Grim's classically cut clothes in ethnic and vintage fabrics really pop—and truly capture the spirit of the Mission. Deep reds with rosebuds and rich purple leopard prints are just a few of the patterns you'll see hanging from the lively rails. ✉ *1038 Valencia St., between 21st and 22nd Sts., Mission* ☏ *415/206–0500* ⊕ *www.godemago.com.*

Schauplatz. A narrow store on a hip Mission block, Schauplatz sells vintage clothing from the 1920s to the 1980s. Some of the dramatic women's wear—go-go boots, pillbox hats, faux Chanel suits—is suitable for street wear or dress-up, depending on your style, while the menswear tends more toward fashionably retro jackets and button-up

18

shirts from the classic to the gaudy. ⊠ *791 Valencia St., at 19th St., Mission* ☎ *415/864–5665* ⊙ *Closed Tues.*

Self Edge. Hanging from metal rods on perfectly separated wooden hangers are dozens of pairs of Japanese selvage denim. The industrial-weight fabric that makes up these jeans will run you between $180 and $450, but alterers will hem them for free on a vintage chain-stitching machine. ⊠ *714 Valencia St., at 18th St., Mission* ☎ *415/558–0658* ⊕ *www.selfedge.com.*

Sunhee Moon. A rack is designated for each color of the rainbow, and clothes are hung by gradation, making entry into Moon's shops a crayon-color dreamscape. The San Francisco–based designer uses only American-made fabrics and manufactures all of her clothes in the Mission. Her Berkeley aesthetic is coupled with Audrey Hepburn's simple, practical elegance. End result: lots of corduroy, solids accented with an occasionally lively print, and well-placed large buttons. ⊠ *3167 16th St., at Guerrero St., Mission* ☎ *415/355–1800* ⊕ *www.sunheemoon. com.*

FURNITURE, HOUSEWARES, AND GIFTS

Aldea Home. A visit here is like being in someone's home and being able to buy everything you see, from the organic sheets to the chairs to the shampoo in the shower. The aesthetic is modern, with bright references to Mexico, India, Turkey, and Japan. Aldea is the perfect place to find a hostess gift or to deck out a corner that's missing something special. Nearby Aldea Ninos (at 1017 Valencia) sells green products for kids. ⊠ *890 Valencia St., at 20th St., Mission* ☎ *415/865–9807* ⊕ *aldeahome. com.*

Casa Bonampak. This bright, authentic, fair-trade artisan store sells the work of Mexican artists, as well as decorations for various Mexican festivities. If you're looking for traditional sugar skulls, papel picado banners, or even "Dia de los Gigantes" (Day of the Dead Giants) tees, look no further. The friendly owner and welcoming vibe will beckon you in. ⊠ *1051 Valencia St., between Hill and 22nd Sts., Mission* ☎ *415/642– 4079* ⊕ *www.casabonampak.com.*

De Angelis. The trendy vintage furniture sold here will fit right in any space. With items that include Tommi Parzinger wall sconces, Hans Olsen's "Fried Egg" chairs, and even bronze coffee tables, the selection at De Angelis is truly inspirational. ⊠ *573 Valencia St., at 17th St., Mission* ☎ *415/861–9800.*

Fodor'sChoice
★

Paxton Gate. Elevating gardening to an art, this serene shop offers beautiful earthenware pots, amaryllis and narcissus bulbs, decorative garden items, and coffee-table books such as *An Inordinate Fondness for Beetles.* The collection of taxidermy and preserved bugs provides more unusual gift ideas. A couple of storefronts away is too-cute Paxton Gate Curiosities for Kids, jam-packed with retro toys, books, and other stellar finds. ⊠ *824 Valencia St., between 19th and 20th Sts., Mission* ☎ *415/824–1872* ⊕ *www.paxtongate.com.*

Therapy. Housewares range from ever-practical refrigerator magnets to such downright silly items as a soap-on-a-rope tribute to the cartoon character Strawberry Shortcake. A retro theme runs to stationery and other reasonably priced items, and the adjacent annex sells retro-style furniture. ⊠ *545 Valencia St., between 16th and 17th Sts., Mission* ☎ *415/865–0981* ⊕ *www.shopattherapy.com.*

HANDICRAFTS AND FOLK ART

Ruby Gallery. Local artists make all the jewelry, clothing, handbags, candleholders, intricately crafted cards, and other gift items sold at this small cooperative store. The hair accessories—from elegant clips studded with vintage Czech glass to barrettes fashioned out of buttons—are especially charming. ⊠ *3602 20th St., at Valencia St., Mission* ☎ *415/550–8052* ⊕ *www.rubygallery.com.*

Studio 24. The gift shop of the acclaimed Galería de la Raza sells crafts from Mexico and Central and South America. Prints and calendars by Latino artists, Day of the Dead folk art, and masks and wood carvings from Latin America are a few of the objects for sale. ⊠ *2857 24th St., at Bryant St., Mission* ☎ *415/826–8009* ⊕ *www.galeriadelaraza.org* ⊙ *Closed Mon. and Tues.*

MUSIC

Aquarius Records. Owner Windy Chien carries on the tradition in this space, which was *the* punk-rock store in the 1970s. These days it carries a variety of music, including a large selection of experimental electronica, all of it handpicked by the hip staffers. ⊠ *1055 Valencia St., between 21st and 22nd Sts., Mission* ☎ *415/647–2272* ⊕ *www.aquariusrecords.org.*

PAPER AND STATIONERY

Flax art & design. In addition to paints, brushes, and art supplies, this sprawling creators' playground sells beautifully made photo albums and journals, fine pens and pencils, crafts kits, stationery, and inspiring doodads for kids. ⊠ *1699 Market St., at Valencia St., Mission* ☎ *415/552–2355* ⊕ *flaxart.com.*

TOYS AND GADGETS

FAMILY **826 Valencia.** The brainchild of author Dave Eggers is primarily a center established to help kids with their writing skills via tutoring and storytelling events. But the storefront is also "San Francisco's only independent pirate supply store," a quirky space filled with eye patches, spyglasses, and other pirate-themed paraphernalia. Eggers's quarterly journal, *McSweeney's,* and other publications are available here. Proceeds benefit the writing center. ⊠ *826 Valencia St., between 18th and 19th Sts., Mission* ☎ *415/642–5905* ⊕ *826valencia.org.*

POTRERO HILL

ART GALLERIES

Catharine Clark Gallery. Although nationally known artists—like Masami Teraoka and Andy Diaz Hope—display their sculptures, paintings, photographs, and installation artwork here, emerging artists with a Bay Area connection get the spotlight, among them Chester Arnold and Josephine Taylor. ⊠ *248 Utah St., Potrero Hill* ☎ *415/399–1439* ⊕ *cclarkgallery.com* ⊙ *Closed Sun. and Mon.*

18

CLOTHING

Kate's Closet. Designer jeans, antique jewelry, tailored leather jackets, and one-of-a-kind woolen sweater dresses are among the new as well as used items that fill this quaint boutique. Each consignment article is carefully selected, and reasonably priced. Mary, the owner, also sells new clothing crafted by local designers. ✉ *1331 18th St., near Missouri St., Potrero Hill* ☎ *415/624–3736.*

FURNITURE, HOUSEWARES, AND GIFTS

Dandelion. The variety of housewares, bath items, books, and tchotchkes includes something for everyone on your gift list. Cocktail paraphernalia, golf-related books, luxury bath products, and indulgent food items such as Fauchon-brand black-fig preserves are only a sample of what's here. ✉ *55 Potrero Ave., at Alameda St., Potrero Hill* ☎ *415/436–9500* ⊕ *www.dandelionsf.com.*

Fodor's Choice ★ **Heath Ceramics.** Sleek, glossy tiles for the home, newly spun dinnerware in rich earth colors, locally inspired cookbooks, and simple bamboo spoons stand stacked on shelves and tables in this factory showroom. ■ **TIP→ This is worth a stop if you're interested in seeing how plates and bowls are made.** Nearby Blue Bottle Coffee serves coffee and light snacks for people and dogs. ✉ *2900 18th St., at Florida St., Potrero Hill* ☎ *415/361–5552* ⊕ *www.heathceramics.com.*

HANDBAGS, LUGGAGE, AND LEATHER GOODS

Rickshaw Bagworks. This San Francisco based company will custom-make you your favorite bag. Choose from a variety of shapes and sizes to fit your MacBook, iPad, or Kindle. Totes, duffels, and messenger bags can also be designed to fit your unique lifestyle. You can also select from a variety of prints and colors, as well as eco-friendly materials; local artisans in their Dogpatch warehouse craft all bags. ✉ *904 22nd St., between Indiana and Minnesota Sts., Potrero Hill* ☎ *415/904–8368* ⊕ *www.rickshawbags.com.*

HANDICRAFTS AND FOLK ART

Collage Gallery. The studio-gallery showcases handmade purses, painted candlesticks, jewelry, and other items by Bay Area artists. There are also a few small antiques, such as charming Westclox alarm clocks. ✉ *1345 18th St., between Missouri and Texas Sts., Potrero Hill* ☎ *415/282–4401* ⊕ *www.collage-gallery.com.*

SPORTING GOODS

Fodor's Choice ★ **Sports Basement.** This sprawling store rewards intrepid shoppers with significant discounts on name-brand sportswear, accessories, and camping and outdoor gear. Helpful salespeople, more knowledgeable than you would expect at a discount warehouse, will help you find just the right running shoes, biking shorts, or yoga tights. Check out their location in the Presidio on Old Mason Street as well. ✉ *1590 Bryant St., between 15th and 16th Sts., Potrero Hill* ☎ *415/575–3000* ⊕ *www.sportsbasement.com.*

BERNAL HEIGHTS

FURNITURE, HOUSEWARES, AND GIFTS

Succulence Life and Garden. Take a deep breath and exhale into the peacefulness of this indoor-outdoor garden shop bursting with lush, succulent greenery. There are bookcases full of plants, and even a "plant bar" where you can make your own plant/pot blending. There's also a host of classes you can enroll in if you're so inclined; the Vertical Gardening DIY class starts at $65. If you're more of a traditionalist, there's a vibrant nursery in the back that will feed all your gardening needs. ⊠ *402 Cortland Ave., between Wool and Bennington Sts., Bernal Heights* ☎ *415/282–2212* ⊕ *www.thesucculence.com.*

DOGPATCH

FOOD AND DRINK

The Wine House. The highly informed and friendly staffers here are willing to help you find the perfect wine for any occasion. The Burgundy, Bordeaux, and Rhône selections are especially good, and the assortment of California wines is small but well chosen. Prices are reasonable. ⊠ *829 26th St., between Tennessee and 3rd Sts., Dogpatch* ☎ *415/355–9463* ⊕ *www.winesf.com* ☉ *Closed Sun.*

PACIFIC HEIGHTS AND JAPANTOWN

PACIFIC HEIGHTS

BEAUTY

BeneFit Cosmetics. You can find this locally based line of cosmetics and skin-care products at Macy's and Sephora, but it's much more fun to come to one of the eponymous boutiques. No-pressure salespeople dab you with whimsical makeup such as Ooh La Lift concealer and Tinted Love, a stain for lips and cheeks. ⊠ *2117 Fillmore St., between California and Sacramento Sts., Pacific Heights* ☎ *415/567–0242* ⊕ *www.benefitcosmetics.com.*

Kiehl's. Fans swear by this company's high-quality, simply packaged skin- and hair-care products. Its spacious store stocks oceans of lotions, potions, and soaps. ⊠ *1971 Fillmore St., between Wilmot and Pine Sts., Pacific Heights* ☎ *415/359–9260* ⊕ *www.kiehls.com.*

MAC. The makeup is bold and trendy, as are many of its devotees. Mod salespeople are happy to show you creamy lipsticks, glittery powders, and dramatic eye shadows. ⊠ *2011 Fillmore St., at Pine St., Pacific Heights* ☎ *415/885–2966* ⊕ *www.maccosmetics.com.*

CHILDREN'S CLOTHING

Dottie Doolittle. Pacific Heights mothers shop here for charming silk dresses and other special-occasion outfits for their little ones. Less pricey togs for infants, boys to size 12, and girls to size 16, are also for sale. ⊠ *3680 Sacramento St., at Spruce St., Pacific Heights* ☎ *415/563–3244* ⊕ *www.dottiedoolittle.com.*

18

CLOTHING: MEN AND WOMEN

Elizabeth Charles. Parlaying the city's obsession with international designers, this intimate boutique stocks Caroline Constas, Kinder Aggugini, Isabel Marant, and Timo Weiland, with an emphasis on the very finest fabrics. ⊠ *2056 Fillmore St., between California and Pine Sts., Pacific Heights* ☎ *415/440–2100* ⊕ *www.elizabeth-charles.com.*

Erica Tanov. The Bay Area designer's background in lingerie and bedding influences the delicate designs here: wispy cashmere, silk organza and charmeuse, and linen. Sweaters tend to drape and wrap; skirts and pajama-wide pants are often brightened with florals or stripes. ⊠ *2408 Fillmore St., between Jackson and Washington Sts., Pacific Heights* ☎ *415/674–1228* ⊕ *www.ericatanov.com.*

HeidiSays Collections. Fanciful windows brimming with bright and festive prints draw passersby into this store. Perky salespeople help you choose between Elizabeth and James and M Missoni and other fashions. To complete your emblematic San Francisco-chic outfit, head down the street, where the Heidi empire continues with HeidiSays Casual (⊠ *2416 Fillmore St.*) and HeidiSays Shoes (⊠ *2105 Fillmore St.*). ⊠ *2426 Fillmore St., between Washington and Jackson Sts., Pacific Heights* ☎ *415/749–0655* ⊕ *www.heidisays.com.*

FOOD AND DRINK

D&M Wines and Liquors. At first glance this family-owned business appears to be just another neighborhood liquor store, but it's actually a rare and wonderful specialist. In a city obsessed with wine, these spirits devotees distinguish themselves by focusing on rare, small-production Armagnac, Calvados, and Champagne. ⊠ *2200 Fillmore St., at Sacramento St., Pacific Heights* ☎ *415/346–1325* ⊕ *dandm.com.*

FURNITURE, HOUSEWARES, AND GIFTS

Nest. A cross between a Parisian antiques show and a Jamaican flea market, this store could get even the most monochrome New Yorker excited about color. You can turn up the volume on your SF souvenirs with vibrant handmade quilts, Chan Luu jewelry, Les Indiennes hand-blocked cotton fabrics, and M. Sasek's cheerfully illustrated book *This is San Francisco.* ⊠ *2300 Fillmore St., at Clay St., Pacific Heights* ☎ *415/292–6199* ⊕ *www.nestsf.com.*

Sue Fisher King Company. When Martha Stewart or the buyers at Williams-Sonoma need inspiration they come to see how Sue has set her sprawling table or dressed her stately bed. (Her specialty is opulent linens for every room.) And when Pacific Heights residents are looking for an impeccable hostess or bridal gift, they come by for a hand-embroidered velvet pillow or a piece of Nicholas Newcomb Hudson Valley pottery. ⊠ *3067 Sacramento St., between Baker and Broderick Sts., Pacific Heights* ☎ *415/922–7276* ⊕ *www.suefisherking.com.*

JEWELRY AND COLLECTIBLES

Goldberry Jewelers. The former longtime girlfriend of Bob Dylan, Margie Rogerson opened this store to showcase her platinum-only designs. While she carries a large selection of engagement rings, her specialty is colored stones: rubies, sapphires, and emeralds. Their colors really sparkle against the background of this all white and Lucite space. By appointment only. ⊠ *3516 Sacramento St., between Laurel and Locust Sts., Pacific Heights* ☎ *415/921–4389* ⊕ *www.goldberry.com.*

PAPER AND STATIONERY

Paper Source. Beautiful handmade papers, cards, envelopes, ribbons, and bookbinding materials line the walls of this shop, which embodies the Bay Area's do-it-yourself spirit. Assembly is required here and that's the fun of it. ⊠ *1925 Fillmore St., at Pine St., Pacific Heights* ☎ *415/409–7710* ⊕ *www.paper-source.com.*

JAPANTOWN

Unlike shops in the ethnic enclaves of Chinatown, North Beach, and the Mission, the 5-acre Japan Center (⊠ *Bordered by Laguna, Fillmore, and Post Sts. and Geary Blvd.*) is under one roof. The three-block complex includes a reasonably priced public garage and three shop-filled buildings. Especially worthwhile are the Kintetsu and Kinokuniya buildings, where shops sell things like bonsai trees, tapes and records, jewelry, antique kimonos, *tansu* (Japanese chests), electronics, and colorful glazed dinnerware and teapots.

BOOKS

Kinokuniya Bookstore. The selection of English-language books about Japanese culture—everything from medieval history to origami instructions—is one of the finest in the country. Kinokuniya is the city's biggest seller of Japanese-language books. Dozens of glossy Asian fashion magazines attract the young and trendy; the manga and anime books and magazines are wildly popular, too. ⊠ *Kinokuniya Bldg., 1581 Webster St., at Geary Blvd., Japantown* ☎ *415/567–7625* ⊕ *www.kinokuniya. com/us.*

FOOD AND DRINK

Crown & Crumpet Tea Salon. This is the perfect spot for all things British; C&C serves traditional afternoon tea starting at 11 am, complete with cucumber sandwiches and scones. The shop also sells china cups and other teatime accessories such as candies, clocks, and coasters. ⊠ *1746 Post St., 2nd fl., Japantown* ☎ *415/771–4252* ⊕ *www. crownandcrumpet.com.*

HANDICRAFTS AND FOLK ART

Ma-Shi'-Ko Folk Craft. Beautiful Mashiko pottery—rustic pieces fired in a wood kiln and coated with a natural glaze—are the specialty here. The wealth of pottery and antiques, including many ceramic vases and wooden chests, makes a visit here worth the somewhat chilly reception from the proprietor. ⊠ *Kinokuniya Bldg., 1581 Webster St., 2nd fl., at Geary Blvd., Japantown* ☎ *415/346–0748.*

Soko Hardware. Open since 1925, this shop specializes in beautifully crafted Japanese tools for gardening and woodworking. In addition to the usual hardware-store items, you can find seeds for Japanese plants and books about topics such as making shoji screens. ⊠ *1698 Post St., at Buchanan St., Japantown* ☎ *415/931–5510.*

18

Antiques Blitz Tour

Whether hunting for Japanese porcelain or American art-deco lamps, serious antiques hounds could spend days poking around San Francisco. But if you have only one day to indulge your passion, with your walking shoes on your feet and cab fare in hand, you can hit some of the highlights.

Start your day in the city's preeminent antiques neighborhood, tree-lined Jackson Square, centered on Jackson Street between Montgomery and Sansome streets. Although you would do well to pop into any shop on these few blocks, try **Antonio's Antiques**, which has two stories of furniture and objets d'art, most French and Italian, from the 17th and 18th centuries. (Take a cab to its larger SoMa store after leaving if you like what you see here.)

A short cab ride away (or a brief stroll to the Embarcadero and a ride on the F-line Muni streetcar), the more affordable shops lining Market Street appeal to a broader crowd. Ask the cabbie to ferry you south of Market, where the turn-of-the-20th-century Belgian oak beds and French armoires at **Grand Central Station Antiques** on 9th Street draw shoppers with slightly more traditional sensibilities.

It's another cab hop to Japan Center, a three-block indoor shopping center that houses **Ma-Shi'-Ko Folk Craft**. Here antique Japanese ceramics and carved wooden pieces share space with contemporary pottery that has a beautiful organic style. If you haven't collapsed under the weight of your purchases yet, hail one more cab and make your way to 2181A Union Street, where the helpful staff of **Dianne's Estate Jewellery** welcome you into a wonderland of vintage timepieces and early-20th-century rings, many with sapphires and rubies.

MALL

FAMILY **New People.** Japanese pop culture has never been so neatly organized as it is here at this state-of-the-art mini mall divided into four shiny levels: the cinema/café downstairs; MARUQ (selling Tokyo's hot fashion right here in SF!) on the first floor; clothing shops like Baby, the Stars Shine Bright, and Sou-Sou on the second floor; and the Superfrog Gallery on the third floor. Expect to see a rotation of emerging artists in the gallery and make sure you try the superstrong coffee and vegan donuts on sale in the café. ⊠ 1746 Post St., at Webster St., Japantown ☎ 415/525–8630 ⊕ www.newpeopleworld.com.

WESTERN ADDITION

FURNITURE, HOUSEWARES, AND GIFTS

Cookin': Recycled Gourmet Appurtenances. People trek here for the impressive collection of vintage Le Creuset cookware and bakeware in discontinued colors. If you can't make sense of this store's jumble of used cooking items—stacked ceiling-high in some places—ask the helpful owner, who will likely interrogate you about what you're preparing to cook before leading you to the right section, be that the corner with hundreds of ramekins or the area containing a bewildering selection of garlic presses. ⊠ *339 Divisadero St., between Oak and Page Sts., Western Addition* ☎ *415/861–1854.*

SPAS

Like the restaurant scene, spas in San Francisco are focused on natural, organic products and deeply reflect he various neighborhoods around the city.

SOMA

Remède Spa. All treatments at the St. Regis Hotel's très chic spa incorporate a line of high-end French skin-care products. Offerings include custom skin therapy, massage, body scrubs, seaweed wraps, and a variety of mani-pedi, facial, and waxing options. Prices range from $18 for a lip wax to $330 for a four-hands massage. ⊠ *St. Regis Hotel, 125 3rd St., at Mission St., SoMa* ☎ *415/284–4060* ⊕ *remede.com/spa.html.*

HAYES VALLEY

Earthbody. A destination for organic products, cleansing, and relaxation—not to mention massage treatments to melt for—this eco spa offers transformative workshops and rituals that help you heal from within. The Goddess Treatment, a client favorite, includes body exfoliation, a hot-oil scalp treatment, and massage using products infused with wildflower blossoms. ⊠ *534 Laguna St., between Hayes and Fell Sts., Hayes Valley* ☎ *415/552–7200* ⊕ *www.earthbody.net.*

NOB HILL

Nob Hill Spa. Warning: after experiencing this serene and luxurious spa's treatments, you'll start to *expect* champagne after your massage. Unique features include the eucalyptus steam bath and a gorgeous infinity pool that overlooks the city through a glass wall. After your treatments, you can hang here all day: relax in the Zen room, get a green-tea body scrub, or just read on the sundeck. Regulars love the 80-minute Nourishing Seaweed facial, the 50-minute Organic Lavender Sugar Scrub skin-exfoliation treatment, and the Table Thai massage, 80 minutes of pure indulgence. ⊠ *Huntington Hotel, 1075 California St., at Mason St., Nob Hill* ☎ *415/474–5400* ⊕ *www.nobhillspa.com.*

COW HOLLOW

Spa Radiance. Elegant but casual Spa Radiance specializes in facials and draws the occasional celebrity. Try the warm cocoa butter body treatment, or the "Nature's Kiss" spa escape—an organic detox facial followed by a warm lavender salt scrub and hot stone massage. A well-deserved treat is the very fine Swiss Oxygen 52 Vitamin facial. ⊠ *3011 Fillmore St., between Union and Filbert Sts., Cow Hollow* ☎ *415/346–6281* ⊕ *www.sparadiance.com.*

18

PACIFIC HEIGHTS AND JAPANTOWN

International Orange. Treatments at this spa and yoga studio include the signature IO Massage, which incorporates Swedish, Acupressure, Thai and Shiatsu techniques. The more straightforward Hot Stone Massage is done with International Orange's own Anoint Oil—grapeseed oil infused with green tea and scented with white lotus and jasmine flower. For a city spa, this is a large space, but it's tranquil and even has a bamboo garden. ✉ *2044 Fillmore St., 2nd fl., between Pine and California Sts., Pacific Heights* ☎ *415/630–5928* ⊕ *www.internationalorange.com.*

Kabuki Springs & Spa. Traditional sit-down Japanese showers and communal bathing are two out-of-the-ordinary experiences at the Kabuki. The renowned Javanese Lulur Treatment includes a combination massage with jasmine oil, exfoliation with turmeric and ground rice, a yogurt application, and a candlelight soak with rose petals. Men and women are welcome every day for private treatments, but call ahead regarding communal bathing schedules; the baths are coed only on Tuesday. Clothing is optional except on coed days. ✉ *1750 Geary Blvd., at Fillmore St., Japantown* ☎ *415/922–6000* ⊕ *www.kabukisprings.com.*

Therapeia Massage. Massages at this oasis of calm near Japantown include and hot-stone options. Acupuncture and facials are also available. The focus is on cleansing and calming the minds as well as the body. ✉ *1801 Bush St., lower level, Japantown* ☎ *415/885–4450* ⊕ *www.therapeiamassage.com.*

THE BAY AREA

WELCOME TO THE BAY AREA

TOP REASONS TO GO

★ **Bite into the "Gourmet Ghetto":** Eat your way through this area of North Berkeley, starting with a slice of perfect pizza from the Cheese Board (just look for the line).

★ **Find solitude at Point Reyes National Seashore:** Hike beautifully rugged—and often deserted—beaches at one of the most beautiful places on earth, period.

★ **Sit on a dock by the bay:** Admire the beauty of the Bay Area from the rocky, picturesque shores of Sausalito or Tiburon.

★ **Go bar-hopping in Oakland's hippest hood:** Spend an evening swinging through the watering holes of Uptown, Oakland's artsy-hip and fast-rising corner of downtown.

★ **Walk among giants:** Walking into Muir Woods, a mere 12 miles north of the Golden Gate Bridge, is like entering a cathedral built by God.

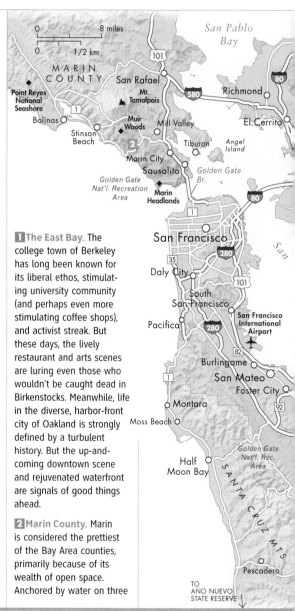

1 The East Bay. The college town of Berkeley has long been known for its liberal ethos, stimulating university community (and perhaps even more stimulating coffee shops), and activist streak. But these days, the lively restaurant and arts scenes are luring even those who wouldn't be caught dead in Birkenstocks. Meanwhile, life in the diverse, harbor-front city of Oakland is strongly defined by a turbulent history. But the up-and-coming downtown scene and rejuvenated waterfront are signals of good things ahead.

2 Marin County. Marin is considered the prettiest of the Bay Area counties, primarily because of its wealth of open space. Anchored by water on three

sides, the county is mostly parkland, including long stretches of undeveloped coastline. The picturesque small towns here—Sausalito, Tiburon, Mill Valley, and Bolinas among them—may sometimes look rustic, but they're mostly in a dizzyingly high tax bracket. There's a reason why people call BMWs "basic Marin wheels."

GETTING ORIENTED

East of the city, across the San Francisco Bay, lie Berkeley and Oakland, in what most Bay Area residents refer to as the East Bay. These two towns have distinct personalities, but life here feels more relaxed than in the city—though every bit as vibrant. Cross the Golden Gate Bridge and head north to reach Marin County's rolling hills and green expanses, where residents enjoy a haute-suburban lifestyle. Farther afield, the wild landscapes of the Muir Woods, Mt. Tamalpais, Stinson Beach, and Point Reyes National Seashore await.

19

Updated by
Denise M. Leto

It's rare for a metropolis to compete with its suburbs for visitors, but the view from any of San Francisco's hilltops shows that the Bay Area's temptations extend far beyond the city limits. East of town are two energetic urban centers, Berkeley and Oakland. Famously radical Berkeley is also comfortably sophisticated, while Oakland has an art and restaurant scene so hip that it pulls San Franciscans to this side of the bay. To the north is Marin County, the beauty queen, with dramatic coastal scenery of breathtaking beauty and chic, affluent villages like Tiburon and Mill Valley.

PLANNING

WHEN TO GO

As with San Francisco, you can visit the rest of the Bay Area comfortably at any time of year, and it's especially nice in late spring and fall. Unlike in San Francisco, though, the surrounding areas are reliably sunny in summer—it gets hotter as you head inland. Even the rainy season has its charms, as hills that are golden the rest of the year turn a rich green and wildflowers become plentiful. Precipitation is usually the heaviest between November and March. Berkeley is a university town, so the rhythm of the school year might affect your visit. It's easier to navigate the streets and find parking near the university between semesters, but there's also less buzz around town.

GETTING HERE AND AROUND

BART TRAVEL

Using public transportation to reach Berkeley or Oakland is ideal. The under- and aboveground BART (Bay Area Rapid Transit) trains make stops in both towns. Trips to either take about a half hour one-way from the center of San Francisco. BART does not serve Marin County.

Contacts BART ☏ 510/465–2278 ⊕ www.bart.gov.

BOAT AND FERRY TRAVEL

For sheer romance, nothing beats the ferry; there's service from San Francisco to Sausalito, Tiburon, and Larkspur in Marin County, and to Alameda and Oakland in the East Bay.

The Golden Gate Ferry crosses the bay to Sausalito from San Francisco's Ferry Building (⊠ *Market St. and the Embarcadero*). Blue & Gold Fleet ferries depart daily for Sausalito and Tiburon from Pier 41 at Fisherman's Wharf; weekday commuter ferries leave from the Ferry Building for Tiburon. The trip to Sausalito takes from 25 minutes to an hour; to Tiburon, it takes from 25 to 55 minutes.

The Angel Island–Tiburon Ferry sails to the island daily from April through October and on weekends the rest of the year.

The San Francisco Bay Ferry runs several times daily between San Francisco's Ferry Building or Pier 41 and Alameda, and Jack London Square in Oakland; one-way tickets cost $6.25. The trip lasts from 20 to 45 minutes, depending on your departure point, and leads to Oakland's waterfront shopping and restaurant district. Purchase tickets on board.

Boat and Ferry Lines Angel Island–Tiburon Ferry ☎ 415/435-2131 ⊕ www.angelislandferry.com. **Blue & Gold Fleet** ☎ 415/705-8200 ⊕ www. blueandgoldfleet.com. **Golden Gate Ferry** ☎ 511 ⊕ www.goldengateferry.org. **San Francisco Bay Ferry** ☎ 510/522-3300 ⊕ sanfranciscobayferry.com.

BUS TRAVEL

Golden Gate Transit buses travel to Sausalito, Tiburon, and Mill Valley from Folsom and Main streets—the Transbay Temporary Terminal—and from other points in San Francisco. For Mt. Tamalpais State Park and West Marin (Stinson Beach, Bolinas, and Point Reyes Station), take one of the many routes to Marin City and transfer there to the West Marin Stagecoach (schedules vary). San Francisco Muni bus 76X runs hourly from Sutter and Sansome streets to the Marin Headlands Visitor Center on weekends and major holidays only. The trip takes about 45 minutes.

19

Though much less convenient than BART, AC Transit buses run between the Transbay Temporary Terminal and the East Bay. AC Transit's F and FS lines stop near the university and 4th Street shopping, respectively, in Berkeley. Lines C and P travel to Piedmont in Oakland. The O bus stops at the edge of Chinatown near downtown Oakland.

Bus Lines AC Transit ☎ 511 ⊕ www.actransit.org. **Golden Gate Transit** ☎ 511 ⊕ www.goldengate.org. **San Francisco Muni** ☎ 311 ⊕ www.sfmta.com. **West Marin Stagecoach** ☎ 415/526-3239 ⊕ www.marintransit.org.

CAR TRAVEL

To reach the East Bay from San Francisco, take Interstate 80 East across the San Francisco–Oakland Bay Bridge. Head east from the University Avenue exit to reach U.C. Berkeley; there's a parking garage on Channing Way near the campus. For Oakland, take Interstate 580 off the Bay Bridge. To reach downtown and the waterfront, take Interstate 980 from Interstate 580 and exit at 12th Street. Both trips take about 30 minutes unless it's rush hour or a weekend afternoon, when you should count on an hour.

Head north on U.S.101 and cross the Golden Gate Bridge to reach all points in Marin by car, essential to visit the outer portions unless you want to spend all day on the bus. From San Francisco, the towns of Sausalito and Tiburon and the Marin Headlands and Point Reyes National Seashore are accessed off U.S. 101. The coastal route, Highway 1, also known as Shoreline Highway, can be accessed off U.S. 101 as well. Follow this road to Mill Valley, Muir Woods, Mt. Tamalpais State Park, Muir Beach, Stinson Beach, and Bolinas. From Bolinas, you can continue north on Highway 1 to Point Reyes. Depending on traffic, it takes from 20 to 45 minutes to get to the Marin Headlands, Sausalito, and Tiburon; driving directly to Point Reyes from San Francisco takes about 90 minutes in moderate traffic if you drive north on U.S. 101 and west on Sir Francis Drake Boulevard. Trips to Muir Woods take from 35 minutes to an hour from San Francisco. Add another 30 minutes for the drive to Stinson Beach (the curving roads make the going slower), 10 more if you continue on to Bolinas. The drive from Bolinas to Point Reyes takes an additional half hour.

RESTAURANTS

The Bay Area is home to popular, innovative restaurants such as Chez Panisse in Berkeley and Commis in Oakland—for which reservations must be made well in advance. Expect an emphasis on locally grown produce, hormone-free meats, and California wines. Many Marin cafés don't serve dinner, and dinner service ends on the early side. (No 10 pm reservations in that neck of the woods.)

HOTELS

Hotels in Berkeley and Oakland tend to be standard-issue, but many Marin hotels package themselves as cozy retreats. Summer in Marin is often booked well in advance, despite weather that can be downright chilly. Check for special packages during this season. *Hotel reviews have been shortened. For full information, visit Fodors.com.*

WHAT IT COSTS				
	$	**$$**	**$$$**	**$$$$**
Restaurants	under $16	$16–$22	$23–$30	over $30
Hotels	under $151	$151–$199	$200–$250	over $250

Restaurant prices are the average cost of a main course at dinner or, if dinner is not served, at lunch. Hotel prices are the lowest cost of a standard double room in high season.

TOURS

Best Bay Area Tours. Morning and afternoon tours of Muir Woods and Sausalito include at least two hours in the redwoods—longer than most tours—before heading on to Sausalito. Tours also make a stop in the Marin Headlands on the way back to the city to enjoy fantastic views. Knowledgeable guides lead small tours in comfortable vans, and hotel pickup is included. ☎ *415/543–8687, 877/705–8687* ⊕ *bestbayareatours. com* ⊠ *From $60.*

Dylan's Tours. Spend three hours exploring San Francisco with some of the friendliest local guides around, then head to Muir Woods for an hour among giant redwoods, with a stop in Sausalito on the way back. Groups are limited to 14 people; past patrons rave about the tour's in-the-know feel. ⊠ *782 Columbus Ave., North Beach, San Francisco* ☎ *415/932–6993* ⊕ *dylanstours.com* ✉ *From $75.*

Extranomical Tours. Take a combination Muir Woods–Sausalito tour with Extranomical, and you can choose to ferry back to San Francisco from Sausalito. Another tour combines a Muir Woods visit with a Wine Country excursion. ☎ *866/231–3752* ⊕ *www.extranomical.com* ✉ *From $77.*

Great Pacific Tour Co. Morning and afternoon tours to Muir Woods and Sausalito run 3½ hours, with hotel pickup, in 14-passenger vans. ☎ *415/626–4499* ⊕ *www.greatpacifictour.com* ✉ *From $65.*

THE EAST BAY

When San Franciscans refer to it, the East Bay often means nothing more than what you can see across the bay from the city—mainly Oakland and Berkeley. There's far more here—industrial-chic Emeryville, the wooded ranchland of Walnut Creek, and sprawling, urban Richmond, to name a few other communities—but Berkeley, anchored by its world-class university, and Oakland, which struggles with violence but has booming arts, nightlife, and restaurant scenes, are the magnets that draw folks across the bay.

BERKELEY

2 miles northeast of Bay Bridge.

The birthplace of the Free Speech Movement, the radical hub of the 1960s, the home of arguably the nation's top public university, and the city whose government condemned the bombing of Afghanistan—Berkeley is all of those things. The city of 100,000 facing San Francisco across the bay is also culturally diverse, a breeding ground for social trends, a bastion of the counterculture, and an important center for Bay Area writers, artists, and musicians. Berkeley residents, students, and faculty spend hours nursing various coffee concoctions while they read, discuss, and debate at any of the dozens of cafés that surround the campus. It's the quintessential university town, and many who graduated years ago still bask in daily intellectual conversation, great weather, and good food. Residents will walk out of their way to go to the perfect bread shop or consult with their favorite wine merchant.

Oakland may have Berkeley beat when it comes to cutting-edge arts, and the city may have forfeited some of its renegade 1960s spirit over the years, but unless a guy in a hot-pink satin body suit, skullcap, and cape rides a unicycle around *your* town, you'll likely find Berkeley offbeat indeed.

19

GETTING HERE AND AROUND

BART is the easiest way to get to Berkeley from San Francisco. Alight at the Downtown Berkeley (not North Berkeley) station, and walk a block up Center Street to get to the western edge of campus. AC Transit buses F and FS lines stop near the university and 4th Street shopping. By car, take I–80 east across the Bay Bridge then take the University Avenue exit through downtown Berkeley to the campus or take the Ashby Avenue exit and turn left on Telegraph Avenue. Once you arrive, explore on foot. Berkeley is very pedestrian-friendly.

ESSENTIALS

Visitor Information Visit Berkeley ⊠ *2030 Addison St., Suite 102, Berkeley* ☎ *510/549–7040* ⊕ *www.visitberkeley.com.*

EXPLORING
TOP ATTRACTIONS

4th Street. Several blocks centering on 4th Street north of University Avenue have evolved from light industrial uses into an upscale shopping and dining district. The compact area is busiest on bright weekend afternoons. Stained Glass Garden, Builders Booksource, and the Apple Store are among shoppers' favorites, along with a slew of boutiques and wonderful paper stores. ■ TIP➔ **A walk through the East Bay Vivarium, at 1827 5th Street, where turtles swim, Amazonian snakes slither, and baby mice (dinner) cower, is better than a walk through the reptile house at the zoo—and it's free.** ⊠ *4th St., between University Ave. and Delaware Sts., Berkeley* ⊕ *www.fourthstreet.com.*

QUICK BITES

Cheese Board Pizza. With a jazz combo playing in the storefront and a long line snaking down the block, Cheese Board Pizza taps into the pulse of the Gourmet Ghetto. The cooperatively owned takeout spot and restaurant draws devoted customers with the smell of just-baked garlic, fresh vegetables, and perfect sauces: one pizza a day, always vegetarian. For just a nibble, the Cheese Board bakery–cheese shop next door sells cookies, muffins, scones, bialys, and the best sourdough baguettes in town. ⊠ *1504–1512 Shattuck Ave., at Vine St., Berkeley* ☎ *510/549–3055* ⊕ *cheeseboardcollective.coop/pizza .*

Fodor's Choice ★

Gourmet Ghetto. The success of Chez Panisse restaurant attracted other food-related enterprises to its stretch of Shattuck Avenue, and the area surrounding the intersection of Shattuck and Vine Street became known as the Gourmet Ghetto. Foodies will do well to spend a couple of hours here, poking around the food shops, grabbing a quick bite, or indulging in a full meal at one of the neighborhood's many excellent eateries.

The line stretches down the block in front of **Cheese Board Pizza,** at 1512 Shattuck, where live jazz bands sometimes serenade the diners that spill out onto the sidewalk and median. Next door is the **Cheese Board Collective**—worker owned since 1971—and its fabulous bakery and extensive cheese counter. Next door to Chez Panisse, César (No. 1515) wine bar and tapas house is a good place for an afternoon quaff or late-night drink.

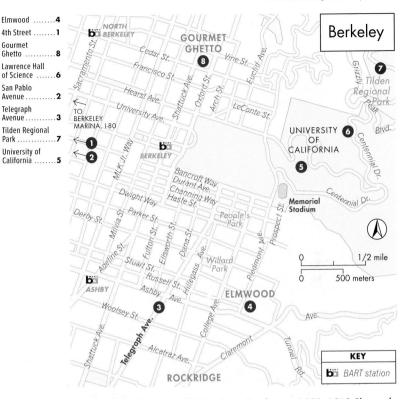

The small food stands of **Epicurious Garden**, at 1509–1513 Shattuck, sell everything from sushi to gelato. Out back, you can find a small terraced garden—the best place to sit—that winds up four levels and ends at the **Imperial Tea Court**. Around the corner just off Vine Street is **Love at First Bite**, a cupcakery that sells scrumptious confections. Across Vine, the **Vintage Berkeley** wine shop occupies the historic former pump house at No. 2113; the offerings here are shrewdly selected and reasonably priced. Coffee lovers of the **Peet's** persuasion may want to pay respects at No. 2124, where the famed roaster got its start; the small café includes a display chronicling Peet's history.

South of Cedar Street in the next block of Shattuck is the art-filled **Guerilla Cafe** (No. 1620), a breakfast and lunch spot beloved for its waffles (the Blue Bottle Coffee doesn't hurt). Also look for the **Local Butcher Shop** (No. 1600), with locally sourced meat and hearty made-to-order sandwiches. A former Ritz-Carlton chef brings white-linen quality to his to-go counter, **Grégoire**, around the corner on Cedar Street (No. 2109). In the block north of Vine Street on Shattuck are popular **Saul's** deli and restaurant and beautiful **Masse's Pastries**. On Thursday, an organic farmers' market thrives here. We could go on, but you get the idea. ⊠ *Shattuck Ave. between Cedar and Rose Sts., North Berkeley* ⊕ *www.gourmetghetto.org.*

FAMILY **Tilden Regional Park.** The **Regional Parks Botanic Garden** is the star of this 2,000-acre park in the hills east of the U.C. Berkeley campus. Botanically speaking, a stroll through the garden, which focuses on native plants of California, provides a whirlwind tour of the entire state. At the garden's visitors center, you can pick up information about Tilden's other attractions, including its picnic spots, Lake Anza swimming site, golf course, and hiking trails (the paved **Nimitz Way,** at Inspiration Point, is a popular hike with wonderful sunset views). ■TIP→ Children love Tilden Park's miniature steam trains; Little Farm, where kids can feed the animals; and the vintage carousel with wooden animals. ⊠ *Regional Parks Botanic Garden, Wildcat Canyon Rd. and South Park Dr., Tilden Park* ☎ *510/544–2747* ⊕ *www.ebparks.org/parks/tilden* ⊠ *Free to park and botanic garden* ⊙ *Park daily 5 am–10 pm; garden daily 8:30–5 (5:30 in summer).*

> ### A TASTING TOUR
>
> For an unforgettable foodie experience, take Lisa Rogovin's **Culinary Walking Tour** (☎ *415/806–5970* ⊕ *www.edibleexcursions.net*). You'll taste your way through the Gourmet Ghetto, learn some culinary history, and meet the chefs behind the food. Tours ($88) take place on Thursday from 11 to 2:15 and Saturday from 10 to 1.

University of California. Known simply as "Cal," the founding campus of California's university system is one of the leading intellectual centers in the United States and a major site for scientific research. Chartered in 1868, the university sits on 178 oak-covered acres split by Strawberry Creek. Bounded by Bancroft Way to the south, Hearst Avenue to the north, Oxford Street to the west, and Gayley Road to the east, Cal has more than 35,000 students and a full-time faculty of 1,600.

Below are a few places of note on campus:

Berkeley Art Museum & Pacific Film Archive. The museum's collection spans five centuries and is strong on mid-20th-century art, particularly abstract expressionist works. The archive is a major venue for foreign, independent, and avant-garde film. BAM/PFA is closed until 2016, when it reopens at a new location: ⊠ *Oxford St. at Center St.* ☎ *510/642–0808 museum, 510/642–1124 film info* ⊕ *www.bampfa.berkeley.edu.* ⊠ *Berkeley* ⊕ *www.berkeley.edu.*

Berkeley Visitor Information Center. You can get your bearings here and find out about campus events. Free 90-minute tours leave from here on weekdays. ⊠ *101 Sproul Hall, Bancroft Way at Telegraph Ave.* ☎ *510/642–5215* ⊕ *visitors.berkeley.edu* ⊙ *Weekdays 8:30–4:30, tours at 10 am (also 1 pm in Apr.).*

Sather Tower. Weekend campus tours leave from this landmark, popularly known as the Campanile, at 10 am on Saturday and 1 pm on Sunday. The 307-foot structure, modeled on St. Mark's Tower in Venice, can be seen for miles. For a view of the campus and beyond, take the elevator up 175 feet, then walk another 38 steps to the observation deck. ⊠ *Elevator $3* ⊙ *Weekdays 10–4, Sat. 10–5, Sun. 10–1:30 and 3–5.*

Berkeley's Political History

Those looking for traces of Berkeley's politically charged past need go no further than Sather Gate. Both the Free Speech Movement and the fledgling political life of actor-turned-politician Ronald Reagan have their roots here. It was next to Sather Gate, on September 30, 1964, that a group of students defied the University of California–Berkeley chancellor's order that all organizations advocating "off-campus issues" (such as civil rights and nuclear disarmament) keep their information tables off campus. Citation of the tablers brought more than 400 sympathetic students into Sproul Hall that afternoon. They stayed until 3 am, setting a precedent of protest that would be repeated in the coming months, with students jamming Sproul Hall in greater numbers each time.

Conservative U.C. president Clark Kerr eventually backed down and allowed student groups to pass out information on campus. By then, the Free Speech Movement had gathered momentum, and the conflict had made a national hero of student leader Mario Savio. Political newcomer Ronald Reagan played on Californians' unease about the unruly Berkeley students in his successful 1966 bid for governor, promising to rein in the "unwashed kooks."

By the end of the 1960s, the cohesion of the groups making up the Free Speech Movement had begun to fray. Some members began questioning the efficacy of sit-ins and other nonviolent tactics that had, until then, been the hallmark of Berkeley student protests. The Black Panthers, headquartered just over the border in Oakland, were ascending into the national spotlight, and their "take no prisoners" approach appealed to some Berkeley activists who had seen little come of their efforts to affect national policy.

By 1969 both Robert Kennedy and Martin Luther King Jr. were dead, and the issue of the day—stopping the flow of troops heading to Vietnam—was not as easy as overpowering a school administration's resistance to free speech. But a more dramatic clash with the university came when it brought in police units to repossess People's Park, a university-owned plot of land at Telegraph Avenue and Haste Street that students and community members had adopted as a park. On the afternoon of May 15, 1969, nearly 6,000 students and residents moved to reclaim the park. In the ensuing riot, police and sheriff's deputies fired both tear gas and buckshot, blinding one observer and killing another. Governor Ronald Reagan ordered the National Guard into Berkeley. Despite a ban on public assembly, crowds continued to gather and march in the days after the first riot. The park changed hands several times in the following tear-gas-filled months, with the fence coming down for the last time in 1972.

A colorful mural on the side of Amoeba Records (Haste Street at Telegraph Avenue) offers the protestors' version of park history. Although the areas around People's Park and Sather Gate may seem quiet now, issues such as affirmative action and tuition increases still bring protests to the steps of Sproul. Protests over civil rights, war, and other inequities march through the center of the campus, though students also gather to rally for sports events, social gatherings, and shows of school spirit.

19

The University of California is the epicenter of Berkeley's energy and activism.

Sproul Plaza. The site of free-speech and civil-rights protests in the 1960s, the plaza remains a platform for political and social activists, musicians, and students. Preachers orate atop milk crates, amateur entertainers bang on makeshift drum sets, and protesters distribute leaflets about everything from marijuana to the Middle East. Walk through at noon for the liveliest show of student spirit. ⊠ *Telegraph Ave. at Bancroft Way.*

University of California Botanical Garden. Thanks to Berkeley's temperate climate, about 13,500 species of plants from all over the world flourish in this 34-acre garden. Free tours are given on Thursdays and weekends at 1:30; the views are breathtaking. ⊠ *200 Centennial Dr.* ☎ *510/643–2755* ⊕ *botanicalgarden.berkeley.edu* ⊠ *$10, free 1st Wed. of month* ⊗ *Daily 9–5, closed 1st Tues. of month.*

WORTH NOTING

Elmwood. Shops and cafés pack this pleasant neighborhood centered on College Avenue, just south of the U.C. campus. You'll know you're here when you see the logo for the beloved art-house cinema and performance space, the **Elmwood theater,** near College and Ashby avenues, though you're just as apt to see a line snaking outside nearby **Ici Ice Cream,** at 2948 College. All the treats here are made on the premises. While you're waiting, check out the architectural details of the nearby pre–World War II storefronts. Century-old shingled houses line the tree-shaded streets nearby. ⊠ *College Ave. between Dwight Way and Alcatraz Ave., Elmwood, Berkeley.*

OFF THE
BEATEN
PATH

Indian Rock Park. An outcropping of nature in a sea of North Berkeley homes, this is an unbeatable spot for a sunset picnic. You know you've reached the rock when you see amateur rock climbers clinging precariously to its side. After-work walkers and cuddling couples, all watching the sun sinking beneath the Golden Gate Bridge, join you at the top. Come early to grab a spot on the rock while it's still light. ✉ *950 Indian Rock Ave., at Shattuck Ave., Berkeley* 🖼 *Free* ☉ *Daily 6 am–10 pm.*

FAMILY **Lawrence Hall of Science.** At this hands-on science museum, kids can look at insects under microscopes, solve crimes using chemical forensics, and explore the physics of baseball. Out front they'll climb on Pheena, a life-size blue-whale model, and clamber over a giant strand of DNA. Out back, it's all about how earthquakes and water have shaped the bay, and from all vantage points sweeping views of the bay and beyond can be had. On weekends come special lectures, demonstrations, and planetarium shows. ✉ *1 Centennial Dr., Berkeley* 📞 *510/642–5132* ⊕ *www.lawrencehallofscience.org* 🖼 *$12, planetarium $4 extra* ☉ *Daily 10–5.*

San Pablo Avenue. Berkeley's diversity is front and center along this evolving north–south artery in West Berkeley, where the old and new stand side by side: sari shops and a Mexican grocery do business near a hipster dive bar, a bait-and-tackle store, a typewriter store, and a dozen cool boutiques, all cheek by jowl in an eight-block microhood that doesn't have a name . . . yet.

Start a block north of University Avenue at the **Albatross Pub** (No. 1822), a neighborhood favorite where grad students have been playing darts and eating free popcorn for 50 years. Tuck into solid Pakistani food at **Indus Village** (No. 1920) and stop by the **Halal Food Market** (No. 1964), then cross University Avenue. Duck into **Mi Tierra Foods** (No. 2082) for piñatas and chorizo—notice the Mission District–like mural—and **Middle East Market** (No. 2054) for rose water and rockin' baklava. **Café V** (No. 2056) has fresh, reliably good, and reasonably priced Vietnamese food, and pretty much everyone loves the thin-crust pies at **Lanesplitter Pizza & Pub** (No. 2033). The coffee at **Local 123** (No. 2049) is strong, delicious, and beautiful, and the back patio is a lovely surprise.

Old-fashioned, family-run **Country Cheese** (No. 2101) has hundreds of cheeses, of course, but it also carries great bulk foods and makes a heck of a sandwich to order. Or grab a table at industrial-cute **Gaumenkitzel** (No. 2121) and tuck in to schnitzel and other traditional German fare. The pierced-and-tattooed set loves **Acme Bar & Company** (No. 2115) for its Bloody Marys and whiskey selection.

As you move south, you'll pass lots of home-decor shops. Witness the reupholstering genius on display at **Mignonne Décor** (No. 2447). One of the Bay Area's oldest salvage shops, **Ohmega Salvage** (Nos. 2400–2407) makes for fun browsing, though its claw-foot tubs and Victorian window frames are pricey.

At the corner of Dwight Way, stop for more caffeine at **Caffè Trieste** (No. 2500), Berkeley's homey branch of North Beach's bohemian coffee bar. Arousing browsing can be had at sex-positive, woman-friendly **Good Vibrations** (No. 2504). Find wonderful gifts at **Juniper Tree**

19

Supplies (No. 2520), with everything for the soap and candle maker, and **Kiss My Ring** (No. 2522), which stocks jewelry designed by the owner. ✉ *San Pablo Ave., between Delaware and Parker Sts., Berkeley.*

Telegraph Avenue. Cafés, bookstores, poster shops, and street vendors line Berkeley's student-oriented thoroughfare, a bustling, if shabby, place to whiff the city's famed counterculture. T-shirt sellers and tarot-card readers come and go on a whim, but **Rasputin Music** (No. 2401), **Amoeba Music** (No. 2455), and **Moe's Books** (No. 2476) are neighborhood landmarks worth checking out. Allen Ginsberg wrote his acclaimed poem "Howl" at **Caffe Mediterraneum** (No. 2475), a relic of 1960s-era café culture that also lays claim to inventing the café latte. **■ TIP→ Panhandlers are omnipresent on Telegraph; take care at night, when things get edgier.** ✉ *South of university from Bancroft Way, Berkeley.*

WHERE TO EAT

Dining in Berkeley is a low-key affair; even in the finest restaurants, most folks dress casually. Late diners be forewarned: Berkeley is an "early to bed" kind of town.

$ SOUTHERN

🍴 **Angeline's Louisiana Kitchen.** The exposed brick walls, maps of Louisiana, ceiling fans, and New Orleans music create a festive atmosphere at Angeline's. Specialties include Voo Doo Shrimp with blue lake beans, crawfish étouffée, and buttermilk fried chicken. The Creole pecan pie is so good you'll be coming back for more. [$] *Average main: $15* ✉ *2261 Shattuck Ave., near Kittredge St., Berkeley* ☎ *510/548–6900* 🌐 *www.angelineskitchen.com* 🕒 *No lunch Mon.*

$ AMERICAN FAMILY

🍴 **Bette's Oceanview Diner.** Buttermilk pancakes are just one of the specialties at this 1930s-inspired diner complete with checkered floors and burgundy booths. Huevos rancheros and lox and eggs are other breakfast options; kosher franks, generous slices of pizza, and a slew of sandwiches are available for lunch. The wait for a seat at breakfast can be quite long; thankfully, 4th Street was made for strolling. **■ TIP→ If you're starving, head to Bette's to Go, next door, for takeout.** [$] *Average main: $10* ✉ *1807 4th St., near Delaware St., 4th Street, Berkeley* ☎ *510/644–3230* 🌐 *www.bettesdiner.com* ✍ *Reservations not accepted* 🕒 *No dinner.*

$$ SPANISH

🍴 **César.** In true Spanish style, dinners are served late at César, whose kitchen closes at 11:30 pm on Friday and Saturday and at 11 pm the rest of the week. Couples spill out from its street-level windows on warm nights, or rub shoulders at the polished bar or center communal table. Founded by a trio of former Chez Panisse chefs, César is like a first cousin to that stalwart eatery right next door, each restaurant recommending the other if there's a long wait ahead. For tapas and perfectly grilled *bocadillos* (small sandwiches), there's no better choice. The bar also makes a mean martini and has an impressive wine list. **■ TIP→ Come early to get seated quickly and to hear your tablemates; the room gets loud when the bar is in full swing.** [$] *Average main: $20* ✉ *1515 Shattuck Ave., at Vine St., North Berkeley* ☎ *510/883–0222* 🌐 *cesarberkeley.com* ✍ *Reservations not accepted.*

$$$$ AMERICAN Fodor's Choice ★

🍴 **Chez Panisse Café & Restaurant.** At Chez Panisse even humble pizza is reincarnated, with innovative toppings of the freshest local ingredients. The downstairs portion of Alice Waters's legendary eatery is noted for its formality and personal service. The daily-changing multicourse dinners are prix-fixe, with the cost slightly lower on weekdays. Upstairs, in the informal café, the crowd is livelier, the prices are lower, and the ever-changing menu is à la carte. The food is simpler, too: penne with new potatoes, arugula, and sheep's-milk cheese; fresh figs with Parmigiano-Reggiano cheese and arugula; and grilled tuna with savoy cabbage, for example. Legions of loyal fans insist that Chez Panisse lives up to its reputation and delivers a dining experience well worth the price. **TIP→ It's wise to make your reservation a few weeks ahead of your visit.** [$] *Average main: $100* ✉ *1517 Shattuck Ave., at Vine St., North Berkeley* ☎ *510/548–5525 restaurant, 510/548–5049 café* 🌐 *www.chezpanisse.com* ✍ *Reservations essential* 🕒 *Closed Sun. No lunch in the restaurant.*

$$ MODERN MEXICAN

🍴 **Comal.** Relaxed yet trendy and surprisingly elegant for this university town, Comal draws a diverse, multigenerational, decidedly casual crowd for creative Mexican-influenced fare and well-crafted cocktails. The menu centers on small dishes that lend themselves to sharing: try the bright and subtle Dungeness crab with avocado, endive, and mandarins; tender and perfectly seasoned heritage pork enchiladas; or quesadillas with hen of the woods mushrooms. If you can't choose from among the more than 100 tequilas and mescals, four different flights offer samples from particular regions or family distilleries. [$] *Average main: $16* ✉ *2020 Shattuck Ave., near University Ave., Downtown, Berkeley* ☎ *510/926–6300* 🌐 *www.comalberkeley.com* 🕒 *No lunch.*

$$ TUSCAN

🍴 **Corso Trattoria.** On the edge of Berkeley's Gourmet Ghetto, this lively spot serves up excellent Florentine cuisine in a spare but snazzy space. The open kitchen at the back dominates the room (which can get smoky at times), and the closely spaced tables add to the festivity of dining here. The seasonal menu might include pan-roasted sturgeon with Brussels sprouts or butter-roasted chicken breast. Side dishes are ordered separately; the baked polenta with mascarpone and Parmesan is a definite crowd pleaser. An extensive Italian wine list complements the menu; save room for the memorable panna cotta. [$] *Average main: $20* ✉ *1788 Shattuck Ave., at Delaware St., North Berkeley* ☎ *510/704–8004* 🌐 *www.trattoriacorso.com* 🕒 *No lunch.*

$$ AMERICAN

🍴 **Gather.** Here organic, sustainable, and all things Berkeley reside harmoniously beneath one tasty roof. This vibrant, well-lit eatery boasts funky lighting fixtures, a variety of shiny wood furnishings, and banquettes made of recycled leather belts. Everything feels contemporary and local, especially the food. Locals foresee doom in the disappearance of the vegan "charcuterie," made of root vegetables, which put the restaurant on the national map; but the stinging nettles pizza is refreshing, and the grilled chicken is oh so juicy. This is a haven for vegetarian, vegan, and gluten-free eaters, but there's plenty for meat eaters to choose from, too. Desserts don't get much better than the chocolate semifreddo with Zinfandel-braised Mission figs and pine nuts.

Innovative Berkeley restaurant Chez Panisse focuses on seasonal local ingredients.

[$] *Average main: $22* ✉ *2200 Oxford St., at Allston Way, Berkeley* ☎ *510/809–0400* 🌐 *www.gatherrestaurant.com.*

$$$ JAPANESE 🍴 **Ippuku.** More Tokyo street chic than standard sushi house, this *izakaya*—the Japanese equivalent of a bar with appetizers—with bamboo-screen booths serves up surprising fare, from chicken tartare to wonderful *yakitori*, skewers such as bacon-wrapped enoki, bacon-wrapped mushrooms, and pork belly. (Anything skewered here is sure to please.) Dinner beats lunch at Ippuku, and savvy diners make reservations and arrive early for the best selection. The bar, which opens onto the street, pours an impressive array of sakes and *shōchū* (liquor distilled from sweet potatoes, rice, or barley). [$] *Average main: $23* ✉ *2130 Center St., Downtown, Berkeley* ☎ *510/665–1969* 🌐 *www.ippukuberkeley.com* 🕒 *No lunch.*

$$$ MEDITERRANEAN 🍴 **Lalime's.** Inside a charming, flower-covered house, this restaurant serves dishes that reflect the entire Mediterranean region. The menu, constantly changing and unfailingly great, depends on the availability of fresh seasonal ingredients. Choices might include grilled ahi tuna, creamy Italian risotto, or grilled lamb chops. The two-level dining room is cheerful and light. Excellent and long-lived but not flashy, the restaurant has a legion of dedicated fans, many middle-aged and up. **■ TIP→ Lalime's is a good second choice if Chez Panisse is booked up.** [$] *Average main: $27* ✉ *1329 Gilman St., at Tevlin St., North Berkeley* ☎ *510/527–9838* 🌐 *www.lalimes.com* ✍ *Reservations essential* 🕒 *Closed Mon. No lunch.*

$ MEXICAN FAMILY 🍴 **Picante.** A barnlike space full of cheerful Mexican tiles and folk-art masks, Picante is a find for anyone seeking good, Cal-Mex food for a song. The masa is freshly ground for the tortillas and tamales (it's fun to watch the tamale maker in action), the salsas are complex, and the flavor combinations are inventive. Try tamales filled with butternut squash and chilies or a simple taco of roasted poblanos and sautéed onions; we challenge you to finish a plate of supernachos. Picante is beloved of Berkeley families with raucous children, as they fit right in to the festival-like atmosphere and are happily distracted by the fountain on the back patio. [$] *Average main: $12* ✉ *1328 6th St., near Camelia St., Berkeley* ☎ *510/525–3121* 🌐 *www.picanteberkeley.com* ✍ *Reservations not accepted.*

$$ AMERICAN FAMILY 🍴 **Rick & Ann's.** Haute comfort food is the focus at this cute diner across from the Claremont hotel. The brunches are legendary for quality and value, and customers line up outside the door before the restaurant opens on the weekend. If you come during prime brunch hours, expect a long wait, but the soft-style eggs are worth it. Pancakes, waffles, and French toast are more flavorful than usual, with variations such as potato-cheese and orange–rice flour pancakes. Lunch and dinner offer burgers, favorites such as Mom's macaroni and cheese, and chicken potpie, but always with a festive twist. Reservations are accepted for dinner and for lunch parties of six or more, but, alas, you can't reserve a table for brunch. [$] *Average main: $16* ✉ *2922 Domingo Ave., at Ashby Ave., Claremont, Berkeley* ☎ *510/649–8538* 🌐 *www.rickandanns.com* 🕒 *No dinner Mon.*

$$$ AMERICAN 🍴 **Rivoli.** Italian-inspired dishes using fresh, mostly organic California ingredients star on a menu that changes every three weeks. Typical meals include line-caught fish, pastas, and inventive offerings such as Rivoli's trademark portobello fritters with aioli. Desserts might include pear granita with gingersnaps or a refreshing Meyer-lemon tart. A lovely back garden and attentive service add to the overall appeal, though some diners find the tables are too closely spaced. The small front bar is a cozy spot for a drink and dessert, but it's standing-room-only on a busy night. [$] *Average main: $26* ✉ *1539 Solano Ave., at Neilson St., Berkeley* ☎ *510/526–2542* 🌐 *www.rivolirestaurant.com* ✍ *Reservations essential* 🕒 *No lunch.*

19

$ AMERICAN FAMILY 🍴 **Saul's.** Well known for its homemade sodas and enormous sandwiches, the Saul's of today uses sustainably sourced seafood, grass-fed beef, and organic eggs. The restaurant is a Berkeley institution, and its loyal clientele swears by the pastrami sandwiches, stuffed-cabbage rolls, and tuna melts. For breakfast, the challah French toast is so thick it's almost too big to bite, and the deli omelets are served pancake style. The high ceilings and red-leather booths add to the friendly, retro atmosphere. ■ **TIP→ Don't overlook the glass deli case, where you can order food to go.** [$] *Average main: $15* ✉ *1475 Shattuck Ave., near Vine St., North Berkeley* ☎ *510/848–3354* 🌐 *www.saulsdeli.com* ✍ *Reservations not accepted.*

WHERE TO STAY

For inexpensive lodging, investigate University Avenue, west of campus. The area can be noisy, congested, and somewhat dilapidated, but it does include a few decent motels and chain properties. All Berkeley lodgings, except for the swanky Claremont, are strictly mid-range.

$$ HOTEL **The Bancroft Hotel.** Lovingly remodeled in 2012, this green boutique hotel—across from the U.C. campus—is fresh, stylish, and completely eco-friendly. **Pros:** closest hotel in Berkeley to campus; friendly staff; many rooms have good views. **Cons:** some rooms are small; bathrooms small and need updating; no elevator. *Rooms from: $155 2680 Bancroft Way, Berkeley 510/549–1000 bancrofthotel.com 22 rooms Breakfast.*

$$$$ HOTEL FAMILY Fodor's Choice ★ **Claremont Resort and Spa.** Straddling the Oakland–Berkeley border, this amenities-rich resort—which celebrates its centennial in 2015—beckons like a gleaming white castle in the hills. **Pros:** amazing spa; supervised child care; solid business amenities; great bay views from some rooms. **Cons:** parking is pricey; resort charge for use of spa, tennis courts, pool, gym; additional fee for breakfast. *Rooms from: $270 41 Tunnel Rd., at Ashby and Domingo Aves., Claremont, Berkeley 510/843–3000, 800/551–7266 www.claremontresort.com 249 rooms, 30 suites No meals.*

$$ HOTEL **Holiday Inn Express.** Convenient to the freeway and 4th Street shopping, this peach-and-beige hotel provides good bang for the buck. **Pros:** good breakfast; short walk to restaurant options on San Pablo and University; free Internet in rooms. **Cons:** area can be noisy and congested with traffic during commute hours; neighborhood can feel sketchy after dark. *Rooms from: $190 1175 University Ave., at Curtis St., Berkeley 510/548–1700, 866/548–1700 www.hiexberkeley.com 69 rooms, 3 suites Breakfast.*

$$ HOTEL **Hotel Durant.** A mainstay of parents visiting their children at U.C. Berkeley, this boutique hotel is also a good option for those who want to be a short walk from Telegraph Avenue. **Pros:** convenient location to Cal and public transit; blackout shades; organic bathrobes. **Cons:** downstairs bar can get noisy during Cal games; parking can be pricey; service can be inept. *Rooms from: $180 2600 Durant Ave., at Bowditch St., Berkeley 510/845–8981 www.hoteldurant.com 143 rooms No meals.*

$$$ HOTEL Fodor's Choice ★ **Hotel Shattuck Plaza.** This historic boutique hotel sits amid Berkeley's downtown arts district, just steps from the U.C. campus and a short walk from the Gourmet Ghetto. **Pros:** central location; near public transit; modern facilities; good views; great restaurant. **Cons:** pricey parking; limited fitness center. *Rooms from: $209 2086 Allston Way, at Shattuck Ave., Downtown, Berkeley 510/845–7300 www.hotelshattuckplaza.com 199 rooms, 17 suites No meals.*

NIGHTLIFE AND PERFORMING ARTS

Berkeley Repertory Theatre. One of the region's highly respected resident professional companies, Berkeley Rep performs classic and contemporary plays. Well-known pieces such as *Crime and Punishment* and *The Arabian Nights* mix with edgier fare like Green Day's *American*

Idiot and Lemony Snicket's *The Composer Is Dead.* The theater's complex is in the heart of downtown Berkeley's arts district, near BART's Downtown Berkeley station. ⊠ *2025 Addison St., near Shattuck Ave., Berkeley* ☎ *510/647–2949* ⊕ *www.berkeleyrep.org.*

Berkeley Symphony Orchestra. The works of 20th-century composers are a focus of this prominent orchestra, but traditional pieces are also performed. BSO plays a handful of concerts each year, in Zellerbach Hall and other locations. ⊠ *1942 University Ave., Suite 207, Berkeley* ☎ *510/841–2800* ⊕ *www.berkeleysymphony.org.*

Cal Performances. The series, running from September through May at Zellerbach Hall and various other U.C. Berkeley venues, offers the Bay Area's most varied bill of internationally acclaimed artists in all disciplines, from classical soloists to the latest jazz, world-music, theater, and dance ensembles. Past performers include Mark Morris Dance Group, the Peking Acrobats, Arlo Guthrie, and Yo-Yo Ma. ⊠ *Zellerbach Hall, Telegraph Ave. and Bancroft Way, Berkeley* ☎ *510/642–9988* ⊕ *calperformances.org.*

Fodor's Choice ★ **Freight & Salvage Coffeehouse.** Some of the most talented practitioners of folk, blues, Cajun, and bluegrass perform in this alcohol-free space, one of the country's finest folk houses. Most tickets cost less than $30. ⊠ *2020 Addison St., between Shattuck Ave. and Milvia St., Berkeley* ☎ *510/644–2020* ⊕ *www.thefreight.org.*

SHOPPING

Fodor's Choice ★ **Amoeba Music.** Heaven for audiophiles, this legendary Berkeley favorite is *the* place to head for new and used CDs, records, cassettes, and DVDs. The dazzling stock includes thousands of titles for all music tastes. The store even has its own record label. There are branches in San Francisco and Hollywood, but this is the original. ⊠ *2455 Telegraph Ave., at Haste St., Berkeley* ☎ *510/549–1125* ⊕ *www.amoeba.com.*

Body Time. Founded in Berkeley in 1970, this local chain uses premium-quality ingredients to create its natural perfumes and skin-care and aromatherapy products. Sustainably harvested essential oils that you can combine and dilute to create your own personal fragrances are the specialty. The Citrus, Lavender-Mint, and China Rain scents are all popular. ⊠ *1950 Shattuck Ave., at Berkeley Way, Berkeley* ☎ *510/841–5818* ⊕ *www.bodytime.com.*

Kermit Lynch Wine Merchant. Credited with taking American appreciation of French wine to a higher level, this small shop is a great place to peruse as you educate your palate. The friendly salespeople can direct you to the latest French bargains. ⊠ *1605 San Pablo Ave., at Dwight Way, Berkeley* ☎ *510/524–1524* ⊕ *kermitlynch.com.*

Moe's Books. The spirit of Moe—the cantankerous, cigar-smoking late proprietor—lives on in this four-story house of books. Students and professors come here to browse the large selection of used books, including literary and cultural criticism, art titles, and literature in foreign languages. ⊠ *2476 Telegraph Ave., near Haste St., Berkeley* ☎ *510/849–2087* ⊕ *moesbooks.com.*

19

Fodor's Choice **Rasputin Music.** A huge selection of new music for every taste draws
★ crowds, and only in a town that also contained Amoeba Music could
Rasputin's stock of used CDs and vinyl be surpassed. ⊠ *2403 Telegraph Ave., at Channing Way, Berkeley* 🕾 *510/848–9004* ⊕ *www.
rasputinmusic.com.*

OAKLAND

East of Bay Bridge.

Often overshadowed by San Francisco's beauty and Berkeley's storied
counterculture, Oakland's allure lies in its amazing diversity. Here you
can find a Nigerian clothing store, a beautifully renovated Victorian
home, a Buddhist meditation center, and a lively salsa club, all within
the same block.

Oakland's multifaceted nature reflects its colorful and often tumultuous
history. Once a cluster of Mediterranean-style homes and gardens that
served as a bedroom community for San Francisco, the city became a
hub of shipbuilding and industry almost overnight when the United
States entered World War II. New jobs in the city's shipyards and fac-
tories attracted thousands of workers, including some of the first female
welders, and the city's neighborhoods were imbued with a proud but
gritty spirit. In the 1960s and '70s this intense community pride gave
rise to such militant groups as the Black Panther Party and the Sym-
bionese Liberation Army, but they were little match for the economic
hardships and racial tensions that plagued Oakland. In many neighborhoods the reality was widespread poverty and gang violence—subjects
that dominated the songs of such Oakland-bred rappers as the late
Tupac Shakur. The highly publicized protests of the Occupy Oakland
movement in 2011 and 2012 and the #BlackLivesMatter movement of
2014 and 2015 illustrated just how much Oakland remains a mosaic
of its past.

The affluent reside in the city's hillside homes, wooded enclaves like
Claremont and Montclair, which provide a warmer, more spacious,
and more affordable alternative to San Francisco, while a constant
flow of newcomers—many from Central America and Asia—ensures
continued diversity, vitality, and growing pains. Many neighborhoods
to the west and south of the city center remain run-down and unsafe,
but a renovated downtown area—sparking a vibrant arts scene—has
injected new energy into the city. Even San Franciscans, often loath to
cross the Bay Bridge, come to Uptown and Temescal for the crackling
arts and restaurant scenes there.

Everyday life here revolves around the neighborhood, with a main business strip attracting both shoppers and strollers. In some areas, such as
high-end Piedmont and Rockridge, you'd swear you were in Berkeley
or San Francisco's Noe Valley or Cow Hollow. Along Telegraph Avenue
just south of 51st Street, Temescal is pulsing with creative culinary
and design energy. These are perfect places for browsing, eating, or
just relaxing between sightseeing trips to Oakland's architectural gems,
rejuvenated waterfront, and numerous green spaces.

GETTING HERE AND AROUND

Driving from San Francisco, take Interstate 80 East across the Bay Bridge, then take Interstate 580 to the Grand Avenue exit for Lake Merritt. To reach downtown and the waterfront, take Interstate 980 from Interstate 580 and exit at 12th Street; exit at 18th Street for Uptown. For Temescal, take Interstate 580 to Highway 24 and exit at 51st Street.

By BART, use the Lake Merritt Station for the Oakland Museum and southern Lake Merritt; the Oakland City Center–12th Street Station for downtown, Chinatown, and Old Oakland; and the 19th Street Station for Uptown, the Paramount Theatre, and the north side of Lake Merritt.

By bus, take the AC Transit's C and P lines to get to Piedmont in Oakland. The O bus stops at the edge of Chinatown near downtown Oakland.

Oakland's Jack London Square is an easy hop on the ferry from San Francisco. Those without cars can take advantage of the free Broadway Shuttle, which runs from the square down Broadway through Chinatown/Old Oakland, downtown, Uptown, and Lake Merritt, all the way to 27th Street. The shuttle runs late on Friday and Saturday nights; its website has full schedule information.

Once you arrive, be aware of how quickly neighborhoods can change. Walking is safe downtown and in the Piedmont and Rockridge areas, but avoid walking west and southeast of downtown.

ESSENTIALS

Shuttle Contact Broadway Shuttle ✉ *Oakland* ⊕ *www.meetdowntownoak. com.*

Visitor Information Visit Oakland ✉ *Jack London Sq., 481 Water St., near Broadway, Oakland* ☎ *510/839–9000* ⊕ *visitoakland.org.*

EXPLORING

TOP ATTRACTIONS

FAMILY
Fodor'sChoice
★

Oakland Museum of California. The museum surveys the state's art, history, and natural wonders in three galleries of absorbing, detailed exhibits. You can travel through myriad ecosystems in the Gallery of California Natural Sciences, from the sand dunes of the Pacific to the coyotes and brush of the Nevada border. Kids love the lifelike wild-animal exhibits, especially the snarling wolverine and the big-eyed harbor seal. The rambling Gallery of California History includes everything from Spanish-era armor to a small but impressive collection of vintage vehicles, including a red, gold, and silver fire engine that battled the flames in San Francisco following the 1906 earthquake. Of particular interest in the Gallery of California Art are paintings by Richard Diebenkorn, Joan Brown, Elmer Bischoff, and David Park, all members of the Bay Area figurative school, which flourished here after World War II. Fans of Dorothea Lange won't want to miss the comprehensive collection of her photographs. ■TIP→ On Friday evening the museum is a lively scene, with live music, food trucks, and half-price admission. ✉ *1000 Oak St., at 10th St., Downtown, Oakland* ☎ *510/238–2200* ⊕ *www.museumca. org* ☑ *$15, $7.50 Thurs. 5–9, free 1st Sun. of month* ☉ *Wed.–Thurs. 11–5, Fri. 11–9, weekends 10–6.*

19

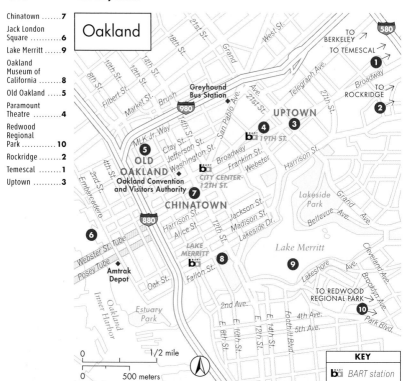

KEY

bø   BART station

Fodor's Choice
★

Paramount Theatre. A glorious art-deco specimen, the Paramount operates as a venue for concerts and performances of all kinds, from the Oakland East Bay Symphony to Tom Waits and Elvis Costello. The popular monthly movie nights start off with a 30-minute Wurlitzer concert preceding classic films such as *Casablanca*. ■ TIP→ The docent-led tours here are fun and informative. ✉ *2025 Broadway, at 20th St., Uptown, Oakland* ☎ *510/465–6400* ⊕ *www.paramounttheatre.com* ✇ *Tour $5* ⊙ *Tour 10 am on 1st and 3rd Sat. of month.*

Rockridge. This upscale neighborhood is one of Oakland's most desirable places to live. Explore the tree-lined streets that radiate out from **College Avenue** just north and south of the Rockridge BART station for a look at California bungalow architecture at its finest. By day College Avenue between Broadway and Alcatraz Avenue is crowded with shoppers buying fresh flowers, used books, and clothing; by night the same folks are back for dinner and locally brewed ales in the numerous restaurants and pubs. With its pricey specialty-food shops, **Market Hall,** an airy European-style marketplace at Shafter Avenue, is a hub of culinary activity. ✉ *Oakland* ⊕ *www.rockridgedistrict.com.*

Fodor's Choice
★

Temescal. Centering on Telegraph Avenue between Piedmont and South Berkeley, Temescal ("sweat house" in the language of the Aztec) is a low-pretension, moneyed-hipster hood with many young families and—gasp—middle-aged folks thrown into of the mix. A critical mass of excellent eateries, from veteran Doña Tomás and favorites Pizzaiola and Aunt Mary's to **Bakesale Betty** (⊠ *5098 Telegraph Ave.*), where folks line up for the fried-chicken sandwich on the one-item menu, and **Doughnut Dolly** (⊠ *482B 49th St.*), who fills her fried treats to order, draws folks from around the Bay Area. Old-time dive bars and check-cashing places share space with newer arrivals like crafty, local children's clothing shop **Ruby's Garden** (⊠ *5026 Telegraph Ave.*) and stalwart **East Bay Depot for Creative Reuse** (⊠ *4695 Telegraph Ave.*), where you might find a bucket of buttons or 1,000 muffin wrappers for $1 among birdcages, furniture, lunch boxes, and ribbon.

Around the corner, **Temescal Alley** (⊠ *49th St.*), a tucked-away lane of tiny storefronts, crackles with the creative energy of the craftspeople who have set up shop there. You can make some surprising finds at Crimson Horticultural Rarities and the fresh home-decor shop Bounty and Feast. ⊠ *Telegraph Ave., between 45th and 51st Sts., Temescal, Oakland* ⊕ *www.temescaldistrict.org.*

Uptown. This is where nightlife and cutting-edge art happens in Oakland, along the formerly gritty, currently crazy-cool Telegraph Avenue/Broadway corridor north of downtown. Dozens of galleries cluster around Telegraph, showing everything from photography and video installations to glasswork and textile arts. On the first Friday of the month, thousands descend for the neighborhood's biggest happening, the gallery walk **Art Murmur** (⊕ *oaklandartmurmur.org*). In addition to galleries open late, Art Murmur has expanded into **First Friday,** a veritable festival featuring food trucks, street vendors, and live music along Telegraph Avenue. Less raucous and more intimate is the **Saturday Stroll,** with member galleries open on Saturday from 1 to 5, often with special events.

Lively restaurants with a distinctly urban vibe make the neighborhood a dining destination; favorites include friendly **Luka's Taproom and Lounge** (⊠ *2221 Broadway*); beautiful art-deco **Flora** (⊠ *1900 Telegraph Ave.*), one of the best brunch places in town; trendy, graffiti-walled **Hawker Fare** (⊠ *2300 Webster St.*), serving Asian street food; elegant **Picán** (⊠ *2295 Broadway*), for upscale Southern comfort food; and the sophisticated **Plum** (⊠ *2216 Broadway*) and its attached bar, just to name a few.

Toss in the bevy of bars, and there's plenty within walking distance to keep you busy for an entire evening: **Cafe Van Kleef** (⊠ *1621 Telegraph Ave.*), the friendly jumble that started it all Uptown; **Bar Three Fifty-Five** (⊠ *355 19th St.*), a house of great cocktails; strikingly beautiful but low-key **Dogwood** (⊠ *1644 Telegraph Ave.*), which has tasty nibbles; and **Somar** (⊠ *1727 Telegraph Ave.*), a bar, music lounge, and gallery in one. Uptown's shopping element is exploding as well, with local goods at the fore; stop by **Oaklandish** (⊠ *1444 Broadway*) for T-shirts, jeans, and everything Oaktown, and **OwlNWood** (⊠ *45 Grand Ave.*) for the coolest collection of vintage and locally designed clothing in town. The Paramount Theatre ⇨ *(see above)*, the Fox Theater ⇨ *(see Nightlife, below)*, and other art-deco architectural gems distinguish

19

this neighborhood. ⊠ *Telegraph Ave. and Broadway from 16th to 26th Sts., Oakland.*

WORTH NOTING

Chinatown. A densely packed, bustling neighborhood, Oakland's Chinatown, unlike its San Francisco counterpart, makes no concessions to tourists. You won't find baskets of trinkets lining the sidewalk and souvenir displays in the shop windows, but supermarkets such as **Yuen Hop Noodle Company and Asian Food Products** (⊠ *824 Webster St.*), open since 1931, overflow with delicacies, and the line for sweets, breads, and towering cakes snakes out the door of **Napoleon Super Bakery** (⊠ *810 Franklin St.*). ⊠ *Between Broadway and Lakeside Dr. and between 6th and 12th Sts., Oakland* ⊕ *www.oakland-chinatown.info.*

Jack London Square. Shops, minor historic sites, restaurants, and the venerable Yoshi's jazz club line Jack London Square, named for the author of *The Call of the Wild, The Sea Wolf,* and other books. London, who was born in San Francisco, also lived in Oakland, where he spent many a day boozing and brawling in the waterfront area, most notably at the tiny **Heinold's First and Last Chance Saloon** (*48 Webster St., at Embarcadero W*). The wonderful saloon has been serving since 1883. Next door is the Klondike cabin in which London spent a summer in the late 1890s. The cabin was moved from Alaska and reassembled here in 1970.

Weekends at the square are lively, with diners filling the many outdoor patios, and shoppers perusing Sunday's farmers' market, from 9 am to 2 pm. ■TIP➡ **The square is worth a peek if you've arrived on the ferry that docks here; but you'll get a better feel for Oakland checking out the Uptown, Rockridge, or Temescal neighborhoods.** ⊠ *Embarcadero W at Broadway, Oakland* ☎ *510/645–9292* ⊕ *www.jacklondonsquare.com.*

Lake Merritt. Joggers and power walkers charge along the 3-mile path that encircles this 155-acre natural saltwater lake in downtown Oakland. Crew teams often glide across the water, and boatmen guide snuggling couples in authentic Venetian gondolas (⊠ *fares start at $60 per couple for 30 minutes* ☎ *510/663–6603* ⊕ *gondolaservizio. com*). **Lakeside Park,** which surrounds the north side of Lake Merritt, has several outdoor attractions, including a small children's park and a waterfowl refuge. The lake is less an attraction than a pleasant backdrop to Oaklanders' everyday life. ■TIP➡ **The nearby Grand Lake neighborhood, centering on the parallel commercial strips of Lakeshore Avenue and Grand Avenue, makes for good browsing and even better eating.** ⊠ *Lakeside Park, Bellevue and Grand Aves., Oakland* ⊕ *www. lakemerritt.org.*

Old Oakland. The restored Victorian storefronts lining four historic blocks, formerly Oakland's main business district, now contain restaurants, cafés, shops, galleries, and a three-block farmers' market that takes place on Friday morning. Architectural consistency distinguishes the area from surrounding streets, lending it a distinct neighborhood feel. Tuscany-inspired **Caffè 817** (⊠ *817 Washington St.*) serves excellent panini and bowls of café latte in an artsy atmosphere. Stop in for a deli sandwich at the Italian grocery **Ratto's International Market** (⊠ *827*

Washington St.), in business for more than a century, or head over to **Pacific Coast Brewing Company** (✉ *902 Washington St.*) for a microbrew on the patio. The **Trappist** (✉ *460 8th St.*) beer bar wins loyalty for its exhaustive selection of Belgian ales. Various pop-up boutiques and permanent shops throughout the neighborhood are reinvigorating the storefront scene. ✉ *Bordered by 7th, 10th, Clay, and Washington Sts., Oakland* 🌐 *old-oakland.com.*

Redwood Regional Park. *Sequoia sempervirens*, or coastal redwoods, grow to 150 feet tall in Redwood Regional Park, one of the few spots in the Bay Area that escaped timber-hungry loggers in the 19th century. The 1,836-acre park has forested picnic spots and dozens of hiking trails, including part of the 31-mile **Skyline National Trail**, which links Redwood to four other parks in the Berkeley–Oakland hills. From downtown Oakland take Interstate 580 east toward Hayward, exit at 35th Avenue/MacArthur Boulevard, and then take 35th Avenue east (which becomes Redwood Road). Watch for a park entrance on the left, 3 to 4 miles down the road. ✉ *7867 Redwood Rd., Oakland* ☎ *888/327–2757* 🌐 *www.ebparks.org/parks/redwood* 🎫 *Free; $5 per vehicle in season at some major entrances, $4 per trailered vehicle* 🕑 *Daily 5 am–10 pm.*

WHERE TO EAT

$$ MEDITERRANEAN

🍴 **À Côté.** This place for Mediterranean food is all about small plates, cozy tables, family-style eating—and truly excellent food. The butternut-squash ravioli, wild-boar chestnut sausage, and duck confit flatbread with apples and cantelet cheese are all fine choices, and you won't find a better plate of *pommes frites* (french fries) anywhere. The restaurant pours more than 40 wines by the glass. Among the tempting desserts here are the lemon pudding cake with lemon cream, huckleberries, and candied pistachios. Heavy wooden tables, cool tiles, and natural light make this a destination for students, families, couples, and the after-work crowd; the heated back patio is warm and welcoming in any weather. [$] *Average main: $20* ✉ *5478 College Ave., at Taft Ave., Rockridge, Oakland* ☎ *510/655–6469* 🌐 *www.acoterestaurant.com* 🕑 *No lunch.*

$ AMERICAN

🍴 **Brown Sugar Kitchen.** Chef and owner Tanya Holland turned an isolated corner in West Oakland into a breakfast and lunch destination. Influenced by her African-American heritage and her culinary education in France—and using local, organic, and seasonal products—she blends sweet and savory flavors like no one else and pairs her dishes with well-chosen wines. The dining room is fresh and bright, with a long, sleek counter, red-leather stools, and spacious booths and tables. **■ TIP→ This is the place to come for chicken and waffles.** [$] *Average main: $15* ✉ *2534 Mandela Pkwy., at 26th St., West Oakland* ☎ *510/839–7685* 🌐 *www.brownsugarkitchen.com* 🕑 *Closed Mon. No dinner.*

$$$ AMERICAN

🍴 **Camino.** Chef-owner Russell Moore cooked at Chez Panisse for two decades before opening this restaurant with co-owner Allison Hopelain that focuses on simple, seasonal, straightforward dishes cooked in an enormous, crackling *camino* (Italian for "fireplace"). The nightly changing menu has only three entrées—each cooked over its own open fire—including one vegetarian option such as eggplant gratin. Everything is made with top-notch ingredients, including local sardines and smelts, grilled lamb and sausage, and Dungeness crab (cooked in the fireplace with rutabagas). Camino is decorated in a Craftsman-meets-refectory style, with brick walls and two long redwood communal tables. ■TIP➔ A gin-based libation with house-made cherry and hibiscus bitters is among the perfectly crafted, seasonally inspired cocktails poured here. $ *Average main: $26* ⊠ *3917 Grand Ave., at Boulevard Way, Grand Lake, Oakland* ☎ *510/547–5035* ⊕ *www.caminorestaurant.com* ⊘ *Closed Tues. No lunch (weekend brunch 10–2).*

$$ ✕ **Chop Bar.** The walls and tables are made of reclaimed wood at this
MODERN small, stylish space whose knowing, tattooed bartenders serve potent
AMERICAN cocktails. A great neighborhood joint for every meal of the day (and brunch on weekends), Chop Bar serves upmarket gastropub grub, including favorites such as oxtail poutine, pork confit with polenta and kale, and burgers that rank among the Bay Area's best. On sunny days when the glass garage door is raised, extending the outdoor seating area out front, you'll feel like an insider who's stumbled upon an industrial neighborhood's cool secret. $ *Average main: $20* ⊠ *247 4th St., at Alice St., Jack London Square, Oakland* ☎ *510/834–2467* ⊕ *www. oaklandchopbar.com.*

$$$$ ✕ **Commis.** A slender, unassuming storefront in Oakland's Piedmont
MODERN neighborhood houses the only East Bay restaurant with a Michelin star.
AMERICAN The room is simple and polished: nothing distracts from the artistry of the fixed multicourse meals ($95, wine pairing $55 additional) chef James Syhabout creates based on the season and his distinctive vision. Dishes might include poached egg yolk with smoked dates and alliums (members of the onion/garlic family) in malt vinegar, or duck roasted on the bone over charcoal with renderings, walnut, and persimmon. Diners don't see the menu until after the meal, the chef's way of ensuring that everyone comes to the table with an open mind. ■TIP➔ This isn't a place to grab a quick bite: meals last about three hours. The service is excellent. $ *Average main: $95* ⊠ *3859 Piedmont Ave., at Rio Vista Ave., Piedmont, Oakland* ☎ *510/653–3902* ⊕ *commisrestaurant.com* ⌂ *Reservations essential* ⊘ *Closed Mon. and Tues. No lunch.*

$$ ✕ **Doña Tomás.** A neighborhood favorite, this spot in Oakland's hot Tem-
MEXICAN escal District serves seasonal Mexican fare to a hip but low-key crowd. Mexican textiles and art adorn walls in two long rooms; there's also a vine-covered patio. Tuck into starters such as quesadillas filled with butternut squash and goat cheese and entrées such as *albondigas en sopa zanahoria* (pork-and-beef meatballs in carrot puree). Some mighty fine tequilas complement the offerings. Brunch is served on weekends. $ *Average main: $19* ⊠ *5004 Telegraph Ave., near 51st St., Temescal, Oakland* ☎ *510/450–0522* ⊕ *www.donatomas.com* ⊘ *Closed Mon. No lunch weekdays. No dinner Sun.*

$ ✕ **Le Cheval Restaurant.** This cavernous restaurant, a lunchtime favorite,
VIETNAMESE is a good place to sample *pho*, Hanoi-style beef noodle soup fragrant with star anise. Other entrées include lemon chicken, cubed beefsteak, and clay-pot snapper. It's hard to spend more than $20 for an entire meal unless you order the seven courses of beef ($28). The complimentary minibowls of soup that are placed on the table as soon as you sit down are a great balm to hungry diners, though the service

is lightning-quick anyway. $ *Average main: $12* ✉ *1019 Clay St., at 11th St., Old Oakland* ☎ *510/763–8495* ⊕ *www.lecheval.com* ⊙ *No lunch Sun.*

$$ ✕ **Luka's Taproom & Lounge.** Hip and urban, with an unpretentious vibe,
AMERICAN Luka's is a real taste of Uptown. Diners nibble on *frites* (fries) any Belgian would embrace and entrées such as crispy-skin salmon or gratinéed mac and cheese. The brews draw them in, too—a nice selection of Trappist ales complements plentiful beers on tap and international bottles—and the DJs in the adjacent lounge keep the scene going late. ■TIP→ **Hungry night owls appreciate the late-night menu, served daily until midnight.** $ *Average main: $19* ✉ *2221 Broadway, at West Grand Ave., Uptown, Oakland* ☎ *510/451–4677* ⊕ *www.lukasoakland.com.*

$$ ✕ **Pizzaiolo.** Apparently no length of a wait can discourage locals who
PIZZA persevere to enjoy the legendary thin-crust, wood-fired pizza served up by Chez Panisse alum Charlie Hallowell in this rustic-chic dining room. Diners—mostly neighborhood hipsters but also young families and foodies of all ages—perch in wooden chairs with red-leather backs; weathered wood floors and brick walls peeking through the plaster create an always-been-here feel. Seasonal pizza options might include wild nettles and pecorino, or rapini and house-made sausage; don't overlook nonpizza dishes such as wild steelhead salmon with fava greens, English peas, and Meyer-lemon butter. Except on Sunday, early risers get to skip the crowds and enjoy Blue Bottle Coffee and pastries from 8 until noon. $ *Average main: $20* ✉ *5008 Telegraph Ave., at 51st St., Temescal, Oakland* ☎ *510/652–4888* ⊕ *www.pizzaiolooakland.com* ⊙ *Closed Sun. No lunch.*

$$ ✕ **Shakewell.** Two veterans of the *Top Chef* TV series opened this stylish
MEDITERRANEAN restaurant in the up-and-coming Lakeshore neighborhood, but hype aside, they're serving up creative and memorable small Mediterranean-influenced dishes. Favorites include the local squid and ink bomba (a paellalike dish baked in a wood-burning oven) and braised pork shoulder with pickled green tomatoes. The name implies an emphasis on cocktails, and you can enjoy a well-crafted one at the popular bar; also be sure to save room for dessert. Hard surfaces plus a lively crowd means the volume can get too high for some. $ *Average main: $20* ✉ *3407 Lakeshore Ave., near Mandana Blvd., Lakeshore, Oakland* ☎ *510/251–0329* ⊕ *www.shakewelloakland.com* ⌫ *Reservations not accepted* ⊙ *Closed Mon. No lunch Tues.–Thurs.*

$$$ ✕ **Wood Tavern.** Expect a warm welcome and a lively atmosphere at this
AMERICAN longtime Rockridge favorite, a neighborhood gem with superb food and
Fodor'sChoice refined service. Classic American fare includes standouts like the pork-
★ belly appetizer, anything marrow, perfect day boat scallops, and one of the best burgers around. For dessert the house-made Nutella–chocolate chip ice cream knocks it out of the park. It's wise to reserve well ahead here, but if you haven't you might score a seat at the bar. $ *Average main: $26* ✉ *6317 College Ave., near 63rd St., Rockridge, Oakland* ☎ *510/654–6607* ⊕ *woodtavern.net* ⊙ *No lunch Sun.*

19

WHERE TO STAY

$$ ⊡ **Best Western Plus Bayside Hotel.** Sandwiched between the serene and
HOTEL scenic Oakland Estuary on one side and train tracks and an eight-lane
freeway on the other, this all-suites property has handsome accommo-
dations with balconies or patios, many overlooking the water. **Pros:**
attractive, budget-conscious choice; free parking; recently renovated;
water views make city bustle seem far away. **Cons:** not near anything
of interest; city-side rooms can be loud. $ Rooms from: $179 ⊠ 1717
Embarcadero, off I–880, at 16th St. exit, Oakland ☎ 510/356–2450
⊕ www.baysidehoteloakland.com ⊷ 81 suites ⦾ Breakfast.

$$$$ ⊡ **Oakland Marriott City Center.** A good choice downtown for business
HOTEL travelers—and not bad for leisure ones, either—the Marriott, conve-
niently located near the Old Oakland and Uptown neighborhoods,
provides comprehensive services and amenities. **Pros:** convenient loca-
tion; ergonomically designed work areas; online discounts often avail-
able off-season and on weekends. **Cons:** low visual appeal; steep fee for
Internet access. $ Rooms from: $269 ⊠ 1001 Broadway, at 11th St.,
Downtown, Oakland ☎ 510/451–4000 ⊕ www.marriott.com ⊷ 481
rooms, 8 suites ⦾ No meals.

$$ ⊡ **Waterfront Hotel.** The only bayfront hotel in town, this thoroughly
HOTEL modern, pleasantly appointed Joie de Vivre property sits among the
appealing restaurants (including the hotel's own) of Jack London
Square. **Pros:** great location; lovely views; dog-friendly. **Cons:** passing
trains can be noisy on city side; parking is pricey; hotel is beginning to
show its age. $ Rooms from: $159 ⊠ 10 Washington St., Jack London
Square, Oakland ☎ 510/836–3800, 800/729–3638 ⊕ www.jdvhotels.
com ⊷ 143 rooms ⦾ No meals.

NIGHTLIFE AND PERFORMING ARTS

Artists have found relatively cheap rent and loft spaces in Oakland,
giving rise to a cultural scene—visual arts, indie music, spoken word,
film—that's definitely buzzing, especially in Uptown (which is pretty
much downtown). Trendy bars and clubs seem to pop up by the week—
everything from artisan breweries to all-out retro dives—and the beer-
garden renaissance has come to Oakland in a big way. Whether you're
an aficionado who likes to discuss the nose and mouthfeel of different
brews or just someone who wants to enjoy a drink outside on a sunny
day, you'll find something to suit you. Oakland's nightlife scene is less
crowded and more intimate than what you'll find in San Francisco.
Music is just about everywhere, though the most popular venues are
downtown.

NIGHTLIFE

Beer Revolution. Hard-core beer geeks: with hundreds of bottled beers and
50 taps, Beer Revolution is for you. Tear yourself away from the beer lists
and grab a table on the patio. ⊠ 464 3rd St., at Broadway, Jack London
Square, Oakland ☎ 510/452–2337 ⊕ www.beer-revolution.com.

Brotzeit Lokal. If you want a water view with your brew, head to this spot
east of Jack London Square and enjoy some wurst or Wiener schnitzel
with your German, Belgian, or California beer. ⊠ 1000 Embarcadero,

near 10th Ave., Jack London Square, Oakland ☎ *510/645–1905* ⊕ *brotzeitbiergarten.com* ⊗ *Closed Mon.*

Fodor's Choice **Café Van Kleef.** Dutch artist Peter Van Kleef's candle-strewn, funky café-

★ bar crackles with creative energy. Van Kleef has a lot to do with the convivial atmosphere; the garrulous owner loves sharing tales about his quirky, floor-to-ceiling collection of pop-culture mementos. The café has a consistently solid calendar of live music, heavy on the jazz side. The drinks are among the stiffest in town. ✉ *1621 Telegraph Ave., between 16th and 17th Sts., Uptown, Oakland* ☎ *510/763–7711* ⊕ *www.cafevankleef.com.*

Fox Theater. Willie Nelson, Counting Crows, Rebelution, and B.B. King have all played at this renovated Mediterranean Moorish–style stunner from 1928 that has good sight lines, a state-of-the-art sound system and acoustics, a bar, and other amenities. ✉ *1807 Telegraph Ave., at 18th St., Uptown, Oakland* ☎ *510/548–3010* ⊕ *www.thefoxoakland.com.*

The Layover Music Bar and Lounge. Bright, bold, and very hip, this hangout filled with recycled furniture is constantly evolving because everything is for sale, from the artwork to the pillows, rugs, and lamps. The busy bar serves up organic cocktails, and depending on the night, the entertainment might include comedy or live or DJ music. ✉ *1517 Franklin St., near 15th St., Uptown, Oakland* ☎ *510/834–1517* ⊕ *www. oaklandlayover.com.*

Lost & Found. The diversions on the welcoming patio here include ping-pong, Hula-Hoops, and cornhole. The beers are great, the solid menu focuses on internationally inspired small bites, and there's a good selection of nonalcoholic drinks. ✉ *2040 Telegraph Ave., at 21st St., Uptown, Oakland* ☎ *510/763–2040* ⊕ *www.lostandfound510.com* ⊗ *Closed Mon.*

Mua. Cuisine, cocktails, and culture—Mua puts it all together in a bright and airy former garage. The chefs serve up beautifully crafted meals like beef bone marrow and garlic prawns; the bartenders shake up elegant cocktails; and a lively crowd enjoys cultural offerings that include poetry readings, art shows, and DJ music. ✉ *2442a Webster St., between 23rd St. and Grand Ave., Uptown, Oakland* ☎ *510/238–1100* ⊕ *www.muaoakland.com.*

19

The Trappist. Grand pillars, brick walls, soft lighting, and the buzz of conversation set a warm and mellow tone inside this Victorian space that's been renovated to resemble a traditional Belgian pub. The setting is definitely a draw, but the real stars are the artisan beers: more than a hundred Belgian, Dutch, and North American ones. The light fare includes panini made with organic ingredients. ✉ *460 8th St., at Broadway, Old Oakland, Oakland* ☎ *510/238–8900* ⊕ *www.thetrappist.com.*

Telegraph. Hipsters hold court at Telegraph, where giant murals and bike wheel rims decorate the largely cement outdoor area, and great burgers pair with beers that change daily. ✉ *2318 Telegraph Ave., at 23rd St., Uptown, Oakland* ☎ *510/444–8353* ⊕ *telegraphoakland.com.*

Fodor's Choice **Yoshi's.** Omar Sosa and Charlie Hunter are among the musicians who

★ play at Yoshi's, one of the area's best jazz venues. Shows start at 8 pm and 10 pm except on Sunday, when they're usually at 7 and 9. The cover runs from $20 to $60. ⊠ *510 Embarcadero St., between Washington and Clay Sts., Jack London Square, Oakland* ☎ *510/238–9200* ⊕ *www.yoshis.com.*

PERFORMING ARTS

California Shakespeare Theater. The Bay Area's largest outdoor theater event showcases three works by the Bard and one by another playwright. Performances take place east of Oakland in Orinda. ⊠ *Bruns Amphitheater, 100 California Shakespeare Theater Way, Orinda* ⊹ *From Oakland, take I–580 or Hwy. 13 to Hwy. 24 W toward Walnut Creek. Exit at Wilder Rd., and turn left* ☎ *510/548–9666 box office* ⊕ *www.calshakes.org* ☉ *Late May–early Oct.*

SPORTS AND THE OUTDOORS

BASEBALL

Oakland A's. Billy Beane of *Moneyball* fame is the general manager of the American League baseball team. Same-day tickets can usually be purchased at the **O.co Coliseum** box office (Gate D). To get to the game, take a BART train to the Coliseum station. ⊠ *O.co Coliseum, 7000 Coliseum Way, off I–880, north of Hegenberger Rd., Oakland* ☎ *510/638–4900* ⊕ *oakland.athletics.mlb.com.*

BASKETBALL

Golden State Warriors. The NBA team plays basketball at **Oracle Arena** from late October into April. BART trains serve the arena; get off at the Coliseum station. Purchase single tickets through Ticketmaster (*800/653–8000, www.ticketmaster.com*). ⊠ *Oracle Arena, 7000 Coliseum Way, off I–880, north of Hegenberger Rd., Oakland* ☎ *888/479–4667 tickets* ⊕ *www.nba.com/warriors.*

FOOTBALL

Oakland Raiders. The National Football League's brawling Oakland Raiders play at **O.co Coliseum.** Tickets are available through Ticketmaster. ⊠ *O.co Coliseum, 7000 Coliseum Way, off I–880, north of Hegenberger Rd., Oakland* ☎ *510/864–5000* ⊕ *www.raiders.com.*

SHOPPING

Pop-up shops and stylish, locally focused stores are proliferating in Old Oakland and Uptown, and Temescal's alleys are decidedly funky. The streets around Lake Merritt and Grand Lake have smaller, less fancy boutiques. College Avenue is great for upscale strolling, shopping, and people-watching.

Diesel. Wandering bibliophiles collect armfuls of the latest fiction and nonfiction at this revered shop. The loftlike space, with its high ceilings and spare design, encourages contemplation, and on chilly days a fire burns in the hearth. Past participants in the excellent authors' events have included Ian Rankin, Annie Leibovitz, Kareem Abdul-Jabbar, and Michael Moore. ⊠ *5433 College Ave., at Kales Ave., Rockridge, Oakland* ☎ *510/653–9965* ⊕ *www.dieselbookstore.com.*

Maison d'Etre. Close to the Rockridge BART station, this store epitomizes the Rockridge neighborhood's funky-chic shopping scene. Look for impulse buys like whimsical watches, imported fruit-tea blends, and funky slippers. ⊠ *5640 College Ave., at Keith Ave., Rockridge, Oakland* ☎ *510/658–2801* ⊕ *maisondetre.com.*

Fodor's Choice **Oaklandish.** This is the place for Oaktown swag. What started out as
★ a collective art project of local pride has become a celebrated brand around the Bay, and proceeds from hip Oaklandish brand T-shirts and accessories still go to support the group's free events and programs. It's good-looking stuff for a good cause. ⊠ *1444 Broadway, near 15th St., Uptown, Oakland* ☎ *510/251–9500* ⊕ *oaklandish.com.*

MARIN COUNTY

Marin is quite simply a knockout—some go so far as to call it spectacular and wild. This isn't an extravagant claim, since more than 40% of the county (180,000 acres), including the majority of the coastline, is parkland. The territory ranges from chaparral, grassland, and coastal scrub to broadleaf and evergreen forest, redwood, salt marsh, and rocky shoreline. It's well worth the drive over the Golden Gate Bridge to explore the Headlands and the stunning beauty of sprawling Point Reyes National Seashore, with more than 80 miles of shoreline.

Regardless of its natural beauty, what gave the county its reputation was Cyra McFadden's 1977 book *The Serial,* a literary soap opera that depicted the county as a bastion of hot-tubbing and "open" marriages. Indeed old-time bohemian, but also increasingly jet-set, Marinites still spend a lot of time outdoors, and surfing, cycling, and hiking are common after-work and weekend activities. Adrenaline junkies mountain bike down Mt. Tamalpais, and those who want solitude take a walk on one of Point Reyes's many empty beaches. The hot tub remains a popular destination, but things have changed since the boho days. Artists and musicians who arrived in the 1960s have set the tone for mellow country towns, but Marin is now undeniably chic, with BMWs supplanting VW buses as the cars of choice.

19

After exploring Marin's natural beauty, consider a stop in one of its lovely villages. Most cosmopolitan is Sausalito, the town just over the Golden Gate Bridge from San Francisco. Across the inlet from Sausalito, Tiburon and Belvedere are lined with grand homes that regularly appear on fund-raising circuits, and to the north, landlocked Mill Valley is a hub of wining and dining and tony boutiques. Book Passage, a noted bookseller in the next town, Corte Madera, hosts regular readings by top-notch authors, and Larkspur, San Anselmo, and Fairfax beyond have walkable downtown areas, each a bit folksier than the next but all with good restaurants and shops and a distinct sense of place.

In general, the farther west of U.S. 101 you go the more countrified things become, and West Marin is about as far as you can get from the big city, both physically and ideologically. Separated from the inland county by the slopes and ridges of giant Mt. Tamalpais, this territory beckons to mavericks, artists, ocean lovers, and other free spirits. Stinson Beach has tempered its isolationist attitude to accommodate out-of-towners, as have Inverness and Point Reyes Station. Bolinas, on the other hand, would prefer you not know its location.

VISITOR INFORMATION

Contact **Marin Convention & Visitors Bureau** ⊠ *1 Mitchell Blvd., Suite B, San Rafael* ☎ *415/925–2060* ⊕ *www.visitmarin.org.*

THE MARIN HEADLANDS

Due west of the Golden Gate Bridge's northern end.

The term *Golden Gate* may now be synonymous with the world-famous bridge, but it originally referred to the grassy, poppy-strewn hills flanking the passageway into San Francisco Bay. To the north of the gate lie the Marin Headlands, part of the Golden Gate National Recreation Area (GGNRA) and among the most dramatic scenery in these parts. Windswept hills plunge down to the ocean, and creek-fed thickets shelter swaying wildflowers.

GETTING HERE AND AROUND

Driving from San Francisco, head north on U.S. 101. Just after you cross the Golden Gate Bridge, take the Alexander Avenue exit. From there take the first left (signs read "San Francisco/U.S. 101 South"), go through the tunnel under the freeway, and turn right up the hill where the sign reads "Forts Barry and Cronkhite." Muni bus 76X runs hourly from Sutter and Sansome streets to the Marin Headlands Visitor Center on weekends and major holidays only. Once here, you can explore this beautiful countryside on foot.

EXPLORING

TOP ATTRACTIONS

FAMILY

Fodor'sChoice

★

Marin Headlands. The headlands stretch from the Golden Gate Bridge to Muir Beach. Photographers perch on the southern headlands for spectacular shots of the city, with the bridge in the foreground and the skyline on the horizon. Equally remarkable are the views north along the coast and out to sea, where the Farallon Islands are visible on clear days.

The headlands' strategic position at the mouth of San Francisco Bay made them a logical site for World War II and cold-war military installations. Today you can explore the crumbling concrete batteries where naval guns protected the approaches from the sea. The headlands' main attractions are centered on Forts Barry and Cronkhite, which lie just across Rodeo Lagoon from each other. Fronting the lagoon is Rodeo Beach, a dark stretch of sand that attracts sand-castle builders and dog owners. The beaches at the Marin Headlands are not safe for swimming. ■TIP➔ The giant cliffs are steep and unstable, so hiking down them can be dangerous. Stay on trails.

The visitor center is a worthwhile stop for its exhibits on the area's history and ecology, and kids enjoy the "please touch" educational sites and small play area inside. You can pick up guides to historic sites and wildlife at the center, as well as the park's newspaper, which has a schedule of guided walks. ⊠ *Visitor Center, Fort Barry Chapel, Fort Barry, Bldg. 948, Field and Bunker Rds., Sausalito* ☎ *415/331–1540* ⊕ *www.nps.gov/goga/marin-headlands.htm* ☉ *Park sunrise–sunset visitor center daily 9:30–4:30.*

FAMILY **Marine Mammal Center.** If you're curious about the rehabilitation of sea mammals from the Pacific—and the human practices that endanger them—stop by this facility for rescued seals, sea lions, dolphins, and otters. An observation area overlooks the pools where the animals convalesce, and nearby plaques describe what you're seeing. ■TIP→ You'll learn even more—and get closer to the animals—on a worthwhile, docent-led tour. ✉ *Fort Cronkhite, 2000 Bunker Rd., off U.S. 101's Alexander Ave. exit, Sausalito* ☎ *415/289–7325* ⊕ *www. marinemammalcenter.org* ⊠ *Center free, tour $9* ◷ *Daily 10–5.*

Fodor'sChoice **Nike Missile Site SF-88-L.** The only accessible site of its kind in the United
★ States provides a firsthand view of menacing cold war–era Hercules missiles and missile-tracking radar, the country's "last line of defense" against Soviet nuclear bombers. It's worth timing your visit to take the guided tour, whose highlight is a visit to the missile-launching bunker. ■TIP→ On the first Saturday of the month the site holds an open house at which some of the docents leading walking tours are Nike veterans who describe their experiences. ✉ *Field Rd., off Bunker Hill Rd.* ☎ *415/331–1453* ⊕ *www.nps.gov/goga/nike-missile-site.htm* ⊠ *Free* ◷ *Thurs.–Sat. 12:30–3:30; guided tour at 12:45, 1:45, and 2:30* ◷ *Site sometimes closes during inclement weather.*

FAMILY **Point Bonita Lighthouse.** A restored beauty that still guides ships to safety with its original 1855 refractory lens, the lighthouse anchors the southern headlands. Half the fun of a visit is the steep ½-mile walk from the parking area through a rock tunnel, across a suspension bridge, and down to the lighthouse. Signposts along the way detail the bravado of surfmen, as the early lifeguards were called, and the tenacity of the "wickies," the first keepers of the light. ✉ *End of Conzelman Rd.* ⊕ *www.nps.gov/goga/pobo.htm* ⊠ *Free* ◷ *Sat.–Mon. 12:30–3:30.*

WORTH NOTING

Hawk Hill. Craggy Hawk Hill is the best place on the West Coast to watch the migration of eagles, hawks, and falcons as they fly south for winter: as many as 1,000 birds have been sighted in a single day. The main migration period is from September through November, and the viewing area is about 2 miles up Conzelman Road from U.S. 101; look for a Hawk Hill sign and parking right before the road becomes one way. In September and October, on rain- and fog-free weekends at noon, enthusiastic docents from the Golden Gate Raptor Observatory give free lectures on Hawk Hill, and a raptor-banding demonstration follows at 1 pm. ✉ *Conzelman Rd., Sausalito* ⊕ *www.ggro.org.*

Headlands Center for the Arts. The center's main building, formerly the army barracks, exhibits contemporary art in a rustic natural setting; the downstairs "archive room" contains objects found and created by residents, such as natural rocks, interesting glass bottles filled with collected items, and unusual masks. Stop by the industrial gallery space, two flights up, to see what the resident visual artists are up to—most of the work is quite contemporary. ✉ *Fort Barry, 944 Simmonds Rd., Sausalito* ☎ *415/331–2787* ⊕ *www.headlands.org* ◷ *Sun.–Thurs. noon–5.*

19

Kayakers enjoy a sunny day on the Sausalito waterfront.

SAUSALITO

2 miles north of Golden Gate Bridge.

Bougainvillea-covered hillsides and an expansive yacht harbor give Sausalito the feel of an Adriatic resort. The town sits on the northwestern edge of San Francisco Bay, where it's sheltered from the ocean by the Marin Headlands; the mostly mild weather here is perfect for strolling and outdoor dining. Nevertheless, morning fog and afternoon winds can roll over the hills without warning, funneling through the central part of Sausalito once known as Hurricane Gulch.

South on Bridgeway (toward San Francisco), which snakes between the bay and the hills, a waterside esplanade is lined with restaurants on piers that lure diners with good seafood and even better views. Stairs along the west side of Bridgeway climb the hill to wooded neighborhoods filled with both rustic and opulent homes. As you amble along Bridgeway past shops and galleries, you'll notice the absence of basic services. If you need an aspirin or some groceries (or if you want to see the locals), you'll have to head to Caledonia Street, which runs parallel to Bridgeway, north of the ferry terminus and inland a couple of blocks. The streets closest to the ferry landing flaunt their fair share of shops selling T-shirts and kitschy souvenirs. Venture into some of the side streets or narrow alleyways to catch a bit more of the town's taste for eccentric jewelry and handmade crafts.

■TIP➡ The ferry is the best way to get to Sausalito from San Francisco; you get more romance (and less traffic) and disembark in the heart of downtown.

Sausalito developed its bohemian flair in the 1950s and '60s, when creative types, led by a charismatic Greek portraitist named Varda, established an artists' colony and a houseboat community here (this is Otis Redding's "Dock of the Bay"). Today more than 450 houseboats are docked in Sausalito, which has since also become a major yachting center. Some of these floating homes are ragged, others deluxe, but all are quirky (one, a miniature replica of a Persian castle, even has an elevator inside). For a close-up view of the community, head north on Bridgeway—Sausalito's main thoroughfare—from downtown, turn right on Gate Six Road, park where it dead-ends at the public shore, and enter through the unlocked gates. Keep a respectful distance; these are homes, after all, and the residents become a bit prickly from too much ogling.

GETTING HERE AND AROUND

From San Francisco by car or bike, follow U.S. 101 north across the Golden Gate Bridge and take the first exit, Alexander Avenue, just past Vista Point; continue down the winding hill to the water to where the road becomes Bridgeway. Golden Gate Transit buses 10 and 2 will drop you off in downtown Sausalito, and the ferries dock downtown as well. The center of town is flat, with plenty of sidewalks and bay views. It's a pleasure and a must to explore on foot.

ESSENTIALS

Visitor Information Sausalito Chamber of Commerce ⊠ *780 Bridgeway, Sausalito* ☎ *415/332–0505* ⊕ *www.sausalito.org.*

EXPLORING

FAMILY **Bay Area Discovery Museum.** Sitting at the base of the Golden Gate Bridge, this indoor-outdoor museum offers entertaining and enlightening hands-on exhibits for children under eight. Kids can fish from a boat at the indoor wharf, imagine themselves as marine biologists in the Wave Workshop, and play outdoors at Lookout Cove (made up of scaled-down sea caves, tidal pools, and even a re-created shipwreck). At Tot Spot, toddlers and preschoolers dress up in animal costumes and crawl through miniature tunnels. ■ TIP→ From San Francisco, take U.S. 101's Alexander Avenue exit and follow signs to East Fort Baker. ⊠ *557 McReynolds Rd., at East Rd. off Alexander Ave., Sausalito* ☎ *415/339–3900* ⊕ *www.baykidsmuseum.org* ☞ *$12, free 1st Wed. of month* ⊙ *Tues.–Sun. 9–5.*

FAMILY **Bay Model.** An anonymous-looking World War II shipyard building holds a great treasure: a sprawling (more than 1½ acres), walkable model of the entire San Francisco Bay and the San Joaquin–Sacramento River delta, complete with flowing water. The U.S. Army Corps of Engineers uses the model to reproduce the rise and fall of tides, the flow of currents, and the other physical forces at work on the bay. ⊠ *2100 Bridgeway, at Marinship Way, Sausalito* ☎ *415/332–3870 recorded information, 415/332–3871 operator assistance* ⊕ *www.spn.usace. army.mil* ☞ *Free* ⊙ *Late May–early Sept., Tues.–Fri. 9–4, weekends 10–5; early Sept.–late May, Tues.–Sat. 9–4.*

Drinking Fountain. On the waterfront between the Hotel Sausalito and the Sausalito Yacht Club is an unusual historic landmark—a drinking

19

0   5 mi

0   5 km

fountain. It's inscribed with "Have a drink on Sally" in remembrance of Sally Stanford, the former San Francisco madam who became the town's mayor in the 1970s. Sassy Sally, as they called her, would have appreciated the fountain's eccentric custom attachment: a knee-level basin that reads "Have a drink on Leland," in memory of her beloved dog. ⊠ *Sausalito.*

Hamburgers. Patrons queue up daily for a sandwich made from the hand-formed beef patties sizzling on the wheel-shaped grill here. Brave the line (it moves fast), get your food to go, and head to the esplanade to enjoy the sweeping views. ⊠ *737 Bridgeway, at Humboldt Ave., Sausalito* ☎ *415/332-9471* ⊘ *No dinner.*

Plaza Viña del Mar. The landmark Plaza Viña del Mar, named for Sausalito's sister city in Chile, marks the center of town. Flanked by two 14-foot-tall elephant statues (created in 1915 for the Panama-Pacific International Exposition), its fountain is a great setting for snapshots and people-watching. ⊠ *Bridgeway and Park St., Sausalito.*

Sausalito Visitors Center and Historical Exhibit. The local historical society operates the center, where you can get your bearings, learn some history, and find out what's happening in town. ⊠ *780 Bridgeway, at Bay*

St., Sausalito ☎ *415/332–0505* 🌐 *www.sausalitohistoricalsociety.com* 🕓 *Tues.–Sun. 11:30–4.*

WHERE TO EAT

$ INTERNATIONAL

🍴 **Avatar's.** "Purveyors of ethnic confusions," this Marin minichain offers Indian fusion combinations such as Punjabi burritos and pumpkin enchiladas that locals revere. The outgoing chef makes a big impression; tell him your preferences, sensitivities, and whims, and he'll create something spectacular and promise you'll want to lick the plate. The creativity of the food and the low prices more than make up for the uninspired space. [$] *Average main: $13* ✉ *2656 Bridgeway, at Coloma St., Sausalito* ☎ *415/332–8083* 🌐 *www.enjoyavatars.com* 🕓 *Closed Sun.*

$$ SEAFOOD FAMILY Fodor's Choice ★

🍴 **Fish.** When locals want fresh seafood, they head to this gleaming dockside fish house a mile north of downtown. Order at the counter—cash only—and then grab a seat by the floor-to-ceiling windows or at a picnic table on the pier, overlooking the yachts and fishing boats. Most of the sustainably caught fish is hauled in from the owner's boats, docked right outside. Try the ceviche, crab Louis, cioppino, barbecue oysters, or anything fresh that's being grilled over the oak-wood fire. Outside, kids can doodle with sidewalk chalk on the pier. [$] *Average main: $20* ✉ *350 Harbor Dr., off Bridgeway, Sausalito* ☎ *415/331–3474* 🌐 *www.331fish.com* ✍ *Reservations not accepted* 💳 *No credit cards.*

$$$ FRENCH

🍴 **Le Garage.** Brittany-born Olivier Souvestre serves traditional French bistro fare in a relaxed, sidewalk café–style bayside setting. The menu is small, but the dishes are substantial in flavor and presentation. Standouts include frisée salad with poached egg, bacon, croutons, and pancetta vinaigrette; steak frites with a shallot confit and crispy fries; and a chef's selection of cheese or charcuterie with soup and mixed greens. The restaurant only seats 35 inside and 15 outside, so to avoid a long wait for lunch, arrive before 11:30 or after 1:30. [$] *Average main: $23* ✉ *85 Liberty Ship Way, off Marinship Way, Sausalito* ☎ *415/332–5625* 🌐 *www.legaragebistrosausalito.com* ✍ *Reservations essential* 🕓 *No dinner Sun.*

$ SCANDINAVIAN

🍴 **Lighthouse Cafe.** A cozy spot with a long coffee bar and dose of Scandinavian flair, this local establishment has been a favorite breakfast (served all day) and brunch destination for decades. The hearty Norwegian salmon omelet with spinach and cream cheese always hits the spot, as do the fruit pancakes and, for lunch, grilled burgers, sandwiches, and Danish specials such as meatballs with potato salad. Expect a wait. [$] *Average main: $12* ✉ *1311 Bridgeway, near Turney St., Sausalito* ☎ *415/331–3034* 🌐 *www.lighthouse-restaurants.com* ✍ *Reservations not accepted* 🕓 *No dinner.*

$$$ ITALIAN

🍴 **Poggio.** One of Sausalito's few restaurants to attract food-savvy locals and tourists, Poggio serves modern Tuscan-style cuisine in a handsome, open-wall space that spills onto the street. Expect dishes such as grilled chicken with roasted beets and sunchokes, braised artichokes with polenta, featherlight gnocchi, and pizzas from the open kitchen's wood-fired oven. Daily breakfast includes fresh-made pastries, house-made granola, and panini such as ham and eggs or prosciutto and provolone. [$] *Average main: $23* ✉ *777 Bridgeway, at Bay St.,*

Sausalito ☎ 415/332–7771 🌐 www.poggiotrattoria.com ✍ Reservations essential.

$$$ JAPANESE Fodor's Choice ★ 🍴 **Sushi Ran.** Sushi aficionados swear that this stylish restaurant—in business for three decades—is the Bay Area's best option for raw fish, but don't overlook the excellent Pacific Rim fusions, a melding of Japanese ingredients and French cooking techniques, served up in unusual presentations. Because Sushi Ran is so highly ranked among area foodies, book from two to seven days in advance for dinner. Otherwise, expect a long wait, which you can soften by sipping one of the 45 by-the-glass sakes from the outstanding wine-and-sake bar. ■ **TIP→ If you arrive without a reservation and can't get a table, you can sometimes dine in the noisy bar.** [$] *Average main: $25* ✉ *107 Caledonia St., at Pine St., Sausalito* ☎ *415/332–3620* 🌐 *www.sushiran.com* ✍ *Reservations essential* ⊗ *No lunch weekends.*

WHERE TO STAY

$$$$ HOTEL 🏨 **Casa Madrona.** What began as a small inn in a 19th-century landmark mansion has expanded over the decades to include a contemporary section and hillside cottages, along with a full-service spa, all tiered down a hill in the center of Sausalito. **Pros:** elegant furniture; spacious rooms; central location. **Cons:** stairs required to access some cottages; breakfast is not included. [$] *Rooms from: $300* ✉ *801 Bridgeway, Sausalito* ☎ *415/332–0502, 800/567–9524* 🌐 *www.casamadrona.com* 🛏 *56 rooms, 1 suite, 7 cottages* 🍽 *No meals.*

$$$$ HOTEL 🏨 **Cavallo Point.** Set in the Golden Gate National Recreation Area, this luxury hotel and resort with a one-of-a-kind location on a former army post contains well-appointed eco-friendly rooms. **Pros:** stunning views; activities include a cooking classes, yoga classes, and nature walks; spa with a tea bar; art gallery; accommodating staff. **Cons:** isolated from urban amenities. [$] *Rooms from: $429* ✉ *601 Murray Circle, Fort Baker, Sausalito* ☎ *415/339–4700* 🌐 *www.cavallopoint.com* 🛏 *68 historic and 74 contemporary guest rooms* 🍽 *No meals.*

$$ B&B/INN 🏨 **Hotel Sausalito.** Handmade furniture and tasteful original art and reproductions give this well-run inn the feel of a small European hotel. **Pros:** great staff; central location; solid midrange hotel. **Cons:** no room service; some rooms feel cramped. [$] *Rooms from: $180* ✉ *16 El Portal, Sausalito* ☎ *415/332–0700, 888/442–0700* 🌐 *www.hotelsausalito.com* 🛏 *14 rooms, 2 suites* 🍽 *No meals.*

$$$$ B&B/INN 🏨 **The Inn Above Tide.** This is the only hotel in the Bay Area with balconies literally hanging over the water, and each of its rooms has a perfect-10 view that takes in wild Angel Island as well as the city lights across the bay. **Pros:** great complimentary breakfast; minutes from restaurants and attractions; central but tranquil setting. **Cons:** costly parking; some rooms are on the small side. [$] *Rooms from: $370* ✉ *30 El Portal, Sausalito* ☎ *415/332–9535, 800/893–8433* 🌐 *www.innabovetide.com* 🛏 *26 rooms, 5 suites* 🍽 *Breakfast.*

PERFORMING ARTS

Sausalito Art Festival. This annual juried fine-arts show, held over Labor Day weekend, attracts more than 30,000 people to the Sausalito waterfront; Blue & Gold Fleet ferries from San Francisco dock at the pier adjacent to the festival. ⊠ *Sausalito* ☎ *415/332–3555* ⊕ *www. sausalitoartfestival.org* ⌕ *$25.*

SPORTS AND THE OUTDOORS

KAYAKING

Sea Trek Ocean Kayaking and SUP Center. The center (SUP stands for stand-up paddleboarding) offers guided half-day sea-kayaking trips underneath the Golden Gate Bridge and full- and half-day trips to Angel Island, both for beginners. Trips for experienced kayakers, classes, and rentals are also available. ■ TIP➔ Starlight and full-moon paddles are particularly popular. ⊠ *Bay Model parking lot, off Bridgeway and Marinship Way, Sausalito* ☎ *415/332–8494* ⊕ *www.seatrek.com* ⌕ *From $20 per hr for rentals, $65 for 3-hr guided trip.*

SAILING

SF Bay Adventures. This outfit's expert skippers conduct sunset and full-moon sails around the bay, as well as fascinating eco- and whale-watching tours with the possibility of viewing great white sharks. If you're interested, the company can arrange for you to barbecue on Angel Island or even spend the night in a lighthouse. ⊠ *60 Liberty Ship Way, Suite 4, Sausalito* ☎ *415/331–0444* ⊕ *www.sfbayadventures.com.*

TIBURON

2 miles north of Sausalito, 7 miles north of Golden Gate Bridge.

On a peninsula that was called Punta de Tiburon (Shark Point) by the Spanish explorers, this beautiful Marin County community retains the feel of a village—it's more low-key than Sausalito—despite the encroachment of commercial establishments from the downtown area. The harbor faces Angel Island across Raccoon Strait, and San Francisco is directly south across the bay—which makes the views from the decks of harbor restaurants a major attraction. Since its incarnation, in 1884, when ferries from San Francisco connected the point with a railroad to San Rafael, the town has centered on the waterfront. ■ TIP➔ The ferry is the most relaxing (and fastest) way to get here, particularly in summer, allowing you to skip traffic and parking problems. If visiting midweek, keep in mind that many shops close either Tuesday or Wednesday, or both.

GETTING HERE AND AROUND

Blue & Gold Fleet ferries travel between San Francisco and Tiburon daily. By car, head north from San Francisco on U.S. 101 and get off at CA 131/Tiburon Boulevard/East Blithedale Avenue (Exit 447). Turn right onto Tiburon Boulevard and drive just over 4 miles to downtown. Golden Gate Transit serves downtown Tiburon from San Francisco; except during evening rush hour you'll need to transfer in Mill Valley, making the bus an inconvenient option. Tiburon's Main Street is made for wandering, as are the footpaths that frame the water's edge.

ESSENTIALS

Visitor Information Tiburon ⊠ *Town Hall, 1505 Tiburon Blvd., Tiburon* ☎ *415/435–7373* ⊕ *www.townoftiburon.org.*

EXPLORING

Ark Row. Past the pink-brick bank building, Main Street is known as Ark Row and has a tree-shaded walk lined with antiques and specialty stores. Some of the buildings are actually old houseboats that floated in Belvedere Cove before being beached and transformed into stores. **■ TIP→ If you're curious about architectural history, the Tiburon Heritage & Arts Commission has a self-guided walking-tour map, available online and at local businesses.** ✉ *Ark Row, parallel to Main St., Tiburon* 🌐 *tiburonheritageandarts.org.*

Old St. Hilary's Landmark and Wildflower Preserve. The architectural centerpiece of this attraction is a stark-white 1886 Carpenter Gothic church that overlooks the town and the bay from its hillside perch. Surrounding the church, which was barged over from Strawberry Point in 1957, is a wildflower preserve that's spectacular in May and June, when the rare black or Tiburon jewelflower blooms. Expect a steep walk uphill to reach the preserve. **■ TIP→ The hiking trails behind the landmark wind up to a peak that has views of the entire Bay Area (great photo op).** ✉ *201 Esperanza St., off Mar West St. or Beach Rd., Tiburon* ☎ *415/435–1853* 🌐 *landmarkssociety.com* 🎟 *Preserve free, $3 church tour* 🕒 *Preserve daily dawn–dusk; church Apr.–Oct., Sun. 1–4.*

WHERE TO EAT

$$$$ AMERICAN

🍴 **The Caprice.** For more than 50 years this Tiburon landmark that overlooks the bay has been the place to come to mark special occasions. The views are spectacular, and soft-yellow walls and starched white tablecloths help to make the space bright and light. Elegant comfort food is the specialty, with choices like seared day-boat scallops or pan-roasted filet mignon. Polishing off the warm chocolate cake with almond ice cream while gazing out at the sunset and porpoises bobbing in the waves below is a near perfect end to the evening. [$] *Average main: $31* ✉ *2000 Paradise Dr., Tiburon* ☎ *415/435–3400* 🌐 *www.thecaprice.com* 🕒 *No lunch.*

$$ SICILIAN

🍴 **Luna Blu.** This lively sliver of an Italian restaurant focusing on seafood has made a splash on the Tiburon dining scene, with locals raving about the food, the service, and the views. It's hard to beat a seat on the heated patio overlooking the bay, but the high-sided booths inside are appealing as well. Chef Renzo Azzarello's Sicilian childhood and training show in dishes such as spaghetti with sea urchin, sausage- and bell pepper-stuffed ravioli with porcini sauce, and braised veal shank; the towering burger served at lunch is a winner. Service is friendly, efficient, and informed. [$] *Average main: $21* ✉ *35 Main St., Tiburon* ☎ *415/789–5844* 🕒 *Closed Tues.*

$ AMERICAN FAMILY

🍴 **New Morning Cafe.** Omelets and scrambles are served all day long at this homey café. If you're past morning treats, choose from the many soups, salads, and sandwiches. The café is open from 6:30 until 2:30 on weekdays, until 4 on weekends. [$] *Average main: $13* ✉ *1696 Tiburon Blvd., near Main St., Tiburon* ☎ *415/435–4315* 🕒 *No dinner.*

$$$ AMERICAN

🍴 **Sam's Anchor Cafe.** Open since 1921, this casual dockside restaurant with mahogany wainscoting is the town's most famous eatery. Most people flock to the deck here for beer, bay views, and seafood. The lunch menu has the usual suspects—burgers, sandwiches, salads, fried fish with tartar sauce—and you'll sit on plastic chairs at tables covered with blue-and-white-checked oilcloths. At night you can find standard seafood dishes with vegetarian and meat options. Mind the seagulls; they know no restraint. **TIP→ Expect a wait for outside tables on sunny summer days or weekends; reservations aren't taken for deck seating or weekend lunch.** [$] *Average main: $23* ✉ *27 Main St., Tiburon* ☎ *415/435–4527* 🌐 *www.samscafe.com.*

WHERE TO STAY

$$$$ HOTEL **The Lodge at Tiburon.** A block from Main Street and framed by stone pillars and sloped rooftops, the Lodge at Tiburon has the feel of a winter ski chalet, though the outdoor pool and its cabanas provide a summery counterpoint. **Pros:** free parking; spacious work desks in each room; room service from the Tiburon Tavern. **Cons:** breakfast not included; some rooms have a few too many mirrors; no bay views. [$] *Rooms from: $299* ✉ *1651 Tiburon Blvd., at Beach St., Tiburon* ☎ *415/435–3133* 🌐 *lodgeattiburon.com* 🛏 *101 rooms, 2 suites* 🍴 *No meals.*

$$$$ B&B/INN **Waters Edge Hotel.** Checking into this elegant hotel feels like tucking away into an inviting retreat by the water—the views are stunning and the lighting is perfect. **Pros:** complimentary wine and cheese for guests every evening; restaurants/sights are minutes away; free bike rentals for guests. **Cons:** downstairs rooms lack privacy and views; except for breakfast delivery, no room service; fitness center is off-site; not a great place to bring small children. [$] *Rooms from: $279* ✉ *25 Main St., off Tiburon Blvd., Tiburon* ☎ *415/789–5999, 877/789–5999* 🌐 *www.marinhotels.com* 🛏 *23 rooms* 🍴 *Breakfast.*

MILL VALLEY

2 miles north of Sausalito, 4 miles north of Golden Gate Bridge.

Chic and woodsy Mill Valley has a dual personality. Here, as elsewhere in the county, the foundation is a superb natural setting. Virtually surrounded by parkland, the town lies at the base of Mt. Tamalpais and contains dense redwood groves traversed by countless creeks. But this is no lumber camp. Smart restaurants and chichi boutiques line the streets, and more rock stars than one might suspect live here.

The rustic village flavor isn't a modern conceit but a holdover from the town's early days as a logging camp. In 1896 the Mill Valley and Mt. Tamalpais Scenic Railroad—called "the crookedest railroad in the world" because of its curvy tracks—began transporting visitors from Mill Valley to the top of Mt. Tam and down to Muir Woods, and the town soon became a vacation retreat for city slickers. The trains stopped running in the 1940s, but the old railway depot still serves as the center of town: the 1924 building has been transformed into the popular Depot Bookstore & Cafe, at 87 Throckmorton Avenue.

The small downtown area has the constant bustle of a leisure community; even at noon on a Tuesday, people are out shopping for fancy cookware and lacy pajamas.

GETTING HERE AND AROUND

By car from San Francisco, head north on U.S. 101 and get off at CA 131/Tiburon Boulevard/East Blithedale Avenue (Exit 447). Turn left onto East Blithedale and continue west to Throckmorton Avenue; turn left to reach Lytton Square, then park. Golden Gate Transit buses serve Mill Valley from San Francisco. Once here, explore the town on foot; it's great for strolling.

ESSENTIALS

Visitor Information Mill Valley Chamber of Commerce ✉ *85 Throckmorton Ave., Mill Valley* ☎ *415/388–9700* 🌐 *www.enjoymillvalley.com.*

EXPLORING

FAMILY **Lytton Square.** Mill Valley locals congregate on weekends to socialize in the many coffeehouses near the town's central square (which is unmarked), but it bustles most any time of day. Shops, restaurants, and cultural venues line the nearby streets. ✉ *Miller and Throckmorton Aves., Mill Valley.*

OFF THE BEATEN PATH **Marin County Civic Center.** A wonder of arches, circles, and skylights about 8 miles north of Mill Valley, the civic center was Frank Lloyd Wright's last major architectural undertaking. Docent-led tours ($5) leave from the gift shop, on the second floor, on Wednesday morning at 10:30. The center's website has self-guided tour map that's also available at the gift shop. ■ **TIP→ Photographs on the first floor depict Marin County homes Wright designed.** ✉ *3501 Civic Center Dr., off N. San Pedro Rd., San Rafael* ☎ *415/473–3762 for docent tour* 🌐 *www.marincounty.org/depts/cu/visitor-services* 🎫 *Free* 🕒 *Weekdays 8–5.*

WHERE TO EAT

$$$ AMERICAN 🍴 **Buckeye Roadhouse.** This is Mill Valley's secret den of decadence, where house-smoked meats and fish, grilled steaks, and old-fashioned dishes such as brisket bring the locals coming back for more. The restaurant also serves beautiful organic salads and desserts so heavenly—like the s'more pie—you'll just about melt into the floor. The look of the 1937 roadhouse is decidedly hunting-lodge chic, with a river-rock fireplace, topped by a trophy fish, dominating one wall. The busy but cozy bar with elegant mahogany paneling and soft lighting is a good place to quench your thirst for a Marin martini or Napa Valley Merlot. [$] *Average main: $24* ✉ *15 Shoreline Hwy., off U.S. 101, Mill Valley* ☎ *415/331–2600* 🌐 *buckeyeroadhouse.com* ✍ *Reservations essential.*

$ MEXICAN FAMILY 🍴 **Joe's Taco Lounge.** A funky, bright lounge (and it really does feel like someone's lounge), this is a fun place to go for a casual, cheap, and delicious Mexican meal. There are all sorts of colorful relics on the walls, and chili-pepper lights adorn the windows. The signature dishes are fish tacos and snapper burritos—which are generous in both size and flavor. The organic burger with spicy "firecracker" fries and the fire-grilled corn on the cob are also yummy. Choose from a wide selection of Mexican beers, or go for a refreshing agave wine margarita. Between 5 and 7 pm, Joe's is popular with families. [$] *Average main: $11* ✉ *382 Miller Ave., and Montford Ave., Mill Valley* ☎ *415/383–8164* 🌐 *www.joestacolounge.com.*

$$$ MODERN AMERICAN 🍴 **Molina.** A suave yet homey design, a convivial vibe buoyed by an all-vinyl soundtrack, and vibrant, impeccable cuisine have turned this snug neighborhood spot into something approaching a destination restaurant. Owner-chef (and DJ) Todd Shoberg aims to please and usually succeeds, most especially with the food, a dozen small plates and five or so entrées that showcase local meat and produce. Smaller dishes have included heirloom broccoli with kumquats and farro, and game hen and king salmon from Bodega Bay have appeared as mains. Molina is on the small side and can get noisy when packed. Sunday brunch is also served. [$] *Average main: $26* ✉ *17 Madrona St., near Throckmorton Ave., Mill Valley* ☎ *415/383–4200* 🌐 *molinarestaurant.com* 🕒 *No lunch.*

$ BURGER FAMILY 🍴 **Pearl's Phat Burgers.** Families, couples, and teenagers flock to Pearl's for juicy, grass-fed organic burgers stacked high with tomatoes, lettuce, bacon, and cheese; sweet-potato fries that are not too crispy and not too soft; and thick, creamy milk shakes. The food here is among the freshest, biggest, and fastest in town. No wonder there's always a line out the door. [$] *Average main: $14* ✉ *8 E. Blithedale Ave., at Sunnyside Ave., Mill Valley* ☎ *415/381–6010.*

$ PIZZA FAMILY 🍴 **Tony Tutto Pizza.** Possibly the best pies in Marin—all vegetarian and mostly organic—are to be had in this simple, pleasant eatery where the focus is all on the food. The owner spent decades in the music business, which you'll see reflected in the menu. Try the Peter, Paul & Pesto, A Love Supreme (margherita), or Whiter Shade of Pale (three cheeses). Choose from the extensive beer list and good wine selection and grab an outdoor table under the heat lamps. Service is warm and welcoming. [$] *Average main: $13* ✉ *246 E. Blithedale Ave., near Sycamore Ave., Mill Valley* ☎ *415/383–8646* 🌐 *www.tonytuttopizza.com* 💳 *No credit cards* 🕒 *Closed Mon. and Tues.*

WHERE TO STAY

$$$$ B&B/INN 🏨 **Mill Valley Inn.** The only hotel in downtown Mill Valley has smart-looking rooms done up in Tuscan colors of ocher and olive, with handcrafted beds, armoires, and lamps by local artisans. **Pros:** minutes from local shops and restaurants; great complimentary continental breakfast; free parking; free mountain bikes. **Cons:** some rooms are noisy; dark in winter because of surrounding trees; some rooms are not accessible via elevator. [$] *Rooms from: $279* ✉ *165 Throckmorton Ave., near Miller Ave., Mill Valley* ☎ *415/389–6608, 800/595–2100* 🌐 *www.marinhotels.com* 🛏 *22 rooms, 1 suite, 2 cottages* 🍽 *Breakfast.*

$$$$ B&B/INN Fodor's Choice ★ 🏨 **Mountain Home Inn.** Abutting 40,000 acres of state and national parks, the inn sits on the skirt of Mt. Tamalpais, where you can follow hiking trails all the way to Stinson Beach. **Pros:** amazing deck and views; peaceful, remote setting. **Cons:** nearest town is a 20-minute drive away; restaurant can get crowded on sunny weekend days; some complain the hotel and service don't live up to the views and price point. [$] *Rooms from: $279* ✉ *810 Panoramic Hwy., at Edgewood Ave., Mill Valley* ☎ *415/381–9000* 🌐 *www.mtnhomeinn.com* 🛏 *10 rooms* 🍽 *Breakfast.*

NIGHTLIFE AND PERFORMING ARTS

NIGHTLIFE

Mill Valley Beerworks. A great place to rest your feet after shopping or hiking, Beerworks serves more than 100 local, national, and international beers, from ale to port to lager. For food, you'll find offerings such as a cheese plate, olives, grilled squid, and pappardelle. ✉ *173 Throckmorton Ave., at Madrona St., Mill Valley* ☎ *415/888–8218* ⊕ *millvalleybeerworks.com.*

PERFORMING ARTS

Sweetwater Music Hall. With the help of part-owner Bob Weir of the Grateful Dead, this renowned club reopened in an old Masonic Hall in 2012. Famous as well as up-and-coming bands play on most nights, and local stars such as Bonnie Raitt and Huey Lewis have been known to stop in for a pickup session. ✉ *19 Corte Madera Ave., between Throckmorton and Lovell Aves., Mill Valley* ☎ *415/388–3850* ⊕ *www.sweetwatermusichall.com.*

MUIR WOODS NATIONAL MONUMENT

12 miles northwest of the Golden Gate Bridge.

Climbing hundreds of feet into the sky, *Sequoia sempervirens* are the tallest living things on Earth. One of the last remaining old-growth stands of these redwood behemoths, Muir Woods is nature's cathedral: imposing, awe-inspiring, reverence-inducing, and not to be missed.

GETTING HERE AND AROUND

Driving to Muir Woods, especially in summer and early fall, causes epic traffic jams around the tiny parking areas and miles-long walks to reach the entrance. Do yourself (and everyone else) a favor and take a shuttle instead, if you can. On weekends and holidays, Memorial Day through Labor Day, Marin Transit's Route 66 shuttle (✉ *$5 round-trip* ⊕ *www.marintransit.org*) is timed to meet boats at Sausalito's ferry landing four times daily en route to Muir Woods. The shuttle also runs every half hour from the Manzanita Park-and-Ride three miles north of the ferry. To get there, take the Highway 1 exit off U.S. 101 (look for the lot under the elevated freeway), or take connecting bus service from San Francisco with Golden Gate Transit. To drive directly from San Francisco by car, take U.S. 101 north across the Golden Gate Bridge to the Mill Valley/Stinson Beach exit, then follow signs to Highway 1 north. Once here, you can wander by foot through this pristine patch of nature.

EXPLORING

FAMILY

Fodor'sChoice

★

Muir Woods National Monument. Walking among some of the last old-growth redwoods on the planet, trees hundreds of feet tall and a millennium or more old, is magical, an experience like few others to clearly illustrate our tiny place in a bigger world. Ancestors of redwood and sequoia trees grew throughout what is now the United States 150,000,000 years ago. Today the *Sequoia sempervirens* can be found only in a narrow, cool coastal belt from Monterey to Oregon. The 550 acres of Muir Woods National Monument contain some of the most majestic redwoods in the world—some more than 250 feet tall. (To see the real giants, though, you'll have to head north to Humboldt County,

where the tallest redwood, in Redwood National Park, has been measured at 380 feet.) The Marin stand was saved from destruction in 1905, when it was purchased by a couple who donated it to the federal government. Three years later it was named after naturalist John Muir, whose environmental campaigns helped to establish the national park system. His response: "Saving these woods from the ax and saw is in many ways the most notable service to God and man I have heard of since my forest wandering began."

Muir Woods, part of the Golden Gate National Recreation Area, is a pedestrian's park. Old paved trails have been replaced by wooden walkways, and the trails vary in difficulty and length. Beginning from the park headquarters, an easy 2-mile, wheelchair-accessible **loop trail** crosses streams and passes ferns and azaleas, as well as magnificent redwood groves. Among the most famous are **Bohemian Grove** and the circular formation called **Cathedral Grove.** On summer weekends visitors oohing and aahing in a dozen languages line the trail. If you prefer a little serenity, consider the challenging **Dipsea Trail,** which climbs west from the forest floor to soothing views of the ocean and the Golden Gate Bridge. For a complete list of trails, check with rangers, who can also help you pick the best one for your ability level.

■ TIP→ The weather in Muir Woods is usually cool and often wet—after all, these giants survive on fog drip—so wear warm clothes and shoes appropriate for damp trails. Picnicking and camping aren't allowed, and pets aren't permitted. Crowds can be large, especially from May through October, so try to come early in the morning or late in the afternoon. The **Muir Woods Visitor Center** has books and exhibits about redwood trees and the woods' history; the café here serves locally sourced, organic food, and the gift shop has plenty of souvenirs. ✉ *1 Muir Woods Trail, off Panoramic Hwy., Mill Valley* ☎ *415/388–2595 park information, 415/526–3239 shuttle information* ⊕ *www.nps.gov/ muwo* ✉ *$7* ☉ *Daily 8 am–sunset.*

MT. TAMALPAIS STATE PARK

16 miles northwest of Golden Gate Bridge.

The view of Mt. Tamalpais from all around the bay can be a beauty, but that's nothing compared to the views *from* the mountain, which range from jaw-dropping to spectacular and take in San Francisco, the East Bay, the coast, and beyond—on a clear day, all the way to the Farallon Islands, 26 miles away.

GETTING HERE AND AROUND

By car, take the Highway 1–Stinson Beach exit off U.S. 101 and follow the road west and then north. From San Francisco, the trip can take from 30 minutes up to an hour, depending on traffic. By bus, take Golden Gate Transit's 10, 70 or 80 to Marin City; in Marin City transfer to the West Marin Stagecoach (☎ *415/226–0855* ⊕ *www. marintransit.org/stage.html*). Once here, the only way to explore is on foot or by bike.

EXPLORING

Mt. Tamalpais State Park. Although the summit of Mt. Tamalpais is only 2,571 feet high, the mountain rises practically from sea level, dominating the topography of Marin County. Adjacent to Muir Woods National Monument, Mt. Tamalpais State Park affords views of the entire Bay Area and the Pacific Ocean to the west. The mountain was sacred to Native Americans, who saw in its profile—as you can see today—the silhouette of a sleeping Indian maiden. Locals fondly refer to it as the "Sleeping Lady." For years the 6,300-acre park has been a favorite destination for hikers. There are more than 200 miles of trails, some rugged but many developed for easy walking through meadows, grasslands, and forests and along creeks. Mt. Tam, as it's called by locals, is also the birthplace (in the 1970s) of mountain biking, and today many spandex-clad bikers whiz down the park's winding roads.

The park's major thoroughfare, Panoramic Highway, snakes its way up from U.S. 101 to the **Pantoll Ranger Station.** The office is staffed sporadically, depending on funding. From the ranger station, Panoramic Highway drops down to the town of Stinson Beach. Pantoll Road branches off the highway at the station, connecting up with Ridgecrest Boulevard. Along these roads are numerous parking areas, picnic spots, scenic overlooks, and trailheads. Parking is free along the roadside, but there's a fee at the ranger station and at some of the other parking lots ($8).

The **Mountain Theater,** also known as the Cushing Memorial Amphitheatre, is a natural amphitheater with terraced stone seats (for nearly 4,000 people) constructed in its current form by the Civilian Conservation Corps in the 1930s.

The **Rock Spring Trail** starts at the Mountain Theater and gently climbs about 1¾ miles to the **West Point Inn,** once a stop on the Mt. Tam railroad route. Relax at a picnic table and stock up on water before forging ahead, via Old Railroad Grade Fire Road and the Miller Trail, to Mt. Tam's Middle Peak, about 2 miles uphill.

Starting from the Pantoll Ranger Station, the precipitous **Steep Ravine Trail** brings you past stands of coastal redwoods and, in the springtime, numerous small waterfalls. Take the connecting **Dipsea Trail** to reach the town of Stinson Beach and its swath of golden sand. ■TIP➔ If you're too weary to make the 3½-mile trek back up, Marin Transit Bus 61 takes you from Stinson Beach back to the ranger station. ⊠ *Pantoll Ranger Station, 3801 Panoramic Hwy., at Pantoll Rd.* ☎ *415/388–2070* ⊕ *www.parks.ca.gov.*

PERFORMING ARTS

FAMILY **Mountain Play.** Every May and June, locals tote overstuffed picnic baskets to the Mountain Theater to see the Mountain Play, popular musicals such as *The Music Man* and *My Fair Lady.* ⊠ *Mt. Tamalpais, Richardson Blvd. off Panoramic Hwy.* ☎ *415/383–1100* ⊕ *www.mountainplay. org* ⊠ *$40.*

BEACH TOWNS

The winds whip wildly around Marin County's miles of coastline. If you've never heard sand "sing" as the wind rustles through it you're in for a treat—though when it lands in your sandwich you might not rejoice. But when the weather's calm and sunny as you stroll Stinson Beach—or you're communing with nature at rocky Muir Beach—you'll realize this landscape is ever so choice.

GETTING HERE AND AROUND

If you're driving, take the Highway 1–Stinson Beach exit off U.S. 101 and follow Highway 1, also signed as Shoreline Highway, west and then north. Public transit serves Stinson Beach and Bolinas but not Muir Beach.

MUIR BEACH

12 miles northwest of Golden Gate Bridge, 6 miles southwest of Mill Valley.

Except on the sunniest of weekends Muir Beach is relatively quiet. But this craggy cove has seen its share of history. Sir Francis Drake disembarked here five centuries ago, rock star Janis Joplin's ashes were scattered here among the sands, and this is where author Ken Kesey hosted the second of his famed Acid Tests.

GETTING HERE AND AROUND

A car is the best way to reach Muir Beach. From Highway 1, follow Pacific Way southwest ¼ mile.

EXPLORING

Green Gulch Farm Zen Center. Giant eucalyptus trees frame the long and winding road that leads to this tranquil retreat. Meditation programs, workshops, and various events take place here, and there's an extensive organic garden. Visitors are welcome to roam the acres of gardens that reach down toward Muir Beach. ■ TIP➔ Follow the main dirt road to a peaceful path (birds, trees, ocean breezes) that meanders to the beach. ✉ *1601 Shoreline Hwy., at Green Gulch Rd., Muir Beach* ☎ *415/383–3134* ⊕ *www.sfzc.org* ✉ *Free* ☾ *Tues.–Sat. 9–noon and 2–4, Sun. 9–10 am.*

BEACHES

FAMILY   **Muir Beach.** Small but scenic, this beach—a rocky patch of shoreline off Highway 1 in the northern Marin Headlands—is a good place to stretch your legs and gaze out at the Pacific. Locals often walk their dogs here; families and cuddling couples come for picnicking and sunbathing. At one end of the sand are waterfront homes (and where nude sunbathers lay their towels), and at the other are the bluffs of the Golden Gate National Recreation Area. **Amenities:** parking (free); toilets. **Best for:** solitude; nudists; walking. ✉ *190 Pacific Way, off Shoreline Hwy., Muir Beach* ⊕ *www.nps.gov/goga/planyourvisit/muirbeach.htm.*

Shutterbugs rejoice in catching a scenic Muir Beach sunset.

WHERE TO STAY

$$$
B&B/INN
Pelican Inn. From its slate roof to its whitewashed plaster walls, this inn looks so Tudor that it's hard to believe it was built in the 1970s, but the Pelican is English to the core, with its smallish guest rooms upstairs (no elevator), high half-tester beds draped in heavy fabrics, and bangers and grilled tomatoes for breakfast. **Pros:** five-minute walk to beach; great bar and restaurant; peaceful setting. **Cons:** 20-minute drive to nearby attractions; some rooms are quite small. $ *Rooms from: $222* ✉ *10 Pacific Way, off Hwy. 1, Muir Beach* ☎ *415/383–6000* ⊕ *www. pelicaninn.com* ⟿ *7 rooms* ⊚| *Breakfast.*

STINSON BEACH

20 miles northwest of Golden Gate Bridge.

This laid-back hamlet is all about the beach, and folks come from all over the Bay Area to walk its sandy, often windswept shore. Ideal day trip: a morning Mt. Tam hike followed by lunch at one of Stinson's unassuming eateries and leisurely beach stroll.

GETTING HERE AND AROUND

If you're driving, take the Highway 1–Stinson Beach exit off U.S. 101 and follow the road west and then north. The journey from San Francisco can take from 35 minutes to more than an hour, depending on traffic. By bus, take the 10, 70, or 80 to Marin City; in Marin City transfer to the West Marin Stagecoach. The intimate town is perfect for casual walking.

BEACHES

FAMILY **Stinson Beach.** When the fog hasn't rolled in, this expansive stretch of sand is about as close as you can get in Marin to the stereotypical feel of a Southern California beach. There are several clothing-optional areas, among them a section called Red Rock Beach. ⚠ Swimming at Stinson Beach is recommended only from early May through September, when lifeguards are on duty, because the undertow can be strong and shark sightings, although infrequent, aren't unheard of. On any hot summer weekend, every road to Stinson is jam-packed, so factor this into your plans. The down-to-earth town itself—population 600, give or take—has a surfer vibe, with a few good eating options and pleasant hippie-craftsy browsing. **Amenities:** food and drink; lifeguards; parking (free); showers; toilets. **Best for:** nudists; sunset; surfing; swimming; walking. ⊠ *Hwy. 1, Stinson Beach* ⊕ *www.stinsonbeachonline.com.*

WHERE TO EAT AND STAY

$$ ✕ **Parkside Cafe.** The Parkside is popular for its beachfront snack bar
AMERICAN (cash only), but inside is Stinson Beach's best restaurant, with clas-
FAMILY sic offerings such as clam chowder, Dungeness crab, and rock-shrimp risotto. Breakfast is served until 2 pm. Creeping vines on the sunny patio shelter diners from the wind; for a cozier ambience eat by the fire in the dining room. $ *Average main: $20* ⊠ *43 Arenal Ave., off Shoreline Hwy., Stinson Beach* ☎ *415/868–1272* ⊕ *www.parksidecafe.com.*

$$ ✕ **Sand Dollar Restaurant.** The town's oldest restaurant still attracts all
AMERICAN the old salts from Muir Beach to Bolinas, but these days they sip whiskey at an up-to-date bar or beneath market umbrellas on the spiffy deck. The food is good—try the fish tacos—but the big draw is the lively atmosphere. Musicians play on Sunday in summer, and on sunny afternoons the deck gets so packed that people sit on the fence rails sipping beer. $ *Average main: $20* ⊠ *3458 Shoreline Hwy., Stinson Beach* ☎ *415/868–0434* ⊕ *www.stinsonbeachrestaurant.com.*

$ ⛱ **Sandpiper Lodging.** Recharge, rest, and enjoy the local scenery at this
B&B/INN ultra-popular lodging that books up months, even years, in advance.
FAMILY **Pros:** bright rooms; lush gardens; minutes from the beach. **Cons:** walls are thin; some guests say motel rooms are overpriced. $ *Rooms from: $145* ⊠ *1 Marine Way, at Arenal Ave., Stinson Beach* ☎ *415/868–1632* ⊕ *www.sandpiperstinsonbeach.com* ⟿ *6 rooms, 4 cabins, 1 cottage* ⊘| *No meals.*

$ ⛱ **Stinson Beach Motel.** Built in the 1930s, this motel surrounds three
B&B/INN courtyards that burst with flowering greenery, and rooms are clean, simple, and summery. **Pros:** minutes from the beach; cozy, unpretentious rooms; kitchenettes in cottages. **Cons:** smaller rooms are cramped. $ *Rooms from: $140* ⊠ *3416 Shoreline Hwy., Stinson Beach* ☎ *415/868–1712* ⊕ *www.stinsonbeachmotel.com* ⟿ *6 rooms, 2 cottages* ⊘| *No meals.*

EN
ROUTE **Martin Griffin Preserve.** A 1,000-acre wildlife sanctuary along the Bolinas Lagoon, this Audubon Canyon Ranch preserve gets the most traffic during late spring, when great blue herons and egrets nest in the evergreens covering the hillside. It's spectacular to see these large birds in white and gray, dotting the tops of the trees. Quiet trails through the rest of the preserve offer tremendous vistas of the Bolinas Lagoon and

Stinson Beach—and fabulous birding. On weekends, "Ranch Guides" are posted throughout to point out nests—scopes are provided—and answer questions. During the week, check in at the small bookstore and take a self-guided tour. ✉ *4900 Shoreline Hwy. 1, between Stinson Beach and Bolinas, Stinson Beach* ☎ *415/868–9244* 🌐 *www.egret.org* 🎟 *Free* 🕑 *Closed mid-Dec.–mid-Mar.*

BOLINAS

7 miles north of Stinson Beach.

The tiny town of Bolinas wears its 1960s idealism on its sleeve, attracting potters, poets, and peace lovers to its quiet streets. With a funky gallery, a general store selling organic produce, a café, and an offbeat saloon, the main thoroughfare, Wharf Road, looks like a hippie-fied version of Main Street, USA.

GETTING HERE AND AROUND

Bolinas isn't difficult to find, though locals notoriously remove the street sign for their town from the highway: heading north from Stinson Beach, follow Highway 1 west and then north. Make a left at the first road just past the Bolinas Lagoon (✉ *Olema–Bolinas Rd.*), and then turn left at the stop sign. The road dead-ends smack-dab in the middle of town. By bus, take the 10, 70, or 80 to Marin City; in Marin City, transfer to the West Marin Stagecoach. Walking is the only way to see this small town.

WHERE TO EAT

$$ AMERICAN 🍴 **Coast Cafe.** Decked out in a nautical theme with surfboards and buoys, the dining room at the Coast serves dependably good American fare, including specials such as shepherd's pie, local fresh fish, grass-fed steaks, and gorgeous salads. Live music accompanies dinner on Thursday and Sunday. On weekends, the café is open for brunch. [$] *Average main: $16* ✉ *46 Wharf Rd., off Olema–Bolinas Rd., Bolinas* ☎ *415/868–2298* 🕑 *Closed Mon.*

19

POINT REYES NATIONAL SEASHORE

Bear Valley Visitor Center is 12 miles north of Bolinas.

With sandy beaches stretching for miles, a dramatic rocky coastline, a gem of a lighthouse, and idyllic, century-old dairy farms, Point Reyes National Seashore is one of the most varied and strikingly beautiful corners of the Bay Area.

GETTING HERE AND AROUND

From San Francisco, take U.S. 101 north, head west at Sir Francis Drake Boulevard (Exit 450B), and follow the road just under 20 miles to Bear Valley Road. From Stinson Beach or Bolinas, drive north on Highway 1 and turn left on Bear Valley Road. If you're going by bus, take one of several Golden Gate Transit buses to Marin City; in Marin City transfer to the West Marin Stagecoach (you'll switch buses in Olema). Once at the visitor center, the best way to get around is on foot.

EXPLORING

FAMILY   **Bear Valley Visitor Center.** A life-size orca model hovers over the center's engaging exhibits about the wildlife and history of the Point Reyes National Seashore. The rangers at the barnlike facility are fonts of information about beaches, whale-watching, hiking trails, and camping. Winter hours may be shorter and summer weekend hours may be longer; call or check the website for details. ⊠ *Bear Valley Visitor Center Access Rd., west of Hwy. 1* ☏ *415/464–5100* ⊕ *www.nps.gov/ pore/planyourvisit* ⊙ *Weekdays 10–5, weekends 9–5.*

FAMILY   **Duxbury Reef.** Excellent tide pooling can be had along mile-long Duxbury Reef, the largest shale intertidal reef in North America. Look for sea stars, barnacles, sea anemones, purple urchins, limpets, sea mussels, and the occasional abalone. But check a tide table (⊕ *www.wrh. noaa.gov/mtr/marine.php*) or the local papers if you plan to explore the reef—it's accessible only at low tide. The reef is a 30-minute drive from the Bear Valley Visitor Center. Take Highway 1 south from the center, turn right at Olema–Bolinas Road (keep an eye peeled; the road is easy to miss), left on Horsehoe Hill Road, right on Mesa Road, left on Overlook Drive, and then right on Elm Road, which dead-ends at the Agate Beach County Park parking lot.

FAMILY   **Point Blue Conservation Science.** Birders adore Point Blue, which lies in the southernmost part of Point Reyes National Seashore and is accessed through Bolinas. (Those not interested in birds might find it ho-hum.) The unstaffed Palomarin Field Station, open daily from sunrise to sunset, has excellent interpretive exhibits, including a comparative display of real birds' talons. The surrounding woods harbor more than 200 bird species. As you hike the quiet trails through forest and along ocean cliffs, you're likely to see biologists banding birds to aid in the study of their life cycles. ■**TIP**➔ Visit Point Blue's website to find out when banding will occur; it's a fun time to come here. ⊠ *Mesa Rd., Bolinas* ☏ *415/868–0655* ⊕ *www.pointblue.org* ⊴ *Free* ⊙ *Daily sunrise–sunset.*

FAMILY   **Point Reyes Lighthouse.** In operation since December 1, 1870, this light-
Fodor's Choice   house is one of the premier attractions of the Point Reyes National
★   Seashore. It occupies the tip of Point Reyes, 22 miles from the Bear Valley Visitor Center, a scenic 45-minute drive over hills scattered with longtime dairy farms. The lighthouse originally cast a rotating beam lighted by four wicks that burned lard oil. Keeping the wicks lighted and the 6,000-pound Fresnel lens soot-free in Point Reyes's perpetually foggy climate was a constant struggle that reputedly drove the early attendants to alcoholism and insanity.

■**TIP**➔ The lighthouse is one of the best spots on the coast for watching gray whales. On both legs of their annual migration, the magnificent animals pass close enough to see with the naked eye. Southern migration peaks in mid-January, and the whales head back north in March; see the slower mothers and calves in late April and early May.

On busy whale-watching weekends (from late December through mid-April), buses shuttle visitors from the Drakes Beach parking lot to the top of the stairs leading down to the lighthouse (*Bus $7, admission free*) and the road is closed to private vehicles. However you've arrived, consider whether you have it in you to walk down—and up—the 308 steps to the lighthouse. The view from the bottom is worth the effort, but the whales are visible from the cliffs above the lighthouse. ✉ *Visitor Center, Western end of Sir Francis Drake Blvd., Inverness* ☎ *415/669–1534* ⏱ *Fri.–Mon. 10–4:30; weather lens room mid-Apr.–Dec., Fri.–Mon. 2:30–4 except during very windy weather.*

Fodor'sChoice **Point Reyes National Seashore.** One of the Bay Area's most spectacular
★ treasures and the only national seashore on the West Coast, the 66,500-acre Point Reyes National Seashore encompasses hiking trails, secluded beaches, and rugged grasslands as well as Point Reyes itself, a triangular peninsula that juts into the Pacific. The town of **Point Reyes Station** is a one-main-drag affair with some good places to eat and gift shops that sell locally made and imported goods.

When explorer Sir Francis Drake sailed along the California coast in 1579, he missed the Golden Gate and San Francisco Bay, but he did land at what he described as a convenient harbor. In 2012 the federal government finally officially recognized Drake's Bay, which flanks the point on the east, as that harbor, designating the spot a National Historic Landmark and silencing competing claims in the 433-year-old controversy. Today Point Reyes's hills and dramatic cliffs attract other kinds of explorers: hikers, whale-watchers, and solitude seekers.

The infamous San Andreas Fault runs along the park's eastern edge and up the center of Tomales Bay; take the short **Earthquake Trail** from the visitor center to see the impact near the epicenter of the 1906 earthquake that devastated San Francisco. A ½-mile path from the visitor center leads to **Kule Loklo,** a reconstructed Miwok village that sheds light on the daily lives of the region's first inhabitants. From here, trails also lead to the park's free, hike-in campgrounds (camping permits are required).

■ TIP➔ In late winter and spring, take the short walk at Chimney Rock, just before the lighthouse, to the Elephant Seal Overlook. Even from the cliff, the male seals look enormous as they spar, growling and bloodied, for resident females.

You can experience the diversity of Point Reyes's ecosystems on the scenic **Coast Trail,** which starts at the Palomarin Trailhead, just outside Bolinas. From here, it's a 3-mile trek through eucalyptus groves and pine forests and along seaside cliffs to beautiful and tiny Bass Lake. To reach the Palomarin Trailhead, take Olema–Bolinas Road toward Bolinas, follow signs to Point Blue Conservation Science, and then continue until the road dead-ends.

The 4.7-mile-long (one-way) **Tomales Point Trail** follows the spine of the park's northernmost finger of land through a Tule Elk Preserve, providing spectacular ocean views from the high bluffs. Expect to see elk, but keep your distance from the animals. To reach the fairly easy hiking trail, look for the Pierce Point Road turnoff on the right, just north of the town of Inverness; park at the end of the road by the old ranch buildings. ✉ *Bear Valley Visitor Center, Bear Valley Visitor Center Access Rd., off Hwy. 1, Point Reyes Station* ☎ *415/464–5100* ⊕ *www.nps.gov/pore.*

19

WHERE TO EAT

$
ECLECTIC

✕**Café Reyes.** In a triangular, semi-industrial room with glazed concrete floors and ceilings high enough to accommodate several full-size market umbrellas, you can mix and match Californian and international flavors. Wood-fired pizzas are the specialty, the sandwiches and salads come in generous portions, and regulars rave about the oysters. ■ TIP➔ On nice days, head for the outdoor patio. $ *Average main: $15* ✉ *11101 Hwy. 1, Point Reyes Station* ☎ *415/663–9493* ⊙ *Closed Mon. and Tues.*

$$
ITALIAN
Fodor's Choice
★

✕**Osteria Stellina.** The vaguely industrial-chic overtones of this West Marin star's otherwise rustic-contemporary decor hint at the panache that enlivens chef-owner Christian Caiazzo's "Point Reyes Italian" cuisine. The emphasis on locally sourced ingredients makes for ingenious combinations—oysters harvested a just a few miles away, for instance, anchor a pizza with leeks braised in cream from Marin and Sonoma cows and garnished with parsley and lemon thyme. Pastas and pizzas dominate the menu, which might contain as few as two entrées for lunch and a handful for dinner. The hit at lunch, tomato minestra, is a lightly spiced seafood concoction reminiscent of gumbo; dinner might include osso buco that pairs Niman Ranch veal with Marin-grown kale, or braised goat with greens from Stellina's own farm. $ *Average main: $19* ✉ *11285 Hwy. 1, at 3rd St., Point Reyes Station* ☎ *415/663–9988* ⊕ *www.osteriastellina.com* ⊙ *Closed Thurs. in winter.*

$$$$
MODERN
AMERICAN

✕**Sir and Star at the Olema.** With a decor that incorporates taxidermied animals, service that some Marinites find uneven if not indifferent, and outré menu items such as goat shin, Sir and Star elicits both rants and raves, often from diners sharing the same table. If you're up Point Reyes way, though, and ready for an indoor adventure to match your outdoor one, this restaurant by Margaret Gradé and Daniel DeLong, the owners of nearby Manka's Inverness Lodge, is worth checking out. The menu changes seasonally, and the ingredients are often so local a dish might be named A Neighbor's Quail (or duck) or Fritters of Coastal Kale. $ *Average main: $35* ✉ *10000 Sir Francis Drake Blvd., at Hwy. 1, Olema* ☎ *415/663–1034* ⊕ *sirandstar.com* ⬧ *Reservations essential* ⊙ *Closed Mon. and Tues. No lunch.*

$$
AMERICAN

✕**Station House Cafe.** In good weather, hikers fresh from the park fill the Station House's garden to enjoy alfresco dining, and on weekends there's not a spare seat on the banquettes in the dining room, so prepare for a wait. If you come for dinner, your meal will kick off with the café's signature popovers, then the focus is on local, seasonal, and sustainable food: oyster shooters, Niman Ranch braised lamb, Californian white sea bass, and sweet bread pudding are standbys. The place is also open for breakfast and lunch, and there's a full bar. $ *Average main: $21* ✉ *11180 Hwy. 1, at 2nd St., Point Reyes Station* ☎ *415/663–1515* ⊕ *www.stationhousecafe.com* ⊙ *Closed Wed.*

$$$
AMERICAN
FAMILY

✕**Tomales Bay Foods.** A renovated hay barn off the main drag houses this collection of upscale food shops, a favorite stopover among Bay Area foodies. Watch workers making Cowgirl Creamery cheese, then buy some at a counter that sells exquisite artisanal cheeses from around the world. Tomales Bay Foods showcases local organic fruits and vegetables

and premium packaged foods, and the **Cowgirl Cantina** turns the best ingredients into creative sandwiches, salads, and soups. You can eat at a small café table or the picnic areas outside. $ *Average main: $23* ✉ *80 4th St., at B St., Point Reyes Station* ☎ *415/663–9335 cheese shop* ☽ *Closed Mon. and Tues. No dinner.*

WHERE TO STAY

$$
B&B/INN
FAMILY

⌕ **Cottages at Point Reyes Seashore.** Amid a 15-acre valley on the north end of town, this secluded getaway offers spacious one- and two-bedroom cabins with fireplaces and patios perfect for sunset barbecues and leisurely breakfasts. **Pros:** spacious accommodations; great place to bring kids. **Cons:** 3-plus miles from downtown Inverness; small pool. $ *Rooms from: $160* ✉ *13275 Sir Francis Drake Blvd., Inverness* ☎ *415/669–7250, 800/406–0405* ⊕ *www.cottagespointreyes.com* ⌁ *20 cabins* ⎮○⎮ *No meals.*

$$$$
B&B/INN

⌕ **Manka's Inverness Lodge.** Chef-owner Margaret Gradé takes rustic fantasy to extravagant heights in her 1917 hunting lodge and cabins, where mica-shaded lamps cast an amber glow, and bearskin rugs warm wide-planked floors. **Pros:** extremely romantic; remote and quiet. **Cons:** no on-site restaurant; sounds from neighboring rooms are easily heard; some question the value for the price. $ *Rooms from: $365* ✉ *30 Callendar Way, at Argyle Way, Inverness* ☎ *415/669–1034* ⊕ *www.mankas. com* ⌁ *5 rooms, 2 suites, 1 boathouse, 2 cabins* ⎮○⎮ *No meals.*

$$
B&B/INN

⌕ **Ten Inverness Way.** This is the kind of down-to-earth place where you sit around after breakfast and share tips for hiking Point Reyes or linger around the living room and its stone fireplace and library. **Pros:** great base for exploring the nearby wilderness; peaceful garden and friendly staff; exceptional breakfast. **Cons:** some rooms are on the small side; poor cell-phone reception. $ *Rooms from: $180* ✉ *10 Inverness Way, Inverness* ☎ *415/669–1648* ⊕ *www.teninvernessway.com* ⌁ *5 rooms* ⎮○⎮ *Breakfast.*

SPORTS AND THE OUTDOORS

HORSEBACK RIDING

Five Brooks Stable. Tour guides here lead private and group horse rides lasting from one to six hours; trails from the stable wind through Point Reyes National Seashore and along the beaches. ✉ *8001 Hwy. 1, north of town, Olema* ☎ *415/663–1570* ⊕ *www.fivebrooks.com* ⌁ *From $40.*

KAYAKING

Blue Waters Kayaking. This outfit rents kayaks and stand-up paddleboards and offers tours and lessons. Make a reservation for rentals to guarantee availability. ✉ *Tomales Bay Resort, 12944 Sir Francis Drake Blvd., Inverness* ☎ *415/669–2600* ⊕ *www.bwkayak.com* ⌁ *From $25.*

THE WINE
COUNTRY

WELCOME TO WINE COUNTRY

TOP REASONS TO GO

★ **Biking:** Cycling is one of the best ways to see the Wine Country—the Russian River and Dry Creek valleys, in Sonoma County, are particularly beautiful.

★ **Browsing the farmers' markets:** Many towns in Napa and Sonoma have seasonal farmers' markets, each rounding up an amazing variety of local produce.

★ **Wandering di Rosa:** Though this art and nature preserve is just off the busy Carneros Highway, it's a relatively unknown treasure. The galleries and gardens are filled with hundreds of artworks.

★ **Canoeing on the Russian River:** Trade in your car keys for a paddle and glide down the Russian River in Sonoma County. From May through October is the best time to be on the water.

★ **Touring wineries:** Let's face it: this is the reason you're here, and the range of excellent sips to sample would make any oeno-phile (or novice drinker, for that matter) giddy.

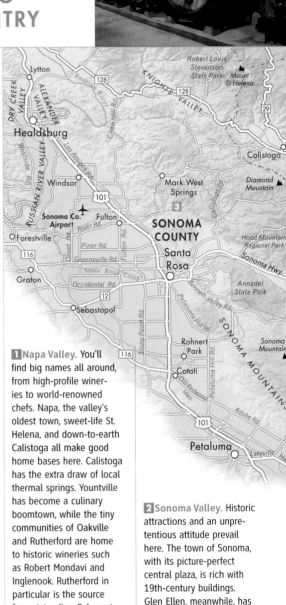

1 Napa Valley. You'll find big names all around, from high-profile wineries to world-renowned chefs. Napa, the valley's oldest town, sweet-life St. Helena, and down-to-earth Calistoga all make good home bases here. Calistoga has the extra draw of local thermal springs. Yountville has become a culinary boomtown, while the tiny communities of Oakville and Rutherford are home to historic wineries such as Robert Mondavi and Inglenook. Rutherford in particular is the source for outstanding Cabernet Sauvignon.

2 Sonoma Valley. Historic attractions and an unpre-tentious attitude prevail here. The town of Sonoma, with its picture-perfect central plaza, is rich with 19th-century buildings. Glen Ellen, meanwhile, has a special connection with author Jack London.

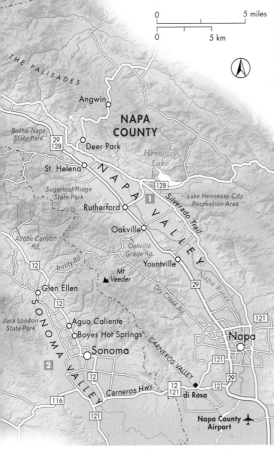

0	5 miles
0	5 km

THE PALISADES

Angwin

NAPA COUNTY

Bothe-Napa State Park

29
128

Deer Park

Hennessy Lake

St. Helena

N A P A

128

Sugarloaf Ridge State Park

Lake Hennessy City Recreation Area

Rufherford

Silverado Trail

1

Oakville

Adobe Canyon Rd.

Oakville Grade Rd.

V A L L E Y

12

Trinity Rd.

Yountville

Mt Veeder

Dry Creek Rd.

Napa River

29

Glen Ellen

12

S

Jack London State Park

Agua Caliente

Boyes Hot Springs

121

O

Sonoma

N

CARNEROS VALLEY

Napa

O

M

A

12

121

V

12

121

29

A

Carneros Hwy.

12
121

12

116

di Rosa

L

L

E

Y

121

Napa County Airport

GETTING ORIENTED

The Napa and Sonoma valleys run roughly parallel, northwest to southeast, and are separated by the Mayacamas Mountains. Northwest of the Sonoma Valley are several more important viticultural areas in Sonoma County, including the Dry Creek, Alexander, and Russian River valleys. The Carneros region, which spans southern Sonoma and Napa counties, is just north of San Pablo Bay.

20

3 Elsewhere in Sonoma. The winding, rural roads here feel a world away from Napa's main drag. The Russian River, Dry Creek, and Alexander valleys are all excellent places to seek out Pinot Noir, Zinfandel, and Sauvignon Blanc. The small town of Healdsburg gets lots of attention, thanks to its terrific restaurants, bed-and-breakfasts, and chic boutiques.

Updated by
Daniel Mangin

Life is lived well in California's premiere wine region, where eating and drinking are cultivated as high arts, and the hotels, inns, and spas rival the world's top resorts for luxury and pampering. Ivy-draped wineries anchor highways and meandering back roads, and boutique operations flourish amid vineyard-blanketed hills. Marquee chefs preside over big-name restaurants whose dishes really *are* as gorgeous as they look in magazine spreads. There's so much to enjoy here: the natural setting is splendid, the architecture divine, the hospitality nearly always sublime.

The Wine Country is also rich in history. In Sonoma you can explore California's Spanish and Mexican pasts at the Sonoma Mission, and the origins of modern California wine making at Buena Vista Winery. Some wineries, among them St. Helena's Beringer and Rutherford's Inglenook, have cellars or tasting rooms dating to the late 1800s. Calistoga is a flurry of late-19th-century Steamboat Gothic architecture, though the town's oldest-looking building, the medieval-style Castello di Amorosa, is a 21st-century creation.

Tours at the Napa Valley's Beringer, Mondavi, and Inglenook—and at Buena Vista in the Sonoma Valley—provide an entertaining overview of Wine Country history. The tour at the splashy visitor center at St. Helena's Hall winery will introduce you to 21st-century wine-making technology, and over in Glen Ellen's Benziger Family Winery you can see how its vineyard managers apply biodynamic farming principles to grape growing. At numerous facilities you can play winemaker for a day at seminars in the fine art of blending wines. If that strikes you as too much effort, you can always pamper yourself at a luxury spa.

To delve further into the fine art of Wine Country living, pick up a copy of *Fodor's Napa and Sonoma*.

PLANNING

WHEN TO GO

High season extends from late May through October, with "crush"—the period when grapes are harvested and crushed—being the best time to see winery workers in action. Crush usually takes place in September and October, sometimes earlier or later depending on the weather. In summer expect hot and dry days, roads jammed with cars, and heavy traffic at tasting rooms. Wine auctions and art and food fairs occur from spring through November. During high season it's wise to book smaller hotels at least a month in advance. To avoid crowds, visit wineries during the week (Tuesday and Wednesday are usually the slowest days). Because many wineries close as early as 4 or 4:30—and only a handful are open past 5—you'll need to get a reasonably early start if you want to fit in more than one or two.

GETTING HERE AND AROUND

AIR TRAVEL

Wine Country regulars often bypass San Francisco and Oakland and fly into Santa Rosa's Charles M. Schulz Sonoma County Airport (STS) on Alaska Airlines, which has nonstop flights from San Diego, Los Angeles, Portland, and Seattle. Avis, Budget, Enterprise, Hertz, and National rent cars here. ■ TIP➔ **Alaska allows passengers flying out of STS to check up to one case of wine for free.**

BUS TRAVEL

Bus travel is an inconvenient way to explore the Wine Country, though it is possible. Take Golden Gate Transit from San Francisco to connect with Sonoma County Transit buses. VINE connects with BART commuter trains in the East Bay and the San Francisco Bay Ferry in Vallejo (⇨ *see Ferry Travel, below*). VINE buses serve the Napa Valley and connect the towns of Napa and Sonoma.

Bus Lines Golden Gate Transit ☎ 415/455–2000 ⊕ www.goldengatetransit. org. **Greyhound** ☎ 800/231–2222 ⊕ www.greyhound.com. **Sonoma County Transit** ☎ 707/576–7433, 800/345–7433 ⊕ www.sctransit.com. **VINE** ✉ Soscol Gateway Transit Center, 625 Burnell St., Napa ☎ 707/251–2800, 800/696–6443 ⊕ www.ridethevine.com.

20

CAR TRAVEL

Driving your own car is by far the most convenient way to get to and explore the Wine Country. In light traffic, the trip from San Francisco or Oakland to the southern portion of either Napa or Sonoma should take about an hour. Distances between Wine Country towns are fairly short, and in normal traffic you can drive from one end of the Napa or Sonoma valley to the other in less than an hour. Although this is a mostly rural area, the usual rush hours still apply, and high-season weekend traffic can often be slow.

Five major roads serve the region. U.S. 101 and Highways 12 and 121 travel through Sonoma County. Highway 29 and the parallel, more scenic, and often less crowded Silverado Trail travel north–south between Napa and Calistoga.

The easiest way to travel between the Napa Valley and Sonoma County is along Highway 12/121 to the south, or Highway 128 to the north. Travel between the middle sections of either area requires taking the slow, winding drive over the Mayacamas Mountains on the Oakville Grade, which links Oakville, in Napa, and Glen Ellen, in Sonoma.

■ TIP➔ If you're wine tasting, either select a designated driver or be careful of your wine intake—the police keep an eye out for tipsy drivers.

From San Francisco to Napa: Cross the Golden Gate Bridge, then go north on U.S. 101. Head east on Highway 37 toward Vallejo, then north on Highway 121, aka the Carneros Highway. Turn left (north) when Highway 121 runs into Highway 29.

From San Francisco to Sonoma: Cross the Golden Gate Bridge, then go north on U.S. 101, east on Highway 37 toward Vallejo, and north on Highway 121. When you reach Highway 12, take it north to the town of Sonoma. For Sonoma County destinations north of Sonoma Valley stay on U.S. 101, which passes through Santa Rosa and Healdsburg.

From Berkeley and Oakland: Take Interstate 80 north to Highway 37 west, then on to Highway 29 north. For the Napa Valley, continue on Highway 29; to reach Sonoma County, head west on Highway 121.

FERRY TRAVEL

From late April through October the San Francisco Bay Ferry sails from the Ferry Building and Pier 41 in San Francisco to Vallejo, where you can board VINE Bus 11 to the town of Napa. Buses sometimes fill in for the ferries.

Contact **San Francisco Bay Ferry** ☎ 510/522-3300 ⊕ sanfranciscobayferry. com.

RESTAURANTS

Farm-to-table Modern American cuisine is the prevalent style in the Napa Valley and Sonoma County, but this encompasses both the delicate preparations of Thomas Keller's highly praised The French Laundry and the upscale comfort food served throughout the Wine Country. The quality (and hype) often means high prices, but you can also find appealing, inexpensive eateries, especially in the towns of Napa, Calistoga, Sonoma, and Santa Rosa, and many high-end delis prepare superb picnic fare. At pricey restaurants you can save money by having lunch instead of dinner.

With a few exceptions (noted in individual restaurant listings), dress is informal. Where reservations are indicated as essential, book a week or more ahead in summer and early fall.

HOTELS

The fanciest accommodations are concentrated in the Napa Valley towns of Yountville, Rutherford, St. Helena, and Calistoga; Sonoma County's poshest lodgings are in Healdsburg. The spas, amenities, and exclusivity of high-end properties attract travelers with the means and desire for luxury living. The cities of Napa and Santa Rosa are the best bets for budget hotels and inns, but even at a lower price point you'll still find a touch of Wine Country glamour. On weekends, two- or even three-night minimum stays are commonly required at smaller lodgings.

Book well ahead for stays at such places during the busy summer or fall season. If your party will include travelers under age 16, inquire about policies regarding younger guests; some smaller lodgings discourage (or discreetly forbid) children. *Hotel reviews have been shortened. For full information, visit Fodors.com.*

Accommodations Listings Napa Valley Hotels & Resorts ☎ *707/251-9188, 855/333-6272* ⊕ *www.visitnapavalley.com/napa_valley_hotels.htm.* **Sonoma Hotels & Lodging** ⊕ *www.sonomacounty.com/hotels-lodging.*

WHAT IT COSTS			
$	$$	$$$	$$$$
Restaurants	under $16	$16–$22	$23–$30	over $30
Hotels	under $201	$201–$300	$301–$400	over $400

Restaurant prices are the average cost of a main course at dinner or, if dinner is not served, at lunch. Hotel prices are for the lowest cost of a standard double room in high season.

TASTINGS AND TOURS

Many wineries require reservations for tours, seminars, and tastings, which in most cases are made through booking websites such as Cellar-Pass and VinoVisit. A good scheduling strategy is to book appointment-only wineries in the morning, saving the ones that allow walk-ins until the afternoon. That way, if lunch or other winery visits take longer than expected you won't be stressed about having to arrive at later stops at a precise time.

Booking Websites CellarPass ☎ *707/255-4390* ⊕ *www.cellarpass.com.* **VinoVisit** ☎ *888/252-8990* ⊕ *www.vinovisit.com.*

Many visitors prefer to leave the scheduling and driving to seasoned professionals. Whether you want to tour wineries in a van or bus along with other passengers or spring for a private limo, there are plenty of operators who can accommodate you. Tours generally last from five to seven hours and stop at four or five wineries. Rates vary from $80 per person to $250 or more, depending on the vehicle and whether the tour includes other guests. On most tours, at least one stop includes a behind-the-scenes look at production facilities and the chance to meet winemakers or others involved in the wine-making process. Most tour operators will pick you up at your hotel or a specified meeting place. You can also book a car and driver by the hour for shorter trips. Rates for limo generally run from $50 to $85 per hour, and there's usually a two- or three-hour minimum. ■ **TIP➜ Some tours include lunch and tasting and other fees, but not all do, so ask.**

Fodor's Choice ★ **Perata Luxury Tours & Car Services.** Perata's customized private tours, led by well-trained, knowledgeable drivers, are tailored to its patrons' interests—you can create your own itinerary or have your guide craft one for you. Tours, in luxury SUVs, cover Napa and Sonoma. The options include exclusive, appointment-only boutique wineries. ☎ *707/227–8271* ⊕ *www.perataluxurycarservices.com* ✉ *From $325 per day, plus fuel surcharge ($25–$35), tasting fees, and 18% gratuity charge.*

Fodor's Choice **Platypus Wine Tours.** The emphasis at Platypus is on "fun" experiences at
★ off-the-beaten-path wineries. Expect intimate winery experiences with
jolly, well-informed guides. You can join an existing tour with other
guests or book a private one. ☏ *707/253–2723* ⊕ *www.platypustours.
com* ✉ *From $99, excluding tasting fees.*

Woody's Wine Tours. The amiable, well-informed Woody Guderian favors
small wineries but will customize a tour to suit your taste and budget. In addition to winery tours in both Napa and Sonoma, Woody
also conducts tours of local craft breweries. ☏ *707/396–8235* ⊕ *www.
woodyswinetours.com* ✉ *From $80 per hr, excluding tasting fees.*

VISITOR INFORMATION

Pretrip Planning Visit Napa Valley ☏ *707/251–5895* ⊕ *www.visitnapavalley.
com.* **Visit Sonoma** ☏ *707/522–5800, 800/576–6662* ⊕ *www.sonomacounty.
com.*

Visitor Centers California Welcome Center ⊠ *9 4th St., at Wilson St., Santa
Rosa* ☏ *800/404–7673* ⊕ *www.visitcalifornia.com/california-welcome-centers/
santa-rosa.* **Napa Valley Welcome Center** ⊠ *600 Main St., at 5th St., Napa*
☏ *707/251–5895* ⊕ *www.visitnapavalley.com/welcome_centers.htm.* **Sonoma
Valley Visitors Center** ⊠ *453 1st St. E, east side of Sonoma Plaza, Sonoma*
☏ *707/996–1090, 866/996–1090* ⊕ *www.sonomavalley.com.*

THE NAPA VALLEY

With more than 500 wineries and many of the biggest brands in the
business, the Napa Valley is the Wine Country's star. With a population
of about 79,000, Napa, the valley's largest town, lures with its cultural
attractions and (relatively) reasonably priced accommodations. A few
miles farther north, compact Yountville is densely packed with top-notch
restaurants and hotels, and Rutherford and Oakville are renowned for
their Cabernet Sauvignon–friendly soils. Beyond them, St. Helena teems
with elegant boutiques and restaurants, and casual Calistoga, known for
spas and hot springs, has the feel of an Old West frontier town.

NAPA

46 miles northeast of San Francisco.

Visitors who glimpse Napa's malls and big-box stores from Highway 29
often speed past the town on the way to the more seductive Yountville
or St. Helena. But Napa has evolved into a destination in its own right.
After spending many years as a blue-collar burg detached from the Wine
Country scene, Napa has reshaped its image. A walkway that follows
the Napa River has made downtown more pedestrian-friendly, and each
year high-profile new restaurants pop up. The nightlife options are arguably the valley's best, shopping is chic and varied, and the Oxbow Public
Market, a complex of high-end food purveyors, is popular with locals
and tourists. An magnitude 6.0 earthquake in August 2014 briefly slowed
Napa's momentum, but the town bounced back admirably and you'll see
little evidence of the damage (an estimated $380 million valley-wide) the
temblor caused.

Continued on page 400

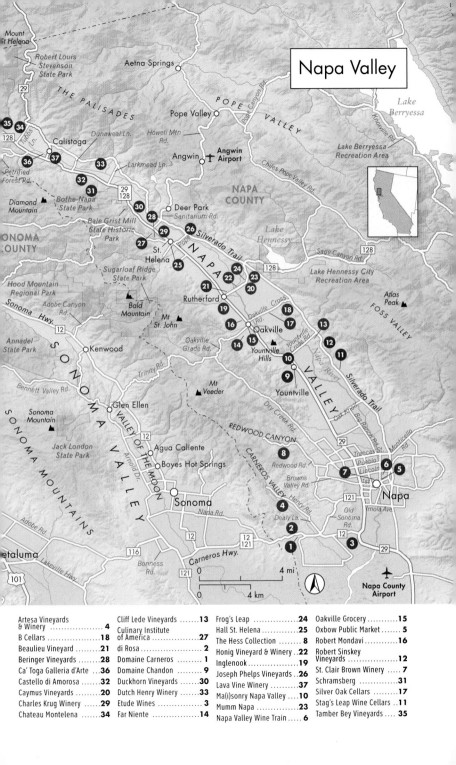

Napa Valley

Mount
St Helena

Robert Louis
Stevenson
State Park

THE PALISADES

Aetna Springs

POPE VALLEY

Pope Valley

Lake
Berryessa

35 **34**
128
Calistoga

Dunaweal Ln.

Howell Mtn
Rd.

Angwin **Angwin
Airport**

Angwin

Lake Berryessa
Recreation Area

36

37

33

Larkmead Ln.

Chiles Pope Valley Rd.

NAPA
COUNTY

Petrified
Forest Rd.

32

31

29
128

Diamond
Mountain

Bothe-Napa
State Park

30

Deer Park

Sanitarium Rd.

Bale Grist Mill
State Historic
Park

28

SONOMA
COUNTY

29

27

26

Silverado Trail

128

Lake
Hennessy

Sage Canyon Rd.

128

St.
Helena

25

Sugarloaf Ridge
State Park

Lake Hennessy City
Recreation Area

Hood Mountain
Regional Park

Adobe Canyon
Rd.

Bald
Mountain

Mt
St. John

21

Rutherford

22 **24**
23
20

Atlas
Peak

FOSS VALLEY

Sonoma Hwy.

12

Annadel
State Park

Kenwood

19

Oakville Cross
Rd.

18
17

13

16

Oakville

Oakville
Grade Rd.

14 **15**

Yountville
Hills

Yountville Cross Rd.

12

11

Napa River

Silverado Trail

Trinity Rd.

10

Mt
Veeder

9

Yountville

Bennett Valley Rd.

SONOMA VALLEY

Glen Ellen

VALLEY OF THE MOON

Dry Creek Rd.

REDWOOD CANYON

Oak Knoll

Big Ranch Rd.

Monticello Rd.

Sonoma
Mountain

Jack London
State Park

Arnold Dr.

Agua Caliente

Boyes Hot Springs

CARNEROS VALLEY

Henry Rd.

29

Trancas
Pueblo
Lincoln
St.

7

6 **5**

8

Redwood Rd.

SONOMA MOUNTAINS

Sonoma

Nana Rd.

Browns
Valley Rd.

4

Dealy La.

Old
Sonoma
Rd.

121

Napa

Imola Ave.

Adobe Rd.

12

2

12
121

3

etaluma

Lakeville Hwy.

101

116

Bonness
Rd.

121

Carneros Hwy.

1

4 mi

12
681

29

**Napa County
Airport**

0   4 km

WINE
TASTING *in*
NAPA *and*
SONOMA

Whether you're a serious wine collector making your annual pilgrimage to Nothern California's Wine Country or a newbie who doesn't know the difference between a Merlot and Mourvèdre but is eager to learn, you can have a great time touring Napa and Sonoma wineries. Your gateway to the wine world is the tasting room, where staff members are happy to chat with curious guests.

VISITING WINERIES

Tasting rooms range from the grand to the humble, offering everything from a few sips of wine to in-depth tours of facilities and vineyards. Many are open for drop-in visits, usually daily from around 10 am to 5 pm. Others require guests to make reservations. First-time visitors frequently enjoy the history-oriented tours at Charles Krug and Inglenook, or ones at Mondavi and J Vineyards that highlight the process as well. The environments at some wineries reflect their founders' other interests: art and architecture at Artesa and Hall St. Helena, movie making at Francis Ford Coppola, and medieval history at the Castello di Amorosa.

Many wineries describe their pourers as "wine educators," and indeed some of them have taken online or other classes and have passed an exam to prove basic knowledge of appellations, grape varietals, vineyards, and wine-making techniques. The one constant, however, is a deep, shared pleasure in the experience of wine tasting. To prepare you for winery visits, we've covered the fundamentals: tasting rooms, fees and what to expect, and the types of tours wineries offer.

Fees. In the past few years, tasting fees have skyrocketed. Most Napa wineries charge $20 or $25 to taste four or so wines, though $35, $45 or even $65 fees aren't unheard of. Sonoma wineries are often a bit cheaper, in the $10 to $25 range, and you'll still find the occasional freebie.

Some winery tours are free, in which case you're usually required to pay a separate fee if you want to taste the wine. If you've paid a fee for the tour—generally from $20 to $40—your wine tasting is usually included in that price.

(opposite page) Carneros vineyards in autumn, Napa Valley. (top) Pinot Gris grapes. (bottom) Bottles from Far Niente winery.

MAKING THE MOST OF YOUR TIME

■**Call ahead.** Some wineries require reservations to visit or tour. It's wise to check before visiting.

■**Come on weekdays.** Especially between June and October, try to visit on weekdays to avoid traffic-clogged roads and crowded tasting rooms. For more info on the best times of year to visit, see this chapter's Planner.

■**Get an early start.** Tasting rooms are often deserted before 11 am or so, when most visitors are still lingering over a second cup of coffee. If you come early, you'll have the staff's undivided attention. You'll usually encounter the largest crowds between 3 and 5 pm.

(top) Sipping and swirling in the DeLoach tasting room. (bottom) Learning about barrel aging at Robert Mondavi Winery.

■**Schedule strategically.** Visit appointment-only wineries in the morning and ones that allow walk-ins in the afternoon. It'll spare you the stress of being "on time" for later stops.

■**Hit the Trail.** Beringer, Mondavi, and other high-profile wineries line heavily trafficked Highway 29, but the going is often quicker on the Silverado Trail, which runs parallel to the highway to the east. You'll find famous names here, too, among them the sparkling wine house Mumm Napa Valley, but the traffic is often lighter and sometimes the crowds as well.

Domaine Carneros.

AT THE BAR

In most tasting rooms, you'll be handed a list of the wines available that day. The wines will be listed in a suggested tasting order, starting with the lightest-bodied whites, progressing to the most intense reds, and ending with dessert wines. If you can't decide which wines to choose, tell the server what types of wines you usually like and ask for a recommendation.

The server will pour you an ounce or so of each wine you select. As you taste it, feel free to take notes or ask questions. Don't be shy—the staff are there to educate you about the wine. If you don't like a wine, or you've simply tasted enough, feel free to pour the rest into one of the dump buckets on the bar.

TOURS

Tours tend to be the most exciting (and the most crowded) in September and October, when the harvest and crushing are underway. Tours typically last from 30 minutes to an hour and give you a brief overview of the winemaking process. At some of the older wineries, the tour guide might focus on the history of the property.

■ TIP➔ If you plan to take any tours, wear comfortable shoes, since you might be walking on wet floors or dirt or gravel pathways or stepping over hoses or other equipment.

MONEY-SAVING TIPS

■ Many hotels and B&Bs distribute coupons for free or discounted tastings to their guests—don't forget to ask.

■ If you and your travel partner don't mind sharing a glass, servers are happy to let you split a tasting.

■ Some wineries will refund all or part of the tasting fee if you buy a bottle. Usually one fee is waived per bottle purchased, though sometimes you must buy two or three.

■ Almost all wineries will also waive the fee if you join their wine club program. However, this typically commits you to buying a certain number of bottles on a regular basis, so be sure you really like the wines before signing up.

Preston of Dry Creek bottles only estate-grown grapes.

TOP 2-DAY ITINERARIES

First-Timer's Napa Tour

Start: Oxbow Public market, Napa. Get underway by browsing the shops selling wines, spices, locally grown produce, and other fine foods, for a taste of what the Wine Country has to offer.

Inglenook, Rutherford. The tour here is a particularly fun way to learn about the history

of Napa winemaking—and you can see the old, atmospheric, ivy-covered château.

Frog's Leap, Rutherford. Friendly, unpretentious, and knowledgeable staff makes this place great for wine newbies. (Make sure you get that reservation lined up.)

Dinner and Overnight: St. Helena. Splurge at Meadowood Napa Valley and you won't need to leave the property for

Domaine Carneros

di Rosa Preserve

121
12

Old Sonoma Rd.

Oxbow Public Market

Napa
29

NAPA COUNTY

Rober Mondav

Far Niente

Yountville

Oakville

KEY
First-Timer's Napa Tour
Wine Buff's Tour

Silverado Trail

Stag's Leap Wine Cellars

Wine Buff's Tour

Start: Stag's Leap Wine Cellars, Yountville. Famed for its cabernet sauvignon and Bordeaux blends.

Beaulieu Vineyard, Rutherford. Pony up the extra fee to visit the reserve tasting room to try the flagship Cabernet Sauvignon.

Mumm Napa, Rutherford. Come for the bubbly—which is available in a variety of tastings—stay for the photography exhibits.

Dinner and Overnight: Yountville. Have dinner at one of the Thomas Keller restaurants. Splurge at Bardessono; save at

Maison Fleurie.

Next Day: Robert Mondavi, Oakville. Spring for the reserve room tasting so you can sip the top-of-the-line wines, especially the stellar Cabernet Sauvignon. Head across Highway 29 to the Oakville Grocery to pick up a picnic lunch.

an extravagant dinner at its restaurant. Save at El Bonita Motel with dinner at Gott's.

Next Day: Poke around St. Helena's shops, then drive to Yountville for lunch.

di Rosa, Napa.
Call ahead to book a one- or two-hour tour of the acres of gardens and galleries, which

are chock-full of thousands of works of art.

Domaine Carneros, Napa.
Toast your trip with a glass of outstanding bubbly.

Sonoma Backroads

Start: Iron Horse Vineyards, Russian River Valley.
Soak up a view of vine-covered hills and Mount St. Helena while sipping a sparkling wine or Pinot Noir at this beautifully rustic spot.

Hartford Family Winery, Russian River Valley.
A terrific source for Pinot Noir and Chardonnay, the stars of this valley.

Dinner and Overnight: Forestville. Go all out with a stay at the Farmhouse Inn, whose award-winning restaurant is one of the best in all of Sonoma.

Next Day: Westside Road, Russian River Valley.
This scenic route, which follows the river, is crowded with worthwhile wineries like Gary Farrell and Rochioli—but it's not crowded with visitors. Pinot fans will find a lot to love. Picnic at Rochioli and enjoy the lovely view.

Matanzas Creek Winery, near Santa Rosa.
End on an especially relaxed note with a walk through the lavender fields (best in June).

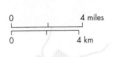

Far Niente, Oakville.
You have to make a reservation and the fee for the tasting and tour is steep, but the

payoff is an especially intimate winery experience. You'll taste excellent Cabernet and Chardonnay, then end your trip on a sweet note with a dessert wine.

WINE TASTING 101

TAKE A GOOD LOOK.

Hold your glass by the stem, raise it to the light, and take a close look at the wine. Check for clarity and color. (This is easiest to do if you can hold the glass in front of a white background.) Any tinge of brown usually means that the wine is over the hill or has gone bad.

BREATHE DEEP.

1. Sniff the wine once or twice to see if you can identify any smells.

2. Swirl the wine gently in the glass. Aerating the wine this way releases more of its aromas. (It's called "volatilizing the esters," if you're trying to impress someone.)

Sniff

3. Take another long sniff. You might notice that experienced wine tasters spend more time sniffing the wine than drinking it. This is because this step is where the magic happens. The number of scents you might detect is almost endless, from berries, apricots, honey, and wildflowers to leather, cedar, or even tar. Does the wine smell good to you? Do you detect any "off" flavors, like wet dog or sulfur?

Sip

AT LAST! TAKE A SIP.

1. Swirl the wine around your mouth so that it makes contact with all your taste buds and releases more of its aromas. Think about the way the wine feels in your mouth. Is it watery or rich? Is it crisp or silky? Does it have a bold flavor, or is it subtle? The weight and intensity of a wine are called its body.

2. Hold the wine in your mouth for a few seconds and see if you can identify any developing flavors. More complex wines will reveal many different flavors as you drink them.

SPIT OR SWALLOW.

The pros typically spit, since they want to preserve their palate (and sobriety!) for the wines to come, but you'll find that swallowers far outnumber the spitters in the winery tasting rooms. Whether you spit or swallow, notice the flavor that remains after the wine is gone (the finish).

DODGE THE CROWDS

To avoid bumping elbows in the tasting rooms, look for wineries off the main drags of Highway 29 in Napa and Highway 12 in Sonoma. The back roads of the Russian River, Dry Creek, and Alexander valleys, all in Sonoma, are excellent places to explore. In Napa, try the northern end. Also look for wineries that are open by appointment only; they tend to schedule visitors carefully to avoid a big crush at any one time.

HOW WINE IS MADE

1. CRUSHING
Harvested grapes go into a stemmer-crusher, which separates stems from fruit and crushes the grapes to release "free-run" juice.

2. PRESSING
Remaining juice is gently extracted from grapes. Usually done by pressing grapes against the walls of a tank with an inflatable bladder.

3. FERMENTING
Extracted juice (and also grape skins and pulp, when making red wine) goes into stainless-steel tanks or oak barrels to ferment. During fermen-tation, sugars convert to alcohol.

4. AGING
Wine is stored in stainless-steel or oak casks or barrels, or sometimes in concrete vessels, to develop flavors.

5. RACKING
Wine is transferred to clean barrels; sediment is removed. Wine may be filtered and fined (clarified) to improve its clarity, color, and sometimes flavor.

6. BOTTLING
Wine is bottled either at the winery or at a special facility, then stored again for bottle-aging.

WHAT'S AN APPELLATION?

A specific region with a particular set of grape-growing conditions, such as soil type, climate, and elevation, is called an appellation. What makes things a little confusing is that appellations, which are defined by the Alcohol and Tobacco Tax and Trade Bureau, often overlap. California is an appellation, for example, but so is the Napa Valley. Napa and Sonoma counties are each county appellations, but they, too, are divided into even smaller regions, usually called subappellations or AVAs (American Viticultural Areas). You'll hear a lot about these AVAs from the staff in the tasting rooms; they might explain, for example, why the Russian River Valley AVA is such an excellent place to grow Pinot Noir grapes.

By law, if the label on a bottle of wine lists the name of an appellation, then at least 85% of the grapes in that wine must come from that appellation.

Wine and contemporary art find a home at di Rosa.

GETTING HERE AND AROUND

Downtown Napa lies a mile east of Highway 29—take the 1st Street exit and follow the signs. Ample parking, much of it free for the first three hours and some for the entire day, is available on or near Main Street. Several VINE buses serve downtown and beyond.

EXPLORING

TOP ATTRACTIONS

Fodor'sChoice ★ **Artesa Vineyards & Winery.** From a distance the modern, minimalist architecture of Artesa blends harmoniously with the surrounding Carneros landscape, but up close its pools, fountains, and the large outdoor sculptures by resident artist Gordon Huether of Napa make a vivid impression. So, too, do the wines crafted by Mark Beringer, who focuses on Chardonnay and Pinot Noir but also produces Cabernet Sauvignon and other limited-release wines such as Albariño and Tempranillo. You can taste wines by themselves or paired with chocolate ($50), cheese ($60), and tapas ($60). ■TIP➔ **The main tour, conducted daily, explores wine making and the winery. A Friday-only tour covers the art, and from June through October there's a vineyard tour.** ⌧ *1345 Henry Rd., off Old Sonoma Rd. and Dealy La., Napa* ☎ *707/224–1668* ⊕ *www.artesawinery.com* ✉ *Tastings $20–$60, tours $30–$45* ☉ *Daily 10–5, winery tour daily at 11 and 2, art tour Fri. at 10:30; reservations required for some tastings and tours.*

Fodor'sChoice ★ **di Rosa.** About 2,000 works from the 1960s to the present by Northern California artists are displayed on this 217-acre art property. They can be found not only in galleries and in the former residence of its late founder, Rene di Rosa, but also on every lawn, in every courtyard, and even on the lake. Some works were commissioned especially for di Rosa, among them Paul Kos's meditative *Chartres Bleu*, a video installation in a chapel-like setting that replicates a stained-glass window from the cathedral in Chartres, France. ■TIP➔ You can view the current temporary exhibition and a few permanent works at the Gatehouse Gallery, but to experience the breadth of this incomparable collection you'll need to book a tour. ⊠ *5200 Sonoma Hwy./Hwy. 121, Napa* ☎ *707/226–5991* ⊕ *www.dirosaart.org* ⊠ *Gatehouse Gallery $5, tours $12–$15* ⊗ *Wed.–Sun. 10–4.*

Fodor's Choice **Domaine Carneros.** A visit to this majestic château is an opulent way
★ to enjoy the Carneros District—especially in fine weather, when the vineyard views are spectacular. The château was modeled after an 18th-century French mansion owned by the Taittinger family. Carved into the hillside beneath the winery, the cellars produce delicate sparkling wines reminiscent of those made by Taittinger, using only Los Carneros AVA grapes. The winery sells full glasses, flights, and bottles of its wines, which also include Chardonnay, Pinot Noir, and other still wines. Enjoy them all with cheese and charcuterie plates, caviar, or smoked salmon. Seating is in the Louis XV–inspired salon or on the terrace overlooking the vines. The tour here covers traditional methods of making sparkling wines. ⊠ *1240 Duhig Rd., at Hwy. 121, Napa* ☎ *707/257–0101, 800/716–2788* ⊕ *www.domainecarneros.com* ⊠ *Tastings $10–$40, tour $40* ⊗ *Daily 10–5:45; tour daily at 11, 1, and 3.*

Fodor's Choice **The Hess Collection.** About 9 miles northwest of Napa, up a winding
★ road ascending Mt. Veeder, this winery is a delightful discovery. The limestone structure, rustic from the outside but modern and airy within, contains Swiss owner Donald Hess's world-class art collection, including large-scale works by contemporary artists such as Andy Goldsworthy, Anselm Kiefer, and Robert Rauschenberg. Cabernet Sauvignon is a major strength, and the 19 Block Cuvée, Mount Veeder, a Cabernet blend, shows off the Malbec and other estate varietals. ■TIP➔ Food-wine pairings include one with chocolates that go well with the Mount Veeder Cabernet Sauvignon. ⊠ *4411 Redwood Rd., west off Hwy. 29 at Trancas St./Redwood Rd. exit, Napa* ☎ *707/255–1144* ⊕ *www. hesscollection.com* ⊠ *Art gallery free, tastings $20–$85* ⊗ *Daily 10–5:30; guided tours daily 10:30–3:30.*

Fodor's Choice **Oxbow Public Market.** The market's two dozen shops, wine bars, and arti-
★ sanal food producers provide an introduction to Napa Valley's wealth of foods and wines. Swoon over decadent charcuterie at the Fatted Calf, slurp bivalves at Hog Island Oyster Company, or chow down on tacos with homemade tortillas at C Casa. Afterward, sip wine at Ca' Momi Enoteca or sample the barrel-aged cocktails and handcrafted vodka of the Napa Valley Distillery. The owner of C Casa also runs Cate & Co., a bakeshop that makes going gluten-free an absolute delight. ■TIP➔ Locals head to Model Bakery around 3 pm for hot-from-the-oven "late bake" bread. ⊠ *610 and 644 1st St., at McKinstry St., Napa* ⊕ *www. oxbowpublicmarket.com* ⊠ *Free* ⊗ *Weekdays 9–9, weekends 10–9; merchants hrs vary.*

20

Climbing ivy and lily pads decorate the Hess Collection's rustic exterior.

Fodor's Choice
★ **St. Clair Brown Winery.** Tastings at this women-run "urban winery" a few blocks north of downtown take place in an intimate, light-filled greenhouse or the colorful culinary garden outside. Winemaker Elaine St. Clair, well regarded for her stints at Domaine Carneros and Black Stallion, produces elegant wines—crisp yet complex whites and smooth, French-style reds among whose stars are the Cabernet Sauvignon and a Syrah from grapes grown in the Coombsville appellation. The wines are paired with addictive appetizers that include almonds roasted with rosemary, cumin, and Meyer lemon juice. ■TIP→ You can sip single wines by the glass or half glass, or opt for the four-wine sampler. ⊠ *816 Vallejo St., off Soscol Ave., Napa* ☎ *707/255–5591* ⊕ *www.stclairbrownwinery.com* ✉ *Tastings $4–$20* ☉ *Daily 11–8.*

WORTH NOTING

Etude Wines. You're apt to see or hear hawks, egrets, Canada geese, and other wildlife on the grounds of Etude, known for its sophisticated Pinot Noirs. Though the winery and its light-filled tasting room are in Napa County, the grapes for its flagship Carneros Estate Pinot Noir come from the Sonoma portion of Los Carneros, as do the ones for the rarer Heirloom Carneros Pinot Noir. Chardonnay, Pinot Blanc, Pinot Noir, and other wines made by Jon Priest are poured daily in the tasting room. On Friday and the weekend, Pinot Noirs from California, Oregon, and New Zealand are compared at seated The Study of Pinot Noir seminars ($45). ■TIP→ Single-vineyard Napa Valley Cabernets are another Etude specialty; the Rutherford and Oakville ones are particularly good. ⊠ *1250 Cuttings Wharf Rd., 1 mile south of Hwy. 121, Napa* ☎ *877/586–9361* ⊕ *www.etudewines.com* ✉ *Tastings $15–$45* ☉ *Daily 10–4:30; Study of Pinot Noir tastings Fri.–Sun. at 10, 1, and 3 by appointment.*

Napa Valley Wine Train. Several century-old restored Pullman railroad cars and a two-story 1952 Vista Dome car with a curved glass roof travel a leisurely, scenic route between Napa and St. Helena. All trips include a well-made lunch or dinner; for all lunches and Saturday dinner you can combine your trip with a winery tour. Murder-mystery plays and dinners with vintners and winemakers are among the regularly scheduled special events. ■ TIP→ It's best to make this trip during the day, when you can enjoy the vineyard views. ⊠ *1275 McKinstry St., off 1st St., Napa* ☎ *707/253–2111, 800/427–4124* ⊕ *www.winetrain.com* ✉ *From $124* ⏰ *Lunch: Jan. and Feb., Fri.–Sun. 11:30; Mar.–Dec., daily 11:30. Dinner: May–Sept., Fri.–Sun. 6:30; Oct., Fri. and Sat. 6:30; Nov.–Mar., Sat. 6:30; Apr., Fri. and Sat. 6:30.*

WHERE TO EAT

$$
MODERN
AMERICAN
Fodor'sChoice
★

✕ **The Boon Fly Café.** This small spot melds rural charm with industrial chic. Outside, swings occupy the porch of a modern red barn; inside, things get sleek with high ceilings and galvanized-steel tabletops. The menu of three squares a day updates American classics such as fried chicken (free-range in this case), burgers (but with Kobe beef), and shrimp and grits. The flatbreads, including a super-creamy smoked salmon one made with fromage blanc, Parmesan, and lemon crème fraîche, are worth a try. Chicken and waffles and other daily specials draw locals, too, and there's a varied selection of wines by the glass. ■ TIP→ Open all day, The Boon Fly makes a convenient mid-morning or late-afternoon stop. $ *Average main: $22* ⊠ *Carneros Inn, 4048 Sonoma Hwy., Napa* ☎ *707/299–4870* ⊕ *www.boonflycafe.com.*

$$$
AMERICAN
Fodor'sChoice
★

✕ **Bounty Hunter Wine Bar & Smokin' BBQ.** A triple threat, Bounty Hunter is a wine store, wine bar, and restaurant in one. You can stop by for just a glass—about 40 choices are available in both 2- and 5-ounce pours—or a bottle, but it's best to come with an appetite. Every dish on the small menu is a standout, including the pulled-pork and beef brisket sandwiches served with three types of barbecue sauce, the signature beer-can chicken (only Tecate will do), and meltingly tender St. Louis–style ribs. The space is whimsically rustic, with stuffed game trophies mounted on the wall and leather saddles standing in for seats at a couple of tables. $ *Average main: $26* ⊠ *975 1st St., near Main St., Napa* ☎ *707/226– 3976* ⊕ *www.bountyhunterwinebar.com* ⚞ *Reservations not accepted.*

$$$$
STEAKHOUSE
Fodor'sChoice
★

✕ **Cole's Chop House.** When only a thick, perfect steak will do, popular Cole's is the best choice in town. The prime steaks—New York and porterhouse—are dry-aged by Allen Brothers of Chicago, purveyors to America's top steak houses. New Zealand lamb chops are the house's non-beef favorite, and seasonal additions might include veal chops. Inside an 1886 stone building, Chops hews to tradition with the starters and sides. Expect oysters Rockefeller, creamed spinach, grilled asparagus with hollandaise, and other standbys, all prepared with finesse. The wine list is borderline epic, with the best of the Napa Valley amply represented. $ *Average main: $38* ⊠ *1122 Main St., at Pearl St., Napa* ☎ *707/224– 6328* ⊕ *www.coleschophouse.com* ⚞ *Reservations essential* ⏰ *No lunch.*

20

$$$$ MODERN AMERICAN Fodor's Choice ★ 🍴 **La Toque.** Chef Ken Frank's La Toque is the complete package: his imaginative Modern American cuisine is served in an elegant dining space, complemented by an astutely assembled wine lineup that in 2014 earned a coveted *Wine Spectator* Grand Award, bestowed on only 74 establishments worldwide. Built around seasonal local ingredients, the menu changes frequently, but Rosti potato with Israeli Russian Osetra caviar routinely appears as a starter, and Moroccan-spiced Liberty Farm duck breast and Wagyu beef served with Frank's variation on poutine are oft-seen entrées. Four-course ($80) and five-course ($98) tasting menus are offered, but for a memorable occasion consider letting the chef and sommelier surprise you via the chef's table tasting menu ($195, $95 additional for wine pairings). [$] *Average main: $80* ✉ *Westin Verasa Napa, 1314 McKinstry St., off Soscol Ave., Napa* ☎ *707/257–5157* 🌐 *www.latoque.com* ⏲ *No lunch.*

$$$$ JAPANESE 🍴 **Morimoto Napa.** *Iron Chef* star Masuharu Morimoto is the big name behind this downtown Napa hot spot. Organic materials such as twisting grapevines above the bar and rough-hewn wooden tables seem simultaneously earthy and modern, creating a fitting setting for the gorgeously plated Japanese fare, from sashimi served with grated fresh wasabi to elaborate concoctions that include sea-urchin carbonara, made with udon noodles. Everything's delightfully overdone, right down to the desserts. **■ TIP→ For the full experience, leave the choice up to the chef and opt for the omakase menu ($120–$160).** [$] *Average main: $44* ✉ *610 Main St., at 5th St., Napa* ☎ *707/252–1600* 🌐 *www.morimotonapa.com.*

$$$ MODERN AMERICAN Fodor's Choice ★ 🍴 **Torc.** *Torc* means "wild boar" in an early Celtic dialect, and chef Sean O'Toole occasionally incorporates his restaurant's namesake beast into dishes at his eclectic downtown restaurant. Bolognese sauce, for example, might include ground wild boar, tomato, lime, and cocoa. O'Toole has helmed kitchens at top New York City, San Francisco, and Yountville establishments. Torc is the first restaurant he's owned, and he crafts meals with style and precision that are reflected in the gracious service and classy, contemporary decor. **■ TIP→ The Bengali sweet potato–pakora appetizer, which comes with a dreamy-creamy yogurt-truffle dip, has been a hit since day one.** [$] *Average main: $25* ✉ *1140 Main St., at Pearl St., Napa* ☎ *707/252–3292* 🌐 *www.torcnapa.com* ⏲ *No lunch weekdays.*

$$$ SPANISH Fodor's Choice ★ 🍴 **ZuZu.** The focus at festive ZuZu is on tapas, paella, and other Spanish favorites. Diners down *cava* (Spanish sparkling wine) or sangria with dishes that might include white anchovies with boiled egg and rémoulade on grilled bread. Locals revere the paella, made with Spanish Bomba rice. Latin jazz on the stereo helps make this place a popular spot for get-togethers. In fall 2014, ZuZu's owners opened **La Taberna,** three doors south at 815 Main Street, a bar for *pintxos* (small bites) and cocktails. The signature dish: suckling pig, which goes well with the beers, wines, and other libations. [$] *Average main: $29* ✉ *829 Main St., near 3rd St., Napa* ☎ *707/224–8555* 🌐 *www.zuzunapa.com* ✍ *Reservations not accepted* ⏲ *No lunch weekends.*

WHERE TO STAY

$$$ HOTEL Fodor's Choice ★ 🏨 **Andaz Napa.** Part of the Hyatt family, this boutique hotel with an urban-hip vibe has luxurious rooms with flat-screen TVs, laptop-size safes, and white-marble bathrooms stocked with high-quality bath products. **Pros:** proximity to downtown restaurants, theaters, and tasting rooms; access

to modern fitness center; complimentary beverage upon arrival; complimentary snacks and nonalcoholic beverages in rooms. **Cons:** parking can be a challenge on weekends; unremarkable views from some rooms. $ *Rooms from: $309* ✉ *1450 1st St., Napa* ☎ *707/687–1234* ⊕ *andaznapa.com* ⤙ *137 rooms, 4 suites* ⦵ *No meals.*

$$$$
RESORT
Fodor's Choice
★

⛱ **Carneros Inn.** Freestanding board-and-batten cottages with rocking chairs on each porch are simultaneously rustic and chic at this luxurious property. **Pros:** cottages have lots of privacy; beautiful views from hilltop pool and hot tub; heaters on private patios; excellent Boon Fly Café is open all day. **Cons:** a long drive to destinations up-valley; smallish rooms with limited seating options. $ *Rooms from: $600* ✉ *4048 Sonoma Hwy./Hwy. 121, Napa* ☎ *707/299–4900, 888/400–9000* ⊕ *www.thecarnerosinn.com* ⤙ *76 cottages, 10 suites* ⦵ *No meals.*

$$
B&B/INN
Fodor's Choice
★

⛱ **Inn on Randolph.** A few calm blocks from the downtown action, the restored Inn on Randolph is a sophisticated haven celebrated for its gluten-free breakfasts and snacks. **Pros:** quiet; gourmet breakfasts; sophisticated decor; romantic setting. **Cons:** a bit of a walk from downtown. $ *Rooms from: $285* ✉ *411 Randolph St., Napa* ☎ *707/257–2886* ⊕ *www.innonrandolph.com* ⤙ *5 rooms, 5 cottages* ⦵ *Breakfast.*

$$
B&B/INN

⛱ **Napa River Inn.** Part of a complex of restaurants, shops, a nightclub, and a spa, this waterfront inn is within easy walking distance of downtown hot spots. **Pros:** wide range of room sizes and prices; near downtown action; pet friendly. **Cons:** river views could be more scenic; some rooms get noise from nearby restaurants. $ *Rooms from: $249* ✉ *500 Main St., Napa* ☎ *707/251–8500, 877/251–8500* ⊕ *www.napariverinn.com* ⤙ *65 rooms, 1 suite* ⦵ *Breakfast.*

$$$
HOTEL
Fodor's Choice
★

⛱ **Senza Hotel.** Exterior fountains, gallery-quality outdoor sculptures, and decorative rows of grapevines signal the Wine Country–chic aspirations of this boutique hotel operated by the owners of Hall St. Helena winery. **Pros:** high-style fixtures; fireplaces in all rooms; Wine Country–chic atmosphere. **Cons:** just off highway; little of interest within walking distance; some bathrooms have no tub. $ *Rooms from: $369* ✉ *4066 Howard La., Napa* ☎ *707/253–0337* ⊕ *www.senzahotel.com* ⤙ *41 rooms* ⦵ *Breakfast.*

NIGHTLIFE AND PERFORMING ARTS

Fodor's Choice
★

1313 Main. Cool, sexy 1313 Main attracts a youngish crowd for top-drawer spirits and sparkling and still wines. The on-site **LuLu's Kitchen** serves bar food—past favorites have included coq au vin wings and corn and shiso fritters—and wild salmon, steak, and other entrées. ✉ *1313 Main St., at Clinton St., Napa* ☎ *707/258–1313* ⊕ *www.1313main.com.*

City Winery Napa. A makeover transformed the 1879 Napa Valley Opera House into a combination wine bar, restaurant, and live-music venue that features top singer-songwriters and small acts. Many of the three dozen wines on tap are exclusive to the club from prestigious area wineries. ✉ *1030 Main St., near 1st St., Napa* ☎ *707/260–1600* ⊕ *www.citywinery.com/napa.*

Uptown Theatre. This top-notch live-music venue, a former movie house, attracts Ziggy Marley, Ani DiFranco, Napa Valley resident and winery owner Boz Scaggs, and other performers. ✉ *1350 3rd St., at Franklin St., Napa* ☎ *707/259–0123* ⊕ *www.uptowntheatrenapa.com.*

20

YOUNTVILLE

9 miles north of the town of Napa.

These days Yountville is something like Disneyland for food lovers. You could stay here for a week and not exhaust all the options—several of them owned by The French Laundry's Thomas Keller—and the tiny town is full of small inns and high-end hotels that cater to those who prefer to walk (not drive) after an extravagant meal. It's also well located for excursions to many big-name Napa wineries, especially those in the Stags Leap District, from which big, bold Cabernet Sauvignons helped make the Napa Valley's wine-making reputation.

GETTING HERE AND AROUND

Downtown Yountville sits just off Highway 29. Approaching from the south take the Yountville exit—from the north take Madison—and proceed to Washington Street, home to the major shops and restaurants. Yountville Cross Road connects downtown to the Silverado Trail, along which many noted wineries do business. The free Yountville Trolley serves the town daily from 10 am to 7 pm (on-call service until 11 except on Sunday).

Contact Yountville Trolley ⊠ *Yountville* ☏ *707/944-1234 10 am-7 pm, 707/312-1509 7 pm-11 pm* ⊕ *www.ridethevine.com/yountville-trolley.*

EXPLORING

TOP ATTRACTIONS

Fodor'sChoice
★

Cliff Lede Vineyards. Inspired by his passion for classic rock, owner and construction magnate Cliff Lede named his Stags Leap vineyard blocks after hits by the Grateful Dead and other bands, but the vibe at his efficient, high-tech winery is anything but laid-back. It's worth taking the estate tour to learn about the agricultural science that informs vineyard management here, and to see the production facility in action. Architect Howard Backen designed the winery and its tasting room, where Lede's Sauvignon Blanc, Cabernet Sauvignons, and other wines, along with some from sister winery Fel, which produces much-lauded Anderson Valley Pinot Noirs, are poured. ■ TIP➜ Walk-ins are welcome at the tasting bar, but appointments are required for the veranda outside and a nearby gallery that often displays rock-related art. ⊠ *1473 Yountville Cross Rd., off Silverado Trail, Yountville* ☏ *707/944-8642* ⊕ *cliffledevineyards.com* ☞ *Tastings $25–$45; estate tour and tasting $75* ☽ *Daily 10–4.*

Domaine Chandon. On a knoll shaded by ancient oak trees, this French-owned maker of sparkling wines claims one of Yountville's prime pieces of real estate. Chandon is best known for bubblies, but the still wines—Cabernet Sauvignon, Chardonnay, Pinot Meunier, and Pinot Noir—are also worth a try. You can sip by the flight or the glass at the bar or begin there and sit at tables in the lounge and return to the bar as needed; in good weather, tables are set up outside. Tours, which cover Chandon's French and California histories and the basics of making sparkling wines, end with a seated tasting. For the complete experience, order a cheese board or other hors d'oeuvres on the lounge menu. ⊠ *1 California Dr., off Hwy. 29, Yountville* ☏ *707/204-7530, 888/242-6366* ⊕ *www.chandon.com* ☞ *Tastings $10–$22, tours $40* ☽ *Daily 10–5; tour times vary.*

Fodor's Choice ★ **Ma(i)sonry Napa Valley.** An art-and-design gallery that also pours the wines of two dozen limited-production wineries, Ma(i)sonry occupies an atmospheric stone manor house constructed in 1904. Tasting flights can be sampled in fair weather in the beautiful garden, in a private nook, or at the communal redwood table, and in any weather indoors among the contemporary artworks and well-chosen *objets*—which might include 17th-century furnishings, industrial lamps, or slabs of petrified wood. ■ **TIP→ Walk-ins are welcome space permitting, but during summer, at harvesttime, and on weekends and holidays it's best to book in advance.** ✉ *6711 Washington St., at Pedroni St., Yountville* ☎ *707/944–0889* 🌐 *www.maisonry.com* 🎟 *Tasting $15–$35* 🕘 *Sun.–Thurs. daily 10–6, Fri. and Sat. daily 10–7; check for later hrs in summer and early fall.*

WORTH NOTING

Fodor's Choice ★ **Robert Sinskey Vineyards.** Although the winery produces a well-regarded Stags Leap Cabernet Sauvignon, two supple red blends called Marcien and POV, and white wines, Sinskey is best known for its intense, brambly Carneros District Pinot Noirs. All the grapes are grown in organic, certified biodynamic vineyards. The influence of Robert's wife, Maria Helm Sinskey—a chef and cookbook author and the winery's culinary director—is evident during the tastings, which are accompanied by a few bites of food with each wine. ■ **TIP→ The Perfect Circle Tour ($75) takes in the winery's gardens and ends with a seated pairing of food and wine.** ✉ *6320 Silverado Trail, at Yountville Cross Rd., Napa* ☎ *707/944–9090* 🌐 *www.robertsinskey.com* 🎟 *Tasting $25, tour $75* 🕘 *Daily 10–4:30; tours by appointment weekdays at 11, weekends at 1.*

Stag's Leap Wine Cellars. A 1973 Stag's Leap Cabernet Sauvignon put this winery and the Napa Valley on the enological map by placing first in the famous Paris tasting of 1976. The grapes for that wine came from a vineyard visible from the new stone-and-glass Fay Outlook & Visitor Center, which opened in 2014. The tasting room has broad views of a second fabled Cabernet vineyard (Fay) and the promontory that gives both the winery and the Stags Leap District AVA their names. ■ **TIP→ A $40 tasting includes the top-of-the-line estate-grown Cabernets, which sell for more than $100; a $25 tasting of more modestly priced wines is also available.** ✉ *5766 Silverado Trail, at Wappo Hill Rd., Napa* ☎ *707/944–2020, 866/422–7523* 🌐 *www.cask23.com* 🎟 *Tastings $25–$40, tour with food and wine pairing $95* 🕘 *Daily 10–4:30; tours by appointment.*

WHERE TO EAT

$$$$ MODERN AMERICAN Fodor's Choice ★ 🍴 **Ad Hoc.** At this casual spot, superstar chef Thomas Keller offers a single, fixed-price menu ($52) nightly, with a small lineup of decadent brunch items served on Sunday. The dinner selection might include braised beef short ribs and creamy polenta, or a delicate panna cotta with a citrus glaze. The dining room is warmly low-key, with zinc-top tables, wine served in tumblers, and rock and jazz on the stereo. Call a day ahead to find out the next day's menu. ■ **TIP→ From Thursday through Saturday, except in winter, you can pick up a boxed lunch to go—the buttermilk fried chicken one is delicious—at the on-site and aptly named Addendum.** [$] *Average main: $52* ✉ *6476 Washington St., at Oak Circle, Yountville* ☎ *707/944–2487* 🌐 *www.adhocrestaurant.com* ✍ *Reservations essential* 🕘 *No lunch Mon.–Sat. No dinner Tues. and Wed.*

$$$ ✕**Bistro Jeanty.** French classics and obscure delicacies tickle patrons'

FRENCH   palates at chef Philippe Jeanty's genteel country bistro. Jeanty prepares

Fodor'sChoice   the greatest hits—escargots, cassoulet, *daube de boeuf* (beef stewed in

★   red wine)—with the utmost precision and turns out pike dumplings and lamb tongue with equal élan. Regulars often start with the extraordinary, rich tomato soup in a flaky puff pastry before proceeding to sole meunière, slow-roasted pork shoulder, or coq au vin (always choosing the simple, suggested side: thin egg noodles cooked with just the right amount of butter and salt). Chocolate pot de crème, warm apple tart tartin, and other authentic desserts complete the French sojourn. $ *Average main: $27* ✉ *6510 Washington St., at Mulberry St., Yountville* ☎ *707/944–0103* ⊕ *www.bistrojeanty.com.*

$$$ ✕**Bottega.** The food at chef Michael Chiarello's trattoria is simultane-

ITALIAN   ously soulful and inventive, transforming local ingredients into regional Italian dishes with a twist. The antipasti shine: you can order grilled short-rib meatballs, house-made charcuterie, or incredibly fresh fish. Potato gnocchi might be served with pumpkin *fonduta* (Italian-style fondue) and roasted root vegetables, and hearty main courses such as a grilled acorn-fed pork shoulder loin with a honey-mustard glaze might be accompanied by cinnamon stewed plums and crispy black kale. The vibe is festive, with exposed-brick walls and an open kitchen, but service is spot-on, and the wine list includes interesting choices from Italy and California. $ *Average main: $26* ✉ *V Marketplace, 6525 Washington St., near Mulberry St., Yountville* ☎ *707/945–1050* ⊕ *www. botteganapavalley.com* ☉ *No lunch Mon.*

$$$ ✕**Bouchon.** The team that created The French Laundry is also behind this

FRENCH   place, where everything—the lively and crowded zinc-topped bar, the

Fodor'sChoice   elbow-to-elbow seating, the traditional French onion soup—could have

★   come straight from a Parisian bistro. Roast chicken with sautéed chicken livers and button mushrooms, and steamed mussels served with crispy, addictive *frites* (french fries) are among the dishes served. ■ **TIP➜ The adjacent Bouchon Bakery sells marvelous macaroons (meringue cookies) in many flavors, along with brownies, pastries, and other baked goods.** $ *Average main: $27* ✉ *6534 Washington St., near Humboldt St., Yountville* ☎ *707/944–8037* ⊕ *www.bouchonbistro.com* ⏍ *Reservations essential.*

$$ ✕**Ciccio.** High-profile French and modern-American establishments may

MODERN ITALIAN   dominate the Yountville landscape, but recent arrival Ciccio instantly

Fodor'sChoice   endeared itself with locals and visitors seeking inventive, reasonably

★   priced—in this case, modern Italian—cuisine. Inside a remodeled former grocery store that retains a down-home feel, executive chef Polly Lappetito, formerly of the Culinary Institute of America, turns out pizzas and entrées, some of whose vegetables and herbs come from the garden of the owners, Frank and Karen Altamura. Seasonal growing cycles dictate the ever-changing menu; Tuscan kale and white-bean soup, wood-fired sardines with salsa verde, and a mushroom, Taleggio, and crispy-sage pizza are among the recent offerings. Frank and Karen own Altamura Vineyards, whose wines are featured here, but their Napa Valley neighbors are also represented, and there's a Negroni cocktail bar. $ *Average main: $19* ✉ *6770 Washington St., at Madison*

St., Yountville ☎ *707/945–1000* ⊕ *www.ciccionapavalley.com* ⚱ *Reservations not accepted* ⊘ *Closed Mon. and Tues. No lunch.*

$$$$ ✕ **The French Laundry.** An old stone building laced with ivy houses the most
AMERICAN acclaimed restaurant in the Napa Valley—and, indeed, one of the most
Fodor's Choice highly regarded in the country. The two nine-course prix-fixe menus (both
★ $295), one of which highlights vegetables, vary, but "oysters and pearls,"
a silky dish of pearl tapioca with oysters and white sturgeon caviar, is
a signature starter. Some courses rely on luxe ingredients like *calotte*
(cap of the rib eye), while others take humble foods such as fava beans
and elevate them to art. Many courses also offer the option of "supplements"—sea urchin, for instance, or black truffles. ■TIP➔ Reservations
are hard-won here; to get one call two months ahead to the day at 10 am,
on the dot. $ *Average main: $295* ✉ *6640 Washington St., at Creek St.,
Yountville* ☎ *707/944–2380* ⊕ *www.frenchlaundry.com* ⚱ *Reservations
essential* ⓙ *Jacket required* ⊘ *No lunch Mon.–Thurs.*

$$$ ✕ **Mustards Grill.** Cindy Pawlcyn's Mustards fills day and night with fans
AMERICAN of her hearty cuisine. The menu mixes updated renditions of traditional
American dishes (what Pawlcyn dubs "deluxe truck stop classics")—
among them barbecued baby back pork ribs and a lemon-lime tart piled
high with browned meringue—with more fanciful choices such as sweet
corn tamales with tomatillo-avocado salsa and wild mushrooms. A
black-and-white marble tile floor and upbeat artworks keep the mood
jolly. $ *Average main: $27* ✉ *7399 St. Helena Hwy./Hwy. 29, 1 mile
north of Yountville, Napa* ☎ *707/944–2424* ⊕ *www.mustardsgrill.com.*

$$$ ✕ **Redd.** The minimalist dining room here seems a fitting setting for chef
MODERN Richard Reddington's up-to-date menu. The culinary influences include
AMERICAN California, Mexico, Europe, and Asia, but the food always feels modern
Fodor's Choice and never fussy. The glazed pork belly with apple puree, set amid a pool
★ of soy caramel, is a prime example of the East-meets-West style. The
seafood preparations—among them petrale sole, clams, and chorizo
poached in a saffron-curry broth—are deft variations on the original
dishes. For the full experience, consider the five-course tasting menu
($80 per person, $125 with wine pairing). ■TIP➔ For a quick bite,
order small plates and a cocktail and sit at the bar. $ *Average main:
$30* ✉ *6480 Washington St., at Oak Circle, Yountville* ☎ *707/944–2222*
⊕ *www.reddnapavalley.com* ⚱ *Reservations essential.*

$$ ✕ **Redd Wood.** Chef Richard Reddington's casual restaurant specializes
ITALIAN in thin-crust wood-fired pizzas and contemporary variations on rustic
Italian classics. The nonchalance of the industrial decor mirrors the
service, which is less officious than elsewhere in town, and the cuisine
itself. A dish such as glazed beef short ribs, for instance, might seem
like yet another fancy take on a down-home favorite until you realize
how cleverly the sweetness of the glaze plays off the creamy polenta
and the piquant splash of salsa verde. Redd Wood does for Italian comfort food what nearby Mustards Grill does for the American version:
it spruces it up but retains its innate pleasures. $ *Average main: $22*
✉ *North Block Hotel, 6755 Washington St., at Madison St., Yountville*
☎ *707/299–5030* ⊕ *www.redd-wood.com.*

20

WHERE TO STAY

$$$$
RESORT
Fodor's Choice
★

Bardessono. Although Bardessono bills itself as the "greenest luxury hotel in America," there's nothing spartan about its accommodations; arranged around four landscaped courtyards, the rooms have luxurious organic bedding, gas fireplaces, and huge bathrooms with walnut floors. **Pros:** large rooftop lap pool; exciting restaurant; excellent spa, with in-room treatments available; polished service. **Cons:** expensive; limited view from some rooms. $ *Rooms from: $650* ⊠ *6526 Yount St., Yountville* ☎ *707/204–6000* ⊕ *www.bardessono.com* ⤳ *56 rooms, 6 suites* ⦿ *No meals.*

$$
B&B/INN

Lavender Inn. On a quiet side street around the corner from The French Laundry restaurant, the Lavender Inn feels at once secluded and centrally located. **Pros:** reasonable rates for Yountville; in residential area but close to restaurants and shops; friendly staff. **Cons:** hard to book in high season; lacks amenities of larger properties. $ *Rooms from: $275* ⊠ *2020 Webber St., Yountville* ☎ *707/944–1388, 800/533–4140* ⊕ *www.lavendernapa.com* ⤳ *9 rooms* ⦿ *Breakfast.*

$$$
HOTEL

Napa Valley Lodge. Clean rooms in a convenient setting draw travelers willing to pay more than at comparable lodgings in the city of Napa to be within walking distance of Yountville's tasting rooms, restaurants, and shops. **Pros:** clean rooms; helpful staff; filling continental breakfast; large pool area; cookies, tea, and coffee in lobby. **Cons:** no elevator; lacks amenities of other Yountville properties. $ *Rooms from: $340* ⊠ *2230 Madison St., Yountville* ☎ *707/944–2468, 888/944–3545* ⊕ *www.napavalleylodge.com* ⤳ *54 rooms, 1 suite* ⦿ *Breakfast.*

$$$$
HOTEL

North Block Hotel. With a chic Tuscan style, this 20-room hotel has dark-wood furniture and soothing decor in brown and sage. **Pros:** extremely comfortable beds; attentive service; room service by Redd Wood restaurant. **Cons:** outdoor areas get some traffic noise. $ *Rooms from: $420* ⊠ *6757 Washington St., Yountville* ☎ *707/944–8080* ⊕ *northblockhotel.com* ⤳ *20 rooms* ⦿ *No meals.*

SPORTS AND THE OUTDOORS

BALLOONING

Napa Valley Aloft. Between 8 and 12 passengers soar over the Napa Valley in balloons that launch from downtown Yountville. The rates include preflight refreshments and a huge breakfast. ⊠ *V Marketplace, 6525 Washington St., near Mulberry St., Yountville* ☎ *707/944–4400, 855/944–4408* ⊕ *www.nvaloft.com* ✉ *From $220.*

BIKING

Fodor's Choice
★

Napa Valley Bike Tours. With dozens of wineries within 5 miles, this shop makes a fine starting point for vineyard and wine-tasting excursions. The outfit also rents bikes. ⊠ *6500 Washington St., at Mulberry St., Yountville* ☎ *707/944–2953* ⊕ *www.napavalleybiketours.com* ✉ *From $99.*

SPAS

Fodor's Choice
★

The Spa at Bardessono. Many of this spa's patrons are hotel guests who take their treatments in their rooms' large, customized bathrooms—all of them equipped with concealed massage tables—but the main facility is open to guests and nonguests alike. An in-room treatment popular with couples starts with massages in front of the fireplace and ends with a whirlpool bath and a split of sparkling wine. For the two-hour Yountville Signature treatment, which can be enjoyed in-room or at the spa, a shea butter–enriched sugar scrub is applied, followed by a massage with antioxidant Chardonnay grape seed oil and a hydrating hair and scalp treatment. The spa engages massage therapists skilled in Swedish, Thai, and several other techniques. In addition to massages, the services include facials, waxing, and other skin-care treatments as well as manicures and pedicures. ⊠ *Bardessono Hotel, 6526 Yount St., at Mulberry St., Yountville* ☎ *707/204–6050* ⊕ *www.bardessono.com/ spa* ⌸ *Treatments $65–$600* ⊗ *Spa 9–6, in-room service 8–8.*

SHOPPING

V Marketplace. The clothing boutiques, art galleries, and gift stores amid this vine-covered market include celebrity chef Michael Chiarello's **NapaStyle,** which sells cookbooks, kitchenware, and prepared foods that are perfect for picnics. The aromas alone will lure you into **Kollar Chocolates,** whose not-too-sweet, European-style chocolates are made on-site with imaginative ingredients. ⊠ *6525 Washington St., near Mulberry St., Yountville* ☎ *707/944–2451* ⊕ *www.vmarketplace.com.*

OAKVILLE

2 miles northwest of Yountville.

A large butte that runs east–west just north of Yountville blocks the cooling fogs from the south, facilitating the myriad microclimates of the Oakville AVA, home to several high-profile wineries.

GETTING HERE AND AROUND

Driving along Highway 29, you'll know you've reached Oakville when you see the Oakville Grocery on the east side of the road. You can reach Oakville from the Sonoma County town of Glen Ellen by heading east on Trinity Road from Highway 12. The twisting route, along the mountain range that divides Napa and Sonoma, eventually becomes the Oakville Grade. The views on this drive are breathtaking, though the continual curves make it unsuitable for those who suffer from motion sickness.

EXPLORING

TOP ATTRACTIONS

Fodor's Choice ★

B Cellars. The chefs hold center stage in this tasting room's large open kitchen, and with good reason: creating food-friendly wines is B Cellars's raison d'être. Founded in 2003, the winery moved from Calistoga to its new Oakville facility, all steel beams, corrugated metal, and plate glass, in 2014. The flagship wines are a Chardonnay, Sauvignon Blanc, and Viognier blend and three red blends. One of the latter is a robust "super Tuscan" made with Cabernet Sauvignon, Sangiovese, Petite Sirah, and Syrah. You can taste the blends and other wines—among them single-vineyard Cabernets whose grapes come from top Napa Valley vineyards—at appointment-only seated tastings involving good-size bites from the kitchen that prove just how admirably winemaker Kirk Venge fulfills the B Cellars mission. ⊠ *703 Oakville Cross Rd., west of Silverado Trail, Oakville* ☎ *707/709–8787* ⊕ *www.bcellars.com* ⌸ *Tastings $45–$125* ⊗ *Daily 10–5 by appointment.*

20

Far Niente's wine cellars have a touch of ballroom elegance.

Far Niente. Though the fee for the combined tour and tasting is high, guests at Far Niente are welcomed by name and treated to a glimpse of one of the Napa Valley's most beautiful properties. Small groups are escorted through the historic 1885 stone winery, including some of the 40,000 square feet of aging caves, for a lesson on the labor-intensive method of making Far Niente's flagship wines: a Cabernet Sauvignon blend and a Chardonnay. The next stop is the Carriage House, which holds a gleaming collection of classic cars. The seated tasting of wines and cheeses that follows concludes on a sweet note with Dolce, a late-harvest wine made from Semillon and Sauvignon Blanc grapes. ✉ *1350 Acacia Dr., off Oakville Grade Rd., Oakville* ☎ *707/944–2861* ⊕ *www. farniente.com* 🍷 *Tasting and tour $65* ⊗ *Daily 10–3 by appointment.*

Silver Oak Cellars. In what may been its decade's most addlepated prognostication, the first review of Silver Oak's Napa Valley Cabernet Sauvignon declared the debut 1972 vintage not all that good—and overpriced at $6 a bottle. Oops. The celebrated Bordeaux-style Cabernet blend, still the only Napa Valley wine bearing its winery's label each year, evolved into a cult favorite, and its only two creators, the late Justin Meyer and current winemaker Daniel Baron, received worldwide recognition for their artistry. At the august Oakville tasting room, constructed out of reclaimed stone and other materials from a 19th-century Kansas flour mill, you can sip the current Napa Valley vintage, the current 100% Cabernet from Silver Oak's Alexander Valley operation, and some library wines ($20). Tours, private tastings, and food-wine pairings elevate the experience. ✉ *915 Oakville Cross Rd., off Hwy. 29, Oakville* ☎ *707/942–7022* ⊕ *www.silveroak.com* 🍷 *Tastings $20–$60, tour $30*

⊙ *Tasting Mon.–Sat.–5, Sun. 11–5; tour Mon.–Thurs. 10 and 1, Fri. and Sat. 10, 1, and 3, Sun. 11 and 1; no appointment required for current-release ($20) tasting; all other tastings and the tour by appointment.*

WORTH NOTING

Oakville Grocery. Built in 1881 as a general store, Oakville Grocery carries high-end groceries and prepared foods. On busy summer weekends the place is often packed with customers stocking up on picnic provisions: meats, cheeses, breads, and gourmet sandwiches. During the week this is a mellow pit stop where you can sit on a bench out front and sip an espresso or head out back and have a picnic. ■ TIP➔ **Patrons dropping by for savory breakfast burritos, scones and muffins, and high-test coffee drinks keep Oakville bustling until right before lunchtime.** ✉ *7856 St. Helena Hwy./Hwy. 29, at Oakville Cross Rd., Oakville* ☎ *707/944–8802* ⊕ *www.oakvillegrocery.com.*

Robert Mondavi Winery. The arch at the center of the sprawling Mission-style building frames the lawn and the vineyard behind, inviting a stroll under the arcades. You can head for one of the two tasting rooms, but if you've not toured a winery before, the 90-minute Signature Tour and Tasting ($30) is a good way to learn about enology, as well as the late Robert Mondavi's role in California wine making. Those new to tasting and mystified by all that swirling and sniffing should consider the 45-minute Wine Tasting Basics experience ($20). Serious wine lovers can opt for the one-hour $55 Exclusive Cellar tasting, during which a server pours and explains limited-production, reserve, and older-vintage wines. ■ TIP➔ **Concerts, mostly jazz and R&B, take place in summer on the lawn; call ahead for tickets.** ✉ *7801 St. Helena Hwy./Hwy. 29, Oakville* ☎ *888/766–6328* ⊕ *www.robertmondaviwinery.com* 🍷 *Tastings $20–$55, tours $20–$50* ⊙ *Daily 10–5; tour times vary.*

RUTHERFORD

2 miles northwest of Oakville.

With its singular microclimate and soil, Rutherford is an important viticultural center, with more big-name wineries than you can shake a corkscrew at. Cabernet Sauvignon is king here. The well-drained, loamy soil is ideal for those vines, and since this part of the valley gets plenty of sun, the grapes develop exceptionally intense flavors.

GETTING HERE AND AROUND

Wineries around Rutherford are dotted along Highway 29 and the parallel Silverado Trail north and south of Rutherford Road/Conn Creek Road, on which wineries can also be found.

EXPLORING

TOP ATTRACTIONS

Fodor's Choice ★ **Caymus Vineyards.** For a winery whose claims to fame include producing Special Selection Cabernet Sauvignon, the only two-time *Wine Spectator* Wine of the Year honoree, Caymus remains a remarkably accessible spot to taste current and past vintages of the celebrated wine. Chuck Wagner started making wine on this property in 1972 and still oversees Caymus production. His children craft most of the other wines in the

20

Wagner Family of Wines portfolio, including the oaked and unoaked Mer Soleil Chardonnays and the Belle Glos Pinot Noirs. ■TIP→ **You can sample Caymus and other wines at the often crowded tasting bar for $25—in good weather, wines are also poured outside—but to taste library wines and learn more about the winery's history, consider booking a private tasting.** ⊠ *8700 Conn Creek Rd., off Rutherford Rd., Rutherford* ☎ *707/967–3010* ⊕ *www.caymus.com* ✉ *Tastings $25–$40* ☉ *Daily 9:30–4:30, last tasting at 4; private tasting by appointment.*

FAMILY

Fodor'sChoice

★

Frog's Leap. John Williams, owner of Frog's Leap, maintains a sense of humor about wine that translates into an entertaining yet informative experience—if you're a novice, the tour here is a fun way to begin your education. You'll taste wines that might include Zinfandel, Merlot, Chardonnay, Sauvignon Blanc, and an estate-grown Cabernet Sauvignon. The winery includes a barn built in 1884, 5 acres of organic gardens, an eco-friendly visitor center, and a frog pond topped with lily pads. ■TIP→ **The tour is highly recommended, but you can also just sample wines either inside or on a porch overlooking the garden.** ⊠ *8815 Conn Creek Rd., Rutherford* ☎ *707/963–4704, 800/959–4704* ⊕ *www.frogsleap.com* ✉ *Tastings $15–$20, tour $20* ☉ *Tastings daily 10–4 by appointment only; tours weekdays at 10:30 and 2:30 by appointment.*

Inglenook. Filmmaker Francis Ford Coppola began his wine-making career in 1975, when he bought part of the historic Inglenook estate. Over the next few decades he reunited the original property acquired by Inglenook founder Gustave Niebaum, remodeled Niebaum's ivy-covered 1880s château, and purchased the rights to the Inglenook name. Various tours cover the estate's history, the local climate and geology, the sensory evaluation of wine, and the evolution of Coppola's signature wine, Rubicon, a Cabernet Sauvignon–based blend. Some tastings are held in an opulent, high-ceilinged room, others in a wine-aging cave. ■TIP→ **You can taste wines by the glass (or the bottle) at The Bistro, an on-site wine bar with a picturesque courtyard.** ⊠ *1991 St. Helena Hwy./Hwy. 29, Rutherford* ☎ *707/968–1100, 800/782–4266* ⊕ *www.inglenook.com* ✉ *Tastings $45–$60, tours $50–$85* ☉ *Daily 10–5; call for tour times.*

Mumm Napa. In well-known Mumm's light-filled tasting room or adjacent outdoor patio you can enjoy bubbly by the flute or the flight, but the sophisticated sparkling wines, elegant setting, and vineyard views aren't the only reasons to visit. An excellent gallery displays 27 original Ansel Adams prints and presents temporary exhibitions by acclaimed photographers. Winery tours cover the major steps making sparklers entails. For a leisurely tasting of several vintages of the top-of-the-line DVX wines, served with cheeses, nuts, and fresh and dried fruit, book an Oak Terrace tasting ($40; reservations recommended on Friday and weekends). ■TIP→ **Carlos Santana fans may want to taste the sparklers the musician makes in collaboration with Mumm's winemaker, Ludovic Dervin.** ⊠ *8445 Silverado Trail, 1 mile south of Rutherford Cross Rd., Rutherford* ☎ *707/967–7700, 800/686–6272* ⊕ *www.mummnapa.com* ✉ *Tastings $8–$40, tour $25 (includes tasting)* ☉ *Daily 10–4:45; tour daily at 10, 11, 1, and 3.*

Frog's Leap's picturesque country charm extends all the way to the white picket fence.

WORTH NOTING

Beaulieu Vineyard. The influential André Tchelistcheff (1901–94), who helped define the California style of wine making, worked his magic here for many years. BV, founded in 1900 by Georges de Latour and his wife, Fernande, is known for its widely distributed Chardonnay, Pinot Noir, and Cabernet Sauvignon wines, but many others are produced in small lots and are available only at the winery. The most famous of the small-lot wines is the flagship Georges De Latour Cabernet Sauvignon, first crafted by Tchelistcheff himself in the late 1930s. ■TIP➜ The engaging historic tour ($35) includes a peek at Prohibition-era artifacts and tastes of finished wines and ones still aging in their barrels. ⊠ *1960 St. Helena Hwy./Hwy. 29, Rutherford* ☎ *707/967–5233, 800/264–6918 Ext. 5233* ⊕ *www.bvwines.com* 🍷 *Tastings $20–$75, tour $35* ☉ *Daily 10–5.*

20

FAMILY | **Honig Vineyard & Winery.** Sustainable farming is the big story at this family-run winery. Michael Honig, the grandson of founder Louis Honig, helped write the code of sustainable practices for the California Wine Institute and was a key player in developing the first certification programs for state wineries. The tour here, offered seasonally, focuses on the Honig family's environmentally friendly farming and production methods, which include the use of solar panels to generate a majority of the winery's power. The family produces only Cabernet Sauvignon and Sauvignon Blanc. You can taste whites and reds at a standard tasting for $20; the reserve tasting ($50) pairs single-vineyard Cabernets with small bites. ⊠ *850 Rutherford Rd., near Conn Creek Rd., Rutherford* ☎ *800/929–2217* ⊕ *www.honigwine.com* 🍷 *Tastings $20–$50; tour $30* ☉ *Daily 10:30–4:30 (reserve tasting daily Mon.–Sat.), tour spring–fall Mon.–Thurs. at 10; tastings and tour by appointment.*

WHERE TO EAT AND STAY

$$$$ MODERN AMERICAN Fodor's Choice ★ 🍴 **Restaurant at Auberge du Soleil.** Possibly the most romantic roost for a dinner in all the Wine Country is a terrace seat at the Auberge du Soleil's illustrious restaurant, and the Mediterranean-inflected cuisine more than matches the dramatic vineyard views. The prix-fixe dinner menu ($105 for three courses, $125 for four; $150 for the six-course tasting menu), which relies largely on local produce, might include veal sweetbreads with hearts of palm and chanterelles in an orange glaze or prime beef pavé with white corn, potato croquettes, and a caramelized shallot sauce. The service is polished, and the wine list is comprehensive. **■ TIP→ With a menu that embraces everything from muffins and gnocchi to Cabernet-braised short rib and (in season) a Maine lobster omelet, the weekend brunch here is delightfully over-the-top.** [$] *Average main: $105* ✉ *Auberge du Soleil, 180 Rutherford Hill Rd., off Silverado Trail, Rutherford* ☎ *707/963–1211, 800/348–5406* 🌐 *www.aubergedusoleil.com* ✍ *Reservations essential.*

$$$ AMERICAN Fodor's Choice ★ 🍴 **Rutherford Grill.** Dark-wood walls, subdued lighting, and red-leather banquettes make for a perpetually clubby mood at this trusty Rutherford hangout. Many entrées—steaks, burgers, fish, succulent rotisserie chicken, and barbecued pork ribs—emerge from an oak-fired grill operated by master technicians. So, too, do starters such as the grilled jumbo artichokes and the iron-skillet corn bread, a ton of butter being the secret of success with both. The French dip sandwich is a local legend, and the wine list includes rare selections from Caymus and other celebrated producers at (for Napa) reasonable prices. You can also opt for a well-crafted cocktail. **■ TIP→ In good weather the patio, popular for its bar, fireplace, and rocking chairs, is open for full meal service or drinks and appetizers.** [$] *Average main: $25* ✉ *1180 Rutherford Rd., at Hwy. 29, Rutherford* ☎ *707/963–1792* 🌐 *www.rutherfordgrill.com* ✍ *Reservations essential.*

$$$$ RESORT Fodor's Choice ★ 🏨 **Auberge du Soleil.** Taking a cue from the olive-tree-studded landscape, this hotel with a renowned restaurant and spa cultivates a luxurious look that blends French and California style. **Pros:** stunning views over the valley; spectacular pool and spa areas; the most expensive suites are fit for a superstar. **Cons:** stratospheric prices; least expensive rooms get some noise from the bar and restaurant. [$] *Rooms from: $850* ✉ *180 Rutherford Hill Rd., Rutherford* ☎ *707/963–1211, 800/348–5406* 🌐 *www.aubergedusoleil.com* 🛏 *31 rooms, 21 suites* 🍽 *Breakfast.*

ST. HELENA

2 miles northwest of Oakville.

Downtown St. Helena is a symbol of how well life can be lived in the Wine Country. Sycamore trees arch over Main Street (Highway 29), a funnel of outstanding restaurants and tempting boutiques. At the north end of town looms the hulking stone building of the Culinary Institute of America. Weathered stone and brick buildings from the late 1800s give off that gratifying whiff of history.

The town got its start in 1854, when Henry Still built a store. Still wanted company, so he donated land lots on his town site to anyone who wanted to erect a business. Soon he was joined by a wagon shop, a shoe shop, hotels, and churches. Dr. George Crane planted a vineyard in 1858, and was the first to produce wine in commercially viable quantities. A German winemaker named Charles Krug followed suit a couple of years later, and other wineries soon followed.

GETTING HERE AND AROUND

Downtown stretches along Highway 29, called Main Street here. Many wineries lie north and south of downtown along Highway 29. More can be found off Silverado Trail, and some of the most scenic spots are on Spring Mountain, which rises southwest of town.

EXPLORING

TOP ATTRACTIONS

Fodor's Choice
★
Charles Krug Winery. A historically sensitive renovation of its 1874 Redwood Cellar Building transformed the former production facility of the Napa Valley's oldest operating winery into an epic hospitality center with a tasting room and a café. Charles Krug, a Prussian immigrant, established the winery in 1861 and ran it until his death in 1892. Italian immigrants Cesare Mondavi and his wife, Rosa, purchased Krug in 1943, and operated it with their sons Peter and Robert (who later opened his own winery). Krug, still run by Peter's family, specializes in small-lot Yountville and Howell Mountain Cabernet Sauvignons and makes Chardonnay, Merlot, Pinot Noir, Sauvignon Blanc, Zinfandel, and a Zinfandel Port. ■TIP→ The café sells food to eat inside or at oak-shaded picnic tables (reservations recommended). ✉ *2800 Main St./Hwy. 29, across from Culinary Institute of America, St. Helena* ☎ *707/967–2229* ⊕ *www.charleskrug.com* ✉ *Tastings $20–$50, tours $60 (includes tasting)* ☉ *Daily 10:30–5; tours by appointment Mon.– Thurs. 10:30 and 12:30, Fri.–Sun. 10:30.*

Duckhorn Vineyards. Merlot's moment in the spotlight may have passed, but you wouldn't know it at Duckhorn, whose fans gladly pay from $50 to nearly $100 a bottle for some of the world's finest wines from this varietal. You can taste Merlot, Sauvignon Blanc, Cabernet Sauvignon, and other wines in the airy, high-ceilinged tasting room, which looks like a sleek restaurant; you'll be seated at a table and served by staffers who make the rounds to pour. In fair weather, you may do your sipping on a fetching wraparound porch overlooking a vineyard. ■TIP→ You don't need a reservation on weekdays to taste the current releases ($30), but you do on weekends, and they're required all the time for private and semiprivate tastings. ✉ *1000 Lodi La., at Silverado Trail N, St. Helena* ☎ *707/963–7108* ⊕ *www.duckhorn.com* ✉ *Tastings $30–$75* ☉ *Daily 10–4.*

Fodor's Choice
★
Hall St. Helena. The award-winning Cabernet Sauvignons, Merlots, and an impeccable Syrah produced here are works of art—and of up-to-the-minute organic-farming science and wine-making technology. A glass-walled tasting room allows you to see in action some of the high-tech equipment director of winemaking Steve Leveque employs to craft the wines, which also include Cabernet Franc and late-harvest Sauvignon Blanc. The main guided tour provides a closer-up look at the facility and covers the winery's history and architecture and the three-dozen works—inside and out—by Patrick Dougherty, John Baldessari, Jesús

20

Moroles, and other major contemporary artists. ■TIP➤ The well-conceived seminars here include ones about the artworks, demystifying food and wine, and collecting Cabernet Sauvignons. ✉ *401 St. Helena Hwy./Hwy. 29, near White La., St. Helena* ☎707/967–2626 ⊕ *www.hallwines.com* ✑*Tastings $30–$100; tours $40–$75* ⊙ *Daily 10–5:30.*

Fodor'sChoice   **Joseph Phelps Vineyards.** An appointment is required for tastings at the
★   winery started by the legendary Joseph Phelps—his son Bill now runs the operation—but it's well worth the effort. Phelps makes fine whites, but the blockbuster wines are reds, particularly the Cabernet Sauvignon and the flagship Bordeaux-style blend called Insignia. The luscious-yet-subtle Insignia sells for more than $200 a bottle. Luckily, all tastings include the current vintage. The 90-minute seminars include one on wine-and-cheese pairing and another focusing on blending. Participants in the latter mix the various varietals that go into the Insignia blend. A new tasting room debuts in 2015 following a major renovation project. ✉ *200 Taplin Rd., off Silverado Trail, St. Helena* ☎ *707/963–2745, 800/707–5789* ⊕ *www. josephphelps.com* ✑ *Tastings and seminars $60–$150 by appointment* ⊙ *Weekdays 10–4, weekends 10–3; tastings by appointment.*

WORTH NOTING

Beringer Vineyards. Arguably the Napa Valley's most beautiful winery, the 1876 Beringer Vineyards is also the oldest continuously operating property. In 1884 Frederick and Jacob Beringer built the Rhine House Mansion as Frederick's family home. Today it serves as the reserve tasting room, where you can sample wines surrounded by Belgian art-nouveau hand-carved oak and walnut furniture and stained-glass windows. The assortment includes a limited-release Chardonnay, a few big Cabernets, and a Sauterne-style dessert wine. A less expensive tasting takes place in the original stone winery. ■TIP➤ The one-hour Taste of Beringer tour ($40), which includes a tasting with small food bites, provides a good overview of the valley's wine-making history. ✉ *2000 Main St./Hwy. 29, near Pratt Ave., St. Helena* ☎707/963–8989, *866/708–9463* ⊕ *www.beringer.com* ✑ *Tastings $20–$50, tours $25– $40* ⊙ *June–mid-Oct., daily 10–6; mid-Oct.–May, daily 10–5; many tours daily, call or check website for times.*

Culinary Institute of America. The West Coast headquarters of the country's leading school for chefs are in the 1889 Greystone Winery, an imposing building that once was the world's largest stone winery. On the ground floor you can check out the quirky Corkscrew Museum and browse a shop stocked with gleaming gadgets and many cookbooks. At the adjacent Flavor Bar you can sample various ingredients (for example, chocolate or olive oil). Plaques upstairs at the Vintners Hall of Fame commemorate winemakers past and present. Beguiling one-hour cooking demonstrations (reservations required) take place on weekends. The student-run Bakery Café by Illy serves soups, salads, sandwiches, and baked goods; the Institute also operates a full restaurant. ✉ *2555 Main St./Hwy. 29, St. Helena* ☎707/967–1100 ⊕ *www.ciachef. edu* ✑ *Museum and store free, cooking demonstrations $20, tastings $10–$15, tour $10* ⊙ *Museum and store daily 10:30–6 (Mon.–Thurs. 11–5 in winter); tour 11:45, 2:45, 5.*

WHERE TO EAT

$$$ MODERN AMERICAN Fodor's Choice ★ 🍴 **Archetype.** Chef Ryder Zetts earned instant raves for his fancifully updated "Americana" cuisine at this establishment designed and owned by winery architect Howard Backen. The cream-color decor, twirling ceiling fans, and rattan settees and chairs set an upscale-homey tone in the main dining area and on the screened-in front porch. Seasonal appetizers might include textbook fried green tomatoes—but with burrata cheese—or peaches with Surryano ham served with creamily addictive mascarpone-pepper jelly. For lunch expect sandwiches such as smoked salmon pepped up by quick-pickled cucumbers. Dinner glides into a more serious realm with, perhaps, bacon-crusted Alaskan halibut or leg of lamb with lamb merguez sausage. **TIP→ The $5 happy hour (daily from 5 to 7) and Monday burger night are popular with locals.** [$] *Average main: $27* ✉ *1429 Main St., near Adams St., St. Helena* ☎ *707/968–9200* 🌐 *www.archetypenapa.com.*

$$ MODERN AMERICAN Fodor's Choice ★ 🍴 **Cindy's Backstreet Kitchen.** At her St. Helena outpost, Cindy Pawlcyn serves variations on the comfort food she made popular at Mustards Grill, but spices things up with dishes influenced by Mexican, Central American, and occasionally Asian cuisines. Along with mainstays such as meat loaf with garlic mashed potatoes and beef and duck burgers served with flawless fries, the menu might include a rabbit tostada or chicken served with avocado salsa and a two-cheese stuffed green chili. Two dessert favorites are the high-style yet homey warm pineapple upside-down cake and the nearly ethereal parfait. [$] *Average main: $22* ✉ *1327 Railroad Ave., at Hunt St., 1 block east of Main St., St. Helena* ☎ *707/963–1200* 🌐 *www.cindysbackstreetkitchen.com.*

$$ MODERN AMERICAN 🍴 **Farmstead at Long Meadow Ranch.** Housed in a former barn, Farmstead revolves around an open kitchen where chef Stephen Barber cooks with as many local and organic ingredients as possible. Many of them—including grass-fed beef and lamb, fruits and vegetables, eggs, extra-virgin olive oil, wine, and honey—come from the property of parent company Long Meadow Ranch. Entrées might include grilled rainbow trout with wild mushrooms, or potato gnocchi with beef ragout, herbs, and Parmesan. Tuesday is the popular panfried chicken night—$37 for a three-course meal. **TIP→ The weekday happy hour, from 4 to 6 (good eats, too), is often hoppin'.** [$] *Average main: $20* ✉ *738 Main St., at Charter Oak Ave., St. Helena* ☎ *707/963–4555* 🌐 *www.longmeadowranch.com/farmstead-restaurant.*

$$$ MODERN AMERICAN Fodor's Choice ★ 🍴 **Goose & Gander.** The pairing of food and drink at intimate Goose & Gander is as likely to involve cocktails as it is wine. Main courses such as wild king salmon with roasted delicata squash, lentils, applewood-smoked bacon, and celery root velouté work well with starters that in season might include cream of mushroom soup made from both wild and cultivated varieties. You can enjoy your meal with a top-notch Chardonnay or Pinot Noir—or a Manhattan made with three kinds of bitters and poured over a hand-carved block of ice. On cold days a fireplace warms the main dining room, and in good weather the outdoor patio is a fetching spot to dine alfresco. **TIP→ Year-round the basement bar is a good stop for a drink.** [$] *Average main: $25* ✉ *1245 Spring St., at Oak St., St. Helena* ☎ *707/967–8779* 🌐 *www.goosegander.com.*

$ × **Gott's Roadside.** A 1950s-style outdoor hamburger stand goes upscale
AMERICAN at this spot whose customers brave long lines to order breakfast sandwiches, juicy burgers, root-beer floats, and garlic fries. Choices not
available a half century ago include the ahi tuna burger and the chili
spice–marinated chicken breast served with Mexican slaw. ■TIP→ Arrive early or late for lunch, or all of the shaded picnic tables on the
lawn might be filled. A second branch does business at Napa's Oxbow
Public Market. $ *Average main: $12* ⊠ *933 Main St./Hwy. 29, St. Helena* ☎ *707/963–3486* ⊕ *www.gotts.com* ⌁ *Reservations not accepted*
$ *Average main: $12* ⊠ *Oxbow Public Market, 644 1st St., at McKinstry St., Napa* ☎ *707/224–6900* ⌁ *Reservations not accepted.*

$$$$ × **Press.** Few taste sensations surpass the combination of a sizzling steak
MODERN and a Napa Valley red, a union that the chef and sommeliers here cel-
AMERICAN ebrate with a reverence bordering on obsession. Beef from carefully
Fodor'sChoice selected local and international purveyors is the star—especially the
★ rib eye for two—but chef Trevor Kunk also prepares pork chops and
free-range chicken and veal on his cherry-and-almond-wood-fired grill
and rotisserie. Kunk, hired in 2014, has added vegetarian offerings that
include a roasted carrot "hot dog" and fried-green-tomato sandwiches.
The cellar holds thousands of wines; if you recall having a great steak
with a 1985 Mayacamas Mt. Veeder Cab, you'll be able to re-create, and
perhaps exceed, the original event. Press's bartenders know their way
around both rad and trad cocktails. $ *Average main: $48* ⊠ *587 St. Helena Hwy./Hwy. 29, at White La., St. Helena* ☎ *707/967–0550* ⊕ *www.
pressthelena.com* ⌁ *Reservations essential* ⊙ *Closed Tues. No lunch.*

$$$$ × **The Restaurant at Meadowood.** Chef Christopher Kostow has garnered
MODERN rave reviews—and three Michelin stars for several years running—for
AMERICAN creating a unique dining experience. After you reserve your table, you'll
Fodor'sChoice have a conversation with a reservationist about your party's desired culi-
★ nary experience and dietary restrictions. Inspired by this conversation,
chef Kostow will transform seasonal local ingredients, some grown on
or near the property, into an elaborate, multicourse experience. If you
choose the Tasting Menu option ($225 per person, $450 with wine pairings), you'll enjoy your meal in the romantic dining room, its beautiful
finishes aglow with warm lighting. Choose the Counter Menu ($500,
$850 with wine pairings), and you and up to three guests can sit inside
the kitchen and watch Kostow's team prepare your meal. ■TIP→ The
restaurant also offers a limited, three-course menu ($90) at its bar. $ *Average main: $225* ⊠ *900 Meadowood La., off Silverado Trail N, St. Helena*
☎ *707/967–1205, 800/458–8080* ⊕ *www.therestaurantatmeadowood.
com* ⌁ *Reservations essential* ⊙ *Closed Sun. No lunch.*

$$$$ × **Terra.** For old-school romance and service, many diners return year
MEDITERRANEAN after year to this quiet favorite in an 1884 fieldstone building. Chef Hiro
Fodor'sChoice Sone gives an unexpected twist to Italian and southern French cuisine,
★ though for a few standouts, among them the signature sake-marinated
black cod in a *shiso* broth, he draws on his Japanese background.
Homey yet elegant desserts, courtesy of Sone's wife, Lissa Doumani,
might include a chocolate mousseline with chocolate peanut butter
crunch and toasted marshmallow. Meals here are prix-fixe—$78 for
four courses where diners choose from the menu, $93 for five, and $105

for six. ■TIP→ Next door, Bar Terra serves cocktails, local wines, and a menu of lighter dishes—the succulent fried rock shrimp served with chive-mustard sauce is a local favorite. $ *Average main: $78* ⊠ *1345 Railroad Ave., off Hunt Ave., St. Helena* ☏ *707/963–8931* ⊕ *www. terrarestaurant.com* ☾ *Closed Tues. No lunch.*

WHERE TO STAY

$ **El Bonita Motel.** For budget-minded travelers the tidy rooms at this HOTEL roadside motel are pleasant enough, and the landscaped grounds and picnic tables elevate this property over similar places. **Pros:** cheerful rooms; hot tub; microwaves and mini-refrigerators. **Cons:** road noise is a problem in some rooms. $ *Rooms from: $130* ⊠ *195 Main St./Hwy. 29, St. Helena* ☏ *707/963–3216, 800/541–3284* ⊕ *www.elbonita.com* ↺ *48 rooms, 4 suites* ⦿| *Breakfast.*

$$$ **Harvest Inn by Charlie Palmer.** Although this inn sits just off Highway HOTEL 29, its patrons remain mostly above the fray, strolling 8 acres of land- Fodor's Choice scaped gardens, enjoying views of the vineyards adjoining the prop- ★ erty, partaking in spa services, and drifting to sleep in beds adorned with fancy linens and down pillows. **Pros:** garden setting; spacious rooms; well-trained staff. **Cons:** some lower-priced rooms lack elegance; high weekend rates. $ *Rooms from: $359* ⊠ *1 Main St., St. Helena* ☏ *707/963–9463, 800/950–8466* ⊕ *www.harvestinn.com* ↺ *69 rooms, 5 suites* ⦿| *Breakfast.*

$$$$ **Meadowood Napa Valley.** Founded in 1964 as a country club, Meado- RESORT wood has evolved into a five-star resort, a gathering place for Napa's Fodor's Choice wine-making community, and a celebrated dining destination. **Pros:** ★ superb restaurant; pleasant hiking trails; gracious service. **Cons:** very expensive; far from downtown St. Helena. $ *Rooms from: $650* ⊠ *900 Meadowood La., St. Helena* ☏ *707/963–3646, 800/458–8080* ⊕ *www. meadowood.com* ↺ *85 rooms, suites, and cottages* ⦿| *No meals.*

CALISTOGA

3 miles northwest of St. Helena.

With false-fronted, Old West–style shops and 19th-century inns and hotels lining its main drag, Lincoln Avenue, Calistoga comes across as more down-to-earth than its more polished neighbors. Don't be fooled, though. On its outskirts lie some of the Wine Country's swankest (and priciest) resorts and its most fanciful piece of architecture, the medieval-style Castello di Amorosa winery.

Calistoga was developed as a spa-oriented getaway from the start. Sam Brannan, a gold rush–era entrepreneur, planned to use the area's natural hot springs as the centerpiece of a resort complex. His venture failed, but old-time hotels and bathhouses—along with some glorious new spas—still operate. You can come for an old-school mud bath, or go completely 21st century and experience lavish treatments based on the latest innovations in skin and body care.

GETTING HERE AND AROUND

Highway 29 heads east (turn right) at Calistoga, where in town it is signed as Lincoln Avenue. If arriving via the Silverado Trail, head west at Highway 29/Lincoln Avenue.

20

EXPLORING
TOP ATTRACTIONS

Castello di Amorosa. An astounding medieval structure complete with drawbridge and moat, chapel, stables, and secret passageways, the Castello commands Diamond Mountain's lower eastern slope. Some of the 107 rooms contain replicas of 13th-century frescoes (cheekily signed [the-artist's-name].com), and the dungeon has an actual iron maiden from Nuremberg, Germany. You must pay for a tour to see most of Dario Sattui's extensive eight-level property, though basic tastings include access to part of the complex. Wines of note include several Italian-style wines, including La Castellana, a robust "super Tuscan" blend of Cabernet Sauvignon, Sangiovese, and Merlot; and Il Barone, a praiseworthy cab made largely from Diamond Mountain grapes. ■TIP→ The two-hour food-and-wine pairing ($75) by sommelier Mary Davidek is among the Wine Country's best. ✉ 4045 N. St. Helena Hwy./Hwy. 29, near Maple La., Calistoga ☎ 707/967–6272 ⊕ www.castellodiamorosa.com ⧉ Tastings $20–$30, tours (with tastings) $35–$75 ⊘ Mar.–Oct., daily 9:30–6; Nov.–Feb., daily 9:30–5; tours and food-wine pairings by appointment.

Ca' Toga Galleria d'Arte. The boundless wit, whimsy, and creativity of the Venetian-born Carlo Marchiori, this gallery's owner-artist, finds expression in paintings, watercolors, ceramics, sculptures, and other artworks. Marchiori often draws on mythology and folktales for his inspiration. A stop at this magical gallery may inspire you to tour **Villa Ca' Toga,** the artist's fanciful Palladian home, a tromp l'oeil tour de force that can be toured from May through October on Saturday only, at 11 am. ✉ 1206 Cedar St., near Lincoln Ave., Calistoga ☎ 707/942–3900 ⊕ www.catoga.com ⊘ Closed Tues. and Wed.

Chateau Montelena. Set amid a bucolic northern Calistoga landscape, this winery helped establish the Napa Valley's reputation for high-quality wine making. At the legendary Paris tasting of 1976, the Chateau Montelena 1973 Chardonnay took first place, beating out four white Burgundies from France and five other California Chardonnays. The 2008 movie *Bottle Shock* immortalized the event, and the winery honors its four decades of classic wine making with a special Beyond Paris & Hollywood tasting of the winery's Napa Valley Chardonnays ($40). You can also opt for a Current Release Tasting ($25) or a Limited Release Tasting ($50) that includes some stellar Cabernet Sauvignons. ✉ 1429 Tubbs La., off Hwy. 29, Calistoga ☎ 707/942–5105 ⊕ www.montelena. com ⧉ Tastings $20–$50, tours $40; appointment required and restrictions apply for some tastings and tours ⊘ Daily 9:30–4.

Fodor'sChoice ★ **Schramsberg.** Founded in 1865, Schramsberg produces sparkling wines made using the *méthode traditionnelle*, also known as *méthode champenoise*. A fascinating tour precedes tastings. In addition to glimpsing the winery's historic architecture, you'll visit caves, some dug in late 19th century by Chinese laborers, where 2 million–plus bottles are stacked in gravity-defying configurations. Tastings include generous pours of very different bubblies. To learn more about them, consider the three-day **Camp Schramsberg,** held in fall and spring. Fall participants harvest grapes and learn about food and wine pairing, riddling (the process of turning the bottles every few days to nudge the sediment into the neck of the bottle), and other topics. In spring the focus is on blending. ✉ *1400 Schramsberg Rd., off Hwy. 29, Calistoga* ☎ *707/942–4558, 800/877–3623* ⊕ *www.schramsberg.com* ⊠ *Tasting and tour $60* ⊙ *Tours at 10, 10:30, 11:30, 12:30, 1:30, and 2:30 by appointment.*

WORTH NOTING

Dutch Henry Winery. The casual style and lack of crowds at this pet-friendly winery make it a welcome change of pace from some of its overly serious neighbors. Towering oak barrels hold excellent Cabernet Sauvignon, Pinot Noir, Zinfandel, Syrah, and other single-varietal wines, along with a well-regarded Bordeaux blend called Argos. Dutch Henry also sells a Sauvignon Blanc and a charming Rosé. A current-release tasting will introduce you to these wines; you can also visit the wine caves on one of two tours that include tastings. ⊠ *4310 Silverado Trail, near Dutch Henry Canyon Rd., Calistoga* ☎ *707/942–5771* ⊕ *www.dutchhenry.com* ⊠ *Tasting $25, tours $35–$50* ⊙ *Daily 10–4:30, tours by appointment.*

Lava Vine Winery. The owners and staff of this jolly spot pride themselves on creating a family- and dog-friendly environment, and you're apt to hear rock, pop, and other tunes as you taste small-lot wines that include Cabernet Sauvignon, Chenin Blanc, Syrah, and Port. The wry Pete might even start playing the banjo. ■TIP→ **If they're available and you like mighty reds, be sure to taste the Suisun Valley Petite Sirah and the Knights Valley Reserve Cabernet.** ⊠ *965 Silverado Trail N, Calistoga* ☎ *707/942–9500* ⊕ *www.lavavine.com* ⊠ *Tasting $10* ⊙ *Daily 10–5.*

Tamber Bey Vineyards. Endurance riders Barry and Jennifer Waitte share their passion for horses and wine at their glam-rustic winery north of Calistoga. Their 22-acre Sundance Ranch remains a working equestrian facility, but the site has been revamped to include a state-of-the-art winery with separate fermenting tanks for grapes from Tamber Bey's vineyards in Yountville, Oakville, and elsewhere. The winemakers produce two Chardonnays and a Sauvignon Blanc, but the winery's stars are several subtly powerful reds, including the flagship Cabernet Sauvignon, a Merlot, and blends dominated by Cabernet Franc, Cabernet Sauvignon, and Petit Verdot. ■TIP→ **Appointments are required, but even on a few-minutes' notice they're generally easy to get.** ⊠ *1251 Tubbs La., at Myrtledale Rd., Calistoga* ☎ *707/942–2100* ⊕ *www.tamberbey.com* ⊠ *Tastings $25–$55, tour and tasting $45* ⊙ *Daily 10–5, by appointment only.*

WHERE TO EAT

$$$
ITALIAN
Fodor'sChoice
★

✕ **Hotel D'Amici.** Italian and Italian-American influences abound at this restaurant operated by the Pestoni family, owners of Rutherford Grove Winery. A wall painted by San Francisco muralist Brian Barneclo riffs off Federico's Fellini's film 8½; photos of Pestonis making Napa Valley wine (since 1892) are everywhere; and, perhaps most importantly, chef Joe Venezia is a protégé of the late cookbook author Marcella Hazan. Like Hazan, Venezia seeks out top-quality ingredients, strives for simplicity, and cooks sauces and his meals' other components long enough to permit the flavors to meld. He prepares all the classics, including gnocchi, spaghetti with seafood, and veal scaloppine, with finesse. Pestoni and other California vintages dominate the wine list, and there are Italian selections. $ *Average main: $24* ✉ *1440 Lincoln Ave., near Washington St., Calistoga* ☎ *707/942–1400* ⊕ *www.hoteldamici.com.*

$$$ ✗ **Jolē.** Local produce plays a starring role at this modern American res-
MODERN taurant, not surprising as chef Matt Spector is one of the area's biggest
AMERICAN proponents of farm-to-table dining. Depending on when you visit, you might enjoy roasted cauliflower served with almonds, dates, capers, and balsamic; kale stew with Tasso ham, kabocha squash, and fingerling potatoes; and molasses-glazed quail with farro risotto, roasted pumpkin, and a maple-bourbon demi-glace. The menu is available à la carte, and there are four-, five-, and six-course prix-fixe options. With about four dozen wines by the glass, it's easy to find something to pair with each course. There's also a full bar, with a happy hour daily from 4 pm to 6 pm. $ *Average main: $25* ✉ *Mount View Hotel, 1457 Lincoln Ave., near Fair Way, Calistoga* ☎ *707/942–9538* ⊕ *jolerestaurant.com* ⊘ *No lunch.*

$$$$ ✗ **Solbar.** Chef Brandon Sharp is known around the region for his subtle
MODERN and sophisticated take on Wine Country cooking. As befits a restau-
AMERICAN rant at a spa resort, the menu here is divided into "healthy, lighter
Fodor's Choice dishes" and "hearty cuisine." On the lighter side, the lemongrass-
★ poached petrale sole comes with jasmine rice and hearts of palm. On the heartier side you might find a rib-eye steak served with Kennebec potatoes, creamed spinach, and sauce bordelaise. The service at Solbar is uniformly excellent, and in good weather the patio is a festive spot for breakfast, lunch, or dinner. $ *Average main: $31* ✉ *Solage Calistoga, 755 Silverado Trail, at Rosedale Rd., Calistoga* ☎ *877/684–9146* ⊕ *www.solagecalistoga.com/solbar.*

WHERE TO STAY

$$$$ ⛺ **Calistoga Ranch.** Spacious cedar-shingle lodges throughout this posh,
RESORT wooded property have outdoor living areas, and even the restaurant,
Fodor's Choice spa, and reception space have outdoor seating and fireplaces. **Pros:**
★ almost half the lodges have private hot tubs on the deck; lovely hiking trails on the property; guests have reciprocal privileges at Auberge du Soleil and Solage Calistoga. **Cons:** innovative indoor-outdoor organization works better in fair weather than in rain or cold. $ *Rooms from: $720* ✉ *580 Lommel Rd., Calistoga* ☎ *707/254–2800, 800/942–4220* ⊕ *www.calistogaranch.com* ⏎ *50 guest lodges* ⦿❘ *No meals.*

$$ ⛺ **Indian Springs Resort and Spa.** Stylish Indian Springs—operating as
RESORT a spa since 1862—ably splits the difference between laid-back style and ultrachic touches. **Pros:** palm-studded grounds with outdoor seat-
ing areas; on-site restaurant; stylish for the price; enormous mineral pool; free touring bikes. **Cons:** lodge rooms are small; service could be more polished. $ *Rooms from: $259* ✉ *1712 Lincoln Ave., Calistoga* ☎ *707/942–4913* ⊕ *www.indianspringscalistoga.com* ⏎ *77 rooms, 18 suites, 18 cottages, 3 houses* ⦿❘ *No meals.*

$$ ⛺ **Luxe Calistoga.** Extravagant hospitality defines the Napa Valley's lux-
B&B/INN ury properties, but this inn takes the prize in the small-lodging category.
Fodor's Choice **Pros:** attentive owners; marvelous breakfasts; good restaurants, tasting
★ rooms, and shopping within walking distance. **Cons:** the hum (and sometimes scent) of street traffic is ever-present. $ *Rooms from: $269* ✉ *1139 Lincoln Ave., Calistoga* ☎ *707/942–9797* ⊕ *luxecalistoga.com* ⏎ *5 rooms* ⦿❘ *Breakfast.*

All it needs is a fair maiden: Castello di Amorosa's re-created castle.

$$ B&B/INN Fodor's Choice ★ 🏨 **Meadowlark Country House.** Two charming European gents run this laid-back but sophisticated inn on 20 wooded acres just north of downtown. **Pros:** charming innkeepers; tasty sit-down breakfasts; welcoming vibe that attracts diverse guests. **Cons:** clothing-optional pool policy isn't for everyone. [$] *Rooms from: $210* ✉ *601 Petrified Forest Rd., Calistoga* ☎ *707/942–5651, 800/942–5651* 🌐 *www.meadowlarkinn.com* 🛏 *5 rooms, 3 suites, 1 cottage, 1 guesthouse* 🍴 *Breakfast.*

$$$$ RESORT Fodor's Choice ★ 🏨 **Solage Calistoga.** The aesthetic at this 22-acre property is Napa Valley barn meets San Francisco loft, so the rooms have high ceilings, polished concrete floors, recycled walnut furniture, and all-natural fabrics in soothingly muted colors. **Pros:** great service; complimentary bikes; separate pools for kids and adults. **Cons:** the vibe may not suit everyone. [$] *Rooms from: $548* ✉ *755 Silverado Trail, Calistoga* ☎ *855/942–7442, 707/226–0800* 🌐 *www.solagecalistoga.com* 🛏 *83 rooms, 6 suites* 🍴 *No meals.*

SPAS

Fodor's Choice ★ **Spa Solage.** This eco-conscious spa has reinvented the traditional Calistoga mud and mineral water therapies. Case in point: the hour-long "Mudslide," a three-part treatment that includes a mud body mask (in a heated lounge), a soak in a thermal bath, and a power nap in a sound/vibration chair. The mud here is a mix of clay, volcanic ash, and essential oils. Traditional spa services—combination Shiatsu-Swedish and other massages, full-body exfoliations, facials, and waxes—are available, as are fitness and yoga classes. ✉ *755 Silverado Trail, at Rosedale Rd., Calistoga* ☎ *707/226–0825, 855/790–6023* 🌐 *www.solagecalistoga.com/spa* 🎫 *Treatments $98–$470* ⏲ *Daily 8–8.*

SPORTS AND THE OUTDOORS

Calistoga Bikeshop. Options here include regular and fancy bikes that rent for $18 an hour and up, and there's a self-guided Cool Wine Tour ($90) that includes tastings at three or four small wineries. ✉ *1318 Lincoln Ave., near Washington St., Calistoga* ☎ *707/942–9687* ⊕ *www. calistogabikeshop.net.*

THE SONOMA VALLEY

The birthplace of modern California wine making—Count Aragon Haraszthy opened Buena Vista Winery here in 1857—Sonoma Valley seduces with its unpretentious attitude and pastoral landscape. Tasting rooms, restaurants, and historical sites, among the latter the last mission established in California by Franciscan friars, abound near Sonoma Plaza. Beyond downtown Sonoma, the wineries and attractions are spread out along gently winding roads. Sonoma County's half of the Carneros District lies within Sonoma Valley, whose other towns of note include Glen Ellen and Kenwood. Sonoma Valley tasting rooms are often less crowded than those in Napa or northern Sonoma County, especially midweek, and the vibe here, though sophisticated, is definitely less sceney.

ESSENTIALS

Contact Sonoma Valley Visitors Bureau ☎ *707/996–1090, 866/996–1090* ⊕ *www.sonomavalley.com.*

SONOMA

14 miles west of Napa, 45 miles northeast of San Francisco.

One of the few towns in the valley with multiple attractions not related to food and wine, Sonoma has plenty to keep you busy for a couple of hours before you head out to tour the wineries. And you needn't leave town to taste wine. There are more than two dozen tasting rooms within steps of the plaza, some of which pour wines from more than one winery. The valley's cultural center, Sonoma, founded in 1835 when California was still part of Mexico, is built around a large, tree-filled plaza.

GETTING HERE AND AROUND

Highway 12 (signed as Broadway near Sonoma Plaza) heads north into Sonoma from Highway 121 and south from Santa Rosa into downtown Sonoma, where (signed as West Spain Street) it travels east to the plaza. Parking is relatively easy to find on or near the plaza, and you can walk to many restaurants, shops, and tasting rooms. Signs on East Spain Street and East Napa Street point the way to several wineries a mile or more east of the plaza.

EXPLORING

TOP ATTRACTIONS

Fodor's Choice ★   **Gundlach Bundschu.** Visitors may mispronounce this winery's name ("gun lock bun shoe" gets you close), but still they flock here to sample polished wines served by friendly pourers. Most of the winery's land has been in the Bundschu family since 1858. Cabernet Franc, Cabernet Sauvignon, Chardonnay, Merlot, and Tempranillo wines all are available in the standard $10 tasting. Add $10 to taste the signature Vintage Reserve red blend. For a more comprehensive experience, take the farm tour ($30), which ends with a cave tasting, or head into the vineyard ($50; available only between May and October). The Heritage Pairing ($75), involving gourmet bites and limited-release wines, takes place on weekends by appointment. ■TIP➔ On summer Fridays and weekends you can taste at vineyard-view tables outdoors. ⊠ *2000 Denmark St., at Bundschu Rd., off 8th St. E, Sonoma* 🕾 *707/938–5277* ⊕ *www. gunbun.com* 🖭 *Tastings $10–$25, tours $30–$50; food-wine pairing $75* ⊙ *June–mid-Oct., daily 11–5:30; mid-Oct.–May, daily 11–4:30; food-wine pairing weekends by appointment.*

Fodor's Choice
★

Patz & Hall. Sophisticated single-vineyard Chardonnays and Pinot Noirs are the trademark of this respected winery that relocated from Napa to Sonoma in 2014. It's a Wine Country adage that great wines are made in the vineyard—the all-star fields represented here include Hyde, Durell, and Gap's Crown—but winemaker James Hall routinely surpasses peers with access to the same fruit, proof that discernment and expertise (Hall is a master at oak aging) play a role, too. Seated tastings hosted by knowledgeable pourers take place in a fashionable single-story residence 3 miles southeast of Sonoma Plaza. You can taste at the bar and on some days on the vineyard-view terrace beyond it, but to learn how food friendly these wines are, consider the Salon Tasting, at which they're paired with gourmet bites crafted with equal finesse. ⊠ *21200 8th St. E, near Peru Rd., Sonoma* 🕾 *707/265–7700* ⊕ *www.patzhall. com* 🖭 *Tastings $25–$75* ⊙ *Thurs.–Mon. 10–4, by appointment.*

Fodor's Choice
★

Ram's Gate Winery. Stunning views, ultrachic architecture, and wines made from grapes grown by acclaimed producers make a visit to Ram's Gate an event. The welcoming interior spaces—think Restoration Hardware with a dash of high-style whimsy—open up to the entire western Carneros. During fine weather you'll experience (in comfort) the cooling breezes that sweep through the area while sipping sophisticated wines, mostly Pinot Noirs and Chardonnays, but also Sauvignon Blanc, Cabernet Sauvignon, Syrah, late-harvest Zinfandel, and even a sparkler. With grapes sourced from the Sangiacomo, Hudson, and other illustrious vineyards, winemaker Jeff Gaffner focuses on creating balanced vintages that express what occurred in nature that year. One food-wine pairing ($60) includes tapas, wine tasting, and a winery tour; the other ($125; Thursday and Friday only) focuses on food and wine education. ⊠ *28700 Arnold Dr./Hwy. 121, Sonoma* 🕾 *707/721–8700* ⊕ *www.ramsgatewinery.com* 🖭 *Tasting $20–$125* ⊙ *Thurs.–Mon. 10–6 by appointment.*

20

Fodor's Choice
★

Scribe. Andrew and Adam Mariani, sons of California walnut growers, established Scribe in 2007 on land first planted to grapes in 1858 by Emil Dresel, a German immigrant. Dresel's claims to fame include cultivating Sonoma's first Riesling and Sylvaner, an achievement the brothers honor by growing both these varietals on land he once farmed. Using natural wine-making techniques they craft bright, terroir-driven wines from those grapes, along with Chardonnay, Pinot Noir, Syrah, and Cabernet Sauvignon. Tastings take place at weathered picnic tables on an oak-shaded knoll overlooking some of Scribe's vineyards. A 1915 Mission Revival–style hacienda nearby is being restored for use as a

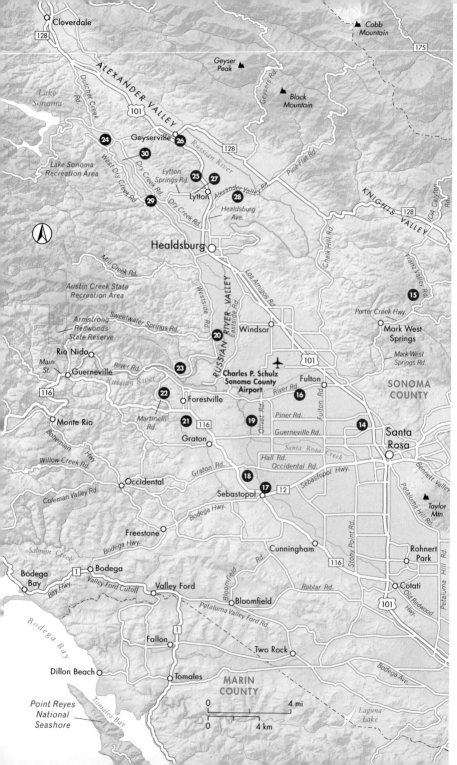

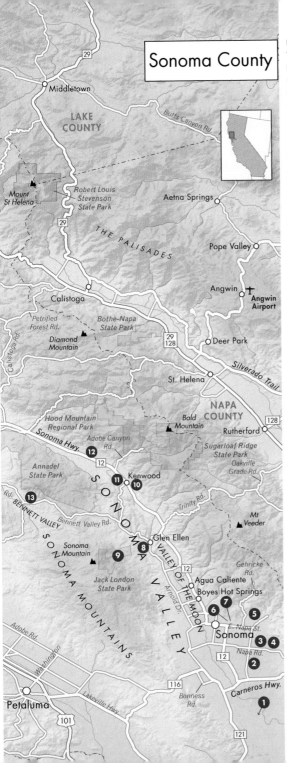

Sonoma County

tasting space. During Prohibition it served as a hideout for bootleggers, and its basement harbored a speakeasy, two of many intriguing tales associated with this historic property. ✉ *2100 Denmark St., off Napa Rd., Sonoma* ☎ *707/939–1858* ⊕ *scribewinery.com* ✉ *Tasting price varies; contact winery* ⊗ *Daily by appointment.*

Sonoma Mission. The northernmost of the 21 missions established by Franciscan friars in California, Sonoma Mission was founded in 1823 as Mission San Francisco Solano. It serves as the centerpiece of **Sonoma State Historic Park,** which includes several other sites in Sonoma and nearby Petaluma. Some early mission structures were destroyed, but all or part of several remaining buildings date to the days of Mexican rule over California. These include the **Sonoma Barracks,** a half block west of the mission at 20 East Spain Street, which housed troops under the command of General Mariano Guadalupe Vallejo, who controlled vast tracks of land in the region. The modest museum contains displays about the missions and information about the other historic sites. ✉ *114 E. Spain St., at 1st St. E, Sonoma* ☎ *707/938–9560* ⊕ *www.parks.ca.gov/?page_id=479* ✉ *$3, includes same-day admission to other historic sites* ⊗ *Daily 10–5.*

Fodor's Choice
★

Walt Wines. You could spend a full day sampling wines in the tasting rooms bordering Sonoma Plaza, but one not to miss is Walt, which specializes in Pinot Noir and makes two Chardonnays. Fruit-forward yet subtle, the Pinots win over even the purists who pine for the genre's days of lighter, more perfumey vintages. Some of the Pinots come from Sonoma County grapes but others are from ones grown in Mendocino County (just north of Sonoma County), California's Central Coast, and Oregon's Willamette Valley. Critics routinely bestow high ratings on all these wines. ✉ *380 1st St. W, at W. Spain St., Sonoma* ☎ *707/933–4440* ⊕ *www.waltwines.com* ✉ *Tastings $20* ⊗ *Daily 11–6.*

WORTH NOTING

Buena Vista Winery. The site where modern California wine making got its start has been transformed into an entertaining homage to the accomplishments of the 19th-century wine pioneer Count Agoston Haraszthy. Tours pass through the original aging caves dug deep into the hillside by Chinese laborers, and banners, photos, and artifacts inside and out convey the history made on this site. Reserve tastings ($40) include library and current wines, plus ones still aging in barrels. The stylish former press house (used for pressing grapes into wine), which dates to 1862, hosts the standard tastings. ■TIP➔ **Chardonnays and Pinot Noirs from Los Carneros AVA are this winery's strong suits.** ✉ *18000 Old Winery Rd., off E. Napa St., Sonoma* ☎ *800/926–1266* ⊕ *www.buenavistawinery.com* ✉ *Tastings $15–$40; tours $10–$35* ⊗ *Daily 10–5; tours by appointment.*

WHERE TO EAT

$$$
AMERICAN
Fodor's Choice
★

✕ **Cafe La Haye.** In a postage-stamp-size open kitchen, the skillful chef turns out main courses that star on a small but worthwhile seasonal menu emphasizing local ingredients. Chicken, beef, pasta, and fish get deluxe treatment without fuss or fanfare—the daily roasted chicken and the risotto specials are always good. Butterscotch pudding is a homey signature dessert. The dining room is compact, but the friendly owner, always there to greet diners, maintains a particularly welcoming vibe. [$] *Average main: $24* ✉ *140 E. Napa St., at 1st St. E, Sonoma* ☎ *707/935–5994* 🌐 *www.cafelahaye.com* 🕒 *Closed Sun. and Mon. No lunch.*

$$$ MODERN AMERICAN Fodor's Choice ★ 🍴 **El Dorado Kitchen.** The visual delights at this winning restaurant include its clean lines and handsome decor, but the eye inevitably drifts westward to the open kitchen, where chef Armando Navarro and his diligent crew craft flavorful dishes full of subtle surprises. Focusing on locally sourced ingredients, the menu might include bomba-rice paella awash with seafood and linguica sausage, or duck confit accompanied by farro salad, kale, mushrooms, and almonds. Even a simple dish like truffle-oil fries, liberally sprinkled with Parmesan, charms with its combination of tastes and textures. The noteworthy desserts include profiteroles with toasted marshmallow and chocolate ganache, and cornbread French toast with strawberries and buttermilk sherbet. [$] *Average main: $26* ✉ *El Dorado Hotel, 405 1st St. W, at W. Spain St., Sonoma* ☎ *707/996–3030* 🌐 *www.eldoradosonoma.com/restaurant.*

$$$ AMERICAN Fodor's Choice ★ 🍴 **Harvest Moon Cafe.** It's easy to feel like one of the family at this little restaurant with an odd, zigzagging layout. Diners seated at one of the two tiny bars chat with the servers like old friends, but the husband-and-wife team in the kitchen is serious about the food, much of which relies on local produce. The ever-changing menu might include homey dishes such as grilled pork loin with crispy polenta and artichokes, Niman Ranch rib-eye steak with a tomatillo salsa and Zinfandel reduction, or pan-seared Hawaiian Ono with jasmine rice, and eggplant. Everything is so perfectly executed and the vibe is so genuinely warm that a visit here is deeply satisfying. ■ **TIP→ A spacious back patio with tables arranged around a fountain more than doubles the seating; a heated tent keeps this area warm in winter.** [$] *Average main: $25* ✉ *487 1st St. W, at W. Napa St., Sonoma* ☎ *707/933–8160* 🌐 *www.harvestmooncafesonoma.com* 🕒 *Closed Tues. No lunch.*

$$$ PORTUGUESE 🍴 **LaSalette.** Born in the Azores and raised in Sonoma, chef-owner Manuel Azevedo serves dishes inspired by his native Portugal in this warmly decorated spot. The best seats are on a patio along an alleyway off Sonoma Plaza. Boldly flavored dishes such as pork tenderloin *recheado*, stuffed with olives and almonds and topped with a Port sauce, might be followed by a dish of rice pudding with Madeira-braised figs or a Port from the varied list. ■ **TIP→ The daily seafood specials are well worth a try, especially the whole fish.** [$] *Average main: $24* ✉ *452 1st St. E, near E. Spain St., Sonoma* ☎ *707/938–1927* 🌐 *www.lasalette-restaurant.com.*

20

$$$$ MODERN AMERICAN 🍴 **Oso.** Owner-chef David Bush, who achieved national recognition for his food and wine pairings at St. Francis Winery, struck out on his own in late 2014, opening this restaurant whose name, Spanish for "bear," acknowledges the nearby spot where rebels raised a flag depicting a bear and declared California's independence from Mexico. Bush serves tapas-size dishes à la carte and prepares a five-course tasting menu with optional wine pairings. An early menu included pickled shrimp with a red cabbage, kale, and peanut slaw à la carte and Syrah-braised short ribs for the tasting. Oso's contemporary barlike space's design incorporates materials reclaimed from previous incarnations of its building, erected in the 1890s as a livery stable. ■ **TIP→ Reservations are required for the tasting**

but aren't accepted otherwise. $ *Average main: $32* ✉ *9 E. Napa St., at Broadway, Sonoma* ☎ *707/931–6926* ⊕ *ososonoma.com* ⊘ *No lunch.*

$$$$
AMERICAN
Fodor'sChoice
★

✕ **Santé.** This elegant dining room has evolved into a destination restaurant through its focus on seasonal and locally sourced ingredients. The room is understated, with dark walls and soft lighting, but the food is anything but. Dishes such as the Sonoma Liberty duck breast and confit leg, served with pearl barley "risotto," sweet carrot puree, and maple duck jus, are sophisticated without being fussy. Others, like the sampler of Niman Ranch beef that includes a petite filet mignon, a skirt steak, and braised pavé beef à la bourguignonne, are pure decadence. The restaurant offers a seasonal tasting menu ($149). $ *Average main: $43* ✉ *Fairmont Sonoma Mission Inn & Spa, 100 Boyes Blvd./Hwy. 12, 2½ miles north of Sonoma Plaza, Boyes Hot Springs* ☎ *707/938–9000* ⊕ *www.santediningroom.com* ⊘ *No lunch.*

$
AMERICAN

✕ **Sunflower Caffé.** The food at this casual eatery, mostly salads and sandwiches, is simple but satisfying. Highlights include the smoked duck breast sandwich, served on a baguette and slathered with caramelized onions. A meal of soup and local cheeses is a good option if you just want to nibble. Both the pretty patio, which is in the back, and the sidewalk seating area facing Sonoma Plaza are equipped with heating lamps and get plenty of shade, so they're comfortable in all but the most inclement weather. Cheerful artworks brighten up the interior, where locals hunker over their computers and take advantage of the free Wi-Fi. Omelets and waffles are the stars at breakfast. $ *Average main: $13* ✉ *421 1st St. W, at W. Spain St., Sonoma* ☎ *707/996–6645* ⊕ *www.sonomasunflower.com* ⊘ *No dinner.*

WHERE TO STAY

$$
B&B/INN

⛫ **Inn at Sonoma.** They don't skimp on the little luxuries here: wine and cheese is served every evening in the lobby, and the cheerfully painted rooms are warmed by gas fireplaces. **Pros:** last-minute specials are a great deal; free soda available in the lobby; free Wi-Fi. **Cons:** on a busy street rather than right on the plaza. $ *Rooms from: $220* ✉ *630 Broadway, Sonoma* ☎ *707/939–1340, 888/568–9818* ⊕ *www.innatsonoma.com* ⥁ *27 rooms* ⦿ *Breakfast.*

$$$$
HOTEL
Fodor'sChoice
★

⛫ **MacArthur Place Hotel & Spa.** Guests at this 7-acre boutique property five blocks south of Sonoma Plaza bask in ritzy seclusion in plush accommodations set amid landscaped gardens. **Pros:** secluded garden setting; high-style furnishings; on-site steak house. **Cons:** a bit of a walk from the plaza; some traffic noise audible in street-side rooms. $ *Rooms from: $425* ✉ *29 E. MacArthur St., Sonoma* ☎ *707/938–2929, 800/722–1866* ⊕ *www.macarthurplace.com* ⥁ *62 rooms, 2 cottage suites* ⦿ *Breakfast.*

$
B&B/INN
FAMILY

⛫ **Sonoma Creek Inn.** The small but cheerful rooms at this motel-style inn are individually decorated with painted wooden armoires, cozy quilts, and brightly colored contemporary artwork. **Pros:** clean, well-lighted bathrooms; lots of charm for the price; popular with bicyclists. **Cons:** office not staffed 24 hours a day; a 10-minute drive from Sonoma Plaza. $ *Rooms from: $145* ✉ *239 Boyes Blvd., off Hwy. 12, Sonoma* ☎ *707/939–9463, 888/712–1289* ⊕ *www.sonomacreekinn.com* ⥁ *16 rooms* ⦿ *No meals.*

SPAS

Willow Stream Spa at Fairmont Sonoma Mission Inn & Spa. With 40,000 square feet and 30 treatment rooms, the Wine Country's largest spa provides every amenity you could possibly want, including pools and hot tubs fed by local thermal springs. Although the place bustles with patrons in summer and on some weekends, the vibe is always soothing. The signature bathing ritual includes an exfoliating shower, dips in two mineral-water soaking pools, an herbal steam, a dry sauna, and cool-down showers. Other popular treatments include the warm ginger-oil float, which involves relaxation in a weightless environment, and the perennially popular caviar facial. The most requested room among couples is outfitted with a two-person copper bathtub. ⊠ *100 Boyes Blvd./Hwy. 12, 2½ miles north of Sonoma Plaza, Boyes Hot Springs* ☎ *707/938–9000* ⊕ *www.fairmont.com/sonoma/willow-stream* ⊠ *Treatments $65–$485.*

SHOPPING

Sonoma Plaza is a shopping magnet, with tempting boutiques and specialty food purveyors facing the square or within a block or two.

FodorśChoice ★ **Chateau Sonoma.** The fancy furniture, lighting fixtures, and objets d'art at this upscale shop make it a dangerous place to enter: after just a few minutes you may find yourself reconsidering your entire home's aesthetic. The owner's keen eye for style and sense of whimsy make a visit here a delight. ⊠ *153 W. Napa St., near 2nd St. W, Sonoma* ☎ *707/935–8553* ⊕ *www.chateausonoma.com.*

FodorśChoice ★ **Sonoma Valley Certified Farmers Market.** To discover just how bountiful the Sonoma landscape is—and how talented its farmers and food artisans are—head to Depot Park, just north of the Sonoma Plaza, on Friday morning. From April through October, the market gets extra play on Tuesday evening in Sonoma Plaza. ⊠ *Depot Park, 1st St. W, at Sonoma Bike Path, Sonoma* ☎ *707/538–7023* ⊕ *www.svcfm.org.*

GLEN ELLEN

7 miles north of Sonoma.

Unlike its flashier Napa Valley counterparts, Glen Ellen eschews well-groomed sidewalks lined with upscale boutiques and restaurants, preferring instead its crooked streets, some with no sidewalks at all, shaded with stands of old oak trees. Jack London, who represents Glen Ellen's rugged spirit, lived in the area for many years; the town commemorates him with place names and nostalgic establishments. Hidden among sometimes-ramshackle buildings abutting Sonoma and Calabasas creeks are low-key shops and galleries worth poking through, and several fine dining establishments.

20

GETTING HERE AND AROUND

Glen Ellen sits just off Highway 12. From the north or south, take Arnold Drive west and follow it south less than a mile. The walkable downtown straddles a half-mile stretch of Arnold Drive.

EXPLORING

Fodor's Choice ★ **Benziger Family Winery.** One of the best-known Sonoma County wineries sits on a sprawling estate in a bowl with 360-degree sun exposure, the benefits of which are explored on popular tram tours that depart several times daily. Guides explain Benziger's biodynamic farming practices and give you a glimpse of the extensive cave system. The regular tram tour costs $25; another tour costing $50 concludes with a seated tasting. Noted for its Chardonnay, Cabernet Sauvignon, Merlot, Pinot Noir, and Sauvignon Blanc wines, the winery is a beautiful spot for a picnic. **■ TIP→ Reserve a seat on the tram tour through the winery's website or arrive early in the day on summer weekends and during harvest season.** ✉ *1883 London Ranch Rd., off Arnold Dr., Glen Ellen* ☎ *707/935–3000, 888/490–2739* 🌐 *www.benziger.com* 🎟 *Tastings $15–$40, tours $25–$50* 🕒 *Daily 10–5; tours daily 11–3:30 except noon on the ½ hr (reservation recommended).*

Fodor's Choice ★ **Jack London State Historic Park.** The pleasures are both pastoral and intellectual at the late writer Jack London's beloved Beauty Ranch. You could easily spend the afternoon hiking the 20-plus miles of trails that loop through meadows and stands of oaks, redwoods, and other trees. Manuscripts and personal artifacts depicting London's travels are on view at the House of Happy Walls Museum, which provides a tantalizing overview of the author's life and literary passions. A short hike away lie the ruins of Wolf House, which mysteriously burned down just before the writer was to move in. Also open to the public are a few farm outbuildings and the completely restored Cottage, a wood-framed building where London penned many of his later works. He's buried on the property. ✉ *2400 London Ranch Rd., off Arnold Dr., Glen Ellen* ☎ *707/938–5216* 🌐 *www.jacklondonpark.com* 🎟 *Parking $10 ($5 walk-in or bike), includes admission to museum; cottage $4* 🕒 *Mar.–Nov., park daily 9:30–5, museum 10–5, cottage noon–4; Dec.–Feb., Thurs.–Mon. park 9:30–5, museum 10–5, cottage noon–4.*

WHERE TO EAT

$$ ITALIAN Fodor's Choice ★ 🍴 **Aventine Glen Ellen.** A Wine Country cousin to chef Adolfo Veronese's same-named San Francisco and Hollywood establishments, this Italian restaurant occupies an 1839 sawmill from California's Mexican period. Evidence of the building's early lives—in 1856 it was converted into a gristmill—can be seen in the old-redwood walls and exposed ceiling beams. Veronese's varied menu includes a half dozen pizzas (the seasonal one with black truffle honey, béchamel, and wild arugula is a savory masterpiece), an equal number of pasta dishes, a risotto of the day, and several meat and fish entrées. All are deftly constructed, and the chicken parmigiana has aroused envy among local Sicilian grandmothers. **■ TIP→ In good weather you can dine on a patio that overlooks Sonoma Creek, which powered the mill in days of yore.** [$] *Average main: $19* ✉ *Jack London Village, 14301 Arnold Dr., ¾ mile south of downtown, Glen Ellen* ☎ *707/934–8911* 🌐 *www.aventineglenellen.com* 🕒 *Closed Mon. No lunch.*

$$ FRENCH 🍴 **The Fig Cafe.** The compact menu at this cheerful bistro, a Glen Ellen fixture, focuses on California and French comfort food—pot roast and duck confit, for instance, as well as thin-crust pizza. Steamed mussels

Horseback riding tours loop around Jack London State Historic Park.

are served with terrific crispy fries, which also accompany the sirloin burger. Weekend brunch brings out locals and tourists for French toast, pizza with applewood-smoked bacon and poached eggs, corned-beef hash, and other delights. **■ TIP→ The unusual no-corkage-fee policy makes this a great place to drink the wine you discovered down the road.** [$] *Average main: $18* ✉ *13690 Arnold Dr., at O'Donnell La., Glen Ellen* ☎ *707/938–2130* 🌐 *www.thefigcafe.com* ✍ *Reservations not accepted* ⏲ *No lunch weekdays.*

$$ ECLECTIC Fodor's Choice ★

🍴 **Glen Ellen Star.** Chef Ari Weiswasser honed his craft at The French Laundry, Daniel, and other bastions of culinary finesse, but the goal at his Wine Country boîte is haute-rustic cuisine, much of which emerges from a wood-fired oven that burns a steady 600°F. Pizzas such as the crisp-crusted, richly sauced Margherita thrive in the torrid heat, as do root and other vegetables roasted in small iron skillets. Ditto for entrées that include juicy, tender roasted whole fish. Weiswasser signs each dish with a sauce, emulsion, or sly blend of spices that jazzes things up without upstaging the primary ingredient. The restaurant's decor is equally restrained, with an open-beam ceiling, exposed hardwood floors, and utilitarian seating. **■ TIP→ Many regulars perch on a stool at the kitchen-view counter to watch the chefs at work.** [$] *Average main: $22* ✉ *13648 Arnold Dr., at Warm Springs Rd., Glen Ellen* ☎ *707/343–1384* 🌐 *glenellenstar.com* ✍ *Reservations essential* ⏲ *No lunch.*

WHERE TO STAY

$$ B&B/INN Fodor's Choice ★

🏨 **Gaige House.** Asian objets d'art and leather club chairs cozied up to the lobby fireplace are just a few of the graceful touches in this luxurious but understated bed-and-breakfast. **Pros:** beautiful lounge areas; lots of privacy; excellent service; full breakfasts, afternoon wine and

Hitching a ride on the Benziger Family Winery tram tour

appetizers. **Cons:** sound carries in the main house; the least expensive rooms are on the small side. [$] *Rooms from: $275* ✉ *13540 Arnold Dr., Glen Ellen* ☎ *707/935–0237, 800/935–0237* 🌐 *www.gaige.com* 🛏 *10 rooms, 13 suites* 🍴 *Breakfast.*

$$ B&B/INN Fodor's Choice ★ 🏨 **Olea Hotel.** The husband-and-wife team of Ashish and Sia Patel operate this boutique lodging that's at once sophisticated and down-home country casual. **Pros:** beautiful style; welcoming staff; chef-prepared breakfasts; complimentary wine throughout stay. **Cons:** fills up quickly on weekends; minor road noise in some rooms. [$] *Rooms from: $288* ✉ *5131 Warm Springs Rd., west off Arnold Dr., Glen Ellen* ☎ *707/996–5131* 🌐 *www.oleahotel.com* 🛏 *10 rooms, 2 cottages* 🍴 *Breakfast.*

KENWOOD

3 miles north of Glen Ellen.

Tiny Kenwood consists of little more than a few restaurants and shops and a historic train depot. But hidden in this pretty landscape of meadows and woods at the north end of Sonoma Valley are several good wineries, most just off the Sonoma Highway (Highway 12).

GETTING HERE AND AROUND

To get to Kenwood from Glen Ellen, drive north on Highway 12.

EXPLORING

B Wise Vineyards Cellar. Although the stylish roadside tasting room of this producer of small-lot red wines sits on the valley floor in Kenwood, B Wise's winery and vineyards, 8½ miles to the southeast, occupy a prime spot high in the new Moon Mountain appellation. Owner-winemaker

Brion Wise made his name crafting big, bold Cabernets. One comes from Wise's mountain estate and another from the nearby Monte Rosso Vineyard, some of whose Cabernet vines are among California's oldest. These hearty mountain-fruit Cabs contrast pleasingly with a suppler one from the Napa Valley's Coombsville AVA. Wise also makes estate Syrah, Petite Sirah, Petit Verdot, and Zinfandel wines, along with Sonoma Coast and Willamette Valley (Oregon) Pinot Noirs and several red blends. ✉ 9077 *Sonoma Hwy., at Shaw Ave., Kenwood* ☎ 707/282–9169 ⊕ *www.bwisevineyards.com* 🍷 *Tastings $15–$25* ⊙ *Daily 10:30–5:30.*

Kunde Estate Winery & Vineyards. On your way into Kunde you pass a terrace flanked by fountains, virtually coaxing you to stay for a picnic with views over the vineyard. Best known for its toasty Chardonnays, the winery also makes well-regarded Sauvignon Blanc, Cabernet Sauvignon, Merlot, and Zinfandel wines. Among the Destination wines available only through the winery, the Dunfillan Cuvée, a blend of Cabernet and Syrah grapes, is worth checking out. The free basic tour of the grounds includes the caves, some of which stretch 175 feet below a vineyard. ■ TIP➔ Reserve ahead for the Mountain Top Tasting, a popular tour that ends with a sampling of reserve wines ($40). ✉ 9825 *Sonoma Hwy./ Hwy. 12, Kenwood* ☎ 707/833–5501 ⊕ *www.kunde.com* 🍷 *Tastings $10–$40, tours free–$50* ⊙ *Daily 10:30–5, tours daily at various times.*

St. Francis Winery. Nestled at the foot of Mt. Hood, St. Francis has earned national acclaim for its food-and-wine pairings. With its red-tile roof and dramatic bell tower, the winery's California Mission–style visitor center occupies one of Sonoma's most scenic locations. The charm of the surroundings is matched by the wines, most of them red, including rich, earthy Zinfandels from the Dry Creek, Russian River, and Sonoma valleys. Chef Bryan Jones's five-course small bites and wine pairings ($50)—Liberty duck breast cassoulet with one of the Zins, for example—are offered from Thursday through Monday; pairings with cheeses and charcuterie ($30) are available daily. ✉ 100 *Pythian Rd., off Hwy. 12, Kenwood* ☎ 888/675–9463, 707/833–6146 ⊕ *www.stfranciswinery. com* 🍷 *Tastings $10–$50* ⊙ *Daily 10–5; tour Fri.–Sun at 11:30.*

WHERE TO EAT AND STAY

$

ITALIAN

✕ **Café Citti.** Classical music in the background, a friendly staff, and a roaring fire when it's cold outside keep this roadside café from feeling too spartan. Order dishes such as roast chicken and slabs of tiramisu from the counter and they're delivered to your table, indoors or on an outdoor patio. The array of prepared salads and sandwiches means the café does a brisk business in takeout for picnic packers, but you can also choose pasta made to order. 💲 *Average main: $13* ✉ 9049 *Sonoma Hwy./Hwy. 12, Kenwood* ☎ 707/833–2690 ⊕ *www.cafecitti. com* 🍴 *Reservations not accepted.*

$$$$

B&B/INN

Fodor's Choice

★

Kenwood Inn and Spa. Fluffy featherbeds, wood-burning fireplaces, and French doors opening onto terraces or balconies give the uncommonly spacious guest rooms at this inn a particularly romantic air. **Pros:** large rooms; lavish furnishings; excellent restaurant; rich full breakfast; romantic. **Cons:** road or lobby noise in some rooms; expensive. 💲 *Rooms from: $495* ✉ 10400 *Sonoma Hwy./Hwy. 12, Kenwood*

20

☎ 707/833–1293, 800/353–6966 ⊕ www.kenwoodinn.com ⤳ 25
rooms, 4 suites ⦿ Breakfast.

ELSEWHERE IN SONOMA COUNTY

Sonoma County's northern and western reaches are a study in contrasts.
Trendy hotels, restaurants, shops, and tasting rooms have transformed
Healdsburg into a hot spot. Within a few miles, though, chic yields to
bucolic, with only the occasional horse ranch, apple or peach orchard,
or stand of oaks interrupting the rolling vineyard hills. The Russian
River Valley is the grape-growing star, but Dry Creek and Alexander
valleys and the Sonoma Coast also merit investigation. Office parks and
tract housing diminish Santa Rosa's appeal, but wineries and cultural
attractions, along with solid budget lodgings, can be found within its
borders.

ESSENTIALS

Contacts Sonoma County Tourism Bureau ⊠ 3637 Westwind Blvd., Santa
Rosa ☎ 707/522–5800, 800/576–6662 ⊕ www.sonomacounty.com.

SANTA ROSA

8 miles northwest of Kenwood, 55 miles north of San Francisco.

With more than 170,000 people, Santa Rosa, the Wine Country's largest city, isn't likely to charm you with its malls, office buildings, and
frequent traffic snarls. Its moderately priced lodgings, however, can
come in handy, especially since Santa Rosa is roughly equidistant from
Sonoma, Healdsburg, and notable Russian River wineries.

The location of Santa Rosa's former Northwestern Pacific Railroad
depot—built in 1903 by Italian stonemasons and immortalized in Alfred
Hitchcock's coolly sinister 1943 film Shadow of a Doubt—provides the
name for the revitalized Railroad Square Historic District west of U.S.
101. The depot is now a visitor center, and 4th Street between Wilson
and Davis streets contains restaurants, bar, and antiques and thrift
shops worth checking out, as do nearby lanes.

GETTING HERE AND AROUND

Santa Rosa straddles U.S. 101, the route to take (north) from San
Francisco. From the Sonoma Valley, take Highway 12 north. Sonoma
County Transit buses serve the city and surrounding area.

VISITOR INFORMATION

Contacts Visit Santa Rosa ⊠ 9 4th St., at Wilson St., Santa Rosa, California,
United States ☎ 800/404–7673 ⊕ www.visitsantarosa.com.

EXPLORING

TOP ATTRACTIONS

Fodor's Choice **Martinelli Winery.** In a century-old hop barn with the telltale triple tow-
★ ers, Martinelli has the feel of a traditional country store, but the sophisticated wines made here are anything but old-fashioned. The winery's
reputation rests on its complex Pinot Noirs, Syrahs, and Zinfandels,
including the $125-a-bottle Jackass Hill Vineyard Zin, made with

grapes from 130-year-old vines. You can sip these acclaimed wines—going back a decade or more—during a private Library Tasting ($50). A standard tasting ($10) focuses on current releases, a Chardonnay, three reds, and a Muscat that tastes like honeysuckle. Winemaker Helen Turley set the Martinelli style—fruit forward, easy on the oak, reined-in tannins—in the 1990s. The current winemaker Bryan Kvamme, a Turley protégé, continues the tradition. ✉ *3360 River Rd., east of Olivet Rd., Windsor* ☎ *707/525–0570, 800/346–1627* ⊕ *www.martinelliwinery. com* 🍷 *Tastings $10–$50* ⊙ *Daily 10–5; library tasting and wine-cheese pairing by appointment only with 48-hr notice.*

Fodor's Choice
★

Matanzas Creek Winery. The visitor center at Matanzas Creek sets itself apart with an understated Japanese aesthetic, extending to a tranquil fountain, a koi pond, and a vast field of lavender. The winery makes Sauvignon Blanc, Chardonnay, Merlot, and Pinot Noir wines under the Matanzas Creek name and three equally well-regarded wines—a Bordeaux red blend, a Chardonnay, and a Sauvignon Blanc—with the Journey label. All tours take in the beautiful estate and include tastings. The Signature tour concludes with tastings of limited-production and library wines paired with artisanal cheeses. ■ TIP→ **An ideal time to visit is in May and June, when lavender perfumes the air.** ✉ *6097 Bennett Valley Rd., Santa Rosa* ☎ *707/528–6464, 800/590–6464* ⊕ *www. matanzascreek.com* 🍷 *Tastings $10–$25, tours $10–$35* ⊙ *Daily 10–4:30; estate tour ($10) daily at 10:30, others by appointment at least 48 hrs in advance.*

FAMILY **Safari West.** An unexpected bit of wilderness in the Wine Country, this African wildlife preserve covers 400 acres. A visit begins with a stroll around enclosures housing lemurs, cheetahs, giraffes, and rare birds such as the brightly colored scarlet ibis. Next, climb with your guide onto open-air vehicles that spend about two hours combing the expansive property, where more than 80 species—including gazelles, cape buffalo, antelope, wildebeests, and zebras—inhabit the hillsides. If you'd like to extend your stay, lodging in well-equipped tent cabins is available. ✉ *3115 Porter Creek Rd., off Mark West Springs Rd., Santa Rosa* ☎ *707/579–2551, 800/616–2695* ⊕ *www.safariwest.com* 🍷 *$70–$95 ($32–$35 ages 3–12)* ⊙ *Safaris mid-Mar.–early Sept., 9, 10, 1, 2, and 4; hrs vary rest of yr.*

WORTH NOTING

FAMILY **Charles M. Schulz Museum.** Fans of Snoopy and Charlie Brown will love this museum dedicated to the late Charles M. Schulz, who lived his last three decades in Santa Rosa. Permanent installations include a re-creation of the cartoonist's studio, and temporary exhibits often focus on a particular theme in his work. ■ TIP→ **Children and adults can take a stab at creating cartoons in the Education Room.** ✉ *2301 Hardies La., at W. Steele La., Santa Rosa* ☎ *707/579–4452* ⊕ *www.schulzmuseum. org* 🍷 *$10* ⊙ *Labor Day–Memorial Day, Mon. and Wed.–Fri. 11–5, weekends 10–5; Memorial Day–Labor Day, weekdays 11–5, weekends 10–5.*

DeLoach Vineyards. Best known for its Russian River Valley Pinot Noirs, DeLoach also produces Chardonnays, old-vine Zinfandels, and a few

20

other wines. Some of the reds are made using open-top wood fermentation vats that have been used in France for centuries to intensify a wine's flavor. Tours focus on these and other wine-making techniques and include a stroll through organic gardens and vineyards. You can also take wine-blending a seminar, compare California and French Chardonnays and Pinot Noirs, or (on weekends only) relax with a wood-fired pizza and a glass of wine. **■ TIP→ The sparklers and still wines of the JCB label, whose letters match the initials of its dapper creator, DeLoach's Burgundy-born owner, Jean-Charles Boisset, are poured in a separate tasting room.** ✉ *1791 Olivet Rd., off Guerneville Rd., Santa Rosa* ☎ *707/526–9111* 🌐 *www.deloachvineyards.com* 🎟 *Tastings $15–$100, tour $20* 🕒 *Daily 10–5, tour daily at noon.*

WHERE TO EAT AND STAY

$$$ ECLECTIC Fodor's Choice ★

🍴 **Willi's Wine Bar.** Don't let the name fool you: instead of a sedate spot serving wine and delicate nibbles, you'll find a cozy warren of rooms where boisterous crowds snap up small plates from the globe-trotting menu. Dishes such as the pork-belly pot stickers represent Asia, and duck prosciutto and Moroccan-style lamb chops are two of the Mediterranean-inspired foods. Several cheese and charcuterie plates are among the many using California-sourced ingredients. Wines are available in 2-ounce pours, making it easier to pair each of your little plates with a different glass. **■ TIP→ It can get noisy inside on busy nights, so consider a table on the covered patio.** [$] *Average main: $28* ✉ *4404 Old Redwood Hwy., at Ursuline Rd., Santa Rosa* ☎ *707/526–3096* 🌐 *williswinebar.net* 🕒 *No lunch Sun. and Mon.*

$$ HOTEL Fodor's Choice ★

🏨 **Vintners Inn.** The owners of Ferrari-Carano Vineyards operate this oasis set amid 92 acres of vineyards that's known for its comfortable lodgings. **Pros:** spacious rooms with comfortable beds; jogging path through the vineyards; online deals pop up year-round. **Cons:** occasional noise from adjacent events center. [$] *Rooms from: $265* ✉ *4350 Barnes Rd., Santa Rosa* ☎ *707/575–7350, 800/421–2584* 🌐 *www.vintnersinn.com* 🛏 *38 rooms, 6 suites* 🍽 *No meals.*

RUSSIAN RIVER VALLEY

10 miles northwest of Santa Rosa.

The Russian River flows from Mendocino to the Pacific, but Russian River Valley wine making centers on a triangle with points at Healdsburg, Guerneville, and Sebastopol. Tall redwoods shade the two-lane roads of this scenic area, where, thanks to the cooling marine influence, Pinot Noir and Chardonnay are the king and queen of grapes.

GETTING HERE AND AROUND

Many Russian River Valley visitors base themselves in Healdsburg. You can find noteworthy purveyors of Pinots and Chards by heading west from downtown on Mill Street, which eventually becomes Westside Road. For Forestville and Sebastopol wineries, continue south and west along Westside until it intersects River Road and turn west. Turn south at Mirabel Road and follow it to Highway 116.

ESSENTIALS

Contacts Russian River Wine Road ☎ 707/433–4335, 800/723–6336 ⊕ www. wineroad.com.

EXPLORING

TOP ATTRACTIONS

Fodor'sChoice **Hartford Family Winery.** Pinot Noir lovers appreciate the subtle differ-
★ ences in the wines Hartford's Jeff Stewart crafts from grapes grown in Sonoma County's three top AVAs for the varietal—Los Carneros, Russian River Valley, and the Sonoma Coast—along with one from the Anderson Valley, just north in Mendocino County. The Pinot Noirs win praise from major wine critics, and Stewart also makes highly rated Chardonnays and old-vine Zinfandels. A reserve tasting ($15) includes a flight of six wines; a tour of the winery is part of the seated private library tasting ($40). ■ TIP→ If the weather's good and you've made a reservation, your reserve tasting can take place on the patio outside the opulent main winery building. ⊠ 8075 Martinelli Rd., off Hwy. 116 or River Rd., Forestville ☎ 707/887–8030, 800/588–0234 ⊕ www.hartfordwines.com 🖃 Tastings $15–$40 ⊙ Daily 10–4:30, tours by appointment.

Fodor'sChoice **Iron Horse Vineyards.** A meandering one-lane road leads to this win-
★ ery known for its sparkling wines and estate Chardonnays and Pinot Noirs. The sparklers have made history: Ronald Reagan served them at his summit meetings with Mikhail Gorbachev; George Herbert Walker Bush took some along to Moscow for treaty talks; and Barack Obama has included them at official state dinners. Despite Iron Horse's brushes with fame, a casual rusticity prevails at its outdoor tasting area (large heaters keep things comfortable on chilly days), which gazes out on acres of rolling, vine-covered hills. Regular tours ($25) take place on weekdays at 10 am. ■ TIP→ When his schedule permits, winemaker David Munksgard leads a private tour by truck ($50) at 10 am on Monday. ⊠ 9786 Ross Station Rd., off Hwy. 116, Sebastopol ☎ 707/887–1507 ⊕ www.ironhorsevineyards.com 🖃 Tasting $20, tours $25–$50 (includes tasting) ⊙ Daily 10–4:30, tour (by appointment) weekdays at 10.

Fodor'sChoice **Merry Edwards Winery.** Winemaker Merry Edwards describes the Russian
★ River Valley as "the epicenter of great Pinot Noir," and she produces wines that express the unique characteristics of the soils, climates, and Pinot Noir clones from which they derive. (Edwards's research into Pinot Noir clones is so extensive that there's even one named after her.) The valley's advantages, says Edwards, are warmer-than-average daytime temperatures that encourage more intense fruit, and evening fogs that mitigate the extra heat's potential negative effects. Group tastings of the well-composed single-vineyard and blended Pinots take place throughout the day, and there are five sit-down appointment slots available except on Sunday. Edwards also makes a fine Sauvignon Blanc that's lightly aged in old oak. Tastings end, rather than begin, with this singular white wine so as not to distract guests' palates from the Pinot Noirs. ⊠ 2959 Gravenstein Hwy. N/Hwy. 116, near Oak Grove Ave., Sebastopol ☎ 707/823–7466, 888/388–9050 ⊕ www.merryedwards.

20

DID YOU KNOW?

People often refer to the Wine Country as having a Mediterranean climate. The temperature year-around and precipitation patterns are very similar to those found in Italy and Greece. But there are also a number of micro-climates that provide the prime conditions for a variety of wines.

com 🖥 *Tasting free* 🕑 *Daily 9:30–4:30; call for appointment or drop in and join next available tasting.*

Fodor's Choice **Rochioli Vineyards and Winery.** Claiming one of the prettiest picnic sites
★ in the area, with tables overlooking the vineyards, this winery has an airy little tasting room with an equally romantic view. Production is small and fans on the winery's mailing list snap up most of the bottles, but the winery is still worth a stop. Because of the cool growing conditions in the Russian River Valley, the flavors of the Chardonnay and Sauvignon Blanc are intense and complex, and the Pinot Noir, which helped cement the Russian River's status as a Pinot powerhouse, is consistently excellent. ✉ *6192 Westside Rd., Healdsburg* ☎ *707/433–2305* ⊕ *www.rochioliwinery.com* 🖥 *Tasting $10* 🕑 *Early Jan.–mid-Dec., Thurs.–Mon. 11–4, Tues. and Wed. by appointment.*

WORTH NOTING

Fodor's Choice **The Barlow.** On the site of a former apple cannery, this cluster of build-
★ ings celebrates Sonoma County's "maker" culture with an inspired combination production space and marketplace. The complex contains microbreweries and wine-making facilities, along with areas where people create or sell crafts, large-scale artworks, and artisanal food, herbs, and beverages. There's even a studio where artists using traditional methods are creating the world's largest *thangka* (Tibetan painting). Only club members can visit the anchor wine tenant, Kosta Browne, but La Follette, MacPhail, and other small producers have tasting rooms open to the public. Warped Brewing Company and Woodfour Brewing Company make and sell ales on-site, and you can have a nip of gin or bourbon at Spirit Works Distillery. ■**TIP→ From July through Octo-ber the complex hosts a Thursday-night street fair, with live music and even more vendors.** ✉ *6770 McKinley St., at Morris St., off Hwy. 12, Sebastopol* ☎ *707/824–5600* ⊕ *www.thebarlow.net* 🖥 *Free to complex; tasting fees at wineries, breweries, distillery* 🕑 *Daily, hrs vary.*

Gary Farrell Winery. Pass through an impressive metal gate and wind your way up a steep hill to reach Gary Farrell, a spot with knockout views over the rolling hills and vineyards below. Though its Zinfandels and Chardonnays often excel, the winery is best known for its Russian River Valley Pinot Noirs, crafted these days by Theresa Heredia. At the tasting bar ($15) you can sample Sauvignon Blanc and other winery-only wines; depending on the weather, seated tastings ($25) focusing on single-vineyard Chardonnays and Pinot Noirs take place on an outdoor terrace or indoors near a fireplace. ■**TIP→ The Pinots from the Hallberg and Rochioli vineyards are worth checking out.** ✉ *10701 Westside Rd., Healdsburg* ☎ *707/473–2909* ⊕ *www.garyfarrellwinery. com* 🖥 *Tastings $15–$25, tours $35–$75* 🕑 *Daily 10:30–4:30, tours by appointment.*

WHERE TO EAT

$$$$ ✕ **The Farmhouse Inn.** From the sommelier who assists you with wine
FRENCH choices to the servers who describe the provenance of the black truf-
Fodor's Choice fles shaved over the intricate pasta dishes, the staff matches the qual-
★ ity of this restaurant's French-inspired cuisine. The signature dish, "Rabbit Rabbit Rabbit," a trio of confit of leg, rabbit loin wrapped

in applewood-smoked bacon, and roasted rack of rabbit with a whole-grain mustard sauce, is typical of preparations that are both rustic and refined. The menu is prix-fixe (three courses $79, four $94). **TIP→ The inn is a favorite of wine-industry foodies, so reserve well in advance; if it's full, you might be able to dine in the small lounge.** [$] *Average main: $79* ✉ *7871 River Rd., at Wohler Rd., Forestville* ☎ *707/887–3300, 800/464–6642* 🌐 *www.farmhouseinn.com* ✍ *Reservations essential* ⏲ *Closed Tues. and Wed. No lunch.*

$$$ MODERN AMERICAN 🍴 **Zazu Kitchen + Farm.** "Know the face that feeds you" is the motto at Zazu, and some of the local ingredients in dishes here come from the owners themselves: executive chef Duskie Estes and her husband, John Stewart, the house salumist (specialist in all things pig). Small plates such as *chicharrones* (fried pork rinds), tamarind Petaluma chicken wings, and baby back ribs can add up to a meal, or you can sample a few appetizers before moving on to a bacon burger, porcini noodle and Sebastopol mushroom stroganoff, or a tomahawk steak for two and fries. In good weather the industrial-looking space's huge doors lift up to admit the breeze that often graces the open-air patio, which is surrounded by raised garden beds that supply produce and spices for diners' meals. [$] *Average main: $23* ✉ *The Barlow, 6770 McKinley St., No. 150, off Morris St., Sebastopol* ☎ *707/523–4814* 🌐 *www.zazukitchen.com* ⏲ *Closed Tues. No lunch Mon.*

WHERE TO STAY

$$$$ B&B/INN Fodor's Choice ★ 🏨 **The Farmhouse Inn.** With a rustic-farmhouse-meets-modern-loft aesthetic, this low-key but upscale getaway with a pale-yellow exterior contains spacious rooms filled with king-size four-poster beds, whirlpool tubs, and hillside-view terraces. **Pros:** fantastic restaurant; luxury bath products; full-service spa. **Cons:** mild road noise audible in rooms closest to the street. [$] *Rooms from: $495* ✉ *7871 River Rd., Forestville* ☎ *707/887–3300, 800/464–6642* 🌐 *www.farmhouseinn.com* 🛏 *19 rooms, 6 suites* 🍽 *Breakfast.*

$ HOTEL FAMILY 🏨 **Sebastopol Inn.** The cheerful rooms clustered around this reasonably priced inn's courtyard are steps from The Barlow, a hip collection of restaurants, wine-tasting rooms, brewpubs, galleries, and other spaces. **Pros:** good rates; friendly staff; across from Barlow complex; near noteworthy wineries. **Cons:** no frills; bland decor. [$] *Rooms from: $129* ✉ *6751 Sebastopol Ave., Sebastopol* ☎ *707/829–2500* 🌐 *www.sebastopolinn.com* 🛏 *29 rooms, 2 suites* 🍽 *No meals.*

SPORTS AND THE OUTDOORS

CANOE TRIPS

Burke's Canoe Trips. You'll get a real feel for the Russian River's flora and fauna on a leisurely 10-mile paddle downstream from Burke's to Guerneville. A shuttle bus returns you to your car at the end of the journey, which is best taken from late May through mid-October and, in summer, on a weekday. Summer weekends can be crowded and raucous. ✉ *8600 River Rd., at Mirabel Rd., Forestville* ☎ *707/887–1222* 🌐 *www.burkescanoetrips.com* 🎟 *$65 per canoe.*

HEALDSBURG

17 miles north of Santa Rosa.

Just when it seems that the buzz about Healdsburg couldn't get any more intense, another feature story appears touting the chic hotel and restaurant scene here. Despite the hype, you needn't be a tycoon to enjoy this town. For every ritzy restaurant there's a bakery or grocery where you can find affordable gourmet eats, and luxe lodgings are matched by modest bed-and-breakfasts. The tin-roof bandstand on Healdsburg Plaza hosts free concerts, at which you might hear anything from bluegrass to Sousa marches. Add to that the plaza's fragrant magnolia trees and bright flower beds, and the whole ensemble seems right out of a Norman Rockwell painting. Healdsburg is ideally located at the confluence of the Dry Creek Valley, Russian River Valley, and Alexander Valley AVAs. Tucked behind groves of eucalyptus or hidden high on fog-shrouded hills, the winery buildings are often barely visible.

GETTING HERE AND AROUND

Healdsburg sits just off U.S. 101. Heading north, take the Central Healdsburg exit to reach Healdsburg Plaza; heading south, take the Westside Road exit and pass east under the freeway. Sonoma County Transit Bus 60 serves Healdsburg from Santa Rosa.

WHERE TO EAT

$$$ SPANISH Fodor's Choice ★ 🍴 **Bravas Bar de Tapas.** Spanish-style tapas and an outdoor patio in perpetual party mode make this restaurant headquartered in a restored 1920s bungalow a popular downtown perch. Contemporary Spanish mosaics set a perky tone inside, but unless something's amiss with the weather nearly everyone heads out back for cocktails, sangrias, beers, or flights of sherry (a tapas-bar staple in Spain) to prep the palate for the onslaught of flavors. Reliable items include the paella, Spanish cured ham, *pan tomate* (tomato toast), farm-fried duck eggs, pork-cheek sliders, croquettes, skirt steak, and crispy fried chicken with pickled peppers. ■ **TIP→ On a hot Healdsburg day, the watermelon salad or gazpacho will instantly reset your internal thermostat.** [$] *Average main: $26* ✉ *420 Center St., near North St., Healdsburg* ☎ *707/433–7700* 🌐 *www.starkrestaurants.com/bravas.html.*

$$ ITALIAN Fodor's Choice ★ 🍴 **Campo Fina.** Ari Rosen, the owner of popular Scopa, converted a storefront that once housed a bar notorious for boozin' and brawlin' into a second showcase for his contemporary-rustic Italian cuisine. Sandblasted red brick, satin-smooth walnut tables, and old-school lighting fixtures strike an appropriately retro note for a dinner menu built around pizzas and a few other Scopa gems such as Rosen's variation on his grandmother's tomato-braised chicken with creamy-soft polenta. Locals love Campo Fina for lunch, especially on the outdoor patio, beyond which lies a boccie court that looks out of a movie set. The Sally Peppers sandwich—house-made sausage, provolone, sweet and spicy peppers, and caramelized onions on a ciabatta roll—is a memorable medley. [$] *Average main: $18* ✉ *330 Healdsburg Ave., near North St., Healdsburg* ☎ *707/395–4640* 🌐 *www.campofina.com* ✍ *Reservations essential.*

$$
MODERN
AMERICAN
Fodor'sChoice
★

✕ **Chalkboard.** Unvarnished oak flooring, wrought-iron accents, and a vaulted white ceiling create a polished yet rustic ambience for the playfully ambitious cuisine of chef Shane McAnelly. Starters such as pork-belly biscuits might at first glance seem frivolous, but the silky flavor blend—maple glaze, pickled onions, and chipotle mayo playing off feathery biscuit halves—signals a supremely capable tactician at work. Likewise with vegetable sides such as fried brussels sprouts perched upon a perky kimchi puree, or moist and crispy buttermilk fried quail. House-made pasta dishes favor rich country flavors—the robust Sonoma lamb *sugo* (sauce) with Pecorino-Romano tickles the entire palate—while desserts named The Candy Bar and Donuts O' the Day aim to please (and do). The canny wine selections ably support McAnelly's cuisine. [$] *Average main: $19* ✉ *Hotel Les Mars, 29 North St., west of Healdsburg Ave., Healdsburg* ☎ *707/473–8030* ⊕ *chalkboardhealdsburg.com.*

$
BAKERY
Fodor'sChoice
★

✕ **Downtown Bakery & Creamery.** To catch the Healdsburg spirit, hit the plaza in the early morning to down a cup of coffee and a fragrant sticky bun or a too-darlin' *canelé,* a French-style pastry with a soft custard center surrounded by a dense caramel crust. Until 2 pm you can also go the full breakfast route: pancakes, granola, poached farm eggs on polenta, or perhaps the dandy bacon-and-egg pizza. For lunch there are sandwiches, pizzas, and calzones. [$] *Average main: $8* ✉ *308A Center St., at North St., Healdsburg* ☎ *707/431–2719* ⊕ *www.downtownbakery. net* ⌫ *Reservations not accepted* ⊗ *No dinner.*

$$$
MODERN
AMERICAN
Fodor'sChoice
★

✕ **Partake by K-J.** Kendall-Jackson's downtown restaurant opened with a novel wine-oriented tasting menu that has evolved into a more straightforward appetizers-salads-entrées format, but the emphasis on pairing top-tier Jackson-label wines and food remains. Much of chef Justin Wangler's produce finds its way from K-J's 3-acre Santa Rosa organic farm to diners' tables in a mere few hours. With ingredients this fresh, Wangler wisely displays a light touch: summertime heirloom-tomato dishes, for instance, might have no dressing at all, the same for salads of tender mixed baby greens. Popular appetizers include lamb sliders; duck breast and local salmon are consistent main-course favorites. ■ TIP➜ Tempura maitake mushrooms, the tour de force side, are served with a sweet Korean soy sauce that plays well off the wafflelike notes in the tempura batter. [$] *Average main: $23* ✉ *241 Healdsburg Ave., near Matheson St., Healdsburg* ☎ *707/433–6000* ⊕ *www.partakebykj. com* ⊗ *Restaurant closed Mon. and Tues. No lunch.*

$$
ITALIAN
Fodor'sChoice
★

✕ **Scopa.** At his tiny, deservedly popular eatery, chef Ari Rosen prepares rustic Italian specialties such as *sugo Calabrese* (tomato-braised beef and pork rib) and house-made ravioli stuffed with ricotta. Simple thin-crust pizzas, including one with mozzarella, figs, prosciutto, and arugula, make fine meals, too. Locals love the restaurant for its lack of pretension: wine is served in juice glasses, and the friendly hostess makes the rounds to ensure everyone is satisfied. You'll be packed in elbow-to-elbow with your fellow diners, but for a convivial evening over a bottle of Nebbiolo, there's no better choice. [$] *Average main: $20* ✉ *109A Plaza St., near Healdsburg Ave., Healdsburg* ☎ *707/433–5282* ⊕ *www.scopahealdsburg.com* ⊗ *No lunch.*

20

$$$ MODERN AMERICAN 🍴 **Spoonbar.** Cantina doors that open onto Healdsburg Avenue make this trendy eatery especially appealing in summer, when a warm breeze wafts into the stylish space. Midcentury modern furnishings, concrete walls, and a long communal table fashioned from rough-hewn acacia wood create an urbane setting for contemporary American fare. Chef Louis Maldonado, a 2014 finalist on Bravo TV's *Top Chef* and a champion on the network's *Last Chance Kitchen*, divides his menu into five sections, from which diners mix and match to create a meal. The mains might include lamb rib-eye stuffed with merguez sausage and escargots or barbecue-glazed flounder served with rock shrimp and corn and scallion ragout. **TIP→ The bar, known for inventive seasonal and historical cocktails, is the real draw for many locals.** [$] *Average main: $25* ✉ *h2hotel, 219 Healdsburg Ave., at Vine St., Healdsburg* ☎ *707/433–7222* 🌐 *www.h2hotel.com/spoonbar* ⏲ *No lunch.*

$$$ SEAFOOD Fodor's Choice ★ 🍴 **Willi's Seafood & Raw Bar.** The festive crowd at Willi's likes to enjoy specialty cocktails at the full bar before sitting down to a dinner of small, mostly seafood-oriented plates. The warm Maine lobster roll with garlic butter and fennel conjures up a New England fish shack, while the ceviches and the scallops served with a ginger-lime aioli suggest Latin America. Gluten-, dairy-, nut, and seed-free options are available for diners with dietary restrictions. Desserts are a big deal here, with the key lime cheesecake and caramelized banana split among the most popular. The wine list favors Sonoma County but also includes entries from Australia, France, Greece, Portugal, and other locales. [$] *Average main: $25* ✉ *403 Healdsburg Ave., at North St., Healdsburg* ☎ *707/433–9191* 🌐 *www.willisseafood.net* ☞ *Reservations not accepted Fri.–Sun.*

WHERE TO STAY

$ HOTEL 🏨 **Best Western Dry Creek Inn.** Easy access to downtown restaurants, tasting rooms, and shopping as well as outlying wineries and bicycle trails makes this Spanish Mission–style motel near U.S. 101 a good budget option. **Pros:** laundry facilities; some pet-friendly rooms; frequent Internet discounts. **Cons:** thin walls; highway noise audible in many rooms. [$] *Rooms from: $172* ✉ *198 Dry Creek Rd., Healdsburg* ☎ *707/433–0300, 800/222–5784* 🌐 *www.drycreekinn.com* 🛏 *163 rooms* 🍽 *Breakfast.*

$$$ B&B/INN Fodor's Choice ★ 🏨 **h2hotel.** Eco-friendly touches abound at this hotel, from the plant-covered "green roof" to wooden decks made from salvaged lumber. **Pros:** stylish modern design; popular bar; complimentary bikes. **Cons:** least expensive rooms lack bathtubs; no fitness facilities. [$] *Rooms from: $313* ✉ *219 Healdsburg Ave., Healdsburg* ☎ *707/922–5251* 🌐 *www.h2hotel.com* 🛏 *28 rooms, 8 suites* 🍽 *Breakfast.*

$$$ B&B/INN Fodor's Choice ★ 🏨 **The Honor Mansion.** An 1883 Italianate Victorian houses this photogenic hotel; rooms in the main home preserve a sense of the building's heritage, whereas the larger suites are comparatively understated. **Pros:** homemade sweets available at all hours; spa pavilions by pool available for massages in fair weather. **Cons:** almost a mile from Healdsburg Plaza; walls can seem thin. [$] *Rooms from: $325* ✉ *891 Grove St., Healdsburg* ☎ *707/433–4277, 800/554–4667* 🌐 *www.honormansion.*

com 🛏 *5 rooms, 7 suites, 1 cottage* ⏲ *Closed 2 wks around Christmas* 🍴 *Breakfast.*

$$$$ RESORT 🏨 **Hotel Healdsburg.** Across the street from the tidy town plaza, this spare, sophisticated hotel caters to travelers with an urban sensibility. **Pros:** several rooms overlook the town plaza; comfortable lobby with a small attached bar; extremely comfortable beds. **Cons:** exterior rooms get some street noise; rooms could use better lighting. [$] *Rooms from: $449* ✉ *25 Matheson St., Healdsburg* ☎ *707/431–2800, 800/889–7188* 🌐 *www.hotelhealdsburg.com* 🛏 *49 rooms, 6 suites* 🍴 *Breakfast.*

$$$$ HOTEL Fodor's Choice ★ 🏨 **Hôtel Les Mars.** This Relais & Châteaux property takes the prize for opulence with guest rooms spacious and elegant enough for French nobility, 18th- and 19th-century antiques and reproductions, canopy beds dressed in luxe linens, and gas-burning fireplaces. **Pros:** large rooms; just off Healdsburg's plaza; fancy bath products; room service by Chalkboard restaurant. **Cons:** very expensive. [$] *Rooms from: $675* ✉ *27 North St., Healdsburg* ☎ *707/433–4211* 🌐 *www.hotellesmars.com* 🛏 *16 rooms* 🍴 *Breakfast.*

SPAS

Fodor's Choice ★ **Spa Dolce.** Owner Ines von Majthenyi Scherrer has a good local rep, having run a popular nearby spa before opening this stylish facility just off Healdsburg Plaza. Spa Dolce specializes in skin and body care for men and women, and waxing and facials for women. Curved white walls and fresh-cut floral arrangements set a subdued tone for such treatments as the exfoliating Hauschka body scrub, which combines organic brown sugar with scented oil. There's a romantic room for couples to enjoy massages for two. **■ TIP→ Many guests come just for the facials, which range from a straightforward cleansing to an anti-aging peel.** ✉ *250 Center St., at Matheson St., Healdsburg* ☎ *707/433–0177* 🌐 *www.spadolce.com* 🎟 *Treatments $55–$240* ⏲ *Tues.–Sun. 10–7.*

SPORTS AND THE OUTDOORS

Fodor's Choice ★ **Wine Country Bikes.** This shop in downtown Healdsburg is perfectly located for single or multiday treks into the Dry Creek and Russian River valleys. Bikes, including tandems, rent for $39 to $145 a day. One-day tours start at $149. ✉ *61 Front St., at Hudson St., Healdsburg* ☎ *707/473–0610, 866/922–4537* 🌐 *www.winecountrybikes.com.*

SHOPPING

Healdsburg is a pleasant spot to window shop, with dozens of art galleries, boutiques, and high-end design shops on or near the plaza.

Gallery Lulo. A collaboration between a local artist and jewelry maker and a Danish-born curator, this museumlike gallery presents changing exhibits of exquisite jewelry, sculpture, and objets d'art. ✉ *303 Center St., at Plaza St., Healdsburg* ☎ *707/433–7533* 🌐 *www.gallerylulo.com.*

Fodor's Choice ★ **The Shed.** Inside a glass-front, steel-clad variation on a traditional grange hall, this shop-cum-eatery celebrates local agriculture with specialty foods. It also stocks seeds and plants, gardening and farming implements, cookware, and everything a smart pantry should hold. ✉ *25 North St., west of Healdsburg Ave., Healdsburg* ☎ *707/431–7433* 🌐 *healdsburgshed.com.*

DRY CREEK AND ALEXANDER VALLEYS

With its diverse terrain and microclimates, the Dry Creek Valley supports an impressive range of varietals. Zinfandel grapes flourish on the benchlands, whereas the gravelly, well-drained soil of the valley floor is better known for Chardonnay and, in the north, Sauvignon Blanc. Pinot Noir, Syrah, and other cool-climate grapes thrive on eastern-facing slopes that receive less afternoon sun than elsewhere in the valley. The Alexander Valley, which lies northeast of Healdsburg, is similarly rustic. Wineries here are known for Zinfandels, Chardonnays, and Cabernet Sauvignons, though Cabernet Franc and other less high-profile wines are also made.

GETTING HERE AND AROUND

To reach the Dry Creek Valley from Healdsburg, drive north on Healdsburg Avenue and turn left on Dry Creek Road. West of U.S. 101, you'll see signs pointing the way to wineries on that road and West Dry Creek Road, which runs roughly parallel about a mile to the west. To get to the Alexander Valley from the plaza, drive north on Healdsburg Avenue and veer right onto Alexander Valley Road. Follow it to Highway 128, where many of this appellation's best wineries lie.

EXPLORING
TOP ATTRACTIONS

Fodor's Choice
★

Jordan Vineyard and Winery. A visit to this sprawling property north of Healdsburg revolves around an impressive estate built in the early 1970s to replicate a French château . A seated one-hour Library Tasting of the current Cabernet Sauvignon and Chardonnay releases takes place in the château itself, accompanied by small bites prepared by executive chef Todd Knoll. The tasting concludes with an older vintage Cabernet Sauvignon paired with cheese. The 90-minute Winery Tour & Tasting includes the above, plus a walk through part of the château. ■TIP→ For a truly memorable experience, splurge on the three-hour Estate Tour & Tasting, whose pièce de résistance is a Cabernet tasting at a 360-degree vista point overlooking 1,200 acres of vines, olive trees, and countryside. ⊠ *1474 Alexander Valley Rd., on Greco Rd., Healdsburg* ☎ *800/654–1213, 707/431–5250* ⊕ *www.jordanwinery.com* ⊠ *Library tasting $30, winery tour and tasting $40, estate tour and tasting $120* ☺ *Library tasting mid-Nov.–mid-Apr., Mon.–Sat. 10 and 2, mid-Apr.–mid-Nov., Mon.–Sat. 10 and 2, Sun. 11, 1, and 3; winery tour mid-Nov.–mid-Apr., Mon.–Sat. at 11, mid-Apr.–mid-Nov., Mon.–Sat. at 11, Sun. at 11; estate tour mid-Apr.–mid-Nov. at 9:45 Thurs.–Mon.*

Fodor's Choice
★

Locals Tasting Room. Though trending upscale, downtown Geyserville remains little more than a crossroads with a few shops and restaurants. But if you're serious about wine, Carolyn Lewis's tasting room is alone worth a trek. Connoisseurs come to sample the output of a dozen or so small wineries, most without tasting rooms of their own. There's no fee for tasting—a bargain for wines of this quality—and the extremely knowledgeable staff is happy to pour you a flight of several wines so you can compare, say, different Cabernet Sauvignons. ⊠ *21023A Geyserville Ave., at Hwy. 128, Geyserville* ☎ *707/857–4900* ⊕ *www.tastelocalwines.com* ⊠ *Tasting free* ☺ *Daily 11–6.*

Fodor's Choice
★
Ridge Vineyards. Ridge stands tall among California wineries, and not merely because one of its 1971 Cabernet Sauvignons placed first in a 2006 re-creation of the 1976 Judgment of Paris tasting. The winery built its reputation on Cabernet Sauvignons, Zinfandels, and Chardonnays of unusual depth and complexity, but you'll also find blends of Rhône varietals. Ridge makes wines using grapes from several California locales—including the Dry Creek Valley, Sonoma Valley, Napa Valley, and Paso Robles—but the focus is on single-vineyard estate wines such as the exquisitely textured Lytton Springs Zinfandel blend from grapes grown near the tasting room. In good weather you can taste outside, taking in views of rolling vineyard hills while you sip. ■ TIP➔ The $20 tasting option includes a pour of the top-of-the-line Monte Bello Cabernet Sauvignon blend from grapes grown in the Santa Cruz Mountains. ⊠ 650 Lytton Springs Rd., off U.S. 101, Healdsburg ☎ 707/433–7721 ⊕ www. ridgewine.com ✉ Tastings $5–$20, tours $30–$40 ☉ June–Oct., Mon.–Thurs. 11–4, Fri. and weekends 11–5; Nov.–May, daily 11–4.

Fodor's Choice
★
Truett Hurst Winery. When the weather's fine, few experiences rate more sublime ("pure magic," enthused one recent guest) than sitting on Truett Hurst's sandy, tree-shaded Dry Creek shoreline, sipping a Green Valley Pinot Noir or a Zinfandel Rosé, chatting with friends, and watching the water flow by. In addition to the Rosé, Truett Hurst makes six Zinfandels, a few of which are always poured in the contemporary, high-ceilinged tasting room or on the outdoor patio. The winemaker blends Petite Sirah into some of the Zins and makes a standalone Petite Sirah as well. Picnickers are welcome creekside or on the patio; meats, smoked fish, cheeses, and spreads are available for sale on-site. ■ TIP➔ Bands, sometimes local, sometimes from beyond, liven things up in the tasting room on weekend afternoons. ⊠ 5610 Dry Creek Rd., 2 miles south of Canyon Rd., Healdsburg ☎ 707/433–9545 ⊕ www.truetthurst.com.

WORTH NOTING

Dry Creek Vineyard. Fumé Blanc is king at Dry Creek, where the refreshing white wine is made in the style of those in Sancerre, France. The winery also makes well-regarded Zinfandels, a zesty dry Chenin Blanc, a Pinot Noir, and a handful of Cabernet Sauvignon blends. Many wines sell for less than $30 a bottle (and some even $20), making this a popular stop for wine lovers looking to stock their cellars for a reasonable price. You can picnic on the lawn next to a flowering magnolia tree. Conveniently, a general store and deli is close by. ⊠ 3770 Lambert Bridge Rd., off Dry Creek Rd., Healdsburg ☎ 707/433–1000, 800/864–9463 ⊕ www.drycreekvineyard.com ✉ Tastings $5–$50, tour $20 ☉ Daily 10:30–5, tour 11 and 1 by appointment.

FAMILY **Francis Ford Coppola Winery.** The film director's over-the-top fantasyland is the sort of place the mid-level Mafiosi in his *The Godfather* saga might declare had real class—the "everyday wines" poured here are pretty much beside the point. The fun here is all in the excess, and you may find it hard to resist having your photo snapped standing next to Don Corleone's desk from *The Godfather* or beside memorabilia from other Coppola films, including some directed by his daughter, Sofia. A bandstand reminiscent of one in *The Godfather Part II* is the centerpiece of a large pool area where you can rent a changing room, complete with

20

shower, and spend the afternoon lounging poolside, perhaps ordering food from the adjacent café. A more elaborate restaurant, Rustic, overlooks the vineyards. ✉ *300 Via Archimedes, off U.S. 101, Geyserville* ☎ *707/857–1400* 🌐 *www.franciscoppolawinery.com* 🎟 *Tastings free–$20, tours $20–$75, pool pass $30* 🕐 *Tasting room daily 11–6, restaurant daily 11–9; pool hrs vary seasonally.*

FAMILY Fodor's Choice ★ **Preston of Dry Creek.** The long driveway at convivial Preston, flanked by vineyards and punctuated by the occasional olive tree, winds down to farmhouses encircling a shady yard with picnic tables. Year-round a selection of organic produce grown in the winery's gardens is sold at a small shop near the tasting room; house-made bread and olive oil are also available. Owners Lou and Susan Preston are committed to organic growing techniques and use only estate-grown grapes in their wines, which include a perky Sauvignon Blanc (the best option for a picnic here), Barbera, Petite Sirah, Syrah, Viognier, and Zinfandel. ✉ *9282 W. Dry Creek Rd., at Hartsock Rd. No. 1, Healdsburg* ☎ *707/433–3372* 🌐 *www.prestonvineyards.com* 🎟 *Tasting $10* 🕐 *Daily 11–4:30.*

WHERE TO EAT AND STAY

$$ ITALIAN Fodor's Choice ★ 🍴 **Diavola Pizzeria & Salumeria.** A dining area with hardwood floors, a pressed-tin ceiling, and exposed-brick walls provides a fitting setting for the rustic cuisine at this Geyserville charmer. Chef Dino Bugica studied with several artisans in Italy before opening this restaurant that specializes in pizzas pulled from a wood-burning oven and several types of house-cured meats. A few salads and meaty main courses round out the menu. **■ TIP→ If you're impressed by the antipasto plate, you can pick up some smoked pork belly, pancetta, or spicy Calabrese sausage to take home.** [$] *Average main: $19* ✉ *21021 Geyserville Ave., at Hwy. 128, Geyserville* ☎ *707/814–0111* 🌐 *www.diavolapizzeria.com* ✍ *Reservations not accepted.*

$ HOTEL 🏨 **Geyserville Inn.** Clever travelers give the Healdsburg hubbub and prices the heave-ho but still have easy access to outstanding Dry Creek and Alexander Valley wineries from this modest, well-run inn. **Pros:** pool; second-floor rooms in back have vineyard views; picnic area. **Cons:** occasional noise bleed-through from corporate and other events. [$] *Rooms from: $155* ✉ *21714 Geyserville Ave., Geyserville* ☎ *707/857–4343, 877/857–4343* 🌐 *www.geyservilleinn.com* 🛏 *41 rooms* 🍽 *No meals.*

TRAVEL SMART
SAN FRANCISCO

GETTING HERE AND AROUND

San Francisco encompasses 46.7 square miles. As a major metropolitan hub it has a fantastic public transportation system; however, if you stray from the main thoroughfares public transport can get tricky, and renting a car becomes a more practical option.

All the city's major attractions are easily accessible via Muni (light-rail vehicles), BART (Bay Area Rapid Transit) trains, taxis, and cable cars; or if you have a comfy pair of shoes, you can always walk. It's exactly 8 miles from the west side of the city to the east side. The streets are neatly arranged along two grids that come together at Market Street, and with the area's well-known landmarks—the Golden Gate Bridge (north), Twin Peaks (south), the Bay Bridge (east), and the Pacific Ocean (west)—as a physical compass, it's difficult to lose your way.

The East Bay is also extremely accessible via public transport; BART is a good way to get where you want to go. And the North Bay is only a boat or bike ride away. Both are good choices, depending on the weather. A car only becomes necessary when you want to go farther north, for example, to Napa or Sonoma County. Keep in mind that rush-hour traffic isn't pleasant, so if you do rent a car try to take to the streets between 10 am and 3 pm, or after 7 pm.

▌ AIR TRAVEL

The least expensive airfares to San Francisco are priced for round-trip travel and should be purchased in advance. Airlines generally allow you to change your return date for a fee; most low-fare tickets, however, are nonrefundable. (But if you cancel, you can usually apply the fare to a future trip, within one year, to any destination the airline flies.)

Nonstop flights from New York to San Francisco take about 5½ hours, and with the 3-hour time change, it's possible to leave JFK by 8 am and be in San Francisco by 10:30 am. Some flights may require a midway stop, making the total excursion between 8 and 9½ hours. Nonstop times are approximately 1½ hours from Los Angeles, 3 hours from Dallas, 4½ hours from Chicago, 4½ hours from Atlanta, 11 hours from London, 12 hours from Auckland, and 13½ hours from Sydney.

Airline Contacts American Airlines ☎ 800/223–5436 ⊕ www.aa.com. **Delta Airlines** ☎ 800/221–1212 ⊕ www.delta. com. **Southwest Airlines** ☎ 800/435–9792 ⊕ www.southwest.com. **United Airlines** ☎ 800/864–8331 ⊕ www.united.com.

Smaller Airlines Frontier Airlines ☎ 800/432–1359 ⊕ www.flyfrontier.com. **jetBlue** ☎ 800/538–2583 ⊕ www.jetblue.com.

AIRPORTS

The major gateway to San Francisco is San Francisco International Airport (SFO), 15 miles south of the city. It's off U.S. 101 near Millbrae and San Bruno. Oakland International Airport (OAK) is across the bay, not much farther away from downtown San Francisco (via I–80 east and I–880 south), but rush-hour traffic on the Bay Bridge may lengthen travel times considerably. San Jose International Airport (SJC) is about 40 miles south of San Francisco; travel time depends largely on traffic flow, but plan on an hour and a half with moderate traffic.

Depending on the price difference, you might consider flying into Oakland or San Jose. Oakland's an easy-to-use alternative, because there's public transportation between the airport and downtown San Francisco. Getting to San Francisco from San Jose, though, can be time-consuming and costly via public transportation. Heavy fog is infamous for causing chronic delays into and out of San Francisco. If you're heading to the East or South Bay, make every effort to fly into Oakland or San Jose Airport, respectively.

At all three airports security check-in can take 30 to 45 minutes at peak travel times.

■ TIP→ Count yourself lucky if you have a layover at SFO's International Terminal. The food served by branches of top local eateries beats standard airport fare: Italian pastries from Emporio Rulli, burgers from Burger Joint, seafood and steak from Lark Creek Grill, sushi from Ebisu.

Long layovers needn't only be about sitting around or shopping. You can burn off vacation calories, too. Check out ⊕ www. airportgyms.com for lists of health clubs that are in or near many U.S. and Canadian airports.

Airport Information **Oakland International Airport** (OAK). ☎ 510/563–3300 ⊕ www. flyoakland.com. **San Francisco International Airport** (SFO). ☎ 800/435–9736, 650/821–8211 ⊕ www.flysfo.com. **San Jose International Airport** (SJC). ☎ 408/392–3600 ⊕ www.flysanjose.com.

GROUND TRANSPORTATION

FROM SAN FRANCISCO INTERNATIONAL AIRPORT

Transportation signage at the airport is color-coded by type and is quite clear. A taxi ride to downtown costs $50 to $55. Airport shuttles are inexpensive and generally efficient. Lorrie's Airport Service and SuperShuttle both stop at the lower level near baggage claim and take you anywhere within the city limits of San Francisco. They charge $16 to $18, depending on where you're going. Lorrie's also sells tickets online, at a $2 discount each way; you can print them out before leaving home. SuperShuttle offers some discounts for more than one person traveling in the same party ($17 per person and $10 for each additional passenger), but only if you're traveling to a residential address.

Shuttles to the East Bay, such as Bay-Porter Express, also depart from the lower level; expect to pay between $34 and $42. Inquire about the number of stops a shuttle makes en route to or from the airport; some companies, such as East Bay Express, have nonstop service, but they cost a bit more. Marin Door to Door operates van service to Marin County for $40 to $50 for the first passenger, and $12 for each additional person; you must make reservations by noon the day before travel. Marin Airporter buses cost $21 and require no reservations but stop only at designated stations in Marin; buses leave every 30 minutes, on the half hour and hour, from 5 am to midnight.

You can take BART directly to downtown San Francisco; the trip takes about 30 minutes and costs less than $9. (There are both manned booths and vending machines for ticket purchases.) Trains leave from the international terminal every 15 minutes or 20 minutes, depending on the day or time.

Another inexpensive way to get to San Francisco (though not as convenient as BART) is via two SamTrans buses: No. 292 (55 minutes, $2 from SFO, $4 to SFO) and the KX (35 minutes, $5; only one small carry-on bag permitted). Board the SamTrans buses on the lower level.

To drive to downtown San Francisco from the airport, take U.S. 101 north to the Civic Center/9th Street, 7th Street, or 4th Street/Downtown exits. If you're headed to the Embarcadero or Fisherman's Wharf, take I–280 north (the exit is to the right, just north of the airport, off U.S. 101) and get off at the 4th Street/King Street exit. King Street becomes the Embarcadero a few blocks east of the exit. The Embarcadero winds around the waterfront to Fisherman's Wharf.

FROM OAKLAND INTERNATIONAL AIRPORT

A taxi to downtown San Francisco costs $70 to $75. By airport regulations, you must make reservations for shuttle service. BayPorter Express and other shuttles serve major hotels and provide door-to-door service to the East Bay and San Francisco. SuperShuttle operates vans to San

Francisco and Oakland. Marin Door to Door serves Marin County for a flat $50 for the first passenger, and $12 for each additional person; make reservations by noon the day before travel.

The best way to get to San Francisco via public transit is to take the AIR BART bus ($3) to the Coliseum/Oakland International Airport BART station (BART fares vary depending on where you're going; the ride to downtown San Francisco from here costs $4.05).

If you're driving from Oakland International Airport, take Hegenberger Road east to I–880 north to I–80 west over the Bay Bridge. This will likely take at least an hour.

FROM SAN JOSE INTERNATIONAL AIRPORT

A taxi to downtown San Jose costs about $18 to $22; a trip to San Francisco runs about $150 to $155. South and East Bay Airport Shuttle transports you to the South Bay and East Bay; a ride to downtown San Jose costs $30 for the first passenger, $10 for each additional, and a van to San Francisco costs $110 for the first passenger, $10 for each additional. Reservations are required to the airport, but not from the airport; call from baggage claim before you collect your luggage.

To drive to downtown San Jose from the airport, take Airport Boulevard east to Route 87 south. To get to San Francisco from the airport, take Route 87 south to I–280 north. The trip will take roughly two hours.

At $9.25 for a one-way ticket, there's no question that Caltrain provides the most affordable option for traveling between San Francisco and San Jose's airport. However, the Caltrain station in San Francisco at 4th and Townsend streets isn't in a conveniently central location. It's on the eastern side of the South of Market (SoMa) neighborhood and not easily accessible by other public transit. You'll need to take a taxi or walk from the nearest bus line. From San Francisco it takes

90 minutes and costs $9.25 to reach the Santa Clara Caltrain station, from which a free shuttle runs every 15 minutes, whisking you to and from the San Jose International Airport in 15 minutes.

Contacts American Airporter ☎ 415/202–0733 ⊕ www.americanairporter.com. **BayPorter Express** ☎ 415/467–1800, 510/864–4000 ⊕ www.bayporter.com. **Caltrain** ☎ 800/660–4287 ⊕ www.caltrain.com. **East Bay Express Airporter** ☎ 877/526–0304 ⊕ www.eastbaytransportation.com. **GO Lorrie's Airport Shuttle** ☎ 415/334–9000 ⊕ www.gosfovan.com. **Marin Airporter** ☎ 415/461–4222 ⊕ www.marinairporter.com. **Marin Door to Door** ☎ 415/457–2717 ⊕ www.marindoortodoor.com. **SamTrans** ☎ 800/660–4287 ⊕ www.samtrans.com. **South and East Bay Airport Shuttle** ☎ 800/548–4664 ⊕ www.southandeastbayairportshuttle.com. **SuperShuttle** ☎ 800/258–3826 ⊕ www.supershuttle.com.

▌ BART TRAVEL

BART (Bay Area Rapid Transit) trains, which run until midnight, travel under the bay via tunnel to connect San Francisco with Oakland, Berkeley, and other cities and towns beyond. Within San Francisco, stations are limited to downtown, the Mission, and a couple of outlying neighborhoods.

Trains travel frequently from early morning until evening on weekdays. After 8 pm weekdays and on weekends there's often a 20-minute wait between trains on the same line. Trains also travel south from San Francisco as far as Millbrae. BART trains connect downtown San Francisco to San Francisco International Airport; the ride costs $8.25.

Intracity San Francisco fares are $1.85; intercity fares are $3.80 to $11.65. BART bases its ticket prices on miles traveled and doesn't offer price breaks by zone. The easy-to-read maps posted in BART stations list fares based on destination, radiating out from your starting point of the current station.

During morning and evening rush hour, trains within the city are crowded—even standing room can be hard to come by. Cars at the far front and back of the train are less likely to be filled to capacity. Smoking, eating, and drinking are prohibited on trains and in stations.

Contacts **Bay Area Rapid Transit** (BART). ☏ 415/989–2278 ⊕ www.bart.gov.

BOAT TRAVEL

Several ferry lines run out of San Francisco. Blue & Gold Fleet operates a number of routes, including service to Sausalito ($11 one-way) and Tiburon ($11 one-way). Tickets are sold at Pier 41 (between Fisherman's Wharf and Pier 39), where the boats depart. Alcatraz Cruises, owned by Hornblower Yachts, operates the ferries to Alcatraz Island ($30 including audio tour and National Park Service ranger-led programs) from Pier 33, about a half-mile east of Fisherman's Wharf ($3 shuttle buses serve several area hotels and other locations). Boats leave 10 times a day (14 times a day in summer), and the journey itself takes 30 minutes. Allow roughly 2½ hours for a round-trip jaunt. Golden Gate Ferry runs daily to and from Sausalito and Larkspur ($10.75 and $10 one-way), leaving from Pier 1, behind the San Francisco Ferry Building. The Alameda/Oakland Ferry operates daily between Alameda's Main Street Ferry Building, Oakland's Jack London Square, and San Francisco's Pier 41 and the Ferry Building ($6.25 one-way); some ferries go only to Pier 41 or the Ferry Building, so ask when you board. Purchase tickets on board.

Information **Alameda/Oakland Ferry** ☏ 510/522–3300 ⊕ sanfranciscobayferry.com. **Alcatraz Cruises** ☏ 415/981–7625 ⊕ www. alcatrazcruises.com. **Blue & Gold Fleet** ☏ 415/705–8200 ⊕ www.blueandgoldfleet. com. **Golden Gate Ferry** ☏ 415/923–2000 ⊕ www.goldengateferry.org. **San Francisco Ferry Building** ⊠ 1 Ferry Bldg., at foot of Market St. on Embarcadero ☏ 415/983–8030 ⊕ www.ferrybuildingmarketplace.com.

BUS TRAVEL

Greyhound serves San Francisco with buses from many major U.S. cities; within California, service is limited to hub towns and cities only. The Greyhound depot is located at the Transbay Temporary Terminal, in the SoMa district. Reservations aren't accepted; seating is on a first-come, first-served basis. Cash, traveler's checks, and credit cards are accepted.

Contacts **Greyhound** ⊠ Transbay Temporary Terminal, 200 Folsom St., between Main and Beale Sts., SoMa ☏ 415/495–1569 ⊕ www. greyhound.com.

CABLE-CAR TRAVEL

Don't miss the sensation of moving up and down some of San Francisco's steepest hills in a clattering cable car. Jump aboard as it pauses at a designated stop, and wedge yourself into any available space. Then just hold on.

The fare (for one direction) is $6 (Muni Passport holders only pay a $1 supplement). You can buy tickets on board (exact change isn't necessary) or at the kiosks at the cable-car turnarounds at Hyde and Beach streets and at Powell and Market streets.

The heavily traveled Powell–Mason and Powell–Hyde lines begin at Powell and Market streets near Union Square and terminate at Fisherman's Wharf; lines for these routes can be long, especially in summer. The California Street line runs east and west from Market and California streets to Van Ness Avenue; there's often no wait to board this route.

CAR TRAVEL

Driving in San Francisco can be a challenge because of the one-way streets, snarly traffic, and steep hills. The first two elements can be frustrating enough, but those hills are tough for unfamiliar drivers.

Be sure to leave plenty of room between your car and other vehicles when on a steep slope. This is especially important when you've braked at a stop sign on a steep incline. Whether with a stick shift or an automatic transmission, every car rolls backward for a moment once the brake is released. So don't pull too close to the car ahead of you. When it's time to pull forward, keep your foot on the brake while tapping lightly on the accelerator. Once the gears are engaged, let up on the brake and head uphill.

■**TIP→** Remember to curb your wheels when parking on hills—turn wheels away from the curb when facing uphill, toward the curb when facing downhill. You can get a ticket if you don't do this.

Market Street runs southwest from the Ferry Building, then becomes Portola Drive as it nears Twin Peaks (which lie beneath the giant radio-antennae structure, Sutro Tower). It can be difficult to drive across Market. The major east–west streets north of Market are Geary Boulevard (it's called Geary Street east of Van Ness Avenue), which runs to the Pacific Ocean; Fulton Street, which begins at the back of the Opera House and continues along the north side of Golden Gate Park to Ocean Beach; Oak Street, which runs east from Golden Gate Park toward downtown, then flows into northbound Franklin Street; and Fell Street, the left two lanes of which cut through Golden Gate Park and empty into Lincoln Boulevard, which continues to the ocean.

Among the major north–south streets are Divisadero, which heading south becomes Castro Street at Duboce Avenue and continues to just past César Chavez Street; Van Ness Avenue, which heading south becomes South Van Ness Avenue after it crosses Market Street; and Park Presidio Boulevard, which heading south from the Richmond District becomes Crossover Drive within Golden Gate Park and empties into 19th Avenue.

TRACKING CHEAP GAS

Determined to avoid the worst prices at the pump? Check the website ⊕ *www. sanfrangasprices.com,* which tracks the lowest (and highest) gasoline costs in the Bay Area. It also has a handy price-mapping feature and a master list of local gas stations.

GASOLINE

Gas stations are hard to find in San Francisco; look for the national franchises on major thoroughfares such as Market Street, Geary Boulevard, Mission Street, or California Street. Once you find one, prepare for sticker shock—the fuel is notoriously expensive here.

Aside from their limited numbers and high costs, everything else is standard operation at service stations. All major stations accept credit and ATM cards; self-service pumps are the norm. Most gas stations are open seven days a week until 11 pm or midnight. Many national franchises on well-traveled streets are open 24/7.

PARKING

San Francisco is a terrible city for parking. In the Financial District and Civic Center neighborhoods parking is forbidden on most streets between 3 or 4 pm and 6 or 7 pm. Check street signs carefully to confirm, because illegally parked cars are towed immediately. Downtown parking lots are often full, and most are expensive. The city-owned Sutter-Stockton, Ellis-O'Farrell, and 5th-and-Mission garages have the most reasonable rates in the downtown area. Large hotels often have parking available, but it doesn't come cheap; many charge in excess of $40 a day for the privilege.

Garages 5th & Mission/Yerba Buena Garage ⊠ *833 Mission St., at 5th St., SoMa* ☎ *415/982–8522* ⊕ *www. fifthandmission.com.* **766 Vallejo Garage** ⊠ *766 Vallejo St., at Powell St., North Beach* ☎ *415/989–4490.* **Ellis-O'Farrell Garage** ⊠ *123 O'Farrell St., at Stockton*

St., Union Sq. ☎ *415/986–4800.* **Embarcadero Center Garage** ✉ *1–4, Embarcadero Center, between Battery and Drumm Sts., Financial District* ☎ *415/772–0670* ⊕ *www.embarcaderocenter.com.* **Opera Plaza Garage** ✉ *601 Van Ness Ave., at Turk St., Civic Center* ☎ *415/771–4776.* **Performing Arts Garage** ✉ *360 Grove St., between Franklin and Gough Sts., Civic Center* ☎ *415/252–8238.* **Pier 39 Garage** ✉ *Embarcadero at Beach St., Fisherman's Wharf* ☎ *415/705–5418* ⊕ *www.pier39.com.* **Portsmouth Square Garage** ✉ *733 Kearny St., at Clay St., Chinatown* ☎ *415/982–6353* ⊕ *www.sfpsg.com.* **Sutter-Stockton Garage** ✉ *444 Stockton St., at Sutter St., Union Sq.* ☎ *415/982–7275.* **Wharf Garage** ✉ *2801 Leavenworth St., at Beach St., Fisherman's Wharf* ☎ *415/775–5060.*

ROAD CONDITIONS

Although rush "hours" are 6–10 am and 3–7 pm, you can hit gridlock on any day at any time, especially over the Bay Bridge and leaving and/or entering the city from the south. Sunday-afternoon traffic can be heavy as well, especially over the bridges.

The most comprehensive and immediate traffic updates are available through the city's 511 service, either online at ⊕ *www.511.org* (where webcams show you the traffic on your selected route) or by calling 511. On the radio, tune in to an all-news radio station such as KQED 88.5 FM or KCBS 740 AM/106.9 FM.

Be especially wary of nonindicated lane changes.

San Francisco is the only major American city uncut by freeways. To get from the Bay Bridge to the Golden Gate Bridge, you'll have to take surface streets, specifically Van Ness Avenue, which doubles as U.S. 101 through the city.

RULES OF THE ROAD

To encourage carpooling during heavy traffic times, some freeways have special lanes for so-called high-occupancy vehicles (HOVs)—cars carrying more than one or two passengers. Look for the

TAKE THE 511

Several transportation organizations—the Metropolitan Transportation Commission, the California Highway Patrol, the California Department of Transportation, and more—pool their data into a free, one-stop telephone (☎ 511) and Web (⊕ www.511.org) resource for all nine Bay Area counties. The service provides the latest info on traffic conditions, route, and fares for all public transit and has info about bicycle and other transportation. The phone line operates 24/7 toll-free.

white-painted diamond in the middle of the lane. Road signs next to or above the lane indicate the hours that carpooling is in effect. If the police stop you because you don't meet the criteria for travel in these lanes, expect a fine of more than $480.

Drivers are banned from using handheld mobile telephones while operating a vehicle in California. The use of seat belts in both front and back seats is required in California. The speed limit on city streets is 25 mph unless otherwise posted. A right turn on a red light after stopping is legal unless posted otherwise, as is a left on red at the intersection of two one-way streets. Children must ride in a properly secured child passenger safety restraint in the backseat until they are eight years old or 4 feet 9 inches tall.

CAR RENTALS

When you reserve a car, ask about cancellation penalties, taxes, drop-off charges (if you're planning to pick up the car in one city and leave it in another), and surcharges (for being under or over a certain age, for additional drivers, or for driving across state or country borders or beyond a specific distance from your point of rental). All these things can add substantially to your costs. Request car seats and extras such as GPS when you book.

Rates are sometimes—but not always— better if you book in advance or reserve through a rental agency's website. There are other reasons to book ahead, though: for popular destinations, during busy times of the year, or to ensure that you get certain types of cars (vans, SUVs, exotic sports cars).

■TIP➜ Make sure that a confirmed reservation guarantees you a car. Agencies sometimes overbook, particularly for busy weekends and holiday periods.

Car-rental costs in San Francisco vary seasonally, but generally begin at $50 a day and $275 a week for an economy car with air-conditioning, automatic transmission, and unlimited mileage. This doesn't include tax on car rentals, which is 9.5%. If you dream of driving with the top down, or heading out of town to ski the Sierra, consider renting a specialty vehicle. Most major agencies have a few on hand, but you have a better chance of finding one at Exotic Car Collection by Enterprise or the locally based City Rent-a-Car. The former specializes in high-end vehicles and arranges for airport pickup and drop-off. City Rent-a-Car likewise arranges airport transfers, and also delivers cars to Bay Area hotels. Both agencies also rent standard vehicles at prices competitive with those of the major chains.

■TIP➜ When renting a specialty car, ask about mileage limits. Some companies stick you with per-mile charges if you exceed 100 miles a day.

In San Francisco you must be at least 21 years old to rent a car, but some agencies won't rent to those under 25; check when you book. Super Cheap Car Rental is near the airport and rents to drivers as young as 20.

ALTERNATIVE RENTALS

City Car Share and Zipcar are membership organizations for any person over 21 with a valid driver's license who needs a car only for short-term use. You must join their clubs beforehand, which you can do via their websites. They're especially useful if you only want to rent a car for part of the day (say four to six hours),

find yourself far from the airport, or if you're younger than most rental agencies' 25-years-or-older requirement. The membership fee often allows you to use the service in several metropolitan areas. If using such a service, you can rent a car by the hour as well as by the day.

GoCar rents electric vehicles at Fisherman's Wharf and Union Square. These cars can travel between 25 and 35 mph and are very handy for neighborhood-based sightseeing, but they're not allowed on the Golden Gate Bridge. GoCars are electric, two-seater, three-wheeled, open convertibles with roll bars (so drivers must wear helmets) with GPS audio tours of the city. You can pick up a GoCar at three locations: two in Fisherman's Wharf and one in Union Square.

Automobile Associations American Automobile Association (*AAA*). U.S.: American Automobile Association; most contact with the organization is through state and regional members. ☎ 415/773-1900 ⊕ www.aaa.com. **National Automobile Club** ☎ 800/622-2136 ⊕ www.thenac.com.

Local Agencies City Car Share ☎ 415/995-8588 ⊕ www.citycarshare.org. **City Rent-a-Car** ✉ 1433 Bush St., near Van Ness Ave., Van Ness/Polk ☎ 415/359-1331, 866/359-1331 ⊕ www.cityrentacar.com. **GoCar** ☎ 800/914-6227 ⊕ www.gocartours.com. **Super Cheap Car Rental** ✉ 10 Rollins Rd., at Millbrae Ave. ☎ 650/777-9993 ⊕ www.supercheapcar.com. **Zipcar** ☎ 415/495-7478 ⊕ www.zipcar.com.

Major Agencies Alamo ☎ 800/462-5266 ⊕ www.alamo.com. **Avis** ☎ 800/633-3469 ⊕ www.avis.com. **Budget** ☎ 800/218-7992 ⊕ www.budget.com. **Hertz** ☎ 800/654-3131 ⊕ www.hertz.com. **National Car Rental** ☎ 877/222-9058 ⊕ www.nationalcar.com.

▌ MUNI TRAVEL

The San Francisco Municipal Railway, or Muni, operates light-rail vehicles, the historic F-line streetcars along Fisherman's Wharf and Market Street, trolley buses, and the world-famous cable cars. Light rail travels along Market Street to the Mission District and Noe Valley (J line), the Ingleside District (K line), and the Sunset District (L, M, and N lines); during peak hours (weekdays, 6 am–9 am and 3 pm–7 pm) the J line continues around the Embarcadero to the Caltrain station at 4th and King streets. The T-line light rail runs from the Castro, down Market Street, around the Embarcadero, and south past Hunters Point and Monster Park to Sunnydale Avenue and Bayshore Boulevard. Muni provides 24-hour service on select lines to all areas of the city.

On buses and streetcars the fare is $2.25. Exact change is required, and dollar bills are accepted in the fare boxes. For all Muni vehicles other than cable cars, 90-minute transfers are issued free upon request at the time the fare is paid. These are valid for two additional transfers in any direction. Cable cars cost $6 and include no transfers (⇨ see *Cable-Car Travel*).

One-day ($15), three-day ($23), and seven-day ($29) Passports valid on the entire Muni system can be purchased at several outlets, including the cable-car ticket booth at Powell and Market streets and the visitor information center downstairs in Hallidie Plaza. A monthly ticket is available for $80, and can be used on all Muni lines (including cable cars) and on BART within city limits. The San Francisco CityPass ($86), a discount ticket booklet to several major city attractions, also covers all Muni travel for seven consecutive days.

The San Francisco Municipal Transit and Street Map ($5) is a useful guide to the extensive transportation system. You can buy the map at most bookstores and at the San Francisco Visitor Information Center, on the lower level of Hallidie Plaza at Powell and Market streets.

BUS OPERATORS

Outside the city, AC Transit serves the East Bay, and Golden Gate Transit serves Marin County and a few cities in southern Sonoma County.

Bus and Muni Information San Francisco Municipal Railway System (*Muni*). ☎ 311, 415/701-3000 ⊕ www.sfmta.com.

▌TAXI TRAVEL

Taxi service is notoriously bad in San Francisco, and hailing a cab can be frustratingly difficult in some parts of the city, especially on weekends. Popular nightspots such as the Mission, SoMa, North Beach, the Haight, and the Castro have a lot of cabs but a lot of people looking for taxis, too. Midweek, and during the day, you shouldn't have much of a problem—unless it's raining. In a pinch, hotel taxi stands are an option, as is calling for a pickup. But be forewarned: taxi companies frequently don't answer the phone in peak periods. The absolute worst time to find a taxi is Friday afternoon and evening; plan well ahead, and if you're going to the airport, make a reservation or book a shuttle instead. Most taxi companies take reservations for airport and out-of-town runs but not in-town rides.

Taxis in San Francisco charge $3.50 for the first 0.5 mile (one of the highest base rates in the United States), 55¢ for each additional 0.5 mile, and 55¢ per minute in stalled traffic; a $2 surcharge is added for trips to the airport. There's no charge for additional passengers; there's no surcharge for luggage. For trips outside city limits, multiply the metered rate by 1.5; tolls and tip are extra.

Taxi Companies DeSoto Cab ☎ 415/970-1300 ⊕ www.desotosf.com. Luxor Cab ☎ 415/282-4141 ⊕ www.luxorcab.com. Veteran's Taxicab ☎ 415/552-1300. Yellow Cab ☎ 415/333-3333 ⊕ yellowcabsf.com.

Complaints San Francisco Police Department Taxi Complaints ☎ 415/701-4400.

▌TRAIN TRAVEL

Amtrak trains travel to the Bay Area from some cities in California and the United States. The *Coast Starlight* travels north from Los Angeles to Seattle, passing the Bay Area along the way, but contrary to its name, the train runs inland through the Central Valley for much of its route through Northern California; the most scenic stretch is in Southern California, between San Luis Obispo and Los Angeles. Amtrak also has several routes between San Jose, Oakland, and Sacramento. The *California Zephyr* travels from Chicago to the Bay Area, and has spectacular alpine vistas as it crosses the Sierra Nevada range. San Francisco doesn't have an Amtrak train station but does have an Amtrak bus station, at the Ferry Building, from which shuttle buses transport passengers to trains in Emeryville, just over the Bay Bridge. Shuttle buses also connect the Emeryville train station with downtown Oakland, the Caltrain station, and other points in downtown San Francisco. You can buy a California Rail Pass, which gives you seven days of travel in a 21-day period for $159.

Caltrain connects San Francisco to Palo Alto, San Jose, Santa Clara, and many smaller cities en route. In San Francisco, trains leave from the main depot, at 4th and Townsend streets, and a rail-side stop at 22nd and Pennsylvania streets. One-way fares are $3.25 to $13.25, depending on the number of zones through which you travel; tickets are valid for four hours after purchase time. A ticket is $7.25 from San Francisco to Palo Alto, at least $9.25 to San Jose. You can also buy a day pass ($6.50–$26.50) for unlimited travel in a 24-hour period. It's worth waiting for an express train for trips that last from 1 to 1¾ hours. On weekdays, trains depart three or four times per hour during the morning and evening, twice per hour during daytime noncommute hours, and as little as once per hour in the evening. Weekend trains run once per hour. The system shuts down at midnight. There are no onboard ticket sales. You must buy tickets before boarding the train or risk paying a $250 fine for fare evasion.

Information Amtrak ☎ *800/872–7245* ⊕ *www.amtrak.com.* **Caltrain** ☎ *800/660–4287* ⊕ *www.caltrain.com.* **San Francisco Caltrain station** ✉ *700 4th St., at King St.* ☎ *800/660–4287.*

ESSENTIALS

▮ COMMUNICATIONS

INTERNET

The city of San Francisco now offers free Wi-Fi service in selected parks and areas in and around the city. For a detailed list of locations visit ⊕ *www6.sfgov.org*. All public libraries also provide Internet access and most hotels have a computer stationed in the lobby with free (if shared) high-speed access for guests. Some hotels can charge up to $10 a day to provide a high-speed connection in the room, others offer it free of charge. In addition, many cafés throughout San Francisco, Marin County, and the East Bay offer free Wi-Fi, but a few continue to charge a $5 to $7 fee. For a list of free Wi-Fi spots in San Francisco, check ⊕ *www.openwifispots.com*.

▮ DAY TOURS AND GUIDES

For walking-tour recommendations, see the Experience San Francisco chapter or the pull-out On-the-Go map.

BOAT TOURS

Blue & Gold Fleet operates a bay cruise that lasts about an hour. Tickets may be purchased at Pier 39, near Fisherman's Wharf. The tour, on a ferryboat with outside seating on the upper deck, loops around the bay taking in the Bay Bridge, Alcatraz Island, and the Golden Gate Bridge. An audiotape tells you what you're seeing. Discounts are available for tickets purchased online.

Information Blue & Gold Fleet ☎ *415/705-8200* ⊕ *www.blueandgoldfleet.com*.

BUS AND VAN TOURS

In addition to bus and van tours of the city, most tour companies run excursions to various Bay Area and Northern California destinations, such as Marin County and the Wine Country, as well as to farther-flung areas, such as Monterey and Yosemite. City tours generally last 3½ hours and cost about $50 per person. The bigger outfits operate large buses, which tend to be roomy. Service is more intimate with the smaller companies, however, because they can fit only about 10 people per vehicle; the vans can be a little tight, but with the driver-guide right in front of you, you're able to ask questions easily and won't have to worry about interrupting someone on a microphone, as is the case with the big companies.

Centrally located in North Beach, Dylan's offers guided six hour tours around San Francisco, which then move on to Muir Woods and Sausalito ($75) in modern air-conditioned mini buses. The company also rents out bicycles for $22 for 24 hours—the best price in town.

Great Pacific Tours is a good small company and conducts city tours in passenger vans (starting at $59). Super Sightseeing is also locally owned and operates tours in 28- and 50-passenger buses. For $21 more, both companies can supplement a city tour with a bay cruise. Super Sightseeing can also add a trip to Alcatraz for $21.

Information Dylan's Tours ✉ *782 Columbus Ave.* ☎ *415/932-6993* ⊕ *dylanstours.com*. **Great Pacific Tours** ☎ *415/626-4499* ⊕ *www.greatpacifictour.com*. **Magic Bus San Francisco**. Actors from the Antenna Theater Company lead the tours for this literal time machine that transports visitors back to 1960s San Francisco. The bus provides a space for music and film clips to both educate and entertain; once the bus stops, you arrive at the historic place you just saw on your screen. Tickets are $60 each and tours last two hours. Pickup is at at 280 Geary St. in Union Square, drop off on the Post Street side of Union Square. Book online, and in advance, to guarantee a seat. ☎ *855/969-6244* ⊕ *magicbussf.com*. **Super Sightseeing** ☎ *415/353-5310* ⊕ *www.supersightseeing.com*.

HELICOPTER TOURS

San Francisco Helicopter Tours offers several options that give you a bird's-eye view of the city. Its Vista tour sweeps over the western shoreline, the Presidio, Union Square, AT&T Park, Alcatraz, and the Golden Gate Bridge; the tour lasts 15 to 20 minutes and costs $160 per person. The Vista Grande tour, which lasts 25 to 30 minutes and costs $205, takes in all of the above as well as Sausalito and Marin County. Longer tours, including trips to the Wine Country, also are available. The tours depart from San Francisco International Airport or the Sausalito heliport; a shuttle transports guests to and from the departure point, picking up and dropping off at downtown hotels and Fisherman's Wharf. Book at least 48 hours in advance.

Information San Francisco Helicopter Tours ☎ 800/400–2404, 650/635–4500 ⊕ *www. sfhelicoptertours.com.*

∎ MONEY

San Francisco often finds itself near the top of lists rating the most expensive cities in the United States. Don't let that scare you off; those ratings are usually based on the cost of living. Local real-estate prices are out of this world—but a trip here doesn't have to cost the moon.

Payment methods are those standard to major U.S. cities. Plastic is king; hotels and most stores and restaurants accept credit cards. Small, casual restaurants, though, may be cash-only operations. You can easily find ATMs in every neighborhood, either in bank branches (these have security vestibules that are accessed by your bank card), convenience stores, drugstores, supermarkets, and even some Starbucks coffee shops. Some performing arts venues, hotels, and fine-dining spots will also accept traveler's checks.

Prices throughout this guide are given for adults. Substantially reduced fees are almost always available for children, students, and senior citizens.

CREDIT CARDS

It's a good idea to inform your credit-card company before you travel. Otherwise, the credit-card company might put a hold on your card owing to unusual activity—not a good thing halfway through your trip. Record all your credit-card numbers—as well as the phone numbers to call if your cards are lost or stolen—in a safe place, so you're prepared should something go wrong. Both MasterCard and Visa have general numbers you can call (collect if you're abroad) if your card is lost, but you're better off calling the number of your issuing bank, since MasterCard and Visa usually just transfer you to your bank; your bank's number is usually printed on your card.

Reporting Lost Cards American Express ☎ 800/528–4800 in U.S. ⊕ *www. americanexpress.com.* **Diners Club** ☎ 800/234–6377 in U.S. ⊕ *www.dinersclub. com.* **Discover** ☎ 800/347–2683 in U.S. ⊕ *www.discovercard.com.* **MasterCard** ☎ 800/627–8372 in U.S. ⊕ *www.mastercard. com.* **Visa** ☎ 800/847–2911 in U.S. ⊕ *www. visa.com.*

∎ RESTROOMS

Public facilities are in forest-green kiosks at Pier 39, on Market Street at Powell Street, at Castro and Market streets, and at the Civic Center. The fee to use the facilities is 25¢, although it's free at some places. Since they're self-cleaning, they're usually tolerable. Most public garages have restrooms, and large hotels usually have lobby-level facilities, and chain bookstores are another good bet.

Find a Loo The Bathroom Diaries. The Bathroom Diaries is flush with unsanitized information on restrooms the world over—each one located, reviewed, and rated. ⊕ *www. thebathroomdiaries.com.*

▌ SAFETY

San Francisco is generally a safe place for travelers who observe all normal urban precautions. First, avoid looking like a tourist. Dress inconspicuously, remove badges when leaving convention areas, and know the routes to your destination before you set out. Use common sense and, unless you know exactly where you're going, steer clear of certain neighborhoods late at night, especially if you're walking alone. Below are certain areas to stay on alert, or avoid:

The Tenderloin. Named for a cut of steak, this neighborhood west of Union Square and above Civic Center can be a seedy part of town, with drug dealers, homeless people, hustlers, and X-rated joints. It's roughly bordered by Taylor, Polk, Geary, and Market streets. Avoid coming here after dark, especially if you're walking.

Western Addition. Gang activity makes this a sketchy neighborhood, even in daytime, with occasional outbreaks of gun violence. Don't stray too far off Fillmore Street.

Civic Center. After a show here, walk west to Gough Street; don't head north, east, or south from the Civic Center on foot, and avoid Market Street between 6th and 10th.

Parts of the Mission District. The flat blocks of the Mission range from a bit scruffy to edgy to truly sketchy, with some gang activity. Steer clear of the areas east of Mission Street and south of 24th Street, especially after dark. If you're walking between 16th and 24th streets, head one block west to Valencia, which runs parallel to Mission.

Some areas in Golden Gate Park. These include the area near the Haight Street entrance, where street kids often smoke and deal pot, and around the pedestrian tunnels on the far west end of the park.

Like many large cities, San Francisco has many homeless people. Although most are no threat, some are more aggressive and can persist in their pleas for cash until it feels like harassment. If you feel uncomfortable, don't reach for your wallet.

▌TIP➜ Distribute your cash, credit cards, IDs, and other valuables between a deep front pocket, an inside jacket or vest pocket, and a hidden money pouch. Don't reach for the money pouch once you're in public.

▌ TAXES

The sales tax in San Francisco is 8.75%. Nonprepared foods (from grocery stores) are exempt. The tax on hotel rooms is 14%.

▌ TIME

San Francisco is on Pacific Time. Chicago is 2 hours ahead of San Francisco, New York is 3 hours ahead, and, depending on whether daylight saving time is in effect, London is either 8 or 9 hours ahead and Sydney is 17 or 18 hours ahead.

▌ TIPPING

TIPPING GUIDELINES FOR SAN FRANCISCO	
Bartender	About 15%, starting at $1 a drink at casual places
Bellhop	$1 to $5 per bag, depending on the level of the hotel
Hotel concierge	$5 or more, if he or she performs a service for you
Hotel doorman, room service, or valet	$3–$4
Hotel maid	$5 a day (either daily or at the end of your stay, in cash)
Taxi Driver	15%–20%, but round up the fare to the next dollar amount
Tour Guide	10% of the cost of the tour
Waiter	18%–20%, with 20% being the norm at high-end restaurants; nothing additional if a service charge is added to the bill

■ VISITOR INFORMATION

The San Francisco Convention and Visitors Bureau can mail you brochures, maps, and festivals and events listings. Once you're in town, you can stop by the bureau's information center near Union Square. Information about the Wine Country, redwood groves, and northwestern California is available at the California Welcome Center on Pier 39.

The Berkeley Convention and Visitors Bureau provides an extensive events calendar and detailed suggestions. The Oakland Convention and Visitors Bureau also has an informative website; click on the "Visitors" link to download the free 60-page guide or have it sent by mail. For information about Marin County and the state and national parks within it, visit the Marin County, California Visitors Bureau in San Rafael or online at ⊕ www. visitmarin.org.

The California Travel and Tourism Commission provides free visitor information and itinerary planners for the entire state.

Contacts San Francisco Visitor Information Center ⊠ Hallidie Plaza, lower level, 900 Market St., at Powell St., Union Sq. ☎ 415/391-2000 TDD ⊕ www.onlyinsanfrancisco.com.

Metro Area Berkeley Convention and Visitors Bureau ⊠ 2030 Addison St., Suite 102, Berkeley ☎ 800/847-4823, 510/549-7040 ⊕ www.visitberkeley.com. **Marin County, California Visitors Bureau** ⊠ 1 Mitchell Blvd., Suite B, at Redwood Hwy. ☎ 415/925-2060, 866/925-2060 ⊕ www. visitmarin.org. **San Jose Convention and Visitors Bureau** ⊠ 408 Almaden Blvd., at Balbach St., San Jose ☎ 800/726-5673, 408/295-9600 ⊕ www.sanjose.org.

State California Travel and Tourism Commission ⊠ Sacramento ☎ 877/225-4367, 916/444-4429 ⊕ www.visitcalifornia.com. **California Welcome Center** ⊠ 2nd level, Pier 39, San Francisco ☎ 415/981-1280 ⊕ www. visitcwc.com.

THE FODORS.COM CONNECTION

Before your trip, be sure check out what fellow travelers are saying in Travel Talk Forums on ⊕ www.fodors.com.

ONLINE RESOURCES

This comprehensive website, ⊕ www. sanfrancisco.com, contains links to local restaurants, cultural institutions, and even government agencies in and around the city.

For local politics and news, there's the online presence of the major daily newspaper, ⊕ www.sfgate.com as well as ⊕ www. fogcityjournal.com. Current arts and cultural events are detailed on the extensive events calendar of ⊕ www.sfstation.com or the San Francisco Chronicle's online entertainment pages, ⊕ www.sfgate.com/ entertainment.

For more cost-conscious, on-the-pulse guidance, visit ⊕ sf.funcheap.com. You can browse articles from San Francisco Magazine, a monthly glossy, at ⊕ www. modernluxury.com/san-francisco. The annual summer issues on "bests" (restaurants, activities, and so on) are handy overviews. SF Weekly's site, ⊕ www. sfweekly.com, makes for good browsing. Where's the Wi-Fi? Click on ⊕ www. wififreespot.com to see where you can log on in the Bay Area for free.

INDEX

PHOTO CREDITS

Front cover: Noah Clayton/age fotostock [Description: Golden Gate Bridge in fog]. Back cover (from left to right): Andy Z./Shutterstock; miss karen/Flickr (CC BY 2.0); Brett Shoaf/Artistic Visuals Photography. Spine: holbox / Shutterstock. 1. 2, Philip Dyer/istockphoto. 5, travelstock44/Alamy. Chapter 1: Experience San Francisco: 8-9, Prisma/Bildagentur AG/Alamy. 10, Brett Shoaf/Artistic Visuals Photography. 11(left), Brett Shoaf/Artistic Visuals Photography. 11 (right), elvis santana/iStockphoto.14-17, Brett Shoaf/Artistic Visuals Photography.18 (left), Eli Mordechai/Shutterstock. 18 (top right), Andresr/Shutterstock. 18 (bottom right), Chee-Onn Leong/Shutterstock. 19 (top left), Chris Pancewicz/Alamy. 19 (right), Robert Holmes. 9 (bottom left), Brett Shoaf/Artistic Visuals Photography. 20, Lisa M. Hamilton. 21, Brett Shoaf/Artistic Visuals Photography. 22, Hal Bergman/iStockphoto. 23. Janet Fullwood. 26, wili_hybrid/Flickr. 27 (left), Brett Shoaf/Artistic Visuals. 27 (right), Corbis Photography. 28, Brett Shoaf/Artistic Visuals Photography. 29, travelstock44/Alamy. 31, Brett Shoaf/Artistic Visuals Photography. 32, San Francisco Municipal Railway Historical Archives. Chapter 2: Union Square & Chinatown: 33, Rubens Abboud/Alamy. 35, Chee-Onn Leong/Shutterstock. 36, Steve Rosset/Shutterstock. 38, San Francisco Travel Association/Scott Chernis. 41, Sheryl Schindler/SFCVB. 43, Brett Shoaf/Artistic Visuals Photography. 44 (top), Arnold Genthe. 44 (bottom), Library of Congress Prints and Photographs Division. 45 (left), Sandor Balatoni/SFCVB. 45 (right), Detroit Publishing Company Collection, Photography Collection, Miriam and Ira D. Wallach Division of Art, Prints and Photographs, The New York Public Library, Astor, Lenox and Tilden Foundation. 46, Brett Shoaf/Artistic Visuals Photography. Chapter 3: SoMa and Civic Center: 49, Walter Bibikow/age fotostock. 51, Robert Holmes. 52, Rafael Ramirez Lee/Shutterstock. 53, stephenrwalli/Flickr. 54, Brett Shoaf/Artistic Visuals. Chapter 4: Nob Hill and Russian Hill: 61, SurangaSL / Shutterstock. 63 and 64, Brett Shoaf/Artistic Visuals Photography. Chapter 5: North Beach: 71, photo.ua / Shutterstock. 73 and 74, Brett Shoaf/Artistic Visuals Photography. 76, M & J Miller / age fotostock. Chapter 6: On the Waterfront: 81, Jon Arnold Images/Alamy. 83, Musee Mecanique in San Francisco. 84, Robert Holmes. 88-89. Chee-Onn Leong/Shutterstock. 95, Lewis Sommer/SFCVB. 96, Daniel DeSlover/Shutterstock.97 (left), POPPERFOTO/Alamy. 97 (center and right), wikipedia.org. 99, Eliza Snow/iStockphoto. 100, Steve Rosset/Shutterstock. Chapter 7: The Marina and the Presidio: 101, Carolina Garcia Aranda/iStockphoto. 103, Brett Shoaf/Artistic Visuals Photography. 104, javarman/Shutterstock. 108, CAN BALCIOGLU/Shutterstock. 109 (top), Zack Frank/Shutterstock. 109 (bottom), Steve Holderfield/Shutterstock. Chapter 8: The Western Shoreline: 113 and 115, Robert Holmes. 116, Brett Shoaf/Artistic Visuals Photography. 118, Chee-Onn Leong/Shutterstock. Chapter 9: Golden Gate Park: 121, California Travel and Tourism Co. 122, Robert Holmes. 123 and 124 (top), Brett Shoaf/Artistic Visuals Photography. 124 (center), Robert Holmes. 124 (bottom), Brett Shoaf/Artistic Visuals Photography. 125, Natalia Bratslavsky/iStockphoto. 126, Robert Holmes. 127 (top), Jack Hollingsworth/SFCVB. 127 (center), Robert Holmes. 127 (bottom), Brett Shoaf/Artistic Visuals Photography. 128 (top and bottom), RobertHolmes. 129 (top and bottom), Janet Fullwood. 130 (top), Donna & Andrew/Flickr. 130 (center and bottom), Robert Holmes. Chapter 10: The Haight, the Castro, and Noe Valley: 131, Robert Holmes. 133, Brett Shoaf/Artistic Visuals Photography. 134, SFCVB. 137, aprillilacs, Fodors.com member. 140, Brett Shoaf/Artistic Visuals Photography. Chapter 11: Mission District: 145, Kārlis Dambrāns/Flickr, [CC BY 2.0] 147, Robert Holmes. 148, Brett Shoaf/Artistic Visuals Photography. 150, Held Jürgen/Prisma/age fotostock. 152, Robert Holmes. Chapter 12: Pacific Heights and Japantown: 155, Robert Holmes. 157, ryan + sarah/Flickr. 158, Brett Shoaf/Artistic Visuals Photography. 160. Janet Fullwood. 161. (top) iStockphoto. 161. (bottom) Susanne Friedrich/iStockphoto. 163, Rafael Ramirez Lee/iStockphoto. Chapter 13: Where to Eat: 167, Lisa M. Hamilton. 168, San Francisco Travel Association/Scott Chernis. 169 (top), T photography / Shutterstock. 169 (bottom), Walleyelj | Dreamstime.com 170, Robert Holmes. 178, Nikolay Bachiyski/Flickr (CC BY 2.0). Chapter 14: Where to Stay: 219, Argonaut Hotel. 220, Clift Hotel. Chapter 15: Performing Arts: 245, Erik Tomasson. 246, Max Kiesler/Flickr, [CC BY 2.0]. Chapter 16: Nightlife and the Arts: 257, San Francisco Travel Association/Scott Chernis. 258, Robert Holmes. 266, Rough Guides/Alamy. Chapter 17: Sports and the Outdoors: 281, Rich Vintage Photography/iStockphoto. 282, Robert Holmes. Chapter 18: Shopping and Spas: 291 and 292, Robert Holmes. 314, nito / Shutterstock. Chapter 19: The Bay Area: 327, Robert Holmes. 329 (top), Robert Holmes. 329 (bottom), Jyeshern Cheng/iStockphoto. 330, Brett Shoaf/Artistic Visuals Photography. 338, Caro / Alamy. 342, Nancy Hoyt Belcher / Alamy. 360, Robert Holmes. 371, Robert Holmes. 375, Mark Rasmussen/iStockphoto. 381, S. Greg Panosian/iStockphoto. Chapter 20: The Wine Country: 383, Andrew Zarivny / Shutterstock. 384, iStockphoto. 385, Robert Holmes. 386, Warren H. White. 392, Robert Holmes. 393(top), kevin miller/iStockphoto. 393 (bottom), Far Niente+Dolce+Nickel & Nickel. 394 (top and bottom)Robert Holmes. 395 (top), Domaine Carneros. 395 (bottom), star5112/Flickr. 396 (top left), Rubicon Estate. 396 (top right and bottom) and 397 (top and bottom), Robert

ABOUT OUR WRITERS

 Michele Bigley spends most of her days exploring her favorite city (San Francisco, of course) with her two sons and husband. When not hunting for sand dollars, hiking through eucalyptus groves, or munching on Italian pastries, she writes articles, books, iPhone apps, and essays about her world travels. Michele updated our Where to Stay chapter this edition.

 Christine Ciarmello is a freelance food and travel writer who was previously deputy editor at the West Coast's regional lifestyle magazine, *Sunset*. There, she explored food, wine, and cocktails—as well as travel. She has an obsession with out-the-box hotels, which you can follow on Twitter @cciarm. Previously she was editor-in-chief at *ISLANDS* magazine, where she explored the foods of Asia, Europe, and the Caribbean. A native New Orleanian who spent her formative years eating gumbo and chargrilled oysters, Christine eats out most nights in San Francisco and updated the Where to Eat chapter.

 Longtime Fodor's writer and editor **Denise M. Leto** roams the city out of sheer love for SF, peeking down overgrown alleyways and exploring tucked-away corners from the Tenderloin to the Richmond, often with her three homeschooled kids in tow. She updated all the neighborhood chapters, the Experience chapter, and the Bar Area chapter in this edition. She also wrote our special features on cable cars, Chinatown, Golden Gate Park, Alcatraz, and the Golden Gate Bridge.

 Daniel Mangin returned to California, where he's maintained a home for three decades, after two stints at the Fodor's editorial offices in New York City, the second one as the Editorial Director of Fodors.com and the Compass American Guides. While at Compass he was the series editor for the *California Wine Country* guide and commissioned the *Oregon Wine Country* and *Washington Wine Country* guides. A wine lover whose earliest visits to Napa and Sonoma predate the Wine Country lifestyle, Daniel is delighted by the evolution in wines, wine making, and hospitality. With several dozen wineries less than a half-hour's drive from home, he often finds himself transported as if by magic to a tasting room bar, communing with a sophisticated Cabernet or savoring the finish of a smooth Pinot Noir. He wrote Fodor's full-length *Napa and Sonoma* guidebook and naturally updated the Wine Country chapter for this book.

 Fiona G. Parrott is a Californian native who spent her childhood exploring the raw wilderness of Marin County and her later years exploring the culinary and musical delights of San Francisco. At present she divides her adventure time between wilderness and cityscape, writing about the Bay Area's cutting edge hotspots. She has worked as a veterinarian, actor, watermelon picker, latrine builder, and university lecturer, but writing for Fodor's is one of her most exciting jobs. For this edition she updated the Sports and the Outdoors, Travel Smart, and Shopping chapters.

 Jerry James Stone, author of *Holidazed: A Cocktail Cookbook for Getting Lit on Christmas*, has been eating and drinking his way through San Francisco for years now, focusing on the sustainable food and wine movement. You can find all his vegan and vegetarian recipes at Cooking Stoned (⊕ *www.cookingstoned.tv*). Jerry updated the Nightlife and the Performing Arts chapters in this year's guide. Follow him on Twitter @jerryjamesstone for mouth-watering recipe ideas.

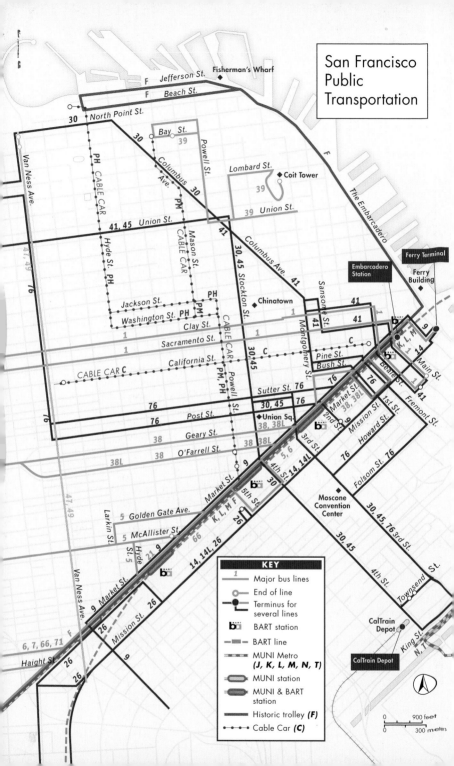